P9-DVJ-026

Handbook of Developmental and Physical Disabilities

(PGPS-148)

Pergamon Titles of Related Interest

Becker / Greenberg EDUCATIONAL REHABILITATION OF THE HANDICAPPED IN THE
GERMAN DEMOCRATIC REPUBLIC & IN THE UNITED STATES OF AMERICA:
An Overview

Harris FAMILIES OF THE DEVELOPMENTALLY DISABLED:
A Guide to Behavioral Intervention

Matson / Mulick HANDBOOK OF MENTAL RETARDATION

Morris / Blatt SPECIAL EDUCATION:
Research and Trends

Wang / Reynolds / Walberg HANDBOOK OF SPECIAL EDUCATION:
Research and Practice

Related Journals

Free sample copies available upon request

ANALYSIS AND INTERVENTION IN DEVELOPMENTAL DISABILITIES

APPLIED RESEARCH IN MENTAL RETARDATION

PERGAMON GENERAL PSYCHOLOGY SERIES
EDITORS
Arnold P. Goldstein, *Syracuse University*
Leonard Krasner, *Stanford University & SUNY at Stony Brook*

Handbook of Developmental and Physical Disabilities

Edited by

Vincent B. Van Hasselt

*California College of Medicine,
University of California, Irvine, Medical Center*

Phillip S. Strain
Michel Hersen

University of Pittsburgh School of Medicine

PERGAMON PRESS

New York · Oxford · Beijing · Frankfurt
São Paulo · Sydney · Tokyo · Toronto

U.S.A.	Pergamon Press, Inc., Maxwell House, Fairview Park, Elmsford, New York 10523, U.S.A.
U.K.	Pergamon Press plc, Headington Hill Hall, Oxford OX3 0BW, England
PEOPLE'S REPUBLIC OF CHINA	Pergamon Press, Room 4037, Qianmen Hotel, Beijing, People's Republic of China
FEDERAL REPUBLIC OF GERMANY	Pergamon Press GmbH, Hammerweg 6, D-6242 Kronberg, Federal Republic of Germany
BRAZIL	Pergamon Editora Ltda, Rua Eça de Queiros, 346, CEP 04011, Paraiso, São Paulo, Brazil
AUSTRALIA	Pergamon Press Australia Pty Ltd., P.O. Box 544, Potts Point, N.S.W. 2011, Australia
JAPAN	Pergamon Press, 5th Floor, Matsuoka Central Building, 1-7-1 Nishishinjuku, Shinjuku-ku, Tokyo 160, Japan
CANADA	Pergamon Press Canada Ltd, Suite No. 271, 253 College Street, Toronto, Ontario, Canada M5T 1R5

First edition 1988

Library of Congress Cataloging in Publication Data
Handbook of developmental and physical disabilities.
(Pergamon general psychology series; 148)
Includes index.
1. Rehabilitation.   2. Physically handicapped.
3. Mentally handicapped.   I. Van Hasselt, Vincent B.
II. Strain, Phillip S.   III. Hersen, Michel.
IV. Series. [DNLM: 1. Handicapped—handbooks.
2. Mental Retardation—rehabilitation—handbooks.
3. Rehabilitation—handbooks. WB 39 H2357]
RM930.H346   1988   617   86—30282

British Library Cataloguing in Publication Data
Van Hasselt, Vincent B.
Handbook of developmental and physical
disabilities.—(Pergamon general psychology series; 148)
1. Pathology.   2. Medicine.
I. Title.   II. Strain, Phillip S.
III. Hersen, Michel.
616   RB111

ISBN 0-08-031595-X

Printed in Great Britain by A. Wheaton & Co. Ltd., Exeter

Contents

Part III. Specific Disabilities

Preface

Over the years a wide variety of professionals have interviewed and conducted research with both the developmentally and physically disabled. In the last few years, however, we have noted heightened activity with such populations. A number of factors have contributed to the burgeoning interest in this area. First, improved medical care has helped to increase the longevity of the disabled and multihandicapped, thus adding to the visibility of the problems. Second, the extremely high economic costs associated with disability have attracted considerable public attention. Third, legal and legislative initiatives proposed by parent advocacy and professional interest groups have functioned to combat long-held negative stereotypes toward both the developmentally and physically disabled. These initiatives have had a dramatic impact on public policy, delivery of health services, and availability of research monies for this field of inquiry. Finally, there now is a greater awareness of the potential for abuse, neglect, or abandonment of children with developmental and physical disabilities.

When we first decided to outline the contents of *Handbook of Developmental and Physical Disabilities*, we were struck by the diversity of the papers and chapters that have appeared in widely scattered publications. The voluminous literature—a result of the rapid expansion of clinical, educational, and investigative endeavors—deals with epidemiological findings, assessment and treatment (psychological and medical), developmental and educational issues, and research considerations. In developing our final outline we were intent on reflecting the great diversity in the field by incorporating views from psychology, psychiatry, medicine, education, special education, and rehabilitation. Thus, in integrating and organizing frequently diverse material, experts in their respective areas have summarized the relevant findings. In this sense, the *Handbook* is cross-categorical and unbiased methodologically, and at the same time articulates the commonalities and distinctive features of the varied disabilities.

The book is divided into three parts and includes 27 chapters. Part I provides an overview of the field that includes an introduction, life-span issues in the disabled, issues in psychological evaluation, and biomedical perspectives. In Part II (General Issues), a variety of important aspects cutting across disability in general have been given careful consideration. These include prevention, family adjustment,

psychosexual adjustment, social integration, research issues, vocational training and rehabilitation, and legal and legislative initiatives. In Part III (Specific
Disabilities), attention to 16 specific developmental and physical disabilities is given
in great detail, with chapters following a
parallel format that includes a description
of the disorder, epidemiological findings,
developmental issues, educational issues,
assessment and treatment, and current
research status.

Many individuals have contributed their
time and expertise to the *Handbook*. First, of
course, we thank our contributors from
many disciplines for agreeing to share their
knowledge. Second, we thank our families
for their support during the course of our
many editorial labors. Third, we extend our

appreciation to Christine M. Sadowski,
Rebecca Aberle, Judith A. Kowolski, Mary
H. Newell, Louise E. Moore, Noelle
Thomas, Jenifer McKelvey, and Mary Jo
Horgan for their technical assistance.
Finally, but hardly least of all, we thank
Jerome B. Frank, our editor at Pergamon
Press, for his long-term support, encour-
agement, and patience in the face of the
inevitable delays confronted during the
process of producing this large handbook.

Vincent B. Van Hasselt
Orange, CA

Phillip S. Strain
Michel Hersen
Pittsburgh, PA

PART 1

Overview

CHAPTER 1

Introduction

Vincent B. Van Hasselt, Phillip S. Strain and Michel Hersen

PREVALENCE

Over the past several years, professionals from a wide range of disciplines have directed increased attention to problems and issues pertaining to disabled persons. Evaluative, rehabilitative, and investigative endeavors designed to eliminate barriers that disabled persons experience have been conducted by a multidisciplinary consortium consisting of educators, psychologists, physicians, social workers, psychiatrists, physical and occupational therapists, rehabilitation specialists, and engineers. There are a number of reasons for the heightened focus on disabled individuals. First, the number of people in the United States with some form of physical or developmental disability has burgeoned in the past few decades. For example, Bowe (1980) estimated that 36 million, or 15% of the population, are disabled. This is consistent with a previous report by the 1976 United States Census Survey of Income and Education, which revealed a figure of 13.6%. Further, there are indications that as many as 10% of children under age 21 are disabled (Gliedman & Roth, 1980). Also, 46% of persons 65 years of age and over report a serious and disabling health impairment (DeJong & Lifchez, 1983). Of particular import is the growing multihandicapped population (Dibedenetto, 1976). These individuals have been referred to by a combination of names for disorders (e.g., deaf-blind, cerebral palsied-deaf, blind-retarded) or by more generic terms, such as developmentally disordered or severely and profoundly handicapped.

The greater number of handicapped persons in general, and those with multiple afflictions in particular, is partly a function

Preparation of this chapter was facilitated by Grant No. G008300135 (National Institute of Handicapped Research) and Contract No. 300-82-0368 (Early Childhood Research Institute) from the U.S. Department of Education. The opinions expressed herein do not necessarily reflect the position or policy of the U.S. Department of Education, and no official endorsement by the Department should be inferred. The authors wish to express their appreciation to Judith A. Kowolski for her assistance in preparation of the manuscript.

of improved prenatal care, decreased infant mortality due to advances in medical and surgical procedures, and strides made in research and treatment of several infant diseases (Mulliken, 1983). However, as Fenderson (1984) points out, "although these improvements . . . help to save lives and prevent untimely death, they also contribute to the increasing number of individuals with significant limitations of function" (p. 527).

ECONOMIC IMPLICATIONS

Another impetus for the upsurge of activity with the disabled is the high economic cost associated with disability. Disabilities are, by definition, chronic disorders that may require many years of care and remediation. Rehabilitation programs can be extremely expensive. For example, a cerebral-palsy day program serving 100 clients may operate on a budget of over half a million dollars per year, or about $5,000 per client (Goldenson, Dunham, & Dunham, 1978). This does not include surgical and medical expenditures. In addition, considerable data have been accrued to document the relationship between disability and low rates of participation in the work force. This finding is most apparent in the elderly and in minority groups (see discussion by Asch, 1984). According to the United States Bureau of Census (1983), only 7% of individuals between ages 35 and 44 have a work disability, while the proportion is increased to 24.1% for those in the 55 to 64 age range. Also, in comparison to an estimated 8.4% of work-disabled whites, 13.4% of blacks have some form of work disability.

Further, state and federal expenditures for support of the disabled have been substantial. In 1977, disability-related payments to working-age individuals amounted to nearly $63.5 billion. Social Security Insurance and Supplemental Security Income programs alone paid $20.6 billion to more than 4 million working-age people with disabilities in 1980 (DeJong & Lifchez, 1983). However, Bowe (1980) and others have argued that the federal government spends 10 times as much on what

have been termed "dependence programs" as on efforts to improve independent functioning in the disabled. The heuristic value of supporting the latter was underscored in the 1981 fiscal report of the Rehabilitation Services Administration. This document showed that the projected lifetime earnings for disabled persons rehabilitated in the previous year would improve by $10.40 for every dollar spent on rehabilitative services designed to promote more self-sufficient and adaptive living. In addition, it was anticipated that these individuals would pay approximately $211.5 million more in combined income, sales, and payroll taxes than if they had not been rehabilitated.

Senator Lowell Weicker, a major Congressional advocate for persons with disabilities, discusses the need for more extensive cost-benefit analyses of government-supported programs that transform "the often dependent and demeaning life-styles of disabled Americans into more meaningful existences. Frequently, these efforts result in getting disabled people off welfare rolls and onto payrolls and tax rolls as well . . . . The American people and the politicians who serve them must be able to see the worth of long-term investments in making society accessible to handicapped persons" (Weicker, 1984, pp. 521–522).

ATTITUDES TOWARD DISABILITY

The problems of inadequate socialization and stereotyping also are major factors accounting for increased assessment and intervention efforts with the disabled. These persons traditionally have been viewed as "flawed" and in need of rehabilitation in order to "bring them up" to normative standards (Jackman, 1983). Moreover, they are considered by many to be helpless, incompetent, unproductive, and dependent. In an analysis conducted over two decades ago, of attitudes of nondisabled persons toward those with disabilities, Siller, Chipman, Ferguson, and Vann (1967) found the following dimensions to be most prevalent: generalized rejection (unpleasant personal reactions), interaction strain, distressed identification (i.e., anxiety by the nonhandicapped regarding their own potential vulnerability), imputed functional limitations, rejection of intimacy, authoritarian virtuousness (viz., appearing to be supportive of the disabled, but actually negative in attitude) and inferred emotional consequences. There is a consensus among professionals that such attitudes continue to prevail among most of the nondisabled population.

The last factor cited by Siller et al. (1967), "inferred emotional consequences," refers to the common view that a disability negatively affects the character and/or emotional status of the disabled person. Wright (1960) used the term "spread" to refer to the belief that people who have a deficit in one area must be inadequate in others. Thus, disability often has been unjustly equated with intellectual limitation or psychological dysfunction. As Lindemann (1981) notes, "This phenomenon of spread may lead to curiously paradoxical perceptions of disabled persons. Those with visible handicaps may be seen as more emotionally maladjusted than, in fact, they are. Those with serious disabilities which are not visible (e.g., diabetes, heart condition) may be assumed to be emotionally healthy, with subsequent surprise should they prove to have significant emotional problems related to their disability" (p. 2). Such generalizations, however, lack empirical support. Indeed, a report by the Task Force on Psychology and the Handicapped (1984) highlights the need to shift our focus from presumed deficits possessed by the disabled to the more harmful and deleterious effects of negative attitudes held by the nonhandicapped, "particularly with respect to expected but imaginary problems the nonhandicapped believe those with disabilities possess" (p. 548). The Task Force concludes that psychological events, such as discrimination, present more serious difficulties to the disabled than physical impairment per se.

SOCIAL DEVELOPMENT

The impact of disability on social development and interpersonal interaction has been articulated at length (cf. Goffman,

1963; Lindemann, 1981; Matson, DiLorenzo, & Andrasik, 1983; Richardson, 1976; Van Hasselt, 1983). After reviewing laboratory and field investigations of behavioral responses of the nonhandicapped toward the handicapped, Asch (1984) concluded that "the presence of someone who actually is or is thought to be disabled arouses in the nonhandicapped person a variety of emotions that, at the very least, hinder ordinary social interaction. Nonhandicapped people prefer to avoid social contact with the disabled or behave more formally and in distorted ways if they are forced to interact with handicapped persons" (p. 532). Along these lines, Richardson (1976) has stated that "no further research is needed to show that it is socially disadvantageous to be physically handicapped in initial social encounters" (p. 32).

In response to the need of many disabled persons for enhanced socialization, psychologists and special educators have designed a variety of social-skills training strategies for several disabled populations. Some of these include the blind and visually impaired (Farkas, Sherick, Matson, & Loebig, 1981; Van Hasselt, Hersen, Kazdin, Simon, & Mastantuono, 1983), deaf (Lemanek, Williamson, Gresham, & Jensen, 1986), mentally retarded (Matson & Zeiss, 1978; Turner, Hersen, & Bellack, 1978), and spinal-cord injured (Dunn, Van Horn, & Herman, 1981), as well as autistic (Ragland, Kerr, & Strain, 1978; Strain, 1983) and multihandicapped (Sisson, Van Hasselt, Hersen, & Strain, 1985) children.

ABUSE

A more recent concern of professionals working with the disabled are preliminary data garnered from aggression and family violence research showing that a disproportionate number of disabled persons may be at high risk for crime, child abuse, and family abandonment (see review by Ammerman, Van Hasselt, & Hersen, in press). Most work in this area has focused on "at risk" handicapped or physically ill children (e.g., Friedrich & Boriskin, 1976; Glaser & Bentovim, 1979; Lynch, 1975). For example, an early study by Gil (1970) showed that 29% of 6,000 confirmed cases of child abuse had some form of developmental disability. A national survey cited by Chotiner and Lehr (1976) revealed that 58% of abused children of Parents Anonymous members had "developmental problems" prior to abuse. While investigations of etiological variables associated with this problem presently are at the nascent stage, the negative stigma attached to disabilities, as well as the high level of social/emotional stress found in families of handicapped or multihandicapped children, are considered possible causative factors (Ammerman et al., in press; Asch, 1984; Glaser & Bentovin, 1979).

LEGISLATIVE INITIATIVES

Another reason for the expansion of direct services and research endeavors for the disabled is the widespread social and legal activism on behalf of the rights of these persons. This is partly an extension of the broader wave of activism and legislative progress for the handicapped witnessed in this country during the 1970s. Indeed, this period was characterized by general recognition of the disabled population as a minority group that historically has been denied its civil rights. In a discussion of changes in educational practices, Kauffman (1981) relates, "The civil rights movement had a profound impact on special education because its message, and the message of court decisions and legislation involving racial discrimination, was clearly that the rights of minorities found protection in the law" (p. 9).

With passage of the Rehabilitation Act of 1973, the handicapped were clearly recognized as being unjustly assigned to devalued status due to their physical characteristics. This act, which is considered a pivotal piece of legislation, prohibited discrimination against qualified handicapped persons in federally funded programs or services. Soon afterward, the Education for All Handicapped Children Act of 1975 was enacted. Under this law, free and appropriate public education was made available to all handicapped children in the least restrictive setting possible. These and other legislative initiatives require that society make the necessary adjustments to provide adequate education, employment, housing, and increased opportunities to handicapped persons so that they may achieve meaningful life goals.

ADVOCACY GROUPS AND PROFESSIONAL INTEREST

Also strongly influential on recent improvements in care and education of handicapped individuals have been parent and child advocacy groups. Organizations such as the National Association for Retarded Citizens and the Association for Children with Learning Disabilities have served as effective mutual support and community action groups and have successfully applied political pressure for new legislation. Similarly, professionals have banded together through a variety of activities and associations and have had an impact on the extent and direction of efforts for the handicapped. For example, the Council for Exceptional Children and its divisions are involved in lobbying to influence teachers and administrators working with disabled children and youth. Also, the growing number of journals (e.g., *Education and Training of the Mentally Retarded, Research in Developmental Disabilities, Journal of the Multihandicapped Person, Journal of Learning Disabilities, Rehabilitation Research*) and college texts devoted to the handicapped reflects the increased professional interest in this field in recent years.

SCOPE OF THE BOOK

Given the vastness of the field of developmental and physical disabilities, coupled with the recently increased legislative and professional attention it has received, we felt that the burgeoning information needed to be included under one cover in the form of a handbook. Indeed, our research revealed that this had not been carried out since the work of Goldenson et al. (1978) almost a decade ago. The objective of this *Handbook*, then, is to examine disability in comprehensive fashion, including articulation of both the general and specific issues that the field is facing. To accomplish this, we have called upon the expertise of individuals from numerous and diverse disciplines. Consequently, the psychological, sociological, legal, legislative, vocational, and medical aspects of disability are accorded their relevant attention.

REFERENCES

Ammerman, R. T., Van Hasselt, V. B., & Hersen, M. (in press). Maltreatment of handicapped children: A critical review. *Journal of Family Violence*.

Asch, A. (1984). The experience of disability: A challenge for psychology. *American Psychologist, 39*, 529–536.

Bowe, F. (1980). *Rehabilitation America*. New York: Harper & Row.

Chotiner, N., & Lehr, W. (Eds.). (1976). *Child abuse and developmental disabilities*. A report from the New England Regional Conference, sponsored by United Cerebral Palsy of Rhode Island and the United Cerebral Palsy Association.

DeJong, G., & Lifchez, R. (1983). Physical disability and public policy. *Scientific American, 48*, 240–249.

Dibedenetto, T. A. (1976). Problems of the deaf retarded: A review of the literature. *Education and Training of the Mentally Retarded, 11*, 164–170.

Dunn, M., Van Horn, E., & Herman, S. (1981). Social skills and spinal cord injury: A comparison of three training procedures. *Behavior Therapy, 12*, 153–164.

Education for All Handicapped Children Act of 1975, Pub. L. No. 94–142, 89 Stat. 775 (1975).

Farkas, G. M., Sherick, R. B., Matson, J. L., & Loebig, M. (1981). Social skills training of a blind child through differential reinforcement. *The Behavior Therapist, 4*, 24–26.

Fenderson, D. A. (1984). Opportunities for psychologists in disability research. *American Psychologist, 39*, 524–528.

Friedrich, M. P. H., & Boriskin, J. A. (1976). The role of the child in abuse: A review of the literature. *American Journal of Orthopsychiatry, 46*, 580–590.

Gil, D. G. (1970). *Violence against children: Physical child abuse in the United States*. Cambridge, MA: Harvard University Press.

Glaser, D., & Bentovim, A. (1979). Abuse and risk to handicapped and chronically ill children. *Child Abuse and Neglect, 3*, 565–575.

Gliedman, J., & Roth, W. (1980). *The unexpected minority: Handicapped children in America*. New York: Harcourt, Brace, Jovanovich.

Goffman, E. (1963). *Stigma: Notes on the management of spoiled identity*. Englewood Cliffs, NJ: Prentice-Hall.

Goldenson, R. M., Dunham, J. R., & Dunham, C. S. (Eds.). (1978). *Disability and rehabilitation handbook*. New York: McGraw-Hill.

Jackman, M. (1983). Enabling the disabled. *Perspectives: The Civil Rights Quarterly, 15*, 23–26.

Kauffman, J. M. (1981). Introduction: Historical trends and contemporary issues in special education in the United States. In J. M. Kauffman & D. P. Hallahan (Eds.), *Handbook of special education*. (pp. 3–23). Englewood Cliffs, NJ: Prentice-Hall.

Lemanek, K. L., Williamson, D. A., Gresham, F. M., & Jensen, B. J. (1986). Social skills training with hearing-impaired children. *Behavior Modification, 10*, 55–71.

Lindemann, J. E. (Ed.). (1981). *Psychological and behavioral aspects of physical disability*. New York: Plenum.

Lynch, M. A. (1975). Ill health and child abuse. *Lancet, 2*, 317.

Matson, J. L., DiLorenzo, T. M., & Andrasik, F. (1983). A review of behavior modification procedures for treating social skill deficits and psychiatric disorders of the mentally retarded. In J. L. Matson & F. Andrasik (Eds.), *Treatment issues and innovations in mental retardation*. New York: Plenum.

Matson, J. L., & Zeiss, R. (1978). Group training of social skills in chronically explosive severely disturbed psychiatric patients. *Behavioral Engineering, 5*, 41–50.

Mulliken, R. K. (1983). Overview. In R. K. Mulliken & J. J. Buckley (Eds.), *Assessment of multihandicapped and developmentally disabled children* (pp. 1–14). Rockville, MD: Aspen.

Ragland, E. U., Kerr, M. M., & Strain, P. S. (1978). Behavior of withdrawn autistic children: Effects of peer social initiations. *Behavior Modification, 2*, 565–578.

Rehabilitation Act of 1973, Pub. L. No. 93–112, 87 Stat. 357 (1973).

Rehabilitation Services Administration. (1981). *Annual report of the Rehabilitation Services Administration* (Publication No. E-80-26000). Washington, DC: U.S. Government Printing Office.

Richardson, S. A. (1976). Attitudes and behavior toward the physically handicapped. *Birth Defects: Original Article Series, 12*, 15–34.

Siller, J. A., Chipman, A., Ferguson, L., & Vann, D. H. (1967). *Studies in reaction of disability: Vol. II. Attitudes of the nondisabled toward the phys-*

ically disabled. New York: New York University School of Education.

Sisson, L. A., Van Hasselt, V. B., Hersen, M., & Strain, P. S. (1985). Peer interventions: Increasing social behaviors in multihandicapped children. *Behavior Modification, 9,* 293–321.

Strain, P. S. (1983). Generalization of autistic children's social behavior change: Effects of developmentally integrated and segregated settings. *Analysis and Intervention in Developmental Disabilities, 3,* 23–34.

Task Force on Psychology and the Handicapped. (1984). Final report of the Task Force on Psychology and the Handicapped. *American Psychologist, 39,* 545–550.

Turner, S. M., Hersen, M., & Bellack, A. S. (1978). Social skills training to teach prosocial behaviors in an organically impaired and retarded patient. *Journal of Behavior Therapy and Experimental Psychiatry, 9,* 253–258.

United States Bureau of the Census. (1976). *Survey of income and education.* Washington, DC: Author.

United States Bureau of the Census. (1983). *Labor force status and other characteristics of persons with a work disability: 1982* (Current Population Reports, Series P-23, No. 127). Washington, DC: U.S. Government Printing Office.

Van Hasselt, V. B. (1983). Social adaptation in the blind. *Clinical Psychology Review, 3,* 87–102.

Van Hasselt, V. B., Hersen, M., Kazdin, A. E., Simon, J., & Mastantuono, A. K. (1983). Training blind adolescents in social skills. *Journal of Visual Impairment and Blindness, 77,* 199–203.

Weicker, L. (1984). Defining liberty for handicapped Americans. *American Psychologist, 39,* 518–523.

Wright, B. (1960). *Physical disability: A psychological approach.* New York: Harper & Row.

CHAPTER 2

Impairments, Handicapping Environments, and Disability: A Life-Span Perspective

Michael A. Smyer, Susan M. McHale, Richard Birkel and Ronald A. Madle

In this chapter, we place the discussion of impairments, handicapping environments, and disability in a life-span perspective. In doing so, we weave together several themes and diverse literature. We begin by considering the definitional issues surrounding three distinct aspects of impaired functioning: impairments, handicaps, and disabilities. These terms often are confused and, at times, substituted for one another; yet each implies a distinct meaning of impairment.

Next we outline the basic elements of a life-span perspective. We use the term "perspective" because those who have developed the conceptual basis of life-span development have repeatedly cautioned that their position does not represent a fully developed theory (e.g., Baltes & Danish, 1980).

In the third section of the chapter, we contrast the life-span perspective with other views of development. One of the elements that a life-span perspective emphasizes is the importance of *context*. A contextual focus necessarily requires a shift away from an exclusive emphasis upon the individual.

Partial support for the preparation of this chapter was provided by Grant No. 2 T32 AG00048-06 from the National Institute on Aging and Grant No. 1 T24 MH17422-02 from the National Institute of Mental Health.

In the final section of the chapter, we highlight several general criteria for assessing the degree, extent, and prognosis of impairment.

DEFINITIONS: IMPAIRMENT, HANDICAP, AND DISABILITY

At the outset of this section we wish to call attention to two problems in current attempts to describe and explain the fluctuations in levels of performance that are characteristic of all individuals over the life course. The first is that terms such as "handicap" and "disability" are cast negatively and presume some decrement in performance from a present standard — a standard that reflects normative evaluations. However, there is no related conceptual framework that describes increments in performance from these same standards. A second problem lies in the fact that when terms such as handicapped, disabled, and impaired are used to describe persons, they tend to identify the source of limitation as intrinsic to the person, pervasive, and more or less permanent. In fact, however, performance levels in particular areas, such as vision, motor abilities, or cognitive skills, do not characterize a person as a whole; nor are these characteristics necessarily permanent or determined wholly by individual factors (Granger, 1984).

In considering these problems, we have chosen to use the following terms and definitions. "Impairment" refers to limitations in functioning or output at the organ-system level. For example, it is useful to talk about "impaired eyesight," "impaired motor coordination," or "impaired blood flow to the brain." Similarly, we prefer to talk about handicapping environments rather than handicapped persons. Finally, we reserve the concept of "disability" for (negative) evaluations of individual capability or performance in specific contexts. A person is likely to suffer a "disability" as a result of the *interaction* of an impairment and a specific context. For example, a person is disabled when, due to impaired heart functioning, she is unable to climb stairs. If all stairs were replaced with elevators, it would not be useful to refer to this person

as disabled any longer. This is more than just a semantic distinction, and it is central to the presentation of a life-span perspective on disability. (For a fuller discussion of these issues, see Gliedman & Roth, 1980.) With these definitions as a point of reference, we now consider the basic elements of a life-span perspective.

LIFE-SPAN DEVELOPMENT: A PERSPECTIVE

Although life-span developmental theory has a long and rich intellectual history (see Baltes & Danish, 1980), contemporary attention to life-span formulations can be traced to a series of conferences and subsequent publications from West Virginia University (e.g., Baltes & Schaie, 1973; Datan & Ginsberg, 1975; Goulet & Baltes, 1970; Nesselroade & Reese, 1973; Turner & Reese, 1980). More recent volumes have continued and expanded the life-span emphasis (e.g., Baltes, 1978; Baltes & Brim, 1979–1984). From these volumes the conceptual and applied elements of a life-span perspective have emerged.

Featherman (1983) has noted that the life-span perspective is not yet a formal theory, with explicit postulates or empirically verifiable hypotheses. Instead, the collection of views and assertions that have come to be labeled life-span development form a guide, or "world view" in Featherman's words, which directs our attention to several elements in the study of constancy and change in human development. Featherman (1983) summarizes the major themes of the perspective:

1. Developmental change occurs over the entire course of life; it is synonymous with aging in the broadest sense. Aging is not limited to any particular time of life; neither is development.
2. Developmental changes in the course of aging reflect biological, social, psychological, physical, and historical events.
3. The multiple determinants of constancy and change in behavior and personality express their influences interactively and cumulatively, defin-

ing life-event or life-history trajectories.

4. Individuals are agents in their own development. Life histories are transactional products of the dialectics among the multiple determinants of development and the motivated, selectively responding person. Generalizations across persons about constancies in human development, especially throughout the last half of life, are few and difficult to formulate.

5. Each new birth cohort potentially ages through a different trajectory of life events, brought about by the impress of sociohistorical change and by individuals' reactions to it. Historically constant generalizations about developmental changes in aging are fewer or greater as a function of the pace and direction of sociohistorical changes, be they evolutionary or revolutionary.

6. Intervention efforts among the aged are effective in changing the course of development, as they are in the young. Behavior and personality apparently remain more malleable throughout the full course of life than becomes apparent in common contemporary social and subcultural settings.

Featherman's summary highlights many of the most important elements of the life-span perspective that are relevant to conceptualizing and working with impaired individuals and their families. It also provides a point of departure for considering several issues inherent in the life-span perspective.

Foremost among these issues is the implicit and explicit view of development. Chandler (1980), for example, notes three sets of assumptions that are questioned by life-span theorists: a monistic view of development, positing a single, universal sequence of growth that ends well before the final portion of the life span and is followed by decrement; a single, universal, and unidirectional sequence in attaining this universal end state of development; and a tacit acknowledgement by both the public and professionals of the ideal end state as well as the process of development. Many of the life-span tenets contradict

these assumptions. Specifically, many have argued that hallmarks of development across the life span are the multidirectional patterns of development that are apparent in many domains (e.g., Baltes, Reese, & Lipsitt, 1980). Closely linked to the variety of patterns of development are the variety of pathways and causes of developmental change. Several scholars have highlighted the influence of historical context (e.g., Elder, 1979), cohort (e.g., Schaie, 1984), familial resources and constraints (e.g., Elder, Liker, & Cross, 1984; Pruchno, Blow, & Smyer, 1984), and personal experience of life events or life stresses (e.g., Callahan & McCluskey, 1983; Reese & Smyer, 1983; Smyer, 1984) among those contributing to the diversity that marks developmental trajectories. To highlight the differences between the life-span perspective and alternative approaches for explaining intra-individual change, we will consider the organismic and mechanistic perspectives, and outline the different implications each has for understanding development and intervention with individuals coping with impairments.

DEVELOPMENTAL MODELS: IMPLICATIONS FOR HANDICAPPED POPULATIONS

Theorists who adopt a life-span perspective have outlined a number of distinctions between this and other approaches to the study of human development (e.g., Lerner, 1985).

The Organismic Position

This perspective, represented by Piaget (1950, 1952) and Freud (1923, 1949), for example, characterizes development as a series of qualitative changes that take place as the individual progresses through a hierarchically organized sequence of stages (Lerner, 1976). This sequence applies universally, being preprogrammed in the species. Differences among individuals can be seen in their rate of progression through the stages, as well as in what final point they achieve. That is, some individuals, perhaps due to a mental or physical impairment, may take longer to move through the stages, or only achieve the beginning steps in the sequence. These individual differences arise because of a person's active role in the developmental process: certain interactions with the physical and social world in combination with a person's current level of functioning promote the movement to more mature stages of development. A final important characteristic of an organismic perspective is that each stage of development applies to all aspects of an individual's functioning. As such, an individual who is impaired cognitively is expected to function socially at the same level. Thus, a deaf child whose language development is delayed also should show delays in cognitive and social realms.

Researchers studying mentally and physically impaired individuals have applied the concepts of stage theory in explaining developmental differences in these populations. Zigler (1966) and Zigler & Harter (1969) suggest that during the heyday of psychoanalysis in this country, Freudian theory was used to "explain" mental retardation. Unusually high rates of crime and illegitimacy in mentally retarded individuals, for instance, were used as evidence that retarded individuals' disabilities stemmed from

> a deficiency in the organization and function of the ego . . . . Not only did the retarded child show impaired development of those ego functions such as reality testing, problem solving, and ability to profit from past experiences, but his ego was seriously handicapped in its capacity to control the demands of the id, e.g., the ability to control aggressive impulses, and to delay gratification. (Zigler & Harter, 1969, p. 1068)

In other words, this impairment was considered to be pervasive, affecting all domains of functioning.

Later theorists have rejected the notion that mental retardation has its basis in a moral or character defect and, similar to those who study the development of children with sensory impairments, explain disabilities as having their basis in cognitive functioning. These researchers have relied on another theorist from the organismic tradition: Jean Piaget. For instance, the stages of development outlined by Piaget have been applied to the study of cognitive and social development of mentally retarded children (e.g., Affleck, 1977; Kahn, 1977) as well as to investigations of development in blind and deaf youngsters (e.g., Fraiberg, 1977; Furth, 1966). These researchers have attempted to document the universality of the Piagetian stages by determining whether children with impairments display the same sequence of stages as do nonimpaired children. In the area of intervention, this approach has been used to argue for providing a systematic sequence of experiences and training for physically or mentally impaired children that would enable them to move through the normal course of development (e.g., Reichler & Schopler, 1976).

The Mechanistic Position

This theoretical perspective also has been used to explain the functioning of individuals coping with impairments and to develop intervention programs for these populations, and is exemplified by the learning and functional analysis approaches (Lerner, 1985). It stands in sharp contrast to the organismic view in that:

1. "Development" is described as involving quantitative rather than qualitative changes.
2. The individual is seen traditionally as a passive recipient of stimulation from the environment, which shapes or determines behavior patterns.
3. Whereas the laws of learning (e.g., those regarding reinforcement and reinforcement contingencies) apply universally, to the extent that individuals have different experiences and reinforcement histories, patterns of behavior will not be universal, but will vary markedly across individuals — even among those at a similar cognitive level.
4. Because behavior patterns are dependent on experiences with the environment, a balance across different

domains of functioning (language, cognitive, social, motor) should not be expected.

Although some writers have attempted to explain the causes of impairments in reinforcement terms without reference to possible biological underpinnings (e.g., Ferster, 1961), most work with populations suffering impairments has focused on intervention procedures (e.g., Azrin & Armstrong, 1973; Palyo, Cooke, Schuler, & Apolloni, 1979). Given the assumptions that there is no one necessary or universal sequence of development and that abilities in one domain (e.g., vision) are not necessarily tied to those in another (e.g., cognition), researchers and professionals who adopt this perspective choose behaviors to instill or modify on the basis of contextual demands. Thus, a mentally retarded child may be toilet trained, the stereotypic behaviors of a schizophrenic adolescent may be extinguished, an autistic child may be taught to produce words or phrases in greeting another person, and a mentally retarded adult may be taught specific motor behaviors as part of vocational training.

The Life-Span Position

The principles that underlie the life-span perspective overlap to some extent with the mechanistic and the organismic traditions, but there are several important differences in substance and emphasis. We have outlined below some of these distinctions that have significant implications for populations coping with impairments.

Universality of Developmental Sequences

The contrast between organismic and mechanistic approaches on this issue is based in each tradition's concepts about the sources of developmental or behavioral change. Specifically, learning theorists see the environment as the source of change, and organismic theorists see interaction with the environment as the means through which the preprogrammed sequence of stages is manifested. In contrast, life-span developmentalists (e.g., Lerner, 1985; Overton, 1984) have adopted

a view midway between these perspectives that has been described as "probabilistic epigenesis," or an "organismic-contextual" view. The underlying assumption here is that individuals and their environments affect one another reciprocally; individuals shape their environments as much as they are shaped by them. Not only do environmental experiences vary by individual and context, but the same experiences later in life will have different effects on the individual because the individual as an organism has changed. So, too, will individuals choose different contexts and experiences due to their past experiences. In short, no one sequence of development is necessary, nor can one be sure that intervening to promote a particular behavior or skill will result in the same outcome for all individuals, because subsequent experiences, which are not predictable, may reinforce or extinguish that training. Thus, for instance, two individuals who spend their childhoods in supportive mainstream school environments may develop very differently as adults. The first may move from a supportive school environment to a group home setting that also supports her needs. In contrast, the other may leave the school environment and find himself in a community that does not offer programs for young adults. In this case there will be discontinuity in the environment and in the individual's subsequent development.

The Importance of Context

A life-span approach differs from an organismic perspective in the idea that patterns of behavior or development will vary depending on context, for instance, home environment, culture, or historical time. It also differs from a mechanistic view in its emphasis on the active role of the individual in choosing and constructing his or her own environment. This emphasis on context, in combination with the notion that development occurs across the life span, has important implications for assessment of persons who must cope with physical and mental impairments, a topic we return to later in this chapter.

In a general way, however, a life-span perspective of context entails several issues. First, the life-span view stresses the notion that which impairments become disabling will vary by context. That is, in certain social groups, at certain historical times, a given condition may or may not be considered disabling.

Second, a life-span view emphasizes the idea that goals for intervention will vary by context. That is, rather than assuming that an individual should be trained to display abilities that comprise a universal developmental sequence, life-span theorists would argue for differential training depending upon the needs and demands of a particular environment. The concept of optimization, promoting an individual's area of greatest skill, which life-span theorists have discussed in the context of development and change in elderly persons, is relevant to disabled populations of all ages. Along these lines, Gold (1975) has argued for optimizing areas of competence in persons with impairments as a means of promoting their integration into the mainstream of society. Gold's argument, labeled the competence-deviance hypothesis, holds that "the more competence an individual has, the more deviance will be tolerated in him by others," with competence being defined as "attributes, skills, etc., which not everyone has, and which are needed and appreciated by someone else," and deviance defined as "aspects of the individual which cause negative attention" (p. 260). In other words, rather than training persons with impairments to look or behave normally, intervention should involve optimizing special areas of ability.

This notion differs from work in the mechanistic tradition, in that multiple levels of analysis and the entire life span are taken into consideration. Thus, the context is not simply the reinforcement contingencies that operate concurrently upon a child's behavior, but the social and political context in which the individual's youth, adulthood, and old age will be spent (Lerner, 1985). For individuals with impairments, this means that early training must take into account the demands of both current and future contexts.

The Timing of Experiences in Development

Within the organismic tradition is a notion that at any given stage, certain experiences are critical in promoting normal growth. That is, "the timing of nature–nurture interaction is crucial for adaptive organism development . . . across normal development, there is a prescribed normative co-occurrence of the variables providing the basis of development" (Lerner, 1985, p. 171). According to the organismic perspective, because the ground plan for development is programmed into the individual, the individual's stage in the sequence of maturation determines which experiences are essential at any given time. This concept, called the critical period hypothesis, holds that an individual must be exposed to certain experiences at certain times during development in order for normal growth to occur. This idea is one basic assumption behind early intervention programs such as preschool education programs (Head Start) for disadvantaged children. At the extreme, this view holds that intervention will not be successful unless it occurs at a specific time during development.

In contrast, the life-span perspective argues against the critical-period notion that optimal organism–environment interactions are invariant across individuals: "there is little use for a concept which prescribes normative co-occurrences of variables. Instead, the qualitative and quantitative changes composing an organism's development derive from variables that co-occur in a probabilistic manner" (Lerner, 1985, p. 172).

The concept of plasticity — that an individual's developmental trajectory can be modified at any point across the life span — is fundamental to the views of many life-span theorists. This perspective is optimistic about the effectiveness of intervention at different points in a person's life and stands in sharp contrast to views that intervention efforts should occur early in life if they are to be successful.

The flip side of this critical-period argument also has implications for individuals with impairments. Specifically, the critical-period notion has been used to argue that if certain experiences occur (early in life) and set the organism on a "normal" course, then development is unlikely to go awry. Thus, if a child with a physical impairment is reared in a warm family environment and has experience in a supportive school program, one may expect the child to become a secure and self-confident adult later in life. On the other hand, given the emphasis life-span researchers place on later life events, from this perspective such an individual would be expected to require special support throughout adult life. That is, feelings of depression or low self-esteem in adults who are experiencing disabilities may arise not only from unresolved childhood experiences, but from significant experiences during adult life that also have the power to influence their sense of well-being.

Stability and Change in Development

With an emphasis on development throughout the life span — even into the very latest stages of life — the life-span perspective comes out clearly on the side of the plasticity of the organism and the malleability of performance and function. This assumption is in contrast to other scholars who argue that beyond a certain early period of plasticity, behavioral functioning and development achieves marked stability fairly quickly in both impaired and unimpaired individuals (e.g., Kopp & McCall, 1982). The issue of stability versus change is not limited to early childhood, however. Much attention has also been focused on the plasticity of behavior, cognition, and personality in late adulthood (e.g., Baltes, Honn, Barton, Orzech, & Lago, 1983; Baltes & Willis, 1982; Costa & McRae, 1980; Nesselroade & Ford, 1985).

Closely linked to the debate on stability and change is a consideration of issues of continuity and discontinuity in development. Here again, life-span scholars posit a controversial view that emphasizes discontinuity in development. This assumption is a natural concomitant of multi-directional, multicausal depictions of development.

As noted, life-span theorists have suggested that another important aspect of developmental trajectories across the life span is selective optimization with compensation (e.g., Baltes, 1984; Baltes, Dittmann-Kohli, & Dixon, 1984). These terms are used to describe the process of individual adaptation to aging. In selective optimization across the life span, individuals increasingly focus their resources (cognitive, psychological, social, physical) into selective and compensatory efforts to accomplish "life mastery and 'successful' aging" (Baltes et al., 1984). These strategies of selective optimization are influenced by and responsive to the range of influences noted above (e.g., historical change, and normative and nonnormative events).

A life-span perspective emphasizes the importance of viewing development within a context. Much of the life-span research is an effort to delineate the influence of context on life-course trajectories. Bronfenbrenner (1979, 1983), whose work traditionally has not been considered within the scope of the life-span school, nonetheless has contributed greatly to an appreciation of the complexity of environmental influences — from the individual's immediate physical environment to the larger sociocultural matrix of shared values and social policy that shape his or her experience of the world (Smyer & Crews, 1985). In the next section we see how the role of context can be extended to assessment of disability.

ASSESSING DISABILITIES AND HANDICAPPING CONDITIONS

Life-span development has multiple causes, including age-graded, history-graded, and nonnormative influences. The individual who attempts to cope with a physical impairment, for example, does so in a context that is uniquely determined by the current constellation of these three sets of forces. As a result, the effects of an impairment vary over the course of the individual's life, under different environmental, economic, and social conditions, and are mediated by a host of idiosyncratic events occurring in the individual's lifetime. Given such complexity, the role of assessment becomes increasingly important at the same time that its scope is broadened. Not only will skills, needs, and aspirations vary over an individual's lifetime, but the skill demands, opportunities, and accessibility of the environment will change in the course of each generation as well. Assessment as a means of guiding action, then, must focus not only on the individual, but on the environment and the degree of congruence between the two as well.

Indeed, a life-span orientation to disability implies a reconceptualization of the very *purpose* of assessment. While it is clear that the individual attempting to cope with an impairment often has a difficult time achieving a good fit in an environment created for those without impairments, the cumulative lifelong effects of such experience have been acknowledged less often. The environmental message of a community that is poorly designed and planned for those with impairments is, "You are not welcome here; this place is dangerous and hostile." In contrast, a town like Berkeley, California, which has demonstrated its concern for the welfare of the physically impaired population with such visible acts as curb cuts, timed stoplights, and ramps provides a message of acceptance and security. Said one individual of his experience in Berkeley, "If they care enough to make things physically accessible, which was never true anywhere else I lived, then probably they will also be more accepting of me personally." Said another: "It is only since coming to Berkeley that I can see myself as a person important to society" (Lifchez, 1979, p. 474).

No longer is it enough to plan for person-environment congruence in some far-distant future; congruence *in the present* and for those at *each developmental level* is the goal.

A life-span orientation, then, broadens our concern to include optimal person-environment fit for those with impairments throughout their lives. A variety of factors is involved in establishing such congruence. We focus here on two classes of contributors: age-graded and history-graded.

Age-Graded Influences

The onset of an impairment — when it first occurs during the life span — has a major effect on the individual's development and well-being. The person suffering a stroke at age 60 may simply opt for early retirement, while the person suffering the same event at age 40 may have to make major, disruptive career adjustments or suffer financially. Thus, the effects of an impairment are mediated by the particular life stage of the individual. In certain cases, the onset of a disabling condition may intensify an already difficult developmental transition (adolescence, for example, or first entry to school), while in other cases the onset of an impairment may actually ease a transition, such as retirement.

The age of onset of an impairment also will determine the number of "life spheres" that are affected and the number of roles the individual is forced to disrupt or alter. An individual who is first faced with a severe impairment during his or her adult, childrearing years may have to alter parental, career, marital, and community roles quite extensively, whereas the individual born with severe impairments may never have the opportunity to invest in such roles.

The age of onset of an impairment also affects the length of time the individual can expect to make special adjustments to the condition. This has implications for the rate and timing of resource expenditure (finances, for example), the scope of life planning necessary, and the development of "secondary disabilities." Many people who acquire a physical impairment early in life, for example, are subject to degenerative disease (high blood pressure, emphysema, osteoarthritis, etc.) earlier than normal. Osteoarthritis, the arthritic condition that stems from the normal degeneration of weight-bearing joints, is likely to occur earlier in life for those whose physical impairments force them to overuse certain areas of their bodies, such as the arms and shoulders in the case of individuals who are partially paralyzed (DeLoach, Wilkins, & Walker, 1983).

Similarly, the side effects, modalities, and length of hospitalization involved in treatment must be considered in the context of the individual's remaining life span. Treatments with serious negative side effects are not likely to be considered in cases where the individual's remaining life span is known to be quite short. Treatment effects also must be considered in the context of the individual's stage of development. Treatment side effects that are likely to adversely affect body image, self-image, and normal activity may best be postponed until after significant life transitions, such as adolescence, are completed if we are particularly concerned with person-environment fit.

It is natural, too, for the individual's concerns to change at different stages in development. For example, a young child with a forearm amputation may resist being fitted for a prosthesis because he finds that he can adapt well without it; but at adolescence his concerns, and hence the degree of fit experienced, are likely to change dramatically. At this stage, the individual, now more concerned with body image and appeal to opposite-sex peers, may demand to be fitted with a prosthesis immediately. Although this change of heart may be predictable, it nonetheless poses a problem in that the teenager has now lost years of adaptive training and experience with a prosthetic arm.

This example leads to the final point in regard to age at onset. Adults who were beset by physical impairment early in life have dealt with the ramifications and problems it brings for considerable time and over different developmental stages. As a result, they have extensive experience in the practical aspects of adjustment as well as hard-gained insight that is of vital use to professionals and peers with lesser experience. In considering the possibilities for improving person-environment congruence, then, we should be particularly conscious of "recycling the resources" of those with lifelong, valuable experience.

History-Graded Influences

Modifications in the context in which adaptation to an impairment must occur result not only from the individual's development, but from technological, scientific, political, and social changes as well. DeLoach and colleagues suggest that technological advances in functional aids and job engineering and modifications make it difficult for professionals to predict the self-care or job potential of any physically or mentally impaired individual (DeLoach, Wilkins, & Walker, 1983). Similarly, changes in social programs and in guiding values and assumptions (paradigms) applied to disability in society will have a major impact on the difficulty or ease of adaptation of the person coping with an impairment. Dealing with the implications of recent and historical changes in scientific and social paradigms for the understanding and treatment of impairment is beyond the scope of this chapter, but the ultimate ramifications of such shifts in values and knowledge can be seen in the specific contexts that exist and are developing for helping those with physical and mental impairments.

Increasingly, positive outcomes for impaired persons are being reported among settings that stress a social development approach to helping and living (Taber, 1980). Taber, in a review of the literature on alternative care for persons with physical and mental impairments, suggests that this approach is characterized by three features: (a) a clear focus on specific role performance or specific features of the social environment that need to be improved, (b) more involvement by nonprofessionals in helping those with impairments, and (c) a definition of modest and immediate goals of change.

The necessity of providing a variety of role experiences for those with physical and mental impairments is particularly important. Recently, Coopersmith (1984), in describing his favorable impression of California's L'Arche community for individuals with physical impairments, summed up his views of how traditional settings often restrict the individual in role options, thus turning a physical impairment into a handicap:

> In families and larger systems with handicapped members, relationships are generally structured and viewed as complementary. The handicapped person is often frozen in such positions as follower, recipient of care, or perpetual learner while the so-called nonhandicapped person serves as leader, caregiver, or teacher. Opportunities for shifting this rigid complementarity or for achieving symmetry are often nonexistent and the reified roles perpetuate one another. (p. 155)

In contrast, the roles and hierarchy at L'Arche community are flexible, giving those with impairments access to leadership and teaching positions. Symmetrical relationships among equals are available to everyone, thus allowing growth and change.

In regard to the second emphasis, we have already stressed the importance of peer counseling and of recycling the valuable resources of experienced individuals within the community of disabled. Such an approach focuses attention on the process by which individuals with physical and mental impairments come to view themselves as "handicapped," and to the salubrious impact of competent role models (Gliedman & Roth, 1980).

Finally, a focus upon modest and immediate goals of change (either in the environment or the person) recognizes that successfully coping with disability is a lifelong process in which the value of ongoing person-environment congruency should not be underestimated. Very often, small adjustments in settings or among persons can produce important and immediate payoffs in personal well-being, feelings of security, and productivity.

SUMMARY

In this chapter we have outlined the relevance of a life-span perspective on human development to research and intervention with individuals with impairments. A topic we have not discussed, however, is how work with persons who are coping with mental and physical impairments can serve to inform students of life-span human development. Gliedman and Roth (1980) for instance, have argued that studying individuals with impairments may provide unique insights about fundamental aspects of development. As these authors note,

> The study of how handicapped children grow up may provide the developmental psychologist with a crucial litmus test, a way to sort out the degree to which today's theories of personality, social behavior, and intellectual growth are culture-bound or culturally unbiased. (pp. 62–64)

Equally important, professionals and lay persons who are concerned about the welfare of those who must cope with a physical or mental impairment require a great deal more information than currently is available. During the past decade, the public has been made aware of the stigmas associated with having a disabling condition, and social programs have been directed at moving persons with physical and mental impairments into the mainstream of education, occupation, and residence. The research community must follow this lead and direct an increased share of its resources to studying what is common and what is unique about the development of those of us who must struggle to adjust to impairments in the context of handicapping environments.

REFERENCES

Affleck, G. (1977). Interpersonal competence of the mentally retarded: A Piagetian perspective. In P. Mittler (Ed.), *Research to practice in mental retardation: Vol. 2. Education and training* (pp. 85–91). Baltimore: University Park Press.

Azrin, N. H., & Armstrong, P. M. (1973). The "mini-meal" — a method for teaching eating skills to the profoundly retarded. *Mental Retardation, 11,* 9–13.

Baltes, P. B. (Ed.) (1978). *Life-span development and behavior: Vol. 1.* New York: Academic Press.

Baltes, P. B. (1984, August). *Life-span developmental psychology: Implications for research and practice.* Invited address presented at the

92nd annual convention of the American Psychological Association, Toronto, Canada.

Baltes, P. B., & Brim, O. G., Jr. (Eds.). (1979–1984). *Life-span development and behavior (Vols. 2–6).* New York: Academic Press.

Baltes, P. B., & Danish, S. J. (1980). Intervention in life-span development and aging: Issues and concepts. In R. R. Turner & H. W. Reese (Eds.), *Life-span developmental psychology: Intervention* (pp. 49–78). New York: Academic Press.

Baltes, P. B., Dittmann-Kohli, F., & Dixon, R. A. (1984). New perspective on the development of intelligence in adulthood: Towards a dual-process conception and a model of selective optimization with compensation. In P. B. Baltes & O. G. Brim, Jr. (Eds.), *Life-span development and behavior: Vol. 6* (pp. 34–76). New York: Academic Press.

Baltes, M., Honn, S., Barton, B., Orzech, M., & Lago, D. (1983). On the social ecology of dependence and independence in elderly nursing home residents: A replication and extension. *Journal of Gerontology, 38,* 556–564.

Baltes, P. B., Reese, H. W., & Lipsitt, L. P. (1980). Life-span developmental psychology. *Annual Review of Psychology, 31,* 65–110.

Baltes, P. B., & Schaie, K. W. (Eds.). (1973). *Life-span developmental psychology: Personality and socialization.* New York: Academic Press.

Baltes, P. B., & Willis, S. L. (1982). Plasticity and enhancement of intellectual functioning in old age: Penn State's Adult Development and Enrichment Project (ADEPT). In F. I. M. Craik & S. E. Trehub (Eds.), *Aging and cognitive processes* (pp. 353–389). New York: Plenum.

Bronfenbrenner, U. (1979). *The ecology of human development: Experiments by nature and design.* Cambridge, MA: Harvard University Press.

Bronfenbrenner, U. (1983). The context of development and the development of context. In R. M. Lerner (Ed.), *Developmental psychology: Historical and philosophical perspectives* (pp. 147–184). Hillsdale, NJ: Lawrence Erlbaum Associates.

Callahan, E. J., & McCluskey, K. A. (Eds.). (1983). *Life-span developmental psychology: Nonnormative life events.* New York: Academic Press.

Chandler, M. J. (1980). Life-span intervention as a symptom of conversion hysteria. In R. R. Turner & H. W. Reese (Eds.), *Life-span developmental psychology: Intervention* (pp. 79–91). New York: Academic Press.

Coopersmith, E. I. (1984). A special "family" with handicapped members: One family therapist's learning from the L'Arche Community. In E. I. Coopersmith (Ed.), *Families with handicapped members.* Rockville, MD: Aspen.

Costa, P. T., & McCrae, R. R. (1980). Still stable after all these years: Personality as a key to some issues in adulthood and old age. In P. B. Baltes & O. G. Brim, Jr. (Eds.), *Life-span development and behavior: Vol. 3* (pp. 65–102). New York: Academic Press.

Datan, N., & Ginsberg, L. H. (Eds.). (1975). *Life-span developmental psychology: Normative life crises.* New York: Academic Press.

DeLoach, C. P., Wilkins, R. D., & Walker, G. W. (1983). *Independent living: Philosophy, process, and services.* Baltimore, MD: University Park Press.

Elder, G. H. (1979). Historical change in life patterns and personality. In P. B. Baltes & O. G. Brim, Jr. (Eds.), *Life-span development and behavior: Vol. 2* (pp. 117–159). New York: Academic Press.

Elder, G. H., Liker, J. K., & Cross, C. E. (1984). Parent–child behavior in the Great Depression: Life course and intergenerational influences. In P. B. Baltes & O. G. Brim, Jr. (Eds.), *Life-span development and behavior: Vol. 6* (pp. 109–158). New York: Academic Press.

Featherman, D. L. (1983). Life-span perspectives in social science research. In P. B. Baltes & O. G. Brim, Jr. (Eds.), *Life-span development and behavior: Vol. 5* (pp. 1–57). New York: Academic Press.

Ferster, C. B. (1961). Positive reinforcement and behavioral deficits in autistic children. *Child Development, 32,* 437–456.

Fraiberg, S. (1977). *Insights from the blind.* New York: Basic Books.

Freud, S. (1923). *The ego and the id.* London: Hogarth.

Freud, S. (1949). *Outline of psychoanalysis.* New York: Norton.

Furth, H. (1966). *Thinking without language: Psychological implications of deafness.* New York: Free Press.

Gliedman, J., & Roth, W. (1980). *The unexpected minority: Handicapped children in America.* New York: Harcourt Brace Jovanovich.

Gold, M. W. (1975). Vocational training. In J. Norti (Ed.), *Mental retardation and developmental disabilities: An annual review: Vol VII.*

Goulet, L. R., & Baltes, P. B. (Eds.). (1970). *Life-span developmental psychology: Research and theory.* New York: Academic Press.

Granger, C. (1984, December). *Goals for rehabilitation of the handicapped elderly: A conceptual approach.* Paper presented at the Conference on Aging and Rehabilitation of the National

Institute of Handicapped Research, Washington, DC.

Kahn, J. (1977). Piaget's theory of cognitive development and its relationship to severely and profoundly retarded children. In P. Mittler (Ed.), *Research to practice in mental retardation: Vol. 2. Education and training* (pp. 77–83). Baltimore: University Park Press.

Kopp, C. B., & McCall, R. B. (1982). Predicting later mental performance for normal, at-risk, and handicapped infants. In P. B. Baltes & O. G. Brim, Jr. (Eds.), *Life-span development and behavior: Vol. 4* (pp. 33–61). New York: Academic Press.

Lerner, R. M. (1976). *Concepts and theories of human development.* Reading, MA: Addison-Wesley.

Lerner, R. M. (1985). Individual and context in developmental psychology: Concepts and theoretical issues. In J. R. Nesselroade & A. Von Eye (Eds.), *Individual development and social change: Explanatory analyses* (pp. 155–187). New York: Academic Press.

Lifchez, R. (1979). The environment as a support system for independent living. *Archives of Physical and Medical Rehabilitation, 60,* 467–476.

Nesselroade, J. R., & Ford, D. H. (1985). P-technique comes of age: Multivariate, replicated, single-subject designs for research on older adults. *Research on Aging, 7,* 46–80.

Nesselroade, J. R., & Reese, H. W. (Eds.). (1973). *Life-span developmental psychology: Methodological issues.* New York: Academic Press.

Overton, W. (1984). World views and their influence on psychological theory and research: Kuhn-Lakatos-Lauden. In H. W. Reese (Ed.), *Advances in child development and behavior.* New York: Academic Press.

Palyo, W. J., Cooke, T. P., Schuler, A. L., & Apolloni, T. (1979). Modifying echolalic speech in preschool children: Training and generalization. *American Journal of Mental Deficiency, 83,* 480–489.

Piaget, J. (1950). *The psychology of intelligence.* London: Routledge & Kegan Paul.

Piaget, J. (1952). *The origins of intelligence in children.* New York: International Universities Press.

Pruchno, R. A., Blow, F. C., & Smyer, M. A. (1984). Life events and interdependent lives. *Human Development, 27,* 31–41.

Reese, H. W., & Smyer, M. A. (1983). The dimensionalization of life events. In E. J. Callahan & K. A. McCluskey (Eds.), *Life-span developmental psychology: Non-normative life events* (pp. 1–33). New York: Academic Press.

Reichler, R. J., & Schopler, E. (1976). Developmental therapy: A program model for providing individual services in the community. In E. Schopler & R. J. Reichler (Eds.). *Psychopathology and child development* (pp. 347–372). New York: Plenum.

Schaie, K. W. (1984). Historical time and cohort effects. In K. A. McCluskey & H. W. Reese (Eds.), *Life-span developmental psychology: Historical and generational effects* (pp. 1–15). New York: Academic Press.

Smyer, M. A. (1984). Life transitions and aging: Implications for counseling older adults. *The Counseling Psycologist, 12,* 17–28.

Smyer, M. A., & Crews, D. E. (1985). "Developmental" intervention and aging: Demographic and economic changes as a context for intervention. In D. A. Kleiber & M. L. Maehr (Eds.), *Advances in motivation and achievement* (pp. 189–215). Guilford, CT: JAI Press.

Taber, M. A. (1980). *The social context of helping: A review of the literature on alternative care for the physically and mentally handicapped.* (DHHS Publication No. ADM 80–842. Washington, DC: U.S. Government Printing Office.

Turner, R. R., & Reese, H. W. (Eds.). (1980). *Life-span developmental psychology: Intervention.* New York: Academic Press.

Zigler, E. F. (1966). Mental retardation: Current issues and approaches. In L. W. Hoffman & M. L. Hoffman (Eds.), *Review of child development research: Vol. 2* (pp. 107–168). New York: Russell Sage.

Zigler, E. F., & Harter, S. (1969). The socialization of the mentally retarded. In D. A. Goslin (Ed.), *Handbook of socialization theory and research* (pp. 1065–1102). Chicago: Rand McNally.

CHAPTER 3

Issues in the Psychological Evaluation of Children

James E. Ysseldyke and Douglas Marston

We have been asked to describe issues in the psychological evaluation of children with developmental and physical disabilities. We have organized our response around what we see as a variety of conceptual, technical, social, political, and economic issues. Within this context we will examine assessment as the process of collecting information for the purposes of (a) specifying and verifying problems and (b) making decisions about individuals (Salvia & Ysseldyke, 1985). Reynolds and Birch (1977) note that assessment is incontrovertibly linked to programming and argue the primary purpose is to develop the best match between diagnosis and effective intervention. In discussing the various issues presented here, this notion will become a predominant theme: assessment does not exist in a vacuum, but is engaged in for several purposes.

Assessment is a practice integral to making decisions about people. In our society there is a fundamental concern for accuracy, justice, and fairness in making decisions about individuals. Many of the issues we describe are issues precisely because of this concern.

CONCEPTUAL ISSUES

Confusion of Purpose

Psychologists have been accused often of engaging in assessment activities with no suitable purpose. Such practice is evidenced when psychologists engage in the ritualistic practice of routine assessment "because it is the thing to do." Whereas assessment should be a process of collecting data for the purpose of making educational or psychological decisions (Salvia & Ysseldyke, 1985), too often it is the process of collecting data for the purpose of collecting data.

Tests are used in educational settings for making referral, screening, classification, instructional, and evaluation decisions. In other settings they are used for making career-planning decisions. Individuals may be provided with test data so they can make decisions about themselves, or a professional may use the data to make decisions for an individual. Assessment data may be used for the purpose of classification in settings other than schools. Individuals are classified for purposes of institutional placement and ascertaining eligibility for specific social services.

It is essential that different kinds of assessment information be collected for the purpose of making the different kinds of decisions. For example, in making decisions about whether or not a person should be classified as mentally retarded, a psychologist will administer an intelligence test. The information derived from the test will be of assistance in the process of making a classification decision. The same information (data on performance on an intelligence test) will be of limited value and assistance in instructional decisions. In this case, it is necessary to know precisely the skills that pupils do and do not have. A major shortcoming in psychological evaluation is the failure on the part of professionals to differentiate their assessment and data collection strategies as a function of the kind of decision to be made.

Thurlow and Ysseldyke (1979) surveyed child-service demonstration centers, model programs for learning-disabled students, for the purpose of identifying the kinds of assessment devices that were used to make different kinds of decisions. They found a general failure on the part of personnel in the model programs to differentiate their assessment strategies and activities. The same tests were used for making eligibility, instructional, and evaluation decisions. Ysseldyke, Algozzine, Regan, and Potter (1980) used a computer-simulated decision-making process to study the kinds of assessment devices administered and assessment data collected by professionals as they made classification and instructional decisions. They found that professionals did not differentiate their assessment devices and activities as a function of the kind of decision to be made.

Thurlow and Ysseldyke (1982) investigated congruence between the kinds of data that teachers need for planning instructional programs and the kinds of data that school psychologists collect. They found that school psychologists did not differentiate their assessment strategies and activities in making classification and instructional planning decisions.

Definitional Dilemmas

One major assessment activity is classification. We classify usually to determine eligibility for services, though often those who classify assume that the practice of doing so helps in making treatment decisions. Two major classification systems are used by those concerned with developmental and physical disabilities: the categorical systems specified by the U.S. Department of Education and the system specified in DSM-III, the *Diagnostic and Statistical Manual* of the American Psychiatric Association. Psychologists are expected to carry out evaluations that will enable them to differentiate people into categories, and the categories are insufficiently or inadequately defined.

Those who use the definitions specified in Public Law 94–142, the Education for All Handicapped Children Act, to assess individuals, must differentiate among students who evidence 11 different kinds of handicapping conditions. Yet, the conditions are imprecisely defined, and it is necessary for states to specify criteria to be used to indicate existence of the conditions. Different states specify different criteria; school districts sometimes use state criteria and sometimes do not; individual psychologists sometimes act in accordance with district criteria and sometimes do not. For example, the most recent federal definition of "specific learning disabilities" is:

a disorder in one or more of the basic psychological processes involved in understanding or in using language, spoken or written, which may manifest itself in an imperfect ability to listen, think, read, write, spell, or do mathematical calculations. The term includes such conditions as perceptual handicaps, brain injury, minimal brain dysfunction, dyslexia, and development aphasia. The term does not include children who have learning problems which are primarily the result of visual, hearing, or motor handicaps, of mental retardation, emotional disturbance, or of environmental, cultural, or economic disadvantage. (USOE, 1977, p. 65083).

Diagnostic personnel are required to identify individuals as learning disabled and to differentiate them from those who are not learning disabled. They have no basis for doing so. They are faced by such impossible tasks as deciding when an ability is imperfect, deciding what a psychological process is, measuring psychological processes, and deciding whether a learning difficulty is due to cultural disadvantage. The definitions of mental retardation, seriously emotionally disturbed, and speech and language impaired are filled with similar vagaries and lead to similar dilemmas in operationalization.

One might quickly be led to think that definitional dilemmas are restricted to mildly handicapping conditions and to conditions that are said to be subjectively determined. It is often argued that such dilemmas are not encountered when professionals must make such so-called objective decisions as to whether or not individuals exhibit vision or hearing problems. All definitions of all handicapping conditions are subjective definitions. Professionals who must make classification decisions must make subjective decisions. For example, the legal definition of blindness specifies that vision must be 20/200 or worse in the better eye. That number is arbitrary. Why not 20/190 or 19/210? The criterion was arrived at subjectively. In determining eligibility for special education, professionals must find evidence of any of 11 conditions of exceptionality. In fact, what professionals are doing is to declare individuals abnormal. Special education is a subsystem of regular education

that exists for the purpose of educating individuals whom school personnel consider to be abnormal (Ysseldyke & Algozine, 1984). This, then, adds one more piece to the definitional dilemma of the psychologist. Perceptions of normal and abnormal change over time; they also change from location to location. This may explain why different kinds of students have been declared eligible for special education services over time, why different kinds of students are considered eligible in different states, and why a student can be considered handicapped in one state and entirely normal in another.

Deciding Where to Begin and How to Proceed

Typically, individuals who are experiencing developmental and/or physical disabilities do not refer themselves to diagnostic personnel. Rather, someone else refers them. Sarason and Doris (1979) state the point well:

The diagnostic process is always a consequence of somebody saying that someone has something wrong with him. We put it this way because frequently it is not the individual who decides to initiate the process. This is the case with children, but there are also times when adults are forced by pressures from others or by legal action to participate in the process. In all of those instances people individually or society in general communicate four ideas: something may be wrong with someone; our lives are being affected; we should find out the source of the trouble; and we should come up with solutions to alter the individual's status and allow us to experience our lives in the way we wish. (p. 128)

When individuals come to the attention of diagnostic specialists, those specialists must decide what they are going to do. Ysseldyke and Algozzine (1983a) describe three fundamental approaches to assessment. These approaches differ as a function of perceived causality of problems and as a function of examiner training and beliefs.

Diagnosing the Learner

Most often, the question in psychological evaluation is "What is wrong with the person?" Tests are administered as part of a process that Sarason and Doris (1979) refer to as a "search for pathology." Tests are administered in an effort to identify within-person deficits, dysfunctions, disorders, or disabilities that may be causing the problems the individual is experiencing. The most common approach to diagnosing the learner consists of administering norm-referenced tests (e.g., intelligence, achievement, or personality tests) and a "profiling" of the learner's strengths and weaknesses relative to those of his or her peers. The practice of diagnosing the learner has been criticized repeatedly and soundly. It is argued that such an approach is technically inadequate (Ysseldyke & Marston, 1982b) and seldom leads to effective instruction (Englemann, Granzin, & Severson, 1979). As such an approach has been criticized, its proponents have made their strategies and techniques more sophisticated. Today, we witness elaborate efforts to specify psycholinguistic, neuropsychological, cognitive, and perceptual strengths and weaknesses. The purpose behind doing so is an alleged increase in the efficiency and effectiveness of prescribing instruction. Engelmann et al. (1979) argue that such approaches are so far removed from instructional reality as to render them of very little value.

Diagnosing Instruction

A fundamentally different approach to assessment is evidenced in efforts in which diagnostic personnel begin assessment with instructional diagnosis. Engelmann et al. (1979) state that "the purpose of instructional diagnosis is to determine aspects of instruction that are inadequate, to find out precisely how they are inadequate, and to imply what must be done to correct their inadequacy" (p. 361). Instructional diagnosis consists of an investigation of the extent to which the principles of learning are being appropriately applied to instruction and to which teachers are engaging in the correct behaviors.

Assessing Opportunity to Learn

Recently, there have been many investigations of the extent to which pupils, both handicapped and nonhandicapped, are actively engaged in responding to instruction (Berliner, 1980; Borg, 1980; Greenwood, Delquadri, Stanley, Terry, & Hall, 1981). Repeatedly, investigators report few opportunities to learn created by very limited actively engaged time. Ysseldyke and Algozzine (1983) recommend that assessment begin by investigating the instruction occurring in classroom situations. Only when it has been demonstrated that students have adequate amounts of time to learn, and that what is being taught is appropriate, is diagnosing the learner recommended. For example, Squires, Huitt, and Segars (1983) have cited several studies that demonstrate if deficiences in prior classroom learning are assessed and remediated, most pupils can learn academic skills typically mastered by only the best pupils (Anderson, 1973; Arlin, 1973; Block, 1970; Ozecelik, 1974).

The Belief That Tests Give Us More Than They Do

No discussion of conceptual issues in psychological evaluation would be complete without at least a superficial treatment of the problems encountered when the users of tests assume the tests give them more than they actually do. Tyler (1984) states the point well when she warns us that tests measure only relative standing on traits common to many people; they do not give information about characteristics unique to individuals. "Tests do not tell us *how* a person thinks, *how* he/she earns scores, or *how* a person learns" (p. 48). Tyler states that

> What test scores give us are *clues* to be followed as we deal with the children and adults for whose welfare we have some responsibility. The scores mean something, but in order to know what, we must consider each individual case in an empathic way, combining test evidence with everything else we know about the person" (p. 50).

INTERPRETING TEST SCORES

When a child is referred for psychological or educational services it is essential that appropriate assessment procedures be employed by the diagnostician. The misuse of test scores is common in psychological assessment. Instances of misuse are most evident when grade equivalents and percentiles are used to interpret test profiles, or when profile analysis or scatter analysis are used to identify individual strengths and weaknesses or to diagnose handicapping conditions.

Percentile and grade equivalent (GE) scores are highly susceptible to overinterpretation. GE scores do not accurately represent scores achieved by students performing below or above grade level, since these scores are only estimates (Jenkins, Deno, & Mirkin, 1979). The use of normal curve equivalent (NCE) scores is a viable alternative, yet use is limited to those times that coincide with the test's norming periods. In practice, grade equivalents and percentile ranks are sometimes averaged. Thorndike and Hagen (1979) point out that GEs and percentile ranks are not equal interval units, and the aggregation or averaging of these scores must be viewed with caution.

Use of subtest scatter is also problematic. Recent federal definitions of learning disabilities specify that a significant discrepancy between a child's ability and his or her actual achievement must be demonstrated. How a child performs on standardized tests of intelligence and achievement has great impact on whether he or she is pronounced learning disabled. Similarly, discrepancy or variability among subtests of intelligence measures, commonly referred to as subtest scatter, is viewed as indicative of learning difficulties (Sattler, 1974).

Neither practice is without severe limitations. First, the reliability of difference scores may be unacceptable (Cronbach & Furby, 1970; Salvia & Clark, 1973). Thorndike and Hagen (1979) cite an example where two tests with high reliabilities (.90) and substantial intercorrelation (.80) produce a reliability of difference score of only .50. This situation is not uncommon in learning disability (LD) assessment, where intelligence and achievement measures with high reliabilities and intercorrelations are used to make decisions that are probably unreliable.

Evidence refuting the use of subtest scatter as indicative of learning disabilities is compelling. In several studies, no significant differences between LD and non-LD children were found on WISC-R verbal-performance discrepancy scores (Kallos, Grabow, & Guarino, 1961; Rudel & Denckla, 1976). In addition, examination of subtest scatter on the WISC-R in normal populations suggests that considerable variability is present (Kaufman, 1976); similar variability has been found for the Woodcock-Johnson Battery (Marston & Ysseldyke, 1984). In sum, the practice of interpreting discrepancy scores as diagnostic indicators of learning disabilities raises many concerns. Certainly, as Hallahan and Bryan (1981) conclude, "It is inadvisable to use discrepancy scores as the sole criterion for designating a child as learning disabled" (p. 143).

TECHNICAL ADEQUACY

One of the fundamental assumptions in the use of assessment information to make decisions about students is that the tests used in the collection of information are technically adequate. To the extent that error is present or tests do not measure what they purport to measure, decision making is adversely affected. One of the major contemporary issues in assessment is the widespread use of technically inadequate tests to make decisions about students. It is specified in Public Law 94–142, the Education for All Handicapped Children Act, that tests must be valid for the purposes for which they are used. A substantive issue in very many recent court cases on assessment of individuals with developmental and physical disabilities has been the validity of the tests used to assess those individuals.

Validity

The concept of validity relates to how well a test measures what it purports to assess (Nunnally, 1967). For example, if a measure of emotional disturbance is valid it must be demonstrated that the procedure is an actual index of this domain. Nunnally delineates four types of validity: face, content, criterion, and construct.

Face validity provides the most superficial evidence of a measure's integrity. "How good the test looks" is accepted as substantiation of the test as a worthwhile measure. While the "appearance" of a test and its format are an obvious factor during test selection, it would hardly rate consideration as the sole criterion in judging the validity of the measure.

A more thorough understanding of a test's validity can be achieved by content validity analysis. Such a process usually involves an examination of the items that are included in the assessment by one of two approaches: expert judgment of inter-item correlational analysis.

The most popular method of determining the validity of a test is the analysis of a measure's criterion validity. One type of criterion validity referred to as predictive validity, relates to how well a test predicts performance on a similar assessment procedure. Typically, this investigation focuses upon the association between two measures as evaluated by Pearson Product-Moment Correlations, partial correlation techniques, and multiple regression methodology. A second type of criterion validity indicates the extent to which a measure may successfully differentiate distinct groupings of clients and is known as divergent validity. Frequently used statistical procedures for this analysis include t-tests, ANOVAs, and discriminant function analysis.

A final means to reviewing a test's veracity is construct validity, an attempt to integrate test performance within a theoretical structure composed of varying psychological constructs. If, for example, one postulates a significant association between the test of interest and variable X while hypothesizing no relationship with variable Y, an examination of the intercorrelations among these constructs within the nomological net (Cronbach & Meehl, 1955) provides confirmation of the test's validity. The most common statistical procedure used to demonstrate construct validity is factor analysis.

While procedures for determining the validity of an assessment device are straightforward, the implementation of such practices is not readily apparent. Salvia and Ysseldyke (1985) conducted an investigation of the validity of many tests used in remedial and special education. Their findings are alarming, for many of the commonly used procedures have questionable validity.

Although many tests may be shown to be inadequate with respect to validity, it could be argued that those devices are not used by psychological and educational professionals. However, such was not the case in a computer simulation study where psychologists and special educators, when given a study, were asked to choose several tests they would employ in their assessment (Ysseldyke et al., 1980). Researchers found that 67% of the tests chosen were not valid measures. The findings are similar to those of other investigators who found the majority of instruments used in diagnosing learning disabilities suspect as valid indicators (Arter & Jenkins, 1979; Coles, 1978; Hammill & Larsen, 1974; Newcomer & Hammill, 1975).

Reliability

The extent to which an assessment procedure provides consistent or accurate data is an index of its reliability. Nunnally (1967) reports that all tests necessarily contain some measurement error. The extent to which these sources of error are minimized determines the ultimate reliability and utility of the assessment procedure. Nunnally outlines several types of reliability that are critical to a test's effectiveness: test-retest reliability, alternate-form reliability, internal consistency, and interjudge reliability.

Test-retest reliability is an index of a test's stability. That is, a client's score, assuming no significant change, should not differ on repeated testings over a short duration. A test's status on this dimension is typically determined by Pearson Product-Moment Correlations between Time 1 and Time 2 test sessions.

Alternate-form reliability assumes significance if parallel forms exist for an assessment procedure. Obviously, one expects congruence in performance among equivalent forms of the same measure. To the extent that this is not true, the accuracy of a test is severely limited. Alternate-form reliability is measured with correlational techniques.

If one assumes that a test contains a homogeneous group of items that are highly related, then internal consistency becomes a relevant factor. Internal consistency is the extent to which individual items on a measure correlate with the total score. Popular methods for assessing internal consistency are the Kuder-Richardson and Coefficient Alpha (Cronbach, 1951).

Finally, interjudge agreement is a relevant feature of many tests, especially those measures of a subjective nature. If there exists the potential for discrepancy among raters, the reliability suffers. For such tests it must be demonstrated that examiners will arrive at similar results and interpretations from test data.

Cronbach (1970) suggests that reliability coefficients approaching .90 are necessary for educational decision making. A less stringent criterion of .80, however, has become common in evaluating psychoeducational assessment methods. In Salvia and Ysseldyke's (1985) review of psychoeducational assessment procedures, several tests were shown to be unreliable. Ysseldyke et al. (1980) examined the adequacy of tests used by psychologists in a computer simulation study. Fifty-nine percent of the measures possessed inadequate reliability. A review of common perceptual-motor tests by Arter and Jenkins (1979) revealed that many of these instruments had not established sufficient evidence of reliability.

Problems in the use of nonreliable tests can be compounded when one uses change and discrepancy scores. In both cases, the overall score is significantly influenced by the reliability of the difference score (Thorndike & Hagen, 1979). As pointed out earlier, if a moderate-to-high intercorre-lation exists between two reliable tests, the resulting difference score is highly unreliable. This measurement phenomenon has extremely negative consequences for traditional assessment practices, such as discrepancy scores, analyzing subtest scores, and measuring progress with pre-post designs.

Summary

Technically inadequate tests are regularly used to make decisions about students. The decisions that are made, placement in set-aside structures like special education classes, or assignments to intensive treatment or intervention may have a significant effect on an individual's life opportunities. Given that there are no technically adequate measures of specific processes or abilities (Salvia & Ysseldyke, 1985) or of socioeconomic or personality functioning (Batsche & Peterson, 1983; Salvia & Ysseldyke, 1985; Walker, 1973), we agree with Martin's (1982) contention that the use of technically inadequate, error-prone measures constitutes unethical assessment.

BIAS IN ASSESSMENT

The U.S.A. and its measurement experts have spent a considerable amount of time debating bias in assessment. We have debated the concept of intelligence (Cattell, 1971; Elkind, 1969; Guilford, 1967; Vernon, 1969; Wechsler, 1971), and the relative contributions to intelligence of genetic and environmental variables (Bayley, 1965; Bereiter, 1969; Bijou, 1971; Bloom, 1964; Cattell, 1971; Hirsch, 1971; Jensen, 1967, 1968a, 1968b, 1969a, 1969b, 1971). Many studies have been carried out to investigate fairness of tests by comparing the performance of groups of individuals on norm-referenced tests (Boone & Adesso, 1974; Goldman & Hewitt, 1976; Jensen, 1974, 1976; Rincon, 1976). Investigations of group differences in performance on psychometric measures have led other investigators to examine the fairness of specific test items as used with members of minority groups (Angoff & Ford, 1971; Fishbein, 1975;

Green, 1971; Lord, 1977; Pine & Weiss, 1976).

We have seen calls for moritoriums on testing, court decisions citing IQ tests as biased against members of minority groups, court orders to discontinue testing, school district searches for *the* fair test, the development of culture-free or culture-fair measures, and the substitution of dynamic assessment and functional assessment for traditional norm-referenced assessment. All of these actions or recommended actions were efforts to address alleged bias in assessment and in the fairness of tests as used with specific groups of individuals.

In 1979 the National Academy of Sciences appointed a Panel on Selection and Placement of Students in Programs for the Mentally Retarded under the auspices of the Committee on Child Development Research and Public Policy of the National Research Council. The panel's mission was twofold: "(1) to determine the factors that account for disproportionate representation of minority students and males in special education programs, especially programs for mentally retarded students, and (2) to identify placement criteria or practices that do not affect minority students and males disproportionately" (Heller, Holtzman, & Messick, 1982, p. ix). The panel analyzed a variety of possible causes of disproportionate placement, including legal and administrative requirements within which special education programs operate, characteristics of instruction and instructional settings provided, characteristics of the students, bias in assessment affected by student characteristics, characteristics of home and family environments, and characteristics of the broader historical and cultural contexts. The panel concluded that "disproportion undoubtedly reflects any or all of these interacting causes, which are likely to be inextricably confounded in any concrete instance" (Messick, 1984, p. 4). The panel ended by rephrasing the initial question. Rather than searching for alternative explanations for bias in assessment, they asked why bias was a problem. The findings of the panel addressed two major issues: the validity of referral and assess-

ment procedures and the quality of the instruction received.

A series of findings from investigations carried out at the University of Minnesota Institute for Research on Learning Disabilities resulted in essentially the same conclusions as those reached by the National Academy of Sciences panel. In a series of investigations of bias in assessment, the Minnesota group concluded that nondiscriminatory assessment is a practical impossibility. Ysseldyke, Algozzine, Regan, and McGue, (1981) demonstrated that even if all forms of test and item bias were eliminated, there would still be a considerable amount of bias in assessment. They reported that the primary factors affecting the decisions that diagnostic personnel made about children were not test scores, but naturally occurring pupil characteristics. They illustrated that factors like children's race, sex, physical appearance, socioeconomic status, and the influence of the parents in the school district directly and in interaction affected the decisions made about students. The Minnesota researchers directed their efforts toward prereferral interventions, increasing academic involvement for handicapped students, and direct and frequent measurement in making instructional decisions (Ysseldyke et al., 1983).

Both the Minnesota researchers and the National Academy panel shifted focus away from tests and bias in tests to effective instruction of handicapped students of all races and ethnic groups. The National Academy of Sciences panel concluded:

> Placement of children in special education programs must be justified continually not only in terms of the validity of the placement but in terms of the value of the program. It should be demonstrable that the special instruction is substantially different from the regular instruction, that it incorporates practices shown to be effective for the problems or disabilities in question, and that it leads to more rapid progress in overcoming these problems and in improving the academic performance of the affected students than would occur in the regular class (Messick, 1984, p. 7)

USING ASSESSMENT INFORMATION IN INSTRUCTIONAL PLANNING

Although many standardized measures of cognitive functioning and achievement may be technically adequate for purposes of identifying students in need of special services, they often are inadequate for instructional planning. Evidence from two surveys reflects these difficulties. Ysseldyke and Shinn (1981) cite a 1961 study of more than 5,000 teachers in which 71% reported that psychological assessments were not helpful. A more recent survey by Thurlow and Ysseldyke (1981) indicates that although a great majority of psychologists believe the information they provide teachers for planning instruction is useful, few resource teachers find it helpful for such purposes.

One explanation for the failure of test information to be useful in instructional planning focuses on the issue of educational relevancy and views standardized tests as insufficient samples of curricula. Jenkins and Pany (1978) did a content analysis of frequently used achievement tests of reading and examined the vocabularies of several popular reading curricula. Their research documents little overlap among the tests and curricula. Specifically, any given standardized achievement test differentially sampled the vocabularies of the various reading series. Thus, reading scores on a given test may be a function of the test administered or the curriculum the pupil is placed in.

In a more recent analysis by Floden, Porter, Schmidt, and Freeman (1980), the test items of four test series in fourth-grade mathematics were analyzed. They noted, "Although . . . the tests are quite similar in some respects, striking differences are also evident" (p. 111). In general, they found considerable variation in the content of the tests and concluded that the tests did not necessarily measure the same achievement, creating the potential for misinterpretation of outcome.

The essential point to be recognized here is that standardized achievement tests are samples of behavior (Salvia & Ysseldyke,

1985). As such, they should be considered limited samples, for they are administered infrequently and do not adequately sample curricular content. The result is a general dissatisfaction among educators who need effective assessment strategies for educational planning.

MEASURING CHANGE

There are major problems in efforts to use standardized aptitude and achievement tests to plan instructional programs. First, these tests usually are administered in a pre-post fashion in order to obtain a difference score representing growth or lack of improvement. Such practice is regarded as a questionable methodology, given the acknowledged unreliability of change scores (Cronbach & Furby, 1970; Thorndike & Hagen, 1979). Second, norm-referenced psychometric measures are designed to assess individual differences, not student learning (Carver, 1974; Hively & Reynolds, 1975; Tyler, 1984). As a result, monitoring client progress on treatment or educational goals and objectives is subject to failure because percentile ranks, grade-equivalent scores, and standard scale scores do not adequately reflect within-individual change.

Given these limitations of standardized tests, it is not surprising that many treatments appear ineffective. For example, gaining access to special services has been labeled a "one-way street" (Goldstein, Arkell, Ashcroft, Hurley, & Lilly, 1975). Once a student is placed in special classes on the basis of test scores that are not designed to measure change, re-entry into regular education may be difficult. The use of these types of standardized tests in measuring pupil progress in special education, then, is not in compliance with the requirements of the least restrictive environment provision of Public Law 94–142 (Jenkins et al., 1979).

DIRECT AND FREQUENT MEASUREMENT

Advocates of alternative assessment systems cite many problems with traditional psychoeducational assessment. Ysseldyke and Algozzine (1983b) note that much of current assessment practice consists of a "search for pathology." This approach is referred to as a child-based categorization model by Goldstein et al. (1975), who state that its primary emphasis is upon describing within-child difficulties. In their report to the Project on the Classification of Exceptional Children (Hobbs, 1975), these authors delineated several deleterious effects of such systems.

First, there is a tendency to produce overgeneralizations about children. Professionals tend to perceive all children placed within a category as alike, a circumstance that ultimately affects educational placement and intervention decisions. The use of IQ is an example in which classification information is often extended beyond the initial intent of the construct. White and Haring (1976) indict categorical classifications because they ignore what a child can do. While students in a given category may share common characteristics, they also possess unique qualities. The result is that when we perceive children as numerical values and test scores we may then operate on biases formed with children previously taught with the same label. Further, the use of obtained scores and interpretation of test profiles may often lead to misjudgments about children's abilities (Cronbach, Gleser, Nanda, & Rajaratnam, 1972).

Ashcroft (1963) provides a solution to the problem of oversimplification of labels, stating that the special educator can use "criteria based on how the children function in school rather than how they perform and are measured on tests" (p. 419). Reynolds (1975) advocates assessment procedures that enhance individual development rather than simply predict or select students.

A second crucial issue is that traditional classification systems ignore the interplay of student and teacher in instruction and assume the cause of instructional problems is the child (Goldstein et al. 1975). This criticism is directed at the practice of using child-based labels that place the blame entirely on the child and fail to acknowledge the significance of environmental

effects. Learning difficulties are not the sole responsibility of the child, but to a large degree are also characteristic of the classroom situation itself (Adelman, 1971).

Alternative assessment approaches have been developed in an attempt to respond to the inadequacies of more traditional approaches. Proponents of a behavioral model have established several methods of assessment that descend from Skinner's (1953) experimental work and are an extension of applied behavior analysis (Baer, Wolf, & Risley, 1968). These approaches are often referred to as a task-analytic or skills-training approach (Howell, Kaplan, & O'Connell, 1979; Mann, 1971). In addition, the behavioral model has fostered several intervention strategies: directive teaching (Stephans, 1976), data-based program modification (Deno & Mirkin, 1977), DISTAR (Engelmann & Bruner, 1974), exceptional teaching (White & Haring, 1976), and precision teaching (Lindsley, 1971).

With respect to behavioral assessment, Lovitt (1976) delineates three essential components: direct measurement, daily measurement, and experimental control. Direct measurement emphasizes the need to measure the behavior that is being taught to the client. The concept is related to Skinner's (1953) work, but it can also be traced to the movement away from standardized norm-referenced tests to criterion-referenced ones.

A student's score on a criterion-referenced measure provides explicit information as to what the individual can or cannot do. Criterion-referenced measures indicate the content of the behavioral repertoire, and the correspondence between what an individual does and the underlying continuum of achievement. Measures which assess student achievement in terms of a criterion standard thus provide information as to the degree of competence attained by a particular student which is independent of reference to the performance of others. (Glaser, 1963, p. 20)

While many standardized achievement tests indirectly measure student skills (Lovitt & Eaton, 1972; Jenkins & Pany,

1978), the behavioral model emphasizes direct measurement.

Another important factor in behavioral assessments is the use of daily or frequent measurement (Lovitt, 1976). An advantage of this methodology is that repeated measurement decreases the possibility of measurement error by eliminating situations where the child has been assessed on an "off day," thus improving reliability (Haring, Lovitt, Eaton, & Hansen, 1978). With the implementation of repeated measurement, time-series data analysis can be effectively utilized in measuring student growth (Glass, Willson, & Gottman, 1975; Hersen & Barlow, 1976).

The last significant aspect of behavioral assessment is experimental control and reflects the importance of determining the functional relationship between the dependent variable (client behavior) and independent behavior (therapy, intervention, or teaching strategy). Utilization of reversal or multiple baseline assessment procedures have become powerful tools in ascertaining the extent of learning and the effectiveness of interventions (Kazdin, 1973). Dunst (1979) argues that the methodology fits Public Law 94–142 requirements, and Jenkins, Deno, and Mirkin (1979) conclude time-series analysis improves the efficacy of the assessment process.

One alternative assessment approach to evolve from the behavioral model is the use of curriculum-based assessment procedures (Deno & Mirkin, 1977; Deno, Mirkin, Chiang, Kuehnle, Lowry, Marston, & Tindal, 1981). The primary characteristics of this methodology have been direct measurement in the child's school curriculum and frequent monitoring with the use of time-series data analysis (Glass, Willson, & Gottman, 1975). Data are collected repeatedly across time, graphed, and analyzed for trends in growth or improvement.

The validity of curriculum-based assessment (CBA) has been established for reading (Deno, Mirkin, & Chiang, 1982; Deno, Marston, Shinn, & Tindal, 1983), written expression (Deno, Marston, & Mirkin, 1981), spelling (Deno, Mirkin, Lowry, & Kuehnle, 1980), and mathematics (Shinn &

Marston, in 1985). Reliability studies of CBA have been conducted by Tindal, Marston, and Deno (1983), Marston and Deno (1981), and Fuchs, Deno, and Marston (1983). In addition, CBA has also been demonstrated to be more sensitive to student growth than standardized tests (Marston, Fuchs, & Deno, 1986), to significantly discriminate categories of exceptional students (Shinn & Marston, 1985), to be effective as a screening and eligibility system for special education (Marston, Mirkin, & Deno, 1984), and to increase student achievement when used by the teacher to guide instruction (Fuchs, Deno, & Mirkin, 1989).

Who is to Test and Decide?

One of the fundamental assumptions in assessment is that individuals are assessed by examiners who are skilled in establishing rapport, test administration, scoring, and interpretation. It is argued that test validity is limited by the extent to which this is true (Newland, 1973; Salvia & Ysseldyke, 1985). Considerable time and effort goes into arguments about who ought to test and make decisions about children (Ysseldyke, 1979). We argue whether diagnoses of emotional functioning ought to be conducted by psychologists or psychiatrists. We debate about who (speech and language pathologists, teachers, psychologists) ought to assess speech functioning and/or language development. We argue about whether special education teachers, remedial reading teachers, or psychologists ought to assess students who experience reading difficulties in school. As is often the case with "ought to" issues, there are more opinions than data.

Rosenthal (1980) reported that children's performance on tests is a function of their degree of familiarity with the person administering the test, as well as of the complexity of the tasks. He reported that unfamiliar examiners strengthen children's performance on easy tasks and weaken their performance on complex tasks. Fuchs, Garwick, Featherstone, and Fuchs (1980) reported that preschool children earned lower scores on complex tasks when they were tested by unfamiliar examiners, but there were no differences in performance of simple tasks as a function of examiner–examinee familiarity. In a replication of this study, however, Fuchs, Featherstone, Garwick, and Fuchs (1981) failed to find differential performance as a function of personal familiarity. Research by DeStefano, Gersten, and Cowen (1977) and by Fuchs et al. (1981) supports the contention that examiners' specialized professional training and expertise vitiates the adverse effects of personal unfamiliarity.

It is not surprising that there is little clarity to the research in this area and we continue to have so many "my turf-your turf" arguments. Readers are reminded that there is no one-to-one correspondence between professional title and competence. We know that there is a reciprocal relationship between examinees and examiners, that individual performance on tests influences and is influenced by examiner training and behavior. We do not know many of the specifics of that interactive relationship.

FUTURE DIRECTIONS

The issues in the psychological evaluation of individuals with developmental and physical disabilities are complex, and there are no simple solutions. Yet, as Ysseldyke and Algozzine (1982) state, *the* critical issue may well be the demand for quick, simple, easy-to-implement solutions to the complex problems we face. Professionals charged with the task of assessing students repeatedly ask questions such as "What test should I use to assess the intelligence of individuals who are both deaf and blind?" or "What battery of tests should be used to identify learning-disabled students?" In response to the demand for quick, simple solutions to complex problems, many claim to have answers. These folks conduct workshop after workshop, training session after training session, essentially saying, "If you do it my way, everything will be O.K." At the same time there has arisen a huge marketing enterprise with promises of *"the* test," culture-fair or -free tests, tests that not only are reliable and valid but that provide

as many as nine IQs in less than 15 minutes, and tests that differentiate learning-disabled from nondisabled students.

In a document entitled "School Psychology: A Blueprint for Training and Practice," Ysseldyke, Reynolds, and Weinberg (1984) address directions for the future of psychological services in school settings that also apply to the issues raised in this chapter. Ysseldyke et al. call for an end to the practice of classifying and categorizing children and a radical reconceptualization of the assessment process, and they specify a set of competencies that psychologists in school settings ought to have.

There is a need to reconceptualize the assessment process by making efforts to identify sources of problems other than those that focus exclusively on the deficits, disorders, or disabilities in individuals who are experiencing academic and behavior problems. It entails operating differently in the assessment of different individuals. Many who assess students concentrate almost exclusively on attempts to find problems within students and use a cookbook approach rather than individualizing their efforts.

Currently, much assessment is directed toward ascertaining the extent to which youngsters *can* be taught. Given the fact that we are in a zero-demission era, one in which individuals cannot be excluded from education, questions of educability are irrelevant. We see individuals going in two directions, however: some are spending an incredible amount of time and energy in efforts designed to make the assessment process increasingly sophisticated; others are shifting their assessment activities to questions of teachability.

For many social, political, economic, and educational reasons, assessment personnel in school settings are moving away from the administration of traditional norm-referenced tests. We see an increase in pre-referral attempts to intervene in students' lives and in instructional programs. In schools, we see enhanced use of curriculum-based measures and efforts to increase academic involvement.

SUMMARY

In this chapter we have analyzed the issues that significantly affect those who are responsible for assessing the physically and developmentally disabled. Society has entrusted us with the obligation to undertake accurate and unbiased evaluations. To this end, the preceding pages discuss issues concerning definitional dilemmas, test interpretation, technical adequacy, bias, instructional planning, and examiner variables.

Although the discussion will not solve the many problems afflicting assessment, increased awareness of these various dimensions should improve assessment. We believe the purpose of assessment has changed over the years, and in considering future directions find we are in agreement with Houts (1977):

As a society, we are beginning to work on a new series of assumptions: that the purpose of education is not to sort people but to educate them; that in a knowledge society, we need to expose as many people as possible to education, not to exclude them from it; that human beings are marvelously variegated in their talents and abilities, and it is the function of education to nurture them wisely and carefully; and not least, that education has an overriding responsibility to respect and draw upon cultural and racial diversity. (p. 18)

REFERENCES

Adelman, H. S. (1971). The not-so-specific learning disability population. *Exceptional Children, 37,* 528–533.

American Psychiatric Association (1980). *Diagnostic and statistical manual of mental disorders: Third Edition.* Washington, D.C.: American Psychiatric Association.

Anderson, L. W. (1973). *Time and school learning.* Unpublished doctoral dissertation, University of Chicago.

Angoff, W. H., & Ford, S. F. (1971). *Item–race interaction on a test of scholastic aptitude.* Princeton, NJ: Educational Testing Service. (ERIC Document Reproduction Service No. ED 058 279)

Arter, J. A., & Jenkins, J. R. (1979). Differential diagnosis-prescriptive teaching: A critical appraisal. *Review of Educational Research, 49,* 517–555.

Ashcroft, S. C. (1963). Blind and partially seeing children. In L. M. Dunn (Ed.), *Exceptional children in the schools.* New York: Holt.

Aslin, M. (1973). *Learning rate and learning rate variance under mastery learning conditions.* Unpublished doctoral dissertation. University of Chicago.

Baer, D. M., Wolf, M., & Risley, T. R. (1968). Some current dimensions of applied behavior analysis. *Journal of Applied Behavior Analysis, 1,* 91–97.

Batsche, G. M. & Peterson, D. W. (1983). School psychology and projective assessment: A growing incompatibility. *School Psychology Review, 12,* 440–445.

Bayley, N. (1965). Comparisons of mental and motor test scores for ages 1–15 months by sex, birth order, race, geographical locations, and education of parents. *Child Development, 36,* 379–411.

Bereiter, C. (1969). The future of individual differences. *Harvard Educational Review, 39,* 162–170.

Berliner, D. (1980). Allocated time, engaged time, and academic learning time in elementary school mathematics instruction. *Focus on Problems in Mathematics, 2,* 27–39.

Bijou, S. W. (1971). Environment and intelligence: A behavioral analysis. In R. Cancro (Ed.), *Intelligence: Genetic and environmental contributions.* New York: Grune & Stratton.

Black, F. W. (1973). Neurological dysfunction and reading disorders. *Journal of Learning Disabilities, 6,* 313–316.

Block, J. H. (1970). *The effects of various levels of performance on selected cognitive, affective, and time variables,* Unpublished doctoral dissertation, University of Chicago

Bloom, B. S. (1964). *Stability and change in human characteristics.* New York: Wiley.

Boone, J. A., & Adesso, V. J. (1974). Racial differences on a black intelligence test. *Journal of Negro Education, 63,* 429–436.

Borg, W. (1980). Time and school learning. In C. Denham, & A. Lieberman (Eds.), *Time to learn.* Washington, DC: National Institute of Education.

Carver, R. P. (1974). Two dimensions of test: Psychometric and edumetric. *American Psychologist, 29,* 512–518.

Cattell, R. B. (1971). The structure of intelligence in relation to the nature–nurture controversy. In R. Cancro (Ed.), *Intelligence: Genetic and environmental influences.* New York: Grune & Stratton.

Coles, G. S. (1978). The learning disabilities test battery: Empirical and social issues. *Harvard Educational Review, 48,* 313–340.

Cronbach, L. J. (1951). Coefficient alpha and the internal structure of tests. *Psychometrika, 16,* 297–334.

Cronbach, L. J. (1970). *Essentials of psychological testing.* New York: Harper & Row.

Cronbach, L. J., & Furby, L. (1970). How we should measure "change": Or should we? *Psychological Bulletin, 1,* 68–80.

Cronbach, L. J., Gleser, G. C., Nanda, H., & Rajaratnam, N. (1972). *The dependability of behavioral measurements: Theory of generalizability for scores and profiles.* New York: Wiley.

Cronbach, L. J., & Meehl, P. E. (1955). Construct validity in psychological tests. *Psychological Bulletin, 52,* 281–302.

Deno, S. L., Marston, D., & Mirkin, P. K. (1981). Valid measurement procedures for continuous evaluation of written expression. *Exceptional Children, 48,* 368–371.

Deno, S. L., Marston, D., Shinn, M., & Tindal, G. (1983). Oral reading fluency: A simple datum for scaling reading disability. *Topics in Learning and Learning Disabilities, 2,* 53–59.

Deno, S. L., & Mirkin, P. K. (1977). *Data-based program modification: A manual.* Reston, VA: The Council for Exceptional Children.

Deno, S. L., Mirkin, P. K., & Chiang, B. (1982). Identifying valid measures of reading. *Exceptional Children, 49,* 36–45.

Deno, S., Mirkin, P., Chiang, B., Kuehnle, K., Lowry, L., Marston, D., & Tindal, G. (1981). Current status of research on the development of a formative evaluation system for learning disabilities programs. In Cruickshank, W. M., & Silver, A. A. (Eds.), *Bridges to tomorrow: Vol. 2, The best of ACLD.* Syracuse, NY: Syracuse University Press.

Deno, S. L., Mirkin, P. K., Lowry, L., & Kuehnle, K. (1980). *Relationships among simple measures of spelling and performance on standardized achievement tests* (Research Report No. 21). Minneapolis: University of Minnesota Institute for Research on Learning Disabilities.

DeStefano, M. A., Gersten, E. L., & Cowen, E. L. (1977). Teachers' views of the treatability of children's school adjustment problems. *Journal of Special Education, 11,* 275–280.

Dunn, L. M., & Markwardt, F. C. (1970). *Peabody individual achievement test.* Circle Pines, MN: American Guidance Service.

Dunst, C. J. (1979). Program evaluation and the Education for All Handicapped Children Act. *Exceptional Children, 46,* 24–33.

Elkind, D. (1969). Piagetian and psychometric conceptions of intelligence. *Harvard Educational Review, 39,* 171–189.

Engelmann, S., & Bruner, E. (1974). *DISTAR reading level 1.* Chicago, IL: Science Research Associates.

Engelmann, S., Granzin, A., & Severson, H. (1979). Diagnosing instruction. *Journal of Special Education, 13,* 355–365.

Fishbein, R. L. (1975). *An investigation of the fairness of the items of a test battery.* Paper presented at the annual meeting of the National Council on Measurement in Education, Washington, DC.

Floden, R., Porter, A., Schmidt, W., & Freeman, D. (1980). Don't they all measure the same thing? In E. Baker, & E. Quellnalz (Eds.), *Educational testing and evaluation.* Beverly Hills, CA: Sage.

Fuchs, L. S., Deno, S. L., & Marston, D. (1983). Improving the reliability of curriculum-based measures of academic skills for psychoeducational decision-making. *Diagnostique, 8,* 135–149.

Fuchs, L. S., Deno, S. L., & Mirkin, P. K. (1984), The effects of frequent curriculum-based measurement and evaluation on pedagogy, student achievement, and student awareness of learning. *American Educational Research Journal, 21,* 449–460.

Fuchs, D., Featherstone, N., Garwick, D. R., & Fuchs, L. S. (1981). *The importance of situational factors and task demands to handicapped children's test performance* (Research Report No. 54). Minneapolis: University of Minnesota Institute for Research on Learning Disabilities.

Fuchs, D., Garwick, D. R., Featherstone, N., & Fuchs, L. S. (1980). *On the determinants and prediction of handicapped childrens' differential test performance with familiar and unfamiliar examiners* (Research Report No. 42). Minneapolis: University of Minnesota Institute for Research on Learning Disabilities.

Glass, G. V., Willson, V. L., & Gottman, J. M. (1975). *Design and analysis of time-series experiments.* Boulder: University of Colorado Press.

Goldman, R. D., & Hewitt, B. N. (1976). Predicting the success of black, Chicano, Oriental and white college students. *Journal of Educational Measurement, 13,* 107–117.

Goldstein, H., Arkell, C., Ashcroft, S. C., Hurley, O. L., & Lilly, S. M. (1975). Schools. In N. Hobbs (Ed.), *Issues in the classification of children.* San Francisco: Jossey-Bass.

Green, D. R. (1971). *Biased tests.* Monterey, CA: CTB/McGraw-Hill.

Greenwood, C., Delquadri, J., Stanley, S., Terry, B., & Hall, R. (1981). *Process-product study of relationships among institutional ecology, student response, and academic achievement.* Unpublished manuscript, University of Kansas, Juniper Gardens Children's Project, Kansas City, KS:

Guilford, J. P. (1967). *The nature of human intelligence.* New York: McGraw-Hill.

Hallahan, D. P., & Bryan, T. H. (1981). Learning disabilities. In J. M. Kauffman & D. P. Hallahan (Eds.), *Handbook of special education.* Englewood Cliffs, NJ: Prentice-Hall.

Hammill, D. D., & Larsen, S. C. (1974). The effectiveness of psycholinguistic training. *Exceptional Children, 41,* 5-14.

Haring, N. G., Lovitt, T. C., Eaton, M. D., & Hansen, C. L. (1978). *The fourth R: Research in the classroom.* Colombus, OH: Charles E. Merrill.

Heller, K. A., Holtzman, W. H., & Messick, S. (Eds.). (1982). *Placing children in special education: A strategy for equity.* Washington, DC: National Academy Press.

Hersen, M., & Barlow, D. H. (1976). *Single-case experimental designs: Strategies for studying behavior change.* New York: Pergamon.

Hirsch, J. (1971). Behavior-genetic analysis and its biosocial consequences. In R. Cancro (Ed.), *Intelligence: Genetic and environmental contributions.* New York: Grune & Stratton.

Hively, W., & Reynolds, M. C. (Eds.). (1975). *Domain-referenced testing in special education.* Reston, VA: The Council for Exceptional Children.

Hobbs, N. (Ed.). (1975). *Issues in the classification of children* (Vols. I & II). San Francisco: Jossey-Bass.

Houts, P. L. (Ed.) (1977). *The myth of measurability.* New York: Hart.

Howell, K. W., Kaplan, J. S., & O'Connell, C. Y. (1979). *Evaluating exceptional children: A task-analysis approach.* Columbus, OH: Charles E. Merrill.

Humphreys, L. G. (1971). Theory of intelligence. In R. Cancro (Ed.), *Intelligence: Genetic and environment contributions.* New York: Grune & Stratton.

Jenkins, J. R., Deno, S. L., & Mirkin, P. K. (1979). Measuring pupil progress toward the least restrictive alternative. *Learning Disability Quarterly, 2,* 81-92.

Jenkins, J. R., & Pany, D. (1978). Standardized achievement tests: How useful for special education? *Exceptional Children, 44,* 448-453.

Jensen, A. R. (1967). Estimation of the limits of heritability of traits by comparison of mono-

zygotic and dizygotic twins. *Proceedings of the National Academy of Sciences, 58,* 149-156.

Jensen, A. R. (1968a). Social class, race, and genetics: Implications for education. *American Educational Research Journal, 5,* 1-42.

Jensen, A. R. (1968b). Patterns of mental ability and socioeconomic status. *Proceedings of the National Academy of Sciences, 60,* 1330-1337.

Jensen, A. R. (1969a). How much can we boost IQ and scholastic achievement? *Harvard Educational Review, 39,* 1-123.

Jensen, A. R. (1969b). Reducing the heredity-environment uncertainty. *Harvard Educational Review, 39,* 209-243.

Jensen, A. R. (1971). The race X sex X ability interaction. In R. Cancro (Ed.), *Intelligence: Genetic and environmental contributions.* New York: Grune & Stratton.

Jensen, A. R. (1974). How biased are culture-loaded tests? *Genetic Psychology Monographs, 90,* 185-224.

Jensen, A. R. (1976). Test bias and construct validity. *Phi Delta Kappan, 58,* 340-346.

Kallos, G. L., Grabow, J. M., & Guarino, E. A. (1961). The WISC profile of disabled readers. *Personnel and Guidance Journal, 39,* 476-478.

Kaufman, A. (1976). A new approach to the interpretation of test scatter on the WISC-R. *Journal of Learning Disabilities, 9,* 33-41.

Kazdin, A. E. (1973). Methodological and assessment considerations in evaluating reinforcement programs in applied settings. *Journal of Applied Behavior Analysis, 6,* 517-531.

Lindsley, O. R. (1971). Precision teaching in perspective: An interview with Ogden R. Lindsley. *Teaching Exceptional Children, 3,* 114-119.

Lord, F. M. (1977). *A study of item bias using characteristic curve theory.* New York: College Entrance Examination Board. (ERIC Document Reproduction Service No. ED 137 486).

Lovitt, T., & Eaton, M. (1972). Achievement RStS versus direct and daily measurement. In G. Senf (Ed.), *Behavior analysis in education.* Lawrence, KS: University of Kansas.

Lovitt, T. C. (1976). Thomas C. Lovitt. In J. M. Kauffman & D. P. Hallahan (Eds.), *Teaching children with learning disabilities: Personal perspective.* Columbus, OH: Charles E. Merrill.

Mann, L. (1971). Psychometric phrenology and the new faculty psychology: The case against ability assessment and training. *Journal of Special Education, 5,* 3-14.

Marston, D., Fuchs, L. S., & Deno, S. L. (1986). Measuring pupil progress: A comparison of standardized achievement tests and curriculum-related measures. *Diagnostique, 11,* 77-90.

Marston, D., & Deno, S. L. (1981). *The reliability of simple, direct measures of written expression.* (Research Report No. 50). Minniapolis, MN: Institute for Research on Learning Disabilities, University of Minnesota.

Marston, D., Mirkin, P. K., & Deno, S. (1984). Curriculum-based measurement: An alternative to traditional screening, referral, and identification. *Journal of Special Education, 18,* 109–118.

Marston, D., & Ysseldyke, J. (1984). Concerns in interpreting subtest scatter on the Woodcock-Johnson Psychoeducational Battery. *Journal of Learning Disabilities, 17,* 588–591.

Martin, R. (1982). Personality assessment. *School Psychology Communique, 16,* 4.

Messick, S. (1984). Assessment in context: Appraising student performance in relation to instructional quality. *Educational Researcher, 13,* 3–8.

Newcomer, P. L., & Hammill, D. D. (1975). ITPA and academic achievement: A survey. *Reading Teacher, 28,* 731–741.

Newland, T. E. (1973). Assumptions underlying psychological testing. *Journal of School Psychology, 11,* 316–322.

Nunally, J. (1967). *Psychometric theory.* New York: McGraw-Hill.

Ozecelik, D. A. (1974). *Student involvement in the learning process.* Unpublished doctoral dissertation, University of Chicago.

Pine, S. M., & Weiss, D. J. (1976). *Effects of item characteristics on test fairness* (Research Report No. 76-5). Minneapolis: University of Minnesota. (ERIC Document Reproduction Service No. ED 134 612). Pub. L. No. 94–142, 89 Stat. 773 (1975) (codified at 20 U.S.C. 1401–1461 (1978)).

Reynolds, M. C. (1975). Trends in special education: Implications for measurement. In W. Hively & M. C. Reynolds (Eds.), *Domain referenced testing in special education.* Reston, VA: The Council for Exceptional Children.

Reynolds, M. C., & Birch, J. W. (1977). *Teaching exceptional children in all of America's schools.* Reston, VA: The council for Exceptional Children.

Rincon, E. L. (1976). Comparison of the cultural bias of the KIT:EXP with the WISC using Spanish-surname children differing in language spoken. *Educational and Psychological Measurement, 36,* 1037–1041.

Rosenthal, R. (1980). *Experimenter effects on behavioral research.* New York: Irvington.

Rudel, R. G., & Denkla, M. B. (1976). Relationship of IQ and reading score to visual, spatial, and temporal matching tasks. *Journal of Learning Disabilities, 9,* 169–178.

Salvia, J., & Clark, J. (1973). Use of deficits to identify the learning disabled. *Exceptional Children, 37,* 305–308.

Salvia, J., & Ysseldyke, J. E. (1985). *Assessment in special and remedial education.* Boston: Houghton Mifflin.

Sarason, S. B., & Doris, J. (1979). *Educational handicap, public policy, and social history.* New York: Free Press.

Sattler, J. M. (1974). *Assessment of children's intelligence.* Philadelphia: W. B. Saunders.

Shinn, M., & Marston, D. (in press). Assessing mildly handicapped, low-achieving and regular education students with curriculum-based assessment. *Remedial and Special Education.*

Skinner, B. F. (1953). *Science and human behavior.* New York: Macmillan.

Stephans, T. M. (1976). *Directive teaching of children with learning and behavioral handicaps* (2nd ed.). Columbus, OH: Charles E. Merrill.

Squires, D. A., Huitt, W. G., & Segars, J. K. (1983). *Effective schools and classrooms. A research-based perspective.* Alexandria, VA: Association for supervision and Curriculum Development.

Thorndike, R. L., & Hagen, E. (1979). *Measurement and evaluation in psychology and education.* New York: Wiley.

Thurlow, M. L., & Ysseldyke, J. E. (1979). Current assessment and decision making practices in model programs for learning disabled students. *Learning Disability Quarterly, 2,* 15–24.

Thurlow, M. L., & Ysseldyke, J. E. (1982). Instructional planning: Information collected by school psychologists *v* information considered useful by teachers. *Journal of School Psychology, 20,* 3–10.

Tindal, G., Marston, D., & Deno, S. L. (1983). *The reliability of direct and repeated measurement* (Research Report No. 109). Minneapolis: University of Minnesota Institute for Research on Learning Disabilities.

Tyler, L. E. (1984). What tests don't measure. *Journal of Counseling and Development, 63,* 48–50.

U.S. Office of Education. (1977, December 29). Assistance to states for education of handicapped students: Procedures for evaluating specific learning disabilities. *Federal Register,* 42(25).

Vernon, P. E. (1969). *Intelligence and cultural environment.* London: Methuen.

Walker, D. K. (1973). *Socioemotional measures for preschool and kindergarten children.* San Francisco: Jossey-Bass.

Wechsler, D. (1971). Intelligence: Definition, theory, and the IQ. In R. Cancro (Ed.), *Intelligence: Genetic and environmental influences.* New York: Grune & Stratton.

White, O. R., & Haring, N. G. (1976). *Exceptional teaching: A multimedia training package* (1st ed.). Columbus, OH: Charles E. Merrill.

White, O. R., & Haring, N. G. (1981). *Exceptional teaching: A multimedia training package* (2nd ed.). Columbus, OH: Charles E. Merrill.

Ysseldyke, J. E. (1979). *My turf–your turf: Who does what in assessment of the handicapped.* Paper presented at the annual meeting of the Council for Exceptional Children, Chicago, April.

Ysseldyke, J. E., & Algozzine, B. (1982). *Critical issues in special and remedial education,* Boston: Houghton-Mifflin.

Ysseldyke, J. E., & Algozzine, B. (1983a). Where to begin in diagnosing reading problems. *Topics in Learning and Learning Disabilities, 2,* 60–69.

Ysseldyke, J. E., & Algozzine, B. (1983b). On making psychoeducational decisions. *Journal of Psychoeducational Assessment, 1,* 187–195.

Ysseldyke, J. E., & Algozzine, B. (1984). *Introduction to special education.* Boston: Houghton Mifflin.

Ysseldyke, J. E., Algozzine, B., Regan, R., & McGue, M. (1981). The influence of tests scores and naturally occurring pupil characteristics on psychoeducational decision making with children. *Journal of School Psychology, 19,* 167–177.

Ysseldyke, J. E., Algozzine, B., Regan, R., & Potter, M. (1980). Technical adequacy of tests used by professionals in simulated decision making. *Psychology in the Schools, 17,* 202–209.

Ysseldyke, J. E., & Marston, D. (1982a). A critical analysis of standardized reading tests. *School Psychology Review, 11,* 259–266.

Ysseldyke, J. E., & Marston, D. (1982b). Gathering decision-making information through the use of non–test-based methods. *Measurement and Evaluation in Guidance, 15,* 58–69.

Ysseldyke, J. E., & Shinn, M. (1981). Psychoeducational evaluation. In J. M. Kauffman & D. P. Hallahan (Eds.), *Handbook of special education.* Englewood Cliffs, NJ: Prentice-Hall.

Ysseldyke, J. E., Thurlow, M. L., Graden, J., Wesson, C., Algozzine, B., & Deno, S. L. (1983). Generalization from five years of research on assessment and decision making. *Exceptional Education Quarterly, 4,* 75–94.

CHAPTER 4

Biomedical Perspectives

Edward J. Nuffield

In considering the widely ranging biological and medical aspects of developmental and physical disabilities, it is necessary to begin by defining the subject matter contained within these entities. The term "disability" is basically an administrative and legal one, referring to the individual's adjustment to a handicap, or impairment, which in turn expresses his or her basic condition. Put another way, disability is what a person does not do; handicap is what a person cannot do (Campbell, 1981). It is clear that the biomedical aspects relate more to the handicaps than to the disabilities of individuals. Nevertheless, the evolution of the concept of disability, especially of developmental disability, is relevant in this context.

The Developmentally Disabled Assistance and Bill of Rights Act of 1975 (PL 94-103) defines developmental disability as follows:

Developmental disability means a disability of a person which

    A. (i) is attributable to mental retardation, cerebral palsy, epilepsy or autism; (ii) is attributable to any other condition of a person found to be closely related to mental retardation because such condition results in similar impairment of intellectual functioning or adaptive behavior to that of mentally retarded persons, or requires treatment and services similar to those required for such persons; or (iii) is attributable to dyslexia resulting from a disability as described in clause (i) or (ii) of this subparagraph.

    B. originates before such a person attains age 18.

    C. has continued or can be expected to contine indefinitely.

    D. constitutes a substantial handicap to such a person's ability to function normally in society.

Apart from the rather indiscriminate use of the terms "disability" and "handicap", this important piece of legislation does help to define the parameters of developmental disability. Of particular importance is the clause pointing to the extended presence of the disability; placing the origin before the age of 18 also helps to limit the range of these conditions. References to mental retardation and other nosological

38

entities merely evades the question of the fundamental nature and extent of these conditions.

A biomedical approach to developmental and physical disabilities needs to focus on the following questions:

1. What biological factors are of etiological significance?
2. What are the physiological and biochemical processes in the development of these conditions?
3. What medical interventions are possible, and what are their potential and actual complications?

In nature, multiple causality is the rule rather than the exception. Hence, the isolation of biological factors of etiological importance does not deny other aspects of causation. Furthermore, ongoing development, normal or deviant, proceeds on the basis of continuous interactions between biological or intrinsic (to the individual) processes and the significant environment, and each of these processes is plastic or responsive to the impact of its counterpart in an ongoing manner (Sameroff & Chandler, 1975; Rutter, 1983). This ongoing interpenetration makes it difficult to isolate biophysical from psychosocial processes in any one condition; nevertheless, a conceptual boundary has to be erected in order to confine the discussion to what has been outlined.

With this caveat in mind, it is possible to identify etiologically significant biological factors as those that affect the organism preconceptually, prenatally, and postnatally in the direction of handicap or disability. It follows that curative or ameliorative interventions can be applied in these three developmental periods. Those that occur preconceptually and prenatally are considered primarily preventive and those after birth as therapeutic, although certain prenatal interventions, such as the surgical correction in utero of neural tube defects, can be considered therapeutic. Until recently, most preventive interventions related to disabilities have consisted of amniocentesis and "therapeutic" abortion, a process that prevents a rise in morbidity statistics at the cost of the loss of the individual.

Prevention may also be classified as primary, secondary, or tertiary (Stark, 1983). Primary prevention preempts the occurrence of the condition through such measures as rubella vaccination of the potential mother or providing Rho GAM for Rh-negative mothers. Removal from exposure to known causes of increases in rates of mutation and avoidance of certain pharmacological substances (e.g., diethylstilbesterol) prior to conception are examples of other primary prevention measures.

Secondary prevention is a way of rectifying an established pathological state; phenylketonuria is the classic example. In such cases the basic genetic fault remains unaltered, but its phenotypic expression is changed.

Tertiary prevention is essentially meliorating or palliative, but includes a number of measures that are considered therapeutic, if not curative, such as pharmacological management of seizures or physical therapy in cases of cerebral palsy.

The number of physical factors affecting the central nervous system (CNS) adversely during the prenatal and postnatal periods is extensive. These factors can be placed in certain groups or classes: (a) infections, (b) chemical toxins, (c) irradiation, and (d) physical trauma. Great progress has been made in the control of bacterial infections and, to a lesser extent, of viral infections and physical trauma. The problems of irradiation and chemical intoxication remain a matter of controversy, especially in terms of their frequency of occurrence. The subject of insults to the fetal brain has recently been called behavioral teratogenesis (Golub & Golub, 1981) and includes topics such as the effects of maternal smoking and alcohol ingestion.

The importance of premature birth, and of neonatal asphyxia, has held up over the decades and led to much research. (For a review of outcome research, see Kopp, 1983, pp. 1129–1155.) In this area much progress has been made in the last few decades, although development continues.

The postnatal physical hazards are infections, trauma, and toxins. In many cases the results of earlier-based defects, such as metabolic errors, manifest themselves through abnormal biochemical mechanisms. It is during this phase that most medical interventions occur. These, however, are unfortunately often only palliative and may lead to their own disadvantageous consequences (e.g., anticonvulsant treatment of seizure disorders, psychotropic treatment of autism).

While the search for specific etiological factors underlying developmental and physical disabilities and their elimination consitute the prime focus of medical biologists, it is true that indirect measures have in the past led to improvements and a decline in the incidence of such disabilities. Warkany (1981), for example, has ascribed the drop in the incidence of cretinism and endemic goiter in certain areas of Switzerland decades before iodized salt was introduced to better communication between communities leading to an exchange of foodstuffs, the introduction of cod liver oil to prevent rickets, and the use of chili saltpeter as fertilizer. All these events masked the specific role of iodine in the prevention of goiter and cretinism.

Since the outcome of developmental disability or malformation is the result of a chain of events, it is possible to interrupt this chain at different points. Prenatal diagnosis and termination of pregnancy is, of course, one of the ways of doing so. Since some 60 to 70% of early (less than five weeks) spontaneous abortions show structural fetal abnormalities, Warkany (1981) has recommended an approach that would "reinforce conditions that naturally eliminate abnormal conceptuses" (p. 186), which he calls supportive theratanasia. How this can be done is a matter for future exploration and research.

Developmental and physical disabilities are a major public health problem, but the biomedical factors, although difficult, are not impossible to surmount. Before analyzing the contemporary picture, it is necessary to examine its historical background.

HISTORY AND DEVELOPMENT

While the presence of developmental disabilities in prehistoric times can be inferred on general grounds, the recovery of skeletal remains makes it possible to pinpoint the existence of certain physical disabilities. Thus, the remains of a man who supposedly lived 45,000 years ago, discovered near the village of Shanidar in Northern Iraq, showed a withered upper right extremity, blindness in the left eye, probably from birth, and an old skull injury on the right side of the head (Solecki, 1971).

The treatment accorded to deformed and obviously defective infants varied during antiquity. In Egypt there is little evidence of infanticide of such individuals (Scheerenberger, 1983). It has been suggested that the cult of Osiris, who was slain and dismembered by his brother, Seth, and resurrected by his wife, Isis, may account for the apparent protection of the congenitally abnormal (Harms, 1976). The ancient Hebrews did not practice infanticide or abortion. The Pentateuch makes no reference to the elimination of the disabled, but rather exhorts assistance to the blind and to the deaf (Leviticus 14: 4, in Scheerenberger, p. 11). On the other hand, the Greeks practiced infanticide on a wide scale. Aristotle (384–322 B.C.) makes it quite clear that "there be a law that no deformed child shall live" (Aristotle, *Politics*, quoted in Scheerenberger, p. 12). In both Sparta and Athens, infanticide was not only confined to the deformed, but probably included neonates of unusual or devious appearance. These societies provide the earliest evidence of negative eugenics.

During the history of imperial Rome one reads for the first time about the practice of mutilating infants and young children for the purpose of begging. Unwanted children were placed at the base of Columna Lactaria, where many were mutilated to increase their value as beggars. Kanner (1964) quotes the attitude of the Stoic philosopher Seneca to the developmentally disabled. It seems to have been one of tolerant distaste, "I have a natural aversion to these monsters" (Kanner, 1964, pp. 5–6). Throughout classical antiquity there was less concern with the cause of physical malformations and disabilities than with the maltreatment of the unfortunates who suffered from them. Early Christianity, however, proscribed infanticide as a heinous crime.

One of the developmental disabilities, namely epilepsy, has been recognized since antiquity and was considered the "sacred disease," though Hippocrates negated that idea, considering that the brain was the cause of the disease, as of many others. He incorporated his ideas about epilepsy into his general theory of humors. During the era of Christianity, however, epileptic attacks were viewed as the result of diabolic possession; the description of the individual cured by Jesus' exorcism is clearly of an epileptic. During the Middle Ages and the Renaissance such supernatural causes competed with more materialistic speculations, such as that of Paulus Bagellardus (Scheerenberger, 1982, p. 28), who attributed epilepsy to an obstruction in the cerebral ventricles. Ambroise Paré, in his treatise *Monstres et Prodiges,* mixed supernatural and anatomical causes to account for congenital abnormalities (Scheerenberger, p. 30).

By the beginning of the 19th century, understanding of the causes of developmental disabilities was still far from what is now taken for granted. Thus Pinel (1806/1962) in his *Treatise on Insanity* quotes "excessive and enervating pleasures; the abuse of spirituous liquors, violent blows on the head, deeply impressed terror, profound sorrow, intense study, tumors within the cavity of the cranium, apoplexy, and excessive use of the lancet in mania."This was a veritable potpourri of plausible and improbable items!

The 19th century saw great advances in terms of description, classification (Down, 1866; Ireland, 1877; Seguin, 1846), and more humane management (it was the era of moral treatment), but an appreciation of biological causes was very limited. Cretinism was recognized as being due to thyroid deficiency and was treated accordingly with thyroid extract. The etiological importance of perinatal factors in cerebral

palsy was illustrated by Little (1862), and for some time cerebral palsy was believed to be invariably the consequence of trauma during the process of birth. We now know this not to be the case.

By the end of the 19th century there were various classificatory schemata of mental retardation based on anatomical criteria. One such categorization, that of Bourneville, was widely accepted. It described eight varieties of "idiocy." Seven of these referred to various malformations of the brain, of which Bourneville (1880) himself had described one, tuberous sclerosis. The eighth category was myxedema due to an absence of the thyroid gland. Most speculations about etiology referred to "hereditary taint," an area poorly understood until the work of Gregor Mendel and the birth of modern genetics.

During the turn of the century, and in the first few decades following, Lombroso's theory of degeneracy dominated concepts of the causation of developmental disabilities. Congenital factors were confused with hereditary ones, and virtually every abnormality present at birth was assumed to have been acquired through transmission from the parents (Barr, 1904). This assumption led to some very negative social policies, and to some interesting, but misleading family studies, such as those of the Jukes, the Kallikaks, and the "Nams" (Scheerenberger, 1983, p. 152). Sterilization of the retarded became widespread, continuing as late as the 1950s. An extreme example of negative social policy was the extermination, through gassing, of tens of thousands of retarded individuals by the Nazis (Grunberger, 1971).

Since the early 1940s there has been a quantum leap in the understanding of specific biological causes of developmental and physical disorders. A whole litany of discoveries could be cited, beginning with the rubella virus afflicting the fetus with congenital deafness, cataracts, heart disease, and overall developmental delay (Gregg, 1941). Even during the previous decade Fölling (1934) discovered phenylketonuria leading to severe mental retardation, the cause being deficiency of the enzyme phenylalanine-4-hydroxylase.

This mechanism was elucidated during the next decade (Jervis, 1954). Other less common amino acidurias were discovered and elucidated in the 1950s: Maple Syrup Urine disease (Menkes, Hurst, & Craig, 1954), argininosuccinic aciduria (Allan, Cusworth, Dent, & Wilson, 1958), and cystathioninuria (Harris, Penrose, & Thomas, 1959). A little later the more important homocystinuria was described by Carson, Cusworth, and Dent (1963).

Of the disorders of carbohydrate metabolism, the important ones are galactosemia, glycogen storage diseases, fructose intolerance, and the group of mucopolysaccharidoses. Galactosemia, although first described in 1908 (Von Reuss), was not understood in terms of its specific enzymatic defect until the work of Kalckar, Anderson, and Isselbacher in 1956. Glycogen storage diseases have been found to be numerous as elucidated by Cori in 1952–1953. Only one variety, described by Pompe (1932), is of clinical importance. Fructose intolerance, to be distinguished from benign fructosuria, and leading to liver damage, attacks of hypoglycemia, and intermittent weakness after fructose ingestion, was first described by Chambers and Pratt (1956). The mucopolysaccharidoses, consisting of at least eight varieties, were described clinically by Hunter (1917) and Hurler (1919). All varieties received the term "gargoylism" by Ellis, Sheldon, and Capon (1936). The exact enzymatic defect leading to accumulation of abnormal metabolites in tissues, including the brain, has been fully elucidated only very recently with the discovery of lysosomal enzymes (Neufeld, 1974).

The gangliosidoses are disorders of lipid metabolism in which lipids accumulate in the nuclear areas of gray matter, often leading to progressive neurological deterioration and premature death. In some of the clinical varieties the specific enzyme deficiency is still not known, but some seven to eight enzymes have been identified (Menkes, 1974). Of these disorders the longest known is Tay-Sachs Disease (Sachs, 1887; Tay, 1880–1881). The deficiency in hexose aminidase was first described by Sandhoff, Andreave, and Jatzkevitz in 1968.

Another metabolic disturbance is hyperuricemia, clinically known as the Lesch-Nyhan syndrome (1964). It was subsequently discovered to be due to a deficiency of hypoxanthine-guanine phosphoribosyl transferase (HGPT) (Seegmiller, Rosenblum, & Kelley, 1967).

Simultaneously with these biochemical advances, there has been striking progress in cytogenetics. Until 1956 it was believed that human cells contained 48 chromosomes (including two sex chromosomes). Tijo and Levan (1956) established that the correct number was 46. Three years later Lejeune, Gauthier, and Turpin (1959) were the first to discover that in Down's syndrome, which constitutes the most commonly recognized clinical form of mental retardation, there are 47 chromosomes, with trisomy 21 the anomaly. Later it was found that translocation of part of chromosome 21 to another chromosome (usually 14 or 22) could lead to identical clinical manifestations (Menkes, 1974). Two other trisomies, those of autosomes 13 and 18, were described by Patau, Smith, Therman, Inhorn, and Wagner (1960) and by Edwards, Harnden, Cameron, Crosse, and Wolff (1960) respectively, and their clinical condition was ascribed to those authors. Both conditions are rare (1:4500/5000 live births), and few cases suffering from either condition survive after 12 months.

More compatible with survival into adulthood is the Cri du Chat syndrome, which occurs due to deletion of the short arm of chromosome 5 (Lejeune, 1964). Deletions of either the long or short arm of other chromosomes, especially 4 and 18, have been found in association with congenital abnormalities by a number of workers (Miller, 1970; Nitowsky, Sindhvanada, Konigsberg, & Weinberg, 1966; Warburton, 1967; Wertelecki, Shindler, & Gerald, 1966). The presence of ring chromosomes first described by Turner, Jennings, Den Dulk, and Stapleton (1962) was also associated by Sparkes, Carrel, and Wright (1967) and by Hoefnagel (1967) with congenital malformations and developmental delay.

Abnormalities of the sex chromosomes were described in the late 1950s for Klinefelter's syndrome and about the same time for Turner's syndrome (Ford, Jones, Miller, & Mittwoch, 1959; Jacobs, Clover, Mayer, Fox, Gerrard, Dunn, & Herbst 1980). The latter is the only monosomy compatible with survival in the human species. Clinically these entities had been described some time earlier (Klinefelter, Reifenstein, & Albright, 1942). While the developmental disabilities associated with these chromosomal abnormalities are usually of minor importance, Klinefelter cases often show minor mental retardation, and cases of Turner's syndrome usually display weakness in spatial organization and sometimes a right–left disorientation (Alexander, Walker, & Money, 1964).

Subsequently, the XYY karyotype was described (Court-Brown, 1968). Mental retardation is not usually associated with this chromosomal variant. On the other hand XXX, tetrasomic X, and pentasomic X cases, as well as XXXY, XXXXY, and XXXYY cases all show varying degrees of developmental delay (Barr, Sergovich, Carr, & Shaver, 1969; Brody, Fitzgerald, & Spiers, 1967; Schlegel, Aspillaga, New, & Gardner, 1965).

Surgical advances in recent history affecting developmental disabilities have been in the area of brain surgery, chiefly relief from hydrocephalus by various shunting procedures. Torkildsen (Scheerenberger, 1983, p. 222) carried out ventriculocisternostomy in the 1940s. Later, ventriculo-vascular or ventriculo-peritoneal shunting replaced the original procedure.

The search for a "magic bullet" to cure all cases of developmental delay proved futile in the 1940s and 1950s (Yannett, 1953). While some of the treatments might have been of use in ameliorating such complications as mental illness for which ECT and lobotomy were proposed, the administration of a brain food was designed to improve basic neuronal functioning. This was attempted in an era when there was as yet little understanding of neurotransmitters, let alone of neuropeptides. Apart from the use of vitamin B (Stevenson & Strauss, 1943) and benzedrine (Cutler, Little, &

Strauss, 1940), the use of glutamic acid stands out as the paradigm of the failed "magic bullet." Albert, Hoch, and Waelsch (1946), Zimmerman, Burgmeister, and Putnam (1949), and Quinn and Durling (1950) all reported promising results. These could not be substantiated (see Kurland & Gilgash, 1953) and the use of glutamic acid fell into disrepute.

A revolution in the pharmacological treatment of mental illness was ushered in during the early 1950s through the discovery of chlorpromazine and reserpine (Delay & Deniker, 1952). An early wave of enthusiasm for the application of these tranquilizers to mentally retarded individuals followed (Wolfson, 1957), but it was soon superseded by disillusionment (Wardell, Rubin, & Ross, 1958). Investigators have recently been more impressed by the potential and actual abuse of these substances than by their beneficial effects. On the other hand, there was resistance to the idea that developmentally disabled persons could also suffer from mental illness. This resistance applied to children as well as to adults. Pioneers in this area were Philips (1966) and Menolascino (1965) in the United States and Reid (1976) in Great Britain.

The watershed in the study and understanding of developmental disabilities was arrived at by the political and legislative actions of the early 1960s, when President Kennedy initiated a special Panel on Mental Retardation (October 11, 1961). One of its offshoots was the creation of mental retardation research centers as set up by Public Law 88–164 to "investigate mental retardation and related aspects of human development." In the past two decades these MRRCs have been in the vanguard of worldwide efforts to advance knowledge in genetic, biochemical, and cellular aspects of developmental disabilities (Begab, 1984). Their endeavors and findings over time constitute a large section of the contemporary scene.

CONTEMPORARY ISSUES

The incidence of developmental and physical disabilities in modern societies is widespread. Prevalence rates for mental retardation are 2 to 3% (Farber, 1968), epilepsy 0.45% (Thompson & O'Quinn, 1979), cerebral palsy 0.2 to 0.25% (Rutter, Graham, & Yule, 1970), specific learning disabilities 2.6% (Thompson & O'Quinn, 1979), specific learning hearing impairment during the developmental years 0.2% (Schein & Delk, 1974), and visual impairment 0.7% (Thompson & O'Quinn, 1979), to mention only a few. The basis for impairment in all these disabilities lies within the realm of biological causation.

Basic scientific findings in cellular biology, genetics, and neurochemistry find application in clinical populations beyond the developmentally disabled, such as the mentally ill and the neurologically impaired in later life (Begab, 1984). The leap from the laboratory to the clinical application of prevention and cure is still a formidable one.

In examining current biomedical concerns, one should consider the following aspects:

1. Etiology
   a. genetic and chromosomal factors
   b. environmental toxins
2. Pathophysiological mechanisms
3. Prevention
   a. primary
   b. secondary
4. Medical management of complications
   a. tertiary prevention

The last two items will be discussed under future implications.

Developmental and physical disabilities are the result of closely intertwined faults in the neurodevelopmental process. Among the developmentally disabled population, multiple conditions are the rule rather than the exception. The combination of seizures, developmental delay, and learning disorder is common. Individuals are categorized separately for legal and administrative purposes, but the biological causality of many of these conditions is shared.

Etiological Factors

A word of caution is in order. What may be considered etiological at one point may turn out to be a pathophysiological mech-

anism at a later date. Thus, the fact that large amounts of phenylpyruvic acid are excreted in the urine as discovered by Fölling (1934) led to the finding that individuals with phenylketonuria (PKU) could not convert phenylalanine to tyrosine (Udenfriend & Bessman, 1953). Blocking this conversion is the absence of phenylalanine hydroxylase. At least part of the extensive pathology of PKU can be explained by this mechanism. The question remains as to why this enzyme is absent. It leads to the inference of a defective gene, confirmed by pedigree studies that indicate the defect is transmitted as an autosomal recessive. Still not understood is how this genetic defect first appeared in the individual's ancestry.

This question leads to a consideration of the causes of genetic mutations. As Penrose (1963) pointed out, in the absence of fresh mutations all genes producing hereditary defects leading to infertility — of which there are many — would eventually die out, though in the case of recessive genes this process is very slow, due to the presence of phenotypically normal and fertile heterozygotes. Thus, the population is in genetic balance. There is, nevertheless, understandable concern that the rate of mutation may increase alarmingly due to new environmental hazards, such as atomic radiation, medical exposure to X-rays, and occupational exposure to chemical toxins. It is believed (Warkany, 1981) that although the hazards of medical exposure to X-rays have been successfully controlled due to the setting up of guidelines by the National Council of Radiation Protection and Measurement (Brent, 1976), those due to chemical exposure are still subject to controversy because adequate controls are very difficult to institute. The results of tests with animals concerning the effects of chemical mutagens may not be valid for human subjects. In order to reach reasonable conclusions for human beings, chemical exposure at a specific point will have to be studied over several generations. Understandably, there is pressure to make decisions within a shorter time frame.

It has to be understood that disabilities are not identical to disease states. Unlike diseases, there is no clear endpoint and therefore no outcome, although the clinical course may conclude with the death of the individual. In describing biomedical tangents one must always keep in mind the functional state of an individual, which at any given time is the result of his or her genetic complement, past experience, current environmental vectors, and developmental stage. To what extent the developmental pace of an individual is governed by genetics and by early environmental factors cannot as yet be determined. Retardation or slowing of the developmental pace in an otherwise perfectly developed individual is largely a theoretical abstraction. Genetic and environmental insults during development are essential factors leading to developmental and physical disability.

Modern genetics has played an important role in elucidating developmental disabilities in the last few decades. Some 2,000 disorders of genetic origin have been catalogued (McKusick, 1971), though not all of these involve delayed development or physical deformity. Direct evidence of a pertinent genetic factor consists of visual demonstration of faulty chromosomes and their products; indirect evidence is obtained from genograms yielding Mendelian ratios and from twin studies comparing monozygous and dizygous pairs.

Technical advances in the examination of chromosomes by modern staining and banding techniques have revealed some of the subtler malformations, such as the discovery of a fragile site on the long arm of the X chromosome (fra X/q27 or 28, see Lubs, 1969). Phenotypic expression of this genetic abnormality is variable, including normal functioning but usually some increase in the occipito-frontal head circumference, an overgrowth of the mandible giving a characteristic "heavy jaw" appearance, and macroorchidism in adults (Partington, 1984). Some authors have suggested a connection between the fragile-X chromosome and infantile autism (August & Lockhart, 1984; Bénézech, Noel, Noel, & Bourgeois, 1983; Meryash, Szymanski, & Park, 1982). A study by Watson et al. (1984) of 76 autistic males indicated a prevalence

of 5.3%, which is not substantially different from that obtained in nonautistic cases of severe retardation (Blomquist, Gustavson, Holmgren, Nordenson, & Sweins, 1982; Carpenter, Leichtman, & Say, 1982; Kinnell & Banu, 1983).

There are difficulties in demonstrating the marker chromosome, and it is important to use the correct medium (Sutherland, 1979b; Neilsen & Tommerup, 1984). It has been found that fluorodioxyuridine (FUdR) enhances the appearance site, and thymidine and folic acid inhibit it (Sutherland, 1979a). The expression of the fragile-X marker appears to diminish with advancing age (Chudley et al. 1983). This also appears to be the case with female carriers (Jacobs et al., 1980; Sutherland, 1979a; Turner, Brookwell, Daniel, Selikowitz, & Zilibowitz, 1980). Turner et al. (1980) found a prevalence of 7% of the marker chromosome in 72 phenotypically normal but mildly retarded girls, indicating a particular phenotypic expression in some female carriers and the importance of genetic screening of other female family members. In view of the in vitro behavior of the chromosome in relation to thymidine and folic acid, Lejeune (1982) has treated patients with large doses of folic acid with positive results.

The most prevalent chromosomal abnormality is trisomy 21, which results in Down syndrome. In about 8 to 10% of cases of Down syndrome there is either translocation or mosaicism. In the vast majority of cases the genetic fault occurs before conception, during meiosis in the gamete, especially the ovum. The only guide one has as to the reason for this normal dysjunction is the advanced age of the mother. The incidence of Down syndrome rises to 0.0275% in mothers over 45 years of age (Penrose, 1963). In a recent study in Manitoba it was found that in 19 of 48 cases, the mother was older than 35 (Hunter, Evans, Thompson, & Ramsey, 1980). However, the percentage of Down syndrome babies born to younger mothers is rising.

Longitudinal studies of Down syndrome infants and young children have indicated that a deceleration of development occurs, beginning between 18 months and four years (Gesell & Amatruda, 1941; Koch, Share, Webb, & Gralicker, 1963). Carr (1975) and Dicks-Mireaux (1966) found the slowing of development to begin even during the first year of life. The problem may be described as an inability to respond to complex visual stimuli; hence, cognitive processing essential to the preoperational phase of development is compromised (Kopp & Parmelee, 1979). The neurochemical processes underlying this difficulty are at present undetermined.

Another well-founded observation of individuals with Down syndrome is their susceptibility to Alzheimer's disease in later life (Dalton, Crapper-McLachlan, & Schlotterer, 1974; Jervis, 1948; Malamud, 1972; Owens, Dawson, & Losin, 1971; Reid & Aungle, 1974). Dalton and Crapper-McLachlan (1984) have found that the prevalence of Alzheimer's disease is 24% and the incidence 9% per year in the population at risk. The reason why some Down syndrome individuals are selected for this degenerative process and others are not remains unknown.

The effects of exogenous toxins on the developing organism, especially the central nervous system, have been studied extensively in experimental animals. A knowledge of embryogenesis is essential in understanding the effects of these substances at different developmental stages (Wilson, 1965).

There are critical periods during which certain parts of the organism, including the central nervous system, are differentially vulnerable. These periods correspond to specific bursts of cell production (Rodier, 1980, 1984). The periods of brain growth (Dobbing & Sands, 1973) consist of elaboration of neuronal cells, proliferation of glia, and the appearance of myelination — all vulnerable to exogenous toxic processes. Exposure to toxic processes may be virtually momentary (e.g., a single X-ray exposure); others are more ongoing (e.g., rubella virus infection).

The placental barrier provides the fetus with protection from many but not all infectious agents. It is also ineffective in preventing harmful chemicals from crossing over. Among infectious organisms, the protozoan *Toxoplasma gondii* is capable of crossing the placental barrier. Among viruses, the cytomegalovirus, rubella, and herpes simplex make up the rest of the TORCH group. Genital herpes is a hazard to the infant during its passage through the birth canal and will show its effects later. The organism responsible for syphilis (*Treponema pallidum*) is unusual in that it is most dangerous during the second trimester rather than earlier.

The list of exogenous chemical agents causing developmental difficulties and morphological deviation is very long. Heavy metals are toxic in early as well as later development. Of these, mercury has antimitotic properties (Sager, Doherty, & Rodier, 1982), lead reduces dendritic contacts and affects the vasculature (Krigman, Mushak, & Bouldin, 1977), and cadmium damages vascular structures (Webster & Valois, 1980). The effects of all of these agents range from loss of the fetus to subtle behavioral changes, such as an altered response to dextroamphetamine (Jason & Kellogg, 1977).

Pharmacological agents tested prior to being introduced as therapeutic drugs are routinely screened for their teratological effects (i.e., to see whether they produce physical abnormalities in offspring). The concept of behavioral teratogenesis (Hutchings, 1978) indicates that certain drugs administered during the fetal period may have subtler effects on development. A combination of both is seen in the fetal alcohol syndrome (Streissguth, Landesman-Dwyer, Martin, & Smith, 1980) and in the fetal hydantoin syndrome. In the fetal alcohol syndrome, Jones and Smith (1973) first described physical abnormalities in facial features. More recently, phenomena such as hyperactivity and learning disabilities also have been considered (Gold & Sherry, 1984). The relationship between maternal alcoholism and certain outcomes in the offspring is complex (El-Guebaly & Offord, 1977) and involves heredity, toxic agents, and postnatal environment.

The effects of pregnant women's exposure to atomic radiation in Hiroshima and Nagasaki have been traced and described over the decades (Blot, 1975; Miller, 1956; Miller & Mulvihill, 1976; Wood, Johnson, & Omori, 1967). There is now good evidence (Otake & Schull, 1984) that the risk of mental retardation is confined to the gestational period of 8 to 15 weeks; this risk corresponds to the known period of maximal neuron proliferation (Dobbing & Sands, 1973).

Endogenous toxic factors include toxemia of pregnancy (Heinonen, Sloane, & Shapiro, 1977; Timonen, Malm, Lokki, & Vara, 1968) and maternal hypertension (Salonen & Heinonen, 1984). Studies of the latter are complicated by an association with antihypertensive drugs.

An interesting toxic factor recognized only fairly recently is the presence of excessive phenylalanine in the blood of pregnant women who were treated successfully for phenylketonuria. This problem has only become germane since these women were able to achieve child-bearing status. A recent survey (Lenke & Levy, 1980) indicated that the degree of mental retardation in the offspring correlated positively with an increase in maternal blood phenylalanine. A high rate of congenital heart disease was also found in the offspring. Dietary treatment of the mother during pregnancy was probably instituted too late; preconceptual dietary treatment, however, might have prevented these physical and mental disabilities.

Perinatal Factors

The main physical hazards during this time are trauma and the premature interruption of intrauterine physiological supports. The former can lead to hypoxia, asphyxia, and intracranial hemorrhage, combined with inadequate pulmonary ventilation, which may be accompanied by hyaline membrane disease; this disease can produce serious brain damage with a variety of pathological outcomes. The point of viability has been put back gradually over the last few years, due to marked improvement in the intensive care of premature infants. Survival of infants as young as 20 weeks of gestational age has been reported. One might expect that the band of obliga-

tory morbidity would have expanded. However, this finding has not yet emerged from the current studies on prematurity (Kopp, 1983). Since 1920, morbidity rates have shown a curvilinear trend, with a peak during the middle period of the 1950s and 1960s and lower rates of morbidity since. Many of the longitudinal studies, however, need to cover a broader span of time in order to demonstrate the true effects of these stresses in surviving children.

Iatrogenic factors also are involved. The most obvious example is the result of excessive oxygen administration in premature infants leading to retrolental fibroplasia (Silverman, 1980). The alleged propensity of obstetricians to do a Cesarean section instead of allowing intrauterine development to conclude naturally may contribute to the deleterious effects of prematurity.

In prematurely delivered infants the neonatal period may be complicated by hypoglycemia and hypocalcemia, the former often due to maternal diabetes. The consequence of both of these conditions may be neonatal seizures with further damaging effects on the developing brain. Neonatal sepsis or bacterial infection, especially meningitis, may lead to seizures and developmental disabilities in later years (Fitzhardinge, Kazemi, Ramsey, & Stern, 1974; Volpe, 1973).

Postnatal Factors

As the organism matures, it becomes more resistant to external physical insults. On the other hand, there are new risk factors, one of the most important of which is head trauma during childhood. These trauma may be due to falls in the home, traffic accidents, and physical abuse by parents or caretakers. Accident proneness indicates that these traumatic events do not occur among children in a random fashion, but may affect certain populations selectively. A number of studies (Hjern & Nylander, 1964; Klonoff, 1971; Rune, 1970) have found psychiatric disorders, family disruption, and poor parental supervision to an excessive degree in cases of childhood head injury. The physical effects of child abuse have been documented extensively, first by Kempe, Silverman, Steele, and Drogenmuller (1962) and by follow-up studies (Elmer, 1967; Martin, Beezley, Conway, & Kempe, 1974). A high incidence of hemiparesis and mental retardation in battered infants exists, particularly if there is skull fracture and subdural hematoma follows the injury. Accompanying this type of trauma are some very negative psychosocial factors that help to determine the extent of the developmental disability. With regard to closed head injuries from any cause, it appears that the duration of posttraumatic amnesia gives the best indication of subsequent cognitive impairment (Chadwick, Rutter, Brown, Shaffer, & Traub, 1981).

While infections, particularly viral ones, may cause serious developmental disabilities in the postnatal period, greater attention has been paid in recent years to environmental toxins. Lead is the substance that has been discussed most frequently in the literature. Lead encephalopathy as an acute condition has been appreciated for some time (Thomas & Blackfan, 1914). Follow-up studies of the survivors of this often fatal condition have indicated developmental delays in the great majority of children (Byers & Lord, 1943; Perlstein & Attala, 1966). In former days, ingestion of lead paints by children exhibiting pica was the chief source of this particular toxin; now airborne sources, such as smelting works and leaded gasoline, may be more important. A recent advance has been the estimation of lead content in hair and in the dentine of deciduous teeth (De la Burdé & Choate, 1972; Needleman & Shapiro, 1974). Serial blood levels, however, are still employed as an index of the lead burden. The effect of lead exposure on cognitive functioning, hyperkinesis, and learning disabilities, while not definitely proven, does suggest a positive association (Needleman et al., 1979). The subject has been reviewed intensively by Rutter (1980).

Other heavy metals have been suspected of contributing to developmental disabilities: cadmium (Marlowe, Errcra, & Jacobs, 1983) and manganese (Collipp, Chen, &

Maitinsky, 1983; Barlow & Kapel, 1979). In all of these cases it is difficult to tease out the direct effects of physical toxins from surrounding psychosocial circumstances.

Pathophysiological Mechanisms

The most extensive area of knowledge bridging genetic causes and phenotypic expression is the so-called inborn error of metabolism. At least 170 of these have been described (McKusick, 1971). A classic example is phenylketonuria. As mentioned before, there is an absence of the enzyme phenylalanine hydroxylase, which converts phenylalanine to tyrosine. The adverse effects of phenylketonuria are attributed to the accumulation of phenylalanine in brain tissue and in other organs. This accumulation leads to delayed migration of neuroblasts, heterotopic gray matter, and defective myelination. There are additional effects, such as interference with the metabolism of tryptophan and tyrosine, the latter leading to defective production of melanin, which explains the fair complexion of many of the affected children. The neurochemical ramifications of this enzyme deficiency are even greater, however. The consequent reduction of tetrahydrobiopterin (BH4) compromises the formation of important neurotransmitters, namely 5-hydroxytryptophan and 3,4-dihydroxyphenylalanine (DOPA) (Scriver & Clow, 1980).

Other metabolic errors, such as those found in maple syrup urine disease, consist of the accumulation of more than one chemical substance. In these cases dietary treatment becomes much more complex.

The lysosomal storage diseases are also caused by enzyme deficiencies leading to the accumulation of normally occurring metabolites and resulting in the distortion of various cells, such as lymphocytes, dermal nerves, and fibroblasts. These effects have been detected by electron microscopy. More refined techniques, such as thin-layer chromatography and high-performance liquid chromatography, can also quantify the abnormally accumulated products (Kolodny & Cable, 1982). Eventually, the presence of these metabolites leads to cell disruption and destruction, with progressive and eventually fatal consequences (Scheerenberger, 1983).

Prevention and Treatment

Most of the professional energy of the biologist has gone into explaining and delineating causes and mechanisms of developmental disabilities rather than into prevention and treatment. Preventive steps have been taken by public health physicians and genetic counselors. The effectiveness of preventive measures depends heavily on ethical considerations and current social policy. Since many disabilities have a genetic basis, the legal and ethical permissibility of genetic screening programs is a major issue (Green & Capron, 1979).

Primary prevention aims at eliminating the conception of an affected individual and can be extended to preventing the birth of such a person. The latter strategy involves amniocentesis and, if necessary, abortion of the detected conceptus. Prenatal diagnosis has been possible for about 20 years and can reveal the presence of all chromosomal abnormalities, some 100 biochemical disorders of metabolism (Milunsky, 1979), and neural tube defects through the estimation of alpha-fetoprotein in amniotic fluid.

It has been demonstrated that 98% of cases with anencephaly and 98% with spina bifida can be detected by a simple amniotic fluid alpha-fetoprotein estimation carried out between 13 and 24 weeks of pregnancy (Wald & Cuckle, 1979). There is a percentage of 0.48 of false positives. Additionally, neural tube defects may be preventable by preconceptual vitamin supplementation for women who have previously given birth to a child with such a defect (Smithells et al., 1981) and run a 5% risk of recurrence (Lawrence, James, Miller, & Campbell, 1980).

With the development of ultrasonographic techniques, it has become possible to diagnose congenital hydrocephalus much earlier and to perform surgery on the fetus in the form of ventriculo-amniotic shunting (Clewell et al., 1982). The performance of such surgical measures is not without its technical and ethical problems.

Enzyme replacement has been of limited use in remediating some developmental diseases. The problem is one of achieving successful uptake by the relevant cells of the central nervous system (Milunsky, 1983). Plasma infusion and infusion of compatible leucocytes have not been very successful in activating the enzyme idouronidase in the mucopolysaccharidoses (Erickson, Sandman, Robertson, & Epstein, 1972; Moser et al., 1974). However, Hobbs et al. (1981) were able to report some success with bone marrow transplantation in a case of Hurler's disease, one of the mucopolysaccharidoses. In spite of sporadic successes, the impact of medical and surgical interventions on developmental disabilities has been minor so far. Corrective measures, such as surgical repair of cleft palate, tenotomy for tendon tightness, and pharmacological control of seizures are, of course, well established.

FUTURE DIRECTIONS

The direction of future advances will be determined as much by public attitudes and consequent policy decisions at the political level as by scientific feasibility. Young and Robinson (1984) have described the public's resistance to certain forms of genetic engineering, such as in vitro fertilization and artificial insemination with donor sperm. On the other hand, the more "negative" undertakings of amniocentesis and genetic screening have met with a measure of approval. Nevertheless, manipulations of genetic material in the form of recombining DNA segments will continue, and eventually lead to some genetic "cures." The use of restriction endonucleases that fragment DNA, and of separation by electrophoresis, can detect DNA sequence alterations and lead to fine "gene mapping." Eventually, replacement by synthesis of a protein fragment or even insertion of a normal gene may lead to a cure of such conditions as the fragile-X syndrome, which is associated with mental retardation (Gerald, 1983). Direct and indirect techniques of gene transfer include injection into individual cells with a micropipette, exposure of cells in a culture dish to a precipitate of DNA, or insertion of a viral particle that then infects a population of cells (Anderson & Fletcher, 1980). These techniques have been carried out successfully in mice, for example, to confer resistance to methotrexate in their bone marrow (Mercola, Stang, Browne, Salser, & Cline, 1980). A beginning has been made with humans in the area of the hemopoetic system, where there are stem cells in the bone marrow that continue to produce abnormal products throughout life. In the case of developmental conditions based on central nervous system abnormalities, the task is much more difficult. Gene insertion would have to target millions of neurones. The answer will come through much earlier detection, that is, during the embryonic phase of development or soon after implantation in utero (Milunsky, 1983). At that early stage, gene insertion can prevent future developmental and physical disabilities.

A potential area for future expansion is the study of the role of neuropeptides affecting the brain. These include melanocyte-stimulating hormone (MSH), MSH release-inhibiting factor 1 (MIF-1), thyrotropin-releasing hormone (TRH), and delta-sleep-inducing hormone (DSIP) (Kastin & Sandman, 1983). MSH has been shown to have beneficial effects on attention, and TRH causes some improvement in depressed individuals. The problem, however, is that the use of peptides in human subjects consitutes something of a shotgun approach to these disabilities (Kastin & Sandman, 1983). The difficulty of activating externally introduced agents at the target site of the neuronal cell or synaptic cleft is relevant to all central nervous system therapy.

Surgical techniques of brain transplantation and grafting are likely to become feasible in the not-too-distant future. Already, successful laboratory experiments have been completed with mature rats in which fetal brain tissue was implanted to replace experimentally damaged *substantia nigra* (Perlow, Hoffer, Seiger, Olson, & Wyatt, 1979). Such replacements will only

be feasible if the chemical pathology can be localized to specific areas of the brain. Localization of this type is becoming more apparent in comparable conditions, such as Alzheimer's disease (Davies, 1978).

Turning to general considerations, there is evidence of continued neural growth and long-term synaptic plasticity in the adult mammalian brain (Bliss & Lomo, 1973). It has been demonstrated that the phosphorylation of pyruvate dehydrogenase increases the strength of the synaptic circuit and may therefore enhance learning and cognition (Blass & Gibson, 1978; Browning, 1984). This area of influencing positively the already developed brain will continue to be explored further.

With regard to prenatal hazards, considerable improvement in combating infections, especially of the rubella virus, can be expected. With stringent immunization measures having their effect, this virus could become extinct.

More difficulties are foreseen in reducing the teratogenic effects of environmental toxins. While awareness of their effects is expanding, it does not necessarily follow that their prevalence will be reduced. Prognosis here depends on future public policy, a matter for social scientists rather than biologists to consider.

SUMMARY

The biological substrate of developmental and physical disabilities is indeed broad and complex. It encompasses much of the fields of cell anatomy, microbiology, genetics, neurophysiology, and neurochemistry, and these areas of knowledge are apt to expand exponentially as a result of recent technical advances. Special emphasis has been given to mental retardation, because it is one of the least specific developmental disabilities and occupies a central position in that cluster of abnormalities.

There have been great advances in the past two decades in elucidating the etiology and the pathogenesis of mental retardation, but very little of that burgeoning knowledge has been applied to attempts at treatment or cure. There is, however, a widespread realization in the scientific community that the course of developmental delay or deviation is not immutable, and we may be on the threshold of a breakthrough in the management of some of the individuals so affected. This hope has tempered the aura of pessimism that has long been pervasive in research and clinical practice.

REFERENCES

Albert, K., Hoch, P., & Waelsch, H. (1946). Preliminary report on the effect of glutamic acid administration in mentally retarded subjects. *Journal of Nervous and Mental Disease, 104,* 263–274.

Alexander, D., Walker, H. T., & Money, J. (1964). Studies in direction sense: 1. Turner's syndrome. *Archives of General Psychiatry, 10,* 337–342.

Allan, J. D., Cusworth, D. C., Dent, C. E., & Wilson, V. K. (1958). A disease, probably hereditary, characterized by severe mental deficiency and a constant gross abnormality of amino acid metabolism. *Lancet, 1,* 182–188.

Anderson, W. F., & Fletcher, J. C. (1980). Gene therapy in human beings: When is it ethical to begin? *New England Journal of Medicine, 303,* 1293–1297.

August, C. J., & Lockhart, L. H. (1984). Familial autism and the Fragile X chromosome. *Journal of Autism and Developmental Disorders, 14,* 197–204.

Barlow, P. J., & Kapel, M. (1979). *Hair metal analysis and its significance to certain disease conditions.* Paper presented at the second annual Trace Minerals Health Seminar, Boston.

Barr, M. (1904). *Mental illness and social policy: The American experience.* Philadelphia: P. Blakiston.

Barr, M. L., Sergovich, F. R., Carr, D. H., & Shaver, E. L. (1969). The triple-X female. *Canadian Medical Association Journal, 101,* 247–251.

Begab, M. J. (1984). Guest editorial on mental retardation research centers. *American Journal of Mental Deficiency, 88,* 461–464.

Bénézech, M., Noel, B., Noel, L., & Bourgeois, M. (1983). Chromosome X Fragile et Darrieration mentale autistique a propos de 23 observations. *Annals Medical-Psychology, 141,* 1006–1010.

Blass, J., & Gibson, G. (1978). Studies in the pathophysiology of pyruvate dehydrogenase deficiency. *Advances in Neurology, 21,* 181–194.

Bliss, T. V. P., & Lomo, T. (1973). Long-lasting potentiation of synaptic transmission in the dentate area of the anesthetized rabbit following stimulation of the perforant path. *Journal of Physiology, 232,* 331–356.

Blomquist, H. K., Gustavson, K. H., Holmgren, G., Nordenson, L., & Sweins, A. (1982). Fragile site X chromosomes and X-linked mental retardation in seventy retarded boys in a North Swedish county: A prevalence study. *Clinical Genetics, 21,* 209–214.

Blot, W. J. (1975). Review of thirty years study of Hiroshima and Nagasaki atomic bomb survivors. II. Biological effects. *Journal of Radiation Research, 16* (Suppl.), 82–88.

Bourneville, D. (1880). Scléreuse tubereuse des convulsions cerebrales. *Archives of Neurology, 1,* 391–394.

Brent, R. L. (1976). Environmental factors: Radiation. In R. L. Brent & M. I. Harris (Eds.), *Prevention of embryonic, fetal, and perinatal disease* (DHEW Publication No. MH 76–853). Bethesda, MD: The John E. Fogarty International Center for Advanced Study in the Health Sciences.

Brody, J., Fitzgerald, M. G., & Spiers, A. S. D. (1967). A female child with five X chromosomes. *Journal of Pediatrics, 70,* 105–109.

Browning, J. (1984). Biochemical studies of synaptic plasticity in the adult mammalian brain. In J. M. Berg & J. M. deJong (Eds.), *Perspectives and progress in mental retardation: Vol. II. Biomedical aspects.* Baltimore: University Park Press.

Byers, R. K., & Lord, E. E. (1943). Late effects of lead poisoning on mental development. *American Journal of Diseases of Children, 66,* 471–494.

Campbell, R. J. (1981). *Psychiatric dictionary* (5th ed.). New York: Oxford University Press.

Carpenter, N. J., Leichtman, M. G., & Say, B. (1982). Fragile X-linked mental retardation: A survey of 65 patients with mental retardation of unknown origin. *American Journal of Diseases of Children, 136,* 392–398.

Carr, J. (1975). *Young children with Down's syndrome.* London: Butterworth.

Carson, N. A. J., Cusworth, D. C., & Dent, G. E. (1963). Homocystinuria: A new inborn error of metabolism associated with mental deficiency. *Archives of Diseases of Childhood, 38,* 425–432.

Chadwick, O., Rutter, M., Brown, G., Shaffer, D., & Traub, M. (1981). A prospective study of children with head injuries: II. Cognitive sequelae. *Psychological Medicine, 11,* 49–61.

Chambers, R. A., & Pratt, R. T. C. (1956). Idiosyncrasy to fructose. *Lancet, 2,* 340–342.

Chudley, A. E., Knoll, J., Gerrard, J. W., Shepel, L., McGahey, E., & Anderson, J. (1983). Fragile (X) X-linked mental retardation: 1. Relationship between age and intelligence and the frequency of expression of Fragile (X) (q. 28). *American Journal of Medical Genetics, 14*, 699–712.

Clewell, W. H., Johnson, M. L., Meier, P. R., Newkirk, J. B., Zide, S. L., Hendee, R. W., Bowes, R. W., Watson, A., Hecht, F., O'Keefe, D., Henry, G., & Shikes, R. H. (1982). A surgical approach to the treatment of fetal hydrocephalus. *New England Journal of Medicine, 306*, 1320–1325.

Collipp, P. J., Chen, S. Y., & Maitinsky, S. (1983). Manganese in infant formulas and learning disability. *Annals of Nutrition and Metabolism, 27*, 488–494.

Cori, G. T. (1952–1953). Glycogen structure and enzyme deficiencies in glycogen storage disease. *Harvey Lectures, 48*, 145–157.

Court-Brown, W. M. (1968). Males with an XYY chromosome complement. *Journal of Medicine and Genetics, 5*, 341–343.

Cutler, M., Little, J., & Strauss, A. (1940). The effect of benzadrine on mentally deficient children. *American Journal of Mental Deficiency, 45*, 59–65.

Daker, M. G., Chidiak, P., Fear, C. N., & Berry, A. C. (1981). Fragile X in a normal male: A cautionary role. *Lancet, 1*, 780.

Dalton, A. J., & Crapper-McLachlan, D. R. (1984). Incidence of memory deterioration in aging persons with Down's syndrome. In J. M. Berg & J. M. DeJong (Eds.) *Proceedings of the Sixth Congress of the International Association for the Scientific Study of Mental Deficiency: Vol. II. Biomedical Perspectives* (pp. 55–62).

Dalton, A. J., Crapper-McLachlan, D. R., & Schlotterer, G. R. (1974). Alzheimer's disease in Down's syndrome: Visual retention deficits. *Cortex, 10*, 366–377.

Davies, P. (1978). Regional distribution of muscarinic acetylcholine receptors in normal and Alzheimer's type dementia brain. *Brain Research, 138*, 385–396.

De La Burdé, B., & Choate, M. S. (1972). Does asymptomatic lead exposure in children have latent sequelae? *Journal of Pediatrics, 81*, 1088–1091.

Delay, J., & Deniker, P. (1952). Le traitement des psychoses par une methode neurolytique derivée de l'hibernotherapie [The treatment of psychoses by a neurolytic method derived from hibernation therapy]. *Congrès des Médicines Aliénistes et Neurologistes de France [Congress of French Alienists and Neurologists], 50*, 497.

Developmentally Disabled Assistance, Bill of Rights Act. PL 94–103, U.S. House of Representatives, (1975).

Dicks-Mireaux, M. J. (1966). Development of intelligence of children with Down's syndrome. *Journal of Mental Deficiency Research, 10*, 89–100.

Dobbing, J., & Sands, J. (1973). Quantitative growth and development of the human brain. *Archives of Diseases in Childhood, 48*, 757–767.

Down, J. L. (1866). Observations on an ethnic classification of idiots. *Reports of Observations at London Hospital, 3*, 259–262.

Edwards, J. H., Harnden, D. G., Cameron, A. H., Crosse, V. M., & Wolff, O. H. (1960). A new trisomic syndrome. *Lancet, 1*, 787.

El-Guebaly, N., & Offord, D. R. (1977). The offspring of alcoholism: A critical review. *American Journal of Psychiatry, 134*, 357–365.

Ellis, R. W. B., Sheldon, W., & Capon, N. B. (1936). Gargoylism. *Quarterly Journal of Medicine, 5*, 119–126.

Elmer, E. (1967). *Children in jeopardy: A study of abused minors and their families*. Pittsburgh: University of Pittsburgh Press.

Erickson, R. P., Sandman, R., Robertson, W. V. W., & Epstein, C. J. (1972). Inefficacy of fresh frozen plasma therapy of mucopolysaccharidosis-II. *Pediatrics, 50*, 693–701.

Farber, B. (1968). *Mental retardation: Its social context and social consequences*. Boston: Houghton-Mifflin.

Fitzhardinge, P. M., Kazemi, M., Ramsey, M., & Stern, L. (1974). Long-term sequelae of neonatal meningitis. *Developmental Medicine and Child Neurology, 16*, 3–10.

Fölling, A. (1934). Uber Ausscheidung von Phenylbrenzträubsaure in den Harn also Stoffwechselanomalie in Verbindung mit Inbezillitat [On the elimination of phenylpyruvic acid in the urine as a metabolic anomaly in association with imbecility]. *Hoppe-Segler Zeitschrift für Physiologische Chemie [Hoppe-Seyer Journal of Physiological Chemistry], 227*, 169–176.

Ford, C. E., Jones, K. W., Miller, D. J., Mittwoch, U., Penrose, L. S., Ridler, M., & Shapiro, A. (1959). The chromosomes in a patient showing both mongolism and the Klinefelter syndrome. *Lancet, 1*, 709–710.

Gerald, P. S. (1983). Chromosomal derangement and treatment prospects. In F. L. Menolascino, R. Neman & J. A. Stark (Eds.), *Curative aspects of mental retardation*, (pp. 27–35). Baltimore: Paul Brookes.

Gesell, A. L., & Amatruda, C. S. (1941). *Developmental diagnosis*. New York: Hoeber.

Gold, S., & Sherry. L. (1984). Hyperactivity, learning disabilities and alcohol. *Journal of Learning Disabilities, 17*, 3-6.

Golub, M. S., & Golub, A. M. (1981). Behavioral teratogenesis. In A. Milunsky, E. A. Friedman & L. Gluck (Eds.), *Advances in perinatal medicine* (Vol. 1). New York: Plenum.

Green, H. P., & Capron, A. M. (1979). Issues of law and public policy in genetic screening. In D. Bergsma (Ed.), *Ethical, social and legal dimensions of screening for human genetic disease* (Vol. 10). New York: Stratton Intercontinental Medical Book Corporation.

Gregg, N. (1941). Congenital cataract following German measles. *Ophthalmological Society of Australia Transactions, 3*, 35-39.

Grunberger, R. (1971). *The 12-year Reich*. New York: Holt, Rinehart & Winston.

Harms, E. (1976). The historic aspects of child psychiatry. In R. Jenkins & E. Harms (Eds.), *Understanding disturbed children*. Seattle: Special Child Publications.

Harris, H., Penrose, L. S., & Thomas, D. H. (1959). Cystothioninuria. *Annals of Human Genetics, 23*, 442-451.

Heinonen, O. P., Sloane, D., & Shapiro, S. (1977). Toxemia of pregnancy and defects of the central nervous system. In D. W. Kaufman (Ed.), *Birth defects and drugs in pregnancy*. Littleton, MS: Publishing Science Group.

Hjern, B., & Nylander, I. (1964). Acute head injuries in children: Traumatology, therapy, and prognosis. *Acta Pediatrica Scandinavia* (Suppl. 152).

Hobbs, J. R., Barrett, A. Y., Chambers, D., James, D. C. O., Hughes-Jones, S. K., Byrom, N., Henry, K., Lucas, C. F., Rogers, T. R., Benson, P. F., Tansley, L. R., Patrick, A. D., Mossman, J., & Young, E. P. (1981). Reversal of clinical features of Hurler's disease and biochemical improvements after treatment by bone-marrow transplantation. *Lancet, 2*, 709-712.

Hoefnagel, D. (1967). A child with group G-ring chromosome. *Humangenetik, 4*, 52-53.

Hunter, C. (1917). A rare disease in two brothers. *Proceedings of the Royal Society of Medicine, 10*, 104-108.

Hunter, G. W., Evans, J. A., Thompson, D. R., & Ramsey, S. (1980). A study of institutionalized mentally retarded patients in Manitoba: 1. Classification and preventability. *Developmental Medicine and Child Neurology, 22*, 145-162.

Hurler, G. (1919). Über einen typ multipler Abartungen, vorwiegend am Skelett-System [A case of multiple anomalies mainly affecting the central nervous system]. *Zeitschrift für Kinderheilkunde [Journal of Pediatrics], 24*, 220-223.

Hutchings, D. E. (1978). In G. Gottlieb (Ed.), *Studies in the develoment of behavior and the nervous system* (p. 7). New York: Academic Press.

Ireland, W. (1877). *On idiocy and imbecility*. London: J. A. Churchill.

Jacobs, P. A., Clover, T. W., Mayer, M., Fox, P., Gerrard, J. W., Dunn, H. O., & Herbst, D. S. (1980). X-linked mental retardation: A study of seven families. *American Journal of Medical Genetics, 7*, 471-489.

Jacobs, P. A., Harnden, D. G., Courtbrown, W. M., Goldstein, J., Close, H. G., McGregor, T. N., McLean, N., & Strong, J. A. (1960). Abnormalities involving the X chromosome in women. *Lancet, 1*, 1213-1215.

Jason, K., & Kellogg, C. (1977). Lead effects on behavioral and neurochemical development in rats. *Federation Proceedings, 308*, 1008.

Jervis, G. A. (1948). Early senile dementia in mongoloid idiocy. *American Journal of Psychiatry, 105*, 102-106.

Jervis, G. A. (1954). Phenylpyruvic oligophrenia (phenylketonuria). *Acta of Research into Nervous and Mental Disease Proceedings, 33*, 259.

Jones, K. L., & Smith, D. W. (1973). Recognition of the fetal alcohol syndrome in early infancy. *Lancet, 2*, 999-1001.

Kalckar, H. M., Anderson, E. P., & Isselbacher, K. J. (1956). Galactosemia: A congenital defect in a nucleotide transferase. *Biochem. Biophys. Acta, 20*, 262-273.

Kanner, L. (1964). *A history of the care and study of the mentally retarded*. Springfield, IL: Charles C. Thomas.

Kastin, A. J., & Sandman, C. A. (1983). Possible role of peptides in mental retardation. In F. J. Menolascino, R. Neman & J. A. Stark (Eds.), *Curative aspects of mental retardation: Biomedical and behavioral advances*. Baltimore: Paul Brookes.

Kempe, C. H., Silverman, F. N., Steele, B. F., & Drogenmuller, W. (1962). The battered-child syndrome. *Journal of the American Medical Association, 181*, 105-112.

Kinnell, H. G., & Banu, S. P. (1983). Institutional prevalence of Fragile X syndrome. *Lancet, 2*, 1427.

Klinefelter, H. F., Reifenstein, E. C., & Albright, F. (1942). Syndrome characterized by gynecamastia, aspermatogenesis without a-leydigism, and increased excretion of follicle-stimulating hormone. *Journal of Clinical Endocrinology, 2*, 615-620.

Klonoff, H. (1971). Head injuries in children: Predisposing factors, accident conditions, and sequelae. *American Journal of Public Health, 61*, 2405–2417.

Kock, R., Share, J., Webb, A., & Gralicker, B. V. (1963). The predictability of Gesell developmental scales in mongolism. *Journal of Pediatrics, 62*, 93–97.

Kolodny, E. G., & Cable, W. J. L. (1982). Inborn errors of metabolism. *Annals of Neurology, 11*, 221–232.

Kopp, C. G. (1983). Risk factors in development. In P. Mussen (Ed.), *Manual of child psychology* (Vol. II, pp. 1081–1188). New York: Wiley.

Kopp, C. B., & Parmelee, A. H. (1979). Prenatal and perinatal influences on behavior. In J. D. Osofsky (Ed.), *Handbook of infant development*. New York: Wiley.

Krigman, M. R., Mushak, P., & Bouldin, T. W. (1977). An appraisal of rodent models of lead encephalopathy. In L. Rosen, H. Shirski & N. Crevevic (Eds.), *Neurotoxicology* (Vol. 1). New York: Raven Press.

Kurland, A., & Gilgash, C. (1953). A study of the effect of glutamic acid on delinquent adult male mental defectives. *American Journal of Mental Deficiency, 57*, 669–680.

Lawrence, K. M., James, N., Miller, M., & Campbell, H. (1980). Increased risk of recurrence of pregnancies complicated by fetal neural tube defects in mothers receiving poor diets, and possible benefit of dietary counselling. *British Medical Journal, 281*, 1592–1594.

Lejeune, J. (1964). Three cases of partial deletion of the short arm of chromosome 5. *Comptes rendus hebdomadaires des scéances de l'Academie des Sciences [Scientific Proceedings of the Academy of Sciences, Paris], 257*, 3068–3070.

Lejeune, J. (1982). Is the Fragile X syndrome amenable to treatment? *Lancet, 1*, 273–274.

Lejeune, J., Gauthier, M., & Turpin, R. (1959). Les chromosomes humains en culture de tissues [Human chromosomes in tissue culture]. *Comptes rendus hebdomadaires des scéances de l'Academie des Sciences [Scientific Proceedings of the Academy of Sciences, Paris], 248*, 602–607.

Lenke, R. R., & Levy, H. L. (1980). Maternal phenylketonuria and hyperphnylalaninemia: An international survey of the outcome of untreated and treated pregnancies. *New England Journal of Medicine, 303*, 1202–1208.

Lesch, M., & Nyhan, W. L. (1964). A familial disorder of uric acid metabolism and central nervous system function. *American Journal of Medicine, 36*, 561–564.

Little, W. (1862). On the influence of abnormal parturitions, difficult labors, premature birth and asphyxia neonatorum on the mental and physical condition of the child, especially in relation to deformities. *Obstetrical Transactions, 3*, 293–346.

Lubs, H. A. (1969). A marker X chromosome. *American Journal of Human Genetics, 21*, 231–244.

Malamud, N. (1972). Neuropathology of organic brain syndromes associated with aging. In C. M. Gaitz (Ed.), *Aging and the brain* (3rd ed.). New York: Plenum.

Marlowe, M., Errera, J., & Jacobs, J. (1983). Increased lead and cadmium burdens among mentally retarded children and children with borderline intelligence. *American Journal of Mental Deficiency, 87*, 477–483.

Martin, H. P., Beezley, P., Conway, P. F., & Kempe, C. H. (1974). The development of abused children. In I. Shulman (Ed.), *Advances in pediatrics* (Vol, 21, pp. 25–73). Chicago: Year Book Medical Publishers.

McKusick, V. A. (1971). *Mendelian inheritance in man: Catalogs of autosomal dominant, autosomal recessive, and X-linked phenotypes* (3rd ed.). Baltimore: The Johns Hopkins University Press.

Menkes, J. M. (1974). *Textbook of child neurology*. Philadelphia: Lea & Febiger.

Menkes, J. M., Hurst, P. L., & Craig, J. M. (1954). A new syndrome: Progressive familial infantile cerebral dysfunction associated with unusual urinary substance. *Pediatrics, 14*, 462–469.

Menolascino, F. J. (1965). Emotional disturbance and mental retardation. *American Journal of Mental Deficiency, 70*, 248–256.

Mental Retardation Research Centers Act. Public Law, 88–164, (1963).

Mercola, K. E., & Cline, M. J. (1980). The potentials of inserting new genetic information. *New England Journal of Medicine, 303*, 1297–1300.

Mercola, K. E., Stang, H. D., Browne, J., Salser, W., & Cline, M. J. (1980). Insertion of a new gene of viral origin into bone marrow cells of mice. *Science, 208*, 1033–1035.

Meryash, D. L., Szymanski, L. S., & Park, G. S. (1982). Infantile autism associated with the Fragile X syndrome. *Journal of Autism and Developmental Disorders, 12*, 295–301.

Miller, O. J., Breg, W. R., Warburton, D., Miller, D. A., de Capoa, A., Allderdice, P. W., Davis, J., Klinger, H. P., McGilvray, E., & Allen, F. H. (1970). Partial deletion of the short arm of chromosome 4 (4p-): Clinical studies in five unrelated patients. *Journal of Pediatrics, 75*, 792–798.

Miller, R. W. (1956). Delayed effects occurring within the first decade after exposure of young individuals to the Hiroshima atomic bomb. *Pediatrics, 18,* 1–18.

Miller, R. W., & Mulvihill, J. J. (1976). Small head size after atomic irradiation. *Teratology, 14,* 355–358.

Milunsky, A. (1979). *Genetic disorders and the fetus: Diagnoses, prevention, and treatment.* New York: Plenum.

Milunsky, A. (1983). Genetic aspects of mental retardation: From prevention to cure. In F. J. Menalascino, R. Newman & J. A. Shark (Eds.), *Curative aspects of mental retardation: Biochemical and behavioral advances.* Baltimore: Paul Brookes.

Moser, H. W., O'Brien, J. S., Atkins, I., Fuller, T. C., Klinman, A., Janowska, S., Russell, P. C., Partsocas, C. S., Cosini, B., & Bulaney, I. T. (1974). Infusion of normal HL-A identical leucocytes in San Filippo disease type B. *Archives of Neurology, 31,* 329–337.

Needleman, H. L., Gunnoe, C., Leviton, A., Reed, R., Peresie, H., Maher, C., & Barrett, P. (1979). Deficit in psychologic and classroom performance of children with elevated dentive lead levels. *New England Journal of Medicine, 300,* 689–695.

Needleman, H. L., & Shapiro, I. M. (1974). Dentive lead levels in asymptomatic Philadelphia school children: Subclinical exposure in high and low risk groups. *Environmental Health Perspectives, 7,* 27–31.

Neufeld, E. F. (1974). The biochemical basis of mucopolysaccharidoses and mucolipidoses. *Progress in Medical Genetics, 10,* 81–101.

Nielsen, K. B., & Tommerup, N. (1984). Cytogenetic investigations in mentally retarded and normal males from 14 families with the Fragile site at Xq 28. Results of folic acid treatment on Fragile (X) expression. *Human Genetics, 66,* 225–229.

Nitowsky, H. M., Sindhvanada, N., Konigsberg, U. R., & Weinberg, T. (1966). Partial 18 monosomy in the cyclops malformation. *Pediatrics, 37,* 260–264.

Otake, M., & Schull, W. J. (1984). In utero exposure to A-bomb radiation and mental retardation: A reassessment. *British Journal of Radiology, 57,* 409–414.

Owens, S. D., Dawson, J. C., & Losin, S. (1971). Alzheimer's disease in Down's syndrome. *American Journal of Mental Deficiency, 75,* 606–612.

Partington, M. W. (1984). The Fragile X syndrome II: Preliminary data in growth and development in males. *American Journal of Medicine and Genetics, 17,* 175–194.

Patau, K., Smith, D. W., Therman, E., Inhorn, S. L., & Wagner, H. P. (1960);. Multiple congenital anomaly caused by an extra autosome. *Lancet, 1,* 790–791.

Penrose, L. S. (1963). *The biology of mental defect.* London: Sidgwick & Jackson.

Perlow, M. J., Hoffer, B. J., Seiger, A., Olson, L., & Wyatt, R. J. (1979). Brain grafts reduce motor abnormalities produced by destruction of nigrostriatal dopamine systems. *Science, 204,* 643–647.

Perlstein, M. A., & Attala, R. (1966). Neurologic sequelae of phenbism in children. *Clinical Pediatrics, 5,* 292–298.

Philips, I. (1966). Children, mental retardation and emotional disorder. In I. Philips (Ed.), *Prevention and treatment in mental retardation.* New York: Basic Books.

Pinel, P. (1962). *A treatise on insanity.* (D. D. Davis, Trans.). New York: Hofner. Facsimile of the 1806 edition.

Pompe, J. C. (1932). Over idiopathische Hypertrophie van het Hart [On idiopathic cardiac hypertrophy]. *Nederland. T. Geneesk [Dutch Journal of Genetics], 76,* 304–311.

Quinn, K., & Durling, D. (1950). Twelve-month study of glutamic acid therapy in different clinical types in an institution for the mentally deficient. *American Journal of Mental Deficiency, 54,* 321–332.

Reid, A. H. (1976). Psychiatric disturbances in the mentally handicapped. *Proceedings of the Royal Society of Medicine, 69,* 509–512.

Reid, A. H., & Aungle, P. G. (1974). Dementia in aging mental defectives. *Journal of Mental Deficiency Research, 18,* 15–23.

Rodier, P. M. (1980). Chronology of neuron development: Animal studies and their clinical implications. *Developmental Medicine and Child Neurology, 22,* 525–545.

Rodier, P. M. (1984). Exogenous sources of malformations in development: CNS malformations and developmental processes. In E. S. Gollin (Ed.), *Malformations of development: Biological and psychological sources and consequences,* pp. 289–293. New York: Academic Press.

Rune, V. (1970). Acute head injuries in children. *Acta Pediatrica Scandinavica* (Suppl. 209).

Rutter, M. (1980). Raised lead levels and impaired cognitive/behavioral functioning: A review of the evidence. *Developmental Medicine and Child Neurology, 22* (Suppl. 43).

Rutter, M. (1983). Issues and prospects in developmental neuropsychiatry. In M. Rutter (Ed.), *Developmental neuropsychiatry.* New York: Guilford.

Rutter, M., Graham, P., & Yule, W. A. (1970). *A neuropsychiatric study in childhood clinics in developmental medicine* (Vols. 52–53). London: Heinemann.

Sachs, B. (1887). An arrested cerebral development with special reference to its cortical pathology. *Journal of Nervous and Mental Disease, 15,* 541.

Sager, P. R., Doherty, R. A., & Rodier, P. M. (1982). Effects of methylmercury in developing mouse cerebellar cortex. *Experimental Neurology, 77,* 179–193.

Salonen, J. F., & Heinonen, O. P. (1984). Mental retardation and mother's hypertension during pregnancy. *Journal of Mental Deficiency Research, 28,* 53–56.

Sameroff, A. J., & Chandler, M. J. (1975). Reproductive risk and the continuum of caretaking causality. In F. D. Horowitz (Ed.), *Review of child development research* (Vol. 4, p. 187). Chicago: University of Chicago Press.

Sandhoff, K., Andreave, V., & Jatzkevitz, H. (1968). Deficient hexose aminodase activity in an exceptional case of Tay-Sachs disease, with additional storage of kidney globoside in visceral organs. *Life Sciences, 7,* 283–288.

Scheerenberger, R. C. (1983). *A history of mental retardation.* Baltimore: Paul Brooks.

Schein, J. D., & Delk, M. T. (1974). *The deaf population in the United States.* Silver Springs, MD: National Association for the Deaf.

Schlegel, R., Aspillaga, M. J., Neu, R., & Gardner, L. I. (1965). Studies in a boy with XXYY chromosomes. *Pediatrics, 36,* 113–115.

Scriver, C. R., & Clow, C. L. (1980). Phenylketonuria: Epitome of human biochemical genetics. *New England Journal of Medicine, 303,* 1336–1342, 1394–1400.

Seegmiller, J. E., Rosenblum, F. M., & Kelley, W. N. (1967). Enzyme defect associated with a sex-linked human neurological disorder and excessive purins synthesis. *Science, 155,* 1682–1685.

Seguin, E. (1846). *Traitement moral, hygiene, et education des idiots, et des autres enfants arrieres* [Moral treatment, hygiene, and education of idiots and other retarded children]. Paris: J. B. Bailliere.

Silverman, L. J., & Metz, A. S. (1973). Numbers of pupils with specific learning disabilities in local public schools in the United States: Spring 1970. *Annals of the New York Academy of sciences, 205,* 310–320.

Silverman, W.A. (1980). *Retrolental fibroplasia: A modern parable.* New York: Grune & Stratton.

Smithells, R. W., Sheppards, S., Schorah, C. J., Seller, M. J., Nevin, N. C., Harris, R., Read, A. P., & Fielding, D. W. (1981). Apparent prevention of neural tube defects by preconceptual vitamin supplementation. *Archives of the Diseases of Childhood, 56,* 911–918.

Solecki, R. (1971). *Shanidar.* New York: Alfred A. Knopf.

Sparkes, R. S., Carrel, R. E., & Wright, S. W. (1967). Absent thumbs with a ring D^2 chromosome: A new deletion syndrome. *American Journal of Human Genetics, 19,* 644–646.

Stark, J. A. (1983). The search for cures of mental retardation. In F. J. Menolascino, R. Neman & J. A. Stark (Eds.), *Curative aspects of mental retardation.* Baltimore: Paul Brooks.

Stevenson, I., & Strauss, A. (1943). The effects of an enriched B^2 (riboflavin) diet on a group of mentally defective children with retardation in physical growth. *American Journal of Mental Deficiency, 48,* 153–156.

Streissguth, A. P., Landesman-Dwyer, S., Martin, J. C., & Smith, D. W. (1980). Teratoganic effects of alcohol in humans and laboratory animals. *Science, 209,* 353–361.

Sutherland, G. R. (1977). Marker X chromosomes and mental retardation. *New England Journal of Medicine, 296,* 1415.

Sutherland, G. R. (1979a). Heritable fragile sites on human chromosomes: I. Factors affecting expression in lymphocyte culture. *American Journal of Human Genetics, 31,* 125–135.

Sutherland, G. R. (1979b). Heritable fragile sites on human chromosomes: III. Detection of fra (X)(q27) in males with X-linked mental retardation and in their female relatives. *Human Genetics, 53,* 23–27.

Tay, W. (1880–1881). Symmetrical changes in the region of the yellow spot in each eye of an infant. *Transactions of the Ophthalmological Society of the United Kingdom, 15,* 541–544.

Thomas, H. M., & Blackfan, A. D. (1914). Recurrent meningitis, due to lead, in a child of 5 years. *Journal of Diseases of Children, 8,* 377–380.

Thompson, R. J., & O'Quinn, A. N. (1979). *Developmental disabilities: Etiologies, manifestations, diagnoses, and treatments.* New York: Oxford University Press.

Tijo, J., & Levan, A. (1956). The chromosome number of man. *Hereditas, 42,* 1–6.

Timonen, S., Malm., E., Lokki, O., & Vara, P. (1968). Factors influencing perinatal mortality and malformations in the newborn. *Annals Pediatrica Fennsica, 14,* 35.

Turner, B., Jennings, A. N., DenDulk, G. M., & Stapleton, T. (1962). A self-perpetuating ring chromosome. *Medical Journal of Australia, 49,* 56–61.

Turner, G., Brookwell, R., Daniel, A., Selikowitz, M., & Zilibowitz, M. (1980). Heterozygous expression of X-linked mental retardation and X-chromosome marker fra (X) (q27). *New England Journal of Medicine, 303,* 662–664.

Turner, G., Daniel, A., & Frost, M. (1980). X-linked mental retardation, macroorchidism and the X-q27 fragile site. *Journal of Pediatrics, 96,* 837–841.

Udenfriend, S., & Bessman, S. P. (1953). Hydroxylation of phenylalanine and antipyrine in phynylpyruvic oligophrenia. *Journal of Biology-Chemistry, 203,* 961–967.

Volpe, J. J. (1973). Neonatal seizures. *New England Journal of Medicine, 289,* 413–416.

Von Reuss, A. (1908). Zuckerausscheidung im Säuglingsalter [Glycosuria in the neonate]. *Wiener Medizinische Wochenschrift [Weekly Viennese Journal of Medicine], 58,* 799–801.

Vorhees, C. V., Brunner, R. L., & Butcher, R. E. (1979). Psychotropic drugs as behavioral teratogens. *Science, 205,* 1220–1225.

Wald, N. J., & Cuckle, H. S. (1979). Second report of the United Kingdom collaborative study on alpha-fetoprotein in relation to neural tube defects: Amniotic fluid alpha-fetoprotein measurements in antenatal diagnosis of anencephaly and open spina bifida in early pregnancy. *Lancet, 2,* 651–662.

Warburton, D., et al. (1967). Distinction between chromosome 4 and chromosome 5 by replication pattern and length of long and short arms. *American Journal of Human Genetics, 19,* 399–402.

Wardell, D., Rubin, H., & Ross, R. (1958). The use of reserpine and chlorpromazine in disturbed, mentally deficient patients. *American Journal on Mental Deficiency, 63,* 330–344.

Warkany, J. (1981). Prevention of congenital malformations. *Teratology, 23,* 175–189.

Watson, M. S., Leckman, J. F., Annex, B., Breg, W. R., Boles, D., Volkmar, F. R., & Cohen, D. J. (1984). Fragile X in a survey of 75 autistic males. *New England Journal of Medicine, 307,* 1462.

Webb, G. C., Roger, J. G., Pitt, D. B., Holliday, J., & Theobald, T. (1981). Transmission of fragile (X) (q27) site from a male. *Lancet,* 1231–1232.

Webster, W. S., & Valois, A. A. (1980). The toxic effects of cadmium on the neonatal mouse CNS. *Journal of Neuropathology and Experimental Neurology, 40,* 247–257.

Wertelecki, W., Shindler, A. M., & Gerald, P. S. (1966). Partial deletion of chromosome 18. *Lancet, 2,* 641–642.

Wilson, J. G. (1965). Embryological considerations in teratology. In J. G. Wilson & J. Warkany (Eds.), *Teratology: Principles and techniques.* Chicago: University of Chicago Press.

Wolfson, I. (1957). Clinical experience with serpasil and thorazine in treatment of disturbed behavior of the mentally retarded. *American Journal of Mental Deficiency, 62,* 276–283.

Wood, J. W., Johnson, K. G., & Omori, Y. (1967). In utero exposure to the Hiroshima atomic bomb: Follow-up at 20 years. *Pediatrics, 39,* 385–392.

Yannett, H. (1953). The progress of medical research in the field of mental deficiency. *American Journal of Mental Deficiency, 57,* 447–452.

Young, G., & Robinson, C. (1984). Attitudes toward genetic engineering: The dilemma of the genetically abnormal child. *Journal of Applied Behavioral Sciences, 20,* 155–166.

Zimmerman, F., Burgemeister, B., & Putnam, T. (1949). The effect of glutamic acid upon the mental and physical growth of mongols. *American Journal of Psychiatry, 105,* 275–287.

PART II

General Issues

CHAPTER 5

Prevention

John D. Cone

Interest in the prevention of developmental disabilities and other handicapping conditions has grown noticeably in the past decade. In large part, this is the result of some very visible successes brought about by years of biomedical and social science research and rapid technological advances in both areas. After defining the conditions to be prevented and providing some conceptual orientation, this chapter describes some of the progress in preventing developmental disabilities in recent years. Accomplishments will be classified roughly in terms of biomedical causes on the one hand and environmental causes on the other. The ethics of prevention are discussed in some detail, with a final section posing ten ethical questions frequently encountered. Throughout the chapter, Caplan's (1964) conceptualizations of primary, secondary, and tertiary prevention are followed; however, the focus is almost exclusively on primary prevention.

ALTERNATE CONCEPTIONS OF DEVELOPMENTAL DISABILITIES

There is no clear consensus concerning what developmental disabilities are. Seltzer (1983) for example, recently provided four major alternatives to defining and classifying mental retardation, the largest single category developmental disability. Each of these is in wide use by different service providers, advocates, consumers, and legislative groups throughout the world.

Mental retardation is the largest subgroup within the general category of developmental disabilities. The classification system presented in *Diagnostic and Statistical Manual of Mental Disorders—III* (DSM-III, see American Psychiatric Association, 1980) strives to be comprehensive and to include multiple dimensions or characteristics in formulating the diagnosis of mental retardation. In this regard, a label or diagnosis reflects the client's mental state, any physical disorder or psychosocial stressors, and some assessment of the highest level of adaptive behavior or functioning achieved during the past year. Each of these general areas is represented in *DSM-III* as an "Axis". The diagnostic system is therefore referred to as "multi-axial". Mental disorders are included on Axes I and II with mental retardation on Axis I and the specific developmental disabilities (e.g., learning disability) on Axis II. Multiple mental handicaps in the same person can be noted by using as many of the Axis I or II diagnoses as needed.

The physical condition of the client is represented by Axis III. Any disorder in physical functioning would be noted by selecting a diagnosis from this axis. Psychosocial stress is represented by Axis IV, which in effect is a global rating of the overall stress to which the client is subject. The 7-point ratings ("none" to "catastrophic") are based on the reactions of normal persons to the stressor. For example, if the client were responding intensely to a stressor that typically was associated with only "minimal" stress by most normal persons, a rating of 2 (minimal) would be assigned. Thus, Axis IV represents the events or stimulus conditions impacting the client, and not the client's reaction to them. It is an effort to describe such events objectively, side-stepping their subjective interpretation by the client. Financial, legal, and marital problems are examples of some of the stressors considered in Axis IV ratings.

The adaptive functioning of the client during the past year is represented on Axis V. Again, a 7-point rating is made on the basis of the highest level of adaptive behavior sustained by the client in three major areas: occupational, social, and leisure. The diagnostician combines the functioning in these areas to arrive at a single rating of adaptive behavior, from "superior" to "grossly impaired".

As with the classification system of the American Association on Mental Deficiency (AAMD), diagnoses using *DSM-III* reflect degrees of impairment. Separate numerical codes (e.g., 317.0, 318.0, etc.) are assigned to mild, moderate, severe, and profound retardation. These diagnoses correspond to intelligence quotients of 50 to 70, 35 to 49, 20 to 34, and less than 20, respectively. When a person is untestable, the diagnosis "unspecified mental retardation" is used.

As Seltzer (1983) notes, despite its multidimensional emphasis, diagnoses using *DSM-III* are likely to rest heavily, if not exclusively, on measures of intellectual functioning because of the reliance on clinical judgment in rating adaptive functioning. Unaided by objective scores from reliable scales of adaptive behavior (e.g., *The Pyramid Scales*; see Cone, 1984), clinicians are likely to be strongly influenced in their Axis IV ratings by the person's individual level of intellectual performance.

The use of AAMD criteria in assigning Axis I categories requires a knowledge of the AAMD classification system. The most widely used approach, especially outside of the medical field, the AAMD classification system became prominent with the publication of Heber's (1959) *Manual on Terminology and Classification*. Mental retardation was defined as "subaverage general intellectual functioning which originates during the developmental period and is associated with impairment in one or more of the following: (1) maturation, (2) learning, and (3) social adjustment" (p. 3). Heber relied on a statistical definition of general intellectual functioning. "Subaverage" was considered to be more than one standard deviation below the mean on a standardized measure of intellectual functioning and thus included scores of 84 and lower. Prior to 1959, it was necessary to have a score of 69 or lower. The change resulted in approximately 15% more people classified as mentally retarded in the newly created "borderline mental retardation" category. A subsequent revision by the AAMD in 1973 deleted this category and returned the "cutoff" score to 70 (Grossman, 1977). The four levels defined in the 1973 revision are mild, moderate, severe, and profound. They correspond to intelligence test scores of 56 to 70, 41 to 55, 26 to 40, and below 25, respectively. The first three ranges represent 2, 3, and 4 standard deviations below the mean, respectively.

The relatively arbitrary nature of statistical definitions such as these, together with the realization that persons with comparable IQ scores reflect widely divergent adaptation to environmental requirements, has led the AAMD to include adaptive behavior as an official part of its diagnosis since 1959. Thus, to be diagnosed as mentally retarded, a person must show general intellectual functioning below 71 *and* deficits in adaptive behavior which are assessed in relation to normal persons of the same age and cultural group as the client.

While the *DSM-III* Axis I diagnoses rest on the AAMD categories, its Axis III classification depends on the medical codes provided in the ninth version of the *International Classification of Diseases (ICD-9)*. Published in 1977, the *ICD-9* requires classification of mental retardation in terms of categories similar to the AAMD system. It also requires associated physical and/or psychiatric conditions to be noted (e.g., "mental retardation following trauma or physical agent" or "mental retardation with chromosomal abnormality"). Unlike AAMD and *DSM-III* systems, assessment of intellectual functioning is based on a combination of various types of information, including clinical impressions and adaptive behavior as well as intelligence tests. As Seltzer (1983) has observed, adaptive behavior and intellectual functioning are not viewed as separate criteria for diagnosing mental retardation in the *ICD-9* system.

The fourth and final major approach to classifying mental retardation specifically, and developmental disabilities in general, is the result of Congressional legislative action. In November 1978, Public Law 95-602, known as the Developmental Disabilities Bill of Rights was enacted. It incorporates a noncategorical, functional definition of developmental disabilities:

> . . . severe, chronic disability of a person which (a) is attributable to a mental or physical impairment or combination of mental and physical impairments; (b) is manifested before the person attains age 22; (c) is likely to continue indefinitely; (d) results in substantial functional limitations in three or more of the following areas of major life activity, (i) self care, (ii) receptive and expressive language, (iii) learning, (iv) mobility, (v) self-direction, (vi) capacity for independent living, and (vii) economic self-sufficiency; and (e) reflects the person's need for a combination and sequence of special, interdisciplinary, or generic care, treatment, or other services which are of lifelong or extended duration and are individually planned and coordinated. (42 USC 6001. Sec. 503)

The definition incorporated in PL 95-602 represents a major shift from the heavy reliance of other definitions on general intellectual functioning. With its emphasis on functional competence, multiple service requirements, chronicity, and age at onset, it clearly indicates that persons of average or above-average intellectual functioning might be classified as developmentally disabled. Moreover, persons with intellectual functioning in the range generally regarded as retarded might *not* be considered developmentally disabled. Thus, from a behavioral standpoint, the noncategorical, functional approach of this definition is laudable. It emphasizes the services needed to improve or maintain the environmental adjustments of developmentally disabled persons. From an administrative standpoint, however, the definition is problematic. It is much more difficult to do epidemiological studies of incidence and prevalence and to direct financial and other resources to appropriate service providers. Moreover, it requires rethinking of preventive approaches based on relatively homogeneous diagnostic entities.

In part, these difficulties are the result of the lack of operational clarity of major elements of the definition (Seltzer, 1983). Such terms as "severe," "chronic," and "substantial" require clarification before reliable diagnostic application of the definition is possible. Difficulties also stem from the relative newness of the definition. With experience and research, it should not be difficult to operationalize these terms and to develop ways of using the definition in making reliable diagnoses. The cooperation of powerful professional organizations will be necessary, however, before the PL 95-602 definition is widely adopted for such purposes. These organizations (e.g., American Psychiatric Association; American Association on Mental Deficiency) have vested interests in their own definitions. Therefore, it is unlikely that widespread adoption will occur in the near future.

IMPLICATIONS FOR PREVENTION

The failure of the professional community to reach consensus on a definition presents major difficulties in organizing a coherent approach to the problem of developmental disabilities. While these difficulties apply to intervention, service-provider training, research, and other areas, they are especially relevant to prevention.

For example, consider epidemiological studies. It we were to isolate areas of relative absence of certain forms of developmental disability in parts of the world and contrast these with areas of relative prevalence, we might obtain clues to the causes of these forms. Without clearly agreed-upon definitions, however, such epidemiological investigations are difficult to conduct.

The problem is most obvious from a biogenetic causation perspective (Rimland, 1969). When a particular biochemical or genetic makeup is suspected as the underlying determinant of a category of disability, it is crucial to identify persons with the disability in accurate and reliable ways. Only persons with the disability should be included. When a social learning or psychogenic hypothesis is being tested, however, the boundaries of the categories are less rigid. It is not expected that a unique set of environmental circumstances will be discovered as causing a particular type of disability; rather, it is accepted that behavior is multiply determined and richly complex. Further, we are unlikely ever to know the precise combination of events that lead to specific forms of disability. What we can ascertain is that certain broadly describable sets of conditions generally will be associated with unsatisfactory outcomes. For example, it is known that conditions associated with poverty lead, on the average, to suboptimal intellectual development.

To some extent, the requirement for precision in defining developmental disabilities for preventive purposes depends on whether primary, secondary, or tertiary prevention is our focus. Primary prevention includes efforts to reduce the incidence of a particular type of disability (Caplan, 1964). Roberts (1970) has suggested that these efforts can be subdivided into: (a) removing the noxious agent, (b) strengthening the host to increase resistance to noxious agents, and (c) preventing contact between host and agent. An example of the first type of effort is ridding the environment of toxic substances (e.g., lead; see Needleman, 1983) that have been shown to be directly related to impaired functioning of the central nervous system. Altering the dietary intake of PKU victims to reduce phenylalanine levels is an example of strengthening the host (see Williamson, Koch, Azen, & Chang, 1981). The third category of primary prevention effort is illustrated by teaching pregnant women to minimize the ingestion of potentially harmful substances, such as alcohol and caffeine, and to avoid smoking cigarettes (Clarren & Smith, 1978; Streissguth, 1983).

It might seem more important to reach a consensus on the definition of disability if reducing its incidence (primary prevention) rather than its prevalence (secondary prevention) was the goal. If prevalence was reduced largely through intervention, and intervention was provided to all who needed it (regardless of the cause of their disability), some definitional ambiguity might be tolerable. This is not the case, however, when intervention involves early detection, which in turn requires early diagnosis. Nonetheless, early detection of *some* problems might be followed by the use of interventions that were not precisely problem-specific.

Modes of intervention are likely to be based on biogenic versus psychogenic factors with more precision required for the former, and relatively less for the latter. Psychogeneticists of a social learning perspective tend to approach behavior similarly, whether it is part of the repertoire of a Down syndrome child or a PKU victim. Such egalitarianism would not characterize the secondary prevention activities of a biogeneticist since biochemical or genetic imbalances suggest treatment in more specific ways.

The same logic might be even more applicable to Caplan's (1964) concept of tertiary prevention. Here, the focus is on reducing residual defects or sequelae of a particular form of disability. By rehabilitative efforts, the effects of the disability on the community adjustment of the individual can be minimized. Augmented education programs for moderately retarded children is a good example of tertiary prevention (Ramey & Bryant, 1983). Biogenic and psychogenic hypotheses of causality seem relatively unimportant when considering tertiary prevention activities. Similarly, high levels of classificatory accuracy are not as critical. Even from an administrative perspective concerned with the allocation of resources to rehabilitative programs for various types of handicaps, it can be argued that some imprecision is tolerable.

To summarize, it has been argued that lack of consensus concerning the definition of developmental disability hampers research aimed at its prevention. The difficulty appears to be greatest for primary prevention efforts, and proportionately less for secondary and tertiary prevention activities. To some extent, the need for definitional precision varies as a function of perspective (biogenic vs. psychogenic).

PREVENTING DEVELOPMENTAL DISABILITIES WITH BIOMEDICAL CAUSES

Some developmental disabilities result solely from the effects of biological factors during the prenatal, perinatal, and subsequent periods. Other developmental disabilities result solely from the effects of environmental factors that theoretically can occur during these same periods, or from the interaction of biological and environmental factors. Some of the most notable prevention successes have involved conditions resulting from biomedical causes. The examples given here, although not comprehensive, permit some contrast with the following section on environmental causes and provide a basis for the discussion of ethical issues in the last section of the chapter.

Rubella

Among the best-known prevention efforts is the campaign to eliminate disabilities resulting from congenital rubella or German measles. Children born to mothers who contracted rubella during pregnancy have an increased risk of blindness, deafness, cardiac difficulties, meningoencephalitis, dysfunction of the reticuloendothelial system, and bone structure problems. The time of occurrence is important, with the first trimester, especially the first two months, being critical (Cooper et al., 1969). According to Singer, Rudolph, Rosenberg, Rawls, and Boniuk (1967), the rubella virus causes inflammation of the brain and interferes with the growth of brain cells in the fetus.

Primary prevention efforts have involved immunization of preschool children. (This is an example of Roberts' [1970] first category of primary prevention efforts, since immunization reduces circulation of the virus in the general population.) Women with no previous history of rubella may also be immunized. Finally, high school girls may have "German measles parties" at which they deliberately expose themselves to an infected friend so as to be immune to the virus at some later time.

There is some advantage to the "measles party" approach, in that there is evidence of a greater immune response following natural infection rather than injection (Horstmann 1971). Moreover, the "reduced circulation of the virus in the population" argument for the mass immunization program begun in 1969 in the United States appears to be of questionable validity. According to Papageorgiou (1980), there has been "little change in the susceptibility rates of women 15 to 40 years old" since implementation of the program. With regard to passive immunization during pregnancy, Papageorgiou recommends confining it to women known to have been exposed to the virus and who elect not to have their pregnancy terminated.

Down Syndrome

The most common form of this condition is an extra chromosome in the 21st position (trisomy 21). While the clinical manifestations of persons with Down syndrome vary widely, most have moderate to severe levels of retardation, a single transverse crease of the palm, short stature, flattened occiput, upward-slanting eyes at the outer corners, and relatively simple fingerprints (Sarason & Doris, 1969). Children born to older women have an increased likelihood of Down syndrome. The incidence is reported to rise from 0.125 to 0.16870 for mothers 18 to 29 years old, to 0.8570 for mothers 35 to 39 years old and 3.970 for mothers over 40 (Benda, 1960). Hook and Fabia (1978) provide yearly rates showing steady increases between 20 and 49 years of age. Though not without some controversy, it is generally concluded that the father's age is not related to the incidence of Down syndrome (cf., Hook, 1982; Penrose, 1962).

The principal prevention strategy has involved analyzing the chromosomal makeup of the fetus by means of amniocentesis. Optimally, the procedure occurs during the 16th week of gestation, with 14 weeks being the lower limit for safety (Warburton, 1980). Approximately 20 to 30 cc of amniotic fluid are withdrawn via a needle inserted in the mother's abdomen. Chromosomal analyses can usually be completed in 3 to 4 weeks following the extraction, approximately half of which are needed for growing cells in a culture. Interestingly, the number of Down syndrome cases found through amniocentesis is greater than would be predicted from the incidence in live births. According to Hook (1978), the discrepancy is due to a high rate of miscarriages among women carrying Down syndrome fetuses beyond 16 weeks. Up to 50% of the fetuses of women over 40 years of age are spontaneously aborted. Another possible contributor is the incomplete recording of the births of Down syndrome babies (Pueschel & Goldstein, 1983).

Amniocentesis has been used to screen for many other chromosomal and biochemically related disorders, including Hurler's syndrome, Tay-Sachs disease, sickle-cell anemia, and neural tube defects. Because of the *relatively* small number of such conditions, however, the most important use of the procedure has been to diagnose Down syndrome, "the most common single cause of mental retardation in our population, accounting for as much as 25 percent of cases of severe defects" (Warburton, 1980, p. 280).

The use of amniocentesis in diagnosing abnormalities associated with developmental disabilities and other handicaps is not without some risk of injury to the mother and fetus. According to Golbus et al. (1979), however, very little risk is involved for either when the procedure is performed in a controlled manner in a hospital setting. There is emerging evidence of some slight increase in spontaneous abortion following amniocentesis. As a result, there is a trend toward reduced use of the procedure in women in the 35 to 40 age range, since the risk for them is less than one percent (Warburton, 1980). For Down syndrome, at least, restricting amniocentesis screening to women over 40 would detect approximately 16% of the cases.

There is also some likelihood that newer, less invasive procedures will be developed to obtain cells from fetuses. Detecting and separating fetal cells in the blood of pregnant women would be one way of accomplishing this (Herzenberg, Bianchi, Schröder, Cann, & Iverson, 1979).

Phenylketonuria

With an incidence of about one per 14,000 newborns (Abuelo, 1983), phenylketonuria (PKU) is the result of a biochemical imbalance associated with high levels of phenylalanine, a protein substance. Excess phenylalanine is toxic to the developing brain, resulting in neurologic abnormalities and retarded cognitive development. The degree of mental retardation in approximately 90% of known cases is usually severe to profound (Penrose, 1962). Overall level of phenylalanine appears unrelated to impairment, however, and it has been reported that 3% of PKU victims are of normal intellectual functioning (Koch, Blaskovics, Wenz, Fishler, & Schaeffer, 1974). Other commonly reported characteristics are a humpbacked curvature of the spine, hyperkinesis, seizures in infancy and early childhood, wide spaces between the teeth, variable skin pigmentation, light-colored hair, blue eyes, abnormal EEGs (Sarason & Doris, 1969), and an unusual or musty body odor (Abuelo, 1983).

PKU is the result of the insufficient production by the liver of the enzyme phenylalanine hydroxylase, which is needed to convert phenylalanine to tyrosine. Since the missing enzyme cannot be provided to victims of PKU, the treatment of choice has been a dietary regimen low in phenylalanine in order to reduce high levels of toxic amino acids to the normal range (Abuelo, 1983).

Dietary treatment of PKU victims is an example of secondary prevention; that is, reducing the debilitating effects of a biochemical imbalance, since the means of prevention are yet unknown. PKU screening programs are in effect in all 50 states of the USA, and their effects have been well established. When excess levels of phenylalanine are detected in the blood of newborns, they are put on a diet that is maintained until at least 4 to 6 years of age. Williamson et al. (1981) reported that children started on a diet at an average age of 3 weeks, whose dietary control was satisfactory, achieved normal intellectual functioning by age 6. At this point, the diet is eliminated, even though the child continues to show excess levels of phenylalanine in the bloodstream. The toxic effects of elevated levels appear to be restricted to the very early years of growth and development. Currently, there is no clear consensus regarding the safe age for terminating dietary treatment. Recent data presented by Koff, Kammerer, Boyle, and Pueschel (1979) failed to detect any significant drop in the intellectual functioning of 30 PKU children whose diets had been terminated between 4 and 6 years of age. These children were periodically reassessed for 41 months after termination.

According to Abuelo (1983), whether the diet can be terminated safely at school age remains a point of some controversy. In addition, other questions arise as successfully treated children mature and approach child-bearing age. Since it is known that maternal phenylketonuria is associated with retardation, will successfully treated PKU females give birth to children with

PKU? Whether reinstitution of dietary restrictions for these women would reduce PKU occurring in their children has yet to be determined. As suggested by Abuelo (1983), a "well planned prospective clinical evaluation of preconceptual dietary treatment is sorely needed" (P. 112).

Cytomegalovirus

With an incidence estimated at 0.4 to 2.4% of live births (Alford, Stagno, & Reynolds, 1975), cytomegalovirus (CMV) is considered "the most frequent and serious form of intrauterine infection" (Lott, 1983, p. 100). A member of the herpes virus family, CMV leaves an estimated 10% of its survivors with neurologic impairment. However, the most severely affected infants represent less than 5% of all newborns infected with CMV (Papageorgiou, 1980). Incidence correlates inversely with maternal age. It is highest in mothers less than 25 years old and much lower in mothers 25 to 35 years of age.

CMV is associated with inflammation of the brain tissue and the meninges (meningoencephalitis). It may cause actual necrosis of brain tissue (Lott, 1983) and inhibit cell division in the developing fetal brain (Papageorgiou, 1980). Microcephaly is commonly associated with CMV, and seizures are often observed in newborns with the disease. Papageorgiou notes that CMV can also result in hearing impairment. As many as 30 to 50 percent of infants born with CMV have a loss of hearing in one or both ears.

The way in which the fetus becomes infected with CMV is not entirely clear. The most seriously affected CMV victims (in terms of mental retardation and neurologic involvement) have usually sustained the infection during the prenatal stage, and not during the birth process itself (Ballard, Drew, Hufnagle, & Riedel, 1979). Infection of the fetus appears to occur during the first or second trimester (Monif, Egan, Held, & Eitzman, 1972). CMV is excreted in the cervix in approximately 3 to 28% of all pregnant women. Moreover, according to Papageorgiou (1980), infections occurring perinatally are "5–10 times more common than intrauterine CMV infections." Hanshaw (1976) has reported that infants congenitally infected with CMV may continue to excrete it in their urine for years following birth. Similar to the high levels of phenylalanine that continue in children born with PKU, CMV appears also to persist. As Papageorgiou notes, however, it is not known whether the continuing presence of CMV is associated with further damage to the infant.

Prevention of CMV has not been as successful as with the other biomedical conditions discussed thus far. A CMV vaccine has been proposed; however, there are many unresolved questions concerning its efficacy and overall safety (Papageorgiou, 1980). Care in the use of blood transfusions can reduce the incidence of CMV transmitted in this manner. The isolation of pregnant women from newborns excreting CMV also is an efficacious strategy. Although therapeutic abortion could be offered, it would be based on insufficient information as to the risk of CMV to the fetus. Because lower socioeconomic status, crowded living conditions, and sexual promiscuity are also associated with CMV (Alford, 1977), general societal improvements in the standard of living would constitute a nonspecific preventive strategy.

DEVELOPMENTAL DISABILITIES WITH ENVIRONMENTAL CAUSES

Developmental disabilities resulting solely from the effects of biological factors represent some of the more notable successes in prevention, with the exception of CMV, which has eluded satisfactory preventive strategies.

Developmental disabilities thought to result largely from interactions between the child and his or her physical and social environment fall into two major classes: severe physical trauma, as might be experienced in an accident or episode of child abuse, and a sustained pattern of inadequate social interactions, primarily with caretakers. Since excellent coverage of the latter is available elsewhere (e.g., Ramey & Bryant, 1983), only chronic disability resulting from injuries sustained as the result of accident and the deliberate actions of others will be presented here, with those leading to developmental disability emphasized. Thus, such injuries must have occurred prior to the age of 22, result in chronic disability of indefinite duration, and lead to sustained functional limitations in three or more areas of major life activity.

Accidental Injury

Each year approximately 75 million persons in the United States are injured seriously enough to warrant medical attention or some restriction in activity (U.S. Department of Health, Education and Welfare, 1978). From age 1 until about age 40, injuries are the most frequent cause of death (Baker & Dietz, 1979). Despite such figures, when "compared with many diseases of far less consequence, the prevention of injuries has received relatively little scientific attention" (Baker & Dietz, 1979, p. 55).

Certain groups have been reliably identified as being at substantially higher risk for injury than others. For example, injuries resulting in death are highest in the elderly. Approximately 0.164% of people aged 75 to 84, compared with 0.086% of people 15 to 24 years of age, are killed by injury (Baker & Dietz, 1979). The likelihood of an injury being fatal is 2½ times greater for males than females. Nonfatal injuries occur 50% more frequently for males than females. People who use alcohol substantially increase their risk of injury. According to Wechsler, Kasey, Thum, and Demone (1969), alcohol was present in the blood of 16 to 56% of emergency room visitors injured on the road, at home, on the job, or in fights. More than 50% of persons killed while driving automobiles have been shown to have blood alcohol levels in the range representing intoxication in most states of the USA (Jones & Joscelyn, 1978).

As with injuries deliberately inflicted (see below), lower socioeconomic status has been associated with a greater number of injuries resulting from accidents. Baker and Dietz (1979) attribute this fact, in part, to employment in higher-risk jobs, unsafe housing, and the use of hazardous products, such as space heaters.

The incidence of developmental disability (as defined in PL 95–602) resulting from accidental injury has not been ascertained. Kraus and his colleagues have reported the incidence of paralysis from spinal cord injury (Kraus, Franti, Riggins, & Richards, & Borhani, 1975). Annegars et al. (1980) have examined the occurrence of epilepsy following head trauma. Given the large number of accidents reported each year, the resulting developmental disabilities must be at least in the tens of thousands.

The prevention of accidental injuries generally has taken the form of altering environmental factors, changing human behavior, or both. Several investigators recently have contrasted environmental and technological solutions with behavioral approaches and concluded in favor of the first (e.g., Baker & Dietz, 1979; Robertson 1986). According to Robertson (1986), accident prevention typically has involved a combination of efforts to change the behavior of people in proximity to a hazard, by means of public education as well as laws or administrative directives. Environmental and technological solutions are frequently excluded, despite the fact that "Virtually all of human injury in the industrialized countries is the result of modification of the elements of the environment by human organizations that concentrate energy in space and time at rates and amounts that injure" (Robertson, 1986, p. 347).

Robertson has reviewed some exemplary efforts to change behavior and concluded that they were not particularly effective. Similarly, Baker and Dietz (1979) commented that solutions to injuries are more promising when approached as an environmental rather than a human behavior problem. For example, high school driver-education programs have long been associated with lower auto insurance premiums for parents because of a supposedly lower frequency of accidents among teenagers who have learned to drive in this way. However, according to more recent studies that have compared students in driver training courses with carefully matched control groups, sub-sequent crash records fail to reveal differences between them (Ray, Weaver, Brink, & Stock, 1982). Although there appear to be no differences in the later driving skills of trained and control students, the net effect of driver-education programs is negative (Robertson & Zador, 1978) because these programs permit more teenagers in a high-accident age category to be on the road. When school districts that dropped such courses have been compared with those retaining them, a substantial reduction in the number of crashes among 16 to 17-year-olds has favored the former (Robertson, 1980).

It would appear, then, that one approach to preventing developmental disabilities due to automobile accidents among teenagers would be to reexamine the practice of permitting earlier licensing of driver-training graduates. The real issue, of course, is the wisdom of focusing preventive efforts on changing human behavior rather than the environment technology. Robertson contends that the technology is available to make most products safer, but that it is ignored. He urges legislation to change this condition. Similarly, Baker and Dietz (1979) recommend that health professionals and others interested in prevention influence decision makers, including legislators, designers, and manufacturers, to initiate injury-reducing policies and practices.

Often overlooked is that the passage of legislation itself is behavior. The behaviors of legislators and those who influence legislation are as subject to scientific analysis and understanding as any other behavior. Behavioral scientists need to give some attention to an experimental analysis of legislative activity (Cone & Hayes, 1980). On a local level, the work of Fawcett and his colleagues with city managers and city councils represent a promising beginning in this direction (Fawcett, Seekins, Whang, Muiv, & de Balcazar, 1984). In other words, even when environmental and technological solutions are developed to reduce injury, they need to be implemented. We know from recent reports of "accidental" chemical and toxic waste spills that regulations are not sufficient. Once governmental bodies such as the Environmental Protection Agency have been successfully influenced to produce appropriate regulatory controls, a behavioral technology will be needed to assure the implementation and sustained effects of these controls.

Injuries Resulting from Child Abuse

The magnitude of family violence is higher than generally realized. According to a survey by Strauss, Gelles, and Steinmetz (1980), 20% of couples interviewed reported they had hit a child with some object. Slightly over 4% admitted actually beating up a child. Kempe (1971) found that 25% of all fractures in 0- to 2-year-olds are the result of abuse. From 10 to 15% of all trauma seen in emergency rooms in children under age 3 is caused by abuse. Further, approximately 0.57% of all children in the United States are sexually, physically, or emotionally abused by parents or caregivers each year (National Center on Child Abuse and Neglect, 1981). The actual incidence is likely to be much higher, given the difficulty in documenting episodes of family violence.

There is general consensus that the effects of child abuse can lead to lifelong deficits, including mental retardation (Hansen, 1980). In an early study, Kempe and his colleagues (Kempe, Silverman, Steele, Droegmueller, & Silver, 1962) studied 302 abuse victims treated at hospitals. Of these, 85 suffered permanent brain injury. In another sample of 447 children identified through legal means, 29 were found to have suffered permanent brain injuries. Smith and Hanson (1974) found that 25% of a sample of 134 abused children in Britain had suffered a fractured skull. Fifteen percent of the sample showed long-term problems, including paraplegia, spasticity, and blindness. According to extrapolations by Hansen (1980), for every death of a child from abuse or neglect, four children are left with long-term incapacitating problems. She estimated that about 440 children a year in New Jersey "may develop some type of central nervous system disturbance as a result of maltreatment by parents or caretakers" (p. 552).

Early reports such as the above were largely the result of uncontrolled surveys. These make it difficult to attribute subsequent developmental problems to child abuse specifically. In the first controlled study in this area, Elmer (1977) failed to find significant differences in developmental problems in matched groups of abused and non-abused control children. The extent of both physical trauma and socioeconomic status were carefully controlled. Elmer's study included measures of school performance as well as physical and neurological development.

With specific attention to parent–child interaction in abusive and neglectful versus control families, Burgess and Conger (1978) failed to find substantial differences between the two groups. Other investigators have reported differences, however. For example, George and Main (1979) found that abused toddlers interacted differently with their caretakers than nonabused toddlers. Abused children threatened or assaulted their caretakers more often, and were more cautious and apprehensive in interactions with other adults. Kinnard (1980), comparing matched groups of 30 abused and 30 nonabused children, reported differences in five areas of emotional growth and development. Wolfe and Mosk (1983) found more parental reports of behavior problems in a group of school-age abused children than in a group of children from a child welfare agency or from the community.

Unfortunately, well-controlled studies definitively linking developmental disabilities with child abuse per se appear to be lacking. As Wolfe and Mosk (1983) have stated, initial research does not provide a sufficient basis for concluding that child abuse is "primarily responsible for the developmental consequences reported among these children" (p. 703). Similarly in a review of controlled studies in this area, Wolfe (1985) recently concluded that few investigations have found significant differences "between abusers and nonabusers on traditional psychological dimensions" (p. 462). He did, however, find patterns of interaction within abusing families to be more aversive and less prosocial than those in nonabusing families.

While the specific effects of child abuse and its probable sequelae remain unclear, there is little argument against the belief that it represents a threat to the healthy development of children and should be prevented. Although several approaches to child abuse prevention have been posted in the literature, there is as yet no consensus concerning the most efficacious strategy. Part of the difficulty stems from the multi-dimensional character of the phenomenon. Unlike the *conditions* discussed earlier in this chapter, child abuse is a *process*. As such, it can actually lead to some of the conditions generally considered to be developmental disabilities (e.g., epilepsy, cerebral palsy).

One tactic for preventing child abuse has been modeled after public health approaches for preventing disease. It involves mass screening to identify parents at risk for abuse. Once identified, such parents would undergo interventions aimed at altering environmental and individual behavioral precursors to abuse. Using the *Michigan Screening Profile of Parenting*, Helfer (1978) has pursued this approach with minimal success. Problems in getting abusive individuals to respond reliably to the questionnaire as well as the very high percentage of false positives, are major difficulties encountered with the individual screening approach.

Earlier, Light (1973) identified similar problems in the use of developmental screening instruments to *identify* child abuse after the fact. He argued that even a very sensitive measure would not be accurate in diagnosing abuse, because of its relatively low base rate of occurrence in the general population (typically assumed to be less than 4%). As Light and later Garbarino (1980) have pointed out, an unacceptably high number of false positives would result. Table 5-1 shows a breakdown of the types of errors that could be expected. From the table it can be seen that the vast majority of classificatory errors are false positives. Indeed, only a miniscule 0.4% of the sample would be abused children who were overlooked. Three times as many cases would be identified as abusive than actually are, however. Given the potential problems with false positives in this area (e.g., self-fulfilling prophecy, stigmatization, litigation), both Light (1973) and Garbarino (1980) argue that such a screening program is not justifiable.

In reviewing studies that have attempted to discover personality traits that might predict abusive behavior, Wolfe (1985) recently concluded that "studies using measures of underlying personality attributes or traits have been unable to detect any patterns associated with child abuse beyond general descriptions of displeasure in the parenting role and stress-related complaints" (p. 1465). Research by Conger and his associates has shown differences between abusive and control families when physical health and variables related to physical and emotional distress, including depression, have been examined (Conger, Burgess, & Barrett, 1979; Lahey, Conger, Atkeson, & Treiber, 1984). Also, when asked about their feelings of competence and frustration as parents, abusive parents reported more problems than controls in a

Table 5-1. Classification of Abuse in the Screening of 1000 Children

	True Status	
Test Results	Abusive (N = 40)	Non-abusive (N = 960)
Abusive	36	96
Nonabusive	4	864

Note. Assumes 4% prevalence and 90% accuracy. From "Preventing Child Maltreatment" by J. Garbarino in *Prevention in Mental Health* edited by R. H. Price, R. F. Ketterer, B. C. Bader, and J. Monahan, 1980, (p.69). Beverly Hills, Sage. Copyright 1980 by Sage. Reprinted by permission.

recent study by Mash, Johnston, and Kovitz (1983).

Wolfe (1985) concluded from his review that there is little support for the hypothesis that abusive parents manifest atypical characterological structures. Rather, the differences that have emerged tend to support a more situation-specific repertoire. Given a number of concomitant socioeconomic, emotional, and physical stressors, abusive parents respond with violence, whereas other parents with comparable exposure to such stressors do not. The different reactions to apparently comparable stimuli is the way in which these conditions are perceived (Wolfe, 1985).

Given the difficulty in finding consistent differences in the psychological makeup of abusive parents, and the various problems associated with screening devices (see Table 5-1), some investigators have recommended a sociological approach to the prevention of child abuse. Garbarino (1980, 1982) has suggested that prevention efforts focus on a "community climate inimical to the growth and maintenance of abusive and neglectful patterns of family life," "social rather than psychological forces," "community development," and the prevention of "social impoverishment of families" (1980, pp. 63–64). In its strongest form, the sociological perspective has been preferred as an alternative to "conventional, individually oriented pre-

vention programs . . . that are 'doomed to failure' (Zigler, 1979)" (Garbarino, 1980, p. 68).

Given the body of research revealing comparable social circumstances for abusing and nonabusing parents, however, the potential utility of the sociological approach is questionable. The concept of "necessary" social conditions is open to some dispute, given the findings of abuse at all levels of educational and socioeconomic status. A multilevel, interdisciplinary approach that combines work with individuals and improved social support is more likely to be useful (Belsky, 1980; Lutzker, 1983). Wolfe (1985) has outlined the components of such an approach. These are presented and supplemented with additional suggestions in Table 5-2. It is evident that a problem as complex as child maltreatment defies a single solution. It is inconceivable that medical science will ever discover a chromosomal aberration or biochemical imbalance that leads to child abuse, strong proponents of a biogenic hypothesis notwithstanding (Rimland, 1969). To date, prevention has been largely secondary, and then tertiary for the seriously injured victims. We can, however, move more strongly toward primary prevention, even if all the answers are not available. Many of the suggestions in Table 5-2 reflect such a before-the-fact emphasis.

Table 5-2. Preventing Child Abuse via Programs Aimed at Social-Community or Individual Change

Social-Community Actions
1. Provide subsidized daycare and preschool programs for every family.
2. Provide volunteer homemaker programs staffed by trained paraprofessionals.
3. Provide infant stimulation programs to facilitate skill development prior to preschool age.
4. Provide "respite" homes and/or "relief parents" who can take over parenting responsibilities in crises or in situations that might develop into crises.
5. Develop a massive public relations effort via legislation and mass media to change the social climate that permits, even promotes, child mistreatment.

Individual Actions
1. Introduce behavioral training in effective adult–child interactions to high school curricula. (Perhaps this could replace driver education courses!)
2. Provide training programs for parents to teach effective child management skills.
3. Provide intervention programs for parents to teach alternative ways of construing environmental and physical stressors.
4. Provide programs to teach effective ways of managing stressors once they have been construed differently.

ETHICAL CONSIDERATIONS IN PREVENTING DEVELOPMENTAL DISABILITIES AND OTHER HANDICAPPING CONDITIONS

Ethical considerations in this area are almost as complex as the area itself. Consider each of the following questions:

1. Does society have a right to subject every newborn to routine screening tests?
2. Does the right to screen apply both to medical (e.g., blood tests) and psychological procedures (e.g., developmental tests)?
3. Should parents found to be at risk on screening tests be required to undergo some form of intervention if it exists?
4. Should parents of developmentally disabled children be required to undergo genetic counseling?
5. Should mothers of defective fetuses be allowed to terminate their pregnancies?
6. Should persons known to have mental, emotional, or physical disabilities be required to undergo sterilization?
7. Should the parents of a developmentally disabled child be allowed to refuse medical treatment that would prolong their child's life?
8. Should abusive parents be required to attend parent-training sessions?
9. Should medical experimentation be permitted on human fetuses?
10. Should all persons be required to engage in certain safety precautions to prevent injury?

These ten questions are only a sample of the major ethical issues encountered in the field of prevention. Many are old questions that have defied answers through many years of discussion and will continue to elude complete resolution. The best we can hope for are contemporary answers that are shaped by the current political and social context.

The question of society's right to subject every newborn to routine screening tests has been answered in the affirmative by current medical practice. We even screen parents before conception (or at least before marriage) with mandatory premarital blood tests. The blood of neonates is routinely checked for evidence of numerous disorders (Guthrie, 1980). As a society, we have determined that the public health benefits are sufficient to outweigh the individual's right to refuse invasive procedures.

When we move from medical to behavioral areas, however, screening is not so easily justified. We have not been willing to require that all infants be screened for developmental delays. Nor have we implemented widespread screening of their homes for evidence of sufficient enrichment. As Coons and Frankenburg (1982) have observed, appropriate procedures must be available before screening can be done ethically. Measures that are simple, quick, economical, relevant to the population, reliable, and accurate must be used. No single measure meeting these requirements has yet been developed. "Simple," "quick," and "economical" have usually been correlated with "unreliable" and "invalid." Reliable and valid measures are usually not economical. Just as routine screening for certain medical conditions was made possible by the development of simple procedures (e.g., the Guthrie tests), routine screening for nonmedically obvious developmental delays must await similar technology.

Because a risk of recurrence exists for certain types of developmental disabilities, it is reasonable to make genetic counseling available to those who might benefit from it. The uncertain effectiveness of genetic counseling in producing reductions in births of defective children to counseled parents (Evers-Kiebooms & Van den Berghe, 1979) makes it premature to require it, however.

The availability of effective prenatal screening procedures (e.g., amniocentesis) makes it possible to detect some conditions associated with developmental disabilities before the fetus comes to term. The right of the mother to terminate such pregnancies has been affirmed by the Supreme Court in *Roe v. Wade*. The apparent increase in public sentiment against legalized abortions, however, might threaten this right in the future.

The general consensus in the early part of this century was that known "defectives" should be sterilized. By 1930, 28 states had sterilization laws for persons with certain criminal behavior and those with mental and physical difficulties (Beyer, 1983). Oliver Wendell Holmes upheld the constitutionality of such legislation in a 1927 U.S. Supreme Court decision, in which he noted that "the principle that sustains compulsory vaccination is broad enough to cover cutting the fallopian tubes . . . three generations of imbeciles are enough" (*Buck v. Bell*, 1927).

When the scientific bases for the eugenics movement that served as the impetus for sterilization laws were largely discredited, interest in such legislation waned (Beyer, 1983). Sterilization of "known defectives" is still prevalent, but it is now more likely to be voluntary than compulsory. The extent to which truly informed and voluntary consent is given is questionable. However, as Beyer has noted, several states have adopted legislation that moves strongly toward making it voluntary.

Parents' refusal of medical treatment for a developmentally defective child has been a point of contention in recent years, partly in response to federal regulations commonly referred to as "Baby Doe" rulings. The general issue of infanticide has confronted us throughout the ages. Interested readers are referred to Damme (1978) for a review. Increased attention to this issue was prompted in the early 1970s by a film entitled "Who Should Survive," by the John F. Kennedy Foundation. It depicts the agony of physicians, nurses, and parents struggling with the decision and subsequent consequences of prohibiting medical treatment that would have saved the life of an infant born with Down syndrome. More recently, a Down syndrome child with a similar, correctible problem was allowed to die when its parents refused corrective surgery in Bloomington, Indiana (Petroskey, 1982). This case gave rise to a United States Department of Health and Human Services notification to all hospitals receiving federal financial aid that it is unlawful to withhold medical care based on the handicapped state of the infant. The warning was based on Section 504 of the Rehabilitation Act of 1973 that prohibits discrimination on the basis of handicap. Subsequent legal decisions have led to some moderation of the DHHS ruling.

Requiring abusive parents to attend parent training classes might at first seem like a good idea, but is fraught with complexities. One might contend that similar intervention is routinely prescribed for persons found driving while intoxicated, whether the driver has injured someone or not. Since abusive parents already have injured someone, such classes certainly seem justifiable.

Although a strong case can be made for mandatory parent training, the "drink driving" analogy is flawed. First, the identification of drunken drivers is easier and more reliable. Second, defining drunken driving as a criminal offense is more straightforward. Courts are understandably reluctant to prosecute aggressively if it is unclear which parent is at fault, or whether the injury might have resulted from an accident. Moreover, the beneficial effects of parent training programs is uncertain for participants attending under legal mandate.

The use of human fetuses for experimentation also has been intensely debated. In recent genetic experimentation, several international panels have discussed the issue. At least two have suggested a 14-day limit on experimentation with embryos. Their thinking was that prior to 14 days of gestation, there is no brain cell development, and therefore the embryo lacks the essence of a human being. As Lamb (1984) has observed, this argument is analogous to defining a person as dead when the central nervous system no longer functions. Consequently, there is some logic to defining life as the point at which the central nervous system begins to function.

The relevance of the experimentation issue to this chapter is that research with the human fetus could possibly lead to the discovery of new ways of preventing developmental disabilities resulting from biomedical causes. Of course, employing a "central nervous system" criterion for other ethical questions might be more problematic.

Finally, the value of requiring all persons to engage in safety precautions to prevent accidental injury has been well documented. Despite arguments that the individual should have the right to choose his or her own protection or lack thereof, there are hundreds of laws and regulations requiring everything from motorcycle helmets to inspections of new electrical wiring. The recent widespread enactment of laws requiring child restraint in moving vehicles is a case in point. Unfortunately, whereas motorcyclists do comply with helmet laws (Robertson, 1976), automobile drivers often fail to restrain their children properly (Williams & Wells, 1981).

SUMMARY

This chapter has reviewed a portion of the literature relevant to the prevention of developmental disabilities and other handicapping conditions. A variety of conditions is included under the rubric of "developmental disabilities." Unfortunately no clear consensus yet exists as to its parameters.

After examining alternate conceptions of mental retardation specifically, and developmental disability in general, the chapter dealt with the prevention of biomedically caused developmental disability. Representative conditions were presented, ranging in degree of preventive success. Problems were noted, even in cases of relatively greater success.

The prevention of developmental disabilities resulting from environmental factors, particularly those leading to severe physical trauma, were covered. Accidental injuries, factors placing one at risk for them, and major prevention strategies were described and critiqued. A combination of environmental and technological and behavior change strategies was recommended.

Injuries resulting from the deliberate actions of others, specifically child abuse, also were reviewed. The incidence of severe head injury alone is sufficient to view child abuse as a major cause of devel-

opmental disability. Strategies for preventing child abuse were discussed, including community-action programs and individual intervention with parents.

Finally, ten ethical questions involved in preventing developmental disabilities and other handicapping conditions were discussed briefly.

A great deal is known about the prevention of developmental disabilities. What is needed at this time is greater recognition by educational, legislative, and funding agencies (e.g., third-party payers) of the value of prevention and the potential economic and intellectual benefits to be accrued from heightened activity in this field.

REFERENCES

Abuelo, D. N. (1983). Genetic disorders. In J. L. Matson & J. A. Mulick (Eds.), *Handbook of mental retardation* (pp. 105–120). New York: Pergamon.

Alford, C. A. (1977). Prenatal infections and psychosocial development in children born into lower socioeconomic settings. In P. Mittler (Ed.), *Research to practice in mental retardation.* Baltimore, MD: University Park Press.

Alford, C. A., Stagno, S., & Reynolds, D. W. (1975). Diagnosis of chronic perinatal infections. *American Journal of Disease in Children, 129,* 455.

American Psychiatric Association. (1980). *Diagnostic and statistical manual of mental disorders—III.* Washington, DC: American Psychiatric Association.

Annegars, J. F., Grabow, J. D., Groover, R. V., Laws, E. R., Elveback, L. R., & Kurland, L. T. (1980). Seizures after head trauma: A population study. *Neurology, 30,* 683.

Baker, S. P., & Dietz, P. E. (1979). Injury prevention. In *Healthy people: The Surgeon General's report on health promotion and disease prevention* DHEW Publication No. PHS 79-55071A, pp. 53–80. Washington, DC: U.S. Government Printing Office.

Ballard, R. A., Drew, W. L., Hufnagle, K. G., & Riedel, P. A. (1979). Acquired cytomegalovirus infection in preterm infants. *American Journal of Diseases in Children, 133,* 482–485.

Belsky, J. (1980). Child maltreatment: An ecological integration. *American Psychologist, 35,* 320–335.

Benda, C. L. (1960). *The child with mongolism.* New York: Grune & Stratton.

Beyer, H. A. (1983). Litigation with the mentally retarded. In J. L. Matson & J. A. Mulick (Eds.), *Handbook of mental retardation* (pp. 79–93). New York: Pergamon.

Buck v. Bell, 274 U.S. 200 (1927).

Burgess, R. L., & Conger, R. D. (1978). Family interaction in abusive, neglectful, and normal families. *Child Development, 49,* 1163–1173.

Caplan, G. (1964). *Principles of preventive psychiatry.* New York: Basic Books.

Clarren, S. K., & Smith, D. W. (1978). The fetal alcohol syndrome. *Journal of Medicine, 298,* 1063–1067.

Cone, J. D. (1984). *The Pyramid Scales: Criterion-referenced measures of adaptive behavior in handicapped persons.* Austin, TX: PRO-ED.

Cone, J. D., & Hayes, S. C. (1980). *Environmental problems/behavioral solutions.* Monterey, CA: Brooks/Cole.

Conger, R., Burgess, R., & Barrett, C. (1979). Child abuse related to life change and perceptions of illness: Some preliminary findings. *Family Coordinator, 28,* 73–78.

Coons, C. E., & Frankenburg, W. K. (1982). Applied biomedical research in mental retardation-prevention. *Applied Research in Mental Retardation, 3,* 221–231.

Cooper, L. Z., Ziring, P. R., Ockerse, A. B., Fedon, B. A., Kiely, B., & Krugman, S. (1969). Rubella. *American Journal of Disease in Children, 118,* 18–29.

Damme, C. (1978). Infanticide: The worth of an infant under law. *Medical History, 22,* 1–25.

Elmer, E. A. (1977). A follow-up study of traumatized children. *Pediatrics, 59,* 273–279.

Evers-Kiebooms, G., & Van Den Berghe, H. (1979). Impact of genetic counseling: A review of published follow-up studies. *Clinical Genetics, 15,* 465–474.

Fawcett, S. B., Seekins, T., Whang, P. L., Muiu, C., & de Balcazar, Y. S. (1984). Creating and using social technologies for community empowerment. *Prevention in Human Services, 3,* 145–171.

Garbarino, J. (1980). Preventing child maltreatment. In R. H. Price, R. F. Ketterer, B. C. Bader, & J. Monahan (Eds.), *Prevention in mental health: Research, policy, and practice* pp. 63–79. Beverly Hills: Sage.

Garbarino, J. (1982). *Children and families in the social environment.* Hawthorne, NY: Aldine.

George, C., & Main, M. (1979). Social interactions of young abused children: Approach, avoidance, and aggression. *Child Development, 50,* 306–318.

Golbus, M. S., Loughman, W. D., Epstein, C. J., Halbash, G., Stephens, J. D., & Hall, B. D. (1979). Prenatal genetic diagnosis in 3000 amniocenteses. *New England Journal of Medicine, 300,* 157–163.

Grossman, H. (Ed.). (1977). *Manual on terminology and classification in mental retardation.* Washington, DC: American Association on Mental Deficiency.

Guthrie, R. (1980). Newborn infant screening and the prevention of mental retardation. In M. K. McCormack (Ed.), *Prevention of mental retardation and other developmental disabilities* (pp. 269–278). New York: Marcel Dekker.

Hansen, C. (1980). Child abuse: A cause and effect of mental retardation. In M. K. McCormack (Ed.), *Prevention of mental retardation and other developmental disabilities* (pp. 549–568). New York: Marcel Dekker.

Hanshaw, J. B. (1976). Cytomegalovirus. In J. S. Remington & J. O. Klein (Eds.), *Infectious diseases of the fetus and newborn infant.* Philadelphia: Saunders.

Heber, R. (1959). *Manual on terminology and classification in mental retardation.* Washington, DC: American Association on Mental Deficiency.

Helfer, R. (1978). *Report on the research using the Michigan Screening Profile of Parenting (MSPP).* Washington, DC: National Center on Child Abuse and Neglect.

Herzenberg, L. A., Bianchi, D. W., Schröder, J., Cann, H. M., & Iverson, G. M. (1979). Fetal cells in the blood of pregnant women: Detection and enrichment by fluorescence-activated cell sorting. *Proceedings of the National Academy of Sciences, 76,* 1453–1455.

Hook, E. B. (1978). Spontaneous deaths of fetuses with chromosomal abnormalities diagnosed prenatally. *New England Journal of Medicine, 299,* 1036–1038.

Hook, E. B. (1982). Epidemiology of Down syndrome. In S. M. Pueschel & J. E. Rynders (Eds.), *Down syndrome: Advances in biomedicine and the behavioral sciences.* Cambridge, MA: The Ware Press.

Hook, E. B., & Fabia, J. J. (1978). Frequency of Down syndrome in live births by single-year maternal age interval: Results of a Massachusetts study. *Teratology, 17,* 223–228.

Horstmann, D. M. (1971). Rubella: The challenge of its control. *Journal of Infectious Diseases, 123,* 640–654.

International Classification of Diseases, 9th revision (1977), Albany, NY: World Health Organization Publications Centre.

Jones, R. K., & Joscelyn, K. B. (1978). *1978 Report on alcohol and highway safety.* Washington, DC: Department of Transportation.

Kempe, C. H. (1971). Pediatric implications of the battered baby syndrome. *Archives of Disease in Childhood, 46,* 28.

Kempe, C. H., Silverman, F. N., Steel, B. F., Droegmueller, W., & Silver, H. (1962). The battered child syndrome. *Journal of the American Medical Association, 181,* 17–24.

Kinard, E. M. (1980). Emotional development in physically abused children. *American Journal of Orthopsychiatry, 50,* 686–696.

Koch, R., Blaskovics, M., Wenz, E., Fishler, K., & Schaeffer, G. (1974). Phenylalanemia and phenylketonuria. In W. L. Nyhan (Ed.), *Hereditable disorders of amino acid metabolism.* New York: Wiley.

Koff, E., Kammerer, B., Boyle, P., & Pueschel, S. M. (1979). Intelligence and phenylketonuria: Effects of diet termination. *Journal of Pediatrics, 94,* 534–537.

Kraus, J. F., Franti, C. E., Riggins, R. S., Richards, D., & Borhani, N. O. (1975). Incidence of traumatic spinal cord lesions. *Journal of Chronic Diseases, 28,* 471–492.

Lahey, B. B., Conger, R. D., Atkeson, B. M., & Treiber, F. A. (1984). Parenting behavior and emotional status of physically abused mothers. *Journal of Consulting and Clinical Psychology, 52,* 1062–1071.

Lamb, E. (1984). Comments made in "Infertility: The great debate," *The Stanford Magazine, 12,* 28–35.

Light, R. (1973). Abused and neglected children in America: A study of alternative policies. *Harvard Educational Review, 43,* 556–598.

Lott, I. T. (1983). Perinatal factors in mental retardation. In J. L. Matson & J. A. Mulick (Eds.), *Handbook of mental retardation,* (pp. 97–104). New York: Pergamon.

Lutzker, J. R. (1983). Project 12-ways: Treating child abuse and neglect from an ecobehavioral perspective. In R. F. Dangel & R. A. Polster (Eds.), *Parent training: Foundations of research and practice,* (pp. 260–297). New York: Guildford.

Mash, E. J., Johnston, C., & Kovitz, K. (1983). A comparison of the mother–child interactions of physically abused and nonabused children during play and task situations. *Journal of Clinical Child Psychology, 12,* 337–346.

Monif, G. R. G., Egan, E. A., Held, B., & Eitzman, D. V. (1972). The correlation of maternal cytomegalovirus infection during varying stages in gestation with neonatal involvement. *Journal of Pediatrics, 80,* 17–20.

National Center on Child Abuse and Neglect. (1981). *Executive summary: National study of the incidence and severity of child abuse and neglect* (DHHS Publication No. OHDS 81-30329).

Washington, DC: U.S. Government Printing Office.

Needleman, H. L. (1983). Environmental pollutants. In C. C. Brown (Ed.), *Childhood learning disabilities and prenatal risk,* (pp. 38–43). New Brunswick, NJ: Johnson & Johnson.

Papageorgiou, P. (1980). Infectious diseases in the intrauterine period of development. In M. K. McCormack (Ed.), *Prevention of mental retardation and other developmental disabilities* (pp. 385–445). New York: Marcel Dekker.

Penrose, L. S. (1962). *The biology of mental defect* (rev. ed.). New York: Grune & Stratton.

Petroskey, D. (1982) Court's involvement makes infant's death noteworthy, *Indianopolis star,* April 27.

Pueschel, S. M., & Goldstein, A., (1983). Genetic counseling. In J. L. Matson & J. A. Mulick (Eds.), *Handbook of mental retardation,* (pp. 259–269). New York: Pergamon.

Ramey, C. T., & Bryant, D. M. (1983). Early intervention. In J. L. Matson & J. A. Mulick (Eds.), *Handbook of mental retardation,* (pp. 467–478). New York: Pergamon.

Ray, H. W., Weaver, J. K., Brink, J. R., & Stock, J. R. (1982). *Safe performance secondary school education curriculum.* Washington, DC: National Highway Traffic Safety Administration.

Rehabilitation Act of 1973: Public Law 93–112, Section 504, 29 U.S.C. 794. Rehabilitation, Comprehensive Services, and Developmental Disabilities Amendments of 1978: Public Law 95-602, 29 U.S.C. 701.

Rimland, B. (1969). Psychogenesis versus biogenesis: The issues and the evidence. In C. S. Plog & W. B. Edgerton (Eds.), *Changing perspectives in mental illness,* (pp. 702–735). New York: Holt, Rinehart & Winston.

Roberts, C. A. (1970). Psychiatric and mental health consultation. *Canadian Journal of Public Health, 51,* 17–24.

Robertson, L. S. (1976). An instance of effective legal regulation: Motorcyclist helmet and daytime headlamp laws. *Law and Society Review, 10,* 456–477.

Robertson, L. S. (1980). Crash involvement of teenaged drivers when driver education is eliminated from high school. *American Journal of Public Health, 70,* 599–603.

Robertson, L. S. (1986). Injury. In L. Michelson & B. Edelstein (Eds.), *Handbook of prevention,* (pp. 343–360). New York: Plenum.

Robertson, L. S., & Zador, P. L. (1978). Driver education and fatal crash involvement of teenaged drivers. *American Journal of Public Health, 68,* 959–965.

Roe v. Wade 93 S. Ct. p.705 (1973).

Sarason, S. B., & Doris, J. (1969). *Psychological problems in mental deficiency* (4th ed.). New York: Harper & Row.

Seltzer, G. B. (1983). Systems of classification. In J. L. Matson & J. A. Mulick (Eds.), *Handbook of mental retardation*, (pp. 143–156). New York: Pergamon.

Singer, D. B., Rudolph, A. J., Rosenberg, H. S., Rawls, W. E., & Boniuk, M. (1967). Pathology of the congenital rubella syndrome. *Journal of Pediatrics, 71,* 665–675.

Smith, S. M., & Hanson, R. (1974). 134 Battered children: A medical and psychological study. *British Medical Journal, 3;* 666–670.

Straus, M. A., Gelles, R. J., & Steinmetz, S. K. (1980). *Behind closed doors: Violence in the American family.* Garden City, NY: Doubleday/Anchor.

Streissguth, A. P. (1983). Smoking and drinking. In C. C. Brown (Ed.), *Childhood learning disabilities and prenatal risk.* (pp. 49–57). New Brunswick, NJ: Johnson & Johnson.

U.S. Department of Health, Education, and Welfare, Public Health Service, Health Resources Administration, National Center for Health Statistics. (March 7 1978). Episodes of persons injured: United States, 1975. *Advance Data.*

Warburton, D. (1980). Amniocentesis in the prevention of mental retardation. In M. K. McCormack (Ed.), *Prevention of mental retardation and other developmental disabilities.* (pp. 279–287). New York: Marcel Dekker.

Wechsler, H., Kasey, E. H., Thum, D., & Demone, Jr., H. W. (1969). Alcohol level and home accidents. *Public Health Reports, 84,* 1043–1050.

Williams, A. F., & Wells, J. A. K., (1981). The Tennessee child restraint law in its third year. *American Journal of Public Health, 71,* 163.

Williamson, M. L., Koch, R., Azen, C., & Chang, C. (1981). Correlates of intelligence test results in treated phenylketonuric children. *Pediatrics, 68,* 161–167.

Wolfe, D. A. (1985). Child-abusive parents: An empirical review and analysis. *Psychological Bulletin, 97,* 462–482.

Wolfe, D. A., & Mosk, M. D. (1983). Behavioral comparisons of children from abusive and distressed families. *Journal of Consulting and Clinical Psychology, 51,* 702–708.

Zigler, E. (1979). Controlling child abuse in America: An effort doomed to failure? In R. Bourne & E. Newberger (Eds.), *Critical perspectives on child abuse.* Lexington, MA: D. C. Heath.

Preparation of this chapter was supported in part by Grant No. G008100025 National Institute of Handicapped Research. I would like to thank Michael L. Murphy for his exceeding patience with me and his consummate skill at the word processor.

CHAPTER 6

Family Adjustment: Issues in Research on Families with Developmentally Disabled Children

Jean Ann Summers

The pervasive emphasis of disability policy in the last decade has been on successfully integrating children and adults with disabilities into the community. With children, the primary focus of intervention is on developing support systems that will allow families to keep their child at home. The emphasis with adults is on developing appropriate levels of independence that include maintaining family ties. Not surprisingly, researchers and service providers have begun to view the family of the person with a disability as a key element in the success of these efforts. Especially during the early years, the family plays an enormous role in shaping the child's future capacity to be an independent adult.

In the process of pursuing greater benefits to the individual with a disability, service providers have become increasingly aware of their responsibilities *beyond* the individual. Families are not merely tools in the service provider's arsenal of interventions. They are also people who share the impact of disability with their family member. They experience the same stigma, the same celebrations of hard-won accomplishment, and many of the same stresses as the person with the disability, in addition to other stresses unique to themselves. Families share the sorrows and also the triumphs that disabilities bring. Thus, service providers are gradually broadening their definition of "client" to include the whole family.

This awakening sense of responsibility on the part of service providers has placed a concomitant demand on researchers to sharpen understanding of the impact of a disability on the family. Effective practice must have a strong theoretical underpinning that gives direction to intervention. Unfortunately, research to date has resulted in more questions than answers. The voluminous body of literature produced over the last three decades is rife with insignificant differences, conflicting results, and methodological problems. In addition, nearly every researcher has a unique definition of "impact" of the disability. Dependent variables range from undefined terms such as "acceptance" or "adjustment" to measures of stress. After a review of this literature the question remains: Just what do we mean by the impact of a disability on families? Apparently nobody knows.

Perhaps an even more important issue to emerge from this research is how to deal with the apparent diversity of family reactions. The plethora of insignificant or conflicting results is in itself an important finding: Some families manage quite well, while others fall apart under similar or seemingly less challenging circumstances. What are the differences between successful and unsuccessful families? Even among families that are coping well, there is a wide diversity of structures and interactional styles. What, aside from their success, do these families have in common? If we could reliably identify successful families, a careful study of them could lead to more effective interventions with unsuccessful families.

HISTORICAL PERSPECTIVES

A discussion of historical perspectives of any issue often carries an implication that each new phase has ushered in successively higher levels of enlightenment and that the older erroneous assumptions have been discarded. Nothing is further from the truth. Ideas evolve more often by building on the past than by reversing older perspectives. The value of historical overview lies in the opportunity it presents to consider the source of current thinking. Thus, the purpose of this section is to discover the contribution of past perspectives of families with disabled children to current assumptions about them. There are three

major lines of thought about families that can be traced to the present: the family as the cause of the disability, the family as a victim of disability, and families as providers of services to people with disabilities.

Families as Villains

The nature–nurture controversy that periodically comes up in discussions of developmental disabilities focuses on families. The combatants in the dispute are proponents of heredity as the main source of disability, versus proponents of environment as the main determinant. Both sides share a common assumption about the cause of disability. The indictments are different, but the accused is the same: the family.

Genes as Genesis

The turn of the century saw a confluence of ideas from biology and the social sciences: Darwin's theory of evolution, Mendel's studies of genetics, and Binet's tests of mental ability. These ideas in turn gave rise to the social Darwinists, who saw human society evolving in accordance with the same laws of selection and survival that Darwin had observed in animals in the wild. Eugenicists went a step further in thinking that humanity could take matters into its own hands by actively encouraging "superior stock" and discouraging "inferior stock" (Scheerenberger, 1983). This notion took a variety of forms, from restricting immigration of people who were "feebleminded" (Sarason and Doris, 1979) to the isolation and sterilization of people with disabilities (Haavik & Menninger, 1981). The ultimate expression of this line of thought was Adolph Hitler's "final solution" — systematic elimination of races of people that he viewed as inferior.

Studies of families during this period were centered around proving the eugenicists' view. Studies like *The Kalikaks* (Goddard, 1912) traced certain families over generations of dissolution, poverty, crime, mental illness, and disabilities.

Services for people with disabilities from about 1900 to the mid-1940s consisted of

removing them from their families and isolating them from the rest of the community. There was an implication that
helping families with problems would
only prolong their agony and do a disserv-
ice to society as a whole (Kerlin, 1889/
1976). As time passed and people realized
the solution was not that simple, attention
turned to new scientific developments,
such as genetic counseling and amniocentesis. While these approaches are much less
judgmental of families and hold great
promise of preventing a number of disabling conditions, professionals must still
be careful to avoid the implication to families that a genetic defect means they are
somehow less worthy as human beings.

Love 'em or Leave 'em

Proponents of environmental causes of
disability, on the other hand, focused on
the problems of an impoverished
emotional or cognitive environment. In
the early part of this century, the environmental position was adopted by many
school systems in large cities. Schools
attempted to "Americanize" children of
immigrants as quickly as possible with
heavy doses of English, Anglo culture, and
patriotism (Sarason & Doris, 1979). Family
cultural heritage was not something to be
proud of, but rather to transcend.

Another facet of the environmental
point of view was provided by the Freud-
ians, who believed that mental disorders
were the result of traumas inflicted on children by their parents. Parents of children
and adults with emotional disordes were
portrayed as cold, rejecting, restrictive, perfectionistic, and demanding (Benson &
Turnbull, 1986). The catch phrase "refriger-
ator mothers" (Bettleheim, 1950) became a
label for parents of autistic children.
Parents of mentally retarded children, on
the other hand, were seen as overprotective
and rejecting (Dingman, Eyeman, &
Windle, 1963).

In the 1960s, the parents-as-cause formulation turned to examining the consequences of cultural deprivation among
welfare families. Research in this decade
focused on insufficient language or cognitive stimulation in poverty-stricken

homes. Attempts to correct the problem
were in the form of intensive early stimulation preschools coupled with parent
training. These programs have undoubtedly been successful, and numerous developmental gains for children have been
documented. Many clinicians now explain
that children with developmental delays
need stimulation beyond what is usually
sufficient for a nondisabled child. The
implication lingers in some quarters, however, that there is something wrong with
these family environments that requires
"fixing" (Benson & Turnbull, 1986).

Families as Victims

A second line of thought about families
with disabled children is that they are the
unfortunate recipients of untold misery
and anguish. Researchers present a litany
of grief, despair, and distress. In the 1950s,
the final stage of adjustment to the reality
of mental retardation was supposed to be
the family's acceptance of institutionalization of their child (Farber, 1960). Studies
documented marital dissolution (Jordan,
1962), sibling disturbances (Farber & Ryckman, 1965; Gath, 1974), chronic depression
in mothers, and socioeconomic stagnation
(Farber, 1968). Reaction to the birth of a
child with a disability was, and still is,
likened to the cycle of grief attending the
death of a loved one, as parents mourn the
loss of their imagined perfect child (Bristor,
1984). Although many of these studies present useful models for clinical intervention
with families in distress, many of the
results are derived from individual case
studies or poor sampling methods (Crnic,
Friedrich, & Greenburg, 1983). The
assumption that the effects of disability are
inevitably negative continues to lead
researchers to focus exclusively on stress
measures and on documenting the effects
of the burden of care.

Families as Service Providers

As a deinstitutionalization movement
has developed, it no longer is customary to
advise families to remove children with
disabilities from their homes. Instead,

parents are urged to keep their children at home or to accept the return of formerly institutionalized sons and daughters to the community. There are few supports available for families of children, which perhaps explains why home placement is the most cost-effective alternative (Wieck & Bruininks, 1980). Parents of institutionalized adults, however, are expected to make a complete reversal of what they long ago had been convinced was the best choice for their child (Avis, 1985; Conroy, 1985). Parents who seek out-of-home placement for their children are given the message that they are less competent and strong than other families (Kupfer, 1982).

Rather than simply keep their child at home, parents are expected to participate in their child's habilitation. They are asked to provide input and approve individualized plans. They are expected to supplement training in schools and residential and vocational programs with home training and motor therapy sessions. And they are expected to be case managers: finding, accessing, and coordinating the various services their child may need. All of this is done to foster the developing independence of the child in the least restrictive environment. There is little thought that the least restrictive environment for the child may be the most restrictive environment for the rest of the family (Benson & Turnbull, 1986).

Summary

These lines of thought form the basis of assumptions that researchers and service providers carry with them into their work: (a) families of children with disabilities are disabled families, (b) the effect of disability is pervasive and bad, and (c) "good" families have reordered their lives around the needs of the child with a disability. These assumptions have had extensive ramifications for the design of service programs and for the lives of families who have come in contact with those programs. The questions in this chapter, however, have more to do with the ways in which such assumptions have shaped research on the impact of disabilities on families.

CONTEMPORARY RESEARCH ISSUES

The assumptions listed above have hampered resolution of two main questions that are (or should be) the focus of research on families with disabled children: What is the impact of disability?; What are the characteristics of successful families? In the case of the first question, the assumption that all effects are negative precludes a comprehensive definition of what is meant by "impact." With regard to the second question, if we subscribe to the assumption that families with disabled children are disabled families, it must be concluded that successful families do not exist. Finally, if it is assumed that families should devote themselves to the well-being of the child with a disability then a successful family would be defined entirely in terms of the person's developmental progress, without regard to the well-being of any other family members. Neither alternative is attractive.

For all their faults, the neat formulations of the past provide comfort and structure to researchers as they design their studies. Discarding them confronts researchers with the harsh reality of a complex world. The problem in defining both impact and success is basically one of multiplicity. There is more than one impact; there is more than one route to success. Moreover, there is no such thing as *the* family; families are diverse entities engaged in varied and complicated interactions that change over time. People change, and so do families. Contemporary issues, then, are centered around the problem of working with multiplicity: inputs or independent variables, changes in time, strategies for success, and outcomes for any given family.

Inputs

Research on families with a disabled member is notoriously abundant with methodological problems. These have been noted in several literature reviews. The majority of articles are case reports and personal family narratives. Murphy (1982) reviewed 50 articles and found only 16 analytical studies. Of these, only 8 included a control group of families with children without disabilities. Hewett (1976) noted an overreliance on research samples drawn from families referred to clinics, resulting in a lack of representation of the total population, including families not actively seeking help. Other methodological problems include employment of measures with poor reliability and validity (Crnic et al., 1983) and the use of subjective, open-ended interviews as a means of gathering data from parents (Blacher, 1984; Wright, Granger, & Sameroff, 1984). Although these studies may have great intuitive power and potential value in suggesting areas for more rigorous research, taken alone they lack both reliability and generalizability.

A major problem in research on families is that they are so highly variable. They vary in size, number of parents, socioeconomic status, ethnic background, religion, social support networks, value system, and communication and problem-solving skills. Disabilities differ in nature, severity, and the caretaking demands they impose. In view of these factors, an adequate sample to measure families on any given dependent variable is almost impossible to assemble. One example of this difficulty is a recent study by Kazak and Marvin (1984) that attempted to measure differences in support networks for families with and without disabilities. Families in the non-disabled control group were selected and matched according to the age of the child in the disability group. Unfortunately, the control group had a median annual income almost $12,000 higher than the disability sample, and in more of the control families both parents were employed. These investigators found that support networks for families of children with disabilities were smaller and more dense (i.e., the networks tended to be closed, cohesive groups). However, the degree to which these findings relate to the presence of a disability is questionable. Although the differences in annual income and dual-job status were not significantly correlated to the major variables, the small sample size (56 families with handicapped children and 53 with-

out) leaves their effects open to question. Families with lower socioeconomic status generally tend to be more isolated (Embry, 1980). Also, there is a good chance that families in which both spouses work have expanded social networks through their jobs. Thus, the impact of disability on a family's social support network has yet to be determined. The point, beyond the issue of social support, is that "when family demographic characteristics are ignored, which has too often been the case in research with families of atypical children, the findings of even the best-designed studies are open to question" (Stoneman & Brody, 1984, pp. 196–197).

The result of these sampling problems is a plethora of conflicting data and nonsignificant findings. One example is a series of studies about the impact of disability on marital adjustment or satisfaction. Some investigators (e.g., Farber, 1960) found significantly more role tension among couples with children with mental retardation. Waisbren (1980), however, reported no significant differences in marital relations among parents of disabled and nondisabled infants. Gath (1977) found no greater or lesser evidence of marital dissolution, but rather that families of children with Down syndrome tended to have either very good or very bad marriages. Both Waisbren and Gath speculated that disability may tend to bring couples with basically sound marriages even closer together, but push couples with other problems farther apart. In an effort by DeMeyer and Goldberg (1983), couples with autistic adolescents had a lower divorce rate than that of the general population in their state (26% versus 40.3%). Again, there is no clear indication of the impact of disability on the quality of parents' marital relationships.

A growing number of investigators are recognizing this problem. Crnic et al. (1983) described the need for research to take into account the multiple inputs that might have an impact on families. Yando and Zigler (1984) also noted that more recent work has begun to use multifactor designs based on a theory of family functioning. These authors also point out that the search for the relationship of demographic variables to families' reaction's to disability may be the wrong approach. Rather, more relevant factors may relate to family relationships and the quality of interactions among members. Investigators of families in general are reaching the same conclusion. For example, Walsh (1982) has noted that in the search for factors defining "normal" or successful families, comparisons of different forms (e.g., single-parent, remarried families, working mothers, homosexual couples, ethnic variations) are of limited value. She states: "Variance within each form was high; some families in each form were more effective than others, which suggests that each form holds the potential for successful adjustment. *Family processes were found to be more important factors than family forms*" (Walsh, 1982, p. 8, italics added).

Family process refers to the family's interactional system. These processes include the rules, roles, and subgroupings that define day-to-day interaction. One element of the family system is cohesion, which is the degree of closeness or distance family members have with one another. Another element is adaptability, or the extent to which families can change to accommodate new situations. Several researchers have called for an emphasis on family systems in studies of families with disabled children (e.g., Simmeonsson & McHale, 1981; Skrtic, Summers, Brotherson, & Turnbull, 1984; Stoneman & Brody, 1984; Summers, Turnbull, & Brotherson, in press).

Family values are another set of variables that may have more importance than demographic factors (Turnbull, Summers, & Brotherson, 1984). Values and beliefs are perceptions of what the world is like, and what it ought to be like. Values play a part in selecting life goals (e.g., success, contentment, a loving family life, independence) and in determining, for example, how to pursue those goals (e.g., people should be honest, open, and straightforward with others) and raise children (e.g., children should be obedient, or be exposed to numerous experiences). Values may also be a factor in a family's ability or willingness to access services (e.g., "we take care of our own") or rely on social support (e.g., "we don't burden others with our troubles").

An example of how values may be salient is shown in a classic study by Farber and Ryckman (1965). These investigators found that middle-class and upper-middle-class families tended to react to the birth of a mentally retarded child as a "tragic crisis" and to exhibit grief and frustration over their child's chances for future accomplishment. These responses were not as often observed in families of lower socioeconomic status. We could speculate that the critical factor might be an achievement ethic held by more families of higher socioeconomic status than by those of lower socioeconomic status. The relationship of values to the impact of disability is an important area for future research.

In the comparison of successful and unsuccessful families, values may also be useful in arriving at a definition of "success." Values shape our life goals, and the achievement of those goals is called success. It may be difficult, if not impossible, to arrive at a value-free definition of success. Thus, it would be unfair to measure family success based on researcher-imposed values, rather than on each family's own definition and goals. Since families are likely to pursue a variety of goals, this shift in emphasis often presents methodological headaches. The effort is worthwhile, however, in order to develop a more relevant body of research.

Changes

The implications of the family life cycle have gained increasing attention from researchers in recent years. Families change over time. Children are born, grow up, leave home; adults pass through youth, mid-life crises, and retirement. At each stage, families tend to adopt different interactional styles that are appropriate to their needs. For example, in a study of 1,000 families, Olson et al. (1983) found that younger families in general tended to be more cohesive and more adaptable, while older families tended to be less cohesive (allowing more individuation) and less adaptable.

For families of children with disabilities, it is becoming apparent that life cycle plays a role in the impact of disability. Suelzle and Keenan (1981) reported that families tended to have less access to services as they became older. Similarly, Birenbaum (1971) found that families with older children became more isolated as they were increasingly unable to maintain the image of "normal" family life. In short, it is clear that families of children with disabilities have both different characteristics and needs. As Murphy (1982) has pointed out, studies that employ samples from all life cycle stages may be masking important factors at each stage.

Another life cycle issue involves the transition from one stage to the next as the family reorganizes its interactional style to accommodate new people and needs. This reorganization process is stressful for any family (Terkelson, 1980), but especially so for families of children with disabilities. Wikler, Wasow, and Hatfield (1981) found that families tended to experience a resurgence of sorrow during times when they were or should have been in the midst of a transition (e.g., child entering school, child's 21st birthday). Life cycle theorists note that families feel even greater stress when the transition occurs at a time other than according to accepted cultural standards (Neugarten, 1976). This finding would explain the stress some families feel as their child becomes an adult and yet remains dependent, they must come to terms with their lifelong responsibilities. The main point is that any study attempting to measure the impact of disability, especially in terms of stress, needs to determine whether the families in the study are going through a life cycle transition (Turnbull, Brotherson, & Summers, 1986).

Coping Strategies

Any action or rethinking a person does that results in reduced feelings of stress is a coping strategy (Pearlin & Schooler, 1978). Studies of coping and coping strategies are therefore aimed at identifying how families successfully handle disability. Stress and coping theorists have identified a variety of strategies people use to cope. These may be classified in five major categories.

Passive Appraisal

Ignoring or refusing to think about a problem in the hope it will go away (Olson et al., 1983).

Reframing

Changing the way one thinks about a problem to make it seem less stressful. This includes such strategies as focusing on the positive contributions — the silver lining on the cloud — and considering the ways in which one's situation is really less difficult than others (positive comparisons) (Turnbull et al., 1984).

Spiritual Support

Explaining the meaning of a problem or situation and reducing stress through fitting the situation into a larger, purposeful framework. This category also includes gaining support from religious teachings (Turnbull, Turnbull, Summers, Brotherson, & Benson, 1986).

Social Support

Relying on friends, extended family, and others for material and emotional support. Social support also includes reduced feelings of stress that come from the knowledge that one is an accepted member of a group (Cobb, 1976).

Professional Support

Utilizing professional services (e.g., therapists, medical assistance, social service agencies) to resolve problems (Olson et al., 1983).

A family may use any one or all of these strategies to tackle the problems of disability. The absence of any one strategy is not necessarily an indicator of stress, since a family may find another strategy more useful for its particular preferences and life-style. For example, many researchers assume that a lack of social support indicates stress. One of the subscales in Holroyd's (1974) Questionnaire on Resources and Stress (QRS) measures the availability of social support and two others measure reframing, or the lack of it (Negative Attitudes, Pessimism). Scores indicating that these strategies are absent cannot be taken as a measure of stress; however, that is exactly the conceptual leap made when they are added with the other subscales to produce an overall stress score.

There are many routes to success, and many ways to cope. Coping strategies may be more effective in some situations than in others. For example, a family awaiting the results of a diagnostic work-up might do well to employ a little passive appraisal, but it would be a poor strategy to use when a child is 4½ and parents are faced with the imminent need to choose from several alternatives for school placement. Passive appraisal in the latter case might reduce feelings of stress but block the family's ability to attend to the task at hand. Thus, research is needed to identify the coping strategies used in different situations, and the results.

The Elusive Outcome

A basic starting point for most research is: What are we looking for? The significance of the dependent variable is the modus operandi of the research design, and its significance is the rationale for undertaking the research in the first place. In many studies of families of children with disabilities, the outcome may unfortunately be defined vaguely or not at all. Broad constructs are used, such as acceptance, adjustment, expectations, or stress, and various investigators define these constructs differently. For example, adjustment is variously defined as reorganization of behavior toward a new object (Bowlby, 1960; Drotar, Baskiewicz, Irvin, Kennell, & Klaus, 1975), reintegration (Howell, 1973), acceptance, finding a solution, gaining knowledge and information (Grays, 1963), realism and mature acceptance (Miller, 1969), or getting on with the tasks of raising the child and finding services (Blacher, 1984). Aside from the fact that these defi-

nitions of adjustment are in themselves vague, it is difficult to make any inferences about common results across investigations.

Other studies use outcome measures that overlap conceptually with the independent variables under consideration. Thus, a number of tautological studies conclude that if x is present, it means x is present. Regarding measures of stress, many instruments measure diverse elements, such as general stress levels, available resources (coping), and the nature of the stressor event. For example, some of the items on the QRS-Short Form (Friedrich, Greenberg, & Crnic, 1983) are disability-specific (i.e., "_____can walk with help"). Consequently, the fact that the QRS successfully discriminates between disabled and nondisabled groups (Friedrich & Friedrich, 1981) is hardly surprising. McCubbin et al. (1980) comment on the problem of circularity:

> Investigations in which the stressors are not kept separate from the dependent variables of family responses are quite common ... The specific hardships associated with the stressor events (not part of the family's response) have been either ignored or obscured, so that it is not always clear whether the family's difficulties and hardships are an inherent part of the stressor. As a result, interpretations of the relationship of stressor to family adjustment tend to be tautological. (p. 857)

Even a "clean" stress measure, however, will not provide a comprehensive portrait of the impact of disability on families. As noted earlier, a family might be effectively reducing stress through the use of one coping strategy or another, but also be failing to accomplish some essential task. In addition, a focus on stress may ignore possible positive outcomes the family is experiencing.

The lingering assumption that all effects of a disability are bad is perhaps one reason that a systematic study of possible benefits has not been made. We do have fragments of evidence that there are, in fact, positive impacts. Studies of siblings of brothers or sisters with disabilities have reported that the siblings were more helpful and tolerant of others (Cleveland & Miller, 1977;

DeMyer, 1979; Grossman, 1972), more often exhibited maturity and a responsible attitude beyond their years (Simmeonsson & McHale, 1981), and more frequently considered devoting their lives to social causes (Farber, 1963) than siblings of children without disabilities. One girl cited family closeness as a special contribution of her sister with a disability: "Because of her difference there was a degree of specialness or closeness that made us all very, very close. We all pitched in and helped each other out and Cathy was the one thing in difficult times that we could focus on" (Klein, 1972, p. 25).

Most of the evidence pointing to the positive contributions of disability is in the form of narrative reports from parents and other family members. In open-ended intensive interviews with 12 families of disabled children with disabilities, Turnbull et al. (1984) found in response to the question, "What are some of the positive contributions_____[disabled person] has made to your family?" most family members described intangible benefits, such as a greater degree of tolerance and patience, a feeling of enhanced self-esteem and competence in coping with day-to-day challenges, and a sense of meaningfulness and purpose in life.

It is thus not inconceivable that families could experience stress in some areas of their lives as a result of the disability, and positive benefits in others. Wikler et al. (1983) observed that the same families reporting periodic feelings of chronic sorrow also reported feeling strengthened by their experiences.

It is increasingly apparent that the impacts of disability, experienced by a single family, may be almost as numerous as the multiple factors contributing to different reactions across families. One promising way of sorting out impacts is to divide family functioning into functional domains and to measure the effects of disability within each one. This strategy is familiar to most professionals in developmental disabilities, since the adaptive behavior of an individual is measured in terms of a number of life categories, such as self-help and socialization. Family functioning (or outcomes) could be conceptualized in terms of the family's ability to meet the needs of each of its members in a variety of areas. Some of those areas, adapted from suggestions by Turnbull et al. (1984), include:

Finances: earning a living, managing the budget

Personal physical care: grooming, health, safety

Domestic care: cooking, cleaning, laundry, household maintenance, transportation

Rest and recuperation: hobbies, sports, or other relaxation activities

Socialization: interaction with others

Affection: love, intimacy, sexual expression

Self-definition: feelings of self-esteem and competency in various roles internal and external to the family

Education: direct teaching and/or emphasis on formalized education

It is clear from this list of family members' needs that a successful family is extremely busy. The tendency of many professionals to focus on the education of the child with the disability could be a source of stress for families if it forces them to neglect other needs. It is also clear that disability might result in stress in some areas (e.g., physical care, education) and successful coping in others (e.g., affection, self-definition). The development of a valid and reliable instrument to measure the degree of stress or coping within distinct domains could provide an operational definition of family success, as well as both general patterns and individual assessments of the impact of disability on families.

FUTURE DIRECTIONS

The issues discussed in this chapter point to a series of steps in future research on families with disabled members. First, we need to develop a method to measure the multiple impacts of disability on families. Such a measure would define several domains of family functioning and evaluate the degree to which each family member feels his or her needs are being met in each area. Second, patterns of coping for successful families (defined as functioning reasonably well in all need areas) must be identified. Since different coping strategies may be useful in disparate situations, this information would be helpful in designing interventions for families who are not coping well. Third, additional work must focus on the changing needs of families over the life cycle. We also must determine heuristic services and professional strategies to diminish the stress of transition, such as helping families to plan for the future. Fourth, the role of values in successful family functioning needs to be examined more closely. What values lead to meeting needs successfully? What values block the family or place it at risk for stress in given areas of functioning? Fifth, the relationship of distinct interactional styles to various functional outcomes warrants further attention. What styles are conducive to successful functioning in different life cycle stages?

Finally, the effects of programs designed to increase family resources must be ascertained. For example, it could be hypothesized that training family members in problem solving and communication skills leads to more balanced levels of cohesion and adaptability, which in turn results in the family's improved ability to meet its needs.

SUMMARY

Despite methodological problems in research on families with disabled children, a negative image of the impact of disability has emerged. Yet, families of disabled children with disabilities share more common features than differences relative to other families in our society. They cover the gamut of family forms, demographic variations, ethnic backgrounds, age groups, and interactional styles. They may encounter the intangible stresses of grief, sorrow, and challenge to their world view. They may also be faced with tangible stresses of economic and physical care responsibilities, social stigma, and frustrating interactions with professionals and the "system". Families may find strength, closeness, meaning, and new direction for their lives in their experiences with disability. Many families tolerate the stresses surrounding disability very well, while others do not.

Thus, the crucial research issue is the definition and fuller understanding of successful families who have experienced disability. It is important to discover how they meet their needs, how they perceive disability, their coping patterns, and the resources they have available to deal with challenges. Such an understanding will lead to an enhanced ability to design interventions and develop support services that will help those with difficulties join the ranks of successful families of children with disabilities.

REFERENCES

Avis, D. W. (1985). Deinstitutionalization jet lag. In H. R. Turnbull & A. P. Turnbull (Eds.), *Parents speak out: Then and now* (pp. 181–191). Columbus, OH: Charles E. Merrill.

Benson, H. & Turnbull A. P. (1986). Approaching families from an individualized perspective. In R. H. Horner, L. M. Voeltz, & H. D. Fredericks (Eds.), *Education of learners with severe handicaps: Exemplary Service Strategies).* Baltimore: Paul H. Brookes Publishing Co.

Bettleheim, B. (1950). *Love is not enough.* Glencoe, NY: Free Press.

Birenbaum, A. (1971). The mentally retarded child in the home and the family life cycle. *Journal of Health and Social Behavior, 12,* 55–65.

Blacher, J. (1984). Sequential stages of adjustment to the birth of a child with handicaps: Fact or artifact? *Mental Retardation, 22,* 55–68.

Bowlby, J. (1960). Grief and mourning in infancy and early childhood. *Psychoanalytic Study of the Child, 15,* 1–9.

Bristor, M. W. (1984). The birth of a handicapped child — A wholistic model for grieving. *Family Relations, 33,* 25–32.

Cleveland, D. W., & Miller, N. (1977). Attitudes and life commitments of older siblings of mentally retarded adults: An exploratory study. *Mental Retardation, 15,* 38–41.

Cobb, S. (1976). Social support as a mediator of life stress. *Psychosomatic Medicine, 38,* 300–314.

Conroy, J. W. (1985). Reactions to deinstitutionalization among parents of mentally retarded persons. In R. H. Bruininks & K. C. Lakin (Eds.), *Living and learning in the least restrictive environment* (pp. 141–152). Baltimore: Paul H. Brookes.

Crnic, K. A., Friedrich, W. N., & Greenburg, M. T. (1983). Adaptation of families with mentally retarded children: A model of stress, coping, and family ecology. *American Journal on Mental Deficiency, 88,* 125–138.

DeMyer, M. K., (1979). *Parents and children in autism.* New York: Wiley.

DeMyer, M. K. & Goldberg, P. (1983). Family needs of the autistic adolescent. In E. Schopler & G. B. Mesibov (Eds.), *Autism in adolescents and adults.* New York: Plenum.

Dingman, H. F., Eyman, R. D., & Windle, C. D. (1963). An investigation of some child-rearing attitudes of mothers with retarded children. *American Journal of Mental Deficiency, 67,* 899–908.

Drotor, D., Backiewicz, A., Irvin, N., Kennell, J., & Klaus, M. (1975). The adaptation of parents to the birth of an infant with a congenital malformation: A hypothetical model. *Pediatrics, 56,* 710–711.

Embry, L. H. (1980). Family support for handicapped preschool children at risk of abuse. In J. J. Gallagher (Ed.), *New Directions for Exceptional Children* (pp. 29–57). San Francisco: Jossey-Bass.

Farber, B. (1960). Family organization and crisis: Maintenance of integration in families with a severely retarded child. *Monographs of the Society for Research in Child Development, 25*(1).

Farber, B. (1963). Interaction with retarded siblings and life goals of children. *Marriage and Family Living, 25,* 96–98.

Farber, B. (1968). *Mental retardation: Its social context and social consequences.* Boston: Houghton-Mifflin.

Farber, B., & Ryckman, D. B. (1965). Effects of severely mentally retarded children on family relationships. *Mental Retardation Abstracts, 2,* 1–17.

Friedrich, W. N., & Friedrich, W. L. (1981). Comparison of psychosocial assets of parents with a handicapped child and their normal controls. *American Journal of Mental Deficiency, 85,* 551–553.

Freidrich, W. N., Greenberg, M. T., & Crnic, K. (1983). A short form of the questionnaire on resources and stress. *American Journal on Mental Deficiency, 88,* 41–48.

Gath, A. (1974). Sibling reactions to mental handicap: A comparison of the brothers and sisters of mongol children. *Journal of Child Psychology and Psychiatry and Allied Disciplines, 15,* 838–843.

Gath, A. (1977). The impact of an abnormal child upon the parents. *British Journal of Psychiatry, 130,* 405–410.

Goddard, H. H. (1912). *The Kalihak family: A study in the heredity of feeblemindedness.* New York: Macmillan.

Grays, C. (1963). At the bedside; The pattern of acceptance in parents of the retarded child. *Tomorrow's Nurse, 4,* 30–34.

Grossman, F. K. (1972). *Brothers and sisters of retarded children: An exploratory study.* Syracuse, NY: Syracuse University Press.

Haavik, S. F., & Menninger, K. A. (1981). *Sexuality, law, and the developmentally disabled person.* Baltimore; Brookes Publishing Co.

Hewett, S. (1976). Research on families with handicapped children — An aid or an impediment to understanding? In D. Bergma & A. E. Pulver (Eds.), *Developmental disabilities: Psychologic and social implications.* The National Foundation, March of Dimes.

Holroyd, J. (1974). The Questionnaire on Resources and Stress; An instrument to measure family response to a handicapped family member. *Journal of Community Psychology, 2,* 92–94.

Howell, S. E. (1973). Psychiatric aspects of habilitation. *Pediatric Clinics of North America, 20,* 203–219.

Jordan, T. E. (1962). Research on the handicapped child and the family. *Merrill-Palmer Quarterly, 8,* 243–260.

Kazak, A. E., & Marvin, R. S. (1984). Differences, difficulties and adaptation: Stress and social networks in families with a handicapped child. *Family Relations, 33,* 67–77.

Kerlin, I. N. (1976). Moral imbecility. In M. Rosen, G. R. Clark, & M. S. Kivitz (Eds.), pp. 303–310. *The history of mental retardation: Collected papers.* Baltimore: University Park Press. Original work published 1889.

Klein, S. D. (1972). Brother to sister/sister to brother. *Exceptional Parent, 3,* 24–27.

Kupfer, F. (1982). *Before and after Zachariah.* New York: Delacorte.

McCubbin, H. I., Joy, C. B., Cauble, A. E., Comeau, J. K., Patterson, J. M., & Needle, R. H. (1980). Family stress and coping: A decade review. *Journal of Marriage and the Family, 42,* 855–871.

Miller, L. G. (1969). Helping parents cope with the retarded child. *Northwest Medicine, 68,* 542–547.

Murphy, M. A. (1982). The family with a handicapped child: A review of the literature. *Developmental and Behavioral Pediatrics, 3,* 73–82.

Neugarten, B. (1976). Adaptations and the life cycle. *The Counseling Psychologist, 6,* 16–20.

Olson, D. H., McCubbin, H. I., Barnes, H., Larsen A., Muken, M., & Wison, M. (1983). *Families: What makes them work.* Beverly Hills: Sage Publications.

Pearlin, L. I., & Schooler, C. (1978). The structure of coping. *Journal of Health and Social Behavior, 19,* 2–21.

Sarason, S. B., & Doris, J. (1979). *Educational handicap, public policy, and social history.* New York: The Free Press.

Scheenberger, R. C. (1983). *A history of mental retardation.* Baltimore: Paul H. Brookes.

Simeonsson, R. J., & McHale, S. (1981). Review: Research on handicapped children: Sibling relationships. *Child Care, Health and Development, 7,* 153–171.

Skrtic, T. M., Summers, J. A., Brotherson, M. J., & Turnbull, A. P. (1984). Severely handicapped children and their brothers and sisters. In J. Blacher (Ed.), *Severely handicapped young children and their families* (pp. 215–246). New York: Academic Press.

Stoneman, Z., & Brody, G. H. (1984). Research with families of severely handicapped children: Theoretical and methodological considerations. In J. Blacher (Ed.), *Severely handicapped young children and their families* (pp. 179–214). New York: Academic Press.

Suelzle, M., & Keenan, V. (1981). Changes in family support networks over the life cycle of mentally retarded persons. *American Journal of Mental Deficiency, 86,* 267–274.

Summers, J. A., Turnbull, A. P., & Brotherson, M. S. (in press). Exceptionality and the family. In E. Lynch & R. Lewis (Eds.), *Introduction to the study of exceptionality.* Glenview, IL: Scott, Foresman.

Terkelson, K. G. (1980). Toward a theory of family life cycle. In E. Carter & M. McGoldrick (Eds.), *The family life cycle: A framework of family therapy* (pp. 21–52). New York: Gardner Press.

Turnbull, A. P., Brotherson, M. J., & Summers, J. A. (1986). Family life cycle: Theoretical and empirical implications and future directions for families with mentally retarded members. In J. J. Gallagher & P. M. Vietze (Eds.), *Families of handicapped persons: Research, programs, and policy issues* (pp. 45–66). Baltimore: Paul H. Brookes.

Turnbull, A. P., Summers, J. A., & Brotherson, M. J. (1984). *Working with families with disabled members: A family systems approach.* Lawrence, KS: Research and Training Center on Independent Living, University of Kansas.

Turnbull, A. P., Turnbull, H. R., Summers, J. A., Brotherson, M. J., & Benson, H. A. (in press). *Families with exceptional children and youth.* Columbus, OH: Charles E. Merrill.

Waisbren, S. E. (1980). Parents' reactions after the birth of a developmentally disabled child. *American Journal of Mental Deficiency, 84,* 345–351.

Walsh, F. (1982). Conceptualizations of normal family functioning. In F. Walsh (Ed.), *Normal family processes.* New York: Guilford.

Wieck, C. A., & Bruininks, R. H. (1980). *The cost of public and community residential care for mentally retarded people in the United States,* Project Report No. 9. Minneapolis: Developmental Disabilities Project on Residential Services and Community Adjustment, University of Minnesota.

Wikler, L. Wasow, M., & Hatfield, E. (1981). Chronic sorrow revisited: Attitude of parents and professionals about adjustment to mental retardation. *American Journal of Orthopsychiatry, 5,* 63–70.

Wikler, L., Wasow, M., & Hatfield, E. (1983). Seeking strengths in families of developmentally disabled children. *Social Work, 21,* 313–315.

Wright, J. S., Granger, R. D., & Sameroff, A. J. (1984). Parental acceptance and developmental handicap. In J. Blacher (Ed.), *Severely handicapped young children and their families* (pp. 51–90). New York: Academic Press.

Yando, R., & Zigler, E. (1984). Severely handicapped children and their families: A synthesis. In J. Blacher (Ed.), *Severely handicapped children and their families.* New York: Academic Press.

CHAPTER 7

Disability and Sexual Adjustment

Barbara Edmonson

In considering the psychosexual adjustment of people with disabilities, it is helpful to review the stages of human development. This process consists of an intertwining of: (a) biological maturation, (b) the development and integration of physical abilities, (c) the development of intellect, (d) growing awareness of the kind of person one is, and (e) a normal progression of desires and interests balanced by the competencies to achieve them.

The biological state—the bones, muscles, neurons, and endocrine system that potentiate movement—is first. As Freud noted, this is a source of the life-enhancing sexual energy that is directed toward certain sequential goals. Children's activity during infancy and childhood foster their physical development and the integration of physiological systems. Their perceptions of what other people are doing in the environment accelerate their experiential learning. Because their activity occurs in a physical and social environment, obstacles to the immediate satisfaction of their desires are sometimes experienced. When these obstacles stimulate new behaviors that prove to be rewarding, the behavioral repertoire is expanded. As conceptual ability grows, children can employ effective behaviors with less trial and error.

The process of working within the limits of a social environment to satisfy one's interests and needs leads to the formation of the executive, psychological part of us—ego or self—the part of the psyche that mediates for the "sexual" or life-enhancing drive and attempts to satisfy it in its sequential manifestation. Depending upon the social ambience and the success of their behavioral efforts, children develop attitudes toward themselves and the world. Some grow into feeling secure, believing that they can cope with difficulties. At the other extreme, some feel unable to attain what is important to them.

THE EFFECTS OF DISABILITY ON DEVELOPMENT

When children have a disability, obstacles to the development of muscle and coordination may occur, as in cases of

91

severe mental retardation, cerebral palsy, or polio. Blindness or impaired vision hampers playful exploration and learning about others by observation. Deafness and hearing impairment take their toll in communication, in obstructing the audible passage of information from others, and in hindering interpersonal play. Goldberg (1981) describes the special problems of the adolescent with a disability in coming to terms with body image and peer-group attitudes. Parental anxiety and overprotection, when they exist, add to the difficulty of achieving emotional and financial independence. In addition to disabilities that may hinder physical and social experiences, Wright (1983) points out that stigmatizing attitudes, so often held by other people, may create a sense of inadequacy, and this self-perception becomes the actual handicap. The healthy normal ego is reasonably confident of being able to satisfy desires and feels adequate in terms of society's yardsticks. The self that lacks confidence will experience anxiety and insecurity and, when unable to satisfy basic drives, can become seriously maladjusted.

In our culture, much has been written about normative adult maturity. Adulthood is presumably attained when one becomes able to care for oneself, achieves an ongoing relationship of intimacy with another person, and assumes responsibility for the care of others (Brown, 1961; Erikson, 1950; Havighurst, 1972). People with serious disabilities are apt to miss out on the informational and social interactional aspects of normal development. Unfortunately, their families, teachers, and health care workers are often unaware of these long-range implications and fail to provide the remedial social training that could facilitate development and add immeasurably to the quality of their lives.

DISABILITY AND SEXUALITY

There is no question that people with disabilities share the sequence of biological urges that others experience. Surveys, case histories, and autobiographies (Bullard & Knight, 1981; Craft, 1980; Edgerton, 1967; Edmonson, McCombs, & Wish, 1979; Ferro

& Allen, 1976; Fitz-Gerald & Fitz-Gerald, 1978; Greengross, 1976; Hahn, 1981; Miller & Morgan, 1980; Robinault, 1978; Robinson, 1979; Wabreck, Wabreck, & Burchell, 1978; Wright 1983) affirm the desire by the mentally retarded, by persons with cerebral palsy, traumatic injury, spina bifida, congenital blindness, and various other disabilities to experience sexual intimacy, marriage, and parenting. At the same time, it is clear from the literature that there are developmental problems within these areas of disability that make it impossible for many, and difficult for all, to attain these goals. Most authors feel that the problems could be ameliorated if schools provided programs to compensate for the experiences that are critically lacking, if parents would do their part toward preparation for responsible sexuality, and if the community network of health, vocational, and social services were adequately funded.

Mental Retardation

People who are mentally retarded must overcome numerous obstacles: They are slow to attain conceptual ability and poor at planning. They have limited social experiences and thus typically lag behind others with respect to socially adaptive behavior. An additional barrier is the misguided belief by many parents, teachers, and other care-givers that if the mentally retarded are sheltered from information they will not develop an interest in sexual behavior. The physical changes of pubescence tend to be somewhat delayed, and while it is likely that the sexual activity of the most severely and profoundly retarded persons will be restricted to masturbation, many studies have demonstrated that most persons who are retarded share the sexual needs and goals of other people. Those who are moderately and mildly retarded seek to engage in normal heterosexual activity, including prepubertal sexual play, dating (Katz, 1970), "necking" and "petting" (Edgerton, 1963; Gebhard, 1973), premarital intercourse (Gebhard, 1973), marriage, and childbearing (Baller, Charles, & Miller, 1967; Edgerton, 1967; Edmonson et al.,

1979; Gebhard, 1973; Heshusius, 1982; Katz, 1970). Most of the moderately retarded adults Edgerton interviewed (1967) felt that to be married was an important indication of normality and status. As with persons who are nonretarded, institutional life has often promoted homosexual relationships (Gebhard, 1973).

In order to prepare retarded children to respond appropriately to their biological and social psychological desires, their caretakers and educators must teach them the multiple components of sexually fulfilling and responsible behavior: good grooming and other skills of independent living; how to dress, present themselves, be assertive, behave as a friend (Katz, 1970; Payne & Patton, 1981), and avoid sexual exploitation; and personal and social responsibility, including the nurturance of others. Such components, of course, are part of a good sex education curriculum for persons with any type of disability, but for the mentally retarded the presentation requires graphic materials, role play, and language that they understand. Various activities should provide opportunities for friendships and "helping networks," so often lacking, that may compensate for failure to marry. All programs of socio-sexual education should emphasize that marriage and parenthood are not essential for status or for happiness; single adults can live good lives, and many married couples elect to have no children. For sources of curricula see Chipouras, Cornelius, Daniels, and Makas (1979), Edmonson (1980), Greenbaum and Noll (n.d.), Moore (1979), and Robinault (1978), among others.

Visual Impairment

Seriously impaired vision can affect the early bonding process between infant and mother. Hicks (1980) refers to the importance of "mutual gaze as a prime element in creating the bond" (p.166) and indicates that the absence of bonding can affect the quality of a child's relationships with others. Children who cannot see what others are doing miss out on the learning aspects of imitative play. In addition, the failure to perceive nonverbal signals in social situations—body movements, gestures, facial expressions—often leads to inappropriate behavior. Because of our cultural dislike of extreme closeness and touching (Dodge, 1979), they are apt to be unaware of the changes that accompany sexual development (Knappett & Wagner, 1976; Scholl, 1974). As an example, Enis and Catarizolo (1972) describe some of the misconceptions of children in a school for the blind with respect to genitalia. Badame (1981) has commented that during adolescence and adulthood, males with severely impaired vision are more handicapped than women because of the cultural expectation of providing transportation for a date. Additional psychosocial effects of blindness are discussed by Scholl (1974) and Torbett (1974), both of whom are advocates of specialized programs of sex education. Chipouras et al. (1979) review some programs and intervention strategies. Additional programs are described by Bidgood (1971), Edmonson (1980), Orlansky and Rhyne (1981), and Robinault (1978). Materials in braille and large print are available from The Sex Education and Information Council of the U.S. (SIECUS).

Neff (1976, 1979) describes the overprotectiveness that is often the approach to children who are deaf and blind, with consequent fear and confusion with respect to the ordinary environment. She urges greater attention to children's overall developmental needs, which she feels are often neglected at the expense of intensive effort to develop speech. Education should help them form a positive self-image and learn gender differences. Among her suggestions is the use of live models, which are used in some other countries, because three-dimensional materials often are not realistic. Among resources are *Sex Education for Deaf-Blind Students* (Cadigan & Geuss, 1981) and others described in Fitz-Gerald and Fitz-Gerald (1979), Robinault (1978) and SIECUS (1984).

Hearing Impairment

Children with impaired hearing miss a great deal of information that normal children acquire from the environment (Fitz-

Gerald & Fitz-Gerald, 1978). Although they can be taught to be socially perceptive, one study suggests that deaf adolescents lack skill in comprehending social cues (Rose, 1975). Robinson (1979) complained of parental overprotection and lack of preparation "to assume the role of a mature sexual adult in society" (p.164). Since most children who are deaf have parents with normal hearing, Robinault (1978) urged that parents familiarize themselves with the stages of development of children's sexual feelings and "develop a vocabulary for communication about sex" (p.36). Books that illustrate signs and phrases for sexuality (Doughten, Minkin, & Rosen, 1978; Woodward, 1979) and additional resource materials are available through SIECUS.

Deaf children who are educated in residential schools for the deaf must cope with parent surrogates, usually female, separation of peer groups by sex, and many restrictions on socializing (Robinson, 1979). Common problems are lack of privacy and very limited time for informal communication with the opposite sex. Homosexuality is not uncommon (Fitz-Gerald & Fitz-Gerald, 1978). Those who know only sign language are cut off from interaction with the hearing (Safilios-Rothschild, 1982). The Fitz-Geralds report significantly fewer marriages by deaf than by hearing persons, and they believe that social isolation and limited heterosexual contacts cause many marital problems. Robinson (1979) commented on the lack of services in the community to help those with hearing disabilities deal with their socio-sexual problems.

Although many schools for deaf children and adolescents in the past have failed to provide socio-sexual education and counseling, this situation is improving. Because reading is typically difficult and audible information is hindered, sex education must be very graphic. The Fitz-Geralds comment that the educator must create an accepting atmosphere, be able to understand "local signs," and be able to communicate clearly and without embarrassment. Resources are referenced in Robinault (1978) and Chipouras et al. (1979). The social-perception training approach of Edmonson, Leach, and Leland (1978) could be modified for use with the hearing impaired.

Physical Disabilities

The degree and type of difficulty that people with physical disabilities experience in attaining sexual maturity depends to some extent upon whether the condition is congenital, as with cerebral palsy and spina bifida; traumatic, as with spinal cord injury; or progressive, such as multiple sclerosis. The development of all such individuals, however, will be affected by the severity of physical "involvement," architectural barriers, their self-perceptions, the attitudes of other people, and their ability to cope with frustration.

As is true of those with congenital disabilities, children with cerebral palsy and spina bifida are often overprotected, as well as hindered in acquiring social skills and in becoming independent of their nuclear families. In addition, they often suffer rejection by adolescent peer groups, lack role models for socio-sexual development (Haraguchi, 1981), and, perhaps most important, view themselves as unfit for and unworthy of sexual intimacy, especially with someone who is not disabled. The real existence of considerable aversion toward an intimate relationship with a disabled person is indicated in studies by Hahn (1981), who also describes some of the pitfalls related to courtship. His presentation of material on the kinds of persons who are unusually attracted to the disabled should be noted. Problems of motor incoordination and sensory deficits that would hamper sexual relationships can often be dealt with (Miller & Morgan, 1979). Wright (1983) has presented autobiographical accounts of several persons who deeply desired a loving relationship and the ability to care for themselves and another. In each case there was a deeply handicapping sense of devaluation, an effort to hide the disability, and pain at some point because of rejection by one who was loved. She sensitively describes "the deep and sometimes overwhelming loneliness" due to the importance assigned in our culture to physical attributes. Rousso (1982) believes that although persons with cerebral palsy are often "socialized into a disabled, asexual role," they can be helped through good counseling to develop a positive body image, requisite social skills, and an understanding and acceptance of their sexuality.

Robinault's (1978) discussion of the special needs and concerns of persons suddenly disabled includes grief and mourning, anxiety about sexual needs and performance, feelings of being devalued, and the attitudes of family members and/or a healthy partner. Although Hahn's (1981) survey of veterans with spinal cord injuries found that half did not expect to get married, Neumann's (1978) review of studies of public attitudes and of a study of interpersonal relationships of applicants for disability benefits is more positive. He believes that our culture lacks the appropriate "social script" with which to "define persons with disabilities as sexual, to promote their desirability as sexual partners, and to provide models" (p. 94). The popular sympathy and interest that was generated by the film *Coming Home* provides some confirmation. Vash (1981) describes some of the practical problems of lovers when one or both has a physical disability. "Paralysis creates one set of problems, pain another, amputations yet another, and neurological impairments affecting erotic sensation and bowel and bladder control produce still more" (p. 79). In addition, "an attendant's help may be necessary to make sexual contact possible."

HISTORY OF ATTITUDES TOWARD DISABILITY AND SEXUALITY

Historically in the Western world people with visible disabilities have been devalued, ignored, mistrusted, exploited and treated in ways that deprive them of the most ordinary pleasures of life. These attitudes have not existed worldwide, as is shown by Edgerton's (1970) lengthy review of diverse practices in nonliterate societies. Wright's (1960) discussion of animal research similarly counters the idea of some general instinctual aversion to the

nonnormal. Her review of Maisel's (1953) data on more than 50 tribes and societies parallels Edgerton's findings, and together they strongly counter a Darwinian notion that communal subsistence requires the elimination of members who are less fit.

In ancient Greece, however, where physical beauty and health were prized and the cardinal virtues were "courage, temperance, justice, and wisdom," Scheerenberger (1983, p. 11) documents the practice of infanticide. Although the god Hephaestus was depicted as crippled, both Plato and Aristotle are cited as prescribing death for infants who were deformed. The Romans, although more diverse in practice, tended also toward cruel treatment.

The score or more of Biblical references to Jesus' attention to "the maimed," "the halt," "the lame," "the blind," and "the mute" suggest that persons with disabilities are worthy and needful and should receive assistance. The messages of Buddha, Confucius, and Mohammed resemble those of Jesus in their compassion and concern for all humankind, including those "weak of understanding" (Scheerenberger, 1983, p. 22).

During the Middle Ages, the high mortality rate and the need for labor in areas of Europe created some acceptance of persons with disabilities, especially where agriculture was a mainstay. However, Scheerenberger states that during those centuries the attitude of the Roman Catholic Church shifted from regarding the disabled as "children of innocence" to "products of sin and the devil" (p. 31). During the period of the Inquisition, many people with epilepsy, mental retardation, or emotional problems were destroyed as persons without souls, or as witches. Others, fortunate to be in a rural area, might become farm labor; those spared of burning in cities might join the legion of beggars or become objects of jest.

According to Scheerenberger, our country's first legal code, adopted by the Massachusetts General Court in 1641, prescribed death as the punishment for homosexual activities, for being a witch, blasphemy, theft, bearing false witness, and other crimes. "The birth of a defective or abnormal child was always suspect, reflecting either God's wrath or the devil" (p. 93). By the early 1800s, Scheerenberger's account indicates that residential service was provided for the "deaf and dumb" and the retarded in one city, but, by and large, through the first half of the 19th century the need for dependable labor led to indenture and slavery. If the mentally retarded, sick, insane, and feeble-minded could not work, they might be placed in an almshouse, workhouse, jail, or mental hospital. There was also the practice of "bidding out," in which the pauper and the disabled person were sold to someone who would provide their care; or they might simply be loaded into a wagon and driven to another town for release.

In mid-19th century, appalled by the miserable conditions she observed in the almshouses and hospitals, Dorothea Dix pleaded with Congress to provide asylums for the mentally ill and mentally retarded. Her plea was for protection and more humane treatment, but certainly not for normalization or acceptance in the community, as she believed association with such persons was injurious. The reform effort that she began attracted some notable contributors. Samuel Gridley Howe (1801–1976), a physician distressed by what he observed of the treatment of "idiots," "the insane," and those who were blind, in 1831 became the director of an asylum for the blind in Massachusetts. This soon became the Perkins Institute and Massachusetts School for the Blind and was followed by establishment of a school for "idiots and feeble-minded youth." Howe, soon joined in the effort to provide education by Harvey Wilbur (1820–1883) and J. B. Richards (1817–1886), wanted to provide education and training to benefit the health, behavior, and happiness of the disabled. Their benign views of the disabled and their belief in education, however, were not shared by a great many others who, like Dix, associated disabilities with "moral defects" and believed that intemperance, venereal disease, and epilepsy were major causes of disabilities.

In the mid-19th century, Malthus aroused concern with his predictions that the population would double every 25 years and soon outgrow nutritional and other resources. His predictions were widely published and in some parts of Europe led to efforts to limit childbirth. Although public reference to contraception was taboo in this country at that time, an American physician, Dr. Knowlton, published a book describing the contraceptive methods that were then known, and it circulated for many years before it was discovered and banned by watchdogs of public morality (Lewisohn, 1958).

Scheerenberger reports that by the 1880s the mentally retarded and epileptics in this country were generally regarded as undesirables who should be removed from society, prohibited from marriage, and made sterile. This attitude drew upon Galton's views of heredity and the Malthusian concern for population growth. It was reinforced by numerous authors who somberly attributed enfeebled judgment, neuroses, crime, and poverty to the degenerative forces of bad heredity. After the turn of the century it was fueled by the publication of Dugdale's account in 1910 of the Jukes, and in 1912 by Goddard's story of the Kallikak family. Even Terman in 1916, Scheerenberger says, regarded the "feeble-minded" as potential criminals or prostitutes. Most states passed laws prohibiting marriage of mentally retarded persons, and sterilization of institutional residents was widely practiced. The 1900s saw an increase in the number of institutions, all built at some distance from communities, in which residents were segregated by sex and considerable effort was expended to prevent any sexual activity, even masturbation.

From 1911 to the 1920s some public schools began to offer special education classes for children with disabilities, but often with the objective of preparing pupils for later life in an institution. The heterogeneity of groupings is shown by the description of one class, which included 2 youngsters with rickets, 6 with convulsions, 1 with epilepsy, 3 who were deaf, 4 with motor uncoordination, and 10 with defective articulation. Teachers had to do the best they could, without special training, in inadequate rooms, and with little in the way of educational resources.

Scheerenberger attributes part of a gradual change in outlook regarding the competence of the disabled to advocacy efforts by Dr. Fernold, superintendent of the Massachusetts state institution. Initially he shared the view that the "feeble-minded" should be removed from society, but after he learned of good adjustments that were made by a number of institutional residents who were released, he became an outspoken advocate for education, humane treatment, and permitting parole of residents from the institutions.

Parole, however, was conjoined with sterilization of those released to the community during their procreative years. After the constitutionality of involuntary sterilization was upheld in 1927 in the case of *Buck v. Bell* (a state's compelling interest in achieving some purpose to be attained by sterilization can override an individual's rights), 25,000 persons are reported to have been sterilized during the 1930s, and the practice continued in 37 states over the next 20 years (Haavik & Menninger, 1981). These authors believe that although such laws still exist in 16 states, 7 of them permitting sterilization of people residing in the community as well as those in institutions, the laws are no longer often enforced.

The 1930s and 1940s saw a 40% increase in institutional placement of the retarded and epileptic. Scheerenberger attributes this trend in part to medical technology: the survival of severely involved infants who previously could not have survived, and the longer life span of most of the disabled. Physicians also commonly urged families to place their handicapped newborn in residential facilities.

By the 1940s and 1950s, much of the work within institutions, including building and grounds maintenance, laundry, food preparation, growing and harvesting crops, care of dairy cattle, and sometimes direct care of patients, was performed by the residents. Institutions were overcrowded and poorly staffed. They provided few programs to prepare residents for a life outside, and it was difficult to find supervised living facilities for those who were eligible for parole or release. But releases were also delayed for the reason that parolees would have to be replaced with more expensive labor.

During this period the situation was improving for the disabled within communities. The Association for Retarded Children, formed by parents in the late 1930s, became a potent political force. They were effective in shifting the public's attitude toward the retarded from fear to sympathy; promoted medical and psychological research; and, with organizations for the hearing and visually impaired, crippled children, the American Association on Mental Deficiency, and similar agencies, they were instrumental in obtaining federal legislation to support teacher training and the expansion of educational and vocational programs. In 1958, PL 85–926 was passed to provide grants to institutions of higher learning and state educational agencies for special education programs for teachers.

In the 1960s and 1970s, during the Kennedy and Johnson administrations, there were major advances. PL 88–164, passed in 1963, supported training personnel for the hard of hearing, speech impaired, visually handicapped, emotionally disturbed, and crippled. In 1966, the Bureau of Education for the Handicapped was created within the U.S. Office of Education to represent handicapped persons and to administer programs. It was the era of the free speech movement, civil rights activism, and the women's movement. It was also, according to Eisenberg, Griggins, and Duval (1982), a time when hospital and institutional clients began to talk with one another, share experiences, frustrations, and desires, and form self-advocacy groups.

Although literature on problems and needs of persons with disabilities existed in the 1950s, as indicated by Wright's (1960) bibliography, the most visible changes have occurred during the 1970s. Chigier (1981) dates the beginning of advocacy in the field of sex and disability from about 1970, with publications such as *Life Together* (Nordqvist, 1972), *Entitled to Love* (Greengross, 1976), and *Not Made of Stone* (Heslinga, Schellen, & Verkvyl, 1974), and the film *Like Other People* (Spastic Society, 1973). The 1970s gave rise to studies and surveys to clarify areas of special concern, sessions on sexuality and disability presented at professional conferences, workshops on sexuality to sensitize professional workers to the needs of the disabled, and the introduction of sex education and family life programs in many schools. The census of 1970 showed that approximately 9% of the population had disabilities. The Vietnam war, in which the United States was heavily engaged from 1969 to 1974, accounted for a large influx of men into hospitals and rehabilitation centers. In addition to the steady annual increment of children with congenital defects, there has been an increasing number of persons seriously injured by automobile accidents, sports activities, toxicity, and disease.

An important step for the disabled was widespread adoption of the principle of "normalization," introduced to this country by Nirje (1970). This principle mandates programs for those with disabilities that provide experiences as close as possible to the mainstream of society. Normalization entails education in a regular rather than special class, insofar as possible, and living at home, with a foster family, or in a group residence in the community rather than in an institution. The decade of the 1970s is notable for efforts to empty institutions and provide a network of services in communities to serve those with disabilities. Legislation was enacted in 1974 to protect handicapped people from discrimination in any program receiving federal financial assistance. In 1975, PL 94–142 required schools to provide free appropriate public education in the least restrictive environment for every child aged 3 to 18 (later, 3 to 21), regardless of the severity of the handicap. The same law also required educators to spell out achievable objectives for each student in detail and to be held accountable for their programs. In 1978, Congress authorized federal funding for Comprehensive Services for Independent Living under Rehabilitation Act amendments.

Obviously, much has occurred to ameliorate problems of people with disabilities. They are still separate and unequal, how-ever, because parents, educators, and other professionals are often ignorant of their special developmental needs, and because those with disabilities often lack opportunities for socialization, mobility, and employment that others enjoy. Eisenberg et al. (1982), in *Disabled People as Second-Class Citizens*, have documented common problems. As enumerated by Falconer (1982), lack of transportation and architectural barriers add to the difficulty of participating in community activities. Many find employment only in sheltered workshops at salaries less than the minimum wage. Lack of income, and the need for personal care attendants, make it impossible for many to find places to live with some independence and privacy. It is difficult to make acquaintances, and even more difficult to form relationships in which they can receive and express affection and love. Marriage is often discouraged, and in some states prohibited by law. Children have been taken away from parents with disabilities on the assumption they would not receive appropriate care. Only in the last 15 to 20 years has a real effort been made to provide housing, transportation, special training, employment, and encouragement toward satisfying sexual needs. In spite of the fact that the laws that have been passed to provide these services, they have been inadequately funded.

Now we are in a time of economic retrenchment, and the future is unclear. Hicks (1982) cites a *New York Times* editorial as evidence of growing concern about costs in relation to the "rights" of the disabled. This editorial asks, how far such rights shall extend: to street signs in Braille, sign language on every TV show, a counselor-guide for every illiterate? Is it our constitutional responsibility to accommodate the needs of a few?

"RIGHTS" OF THE DISABLED

Since 1970, much has been written about the sexual development and needs of people with disabilities. The ubiquity of their problems has led, on the one hand, to a national effort to remove architectural barriers and provide vocational opportunities. The doors of community agencies have been opened to the disabled, many other efforts have been inaugurated to improve the quality of their lives. On the other hand, the recent emphasis on sexual needs, sometimes expressed as "rights," may have intensified controversy with respect to certain goals and programs.

Chigier (1981), an early advocate of sexual rights of persons with disabilities, espoused the following sexual rights for the disabled in the 1972 presentation to the World Congress of Rehabilitation: the right to (a) receive information; (b) be educated; (c) sexually express oneself; (d) marry; (e) be parents; and (f) receive sexual health services from the community, such as genetic counseling, family planning, and sex counseling. Some aspects of these "rights" and their programmatic implications are controversial and will be discussed as issues.

The Right to Receive Information

Although our attitudes toward contraception have changed from the days when Dr. Knowlton was imprisoned for publishing such information, the use of contraceptives is counter to the position of the Roman Catholic Church, and some parents fear that advertising or easy availability will stimulate sexual experimentation by their children. When permitted by state law, Planned Parenthood, health agencies, and physicians may give information about contraception and childbirth to a minor who solicits this information without the permission of a parent. Although lawful in most states, the practice is controversial and distressing to many who see it as interference with parental rights. Information about sexuality, contraception, and childbirth may be imparted to children in authorized programs of sex education in schools, but children of parents who oppose such a program typically are excused from participation.

The Right to Be Educated

To be effective, education for responsible sexuality must begin in the earliest years. However, it is not productive to assert a *right* to sex education from an agency other than the family. Parents have a right to establish family values for their children, and they must be credited with the desire to be protective of and helpful to their children. Parents must want and approve a program if it is to be successful. Parents have the right to transfer their children from a school whose education they disapprove of to a private school, and to express their disapproval of the presentation of sexually related (or any other) educational material in the public school. Although many schools and institutions have been able to implement programs in sex and family life education, others are fearful of parental protests or have failed to gain parental collaboration and authorization. A description of the importance of sex education is presented in Robinault (1978), a book that should be in the library of every facility for people with disabilities. For guidelines to promote collaboration between parents, teachers, and administrators, see *A Resource Guide in Sex Education for the Mentally Retarded* (SIECUS, 1971), Chipouras et al. (1979), Edmonson (1980), and other publications listed in SIECUS bibliographies.

The Right to Sexual Self-Expression

In all cultures, there are social norms and laws with respect to sexual expression. There is no need to refer to statutes concerning incest, child pornography, rape, and sadomasochism, or to the numerous states in which homosexual acts and prostitution are unlawful. Since the 1940s, with the Kinsey Report and subsequent studies of socio-sexual behavior, there is broader acceptance of premarital sex, homosexual attachments, and sex for pleasure rather than for procreation. Sexual relationships are openly presented in movies, books, magazines, and television shows, and are sometimes described in the news. But public display of intimate sexuality is counter to the values of many individuals and subject occasionally to court action.

There is still prejudice and controversy with respect to homosexuality. It is no longer considered an illness or a perversion by the American Psychological Association or the American Medical Association. Some church study committees have made positive statements with respect to homosexual attachments (*Towards a Quaker View of Sex*, 1964; *Human Sexuality: New Directions in American Catholic Thought*, 1977; *Human Sexuality: A Preliminary Study*, The United Church of Christ, 1977), and the Unitarian Universalist Church will perform services of union or marriage. The trend is to accept a sexual liaison between consenting adults as long as it does not injure other parties. Nevertheless, there are penalties for homosexual acts in many states, and such a liaison may lead to efforts to remove children from the household.

By now, the sexuality of people with disabilities has been widely recognized and accepted, but they are confronted by many practical problems or issues. Dunn, Lloyd, and Phelps (1981) have discussed a number of these: the availability of community activities where one might meet people, tactics of approach, communication, the topic of the wheelchair and the injury, clearing up sexual misconceptions, finding a location, sexual positions, and props and aids. The facilitive role of personal attendants or health care professionals is addressed in Vash (1981) and Bullard and Knight (1981). In addition, sexual exploitation of the handicapped is of great current concern (Sequoia Area VIII Board for Developmental Disabilities, 1984).

The Right to Marry

Basically, it is the position of the Supreme Court that the right to marry, establish a home, and bring up children is protected under "the guarantee of liberty" (Haavik & Menninger, 1981, p. 94). However, 37 states and the District of Columbia have laws prohibiting or restricting the marriage of retarded persons. (Jacobs, 1976–1977; Shaman, 1978). The restrictions range from the requirement in Pennsylvania that a judge must decide whether the marriage is in the best interest of the applicants and the public to assuring, in Washington, that the couple is incapable of procreation. Haavik and Menninger add that

in several states such a marriage can be declared void, making children illegitimate. In some states marriage is a crime subject to imprisionment or fine, and in other states any person aiding and abetting such a marriage is subject to punishment. One rationale for such restrictions is that the retarded person does not understand the concept of matrimony and its accompanying responsibilities and cannot therefore give informed consent to the marriage contract. Shuger (1979) discusses the concept of informed consent, pointing out that the label of mental retardation carries a presumption of incompetence even if no court has declared the person to be incompetent. In reviewing the laws, Jacobs (1976–1977) urges revision, commenting, "Mentally disabled persons, as individuals, are entitled to the same constitutional guarantees as all other citizens. The law should treat mentally disabled persons as individuals with varying needs and capacities for love and affection and marital responsibility" (p. 486).

States that formerly prohibited marriage of a person with epilepsy have repealed such laws since 1965 through efforts of the Epilepsy Foundation of America, but five states retain the requirement of involuntary sterilization for an epileptic who marries.

The Right to Be Parents

Although the right to marry would normally imply the right to have children, in the case of the mentally retarded and the epileptic some states withhold permission to marry unless the spouse is sterile or past the age of procreation. Justification for sterilization is based on the assumption that if children were to be born of such a union, they would become a burden to the state. These restrictions apply only to the retarded and the epileptic, and not uniformly to other groups (e.g., alcoholics and abusive parents) who might provide unsatisfactory child care. In fact, retarded couples are often good parents. Thus, students of the law (Haavik & Menninger, 1981; Shuger, 1979) believe these laws violate the equal protection clause of the

United States Constitution and should be modified. Haavik and Menninger provide an overview of studies of parents, in which one or both were retarded. Although the quality of child care was judged satisfactory in many cases, in many others it was not. The survey indicated that "extensive support from social service or health agencies was necessary for the majority . . . to supply their everyday domestic and child care needs" (p. 73). In most instances the children's IQs were higher than those of their retarded parents. Early intervention programs provided for the children, or sometimes for the parents, were shown to add to the childrens' IQ ranges.

Most parents and care-givers believe that moderately and severely retarded persons should not undertake parenthood (Haavik & Menninger, 1981), but because many mildly retarded individuals have been adequate parents, the attitude toward them is more mixed. In general, the authors believe that competence is an individual matter, not wholly correlated with IQ. Child care is affected by level of income, harmoniousness of the marriage, mental health of the parents, the number of children, and available support systems, and all of these factors should be considered when one is counseling a couple about whether to have children.

The few studies of child care cited for families with parents who were blind or deaf also reported some problems, but the authors concluded that "what little evidence there is suggests that modifications and satisfactory adjustments are usually possible" (p. 74).

Contraception

Contraceptives become an issue if provided to a minor by someone other than a parent or when their use is involuntary, as was the case in institutions where women residents were given IUDs. Because procreation is recognized as a constitutional right, an abridgement of this right requires an overriding interest of the state. There is also a pragmatic problem with respect to the voluntary use of contraceptives by retarded women. The methods that do not require foresight, such as IUDs and the

medication depo-provera, are associated with unpleasant side effects, and many retarded women will not follow through with taking the pill daily. Condoms are easily accessible, of course, and males who have sufficient manual dexterity can usually be taught their application. The courts have recognized contraceptives as a less restrictive alternative to sterilization in cases in which a convincing case has been made for the involuntary prevention of childbirth.

Sterilization (vasectomy or tubal ligation) is a relatively simple surgical procedure, but the possible adverse reactions and long-range consequences, as described in Haavik and Menninger (1981), need to be considered and made known to applicants. Sterilization is a religious issue for some persons (Alcorn, 1974) and, as indicated by Edgerton (1967), Haavik and Menninger (1981), Roos (1975), and Sabagh and Edgerton (1962), may have adverse psychological impact upon the individual, especially if the operation was not voluntary. Conversely, however, individuals have viewed sterilization positively (Edgerton, 1967). Although sanctioned by laws in many states, few involuntary sterilizations currently are performed, perhaps for fear that the law might be challenged by today's more aggressive victims, or because it is recognized as a violation of human rights by contemporary hospital and institution administrators.

Haavik and Menninger cited a study by Whitcraft and Jones (1974), in which 86% of 652 professionals and parents of retarded children favored sterilization for retarded persons. They reported that parents sometimes initiate proceedings, fearing that their youngster would not provide adequate care for a child of his or her own. It is currently difficult for a retarded person to obtain voluntary sterilization surgery because, as Shuger (1979) explains, a physician must obtain informed consent before administering nonemergency medical treatment. Informed consent is "knowing, competent, and voluntary" (p. 216). To satisfy the first of these requirements, the nature of the treatment, the risks and discomforts, and the likelihood of success must be described in such a way that the client or legal guardian can understand it. For consent to be "competent," the person must have the mental capacity to grasp the information and make a decision. Unfortunately, many who are mentally retarded have a "yea-saying" proclivity without comprehension of what they are responding to, making it hard to know whether they have understood. The "voluntary" part can easily be compromised by the setting—institution or doctor's office—in which the discussion is held, or by an authoritative individual who is asking for the decision.

The Right to Receive Sexual Health Services from the Community

This issue is less controversial than the previous items, but it may be hard to find a counselor or health care professional who can deal knowledgeably with the sexual concerns of persons with disabilities or with the concerns of their families. Wallace (1980) believes that medical students need broader education in human sexuality than they currently receive and would profit from presentations by individuals who are physically disabled. Cummings (1979) describes the necessary teamwork between health care professionals and the client, and the important goal of sexual rehabilitation. Additional information concerning clients' needs and special programs for the helping professions have been presented by Bernado (1981), Chubon (1981), Greengross (1980), Nordqvist (1980), Schiller (1977), Stewart (1981), Thorn-Gray and Kern (1983), Thornton (1978), Vash (1981), and numerous others. Much helpful information is contained in Bullard and Knight (1981) and Robinault (1978). Specifically helpful with respect to sexual options of persons with severe physical disabilities are books by Mooney, Cole, and Chilgren, (1975), Heslinga et al. (1974), and others referred to in Chipouras et al. (1979).

FUTURE TRENDS

Some types of disability, such as blindness, deafness, and deaf-blindness, are decreasing because of medical knowledge, and mild retardation can be decreased by programs that compensate for conditions of poverty. It is unlikely, however, that visual and auditory disabilities will entirely disappear, or that the incidence of moderate, severe, and profound mental retardation, cerebral palsy, spina bifida, multiple sclerosis, muscular dystrophy, or traumatic injury will decrease. Much of the 9% or more of our disabled population will continue to need public understanding and support in order to attain rewarding intimate relationships and family life.

The progress of the last 15 years in information, services, and growth in public understanding and acceptance will surely continue, despite greater competition for public funds, but progress will be slowed and it will take ingenuity and effort to sustain a minimal level of funding. Hallahan and Kauffman (1978) pointed out that "public support in the form of legislation and the appropriation of funds has been achieved and sustained only by the most arduous and persevering efforts of individuals who are advocates for exceptional children" (p. 22). The organizations that represent this population will now have to intensify their campaigns for public understanding and support. Justification for services will emphasize the economic importance of teaching people to be independent and sexually responsible.

The media, which has helped win acceptance of people with disabilities and acceptance of "alternative life-styles," may reduce the pressure upon people to achieve marriage and procreation as indications of status and maturity. But the positive views that are currently held by many with respect to premarital intercourse, intercourse for pleasure rather than procreation, and homosexual relationships will continue to be opposed on the basis of religious or other principles. Within the Roman Catholic Church, views opposing the official position on contraception and abortion have been aired, and it appears possible, in the long run, that some synthesis of opposing views will emerge. Masturbation, which was once regarded as a sin, is widely accepted as harmless. Homosexual relationships will probably continue to gain social and legal acceptance, insofar as participants demonstrate the responsibility and commitment to others that are presumed to accompany heterosexual marriage. Surely, it is behavior rather than the marriage license that should be recognized as "sexual maturity." Acceptance will be helped by the studies, earlier cited, that have been made by a number of churches.

Unless there is a resolution of the arms race and some drastic shrinking of our nation's financial deficit, it will be hard to maintain public funding for the services that are important for the disabled. Our economic philosophy that people should look out for their own best interests, and the belief that serious effort will earn its appropriate reward, insulates us from the needs, pain, and suffering of others. Although we do rise to great generosity from time to time in the face of a publicized catastrophe, by and large we are not encouraged to incorporate the problems of others into our awareness and behavior in any continuous and productive way. Obviously, parents and families of the handicapped are exceptions, as are the professionals who work in rehabilitation, but in this country relatively few people bear any continuing concern for those who are less privileged or able; hence the annual fund-raising campaigns, television marathons, and dramatizations of need that, for a brief period of time, provoke us into giving some financial aid for research and supportive programs.

SUMMARY

Normal development from infancy to sexual adulthood requires sensory and motor abilities to reach out into and respond to the social environment, develop cognitive structures and communication, and formulate an acceptable and satisfying sexual role. Marriage, parenthood, or at least a caring and nurturant relationship with another are regarded as goals of sexual maturity.

Sensory, motor, and cognitive disabilities hinder children's play and other types of interaction, and often result in impoverished social skills and self-knowledge.

Parents, educators, and others must become aware of the exceptional needs of children with disabilities in order to provide them with compensatory experiences. Because of negative attitudes toward disability, it is difficult for persons with disabilities to share in the casual daily activities of the nondisabled, to form close friendships, and especially intimate heterosexual relationships.

Since the 1960s we have made progress in recognizing the sexuality and special needs of the disabled, partly from the advocacy of organizations and from the growing assertiveness of the disabled themselves. Legislation has provided education, vocational training, counseling, and some facilities for independent living. Professionals who are knowledgeable about socio-sexual problems work to broaden the awareness of others through workshops and public presentations. There is a literature on sexuality and disability, with suggestions for parents, educators, counselors, health care providers, and the disabled themselves. Because of the growth of public understanding, this progress must surely continue, but as cautioned by Safilios-Rothschild (1982), it will take a concerted effort by advocacy agencies and individuals to assure the humanitarian gains that have been so slowly achieved.

REFERENCES

Alcorn, D. A. (1974). Parental views on sexual development and education of the trainable mentally retarded. *The Journal of Special Education, 8,* 119–130.

Badame, R. S. (1981). Social skills: The process of learning to take risks. In D. G. Bullard & S. E. Knight (Eds.), *Sexuality and physical disability: Personal perspectives.* St. Louis: C. V. Mosby.

Baller, W. F., Charles, D. C., & Miller, E. L. (1967). Midlife attainments of the mentally retarded: A longitudinal study. *Genetic Psychology Monographs, 75,* 235–329.

Bernardo, M. L. (1981). Premarital counseling and the couple with disabilities: A review and recommendations. *Rehabilitation Literature, 32,* 213–217.

Bidgood, F. E. (1971). A study of sex education programs for visually handicapped persons. *New Outlook for the Blind, 65,* 318–323.

Brown, J. A. C. (1961). *Freud and the post-Freudians*. Baltimore: Penguin Books.

Bullard, D. G., & Knight, S. E. (Eds.). (1981). *Sexuality and physical disability: Personal perspectives*. St. Louis: C. V. Mosby.

Cadigan, E., & Geuss, R. R. (1981). *Sex education for deaf-blind students*. Watertown, MA: Perkins School for the Blind. (Available from SIECUS, 80 Fifth Ave., New York, NY 10011)

The Catholic Theological Society of America. *Human Sexuality: New directions in American thought*, 1977. New York: Paulist Press.

Chigier, E. (1981). Sexuality and disability: The international perspective. In D. G. Bullard & S. E. Knight (Eds.), *Sexuality and physical disability: Personal perspectives*. St. Louis: C. V. Mosby.

Chipouras, S., Cornelius, D., Daniels, S. M., & Makas, E. (1979). *Who cares? A handbook on sex education and counseling services for disabled people*. Washington, DC: George Washington University.

Chubon, R. A. (1981). Development and evaluation of a sexuality and disability course for the helping professions. *Sexuality & Disability*, 4, 3–14.

Craft, M. (1980). Sex and the handicapped: 1. Change in attitudes. In W. H. G. Armytage, R. Chester, & J. Peel (Eds.), *Changing patterns of sexual behavior*. New York: Academic Press.

Cummings, V. (1979). The role of the psychiatrist in managing the sexual problems of disabled patients. *Sexuality & Disability*, 2, 5–7.

Dodge, L. R. (1979). Sexuality and the blind disabled. *Sexuality & Disability*, 2, 200–205.

Doughten, S. D., Minkin, M. B., & Rosen, L. E. (1978). *Signs for sexuality: A resource manual*. Seattle: Planned Parenthood of Seattle. (Available from SIECUS, 80 Fifth Ave., New York, NY 10011).

Dunn, M., Lloyd, E. E., & Phelps, G. H. (1981). Sexual assertiveness in spinal cord injury, In D. G. Bullard & S. E. Knight (Eds.), *Sexuality and physical disability: Personal perspectives*. St. Louis: C. V. Mosby.

Edgerton, R. B. (1963). A patient elite: Ethnography in a hospital for the mentally retarded. *American Journal of Mental Deficiency*, 68, 372–385.

Edgerton, R. B. (1967). *The cloak of competence*. Berkeley, CA: University of California Press.

Edgerton, R. B. (1970). Mental retardation in non-Western societies: Toward a cross-cultural perspective on incompetence. In H. C. Hayward (Ed.), *Social-cultural aspects of mental retardation: Proceedings of the Peabody-NIMH Conference*. New York: Appleton-Century-Crofts.

Edmonson, B. (1980). Sociosexual education for the handicapped. *Exceptional Education Quarterly*, 1, 67–76.

Edmonson, B., Leach, E. M., & Leland, H. (1978). *Social perceptual training for community living: Prevocational units for retarded youth* (rev. ed.). Freeport, NY: Educational Activities.

Edmonson, B., McCombs, K., & Wish, J. (1979). What retarded adults believe about sex. *American Journal of Mental Deficiency*, 84, 11–18.

Eisenberg, M. G., Griggins, C., & Duval, R. J. (Eds.). (1982). *Disabled people as second-class citizens*. New York: Springer Publishing.

Enis, C. A., & Catarizolo, M. (1972). Sex education in the residential school for the blind. *Education of the Visually Handicapped*, 3, 61–64.

Erikson, E. H. (1950). *Childhood and society*. New York: W. W. Norton.

Falconer, J. (1982). Health care delivery: Problems for the disabled. In M. G. Eisenberg, C. Griggins, & R. J. Duval (Eds.), *Disabled people as second-class citizens*. New York: Springer Publishing.

Ferro, J. M., & Allen, H. A. (1976). Sexuality: The effects of physical impairment. *Rehabilitation Counseling Bulletin*, 20, 148–151.

Fitz-Gerald, D., & Fitz-Gerald, M. (1978). Sexual implications of deafness. *Sexuality & Disability*, 1, 57–69.

Fitz-Gerald, D., & Fitz-Gerald, M. (1979). Sexual implications of deaf-blindness. *Sexuality and Disability*, 2, 212–215.

Gebhard, P. H. (1973). Sexual behavior of the mentally retarded. In F. F. de la Cruz & G. D. LaVeck (Eds.), *Human sexuality and the mentally retarded*. New York: Brunner/Mazel.

Goldberg, R. T. (1981). Toward an understanding of the rehabilitation of the disabled adolescent. *Rehabilitation Literature*, 42, 65–74.

Greenbaum, M., & Noll, S. J. (no date). *Education for adulthood: A curriculum for the mentally retarded*. Staten Island, NY: Staten Island Mental Health Society.

Greengross, W. (1976). *Entitled to love—The sexual need of the handicapped*. London: Malaby Press.

Greengross, W. (1980). Some problems that professionals experience in counseling the disabled. *Sexuality & Disability*, 3, 187–192.

Haavik, S., & Menninger, II, K. A. (1981). *Sexuality, law, and the developmentally disabled person: Legal and clinical aspects of marriage, parenthood, and sterilization*. Baltimore: Paul H. Brookes.

Hahn, H. (1981). The social components of sexuality and disability: Some problems and proposals. *Sexuality & Disability*, 4, 220–233.

Hallahan, D. P., & Kauffman, J. M. (1978). *Exceptional children: Introduction to special education.* Englewood cliffs, NJ: Prentice-Hall.

Haraguchi, R. S. (1981). Developing programs meeting the special needs of physically disabled adolescents. *Rehabilitation Literature, 42,* 75–78.

Havighurst, R. J. (1972). *Developmental tasks and education* (3rd ed.). New York: David McKay.

Heshusius, L. (1982). Sexuality, intimacy, and persons we label mentally retarded: What they think. *Mental Retardation, 20,* 164–168.

Heslinga, K., Schellen, A. M. C. M., & Verkuyl, A. (1974). *Not made of stone.* Springfield, IL: Charles C. Thomas.

Hicks, S. (1980). Relationship and sexual problems of the visually handicapped. *Sexuality & Disability, 3,* 165–177.

Hicks, J. S. (1982). Should every bus kneel? In M. G. Eisenberg, C. Griggins, & R. J. Duval (Eds.), *Disabled people as second-class citizens.* New York: Springer Publishing.

Jacobs, L. G. (1976–1977). The right of the mentally disabled to marry: A statutory evaluation. *Journal of Family Law, 15,* 463–507.

Katz, E. (1970). *The retarded adult at home.* Seattle, WA: Special Child Publications.

Knappett, K., & Wagner, N. N. (1976). Sex education and the blind. *Education of the Visually Handicapped, 8,* 1–5.

Lewisohn, R. (1958). *A history of sexual customs.* New York: Harper & Row.

Maisel, E. (1953). *Meet a body.* New York: Institute for the Crippled and Disabled.

Miller, S., & Morgan, M. (1980). Marriage matters: For people with disabilities too. *Sexuality & Disability, 3,* 203–211.

Mooney, T. A., Cole, T. M., & Chilgren, R. A. (1975). *Sexual options for paraplegics and quadriplegics.* Boston: Little, Brown.

Moore, M. H. (1979). *Developing responsible sexuality: A comprehensive skills program for the handicapped.* New York: Walker Educational Book Corporation.

Neff, J. (1976). How does one handle sex education with a deaf-blind child? *American Annals of the Deaf, 12,* 359–360.

Neff, J. (1979). Another perspective on sexuality and those who are deaf and blind. *Sexuality and Disability, 2,* 206–210.

Neumann, R. J. (1978). Sexuality and the spinal cord injured: High drama or improvisational theater? *Sexuality & Disability, 1,* 93–99.

Nirje, B. (1970). The normalizational principle: Implications and comments. *Journal of Mental Subnormality, 16,* 62–70.

Nordqvist, I. (1972). *Life together.* Stockholm: Swedish Central Committee for Rehabilitation.

Nordqvist, I. (1980), Sexual counseling for disabled persons. *Sexuality & Disability, 3,* 193–198.

Orlansky, M. D., & Rhyne, J. M. (1981). Special adaptations necessitated by visual impairments. In J. M. Kauffman & D. P. Hallahan (Eds.), *Handbook of special education.* Englewood Cliffs, NJ: Prentice-Hall.

Payne, M. R., & Patton, J. R. (1981). *Mental Retardation.* Columbus, OH: C. E. Merrill.

Public Law 85-926. U.S. Code congressional and administrative News. 85th Congress. Second session. 1985. Vol. I. Laws. (pp. 2140–2141). St. Paul, MN: West Publishing.

Public Law 88-164. U.S. Code congressional and administrative News. 88th Congress. First session. 1963. Laws, legislative history, executive orders, proclamations, etc., index, tables (pp. 309–329). St. Paul, MN: West Publishing.

Public Law 94-142. U.S. Code congressional and administrative News. 94th Congress. First session. 1975. Vol. II. Legislative history, proclamations, executive orders, index, tables (pp. 1425–1508). St. Paul, MN: West Publishing.

Robinault, I. P. (1978). *Sex, society and the disabled.* Hagerstown, MD: Harper & Row.

Robinson, L. D. (1979). Sexuality and the deaf culture. *Sexuality & Disability, 2,* 161–168.

Roos, P. (1975, Spring). Psychological impact of sterilization on the individual. *Law & Psychology Review,* 45–56.

Rose, S. (1975). *The use of the Test of Social Inference with deaf adolescents.* Unpublished doctoral dissertation, The Ohio State University, Columbus.

Rousso, H. (1982). Special considerations in counseling clients with cerebral palsy. *Sexuality & Disability, 5,* 78–88.

Sabagh, G., & Edgerton, R. (1962). Sterilized mental defectives look at eugenic sterilization. *Eugenics Quarterly, 9,* 213–216.

Safilios-Rothschild, C. (1982). Social and psychological parameters of friendship and intimacy for disabled people. In M. G. Eisenberg, C. Griggins, & R. J. Duval (Eds.), *Disabled people as second-class citizens.* New York: Springer Publishing.

Scheerenberger, R. C. (1983). *A History of mental retardation.* Baltimore: Paul H. Brookes.

Schiller, P. (1977). *Creative approaches to sex education and counseling.* New York: Associated Press.

Scholl, G. T. (1974). The psychosocial effects of blindness: Implications for program planning in sex education. *New Outlook for the Blind, 68,* 201–209.

Sequoia Area VIII Board for Developmental Disabilities. (1984). *Recommendations and resource information for advocates and service providers on the subject of sexual abuse of persons with developmental disabilities.* (Available from 546 West Shields, Suite A, Fresno, CA 93705).

Shaman, J. M. (1978). Persons who are mentally retarded: Their right to marry and have children. *Family Law Quarterly, 12,* 61–84.

Shuger, N. (1979). The legal rights of handicapped persons with regard to procreation. *Sexuality & Disability, 2,* 216–230.

SIECUS. (1971). *A resource guide in sex education for the mentally retarded.* New York: Sex Information and Education Council of the U.S.

Spastic Society. (1973). *Like other people* [film] Northfield, IL: Perennial Education.

Stewart, T. D. (1981). Sex, spinal cord injury, and staff rapport. *Rehabilitation Literature, 42,* 347–350.

Thorn-Gray, B. E., & Kern, L. H. (1983). Sexual dysfunction associated with physical disability: A treatment guide for the rehabilitation practitioner. *Rehabilitation Literature, 44,* 138–144.

Thornton, C. E. (1978). A nurse-educator in sex and disability. *Sexuality & Disability, 2,* 28–32.

Torbett, D. S. (1974). A humanistic and futuristic approach to sex education for blind children. *New Outlook for the Blind, 68,* 210–215.

Towards a Quaker view of sex (revised ed.). 1964. London: The Friends Home Service Committee.

The United Church of Christ. (1977). *Human Sexuality: A preliminary Study.* New York: United Church Press.

Vash, C. L. (1981). *The psychology of disability.* New York: Springer Publishing.

Wabreck, A., Wabreck, C., & Burchell, R. C. (1978). The tragedy of spina bifida: Spina myelomeningocele. *Sexuality & Disability, 1,* 210–217.

Wallace, D. (1980). Sexuality and the disabled: Implication for the sex education of medical students. *Sexuality & Disability, 3,* 17–25.

Whitcraft, C., & Jones, J. (1974). A survey of attitudes about sterilization of retardates, *Mental Retardation, 12,* 30–33.

Woodward, J. (1979). *Signs of sexual behavior.* Silver Springs, MD: T. J. Publishers. (Available from SIECUS, 80 Fifth Ave., New York, NY 10011)

Wright, B. A. (1960). *Physical disability—A psychological approach.* New York: Harper & Row.

Wright, B. A. (1983). *Physical disability—A psychosocial approach.* New York: Harper & Row.

CHAPTER 8

Social Integration

Luanna H. Meyer and JoAnne Putnam

Few people think about equality when they think about special.

Assigning disabled people to special programs, giving them special buses and special schools, puts the community of disabled people in a ghetto. When the choice is between using the special service or doing without entirely, you really have no choice....

When blacks had no choices about where to live — but could live in only one area of town — that was called a ghetto.

The lack of choice for integrated options for disabled people for transportation, for seating in places of public accommodation, for schooling; the provision of a special entrance, or a ramp at the back door or at the loading dock; of a "special elevator for the handicapped only", a "special restroom", are all signals that our society places disabled people in a ghetto too. (What They Mean is Segregated, 1983, p. 4)

The past several decades have witnessed profound changes in the design of services for persons with disabilities. After a long history of exclusion and isolation of these individuals from nearly all mainstream educational and community environments, professional and public opinion is shifting. Since the passage of Public Law 94-142, for example, federal policy and professional recommendations have increasingly emphasized the provision of educational services for children with disabilities in integrated settings, that is, in proximity to peers who are not handicapped (Biklen, 1985; Certo, Haring, & York, 1984; Stainback & Stainback, 1985; Will, 1983). Past attitudes of sympathy, protection, and care have given way to the current focus upon individual development, personal growth and self-determination, social interdependence, and full participation in the mainstream of society, regardless of the nature or degree of handicapping condition (Bellamy et al., 1984; Brown

This work was supported in part by Contract No. 300-82-0363 from the U.S. Department of Education. The material does not necessarily reflect the position or policies of the U.S. Department of Education, and no official endorsement should be inferred. Order of authorship is alphabetical, and the authors' contributions to the writing of this chapter were equal.

et al., 1984; Guess & Siegel-Causey, 1985; Turnbull & Turnbull, 1985; Voeltz & Evans, 1983). These values are reflected in both model program development efforts and, in some states (e.g., Hawaii, Vermont), state-wide implementation of integrated public school services for all students, including those with the most severe disabilities (Horner, Meyer, & Fredericks, 1986). In contrast, the reality of school and community services in most regions continues to reveal substantive discrepancies with these stated program goals and values. There are historical, fiscal, and administrative reasons for the maintenance of the large congregate care facilities and separate, segregated school services that continue to exist in many parts of the country. The discrepancies and the reasons behind them represent a significant challenge to ongoing research and program development efforts to accomplish the physical and social integration of persons with disabilities into all aspects of community living.

There is not yet complete concensus that the goal of social integration is an appropriate one. Some continue to debate the educability of children with various disabilities, the social validity of integrated educational services, the movement to community living environments, and the wisdom of forcing the demise of institutions and segregated schools (Becker, 1984; Gresham, 1985; Kauffman & Krous, 1981; Silverstein, 1985). Disagreement reflects several points of view and primary concerns: (a) a bias that no change should occur until empirical data clearly favor the superiority of integrated services over segregated ones; (b) a fear that (as has been historically the case) the loss of handicapped-only settings may eventually lead to the loss of services to this population; (c) the conviction that children with disabilities will be rejected and even abused by their nonhandicapped peers in regular schools and in the general community; and (d) logistical, systemic resistance to the dismantling of a separate service delivery structure, which by now represents state and county budget line items, major sources of employment for many individuals and perhaps entire geographic regions, union seniority privi-

leges, physical facilities constructed through public bonds that commit taxpayer funds for years into the future, and the professional careers of numerous, often influential persons who identify with the existence of that separate structure.

The focus of this chapter is social integration in school settings. Ultimately, of course, the achievement of social integration can only be measured by the extent to which persons with disabilities enjoy full access to and participation in all community environments and the activities that typically occur in those environments. Our review presents a comprehensive picture of the efforts and accomplishments reported in school settings including children with disabilities. Perhaps because the educational system is universal and provides ready access to all children who attend, the majority of our research on social integration has occurred in schools. However, there are significant efforts in other community environments as well (e.g., see Lakin & Bruininks, 1985b, and Chapter 21, this volume, for reviews of these developments). Our presentation will touch briefly upon certain of these developments that are most relevant for the social integration of school environments. Following a history of school services for children with disabilities, the majority of the chapter will review contemporary issues and ongoing research and development efforts. Finally, we conclude with a discussion of future directions. Each of these is either implied by our existing data base or is specifically prompted by obvious gaps in this knowledge.

Clearly, social integration is a goal that reflects an overall positive trend in societal values affecting persons with disabilities as rights are recognized and the importance of community to quality of life is acknowledged. At the same time, information on effective systems change and individual intervention strategies is critical if this goal is to be achieved constructively. Data can document positive outcomes, but are also needed to support the design of more effective interventions where results are equivocal or even negative. In the absence of systematic evaluation data to monitor and refine our intevention efforts, the social integration of persons with disabilities may continue to be dismissed as personal bias while the current reality of separate systems remains the predominant pattern of service delivery.

HISTORY AND DEVELOPMENT

The educational mandate of PL 94-142 signaled the recognition of society's responsibility to provide an education for all children, regardless of handicapping condition, and included an emphasis upon doing so in the least restrictive environment, that is, in proximity to nonhandicapped peers. The same forces that were no doubt instrumental in generating this significant school reform were simultaneously effecting major reform in other service areas as well. Within the past 15 years, a dramatic reduction in the population of persons with disabilities living in publicly supported institutional facilities has occurred, and the admission of young children to these congregate care settings has virtually ended (Braddock & Heller, 1985; Hill, Lakin, & Bruininks, 1984). The public policy of deinstitutionalization has been systematically reinterpreted from an initial emphasis upon nearly any alternative to a large institution to a model of normalized, family-scale living environments that are integrated into residential neighborhoods and no longer isolated from community life (Lakin & Bruininks, 1985a). The impetus for these changes in service delivery involves a complex history of events and influences, including newly emerging philosophies and conceptual shifts, parent and consumer activism, and legislative reform, along with litigation and mandates.

Phases in Educational Integration

In the United States, the educational integration of children with handicapping conditions has evolved through four stages that can be roughly delineated as: (a) no educational services, prior to 1800; (b) residential schools, 1820–1900; (c) special schools and classes, 1850–1975; and (d) integration into regular schools and classes, 1975–present.

No Educational Services

Prior to the 1800s, most persons with identifiable handicaps were excluded from participating in educational and other community functions. This period of history typically has been depicted as one of extreme neglect, rejection, and even abuse of individuals with handicaps (Hewett & Forness, 1974; Kanner, 1964; Reynolds & Birch, 1977). Periods or instances of humanistic concern, charity, and even superstitious reverence also have been accounted by historians, though these are noted to be rare (Kanner, 1964; Scheerenberger, 1983). With few exceptions, persons with handicaps were not considered to be worthy of or capable of benefiting from education and training. Thus, they were left to their own devices and received little public assistance.

Residential Schools

The residential school phase began in the early mid-1800s and can be historically linked to general social reform efforts that attempted to redress the neglect and mistreatment of various socially devalued groups. Reformers such as Thomas Gallaudet and Samuel Gridley Howe sought to improve the inhumane treatment of individuals with handicaps by establishing the first residential schools for education and training. In 1817, Gallaudet founded the American Asylum for the Education and Instruction of the Deaf, and in 1855, Howe founded the Massachusetts School for Idiots and Feeble-Minded Youth (sic). These and similar residential schools of this period typically serviced only one category of handicapping condition, such as hearing impairments, visual impairments, or mental handicaps. Preference for placement and services was given to children with relatively mild handicaps, most likely (then as now) because they were believed to have better prospects for making educational and treatment gains, and they were more readily served than either adults or children with more severe and multiple handicapping conditions.

By the late 1800s, residential schools were increasing dramatically in number and size. As Scheerenberger (1983) has noted, "The small, homelike educational establishment was replaced by the large, overcrowded, and underfinanced multi-purpose facility that would typify institutions for generations to come" (p. 123). Isolation and segregation of handicapped persons in institutions (especially those with mental disabilities) received strong support as a social policy in the early 1900s, due in large part to the eugenics movement, which advocated the prevention of procreation by "undesirables" through such social practices (Scheerenberger, 1983).

Special Schools and Classes

The advent of special classes and special schools was ushered in during the latter part of the 19th century as a result of public policy changes that were taking place in regular education. With the enforcement of compulsory education legislation and the implementation of a class-graded instructional system, schools were confronted with the task of educating *all* students in the context of a class-graded, lockstep instructional progression (Sarason & Doris, 1979). Thus, many students of relatively low academic ability — who might otherwise have dropped out of school at an early age or never enrolled at all — were required to attend school for the first time. As these students did not progress in their academic subjects at a typical rate, special classes and day schools were established to educate those who were failing, in the absence of any individualized assistance in regular public school classrooms. Chaves (1977) avers "Special classes came about, then, not for humanitarian reasons but because exceptional children were unwanted in the regular public school classroom. Feelings against mainstreaming, that is, placing exceptional children in regular classrooms, were strong" (p. 30). Only those students considered to be educable and who could physically meet the requirements of school attendance (e.g.,

move about in the school, sit at desks) could enroll in public schools. Children who were nonambulatory, not toilet-trained, or severely cognitively impaired, for example, were still excluded.

The number of special classes and schools declined somewhat during the Depression years, but began to proliferate again in the late 1930s with the provision of increased financial support (Johnson, 1962). A major question facing educators in the 1930s and early 1940s was whether students with handicaps would benefit more from special class placements in the regular school building used by their non-handicapped peers or from segregated, special school placements. It is evident that in the mid-1900s, school systems generally favored regular school, special class programs for students with mild handicaps; those with moderate to severe disabilities were either not served at all or relegated exclusively to special schools and training programs located in institutions. According to statistics reported by Mackie (1969), there was a 400% increase in the number of handicapped students enrolled in public school programs between 1948 and 1966, and in 1963, 90% of these students received instruction in full-time special classes.

Integration in Regular Schools and Classes

The fourth and most recent stage in the educational integration of students with disabilities is taking place in the 1980s: social and academic integration into regular schools and classrooms. Preceded by the civil rights movement of the 1950s and 1960s, influenced greatly by parent and consumer activism that resulted in legislation and litigation supporting services, and fueled by severe academic and professional criticisms of the educational validity of special classes, the trend toward mainstreaming has steadily gained momentum over the past 15 years. Briefly, mainstreaming has involved the placement of students with mild, moderate, or severe disabilities into academic and social situations with their nondisabled peers to the fullest extent possible while still meeting basic educational needs.

Although this trend to increasingly integrate individuals with handicaps into our schools and communities has been continuous, it cannot be described as a steady or linear progression. In 1982, for example, attempts by the current presidential administration and the Department of Education to deregulate certain provisions of PL 94-142 and shift responsibilities from the federal government to the states were met by an unprecedented reaction from parents and advocacy groups protesting such changes. In a series of national hearings, and in submitted written testimony and letters which exceeded that on any other issue in recent history, the overwhelming majority expressed their fears that these proposed changes weakened the legislative assurances of publicly supported educational programs and the quality of those services. As a result, the administration withdrew its proposal and the regulations remained unaltered.

This somewhat rocky political activity has been accompanied by continued professional debate regarding the efficacy of mainstreaming (Polloway, 1984; Strain & Kerr, 1981). In addition to expressed concerns regarding the social acceptance of mildly handicaped students by nonhandicapped peers (e.g., Gresham, 1982), even the potential educability of children with more severe disabilities has been questioned. For example, Kauffman and Krouse (1981) critiqued what they termed the "cult of educability" and argued that the position that all children are educable (as articulated in legislation, court decisions arising from litigation, and extra-judicial interpretations) "may be indefensible on philosophical grounds, undesirable as social policy, and questionable as a moral precept or ethical standard" (p. 54). It is important to note that differences of opinion regarding mainstreaming are evident among persons with disabilities themselves. Some members of the deaf community in particular have advocated that children with severe hearing disabilities be educated with other children experiencing similar disabilities in order to benefit from a sense of community and belonging (Becker, 1984). While these differences of professional,

advocatory, and consumer opinion are unlikely to be resolved by philosophical debate, Baer's (1981) analogy of the educability argument as a "Scottish verdict" may be especially apropos; we cannot prove that all children are capable of learning, nor can we prove that some are incapable of learning. Thus, he suggested that the progressive next step be one of optimism, in which serious efforts to achieve positive outcomes include both creating quality programs and making such programs accessible to all students with disabilities, including those traditionally excluded. Similarly, it may be precipitous to argue against the design of educational and community services to support the social integration of persons with disabilities, based upon the limited achievements of a past time when resources, services, and even public and professional opinion were overwhelmingly biased against integration.

Factors Influencing Social Integration in the 1960s and 1970s

The most dramatic changes with respect to the social integration of all children with handicaps — particularly those with moderate to severe disabilities — have occurred since the 1960s. Efficacy research, expert opinion, parent and professional advocacy groups, legislation and litigation have all helped turn the tide.

Efficacy Research

Studies conducted by researchers during the 1960s and 1970s were important in stimulating educators, scholars, and parents to question the wisdom of placing students with mild handicaps in segregated special classes. Polloway (1984) reported that a computer search for the years 1966–1983 produced more than 600 citations related to the most effective classroom placement for "mildly learning handicapped students". Findings of some of the earlier studies, although mixed, generally indicated that students in regular classes achieved as well as or better than those enrolled in special classes (Budoff & Gottlieb, 1976; Carroll, 1967, 1967; Stanton & Cassidy, 1964). Goldstein, Moss, and Jordan (1965) found that educable mentally retarded students with higher IQ levels performed better in regular classes, and students with lower IQs performed better in special classes. Outcomes regarding social adjustment were varied; some studies supported special class placement on the basis of evidence that handicapped students were rejected by nonhandicapped Peers (Iano, Ayers, Heller, McGettigan, & Walker, 1974; Johnson, 1950); others supported regular class placement (Budoff & Gottlieb, 1976; Meyerowitz, 1962).

Johnson and Meyer (1985) noted that the data on social acceptance and interactions between students with disabilities and their nonhandicapped peers can be interpreted either negatively or positively as a function of whether the mainstreamed children and the environment into which they were mainstreamed were prepared for one another. Where no intervention took place, the results were negative; where an intervention occurred, the outcome data were positive (Gottlieb, 1978, 1981). Johnson, Johnson, and Maruyama (1983) similarly cautioned that interpretation of the results of their meta-analysis of this literature must be viewed as outcomes associated with particular integration contexts. Where the data are negative, these findings reflect the need for research on effective interventions to support heterogeneous educational groupings. Donaldson (1980), in her review of the research on social acceptance and attitudes, also argued that where outcomes were less than optimal, the task of educators should be to identify the socialization factors that are responsible and design alternative interventions. Finally, Asher and Taylor (1981) challenged the validity of the dependent measures used in this social integration research, which they considered to be unduly restrictive and even inappropriate. They maintained that it may not be realistic to expect that children with mild mental retardation would be named as "best friends," for example, by nonhandicapped peers as a function of mainstreaming, and suggested a range of social acceptance measures and outcomes that might be explored as alternative outcome goals.

Hence, Voeltz (1980) began her research on interactions between children with severe disabilities and their nonhandicapped peers with the assumption that as these children were quite different from one another and had few opportunities to learn how to interact, it was naive to expect them to possess the skills and social supports to do so without intervention. Burton and Hirshoren (1979) had argued that the social rejection reported for mildly handicapped children would be even more likely to occur for children with severe disabilities. But in subsequent work, Voeltz and her colleagues were able to document significant positive results as a function of systematic intervention efforts to prepare these children to socially interact with one another, including the development of positive attitudes, friendship patterns, and observed positive interaction behaviors in school settings (Voeltz, 1982; Voeltz & Brennan, 1984).

Research reviews examining the methodological adequacy of efficacy studies on academic outcomes have pointed to serious flaws, including problems with subject selection and assignment to comparison groups, specification of the independent variable, and the choice of outcome measures (Bruininks, Rynders, & Gross, 1974; Cegelka & Tyler, 1970; Strain & Kerr, 1981). Despite their inconclusiveness and possible methodological inadequacies, however, one conclusion seems justified: After considerable investment of pupil and researcher effort, efficacy studies have failed to clearly demonstrate that students in special classes will do better academically or socially than similar students who remain in the regular classroom, with or without additional special education courses. Without this assurance, it has become increasingly difficult for educators to support the continued separation of handicapped from nonhandicapped students via special class and special school placements. Since the 1970s this comparative research on the effects of special versus regular class placements appears to have given way to intervention research to validate effective strategies to deliver specialized services in regular education environments. (This literature will be reviewed in the section on Current Trends.)

Dunn's (1968) paper was perhaps the classic indictment of special classes, which fundamentally challenged the existence of a separate, special education system and served as a powerful stimulus to the mainstreaming movement for mildly handicapped students in particular. Dunn offered two major criticisms of separate special education programs apart from regular class placement. First, he too summarized the equivocal evidence on pupil outcomes as failing to support the superiority of special classes over regular education. Second, Dunn charged that students classified as mildly mentally retarded and served in separate classes disproportionately represented ethnic and racial minority groups. Thus, regardless of any original intent to provide specialized educational servies to students experiencing academic difficulties in regular education, special education appeared to be acting as a de facto tool for racial segregation at a time when *Brown v. Board of Education* was otherwise forcing the ethnic integration of public schools. Given this dual circumstance, Dunn stated that there could be no further justification for special education as a separate educational system.

Professional and Public Opinion

Written and spoken opinions by leaders in the field of special education and in the national political arena also served to change societal attitudes regarding segregation of persons with handicaps. Blatt and Kaplan's (1966) famous exposé of institutional life in their pictorial essay *Christmas in Purgatory* had a dramatic impact. For the first time, people were vividly informed of the deplorable and inhumane conditions existing in institutions for persons with mental handicaps. A year before Blatt and Kaplan's book was published, Senator Robert Kennedy had publicly stated his negative reactions after visiting several New York state institutions, and his message reached millions of Americans through the news media.

The introduction of Nirje's (1969) concept of normalization into the United States by Wolfensberger (1972) and others was also influential in promoting community integration of persons with handicaps. Normalization is defined as the utilization of culturally normative means for establishing and maintaining behaviors and characteristics that are as culturally normal as possible (Wolfensberger, 1972). This key concept was significant because it offered a goal-oriented process by which persons with handicaps would be integrated into communities and asssisted in the fulfillment of human rights.

In the late 1970s, Brown, Nietupski, and Hamre-Nietupski (1976) wrote their now classic paper entitled "The Criterion of Ultimate Functioning". They suggested that goals for students with severe handicaps should be based on the skills needed for adjustment to and participation in current and future integrated educational and community environments. Qualities of the least restrictive environment for students with severe and profound handicaps were articulated, based upon general principles of age-appropriate and integrated educational services that maximized social interactions between students with handicaps and their nonhandicapped peers. Shortly thereafter, Wilcox and Sailor (1980) declared that the goal of social integration was a shared value and proposed that the task confronting educators is to develop effective programs to translate that value into educational and social practices.

*Advocacy, Litigation, and Legislation**

Parent and professional adovocates of civil rights for children with handicaps were activated, in part, by efficacy research, expert opinion, and judicial recognition of the importance of the right to an education for all children, as embodied in the Civil Rights Act of 1954 (*Brown v. Board of Education*). Subsequent to the Civil Rights Act,

* Special thanks are due to Frank Laski, Public Interest Law Center of Philadelphia, who read the first draft of this section and provided helpful input into the legal interpretations of the court decisions that are discussed.

numerous court cases began to focus on the right to inclusion. Javits (in Okun, 1981) reported in 1973 that such litigation was pending in 25 states on 38 due process cases for students with handicaps. Advocacy organizations, such as the National Association for Retarded Citizens, fought for equal educational opportunities for children with handicaps through the courts and via legislative action. The Pennsylvania Association for Retarded Citizens (PARC) was responsible for a landmark case impacting upon persons with handicaps (*PARC v. Commonwealth of Pennsylvania*, 1972). Its outcome established the right of every child to an education and made it the obligation of the schools to provide this education. The subsequent PARC Settlement Agreement of 1982 was revolutionary because it specified what was meant by an appropriate education for learners with severe and profound handicaps, as exemplified in the following excerpt: "Each student assigned to a class for the severely and profoundly impaired must be provided with a program of education and related services which is conducted in age-appropriate schools *attended* also by non-handicapped students, in natural proportions" (*PARC v. Pennsylvania*, 1982, p. 2).

By the 1970s, the social climate was receptive to the concepts presented in Public Law 94-142, the Education for All Handicapped Children Act. Enacted in 1975, the law embodied many judicial principles involving special education, including the right to education, due process, individualized programming, and the least restrictive alternative. Reynolds (1978) referred to this legislation as "an educational Magna Charta for all those children who have been kept out of the mainstream of education for whatever reason" (p. xv). Sections pertaining to the least restrictive alternative and an appropriate public education are central to the social integration of handicapped children. The principle of the least restrictive alternative insures that handicapped children will be educated with nonhandicapped students to the maximum extent possible, while also implying that there are alternative settings in which a child can be placed. Tradition-

ally, the regular classroom has been regarded as the least restrictive educational environment, and a residential, handicapped-only school placement would be considered most restrictive. PL 94-142 requires that states provide a continuum of services that includes these placement options. In contrast, professionals have argued that a continuum of services can be provided to students, *all of which* are located in the least restrictive environment, that is, in the regular school and neighborhood community (Meyer & Evans, 1986). For example, Reynolds and Birch (1982) have suggested that regular classes must become sufficiently diverse to support individualized instruction so that separate educational environments — such as special classes and schools — are no longer viewed as reasonable or the only options for meeting the needs of certain students.

There is now remarkable variability across the country in the extent to which students attend their neighborhood public school with nonhandicapped peers. The U.S. Department of Education Report to Congress (1985) noted that in 1982–1983 the majority of special education students attended school in regular education buildings: 68% received most of their instruction in regular classes, and an additional 25% attended separate classes. Only 7% attended separate schools or hospitals, or received homebound instruction. Overall, less than 5.5% of students aged 7 to 17 were segregated. Yet these optimistic figures are misleading; 67% of these students receive special education services for learning disabilities and speech impairments. If we examine the educational placements of the remaining 33% who have more enduring and severe disabilities, we find that 10 to 55% of these students are segregated. In fact, whether or not a student with severe handicaps will be enrolled in a general attendance or a handicapped-only school appears to be determined primarily by the prevalent pattern of service delivery in a geographic region. Thus, students with severe disabilities who live in Maryland, Missouri, and most areas of New York and Texas are given no other option than attendance in a segregated, handicapped-only school. Students with identical educational needs who live in Vermont, Nebraska, or Hawaii, on the other hand, are likely to receive special education services while attending the same schools as nonhandicapped children. Such marked discrepancies in the abilities of states and school districts to provide integrated services promises to continue to be a major issue.

Some time ago, Gilhool and Stutman (1979) asserted:

> There is no cognizable reason under the statutes for handicapped-only centers, certainly not on the scale they now exist. If a child can come to school at all, even to a self-contained class in a handicapped-only center, he can come to a self-contained class in a normal school. Any teaching technique that can be used in a self-contained class can be used in a regular school building. There are few if any legitimate teaching strategies which require the complete isolation of a child from interaction with other children, and the few such strategies that there may be apply to very few children and for very short periods of time (p. 215).

In addition to the Pennsylvania case discussed earlier in this chapter, there have been two additional federal court decisions that are directly relevant to the integration issue. In *Roncker v. Walters* (1983), the school district was required to provide Neil Roncker, who has severe disabilities, with an educational placement in an integrated setting. Each of the specialized services stated as his program needs was judged to be "portable," that is, easily moved to a regular education building. The judge ruled that the integration question was a substantive and not strictly procedural issue, such that:

> [The integration question] is not one of methodology but rather involves a determination of whether the school district has satisfied the Act's requirement that handicapped children be educated alongside nonhandicapped children to the maximum extent appropriate . . . Since Congress has decided that [interaction with handicapped] children is appropri-

ate, the states must accept that decision, if they desire federal funds.

The Court of Appeals went on to state that even in cases where the services provided by a segregated facility are considered superior, the court must determine whether the services that make that placement superior could feasibly be provided in a nonsegregated setting. That is, in the tradition of the Gilhool and Stutman argument, placement in a segregated school would be inappropriate under PL 94-142 if the needed specialized services could instead be provided in an integrated school. Upon further appeal by the school district, the Supreme Court declined to review the Roncker case, and currently there are major efforts throughout the state of Ohio to replace a system of separate schools with integrated services.

In apparent opposition to the Roncker ruling, the decision of the federal district court in Missouri can be offered as support for the continued existence of an entire state system of separate schools for students with severe handicaps. In *St. Louis Developmental Disabilities Treatment Center Parents Association v. Mallory* (1985), the court found that the maintenance of separate schools in itself was not a violation of PL 94-142 if state procedures to assure individual placements in the least restrictive placement were in effect. Even though nearly all students with severe disabilities in Missouri attend centralized handicapped-only schools, the existence of these state procedures was judged sufficient protection agianst a "systematic challenge" to the maintenance of these schools. Unlike the Roncker case, the St. Louis Court was not asked, nor did it decide, whether placement of any individual children in separate schools had been appropriate. In affirming the district court, the Court of Appeals noted that there was no specific proof regarding which severely handicapped children would benefit from regular school placements, which were unavailable. That particular issue and the application of Roncker to Missouri schools was left for "another day," as the Court of Appeals found "no error in the district court's analysis of the very narrow issues presented at trial regarding the requirements of the Education Act" (*St. Louis v. Mallory*, 1985). The narrow issues which were involved in the distict ruling centered on the plaintiff's failure to demonstrate that Missouri was acting in a discriminatory way toward students with severe disabilities. That is, the court was persuaded that the placement decision process — as described by educational system representatives from the state of Missouri — was based upon a determination of individual needs. As such, this process was in compliance with the federal mandate to individualize services to meet those needs.

PL 94-142 does indeed refer to the need for such a continuum of services, and it can be read to equate this continuum with placement options rather than the provision of more intensive services in integrated settings. It is clear that further recourse to the courts on this issue must be framed in terms of the individualized needs of particular children to support the right to placement in proximity to nonhandicapped peers. Social integration for *all* handicapped children is not unambiguously supported as a substantive goal of the Education for All Handicapped Children Act.

CONTEMPORARY ISSUES

While the legal and philosophical debate continues regarding the social integration of and appropriate educational placement for children with disabilities, there is a parallel literature of empirical work on the development of social competence and interaction skills in these children. In comparison with those who view the issue historically or ideologically, the researchers and practioners who publish in clinical and experimental journals may have approached the issue from a different perspective. Regardless of the extent to which these scientist-practioners were committed (or not) to the social integration of persons with disabilities, their concern clearly has been to investigate intervention strategies that would be effective in generating the mastery of certain skills and accomplish-

ments by persons with disabilities. Yet, the emphasis in this empirical work has shifted from a focus on the individual needs of one or more handicapped children within or across particular disabilities categories to a growing recognition of the critical importance of the social ecology — the characteristics of the environment — on the child's behavior and potential outcome. Strain, Odom, and McConnell (1984) perhaps offer the fundamental critique: The remedial model of special education is not adequate to the task of remediating the social interaction deficits of children with disabilities and may do more to perpetuate these deficits than modify them, if the effects of the social environment are not addressed. While children with disabilities may have particular social skill deficits, the environmental opportunities made available to them will be critical to the remediation of those needs. Strain and his colleagues emphasize that reciprocity is needed for the development of social competence, social opportunities, adaptations, and various modifications to naturally occurring activities, situations, and settings. In particular, they present considerable evidence that exposure to social interactions with nondisabled peers and others in the community is essential to the development of social competence. In addition, exposure to severely disabled persons is equally critical for nonhandicapped individuals if they are to learn social reciprocity.

In this section, we shall review the findings of studies investigating the effects of various environmental modifications and intervention strategies upon the social interaction of children with disabilities. This work is evident in disparate research traditions involving persons with developmental and physical disabilities. For example, there are parallel lines of research in the different journals representing work in child development, regular education curriculum development, special education curriculum development, particular disability categories (e.g., mental retardation, autism), and applied behavior analysis. The sheer volume of this work, along with the theoretical and empirical richness that it reveals clearly implicates a necessity of both future research directions and the involvement of persons with disabilities in the community. Changes in attitudes and a recognition of legal and civil rights are important developments that will support the movement of these individuals to appropriately normalized, integrated environments. In addition, the programmatic efforts described in this section may be pivotal to the long-term outcomes of changes in social policy. The intensive efforts by scientist-practitioners to address and resolve fundamental service delivery issues in these newly developed, socially integrated situations and environments can assure that principles are translated effectively and sensitively into practices that reflect an improved quality of life for persons with disabilities.

Social Competence and Social Integration

The social integration of children with disabilities into schools and communities is a function of both the individual's social competence and the opportunity to participate in those environments. In practice, social competence has been regarded as a requisite criterion for participation in normalized and integrated environments, so that opportunities would be contingent upon the mastery of skills. Where children do not do well, special assistance has typically been made available through individualized instruction in separate environments; when their skills and behavior more closely resemble mainstream expectations of normality, students are returned to the regular classroom. This model has been criticized on several grounds. First, the assumption that an age-graded, lockstep curriculum adequately meets most children's educational needs has been challenged. Criticisms of the achievements of the public school system have been leveled on behalf of children with and without disabilities, including those labeled as gifted. Knoll and Meyer (1987) review these criticisms and argue for increased efforts to adapt general school curricula and provide individualized assistance to all children, rather than maintain separate, specialized environments for each of the various

groupings (see also Reynolds & Birch, 1982). Second, children with disabilities that involve severe learning problems are said to experience great difficulties in generalizing what they have learned to the relevant situations and environments (Horner, Bellamy, & Colvin, 1984; Stokes & Baer, 1977; Stokes & Osnes, 1985). If this is so, the very difference entailed by specialized and separate environments created to facilitate individualized instruction — particularly if those settings include only other persons with similar severe problems — implies that any behavior change may be specific to those "deviant" settings and will not generalize to natural contexts (Meyer & Evans, 1986).

Finally, the remedial model implies that some children may never be integrated into the mainstream of school and community. This would be the case whenever the child's learning difficulties are so severe that it is unlikely that he or she will ever master the requisite number of skills and behaviors at a sufficient rate and level of accuracy to be judged socially competent. Autism, for example, is now viewed as a lifelong disability that involves certain basic cognitive and behavioral deficits across the life span, regardless of quality programming (see Chapter 13, this volume). Although the remedial model of special education may have validity for children who can be expected to improve sufficiently to be judged "normal," this same model entails lifelong exclusion from the community for those whose disabilities make this goal unrealistic. In contrast, Brown (1986) and Donnellan (1984) have called for complete social integration of persons with disabilities, including the design of interventions to meet educational and habilitative needs in normalized and integrated contexts. According to this alternative view, increasingly intensive interventions (curricular modifications, prostheses and adapted equipment, additional staff) would be provided in integrated environments, as opposed to associating the availability of those services with a continuum of increasingly restrictive placements to which the child must move (Meyer & Evans, 1986; Warren & Juhrs, 1984).

Similarly, the remedial model of social skills instruction contrasts with recent emphases upon social reciprocity in natural environments (Strain et al., 1984). Traditional social skills instruction has involved the acquisition or strengthening of discrete topographies of behavior — such as greeting responses — in highly controlled laboratory settings, and often with only very young children (Guralnick, 1978; Lancioni, 1982; Stokes, Baer, & Jackson, 1974). Less attention has been paid to older individuals, the elaboration phases of social interactions, or the occurrence of even isolated responses, such as greeting others in a community environment (Gaylord-Ross, Stremel-Campbell, & Storey, 1986; Renzaglia & Bates, 1983). This early work was important in laying the foundation for the more complex and difficult task of developing social competence in natural settings, but it has been increasingly criticized as an atheoretical and contextually void approach that has failed to result in meaningful demonstrations of social integration outcomes (Beveridge & Brinker, 1980; Gresham, 1981; Odom & Strain, 1984).

In contrast, recent writings on social competence have emphasized irrevocable ties to locale as well as situational and attitudinal features of the environment, and that the construct of social competence involves a judgment by other persons as much as it does the display of various skill topographies (McFall, 1982). Taxonomies of social functions have emphasized the behavior of the individual in relationship to social conventions that vary depending upon the nature of the interaction, location, and numerous other contextual variables (Meyer, Reichle, et al., 1985; Stremel-Campbell, Clark-Guida, & Johnson-Dorn, 1984). This perspective dictates that assessment and clinical interventions must be conducted in the context of the individual's performance in these specific and variable situations (Dodge & Murphy, 1984; Gaylord-Ross, Stremel-Campbell, & Storey, 1986; McFall & Dodge, 1982). In special education, this requires that assessment and instructional planning occur through a three-step process: (a) delineat-ing the sequence of behaviors performed by a person judged to be competent in the particular situation; (b) comparing the performance of the person who needs instruction with the criterion behavior sequence; and (c) designing an intervention program based upon any discrepancies and the individual's particular needs. Various authors have delineated alternative but similar strategies that reflect this approach (Brown et al., 1979; Cone & Hoier, 1985; Dodge, McClaskey, & Feldman, 1985; Dodge & Murphy, 1984; Meyer, McQuarter, & Kishi, 1985; Strain, 1983a). Thus, exposure to and experiences in natural environments with individuals who are not disabled becomes an essential ingredient to the development of social competence and the social integration of persons with disabilities.

Integration Interventions and Outcomes

Once the decision has been made to provide special education services to handicapped children in their neighborhood schools and in regular classrooms, the evidence to date points to the need for systematic intervention efforts to promote positive outcomes for both handicapped and nonhandicapped children (Johnson, Johnson, & Maruyama, 1983; Madden & Slavin, 1983; Wang & Birch, 1984b). In a recent review, Gresham (1982) summarized this information: ". . . mere physical placement of handicapped learners in regular classrooms does not necessarily result in positive consequences" (p. 430). In concurrence, Strain and Shores (1983) replied: "It should surprise no special educator to learn that an absence of instruction leads to an absence of skill!" (p. 272). Voeltz (1984) also maintains that negative outcomes associated with the physical integration of handicapped children into mainstream settings simply indicate the need for intervention, which is as appropriate for educators and other practitioners to address as they would any other curricular need (see also Salend, 1984). In the remainder of this section, we shall review the results of such intervention efforts.

School and Curricular Reform

Students with handicaps who are placed in regular educational environments without systematic intervention do not do well (Devonney, Guralnick, & Rubin, 1974; Fredericks et al., 1978; Semmel, Gottlieb, & Robinson, 1979). Studies of the effects of such placements upon children with mild handicaps (e.g., learning disabilities and mild mental retardation) indicate that they (a) are more socially isolated from their peers than are nonhandicapped students; (b) are less socially accepted than their nonhandicapped peers (Asher & Taylor, 1981; Bryan, 1974; Gresham, 1982; MacMillan, Jones, & Aloia, 1974); and (c) tend to interact more frequently among themselves than with handicapped students in integrated settings (Peterson & Haralick, 1977; Porter, Ramsey, Tremblay, Iaccobo, & Crawley, 1978). Gottlieb (1981) reviewed these findings and questioned the prevalent practice of specialized instruction in "pull out" resource rooms while the remainder of the school day is spent in the regular classroom without assistance. In their discussion of the possible negative impact of such "pull out" practices, Wang and Birch (1984b) stated:

> Administrative changes have occurred in the provision of special education, without the "in-class" programming changes essential for realistic implementation of concepts such as mainstreaming. Under these conditions, exceptional students are unlikely to be full participants in the social and intellectual life of regular classes, and whatever social and attitudinal benefits might accrue are likely to be diluted. (p. 393)

In all fairness, integration outcomes must also be judged in the context of regular schools. Various study reports have called for significant instructional and curricular reform in American public education (Gross & Gross, 1985; National Commission on Excellence in Education, 1983). Goodlad's (1983) in-depth study of 1,016 schools identified several problems: (a) a predominance of whole-class, large-group instruction, with very little instructional variability; (b) little emphasis upon provid-

ing corrective feedback-with-guidance to students or promoting stimulation of concept formation; (c) affectless (either positive or negative) classrooms; and (d) minimal teacher-to-student and student-to-teacher interaction (mostly teacher talking and monitoring of seat work). Biklen (1985) synthesizes this literature on "effective schools" (the term often used) in his summary of various strategies for mainstreaming, consistent with the concerns in general education and special education for excellence and equality. Other authors have also emphasized the common goals, strategies, concerns, and needs of both special and regular education, and questioned the existence of special education as a separate entity apart from the need to individualize instruction for all students (Ysseldyke & Algozzine, 1982). Stainback and Stainback (1984) have specifically proposed the merger of the two systems, based upon both these commonalities and the inefficiency of operating a dual system.

The Adaptive Learning Environments Model (ALEM) is perhaps the most fully developed and validated approach to modifying the regular education curriculum in a way that maximizes both handicapped and nonhandicapped students' opportunities to master basic academic and social skills (Wang & Birch, 1984b). ALEM has been field tested for more than a decade at the University of Pittsburgh and elsewhere in a considerable number of public and private schools as a curricular modification to support students with mildly handicapping conditions and others with learning difficulties in the regular classroom. (Wang and Birch noted in their 1984b report that components of ALEM were in use in over 150 school districts in 28 states.) The model is based upon the following components: (a) a diagnostic-prescriptive monitoring system, (b) delabeling of mainstreamed special students, (c) provision of individualized assistance to all students experiencing learning problems based upon regular performance data, and (d) teaching of self-management skills. School districts may implement the model using either adaptations of the individualized curricula developed at the University of Pittsburgh or locally used texts and curricula that can be adapted for the program (Wang & Birch, 1984b). Wang and Birch (1984a) reported the effects of ALEM on exceptional students (learning disabled, socially and emotionally disturbed, visually impaired, and gifted) placed in full-time mainstream settings or receiving resource room services (partial mainstreaming). The full-time mainstreaming approach using the ALEM model produced more positive effects on observed student behaviors (e.g., interactions with teachers and peers, on-task behavior), achievement, attitudes, and costs of services. Higher fidelity in ALEM program implementation was associated with more favorable outcomes (Wang & Birch, 1984a). Wang and Birch (1984b) provide an overview of the various validation studies and outcomes reported for the ALEM model.

Task Structure and Activity/Materials Modifications

Various authors have maintained that special education stigmatizes persons with severe disabilities and socially separates them from their nonhandicapped peers through involvement in activities that are not age-appropriate. Brown, Nietupski, and Hamre-Nietupski (1976) and Guess and Noonan (1982) note that use of a developmental curriculum model that ignores the student's chronological age and instead focuses upon the construct of mental age can lead to training on preschool tasks that is neither functional in the community for school age and beyond, nor likely to promote interactions with nonhandicapped peers. Bates, Morrow, Pancsofar, and Sedlack (1984) exposed two groups of college students to photographs of the same young woman with Down syndrome engaged in functional activities in integrated environments versus those that were more characteristic of a developmental curriculum. Students who viewed the integrated and functional activities reported significantly higher expectations for the young woman than those who viewed the nonfunctional photographs.

Stokes and Osnes (1985) suggest that social interactions may be facilitated as an indirect consequence of intervention that teach children other nonsocial skills that would place them in more frequent social contact with peers. There has been some work on the effects of different activity contexts and materials on children's social interactions, though most studies include direct social skills training as well. Buell, Stoddard, Harris, and Baer (1968) reported increases in positive social responses, such as touching, verbalization, and playing with other children, as a consequence of teaching a young girl how to use outdoor play equipment that brought her into natural social contact with peers. Similarly, Gaylord-Ross, Haring, Breen, and Pitts-Conway (1984) and Breen, Haring, Pitts-Conway, and Gaylord-Ross (1985) reported increased and generalized social interactions between autistic teenagers and non-handicapped peers and others at school and on job training sites through training in social skills as well as the use of age-appropriate materials and activities (i.e., hand-held video game, a Walkman radio with headphones, chewing gum, and coffee).

In contrast to these investigations of behavior during relatively informal social exchanges with peers, there has been considerable research on the effects of different task structures on student performance and peer interaction. Johnson and Johnson at the University of Minnesota have spent well over a decade developing an empirical data base demonstrating that the goal structures typical of today's school environment can be redesigned to facilitate the acceptance of heterogeneous values, learning styles, and student racial/cultural identities. Unit recently, most of their work was focused upon investigating the different effects of cooperative goal structures in school learning experiences and those that are individualistic or competitive based upon interpersonal attraction and social acceptance among students from different racial and cultural groups. In the cooperative goal structure, the goal is achieved only if all members of the (heterogeneous) group work together to achieve that goal. This model contrasts with individualistic and competitive learning situations that are more typical of academic and extracurricular activities such as sports, in which the goal is to surpass one's own performance or that of others. The Johnsons and their colleagues have extended this work to investigate the effects of cooperative task structures on both social and academic behaviors of heterogeneous groups, including handicapped and nonhandicapped youngsters. Studies with moderately and severely retarded and severely physically handicapped children have been done in elementary and secondary schools and community recreation settings, involving activities as varied as science projects, music education, and group recreation activities, among others (Jellison, Brookes, & Huck, 1984; Johnson, Johnson, DeWeerdt, Lyons, & Zaidman, 1983; Johnson, Rynders, Johnson, Schmidt, & Haider, 1979; Putnam & Rynders, 1985; Rynders, Johnson, Johnson, & Schmidt, 1980). In general, the evidence is that cooperative groups are associated with significantly higher levels of certain positive social and verbal interaction behaviors, greater interpersonal attraction on sociometric outcome measures, and equal and sometimes higher academic gains by students who participate in these integrated experiences. Some research also suggests that cooperative task structures coupled with individualized instruction or reinforcement contingencies may provide even greater benefits for handicapped and nonhandicapped students, in terms of social, behavioral, and achievement gains (Jellison et al., 1984; Madden, Slavin, & Leavey, 1984).

Individual Social Skill Instruction

As we noted earlier in this chapter, contemporary approaches to social competence emphasize that individual needs must be addressed in relevant social contexts. Although a comprehensive review of social skills instruction with handicapped children is beyond the scope of this chapter, we shall briefly review current research in this area that is focused upon preparing children with disabilities to interact with others — particularly their peers. Stokes and Osnes (1985) note that

certain social responses can be critical if they are of such a nature that they are likely to be consistently reinforced from other people in most settings and thus lead to further positive social interaction among those individuals. Gable, Hendrickson, and Strain (1978) described a strategy to identify such critical skills by observing children's social interaction in natural contexts to determine which behaviors reliably elicited a positive response from peers. Using this approach, Hendrickson, Strain, Tremblay, and Shores (1982) identified certain critical social skills that generated a reciprocal interaction promoting further social interaction and play. They taught young children to suggest play activities, offer to share, and provide assistance during play, and were able to demonstrate increased positive social interactions among children as a function of the acquisition and use of these social skills.

It is possible, of course, that children targeted for social skills instruction because of difficulties in this area lack a sufficiently positive social behavior repertoire for this procedure to be useful. That is, the child initially may not exhibit social interaction behaviors that reliably elicit positive attention from peers. Thus, Strain (1983a) identified potential target social behaviors by comparing the interaction of handicapped children who consistently received high sociometric ratings to those children rated low on these measures. The high-rated children shared materials, organized play, assisted with tasks, were affectionate, and responded positively to social initiations by peers, and the low-rated children exhibited more negative social interactions.

Finally, Strain, Odom, and McConnell (1984) caution that teaching social skills to the handicapped child — even if those skills have been identified as important — is only the first step to improving the social status of that child. Some instruction of the child's peers may also be needed to insure that these children notice and respond to the handicapped child's newly acquired social behaviors. Futhermore, teacher intervention may be crucial to shape social interactions through reinforcement and prompting procedures. The next two sections summarize current research findings on the effects of peer- and teacher-mediated interventions.

Peer-Mediated Interventions

There is considerable evidence that with preparation, nonhandicapped peers interact positively with children with disabilities, and that a socially responsive environment may even facilitate the development of certain social skills that are best learned from other children and not from adults (Brinker, 1985; Meyer et al., 1987). Efforts to prepare nonhandicapped peers for and to facilitate these interactions fall into three broad categories:

1. Nonhandicapped "confederate" peers are trained to deliver social initiations and reinforcements to handicapped children in the context of typical interaction.
2. Nonhandicapped children are trained to serve as "peer tutors" and provide direct instruction to their handicapped peers.
3. Nonhandicapped peers are encouraged to develop friendships with their handicapped peers and receive some initial teacher direction and supervision (which is then withdrawn as the children get to know one another) in relatively informal play activities.

Strain and his colleagues have conducted numerous studies to investigate the effects of training nonhandicapped children to initiate and reinforce social interactions with autistic and other handicapped peers (Strain, Kerr, & Ragland, 1981). In two early studies, nonhandicapped children were taught to use specific verbal and gestural interactions with withdrawn preschool children, with mixed generalization results (Strain, 1977; Strain, Shores, & Timm, 1977). Later studies emphasized teaching nonhandicapped students to prompt and reinforce the behavior of peers with disabilities (Strain, 1981), and the generalization of improvements in positive social behaviors by autistic children to other integrated settings. The fact that the behavioral improvements did not general-

ize to segregated settings was attributed to differential levels of social responsiveness of the peers in the two environments (Strain, 1983b). Odom, Hoyson, Jamieson, and Strain (1985) taught nonhandicapped preschool children to make social overtures to three handicapped peers. When needed, the teacher both prompted and reinforced the confederate peers to maintain their interactions. An increase in frequencies of positive social behavior occurred in the intervention classroom, but did not generalize to two additional classrooms until the interventions also were implemented in those settings. Finally, withdrawal of the teacher's token reinforcement system did not adversely affect the interaction level, but a reduction in teacher prompts did. In their discussion of the implications of these findings, Odom and his colleagues question whether "preschool-aged children have adequate social repertoires for independently generating a variety of successful social initiations when interacting with a peer who is consistently unresponsive" (p. 15).

In their review of peer-mediated interventions, Odom and Strain (1984) note that generalization of social interaction behavioral improvements to nontraining peers and maintenance across time remains a problem. Subsequently, Brady et al. (1984), Fox et al. (1984), and Gaylord-Ross et al. (1984) reported the results of a procedure described as "multiple peer exemplar training," in which the nonhandicapped peers who were selected to represent the "range of critical attributes in the stimulus conditions where generalization is to take place" (Gaylord-Ross et al., 1984, p. 234) were sequentially introduced into the peer interaction activity. In each study, this procedure resulted in the eventual generalization of the social behaviors to a peer who had not been involved in the initial training.

In peer tutoring programs, the nonhandicapped student receives systematic training to provide instruction to handicapped students and serves in a role that essentially parallels that of the teacher. Peer tutoring programs in special education were originally promoted as a strategy to attain a more intensive pupil-teacher ratio in school and community set-tings, but they have most recently been advocated as a technique to prepare non-handicapped children to accept and inter-act positively with persons who have dis-abilities (e.g., Kohl, Moses, & Stettner-Eaton, 1984). Such programs are generally evaluated through evidence of the extent to which the nonhandicapped peer tutor reliably exhibits the learned instructional procedures (e.g., delivering cues, prompt-ing, providing reinforcements, and keep-ing data), as well as through skill gains made by the handicapped child who was tutored (e.g., Fenrick & McDonnell, 1980; Kohl, Moses, & Stettner-Eaton, 1983). The major distinction that can be made between peer tutor programs and the various "con-federate" peer training programs just described involves the nature of the activi-ties and the role performed by the peer. Peer tutors interact with handicapped peers in a hierarchical relationship in which they use behavior modification and other techniques to instruct students on the kinds of tasks likely to be listed as major goals on the IEP (e.g., self-help and aca-demic skills). This relationship contrasts rather sharply with the kinds of peer inter-actions that children normally experience, and Krouse, Gerber, and Kauffman (1981) stress the fact that we know little about the long-term effects of peer tutoring. Meyer (1985) has argued that the hierarchical and "professionalized" nature of peer tutor relationships seems unlikely to lead to a normalization of the social status of per-sons with disabilities, and if they are the only peer interaction experiences afforded certain handicapped children, are a poor substitute for mutual sharing and friendships.

In peer interaction programs that emph-asize the development of friendships, chil-dren spend time together engaged in social and leisure activities. Typically referred to by a term such as "Special Friends," this model is based upon the assumption that meaningful social relationships (i.e., friendships) can develop between handi-capped and nonhandicapped children, and that such relationships will endure over time and extend outside of the school day (Voeltz, 1984). Children in these pro-grams are generally matched in ways that parallel friendship patterns, for example, similar ages, same sex, physical accessi-bility to one another (live in the same neighborhood), and shared interests and enjoyment of similar activities. Of course, the children also should like one another. Rather than being taught general instruc-tional or reinforcement techniques, the nonhandicapped child is given personal-ized information about his or her handi-capped peer that is directly relevant to their social interaction, such as how to play a game and which words the handicapped child understands. Both the handicapped and nonhandicapped child receive assist-ance to acquire any social, play, and com-munication skills considered to be essential to their interaction. A detailed trainer's manual has been developed and validated for use in integrated public school environ-ments (Voeltz et al., 1983), and outcome studies show significant positive attitudi-nal and behavioral effects as a function of the program (Voeltz, 1980, 1982; Voeltz & Brennan, 1984). In addition, a large-scale study has been conducted in 10 classrooms in six different schools, involving 60 child dyads to compare this "special friends" approach to peer tutoring. Cole, Vander-cook, and Rynders (in press) report that the percentage occurrence of appropriate play, cooperative play, and positive affect — as measured by an "equity score" reflecting Hartup's (1984) notion of reciprocity in social relationships — significantly fav-ored the special friends program over peer tutoring. Furthermore, on a self-report measure, the nonhandicapped peer tutors reported having significantly less fun and less interest in the relationship than did children who were special friends. To date, this study represents the only carefully controlled investigation of the relative effects of these two recommended approaches to structuring peer interac-tions. Clearly, considerably more data are needed to support the use of one or the other strategy to facilitate the social inte-gration of children with severe and other disabilities.

Teacher Mediation

The approaches discussed above as strategies to prepare children for integration were characterized as peer-mediated to reflect the major role assigned to the nonhandicapped child whether the child was to teach, serve as a model, or simply provide good company and friendship to his or her handicapped peers. Yet, in each of the reports reviewed, the teacher also played a role in training and supervising the children prior to and during the interactions. Odom et al. (1985) presented some data that withdrawal of one component (prompting) of teacher assistance resulted in a decrease in positive social interaction and suggested that preschool children in particular may simply not be able to maintain these interactions without some help from the teacher or another adult.

In our work with school-age children with severe disabilities and their nonhandicapped peers, we have observed that teachers are reluctant to "back away" from continued direction of such interactions (Meyer et al., 1987). They tend to continue indefinitely to instruct nonhandicapped children on how to interact with severely handicapped peers, provide extra assistance to the handicapped children so they can participate more fully, and intensively supervise handicapped students who have severe behavior problems. At the very least, since these children generally do not attend school with nonhandicapped peers in the same classroom, teachers must make some accommodations to their shedules to permit social interactions and shared activities to occur. The teacher also serves as the initial model, provides social reinforcement to the children, and determines the kinds of activities and materials used in the interactions. Each of these variables has been shown to have an impact upon the outcomes associated with heterogeneous groupings (Johnson, Johnson, & Maruyama, 1983).

The University of Minnesota Consortium Institute has conducted a planned series of studies to investigate the impact of variations in teacher instruction and supervision on the quality of interactions between severely handicapped children and their nonhandicapped peers in school settings. Because handicapped children exhibit widely varying behavioral repertoires, some initial teacher direction has been assumed to be essential during the early phases of social integration. Meyer et al. (1987) established a base line of the level of teacher direction that was being provided after autistic children from two public school classrooms and nonhandicapped peers had interacted for more than four months. This level of teacher intrusion was contrasted with a nonintrusive condition in which teacher interventions were kept to a minimum. There were few differences on either positive or negative behaviors of the autistic children as a function of the level of teacher intrusion, and those that did occur favored, for the most part, less teacher involvement. In a partial replication study, the nature of the teacher direction was investigated by comparing teachers' nonspecific verbal attention with verbal instructions that emphasized cooperation. Forty child dyads, consisting of an elementary student with severe to profound retardation and a similar-age regular education peer from several schools, participated in this study (Cole, Meyer, Vandercook, & McQuarter, 1986).

Early positive gains in socially interactive behaviors for the cooperation condition were reversed, with the nonspecific verbal attention group displaying increasingly more positive social interaction as the intervention continued. Cole (1986), interpreting these results to suggest that continued specific verbal intervention is not needed and even interferes with the maintenance of initial positive effects, conducted a subsequent study involving 28 heterogeneous dyads similar to the children in the Cole et al. (1986) report. In this study, the dyad experienced a two-week intervention of either verbal instruction with modeling of cooperative play behavior or noninstructional teacher attention, both followed by four weeks of reduced teacher attention. The children's social interaction was generally quite positive in both conditions, but there were a number of significant differences in play behaviors that favored teacher modeling.

Although we lack comparison data with an "intrusion-free" condition, these studies taken together do provide some support for an initial and brief phase of teacher intervention stressing cooperative play, followed by reduced teacher involvement to facilitate peer interactions between school-age nonhandicapped children and children with severe disabilities. This apparent need for reduced teacher involvement at the elementary age level contrasts with Odom et al. (1985), whose work with preschool children suggests a continuing need for some teacher supervision. This difference may well be attributable to children's behavioral characteristics at different ages rather than specific to interactions between handicapped and nonhandicapped children.

Social Integration and Friendships

The dynamics of social acceptance and peer relationships are variable and complex. Developmental research has documented dramatic changes across the years from childhood to adulthood for both friendship and peer interactions (Epstein, 1983a). Changes in definitions and expectations of friendship vary further as a function of different environmental contexts. The characteristics of school environments and activities can drastically alter children's interactional patterns and, therefore, their friendships (Hansell & Karweit, 1983; Karweit, 1983; Slavin & Hansell, 1983). There are differences in types of friends (friend, "best friend," acquaintance, and so forth) and in the extent to which the relationship is symmetrical or complementary. That is, the status of two children in a friendship may be equal on some criteria and unequal on others, but as long as a mutually satisfactory balance is maintained, the relationship continues (Epstein, 1983a).

Epstein (1983b) summarizes the theoretical perspectives and data on the involvement of individuals in multiple group memberships. Each individual participates in personally meaningful social relationships; some may be quite different from others, and many may be confined to particular environments or activities. Thus, children may have friends in school whom they choose for certain types of activities, and other friends in their neighborhood, at summer camp, and so forth (Epstein, 1983b). Voeltz and Brennan (1984) found that the relationships between nonhandicapped children and those with severe disabilities were described by the nonhandicapped children as being similar to those they enjoyed with their "best" friends, with some differences with the dys-symmetry of the relationship. Voeltz (1982) and Strain (1984) suggested that relationships appeared to take on some of the characteristics of cross-age relationships, which are said to be more common in neighborhood friendships and less likely in an age-graded school system (Rubin, 1980). Such relationships could be viewed as reinforcing to the nonhandicapped child; the social interaction might create less social pressure and lower performance demands than the child's relationships with adults and non-handicapped peers, and it might also enhance the child's self-esteem in playing a "big brother" or "big sister" role. Strain (1984) notes the perception that the handicapped child needs assistance may function to "maintain handicapped children's friend status in the absence of social responsiveness" (p. 26).

In eight years of conducting research on peer interactions in dozens of schools in Hawaii and Minnesota, we have found that large percentages of nonhandicapped children (as many as 40% of the total elementary school enrollment and 15% of secondary school enrollment) actively and voluntarily participate in these interactions. Apparently, they find such relationships personally satisfying, and any differences do not appear to detract from their desirability. Kishi (1985) has completed a series of follow-up interviews with a pilot sample of eight nonhandicapped teenagers who had participated in a special friends program four to six years earlier, and she reports that all students recalled their experiences positively. In describing their relationships with their friends in special education, who were moderately to profoundly retarded with additional motor and sensory impairments, their comments reflect relatively normalized social relationships:

> ... after I got to know them it was easier ... [After] about three weeks, at the most, by then we were getting to be good friends. (p. 5)

> It's just like meeting a new friend. You're not sure what they are like, or what they are going to think, or do. But once you get used to them, it's fun. It's fun being around them. It's fun doing things with them. (p. 5)

> In the beginning when I worked with Sharon, I saw her as someone I could help and someone who needed that help. But after a while, I saw her as just another person. (p. 5)

> When you first start you maybe think they are not much like you or something, but after a while they become just like you. (p. 6)

> I talked with her and played with her ... [Sally] didn't really seem like she was deaf ... she just seemed able to [hear me]. (p. 8)

One disconcerting finding was that none of these relationships had endured, and the children had lost contact with one another. Kishi notes a possible explanation: The special education students with severe handicaps were separated from their peers when they moved on to high school, due to an administrative decision to centralize special education services at one particular secondary school. Even though this school was also integrated, it was different from the neighborhood school that their nonhandicapped friends from elementary school attended. Epstein (1983b) points out that such administrative decisions by school systems have a negative impact upon children's friendships. Children do not have the same resources and abilities as adults to maintain social relationships in spite of such a difficulty as, for example, geographical distance. Similarly, Ladd, Munson, and Miller (1984) reported that the friendships among hearing-impaired and deaf students in a mainstream school program involved little or no out-of-school contact. This finding could indicate that these relationships were limited by choice, but Ladd and his colleagues suggest an alternative explanation: The deaf students attended residential schools for most of their program, away from their families, and may have had little opportunity to reciprocate an invitation such as inviting a friend home, which would be characteristic of such friendships.

FUTURE DIRECTIONS

As Gaylord-Ross and Peck (1985) noted in their review of integration efforts on behalf of students with severe disabilities, the existing data base for this change in public policy is still relatively limited. Even though the decision to integrate is value-based, validated strategies to do so effectively must be grounded in research with a broad range of subjects (age groups and handicapping conditions) and settings (school as well as nonschool contexts). An additional challenge in this area should be evident from the diversity of the contributions summarized in this chapter: Disciplines reflecting varying perspectives are involved in parallel research and program development efforts, and there is scant evidence that these sources of information are being shared across disciplinary and theoretical lines. These parallel and independent research efforts on the social integration of children with mental and physical disabilities have generated similar outcomes, which in itself provides additional support for significant social reform. But the field of disabilities is small enough to allow for reasonable interchange, and it is sobering to reflect on the time lag between Dunn's (1968) fundamental critique and the now burgeoning literature on returning handicapped children to the mainstream. This time period corresponds to a generation of children who, by and large, completed their school careers in segregated settings while the professional community debated issues and continued to study the children in what are now acknowledged to be less than ideal learning and social environments. Nor, as noted earlier in this chapter, is the change in social policy accompanied by universal implementation. In may parts of the country, persons with severe disabilities in particular may expect to be socially isolated from their peers and community throughout their life span.

Thus, we offer three major recommendations for future research and program development efforts to socially integrate persons with disabilities. First, the marked variability across the country with respect to the extent to which handicapped children attend school in integrated versus segregated settings begs further investigation. Biklen (1986) suggests that clinical judgment is a "myth," that is, the operationalization of special services and the decisions regarding placement of individual children are profoundly affected by such noneducational issues as funding patterns. Second, future applied research conducted with handicapped as well as nonhandicapped children, and with their teachers, parents, and community, must reflect a primary concern for ecological and educational validity, in *addition* to experimental validity (Voeltz & Evans, 1983). Policy makers and practitioners have become increasingly cynical about the relevance of research to the real-world contingencies with which they deal daily. Particularly in the area of social integration, which by its very nature demands attention to contextual variables, those who do research and develop curricula must do so in the context of actual public school and community settings if they wish their efforts to have an impact.

Finally, more longitudinal research is needed on the effects of social integration on both handicapped and nonhandicapped children. It is particularly critical to conceptualize social integration goals for children that reflect a concern for normalizing their social status and leading to social acceptance, mutual respect, and friendships. Many children with disabilities are now deprived of meaningful opportunities to interact with persons other than a small number of similarly handicapped peers (not of their own choosing), their families, and paid professionals and other staff members. As important as those interactions may be, they should not preclude participation in other social

relationships and, specifically, friendships. Friendship is a valued commodity for nearly all of us: Where the design of educational services significantly restricts opportunities to develop and experience these rich personal relationships, a coexistence between children's social and skill development needs should be recognized as a compelling, overdue goal.

REFERENCES

Asher, S. R., & Taylor, A. R. (1981). The social outcomes of mainstreaming: Sociometric assessment and beyond. *Exceptional Education Quarterly, 1*, 13–30.

Baer, D. M. (1981). A hung jury and a Scottish verdict. *Analysis and Intervention in Developmental Disabilities, 1*, 91–97.

Bates, P., Morrow, S. A., Pancsofar, E., & Sedlak, R. (1984). The effect of functional vs. nonfunctional activities on attitudes/expectations of nonhandicapped college students: What they see is what we get. *Journal of the Association for Persons with Severe Handicaps, 9*, 73–78.

Becker, N. V. (1984). Being deaf and surprised. In A. J. Brightman (Ed.), *Ordinary moments: The disabled experience* (pp. 51–60). Baltimore: University Park Press.

Bellamy, G. T., Rhodes, L. E., Wilcox, B., Albin, J. M., Mank, D. M., Boles, S. M., Horner, R. H., Collins, M., & Turner, J. (1984). Quality and equality in employment services for adults with severe disabilities. *Journal of the Association for Persons with Severe Disabilities, 9*, 270–277.

Beveridge, M., & Brinker, R. P. (1980). An ecological-developmental approach to communication in retarded children. In M. Jones (Ed.), *Language disorders in children* (pp. 45–67). Lancaster, England: MTP Press.

Biklen, D. (1985). *Achieving the complete school: Strategies for effective mainstreaming.* New York: Teachers College Press.

Biklen, D. (1987). The myth of clinical judgment. *Journal of Social Issues.*

Blatt, B., & Kaplan, F. (1966). *Christmas in purgatory: A photographic essay on mental retardation.* Boston: Allyn and Bacon.

Braddock, D., & Heller, T. (1985). The closure of mental retardation institutions: I. Trends in the U.S. *Mental Retardation, 23*, 168–176.

Brady. M. P., Shores, R. E., Gunter, P., McEvoy, M. A., Fox, J. J., & White, C. (1984). Generalization of an adolescent's social interaction behavior via multiple peers in a classroom setting. *Journal of the Association for Persons with Severe Handicaps, 9,* 278–286.

Breen, C., Haring, T., Pitts-Conway, V., & Gaylord-Ross, R. (1985). The training and generalization of social interaction during breaktime at two job sites in the natural environment. *Journal of the Association for Persons with Severe Handicaps, 10,* 41–50.

Brinker, R. P. (1985). Interactions between severely mentally retarded students and other students in integrated and segregated public school settings. *American Journal of Mental Deficiency, 89,* 587–594.

Brown v. Board of Education (1954), 347 U.S. 483 (1954).

Brown, L. (1986). Foreword: Then and now. In R. H. Horner, L. H. Meyer, & H. D. Fredericks (Eds.), *Education of learners with severe handicaps: Exemplary service strategies* (pp. xi–xiii). Baltimore: Paul H. Brookes.

Brown, L., Branston, M., Hamre-Nietupski, S., Pumpian, I., Certo, N., & Gruenewald, L. (1979). A strategy for developing chronological age-appropriate and functional curricular content for severely handicapped adolescents and young adults. *Journal of Special Education, 13,* 81–90.

Brown, L., Nietupski, J., & Hamre-Nietupski, S. (1976). The criterion of ultimate functioning and public school services for the severely handicapped student. In M. A. Thomas (Ed.), *Hey, don't forget about me: Education's investment in the severely, profoundly and multiply handicapped* (pp. 2–15). Reston, VA: Council for Exceptional Children.

Brown, L., Shiraga, B., York, J., Kessler, K., Strohm, B., Rogan, P., Sweet, M., Zanella, K., VanDeventer, P., & Loomis R. (1984). Integrated work opportunities for adults with severe handicaps: The extended training option. *Journal of the Association for Persons with Severe Handicaps, 9,* 262–269.

Bruininks, R. H., Rynders, J. E., & Gross, T. C. (1974). Social acceptance of mildly retarded pupils in resource rooms and regular classes. *American Journal of Mental Deficiency, 78,* 377–383.

Bryan, T. (1974). Peer popularity of learning disabled children. *Journal of Learning Disabilities, 7,* 621–625.

Budoff, M., & Gottlieb, J. (1976). Special class students mainstreamed: A study of aptitude (learning potential) X treatment interaction. *American Journal of Mental Deficiency, 81,* 1–11.

Buell, J., Stoddard, P., Harris, F. R., & Baer, D. M. (1968). Collateral social development accompanying reinforcement of outdoor play in a preschool child. *Journal of Applied Behavior Analysis, 1,* 167–173.

Burton, T. A., & Hirshoren, A. (1979). Some further thoughts and clarification on the education of severely and profoundly retarded children. *Exceptional Children, 45,* 618–625.

Carroll, A. (1967). The effects of segregated and partially integrated school programs on self concept and academic achievement of educable mental retardates. *Exceptional Children, 34,* 93–99.

Cegelka, W., & Tyler, J. (1970). The efficacy of special class placement for the mentally retarded in proper perspective. *Training School Bulletin, 65,* 33–65.

Certo, N., Haring, N., & York, R. (Eds.). (1984). *Public school integration of severely handicapped students: Rational issues and progressive alternatives.* Baltimore: Paul H. Brookes.

Chaves, I. M. (1977). Historical overview of special education in the United States. In P. Bates, F. L. West, & R. B. Schmerl (Eds.), *Mainstreaming: Problems, potentials, and perspectives* (pp. 25–41). Minneapolis: National Support Systems Project.

Cole, D. A. (1986). Facilitating play in children's peer relationships: Are we having fun yet? *American Educational Research Journal, 23,* 201–215.

Cole, D. A., Meyer, L. H., Vandercook, T., & McQuarter, R. J. (1986). Interactions between peers with and without severe handicaps: Dynamics of teacher intervention. *American Journal of Mental Deficiency, 91,* 160–169.

Cole, D. A., Vandercook, T., & Rynders, J. (1987). Peer interaction programs for children with and without severe disabilities. *American Educational Research Journal,* in press.

Cone, J. D., & Hoier, T. S. (1985). Assessing children: The radical behavioral perspective. In R. Prinz (Ed.), *Advances in behavioral assessment of children and families* (Vol. 2). New York: JAI Press.

Devonney, C., Guralnick, M. J., & Rubin, H. (1974). Integrating handicapped and nonhandicapped preschool children: Effects on social play. *Childhood Education, 50,* 360–364.

Dodge, K. A., McClaskey, C. L., & Feldman, E. (1985). Situational approach to the assessment of social competence in children. *Journal of Consulting and Clinical Psychology, 53,* 344–353.

Dodge, K. A., & Murphy, R. R. (1984). The assessment of social competence in adolescents. In P. Karoly & J. J. Steffan (Eds.), *Adolescent behavior disorders: Current perspectives* (pp. 61–96). Lexington, MA: D. C. Heath.

Donaldson, J. (1980). Changing attitudes toward handicapped person: A review and analysis of research. *Exceptional Children, 46,* 504–514.

Donnellan, A. M. (1984). The criterion of the least dangerous assumption. *Behavioral Disorders, 9,* 141–150.

Dunn, L. M. (1968). Special education for the mildly retarded — Is much of it justifiable? *Exceptional Children, 3,* 371–379.

Epstein, J. L. (1983a). Friends among students in schools: Environmental and developmental factors. In J. L. Epstein & N. Karweit (Eds.), *Friends in school: Patterns of selection and influence in secondary schools* (pp. 3–25). New York: Academic Press.

Epstein, J. L. (1983b). School environment and student friendships: Issues, implications, and interventions. In J. L. Epstein & N. Karweit (Eds.), *Friends in school: Patterns of selection and influence in secondary schools* (pp. 235–253). New York: Academic Press.

Fenrick, N., & McDonnell, J. (1980). Junior high school students as teachers of the severely retarded: Training and generalization. *Education and Training of the Mentally Retarded, 15,* 187–194.

Fox, J. J., Gunter, P., Brady, M. P., Bambara, L., Spiegel-McGill, P., & Shores, R. E. (1984). Using multiple peer exemplars to develop generalized responding of an autistic girl. In R. B. Rutherford & C. M. Nelson (Eds.), *Monograph on behavioral disorders: Severe behavior disorders of children and youth* (Vol. 7, pp. 17–26). Reston, VA: Council for Exceptional Children.

Fredericks, H. D., Baldwin, V., Grove, D., Moore, W., Riggs, C., & Lyons, B. (1978). Integrating the moderately and severely handicapped preschool child into a normal day care setting. In M. Guralnick (Ed.), *Early intervention and integration of handicapped and nonhandicapped children,* (pp. 191–206). Baltimore: University Park Press.

Gable, R. A., Hendrickson, J. M., & Strain, P. S. (1978). Assessment, modification, and generalization of social interaction among severely retarded, multihandicapped children. *Education and Training of the Mentally Retarded, 13,* 279–286.

Gaylord-Ross, R. J., Haring, T. G., Breen, C., & Pitts-Conway, V. (1984). The training and generalization of social interaction skills with autistic youth. *Journal of Applied Behavior Analysis, 17,* 229–247.

Gaylord-Ross, R. J., & Peck, C. A. (1985). Integration efforts for students with severe mental handicaps. In D. Bricker & J. Filler (Eds.), *Severe mental retardation: From theory to prac-* *tice* (pp. 184–207). Reston, VA: Council for Exceptional Children.

Gaylord-Ross, R. J., Stremel-Campbell, K., & Storey, K. (1986). Social skills training in natural contexts. In R. H. Horner, L. H. Meyer, & H. D. Fredericks (Eds.), *Education of learners with severe handicaps: Exemplary service strategies* (pp. 161–187). Baltimore: Paul H. Brookes.

Gilhool, T., & Stutman, E. (1979). Integration of severely handicapped students: Toward criteria for implementing and enforcing the integration imperative of PL 94-142 and Section 504. In *LRE: Developing criteria for the evaluation of the least restrictive environment provision* (p. 191–227). Philadelphia: Research for Better Schools.

Goldstein, H., Moss, J. W., & Jordan, L. J. (1965). *The efficacy of special class training and the development of mentally retarded children.* (U.S. Office of Education Cooperative Research Project No. 619). Urbana, IL: University of Illinois.

Goodlad, J. I. (1983). A study of schooling: Some findings and hypotheses. *Phi Delta Kappan, 64,* 462–470.

Gottlieb, J. (1978). Observing social adaptation in schools. In G. P. Sackett (Ed.), *Observing behavior: Vol. I. Theory and applications in mental retardation* (pp. 285–309). Baltimore: University Park Press.

Gottlieb, J. (1981). Mainstreaming: Fulfilling the promise? *American Journal of Mental Deficiency, 86,* 115–126.

Gresham, F. M. (1981). Social skills training with handicapped children: A review. *Review of Educational Research, 51,* 139–176.

Gresham, F. M. (1982). Misguided mainstreaming: The case for social skills training with handicapped children. *Exceptional Children, 48,* 422–433.

Gresham, F. M. (1985, May). *Social validity of the mainstreaming concept: Insignificant goals, unacceptable treatments, and unimportant effects.* Paper presented at the annual conference of the Association for Behavior Analysis, Columbus, OH.

Gross, B., & Gross, R. (Eds.). (1985). *The great school debate: Which way for American education?* New York: Simon & Schuster.

Guess, D., & Noonan, M. J. (1982). Curricula and instructional procedures for severely handicapped students. *Focus on Exceptional Children, 14,* 1–12.

Guess, D., & Siegel-Causey E. (1985). Behavioral control and education of severely handicapped students: Who's doing what to whom? And why? In D. Bricker & J. Filler (Eds.), *Severe mental retardation: From theory to practice* (pp. 230–244). Reston, VA: Council for Exceptional Children.

Guralnick, M. J. (Ed.). (1978). *Early intervention and the integration of handicapped and nonhandicapped children.* Baltimore: University Park Press.

Hansell, S., & Karweit, N. (1983). Curricular placement, friendship networks, and status attainment. In J. L. Epstein & N. Karweit (Eds.), *Friends in school: Patterns of selection and influence in secondary schools* (pp. 141–161). New York: Academic Press.

Hartup, W. W. (1984). The peer context in middle childhood. In W. A. Collins (Ed.), *Development during middle childhood* (pp. 240–282). Washington, DC: National Academy Press.

Hendrickson, J. M., Strain, P. S., Tremblay, A., & Shores, R. E. (1982). Interactions of behaviorally handicapped children: Functional effects of peer social initiations. *Behavior Modification, 6,* 323–353.

Hewett, F. M., & Forness, S. R. (1974). *Education of exceptional learners.* Boston: Allyn and Bacon.

Hill, B. K., Lakin, K. C., & Bruininks, R. H. (1984). Trends in residential services for people who are mentally retarded: 1977–1982. *Journal of the Association for Persons with Severe Handicaps, 9,* 243–250.

Horner, R. H., Bellamy, G. T., & Colvin, G. T. (1984). Responding in the presence of nontrained stimuli: Implications of generalization error patterns. *Journal of the Association for Persons with Severe Handicaps, 9,* 287–295.

Horner, R. H., Meyer, L. H., & Fredericks, H. D. (Eds.). (1986). *Education of learners with severe handicaps: Exemplary service strategies.* Baltimore: Paul H. Brookes.

Iano, R. P., Ayers, D., Heller, H. B., McGettigan, J. F., & Walker, V. S. (1974). Sociometric status of retarded children in an integrative program. *Exceptional Children, 40,* 267–271.

Jellison, J. A., Brookes, B. H., & Huck, A. M. (1984). Structuring small groups and music reinforcement to facilitate positive interactions and acceptance of severely handicapped students in the regular music classroom. *Journal of Research in Music Education, 32,* 243–264.

Johnson, G. O. (1950). A study of the social position of mentally handicapped children in the regular schools. *American Journal of Mental Deficiency, 55,* 60–89.

Johnson, G. O. (1962). Special education for the mentally handicapped: A paradox. *Exceptional Children, 29,* 62–69.

Johnson, D. W., & Johnson, R. T. (1980). Integrating handicapped students into the mainstream. *Exceptional Children, 47,* 90–98.

Johnson, D. W., Johnson, R. T., & Maruyama, G. (1983). Interdependence and interpersonal attraction among heterogeneous and homogeneous individuals: A theoretical formulation and a meta-analysis of the research. *Review of Educational Research, 53,* 5–54.

Johnson, R. E., & Meyer, L. H. (1985). Program design and research to normalize peer interactions. In M. P. Brady & P. L. Gunter (Eds.), *Integrating moderately and severely handicapped learners: Strategies that work* (pp. 79–101). Springfield, IL: Charles C. Thomas.

Johnson, R. T., Johnson, D. W., DeWeerdt, N., Lyons, V., & Zaidman, B. (1983). Integrating severely adaptively handicapped seventh-grade students into constructive relationships with nonhandicapped peers in science class. *American Journal of Mental Deficiency, 87,* 611–619.

Johnson, R. T., Rynders, J., Johnson, D. W., Schmidt, B., & Haider, S. (1979). Interaction between handicapped and nonhandicapped teenagers as a function of situational goal structuring: Implications for mainstreaming. *American Educational Research Journal, 16,* 161–167.

Kanner, L. (1964). *History and care of the mentally retarded.* Springfield, IL: Charles C. Thomas.

Karweit, N. (1983). Extracurricular activities and friendship selection. In J. L. Epstein & N. Karweit (Eds.), *Friends in school: Patterns of selection and influence in secondary schools* (pp. 131–139). New York: Academic Press.

Kauffman, J. M., & Krouse, J. (1981). The cult of educability: Searching for the substance of things hoped for; the evidence of things not seen. *Analysis and Intervention in Developmental Disabilities, 1,* 53–60.

Kishi, G. S. (1985, December). *Long-term effects of a social interaction program between nonhandicapped and severely handicapped children.* Paper presented at the 12th annual conference of the Association for Persons with Severe Handicaps, Boston.

Knoll, J., & Meyer, L. H. (1987). Integrated schooling and educational quality: Principles and effective practices. In M. Berres & P. Knoblock (Eds.), *Managerial models of mainstreaming* (p. 41–59). Rockville, MD: Aspen.

Kohl, F. L., Moses, L. G., & Stettner-Eaton, B. A. (1983). The results of teaching fifth and sixth graders to be instructional trainers with severely handicapped students. *Journal of the Association for the Severely Handicapped, 8*(4), 32–40.

Kohl, F. L., Moses, L. G., & Stettner-Eaton, B. A. (1984). A systematic training program for teaching nonhandicapped students to be instructional trainers of severely handicapped schoolmates. In N. Certo, N. Haring, & R. York (Eds.), *Public school integration of severely handicapped students: Rational issues and progressive alternatives* (pp. 185–195). Baltimore: Paul H. Brookes.

Krouse, J., Gerber, M., & Kauffman, J. (1981). Peer tutoring: Procedures, promises, and unresolved issues. *Exceptional Education Quarterly, 1*, 107–115.

Ladd, G. W., Munson, H. L., & Miller, J. K. (1984). Social integration of deaf adolescents in secondary-level mainstream programs. *Exceptional Children, 50*, 420–428.

Lakin, K. C., & Bruininks, R. (1985a). Contemporary services for handicapped children and youth. In R. Bruininks & K. C. Lakin (Eds.), *Living and learning in the least restrictive environment* (pp. 3–22). Baltimore: Paul H. Brookes.

Lakin, K. C., & Bruininks, R. H. (Edes.). (1985b). *Strategies for achieving community integration of developmentally disabled citizens.* Baltimore: Paul H. Brookes.

Lancioni, G. (1982). Normal children as tutors to teach social responses to withdrawn mentally retarded schoolmates. *Journal of Applied Behavior Analysis, 15*, 17–40.

Mackie, R. (1969). *Special education in the United States: Statistics 1948–1966.* New York: Teachers College Press.

MacMillan, D. L., Jones, R. L., & Aloia, G. F. (1974). The mentally retarded label: A theoretical analysis and review of research. *American Journal of Mental Deficiency, 79*, 241–261.

Madden, N. A., & Slavin, R. E. (1983). Mainstreaming students with mild handicaps: Academic and social outcomes. *Review of Eductional Research, 53*, 519–569.

McFall, R. M. (1982). A review and reformulation of the concept of social skills. *Behavioral Assessment, 4*, 1–33.

McFall, R. M., & Dodge, K. A. (1982). Self-management and interpersonal skills learning. In P. Karoly & F. H. Kanfer (Eds.), *Self-management and behavior change: From theory to practice* (pp. 353–392). New York: Pergamon.

Meyer, L. H. (1985, December). *Why integration, or why nonhandicapped kids should be friends and not tutors.* Paper presented at the 12th annual conference of the Association for Persons with Severe Handicaps, Boston.

Meyer, L. H., & Evans, I. M. (1986). Modification of excess behavior: An adaptive and functional approach for educational and community contexts. In R. H. Horner, L. H. Meyers, & H. D. Fredericks (Eds.), *Education of learners with severe handicaps: Exemplary service strategies* (pp. 315–350). Baltimore: Paul H. Brookes.

Meyer. L. H., Fox, A., Schermer, A., Ketelsen, D., Montan, N., Maley, K., & Cole, D. (1987). The effects of teacher intrusion on social play interactions between children with autism and their nonhandicapped peers. *Journal of Autism and Developmental Disorders, 17*, 315–332.

Meyer, L. H., McQuarter, R. J., & Kishi, G. S. (1985). Assessing and teaching social interaction skills. In S. Stainback & W. Stainback (Eds.), *Integration of students with severe handicaps into regular schools* (pp. 66–86). Reston, VA: Council for Exceptional Children.

Meyer, L. H., Reichle, J., McQuarter, R., Cole, D., Vandercook, T., Evans, I., Neel, R., & Kishi, G. (1985). *Assessment of social competence (ASC): A scale of social competence functions.* Minneapolis: University of Minnesota Consortium Institute.

Meyerowitz, J. H. (1962). Self-derogations in young retardates and special class placement. *Child Development, 33*, 443–451.

National Commission on Excellence in Education (1983). *A nation at risk: The imperative for educational reform.* Washington, DC: Department of Education.

Nirje, B. (1969). The normalization principle and its human management implications. In R. B. Kugel & W. Wolfensberger (Eds.), *Changing patterns in residential services for the mentally retarded.* Washington, DC: President's Committee on Mental Retardation.

Odom, S. L., Hoyson, M., Jamieson, B., & Strain, P. S. (1985). Increasing handicapped preschoolers' peer social interactions: Cross-setting and component analysis. *Journal of Applied Behavior Analysis, 18*, 3–16.

Odom, S. L., & Strain, P. S. (1984). Peer-mediated approaches to promoting children's social interaction: A review. *American Journal of Orthopsychiatry, 54*, 544–557.

Okun, K. A. (1981). Mainstreaming and the myth of equality. In P. Bates (Ed.), *Mainstreaming: Our current knowledge base.* Minneapolis: University of Minnesota National Support Systems Project.

Pennsylvania Association for Retarded Children (PARC) v. Commonwealth of Pennsylvania, 343 F. Supp. 278 (E.D. Pa. 1972).

Pennsylvania Association for Retarded Citizens v. Commonwealth of Pennsylvania. Consent Decree on Enforcement Petition in Fialkowski et al. v. School District of Philadelphia et al., entered June, 1982.

Peterson, N. L. & Haralick, J. G. (1977). Integration of handicapped and nonhandicapped preschoolers: An analysis of play behavior and social interaction. *Education and Training of the Mentally Retarded, 12,* 235–245.

Polloway, E. A. (1984). The integration of mildly retarded students in the schools: A historical review. *Remedial and Special Education, 5*(4), 18–28.

Porter, R. H., Ramsey, B., Tremblay, A., Iaccobo, M., & Crawley, I. (1978). Social interactions in heterogeneous groups of retarded and normally developing children: An observational study. In G. Sackett (Ed.), *Observing behavior: Theory and applications in mental retardation* (Vol. 1, pp. 311–330). Baltimore: University Park Press.

Putnam, J. W., & Rynders, J. E. (1985). *Effects of teacher instruction on promoting cooperative interactions between moderately-severely mentally handicapped and nonhandicapped children.* Minneapolis: University of Minnesota Consortium Institute.

Renzaglia, A. M., & Bates, P. (1983). Socially appropriate behavior. In M. E. Snell (Ed.), *Systematic instruction of the moderately and severely handicapped* (2nd ed., pp. 314–356). Columbus, OH: Charles E. Merrill.

Reynolds, M. (Ed.). (1978). *Futures of education for exceptional students: Emerging structures.* Reston, VA: Council for Exceptional Children.

Reynolds, M. C., & Birch, J. (1977). *Teaching exceptional children in all of America's schools.* Reston, VA: Council for Exceptional Children.

Reynolds, M. C., & Birch, J. W. (1982). *Teaching exceptional children in all of America's schools* (rev. ed.). Reston, VA: Council for Exceptional Children.

Roncker v. Walters, 700 F.2d 1058 (6th Cir. 1983).

Rubin, Z. (1980). *Children's friendships.* Cambridge, MA: Harvard University Press.

Rynders, J. E., Johnson, R. T., Johnson, D. W., & Schmidt, B. (1980). Producing positive interaction among Down's syndrome and nonhandicapped students through cooperative goal structuring. *American Journal of Mental Deficiency, 85,* 268–273.

St. Louis Developmental Disabilities Treatment Center Parents Association v. Arthur M. Mallory. DC MD 591 F. Supp. 1416, aff'd 767 F.2d 518 (8th. Cir. 1985).

Salend, S. J. (1984). Factors contributing to the development of successful mainstreaming programs. *Exceptional Children, 50,* 409–416.

Sarason, S. B., & Doris, J. (1979). *Educational handicap, public policy, and social history: A broadened perspective on mental retardation.* New York: Free Press.

Scheerenberger, R. C. (1983). *A history of mental retardation.* Baltimore: Paul H. Brookes.

Semmel, M. I., Gottlieb, J., & Robinson, N. M. (1979). Mainstreaming: Perspectives on educating handicapped children in public schools. In D.C. Berliner (Ed.), *Review of research in education* (pp. 223–279). Washington, DC: American Educational Research Association.

Silverstein, R. (1985). The legal necessity for residential schools serving deaf, blind, and multiply impaired children. *Journal of Visual Impairment and Blindness, 79*(4), 145–149.

Slavin, R. E., & Hansell, S. (1983). Cooperative learning and intergroup relationships: Contact theory in the classroom. In J. L. Epstein & N. Karweit (Eds.), *Friends in school: Patterns of selection and influence in secondary schools* (pp. 93–114). New York: Academic Press.

Stainback, S., & Stainback, W. (1985). *Integration of students with severe handicaps into regular schools.* Reston, VA: Council for Exceptional Children.

Stainback, W., & Stainback, S. (1985). A rationale for the merger of special and regular education. *Exceptional Children, 51,* 102–111.

Stanton, J. E., & Cassidy, V. M. (1964). Effectiveness of special classes for educable mentally retarded. *Mental Retardation, 2,* 8–13.

Stokes, T. F., & Baer, D. M. (1977). An implicit technology of generalization. *Journal of Applied Behavior Analysis, 19,* 349–367.

Stokes, T. F., Baer, D. M., & Jackson, R. (1974). Programming the generalization of a greeting response in four retarded children. *Journal of Applied Behavior Analysis, 7,* 599–610.

Stokes, T. F., & Osnes, P. G. (1985). Programming the generalization of children's social behavior. In P. S. Strain, M. J. Guralnick, & H. Walker (Eds.), *Children's social behavior: Development, assessment, and modification.* New York: Academic.

Strain, P. S. (1977). Effects of peer social initiations on withdrawn preschool children. *Journal of Abnormal Child Psychology, 5,* 445–455.

Strain, P. S. (1981). Peer-mediated treatment of exceptional children's social withdrawal. *Exceptional Education Quarterly — Peer Relations of Exceptional Children and Youth, 4,* 93–105.

Strain, P. S. (1983a). Identification of social skills curriculum targets for severely handicapped children in mainstreamed preschools.

Applied Research in Mental Retardation, 4, 369–382.

Strain, P. S. (1983b). Generalization of autistic children's social behavior change: Effects of developmentally integrated and segregated settings. *Analysis and Intervention in developmental Disabilities, 3,* 23–34.

Strain, P. S. (1984). Social behavior patterns of nonhandicapped and developmentally disabled friend pairs in mainstream preschools. *Analysis and Intervention in Developmental Disabilities, 4,* 15–28.

Strain, P. S., & Kerr, M. M. (1981). *Mainstreaming of children in schools.* New York: Academic Press.

Strain, P. S., Kerr, M. M., & Ragland, E. (1981). The use of peer social initiations in the treatment of social withdrawal. In P. Strain (Ed.), *The utilization of classroom peers as behavior change agents* (pp. 101–128). New York: Plenum.

Strain, P. S., Odom, S. L., & McConnell, S. (1984). Promoting social reciprocity of exceptional children: Identification, target behavior selection, and intervention. *Remedial and Special Education, 5,* 21–28.

Strain, P. S., & Shores, R. E. (1983). A reply to "Misguided Mainstreaming". *Exceptional Children, 50,* 271–272.

Strain, P. S., Shores, R. E., & Timm, M. (1977). Effects of peer social initiations on the behavior of withdrawn preschool children. *Journal of Applied Behavior Analysis, 10,* 289–298.

Stremel-Campbell, K., Clark-Guida, J., & Johnson-Dorn, N. (1984). *Pre-language and language communication curriculum for children/youth with severe handicaps.* Monmouth, OR: Teaching Research.

Turnbull, A. P., & Turnbull, R. (1985). Developing independence. *Journal of Adolescent Health Care, 6,* 108–119.

U.S. Department of Education. (1985). *Seventh annual report to Congress on the implementation of Public law 94-142: The Education for All Handicapped Children Act.* Washington, DC : U.S. Government Printing Office.

Voeltz, L. M. (1980). Children's attitudes toward handicapped peers. *American Journal of Mental Deficiency, 84,* 455–464.

Voeltz, L. M. (1982). Effects of structured interactions with severely handicapped peers on children's attitudes. *American Journal of Mental Deficiency, 86,* 380–390.

Voeltz, L. M. (1984). Program and curriculum innovations to prepare children for integration. In N. Certo, N. Haring, & R. York (Eds.), *Public school integration of severely handicapped students: Rational issues and progressive alternatives* (pp. 155–183). Baltimore: Paul H. Brookes.

Voeltz, L. M., & Brennan, J. (1984). Analysis of interactions between nonhandicapped and severely handicapped peers using multiple measures. In J. M. Berg (Ed.), *Perspectives and progress in mental retardation: Vol. I. Social, psychological, and educational aspects* (pp. 61–72). Baltimore: University Park Press.

Voeltz, L. M., & Evans, I. M. (1983). Educational validity: Procedures to evaluate outcomes in programs for severely handicapped learners. *Journal of the Association for the Severely Handicapped, 8,* 3–15.

Voeltz, L. M., Hemphill, N. J., Brown, S., Kishi, G., Klein, R., Freuhling, R., Collie, J., Levey, G., & Kube, C. (1983). *The special friends program: A trainer's manual for integrated school settings* (rev. ed.). Honolulu: University of Hawaii.

Wang, M. C., & Birch, J. W. (1984a). Comparison of a full-time mainstreaming program and a resource room approach. *Exceptional Children, 51,* 33–40.

Wang, M. C., & Birch, J. W. (1984b). Effective special education in regular classes. *Exceptional Children, 50,* 391–398.

Warren, F., & Juhrs, P. (1984). Community philosophy: Continuum of services. *Community News, 1,* 1–2.

What they mean is segregated. (1983, August). *The Disability Rag,* pp. 3–4.

Wilcox, B., & Sailor, W. (1980). Service delivery issues: Integrated educational systems. In B. Wilcox & R. York (Eds.), *Quality education for the severely handicapped: The federal investment* (pp. 277–304). Washington, DC: U.S. department of Education.

Will, M. (1983, November). *Keynote address.* Tenth annual conference of the Association for Persons with Severe Handicaps, San Francisco.

Wolfensberger, W. (1972). *The principle of normalization in human services.* Toronto: National Institute on Mental Retardation.

Ysseldyke, J. E., & Algozzine, B. (1982). *Critical issues in special and remedial education.* Boston: Houghton Mifflin.

CHAPTER 9

Research Issues in Developmental and Physical Disabilities

Scott R. McConnell, Diane Sainato and Bonnie L. Utley

A critical appraisal of research issues in developmental and physical disabilities is truly an enormous task. First, the history of this research literally spans centuries: Down's work in mental retardation during the first half of the 19th century, as well as Itard's early research with blind children during the 18th century, are two notable examples of this rich historical foundation. In addition, research has covered a wide array of conditions, characteristics, or diseases that might be considered disabilities. The 17 chapters on specific disabilities presented in this volume attest to the necessary breadth of this research.

Research efforts in developmental and physical disabilities can be loosely categorized into four overlapping but somewhat distinct areas of inquiry: (a) research into the cause of disabling conditions, (b) assessment of the incidence or prevalence of these conditions in various populations, (c) efforts to prevent the development of a disabling condition, and (d) evaluation of treatment procedures designed to reduce the frequency or severity of existing disabilities. In addition, individuals conducting this research represent a variety of academic disciplines, including medicine, related health sciences (e.g., public health, physical therapy), psychology, vocational rehabilitation, and education. Variability in the specific focus of investigation, as well as heterogeneity in the training and discipline of the investigators, further widens the necessary scope of any review

Preparation of this chapter was supported by Grant No. G00–83–03692 and Contract No. 300–82–0368 from the U.S. Department of Education. The opinions expressed herein do not necessarily reflect the position or policy of the U.S. Department of Education. The authors thank Cathy Johnson for her assistance in the preparation of this manuscript.

of research issues in developmental and physical disabilities.

In spite of differences in objective or discipline, the various aspects of research in developmental and physical disabilities do have important commonalties. Perhaps most important, and most obvious, is the level of agreement in the overall goal for this research. In general, most researchers in developmental and physical disabilities are trying to acquire knowledge that will decrease the frequency and/or severity of disabling conditions. To the degree that this general goal is held and operated upon, all research in developmental and physical disabilities is, or should be, ultimately relevant or useful in the development of effective prevention or treatment strategies.

The relevance of research efforts to the development of more effective intervention procedures has received increased attention in the last decade. This important link between even the most "basic" of research efforts and direct intervention has been termed *educational validity* (Voeltz & Evans, 1983) and *ecological validity* (Brooks & Baumeister, 1977) and is closely linked to the concept of *treatment validity* (Nelson & Hayes, 1979). Simply put, ecological validity is the degree to which any given research project bears a direct relationship to the ongoing development and/or evaluation of prevention or intervention efforts — the degree to which a given investigation contributes progress toward the general goal outlined above.

Because of the current scope of research in developmental and physical disabilities, this chapter will present general issues that are relevant for a wide spectrum of empirical efforts. In addition, because of the socially and personally preceived importance of research efforts that contribute to the amelioration of disabling conditions, a major emphasis of this chapter will be issues that most affect the ecological validity of our work. Taken together, these assumptions lead to several common research goals: (a) identify factors contributing to disabling conditions, (b) develop and validate the best practices for identifying and treating these disabilities, (c)

assemble identified practices into effective and efficient treatment programs, and (d) disseminate information regarding these programs to others.

Much of the research fitting this description is based on direct intervention, as well as on procedures of behavior analysis, behavioral assessment, and educational/behavioral skills training. As a result, much of our discussion will be pertinent to intervention and behavioral research issues. The discussion will include, however, a review of issues relevant to both descriptive and experimental group research.

METHODOLOGICAL ISSUES

There has been steady growth in the methodological sophistication of research in developmental and physical disabilities. This increasing methodological rigor has included the use of more sophisticated experimental designs, the development of more detailed and careful assessment procedures, and better specification of treatment procedures and subject samples. Yet, as the field of disabilities research grows in sophistication and knowledge, we face a continuing need to review and, where necessary, modify our scientific methods. More subtle (and perhaps more difficult) research questions require increasingly sophisticated experimental methods.

While a variety of methodological issues are pertinent to specific types of research, or to research with discrete populations, several general themes emerge: first, issues in experimental design and experimental control; and second, innovations in research design and experimental procedures.

Experimental Design

A wide variety of experimental and quasi-experimental designs have been used throughout the history of research in developmental and physical disabilities. A multitude of basic and advanced texts on experimental design and methods can be found both within individual disciplines and for specific disabilities. Although experimental paradigms are fundamentally selected for their ability to answer a specific research question, traditions in particular areas of research also contribute to the selection of designs.

Over the past three decades, two somewhat distinct research methodologies have emerged in disabilities research. Perhaps most prevalent is the use of group (or traditional) experimental designs (e.g., Campbell & Stanley, 1966; Hays, 1963). At least three features distinguish group designs. First, experimental analysis is based on the comparison of two or more groups on some measure or set of measures. This comparison may be between treatment and control groups, or between clinical (i.e., disabled) and nonclinical samples. Further, this comparison may be made at a single point in time or be repeated (e.g., pre- and post-treatment, longitudinal). Second, comparisons are made through parametric (e.g., Hays, 1963) or nonparametric (e.g., Sigel, 1956) statistical analyses. Comparisons may be between means, distributions, ranges, or ranks, but the basic unit of analysis is the group. Third, group designs may be descriptive or experimental. Descriptive or correlational, designs may examine relationships among measures for a single group (e.g., Gottlieb, Semmel, & Veldman, 1978), or they may compare measures across known groups (Van Hasselt & Hersen, 1984). In experimental designs an independent variable is directly manipulated by the investigator. While descriptive studies offer important foundations for later investigation, only experimental designs provide necessary information for the direct inference of causation.

The second major methodology has been the single case, or behavior analytic, research design (e.g., Hersen & Barlow, 1976; Tawney & Gast, 1984). As with group designs, several key features distinguish the single case experimental method. First, although rarely conducted with a single case, these designs require very few subjects, with each serving as his or her own control. Data are collected repeatedly on a set of dependent measures and graphed in time series fashion. Second, comparisons are primarily made via visual analysis of graphic displays of subjects' data. Changes in either level or trend are identified by comparing one segment of time series data to earlier or later phases of the same series. While statistical analyses have been developed or adapted for single case designs (e.g., Hartmann et al., 1980; Kazdin, 1976), the use of these procedures is questioned on both conceptual (e.g., Baer, 1977) and mathematical (Blumberg, 1984) grounds. Third, single case designs almost invariably include experimenter manipulation of one or more independent variables. Experimental effects are identified by changes in dependent measures that coincide with the introduction or withdrawal of an independent variable.

While group and single case methods previously have been viewed as representing distinct philosophical or experimental foundations, a more accurate description of their differences may be made with reference to the experimental questions one seeks to answer (Hersen & Barlow, 1976; Walker, Hops, & Greenwood, 1984). In general, single case methods offer an intensive, exact, and well-specified analysis of variables controlling the occurrence or nonoccurence of individual behaviors or classes of behavior. Single case designs might be applied for basic analyses of behavioral control (Sidman, 1960) or of environmental effects and treatment effectiveness (Baer, Wolf, & Risley, 1968). Traditional group designs offer more "actuarial" analyses of relationships among measures or the effects of independent variables. As a result, group designs offer descriptions and normative comparisons of subject samples, as well as cost-benefit or cure-rate analyses for treatment programs. In addition, these designs are well-suited for evaluating the efficiency of treatment packages.

Past distinctions between group and single case methods are becoming blurred. For instance, single case designs are now available for evaluating the relative effectiveness of two or more interventions (Barlow & Hayes, 1979; Tawney & Gast, 1984). They are also being adapted to study covariation among "treated" and "untreated" behaviors (e.g., McConnell,

Strain, Lenkner, & Szumowski, 1985; Wahler, 1975), as well as the relative effectiveness of individual components in a comprehensive treatment program (Tawney & Gast, 1984; Walker et al., 1984). Similarly, group designs are now being employed to tentatively identify antecedents and consequences controlling individual behaviors (e.g., Patterson, 1982) and factors that may affect generalization of behaviors in new settings (Sainato & Lyon, 1983).

In spite of continued development in experimental methods in disabilties research, there is a growing need to question whether critical features of basic designs may in fact be limiting progress in the development of efficient and effective treatments. Demonstration of experimental control using single case methodology generally requires reversal of a treatment effect (i.e., withdrawal of treatment designs) or independence of this effect across behaviors, settings, or subjects (i.e., multiple baseline design). As Voeltz and Evans (1983) have persuasively argued, however, these standards for experimental control may have prevented the development of treatment procedures that produce: (a) efficient change across a class of bahaviors, (b) sustained performance or maintenance of treated behaviors, or (c) generalized effects across settings or learners. Group designs, in which experimental effects are observed in measures aggregated across subjects, may obscure important idiosyncratic outcomes. Consequently, variables limiting the development of maximally powerful treatments (i.e., those that eliminate individual differences) may not be identified.

In addition, there is a growing call to examine behavior and behavior change in a broader context. This includes: (a) an examination of the effects of experimental procedures on other behaviors in each subject's repertoire (Willems, 1974), (b) attention to ecological or environmental events associated with behaviors of interest (Landesman-Dwyer, Stein, & Sackett, 1978; Rogers-Warren & Warren, 1977; Willems, 1974), or (c) assessment and programming for covariations in *other persons'* perform-

ance that may effect the generalization or maintenance of a target behavior (McConnell et al., 1985; Patterson, 1982).

Innovations in Research and Assessment

Empirical Research and Development

Walker et al. (1984) have described an empirical research and development effort that combines broad-based naturalistic assessment, intensive single-case experimentation, and group treatment-outcome studies into a single program for the validation of standardized treatment programs for childhood behavior disorders. These investigators and their colleagues at the Center at Oregon for Research on the Behavioral Education of the Handicapped (CORBEH) followed a systematic three-step process that moved from highly controlled, laboratory research to loosely controlled experiments in naturalistic settings. First, single-case experiments were conducted in an experimental classroom setting. This experimentation allowed the investigators to closely track effects of treatment, to identify functional relationships and sources of variability in children's performance, and to systematically vary treatment conditions so that powerful intervention procedures could be identified. This phase of research and development closely followed the "technique building" described by Bergin and Strupp (1972).

Second, single case evaluations of identified treatment procedures were conducted by CORBEH personnel in naturalistic settings (i.e., elementary school classrooms and playgrounds). Working with children similar to those previously enrolled in the experimental classroom, this series of experiments allowed Walker and his associates to refine implementation procedures and replicate the effects of treatment in a criterion setting. As a result, the external validity of treatment was initially established by demonstrating its effectiveness in a natural setting.

Third, field tests of the treatment package were completed. At this point, traditional group designs were used to evaluate the effectiveness of intervention compared to services already available for handicapped children. In addition, all treatment was provided in situ by school district personnel; CORBEH staff members provided training in typical workshop sessions. Thus, field tests further demonstrated the external validity of treatment by evaluating intervention as it would typically be conducted.

The CORBEH model demonstrates careful transition from highly controlled, stipulated environments to more loosely controlled, naturalistic ones. In addition, this model illustrates the careful selection of experimental procedures based on the amount of information known and the specific question to be answered. By systematically progressing from single case experimentation to group treatment-outcome research in school settings, investigators were able to construct powerful treatment programs that were sufficiently effective in practice.

Assessment and Analysis of Generalization Effects

In recent years, disabilities researchers have paid increased attention to the assessment and analysis of variables affecting generalization of treatment outcomes. Treatment effects may generalize over time (also termed maintenance), to the same behavior in other settings, or to other behaviors in the client's repertoire. Any of these generalization effects represent necessary increases in the efficacy, efficiency, and social validity of intervention programs.

As noted above, however, research designs and experimental procedures used in the past tended to focus more closely on the discrete or immediate effects of treatments, with less regard for the generalization of these effects across other dimensions. In fact, experimental procedures may have prevented investigators from attending more closely to issues of generalization. In both single case and group designs, experimental control is of central importance; generalization effects, particularly those across time or behaviors, can be limi-

ted by tight experimental control. For instance, where an investigator is conducting a multiple baseline analysis across three behaviors in a single subject, generalization across those behaviors poses a serious threat to the internal validity of the experiment. Similarly, in group designs, dependent variables are often selected to sample specific effects of treatment; as a result, effects beyond those being tested may not be detected by the investigator. In either case, the demonstration of generalization (and increased effectiveness) of a treatment outcome is restricted.

This increased attention to assessment and analysis of generalization effects has prompted a number of investigators to adapt existing experimental procedures or, in some cases, to develop new ones. One notable example of recent methodological innovations is offered by Kohler and Greenwood (1986) in their discussion of procedures for the identification of natural communities of reinforcement.

In their 1977 paper, Stokes and Baer identified a variety of procedures that hold promise for promoting the generalization of behavior change. One of these procedures, "introduction to natural maintaining contingencies," suggests that target behaviors can be exposed to naturally occurring communities of reinforcement, such that these behaviors become "entrapped" and maintained by natural contingencies rather than by those supplied by the therapist. This phenomenon has received much attention, but save for few examples (see Baer & Wolf, 1970), analyses have not been available.

Kohler and Greenwood (1986) offer five types of necessary evidence for the existence of natural communities of reinforcement. The three most basic types require comprehensive assessment of the behavior of subjects and peers. First, documentation of a naturally occurring reinforcement community requires some significant generalization of the initial treatment effect, whether across time, behaviors, or settings. Second, an investigator must demonstrate that treatment and generalization effects must be maintained over time, after the experimental contingencies or treatment have ended. Third, specific peer behaviors must be reliably associated, either as antecedents or as consequences, with occurrence of target behavior(s) of the subject. This demonstration requires the development and use of broad-based assessment protocols that capture the interactive behavior of both subjects and peers during treatment and nontreatment periods. Taken together, these three types of assessment offer tentative evidence of the existence of a behavioral trap, or generalization due to naturally occurring contingencies.

Conclusive evidence for the presence of behavioral trap follows from systematic analysis, and it is here that Kohler and Greenwood (1986) offer careful recommendations for the adaptation of existing experimental procedures. First, a functional relationship between specific peer behaviors and the target behavior must be demonstrated. This requires manipulation of peer behaviors *independent* of the behavior of the primary subjects, so that the effect of this manipulation can be observed. As such, this procedure represents an extension of more typical behavioral research, whereby the results of direct manipulation by the experimenter are often of primary interest. In this case, however, the independent variable is represented as peer behaviors that are the focus of the experimenter's manipulations. In addition to demonstrating functional relationship between peer behaviors and the target behavior, a systematic replication of the effect of these peer behaviors must be obtained. The investigator must demonstrate that the same peer behaviors will strengthen other behaviors in the subject's repertoire, thus illustrating the reinforcing nature of the indentified peer behaviors.

Like Walker et al. (1984), Kohler and Greenwood's (1984) guidelines rely on existing methodology and research practices, yet provide powerful and important innovations. Both approaches call for greater specificity and breadth in our research efforts. CORBEH's treatment programs were based on research conducted in a highly controlled experimental classroom. Walker and his colleagues then planned systematic replication of treatment packages under increasingly naturalistic conditions as an aspect of their research program. Similarily, Kohler and Greenwood extracted specific aspects of social interaction for further analysis, then recommended more broad-based assessment and the replication of functional relationships with various target behaviors.

Methodological innovations such as these provide for the continued development of disabilities research. Yet, as we suggested earlier, methodological rigor cannot be evaluated outside the context of social validity of research in developmental and physical disabilities.

SOCIAL VALIDITY

Research conducted with persons who are physically and/or developmentally disabled should be evaluated on both experimental and therapeutic criteria. Experimental criteria are related to methodology and focus primarily on evidence that the intervention was responsible for behavior change (internal validity). Therapeutic or clinical criteria are the standards by which a research effort is evaluated to determine if the target behavior, intervention procedures, and treatment outcomes are socially important (social validity). Social validation measures in behavioral research assist in determining the efficacy of treatment for ameliorating clinical and social problems more completely than specific, objective measures alone.

According to both Kazdin (1977) and Wolf (1978), intervention should be validated socially on at least three levels. The first level is social significance of the goals in intervention. Are the specific behavioral goals really what society wants? Are the target behaviors selected for intervention important to individuals in the natural environment? The second level of validation is the social appropriateness of procedures. Do the ends justify the means? That is, do the participants, caregivers, and other consumers consider the treatment procedures acceptable? Of the range of intervention procedures available, was the most acceptable procedure selected? The third level of validation concerns the social importance of the effect of intervention. Are consumers satisfied with the results? Does the degree of behavior change have practical value?

Social validation measures at all three levels can be implemented through either social comparison and subjective evaluation.

Social Comparison

Social comparison requires identification of peers who are similar in both subject variables (e.g., age) and demographic variables (e.g., socioeconomic status) to the client referred for treatment. Identification is followed by systematic measurement of the behavior of interest as exhibited by peers in relevant normalized settings.

Social comparison measures are particularly relevant at both the first and third levels of validation (significance of goals and importance of treatment effects). Data comparing a client's behavior with nondeviant peers provide support (or lack of support) for the necessity of intervention. If intervention is warranted by such a comparison, data on nondeviant peers provide empirically-derived criteria for the degree of change to be targeted in the client. At the third level of validity, social comparison of a client's behavior to that of nondeviant peers can assist clinicians in determining the success of treatment. Table 9-1 contains brief descriptions of several studies in which social comparison measures were used.

Social comparison requires development of normative standards of behavior. Although social comparison helps link research and practice, this process may be problematic in certain circumstances. Should normative behavior exhibited in many classroom environments and residential settings serve as the standard for measuring the importance of behavior change achieved through intervention? Some teachers may focus too heavily on "deportment" at the expense of providing optimal conditions for academic achievement. Some

vocational training programs may prepare clients well with regard to normative production rates, but neglect to provide instruction on social skills or grooming, both of which contribute significantly to successful vocational placement. And finally, intervention may reduce question-asking behavior to the normative of "manageable" in institutional settings, without regard to the range exhibited in less restrictive, community-based settings. Clearly, social comparison alone does not add social validity to a research effort. The use of comparison measures must be preceded by thoughtful selection of target behaviors in accordance with the goals of placement in least restrictive environments. Intervention should be applied only when data indicate that particular behavior is detrimental to a client's successful school, living, and vocational experiences.

In addition to being somewhat arbitrary, normative data can be too stringent for populations unlikely to achieve normal functioning along a particular dimension of behavior. For example, normative data on the rate of walking by physically able adults provide an unfair criterion in goal setting, as well as an inappropriate measure of the effectiveness of treatment aimed at improving the mobility of a person with cerebral palsy or spina bifida. A more appropriate social comparison measure for many individuals with severe disabilities should relate to increased functionality of a target behavior achieved through intervention. For example, intervention may be evaluated by change in a person's independent use of an electric wheelchair in relation to wheelchair mobility provided by an aide.

Subjective Evaluation

Subjective evaluation requires that persons with expertise in a particular area and/ or persons who are familiar with, or who interact with a client in relevant settings, make judgements about qualitative aspects of a client's behavior change. In other words, do significant others (e.g., social workers) discriminate in client behavior following intervention? Whereas social comparison measures are particularly relevant

Table 9-1. Summary of Representative Studies Utilizing Social Comparison Measures

REFERENCE	DESCRIPTION
Menchetti, Rusch, & Lamson (1981)	Participants at a national conference of college/university food service professionals evaluated the acceptability of various employment training techniques. Employers differentially accepted the use of some training procedures based upon worker description (handicapped vs. nonhandicapped). Certain procedures (e.g., yelling) were considered unacceptable under any circumstances.
Minkin et al. (1976)	The conversational abilities of junior high school and university students were ranked according to the amount of questions, positive feedback, and time spent talking. These conversational samples became the standard for measuring the effectiveness of a treatment program designed to improve deficient social communication skills in four court-adjudicated delinquent and predelinquent girls.
Twardosz, Schwartz, Fox, & Cunningham (1979)	Four classes of affectionate behavior (e.g., active, affectionate physical contact) were defined. A set of 15 videotaped segments of a wide range of care-giver–child interactions was prepared. These segments included a variable number of affectionate behaviors. The segments were scored both by trained observers using the behavioral definitions and by community volunteers using a 7-point Likert-type rating scale. Significant relationships were found between the occurrence of specific behaviors measured by the behavioral definitions and the opinions of the community members as measured by the rating scale.
Van Houten (1979)	The author summarizes social validation procedures and proposes a more experimentally based procedure to select standards of competence. The recommended strategy requires manipulation of the behavior of interest over its entire range to determine at which values the behavior is maximally effective in attaining important functional goals.
Walker & Hops (1976)	Observational data were recorded on several behaviors (e.g., attention to task) for both "target" students (i.e., referred for treatment) and regular classroom peers. Normative peer data were used as the standard against which the effects of treatment were compared, both in the treatment setting and following return to the regular classroom.

at both the first and third levels of social validation (significance of goals and importance of treatment effects), subjective evaluation measures are used primarily at the second and third levels of social validation (acceptability of treatment procedures and importance of treatment effects).

Social comparison measures provide additional objective support for the degree of change achieved through intervention. This is unlike the early use of subjective evaluation measures, which did not involve specification of a particular level of performance. Over time, however, there has been movement toward the development of empirically derived evaluation measures. This has resulted in the replacement of global evaluations of improvement with more discrete categorization of the degree of behavior change.

Social comparison measures require objective, well-defined evaluations of non-deviant peers in relevant settings, with a representative sample of data collected to meet strict standards of reliability. Subjective evaluation measures, on the other hand, usually consist of a single observation that is quantified in the form of a questionnaire. Questionnaires used to date range from single-item instruments to multiple-scale surveys. Many questionnaires include items requiring semantic differential ratings where evaluators respond in a Likert-type format. A second common type of questionnaire requires raters to indicate relative agreement or disagreement with a variety of evaluation statements. For meaningful responses to be obtained, great care must be taken during construction of the instrument with regard to its psychometric qualities. Many of the subjective evaluation scales used have been poorly validated and included little or no reliable data. Kazdin's work (1980a, 1980b, 1981) forms one of the only bodies of related research that includes the consistent use of a well validated measurement instrument for evaluating the effects of treatment.

Subjective evaluation measures fall into two general categories: those that reflect clinically or socially important changes in a client, and those that reflect consumer satisfaction with intervention.

Subjective Evaluation of Clinically Significant Behavior Change

The selection of persons to evaluate the significance of behavior change is a critical variable in assessing social validity of research or intervention efforts. It is generally recommended that persons selected to complete subjective evaluations have a particular type of expertise, so their judgments of behavior change have more credibility than those of citizens at large. For example, Voeltz, Wuerch, and Bockhaut (1982) selected a variety of experts to evaluate the effectiveness of their leisure skills training program for severely handicapped youth. The experts included parents and institutional day-program staff. More interesting was

the addition of evaluators from community-based facilities serving mentally retarded young adults as well as nonhandicapped teenage peers. A second example that illustrates meaningful selection of persons for completion of subjective evaluation measures is described by Kolko, Dorsett, and Milan (1981). These investigators selected psychologists, staff from a psychiatric hospital, and undergraduate students to evaluate pre- and post-treatment videotapes showing the effects of a social skills training program conducted with adolescent psychiatric patients.

A second aspect of the selection process is whether or not persons who *interact* with the client should judge the importance of treatment effects. Clearly, people who interact with a client should be able to discriminate meaningful behavior change. There is, however, some evidence that once a client is perceived as deviant, subsequent nondeviant performance is insufficient to overcome the initial perception (Kazdin, 1977). For this reason, some subjective evaluation procedures rely on the opinion of experts not associated with a client. This is done despite the fact that these expert opinions are not necessarily representative of people who have contact with a client. A partial solution to this dilemma may be the emergence of empirically derived subjective evaluations in which well-defined values are assigned to all of the performances to be observed.

Subjective evaluation procedures initially consisted of relative judgments as to the presence or absence of certain behaviors (e.g., affection), as well as global judgments of improvement along a continuum of behavior (e.g., amount of social interaction). Although researchers who have used global evaluations report high agreement among evaluators, there has been a transition to the practice of anchoring subjective evaluations with normative criteria. This is done by familiarizing evaluators with nonproblem peers along the dimension of behavior to be treated. Table 9-2 contains descriptions of several studies that included subjective evaluation of clinically or socially important change in a client.

Table 9-2. Summary of Representative Studies Utilizing Subjective Evaluation Measures

REFERENCE	DESCRIPTION
Kazdin (1980a)	Undergraduate students were provided with audiotaped descriptions of treatments commonly used with children who demonstrate severe behavior problems. The subjects then ranked acceptability of the procedures. Differential Reinforcement of Other Behavior (DRO) was more acceptable than timeout, drugs, or shock. These outcomes changed when descriptions of the *severity* of the behavior were provided. All treatments became more acceptable as severity level increased.
Kazdin (1980b)	Using a similar format of presentation (described above), undergraduate college students distinguished variations of timeout on the basis of their acceptability as treatment alternatives. Nonexclusionary forms of timeout were rated more acceptable than isolation. DRO was more acceptable than any punishment procedure.
Kazdin (1981)	Again, the same format resulted in groups of undergraduate students distinguishing alternative treatments on the basis of their acceptability. DRO was the most acceptable procedure, followed by positive practice, timeout, and drugs. The efficacy of treatment (strong vs. weak) did not influence acceptability, but the presence of adverse side effects did affect ratings.
Porterfield, Herbert-Jackson, & Risley (1976)	The acceptability of a nonexclusionary timeout procedure vs. redirection for treatment of aggression was assessed by having six women, naive to this experiment but experienced with young children, rank audiotapes of classroom activities as pleasant or unpleasant. Tapes contained segments when timeout was and was not in effect. Additionally, all care-givers completed questionnaires rating relative effects of the treatments.
Schreibman, Koegel, Mills, & Burke (1981)	A rating scale was used to assess the reaction of naive judges to videotaped samples of mother–child interaction. The children shown on the tape were autistic and undergoing behavioral treatment. Both pre-treatment and 6-month progress tapes were shown. A 7-point Likert scale was used to rank 17 items, including language and play skills. More global items (e.g., "I like this child") were included, as well as a social distance scale. The latter items required Yes/No answers to quesitons such as "Would you be willing to babysit this child?"

Consumer Satisfaction Measures

McMahon and Forehand (1983) have provided a comprehensive review of the literature regarding consumer satisfaction measures. Their review is not limited to measures of treatment outcome alone, but includes consumer satisfaction with therapists, treatment procedures, and formats of treatment (e.g., large group instruction). They also discuss the maintenance of consumer satisfaction over time. Table 9-3 describes a number of representative studies that have used consumer satisfaction measures.

McMahon and Forehand have critiqued the current status of consumer satisfaction measures. They point out that most of the work carried out on consumer satisfaction to date has been limited to parent training and the Achievement Place model of

Table 9-3. Summary of Representative Studies Utilizing Consumer Satisfaction Measures

REFERENCE	DESCRIPTION
Consumer Satisfaction with Treatment Outcome and / or Therapist	
Eyberg & Johnson (1974)	Two parental verbal report measures were used to supplement other measures of treatment outcome (e.g., parent observation data). The verbal report measures were the Becker Bipolar Adjective Checklist (1960) and the Therapy Attitude Inventory. The former measure was used to reflect changes in parents' perceptions of their children; the latter was constructed to assess parents' satisfaction with the process and outcome of the treatment program.
Forehand, Wells, & Griest (1980)	This study examined four types of social validation in evaluating the effectiveness of a parent training program. Social comparison and subjective evaluation were used, as well as a long-term investigation of consumer satisfaction and social acceptability of treatment procedures. Questionnaires measuring parents' perceptions of their child's and their own adjustments were completed by the parents before and after treatment and at a 2-month follow-up. Consumer satisfaction and social acceptability of treatment were measured by phone interviews in which parents' responded to seven questions (e.g., their feelings toward the child). A 7-point scale was used to quantify the parents' responses.
Rinn, Vernon, & Wise (1975)	Parents of "problem children" were asked to rate the instructors of a class on the principles of applied operant learning and the use of behavior modification as a child-rearing technique, and whether they would recommend the class to others. The first two categories were evaluated on a scale of 1–10; the third measure consisted of a simple Yes/No response.
Consumer Satisfaction with Treatment Procedures	
Foxx & Shapiro (1978)	The acceptability and practicality of a mild timeout procedure were assessed by providing a two-page summary of the procedure to 40 individuals who were experienced with the target population. After reading the summary, the respondents were required to answer five questions and to list all procedures they considered to be more severe or restrictive than the one described.
O'Dell et al. (1982)	Parents' satisfaction with one of four training methods designed to improve their skills in delivering positive reinforcement was assessed using three Likert scale items. The questions required parents to rate on a 7-point scale their overall impression of the training, how well they understood the content, and how likely they were to use the techniques.
Consumer Satisfaction with the Format of Treatment	
Kirigin, Braukmann, Atwater, & Wolf (1982)	Consumer evaluation measures were obtained on Teaching-Family (Achievement Place) vs. Non-Teaching-Family programs. Questionnaires were sent to relevant consumer groups (e.g., juvenile court and social welfare personnel) as well as to youth participants. The questionnaire contained a 7-point Likert scale to obtain ratings of staff effectiveness, cooperation, etc. Additionally, the youth rated program staff on dimensions such as fairness and effectiveness in helping them learn to solve their problems.

REFERENCE	DESCRIPTION
Robin (1981)	Two forms of consumer satisfaction measure were used. The first was an attitude survey measuring satisfaction with treatment, with separate Likert scale completed by parents (16 items) and adolescents (13 items). The second measure of consumer satisfaction was a three-item questionnaire designed to assess expectations for therapeutic change that was distributed to each family member.

treatment for juvenile delinquents. Studies that have involved treatment of children typically rely on consumer satisfaction measures completed by parents or other adults rather than the child. McMahon and Forehand believe this approach to be problematic because of ethical issues regarding children's participation in their own treatment decisions. On the other hand, they describe how difficult it is for young children to respond accurately on a self-report measure; thus, children's contribution to evaluation may be of limited value.

Consumer satisfaction measures have been used quite successfully with adolescents served through the Achievement Place model. In this group, high consumer satisfaction with treatment was correlated with a lower number of crimes and other offenses. Similar results have not been found with other populations, however.

Few investigations have reported measures of consumer satisfaction over time. Fewer still analyzed their data statistically. Those studies that have included descriptive data revealed mixed maintenance effects. Some have indicated declining satisfaction over time; others report continuing satisfaction.

McMahon and Forehand (1983) have concluded that consumer satisfaction measures should not be limited only to clients who complete treatment. They added that someone other than the therapist should conduct the assessment, in order to ensure truthful responses and guarantee anonymity.

Ethical Considerations in the Use of Social Validation Measures

The first ethical consideration in the use of social validation relates to the community standards underlying social comparison measures. As stated earlier, use of social comparison strategies does not automatically increase the social validation of an experiment or intervention. Social comparison should be an outgrowth of a well-developed philosophy of treatment that includes: (a) selection of the least intrusive treatment from the hierarchy of those demonstrated to be effective for a particular problem, (b) selecting for measurement those settings that are the least restrictive for the client, and (c) withholding treatment behaviors that are simply inconvenient or troublesome for a service provider (e.g., maintaining arbitrarily strict standards of "law and order" in the classroom). This final point has been well articulated by Winnett and Winkler (1972).

The second ethical consideration relates to inaccuracy of subjective evaluation data. Some of the reasons why subjective evaluation measures may not always yield accurate data were alluded to in the previous discussion on consumer satisfaction measures (e.g., fear of retaliation if anonymity is lost). These cautions were supported by Berleman, Seaberg, and Steinburn (1972) who showed that both delinquent youth and their parents reported positive changes after an intensive 1- to 2-year delinquency treatment program, even though no positive impact was found on disruptive behavior in school, police contacts, or rate of institutionalization. Berleman et al. (1972) recommended that clients be taught to observe their own behavior so that more accurate decisions about improvements could be made. Although determination of the reliability of verbal descriptions of private events is impossible, clients receiving services must still be considered the best evaluators of their treatment needs, procedural preferences, and post-treatment satisfaction.

TRANSLATING RESEARCH INTO PRACTICE

A major issue confronting researchers, clinicians, and practitioners in the area of developmental disabilities is the translation of research into practice. Research must contribute not only to knowledge of the etiology, incidence, and prevalence of developmental disabilities, but also to the development of effective treatment procedures. Efforts to close the gap between research and practice have been hampered by a number of factors. Traditionally, researchers and practitioners have followed parallel rather than converging pathways. Researchers are trained as scientists whose goals are to answer questions following a logical scientific progression. Conversely, practitioners are taught to be the consumers of such knowledge and to deal with patients, clients, and students in the so-called "real world." This distinction begins early in the education process and is unfortunately reinforced by "patterns of funding, preferential status in academia, and the conviction of many scientists that objectivity in research and program adequacy are mutually exclusive goals" (Begab, 1977, p. 2). It is our conviction that there must be an interdependence between research scientists and practitioners. One might accomplish this task in two ways: in clinical training, and through structuring the clinical environment for research.

Clinical Training

Most practitioners receive limited exposure to research practices during their clinical education. Many clinical training programs require only one or two research courses, and students are prepared to be little more than consumers of research reports. In addition, students have minimal opportunity for "hands on" experience with regard to the empirical verification of a research question. However, teachers and clinicians who work with the develop-

mentally disabled will have to meet new standards in the future (Tawney & Gast, 1984). Informed parents will increasingly demand data on child performance and question the impact that the practitioner has had on behavior change. Practitioners will be at a disadvantage if they are unable to demonstrate empirically the effects of their treatments.

Colleges and universities must begin to train future practitioners to conduct clinically based research. Students should receive additional didactic training and have opportunities to participate in field research. Gradually, through using such "veteran students" as field-based supervisors, these programs would have on-site scientist-practitioners who could model, explain, and reinforce the use of research paradigms in the field. Indeed, Center and Obringer (1984) have stated that special education practitioners were more likely to participate in field research if they had been involved in research during their graduate programs.

Structuring Clinical Environments for Research

Beyond training practitioners to conduct research in the field, we must structure clinical environments for research. In this way, teachers and practitioners might examine questions that would increase their effectiveness and expand the knowledge base in developmental and physical disabilities. The types of research in which clinicians might engage are circumscribed by the nature of the problems or disabilities exhibited by their clients. In addition, practitioners have to work within the resources of their particular settings. For example, the most valuable resource the research-practitioner has on hand are his or her colleagues. These collaborators should have similar interests and complementary skills. Supervisors also may provide needed support (e.g., obtaining a subject pool).

In choosing a research topic, the practitioner should keep in mind the notion of "field-responsive research." This type of research has direct impact on some need demonstrated by a particular client or group of clients. For example, if a clinician works with mentally retarded children and their parents, it may be expedient to develop research questions examining parent training problems that are common to the group.

Here, one must interject a note of caution. Although it may be expedient to fill a treatment need and to conduct research on that particular intervention, the research-oriented practitioner should also make some attempt to have a related theme in his or her work. In this way, much valuable time and effort may be saved in developing one standard observation scheme or other methodology for examining a variety of independent variables. In addition to choosing a programmatic theme for research, the research-practitioner should be realistic. Hartmann, Wood, and Shigetomi (1981) recommend evaluating the financial and logistical requirements of planned research and comparing them to the resources at hand (e.g., materials, equipment, available staff and subjects). They also suggest being careful not to select an unsuitable level of precision or too many variables when designing a project. Rather, the clinical researcher should approach a problem with a small series of interrelated studies, each of which examines one facet of a problem. In summary, for clinically based research to be a rewarding experience, the research-practitioner's dual goal is to provide the client with the most effective and efficient treatment possible and to incorporate that treatment protocol into a research strategy. In this way, both the client and science will be served.

SUMMARY

As stated at the outset, there is enormous breadth in issues related to research in developmental and physical disabilities. Three issues are of central concern for the continued development of ecologically valid, socially important research: innovations in research design and methodology, increased attention to the social validity of intervention, and the ongoing integration of research and practice. Other issues, such as the continued development

of effective assessment procedures and the selection of treatment procedures on the basis of client characteristics, are also important and worthy of future attention.

Honing the conceptual and methodological rigor of disabilities research is clearly an essential task. As a whole, this field has made substantial gains in the identification, prevention, and amelioration of disabling conditions. Through greater attention to and revision in the process of our work, continued progress is assured.

REFERENCES

Baer, D. M. (1977). Perhaps it would be better not to know everything. *Journal of Applied Behavior Analysis, 10,* 167–172

Baer, D. M., Wolf, M. M., & Risley, T. R. (1968). Some current dimensions of applied behavior analysis. *Journal of Applied Behavior Analysis, 1,* 91–97.

Baer, D. M., & Wolf, M. M. (1970). The entry into natural communities of reinforcement. In R. Ulrich, T. Stachnik, & J. Mabry (Eds.). *Control of human behavior* (pp. 319–324). Glenview, IL: Scott Foresman.

Barlow, D. H., & Hayes, S. C. (1979). Alternating treatments design: One strategy for comparing the effects of two treatments. *Journal of Applied Behavior Analysis, 12,* 199–210.

Begab, M. J. (1977). Barriers to the application of knowledge. In P. Mittler (Ed.), *Research to practice in mental retardation* (Vol. 1, pp. 1–30). Baltimore: University Park Press.

Bergin, A., & Strupp, H. (1972). *Changing frontiers in the science of psychotherapy.* New York: Aldine-Atherton.

Berleman, W. C., Seaburg, J. R., & Steinburn, T. W. (1972, September). The delinquency prevention experiment of the Seattle Atlantic Street Center: A final evaluation. *Social Science Review,* pp. 323–346.

Blumberg, C. J. (1984). Comments on "A simplified time-series analysis for evaluating treatment interventions." *Journal of Applied Behavior Analysis, 17,* 539–542.

Brooks, P. K., & Baumeister, A. A. (1977). A plea for consideration of ecological validity in the experimental psychology of mental retardation. *American Journal of Mental Deficiency, 81,* 407–416.

Campbell, D. T., & Stanley, J. C. (1966). *Experimental and quasi-experimental designs for research.* Chicago: Rand-McNally.

Center, D. B., & Obringer, S. J. (1984). Variables affecting productivity in special education researchers. *Teacher Education and Special Education, 7*, 215–220.

Eyberg, S. M., & Johnson, S. M. (1974). Multiple assessment of behavior modification with families: Effects of contingency contracting and order of treated problems. *Journal of Consulting and Clinical Psychology, 42*, 594–606.

Forehand, R., Wells, K. C., & Griest, D. L. (1980). An examination of the social validity of a parent training program. *Behavior Therapy, 11*, 488–502.

Foxx, R.M., & Shapiro, S. T. (1978). The timeout ribbon: A nonexclusionary timeout procedure. *Journal of Applied Behavior Analysis, 11*, 125–136.

Gottlieb, J., Semmel, M. I., & Veldman, D. J. (1978). Correlates of social status among mainstreamed retarded children. *Journal of Educational Psychology, 70*, 396–405.

Hartmann, D. P., Gottman, J. M., Jones, R. R., Gardner, W., Kazdin, A. E., & Vaught, R. (1980). Interrupted time-series analysis and its application to behavioral data. *Journal of Applied Behavior Analysis, 13*, 543–560.

Hartmann, D. P., Wood, D. D., & Shigetomi, C. C. (1981). Guidelines for initiating and maintaining a productive research career. *Behavioral Assessment, 3*, 273–282.

Hays, W. L. (1963). *Statistics for psychologists.* New York: Holt, Rinehart and Winston.

Hersen, M., & Barlow, D. H. (1976). *Single-case experimental designs: Strategies for studying behavior change.* New York: Pergamon.

Kazdin, A. E. (1976). Statistical analyses for single case designs. In M. Hersen & D. H. Barlow (Eds.), *Single-case experimental designs: Strategies for studying behavior change* (pp. 263–316). New York: Pergamon.

Kazdin, A. E. (1977). Assessings the clinical or applied importance of behavior change through social validation. *Behavior Modification, 1*, 427–452.

Kazdin, A. E. (1980a). Acceptability of alternative treatments for deviant child behavior. *Journal of Applied Behavior Analysis, 13*, 259–273.

Kazdin, A. E. (1980b). Acceptability of timeout from reinforcement procedures for disruptive behavior. *Behavior Therapy, 11*, 329–344.

Kazdin, A. E. (1981). Acceptability of child treatment techniques: The influence of efficacy and adverse side effects. *Behavior Therapy, 12*, 493–506.

Kirigin, K. A., Braukmann, C. J., Atwater, J. D., & Wolf, M. M. (1982). An evaluation of teaching-family (achievement place) group homes for juvenile offenders. *Journal of Applied Behavior Analysis, 15*, 1–16.

Kohler, F., & Greenwood, C. R. (1986). Toward a technology of generalization: The identification of natural communities of reinforcement. *The Behavior Analyst, 9*, 19–26.

Kolko, D. J., Dorsett, P. G., & Milan, M. A. (1981). A total assessment approach to the evaluation of social skills training: The effectiveness of an anger control program for adolescent psychiatric patients. *Behavioral Assessment, 3*, 383–402.

Landsman-Dwyer, S., Stein, J. G., & Sackett, G. P. (1978). A behavioral and ecological study of group homes. In G. P. Sackett (Ed.), *Observing behavior: Vol. 1. Theory and applications in mental retardation* (pp. 349–378). Baltimore: University Park Press.

McConnell, S. R., Strain, P. S., Lenkner, D. A., & Szumowski, E. (1985, May). *The effect of child academic behavior on contingent teacher attention: Entry into a complex community of reinforcement.* Paper presented at the Association for Behavior Analysis, Columbus, OH.

McMahon, R. J., & Forehand, R. L. (1983). Consumer satisfaction in behavioral treatment of children: Types, issues, and recommendations. *Behavior Therapy, 14*, 209–225.

Menchetti, B. M., Rusch, F. R., & Lamson, D. S. (1981). Social validation of behavioral training techniques: Assessing the normalizing qualities of competitive employment training procedures. *The Journal of the Association for the Severely Handicapped, 6*, 6–17.

Minikin, N., Braukmann, C. J., Minikin, B. L., Timbers, G. D., Timbers, B. J., Fixsen, D. L., Phillips, E. L., & Wolf, M. M. (1976). The social validation and training of conversational skills. *Journal of Applied Behavior Analysis, 9*, 127–139.

Nelson, R. O., & Hayes, S. C. (1979). Some current dimensions of behavioral assessment. *Behavioral Assessment, 1*, 1–16.

O'Dell, S. L., O'Quin, J. A., Alford, B. A., O'Briant, A. L., Bradlyn, A. S., & Giebenhain, J. E. (1982). Predicting the acquisition of parenting skills via four training methods. *Behavior Therapy, 13*, 194–208.

Patterson, G. R. (1982). *Coercive family processes.* Eugene, OR: Castalia Press.

Porterfield, J. K., Herbert-Jacksen, E., & Risley, T. R. (1976). Contingent observation: An effective and acceptable procedure for reducing disruptive behavior of young children in a group setting. *Journal of Applied Behavior Analysis, 9*, 55–64.

Rinn, R. C., Vernon, J. C., & Wise, M. J. (1975). Training parents of behaviorally disordered children in groups: A three years' program evaluation. *Behavior Therapy, 6*, 378–387.

Robin, A. L. (1981). A controlled evaluation of problem-solving communication training with parent–adolescent conflict. *Behavior Therapy, 12,* 593–609.

Rogers-Warren, A., & Warren, S. (1977). *Ecological perspective in behavior analysis.* Baltimore: University Park Press.

Sainato, D., & Lyon, S. (1983, December). A descriptive analysis of the requirements for independent performance in handicapped and nonhandicapped preschool classrooms. In P.S. Strain (Chair), *Assisting behaviorally handicapped preschoolers in mainstream settings: A report of research from the Early Childhood Research Institute at the University of Pittsburgh.* Symposium presentation at the First Chance Conference, Washington, DC.

Schreibman, L., Koegel, R. L., Mills, J. I., & Burke, J. C. (1981). Social validation of behavior therapy with autistic children. *Behavior Therapy, 12,* 610–624.

Sidman, M. (1960). *Tactics of scientific research.* New York: Basic Books.

Sigel, S. (1956). *Nonparametric statistics for the social sciences.* New York: McGraw-Hill.

Stokes, T. F., & Baer, D. M. (1977). An implicit technology of generalization. *Journal of Applied Behavior Analysis, 10,* 349–367.

Tawney, J. W., & Gast, D. L. (1984). *Single subject research in special education.* Columbus, OH: Charles E. Merrill.

Twardosz, S., Schwartz, S., Fox, J., & Cunningham, J. L. (1979). Development and evaluation of a system to measure affectionate behavior. *Behavioral Assessment, 1,* 177–190.

Van Hasselt, V. B., & Hersen, M. (1984, August). *Assessment of social skills in visually handicapped children.* Paper presented at the American Psychological Association, Toronto.

Van Houten, R. (1979). Social validation: The evolution of standards of competency for target behaviors. *Journal of Applied Behavior Analysis, 12,* 581–591.

Voeltz, L. M., & Evans, I. M. (1983). Educational validity: Procedures to evaluate outcomes in programs for severely handicapped learners. *Journal of the Association for the Severely Handicapped, 8,* 3–15.

Voeltz, L. M., Wuerch, B. B., & Bockhaut, C. H. (1982). Social validation of leisure activities training with severely handicapped youth. *The Journal of the Association for the Severely Handicapped, 7,* 3–14.

Wahler, R. G. (1975). Some structural aspects of deviant child behavior. *Journal of Applied Behavior Analysis, 8,* 27–42.

Walker, H. M., & Hops, H. (1976). Use of normative peer data as a standard for evaluating classroom treatment effects. *Journal of Applied Behavior Analysis, 9,* 159–168.

Walker, H. M., Hops, H., & Greenwood, C. R. (1984). The CORBEH research and development model: Programmatic issues and strategies. In S. Paine, T. Bellamy, & B. Wilcox (Eds.), *Human services that work* (pp. 57–79). Baltimore, MD: Paul H. Brookes.

Willems, E. P. (1974). Behavioral technology and behavioral ecology. *Journal of Applied Behavior Analysis, 7,* 151–165.

Winett, R. A., & Winkler, R. C. (1972). Current behavior modification in the classroom: Be still, be quiet, be docile. *Journal of Applied Behavior Analysis, 5,* 499–504.

Wolf, M. M. (1978). Social validity: The case for subjective measurement, or how applied behavior analysis is finding its heart. *Journal of Applied Behavior Analysis, 11,* 203–215.

CHAPTER 10

Competitive Employment: Overview and Analysis of Research Focus

Thomas R. Lagomarcino and Frank R. Rusch

Interest in integrating persons with mental retardation into the community has increased dramatically in recent years (Novak & Heal, 1980), primarily as a result of growing emphasis on normalization. The principle of normalization has had far-reaching effects as evidenced in recent efforts to enhance competitive employment opportunities for persons who are mentally retarded (Rusch & Mithaug, 1980; Wehman, 1981). Through competitive employment, mentally retarded adults are able to earn a minimum wage by performing valued work in integrated normalized settings.

The purpose of this chapter is threefold: we review studies that have attempted to isolate factors contributing to job terminations of persons with mental retardation, as well as other relevant literature; compare the findings of these studies; and propose recommendations for future research.

FACTORS CONTRIBUTING TO JOB TERMINATIONS

Over the years, researchers have repeatedly attempted to describe the employability of mentally retarded adults. Earlier studies examined the importance of various demographic variables for employability, including such characteristics as home influence (Neff, 1959; Shafter, 1957),

Preparation of this paper was supported in part by Grant No. OEG-0084-30081 from the U. S. Department of Education. The opinions expressed herein do not necessarily reflect the position or policy of the U. S. Department of Education, and no official endorsement should be inferred. Copies can be obtained from the authors, Office of Career Development for Special Populations, College of Education, 1310 South Sixth Street, Champaign, Illinois, 61820.

age (Kolstoe, 1961; Neff, 1959; Shafter, 1957), intelligence (Kolstoe, 1961; Reynolds & Stunkard, 1960; Shafter, 1957), and years of schooling and academic achievement (Kolstoe, 1961; Shafter, 1957). Often these earlier research efforts found no significant differences between "successful" and "unsuccessful" groups, leading Cobb (1972) to note that "there is one clear conclusion to be drawn from this array of studies . . . that no simple formula for prediction is possible" (p. 138). Table 10–1 lists a series of studies that address the reasons mentally retarded adults lose their jobs.

In recent years, studies of the specific characteristics of the mentally retarded population that lead to job failure have shifted to an analysis of feedback from supervisors and co-workers. For example, Fulton (1975) studied 55 mildly mentally retarded adults who had been placed in jobs in the community. The sample included two groups: (a) successful in competitive placement and (b) unsuccessful. The criterion for success was employment in the initial placement for six months or longer. Not successful was defined as losing the initial placement in less than six months. The variables examined were similar to those of many previous studies (e.g., Kolstoe, 1961; Shafter, 1957) and included arithmetic grade level, reading grade level, previous work history, number of days of program services, number of days between program termination and job placement, sex, presence of secondary emotional disability, client's living arrangement (alone or with family), hourly rate, and employer's past history of hiring persons who were handicapped. The only significant difference noted between the two groups was the presence of a secondary emotional disability in one-third of the clients who were unsuccessful in remaining employed. These emotional disabilities included acting out, yelling, and behaving in an unusual or strange manner.

In another investigation, Schalock and Harper (1978) evaluated 52 mildly and moderately mentally retarded adults who had been continuously employed over a two-year period. Results indicated that successful employment was related to age (older clients did better), sensorimotor functioning, visual-auditory processing, and language and symbolic operation. Intelligence was not related to successful employment. The major reason for unsuccessful employment was inappropriate social behavior. Other factors included slow working rate, lack of initiative, poor communication skills, unacceptable personal appearance, and health problems.

Table 10-1. Problem Areas Identified in the Employment of Mentally Retarded Adults

Study	Insufficient Speed/ Accuracy	Extreme Dependence on Supervision	Inappropriate Interaction with Others	Deviant Behavior	Unacceptable Personal Appearance	Poor Attendance/ Tardiness
Fulton (1975)				X		
Schalock & Harper (1978)	X		X	X	X	
Sowers, Thompson, & Connis (1979)	X	X	X	X		
Greenspan & Shoultz (1981)	X		X	X		X
Kochany & Keller (1981)	X		X	X		X
Brickey, Browning, & Campbell (1982)		X	X	X	X	X
Wehman et al. (1982)		X	X	X		
Ford, Dineen, & Hall (1984)	X	X	X	X	X	X

HDPD—F

Sowers, Thompson, and Connis (1979) assessed the success of 17 graduates from the Employment Training Program at the University of Washington (Rusch & Schutz, 1979) who had been placed in 31 different jobs. Of the 13 jobs lost during the first 5 months, 10 were due to lack of speed. Other reasons for job loss were employer's dissatisfaction with quality, poor attitude or lack of motivation, and inability to follow instructions or complete tasks without ongoing supervision. These reasons were compiled from job supervisors' verbal reports. Interestingly, another cause of job failure was the supervisor's inability to provide a job description that outlined the duties of a specific position. Supervisors indicated that successful employment was related to dependability, social skills, and satisfactory work.

A more recent study of the Employment Training Program (Ford, Dineen, & Hall, 1984) involved 82 mentally retarded adults placed in fast-food service jobs. A review of these clients' records indicated that 47% of the reported job losses were due to vocational issues, primarily insufficient speed or failure to complete work within the prescribed time limit (31%). Other difficulties resulting in job loss included poor performance, too much need for supervision, and noncompliance. In 42% of the job losses, social skills were involved. In addition to poor social interaction with employers and co-workers, which accounted for 12% of the job losses, social skills problems also involved emotional outbursts and inappropriate language. Other factors, such as poor attendance, theft, and personal hygiene also were cited as reasons for job termination. In many instances, multiple factors were involved.

Brickey, Browning, and Campbell (1982) examined the employment histories of 53 mildly and moderately mentally retarded adults over a 30-month period. Employers, employees, and/or placement counselors listed 29 different reasons for job separation. Multiple reasons often were given for unsuccessful placements. Major reasons included lack of speed in performing job-related tasks, followed by absenteeism, tardiness, poor relations with peers and supervisors, and inappropriate behaviors. Results also indicated that women were more successful than men.

Kochany and Keller (1981) investigated the causes for failure among clients served by Project Employability (Wehman, 1981), a job placement, training and follow-up program. Subjects for this study consisted of 18 mentally retarded adults who had not yet been hired for or terminated from jobs in the community. The subjects were divided into two groups: clients who were unemployed at the time of the study, but had been previously employed for three weeks or more; and clients who had never been hired or who had been employed for less than three weeks. Results showed that employment failure usually stemmed from multiple factors, primarily maladaptive behaviors, poor attendance, and tardiness. Other reasons were supervisor indecision, critical nonvocational skills (e.g., communication, transportation, time concepts), work incompetence, and lack of agency support.

Subsequent to Kochany and Keller's (1981) study, Wehman (1982) reviewed the results of Project Employability after three years of ongoing services. Of the 63 clients placed in a total of 75 jobs, 42 were employed at the time of the follow-up study. The reasons most often given for job termination included noncompliance in carrying out work tasks, off-task behaviors, and not notifying the employer when the client was unable to work. Bizarre and/or aggressive behaviors and poor quality of work also were cited as causes of job failure.

Greenspan and Shoultz (1981) interviewed co-workers, job placement staff, and former employers to ascertain why 30 mildly and moderately mentally retarded adults were involuntarily terminated from employment. Data were coded according to two categories: social, that is, temperament, character, and social awareness, and nonsocial, including production inefficiency, health problems, and company layoff. Results revealed that social reasons were as important as nonsocial reasons in determining why mentally retarded employees lose their jobs. Although not statistically significant, lack of social awareness was the most frequently cited reason for job loss. Inappropriate conversations, talking too much, verbal abuse, blaming co-workers for problems, and failure to listen to or follow supervisor's instructions also were implicated as causes.

Summary

Results of past research point to several factors that contribute to mentally retarded individuals' loss of jobs. Foremost among these are deviant behavior, inappropriate interactions with supervisors and co-workers, extreme dependence on supervision, insufficient speed and accuracy, poor attendance and/or excessive tardiness, and unacceptable personal appearance. Deviant behavior, followed by inappropriate interactions with supervisors and co-workers was cited more frequently than the other factors, which were primarily nonsocial in nature (e.g., speed, accuracy, attendance).

ON-THE-JOB TRAINING

This section reviews research that has investigated methods of teaching mentally retarded individuals to perform job-related tasks once they have been placed in the job. Findings will be presented relative to the focus of the preceding section, which iden-

tified seven factors relating to job termination among mentally retarded workers (see Table 10-2).

Insufficient Speed and Accuracy

Recent studies have shown a relationship between insufficient speed and accuracy and job termination (Greenspan & Shoultz, 1981; Kochany & Keller, 1981; Schalock & Harper, 1978; Sowers, Thompson, & Connis, 1979). As a result, several investigators have sought to improve the work performance of mentally retarded clients. For example, White and Kennedy (1980) increased the silverware-rolling rate of a 28-year-old moderately mentally retarded adult who was employed as a kitchen helper in a cafeteria. The employee received points for producing a certain number of rolls of silver per minute during two 5-minute periods. Points were later exchanged for special privileges. Results indicated a 100% increase in the rate of silverware rolling. Thus, the employee's on-task behavior reached 100% of the industrial norm for 16 of 18 observations over a 3-month period. This performance level was maintained after the trainer systematically withdrew the point system as well as her presence at the job site.

Keller, Kennedy, and Kochany (1980) taught a 35-year-old severely mentally retarded adult who was employed as a dish-

Table 10-2. Applied Behavior Analytic Studies Conducted with Employed, Mentally Retarded Adults

Study	Insufficient Speed/ Accuracy	Extreme Dependence on Supervision	Inappropriate Interaction with Others
White & Kennedy (1981)	X		
Keller, Kennedy, & Kochany (1981)	X		
Crouch, Rusch, & Karlan (1984)	X		
Rusch, Morgan, Martin, Riva, & Agran (1985)		X	
Schutz, Rusch, & Lamson (1979)			X
Karlan & Rusch (1982)			X
Rusch & Menchetti (1981)			X
Kochany, Simpson, Hills, & Wehman (1981)			X
Stanford & Wehman (1982)			X
Rusch, Weithers, Menchetti, & Schutz (1980)			X

Note: For the categories "Deviant Behavior", "Unacceptable Personal Appearance" and "Poor Attendance/Tardiness," no data were available.

washer in a nursing home to increase his rate of scrubbing pots and pans. Intervention efforts consisted of verbal prompting, visual monitoring of speed using a recording chart, and reinforcement of appropriate speed and performance.

Crouch, Rusch, and Karlan (1984) examined the effectiveness of verbal training procedures (cf. Israel, 1978) on improving the work performance of three moderately mentally retarded kitchen laborers. In this study, work supervisors indicated that the subjects needed to improve their productivity, and certain tasks in particular needed to be performed faster (e.g., sweeping, mopping, setting up the lunch line). Training initially entailed verbal praise of employees for indicating when they started and completed their tasks. A second reinforcement phase involved prompting employees to make the same five time statements as in the previous phase and reinforcing them only for performing tasks at the assigned times. Results of the investigation indicated that reinforcing of employees verbal statements was sufficient for decreasing time spent on completing tasks.

Extreme Dependence on Supervision

As noted above, extreme dependence on supervision has been identified as a major reason for mentally retarded adults' unsuccessful employment (Brickey, Browning, & Campbell, 1982; Sowers, Thompson, & Connis, 1979). Thus, clients' inability to follow verbal instructions of supervisors and initiate tasks independent of supervisor prompts often results in the supervisor devoting excessive time to employees. This additional supervision places stress on the relationship between supervisors and mentally retarded employees, often leading to job termination. In a study designed to enhance client independence on the job, Rusch, Morgan, Martin, Riva, and Agran (1985) introduced self-instruction procedures in the form of verbal rehearsal. Work supervisors were asked to identify three tasks that employees performed only when they were directly supervised (e.g., wiping counters, checking supplies, re-

stocking supplies). Based on this information, the self-instruction trainer teaches subjects to ask and find answers to questions about tasks requiring completion, and to perform tasks through self-instruction and self-reinforcement. Results revealed that subjects were able to rehearse self-instructional strategies, and self-instruction improved their work performance.

Inappropriate Interactions with Supervisors and Co-workers

Recent studies have revealed a relationship between social skills and employment (Greenspan & Shoultz, 1981). Specifically, successful employment has been found to depend on clients' ability to follow verbal directions given by supervisors, greet customers, and interact appropriately with co-workers. Several investigators have reported efforts to teach social skills in employment settings. For example, Schutz, Rusch, and Lamson (1979) examined the efficacy of an employer-validated procedure applied to three moderately mentally retarded adults who verbally abused trainers, co-workers, and supervisors throughout the working day. The validated procedure consisted of a warning and one-day suspension from work contingent upon verbal abuse. Results indicated that these procedures were effective in decreasing verbal abuse.

Following instructions is considered an important skill for mentally retarded workers (Rusch & Mithaug, 1980; Rusch & Schutz, 1979). It requires the employee (a) to indicate to the supervisor that the request has been understood (i.e., acknowledgment) and (b) to complete the task requested (i.e., compliance). Karlan and Rusch (1982) analyzed the relationship between acknowledgment and compliance for two moderately mentally retarded adults. Following baseline assessment, subjects were verbally prompted each time they did not acknowledge a request, given social praise for every instance of acknowledgment, and intermittently praised for compliance. The intervention appeared to affect acknowledgment negatively and compliance positively.

Rusch and Menchetti (1981) examined the effectiveness of an employer-validated training procedure for increasing the compliance of a moderately mentally retarded worker who refused to perform tasks when requested to do so by supervisors, cooks, and co-workers (Schutz, Rusch, & Lamson, 1979). Treatment consisted of instructing the employee to perform four specific steps when a request was made (stop, acknowledge request, perform task, return to original job) and having the employee rehearse the correct responses. The subject was also told that if he failed to comply, the shift supervisor would send him home (Schutz et al., 1979). In this investigation co-workers served as change agents. At the end of a shift the vocational trainer interviewed co-workers to determine if the employee had performed these steps in response to requests. Results suggested that the combination of requiring the employee to practice the correct responses and giving a warning effectively improved compliance. Using a similar procedure, Kochany, Simpson, Hill, and Wehman (1980) increased the duration of a moderately mentally retarded employee's compliant behavior.

Inability to interact with co-workers (Wehman, 1981) and talking at unacceptable times (Greenspan & Shoultz, 1981) also have been identified as a problem behavior of mentally retarded workers. A few studies have attempted to improve the conversational skills of mentally retarded workers. Two of these have included non-handicapped co-workers. For example, Stanford and Wehman (1982) facilitated interactions between two moderately mentally retarded employees and their non-handicapped co-workers during breaks. Subjects were given verbal prompts to socially interact with their co-workers (e.g., "Say hi to Shirley") and were praised if they interacted following a prompt.

An alternating treatment design consisting of alternating data sessions each day between intervention (i.e., prompting for social skills) and baseline (i.e., existing skills without supervision) was used to measure the effects of prompting to increase the frequency of social interactions

Rusch, Weithers, Menchetti, and Schutz (1980) reduced the number of topic repetitions made by a moderately mentally retarded employee during his conversations with co-workers during lunch and dinner breaks. The employee was told that he repeated topics too often and that his co-workers would like this behavior to decrease. Treatment also included advising co-workers to provide feedback when the subject repeated a topic. Rusch et al. found that counseling had an immediate effect on decreasing the employee's topic repetitions. The most effective training strategy consisted of feedback from both the vocational trainer and co-workers to the subject.

SUMMARY

The purpose of this chapter has been to ascertain if job loss factors identified in follow-up studies are similar to those addressed in applied behavior research reported in mainstream mental retardation journals. Applied research efforts identify three major causes for job loss as reported by employers: insufficient speed and/or accuracy, extreme client dependence on supervision, and inappropriate interactions with supervisors and co-workers. Deviant behavior, which elsewhere has been suggested as a primary factor associated with unemployability, has not been emphasized by applied research (e.g., Fulton, 1975; Greenspan & Shultz, 1981). Similarly, applied research has not addressed personal appearance or attendance.

Follow-up investigations, in contrast, suggest speed and/or accuracy, interactions with supervisors and co-workers, and deviant behavior as primary reasons for job loss.

What explanation may be given for the differences between applied research and follow-up studies? The applied research studies reported to date are the result of two competitive employment program (CEP) models that have served as prototypes for the development of long-term, follow-up efforts (cf. Bitter, 1979; Brolin, 1982). As discussed by Wehman (1981) and by Rusch and Mithaug (1980), they have been termed the "supported work model." The supported work model consists of distinct, coordinated efforts to increase the likelihood of employment. The community is first surveyed to identify possible jobs and sources of job-related social and vocational skills training (Rusch, 1983). Community-based (nonsheltered) training sites are then established within work settings, where potential employees are taught to perform the skills necessary for competitive employment. Once individuals are trained in the nonsheltered community work setting, they are placed into targeted jobs. Finally, training and long-term follow-up of decreasing intensity are provided to facilitate maintenance of acquired skills and to provide training unique to the employment site.

During the follow-up phase of the supported work model, placement specialists ask employers, supervisors, and co-workers to participate in evaluating employees' adjustment. This evaluation is usually achieved by rating the employee's performance at several points throughout the first year of employment (White & Rusch, 1983). In addition, Rusch (1983) suggests conducting a monthly evaluation during the first six months. Applied behavior analysis is unique to this approach in that it identifies single, major problems in need of immediate remediation. However, focusing on single difficulties that are more amenable to change also limits the scope of applied research.

In contrast to applied research, supported work model, follow-up studies tend to address the reasons for job loss. Often these investigations use multiple methods of data retrieval to identify why individuals lose their jobs. For example, Greenspan and Shoultz (1981) utilized employer and employee interviews. Interviews might also be conducted with professionals associated with social service agencies involved in community adjustment. Thus, follow-up studies provide multiple reasons for termination, whereas applied research studies focus on single reasons in need of remediation.

Future research is warranted in several areas. Specifically, more work is needed to determine if factors already identified in the literature provide a basis for theoretical arguments in favor of any one reason being accountable for most of the interstudy variation. For example, it is widely accepted that social reasons contribute as much or more to job loss as specific work performance skills, such as speed, task completion, and accuracy (cf. Greenspan & Shoultz, 1981).

Determining the best methods of identifying why mentally retarded individuals lose their jobs is another critical need. To date, no efforts have been made to validate reasons for terminations. The consequent reliance upon single interviewers' data retrieval methods, without systematic training and utilization of several interviewers for the purpose of interviewing key persons (e.g., employers, parents) to provide measures of agreement, may result in perceived versus actual reasons reported for client termination. Without a reliable measure of agreement, the reasons reported for job loss are subject to many validity problems, such as bias, fabrication, or drift.

In summary, this chapter has compared causes of job loss in mentally retarded adults, as suggested by a number of recent follow-up studies, with applied behavior-analytic investigations carried out in competitive employment. Several areas of agreement between the two approaches were identified. Specifically, the importance of speed and/or accuracy and the interactions of employees with supervisors and co-workers were noted. Unlike applied research, the follow-up studies revealed multiple reasons for job termination. This difference may be a result of employers attempting to justify their actions, as well as the data collection methods typically used in this type of work.

REFERENCES

Bitter, J. A. (1979). *Introduction to rehabilitation.* St. Louis, MO: C. V. Mosby.
Brickey, M., Browning, L., & Campbell, K. (1982). Vocational histories of sheltered

workshop employees placed in projects with industries and competitive jobs. *Mental Retardation, 20*(2), 52–57.

Brolin, D. E. (1982). *Vocational preparation of retarded citizens* (2nd ed.). Columbus, OH: Charles E. Merrill.

Cobb, H. (1972). *The forecast of fullfillment: A review of reasearch on the predictive assessment of the adult retarded for social and vocational adjustment.* New York: Teacher's College Press.

Crouch, K., Rusch, F. R., & Karlan, G. R. (1984). Utilizing the correspondence training paradigm to enhance productivity in an employment setting. *Education and Training of the Mentally Retarded, 19,* 268–275.

Ford, L., Dineen, J., & Hall, J. (1984). Is there life after placement? *Education and Training of the Mentally Retarded, 19,* 291–296.

Fulton, R. W. (1975). Job retention of the mentally retarded. *Mental Retardation, 13,* 26.

Greenspan, S., & Shoultz, B. (1981). Why mentally retarded adults lose their jobs: Social competence as a factor in work adjustment. *Applied Research in Mental Retardation, 2,* 23–38.

Israel, A. C. (1978). Some thoughts on correspondence between saying and doing. *Journal of Applied Behavioral Analysis, 11,* 271–276.

Karlan, G. R., & Rusch, F. R. (1982). Analyzing the relationship between acknowledgement and compliance in a nonsheltered work setting. *Education and Training of the Mentally Retarded, 17,* 202–208.

Keller, J., Kennedy, K., & Kochany, L. (1981). Maintaining the employability of a severely retarded food service worker: Use of a changing criterion program. In P. Wehman, *Competitive employment: New horizons for severely disabled individuals* (pp. 70–75). Baltimore: Paul H. Brookes.

Kochany, L., & Keller, J. (1981). An analysis and evaluation of the failures of severely disabled individuals in competitive employment. In P. Wehman, *Competitive employment: New horizons for severely disabled individuals* (pp. 181–198). Baltimore: Paul H. Brookes.

Kochany, L., Simpson, T., Hill, J., & Wehman, P. (1981). Reducing noncompliance and inappropriate verbal behavior in a moderately retarded food service worker: Use of a systematic fading procedure. In P. Wehman, *Competitive employment: New horizons for severely disabled individuals* (pp. 63–68). Baltimore: Paul H. Brookes.

Kolstoe, O. P. (1961). An examination of some characteristics with discrimination between employed and not employed mentally

retarded males. *American Journal of Mental Deficiency, 66,* 472–482.

Neff, W. S. (1959). *The success of a rehabilitation program—A follow-up study of clients of the vocational adjustment center.* Chicago: The Jewish Vocational Service.

Novak, A. R., & Heal, L. W. (Eds.). (1980). *Community integration of developmentally disabled individuals.* Baltimore, MD: Paul H. Brookes.

Reynolds, M. C., & Stunkard, C. L. (1960). *A comparative study of day class vs. institutionalized educable retardates.* (Tech. Rep. No. 192). Minneapolis: University of Minnesota.

Rusch, F. R. (1983). Competitive vocational training. In M. Snell (Ed.). *Systematic instruction of the moderately and severely handicapped* (2nd ed.). Columbus, OH: Charles E. Merrill.

Rusch, F. R., & Menchetti, B. M. (1981). Increasing compliant work behaviors in a nonsheltered work setting. *Mental Retardation, 10,* 107–111.

Rusch, F. R., & Mithaug, D. E. (1980). *Vocational training for mentally retarded adults: A behavior analytic approach.* Champaign, IL: Research Press.

Rusch, F. R., Morgan, T. K., Martin, J. E., Riva, M., & Agran, M. (1985). Competitive employment: Teaching mentally retarded employees self-instructional strategies. *Applied Research in Mental Retardation, 6,* 389–408.

Rusch, F. R., & Schutz, R. P. (1979). Nonsheltered employment of the mentally retarded adult: Research to reality? *Journal of Contemporary Business, 8,* 85–98.

Rusch, F., Weithers, J., Menchetti, B., & Schutz, R. (1980). Social validation of a program to reduce topic repetition in a nonsheltered setting. *Education and Training of the Mentally Retarded, 15,* 208–215.

Schalock, R. L., & Harper, R. S. (1978). Placement from community-based mental retardation programs: How well do clients do? *American Journal of Mental Deficiency, 83,* 240–247.

Schutz, R. P., Rusch, F. R., & Lamson, D. S. (1979). Eliminating unacceptable behavior: Evaluation of an employer's procedure to eliminate unacceptable behavior on the job. *Community Services Forum, 1,* 5–6.

Shafter, A. J. (1957). Criteria for selecting institutionalized mental defectives for vocational placement. *American Journal on Mental Deficiency, 61,* 599–616.

Sowers, J., Thompson, L. E., & Connis, R. T. (1979). The food service vocational training program: A model for training and placement of the mentally retarded. In T. G. Bellamy, G. O'Connor, & C. C. Karan (Eds.),

Vocational habilitation of severely handicapped persons (pp. 201–204). Baltimore, MD: University Park Press.

Stanford, K., & Wehman, P. (1982). Improving the social interactions between moderately retarded and nonretarded coworkers: A pilot study. In P. Wehman & M. Hill (Eds.), *Vocational training and job placement of severely disabled persons* (pp. 141–159). Richmond, VA: Virginia Commonwealth University.

Wehman, P. (1981). *Competitive employment: New horizons for severely disabled individuals.* Baltimore, MD: Paul H. Brookes.

Wehman, P. (1986). Competitive employment in Virginia. In F. R. Rusch (Ed.), *Competitive employment: Supported work models, methods, and issues.* Baltimore, MD: Paul H. Brookes.

Wehman, P., Hill, M., Goodall, P. A., Cleveland, P., Brooke, V., & Pentecost, J. (1982). Job placement and follow-up of moderately and severely handicapped individuals after three years. *Journal of the Association for the Severely Handicapped, 7,* 5–16.

White, D. M., & Rusch, F. R. (1983). Social validation in competitive employment: Evaluating work performance. *Applied Research in Mental Retardation, 4,* 343–354.

White, S. & Kennedy, K. (1981). Improving the work productivity of a mentally retarded woman in a city restaurant. In P. Wehman, *Competitive employment: New horizons for severely disabled individuals* (pp. 68–70). Baltimore: Paul H. Brookes.

Wolfensberger, W. (1972). *Normalization: The principle of normalization in human services.* Toronto, Canada: National Institute on Mental Retardation.

CHAPTER 11

Legal and Legislative Initiatives in Disability

Henry A. Bersani, Jr. and Thomas Nerney

Any good library has a shelf with several volumes that address the issue of laws and people with disabilities. The purpose of this chapter is not to compete with those texts, since we could never fit all the potentially useful information on this topic into one chapter. Instead, our goal is to offer an overview of legal and legislative initiatives in the field of disability, along with a commentary on what it all means. This chapter discusses the history of legal initiatives, the current status of legislative matters, and possible future trends. One word of caution. There is a tendency to think that progress in the field of disability can only be made in the courts and in the legislature. This is not our approach. Progress is made when clinical gains, policy reform, and favorable legislation all occur at the same time.

Spheres of Policy Reform

Although it is popular to use the terms "legal reform" or "legislative reform" interchangeably, there are, in fact, several interrelated spheres of policy reform that need

to be considered: legislation, litigation, appropriation, and regulation.

Legislation refers to statutes or laws that are passed by a legislature, such as the United States Congress or a state legislature. We will discuss several pieces of legislation that have direct bearing on the lives of persons with disabilities. In addition to these specific laws, Appendix 11-1 offers a chronological listing of U.S. legislation affecting persons with disabilities.

Litigation refers to the results of court cases. Legislation is the role of a legislature, and litigation is developed in the judiciary branch of government. As in legislation, litigation may occur at the federal level (United States circuit courts or the United States Supreme Court) or at the state level (state court of appeals or state supreme court).

The stage of *appropriation* is frequently overlooked by advocates for persons with developmental disabilities. Many pieces of legislation set out procedures or initiate projects, but legislation alone does not necessarily guarantee that funds will be available to bring the projects to fruition. Appropriation is a distinct part of the governmental process.

When a law is passed, an appropriate governmental agency, such as the Department of Health and Human Services, is charged with developing the *regulations* needed to implement it. The regulatory agency examines both the statutory language and Congressional intent as reflected in committee reports. On this basis, the agency will develop the regulations and procedures needed to make the law a reality.

For the purposes of this chapter, we will focus primarily on legislation and litigation.

Legal Terms and Nomenclature

The legal profession has its own highly developed vocabulary. Most professionals who work in the field of disability are not expected to be legal experts, but eventually encounter a limited number of legal terms. In order to be a good teacher, rehabilitation worker, or advocate, a minimal legal vocabulary is essential. Appendix 11-2 presents a glossary of basic legal terminology.

The Evolution of a Law Suit

Going to court is only one way to achieve political change. In special education, however, several of the most significant reforms have been the result of court actions. For this reason, it is useful to understand how a court case develops and finally gets to court. Taylor and Biklen (1980) identify three steps in preparing a court case.

First, all of the facts must be identified. In this stage, one who is preparing to sue (the plaintiff) identifies the issues that he or she wishes to rectify, for example, dissatisfaction with a segregated educational setting or denial of special support services.

Once the issue or issues have been identified, the second step is to examine the facts of the case in light of various laws. In the instance of a segregated educational program, the plaintiff might start with an

examination of PL 94-142. In the case of being denied access to special services, the plaintiff could look at the constitutional right of due process, or Section 504 of the Rehabilitation Act of 1973.

The third and final step is to decide on a concrete course of action. Not all injustices require a court case to be resolved. By going through the previous two steps in this process identifying a problem and researching the law, a solution often can be found. A prospective plaintiff may find a solution without going to court. In addition, the threat of legal action is often sufficient to "coax" a service provider or agency to respond to the individual's concerns and in many cases may be at least as powerful as an actual court action. Although state-level court cases can have some effect beyond the state in which the case was decided, national policy change is more likely to occur with cases that are heard at the federal level in the United States Supreme Court. However, only a very small percentage of disputes ever get to that level.

How a Case Gets to Supreme Court

There are several ways in which a case may be heard by the Supreme Court. Two routes are by far the most common, however, and apply best to cases affecting persons with disabilities (Abeson, 1976). These two routes can be described as the state and federal routes.

The state route usually is a three-step process. First, a case is brought to trial at the state level. If either party is dissatisfied with the judgment, an appeal is made. Then the appeal is taken to the state appeals court. If either party is dissatisfied with that decision, they may take it to the state supreme court, which rules on the case. If either party is still dissatisfied with the decision, they may ask that the case be heard by the United States Supreme Court.

The federal route is also a three-step process. A case involving a federal law is tried in a federal district court. If either party is displeased with the decision of that court, they may take the case to the district court of appeals. Then the circuit court of appeals reviews the case and rules on the decision.

Finally, the appeals court's decision may be taken to the Supreme Court by a dissatisfied party.

It is important to note that not all cases sent to the Supreme Court are actually heard before that court. Cases are carefully screened, and in most cases the court decides to let the lower court decision stand. When a case is to be heard by the court, briefs are submitted by both sides, and then oral arguments are heard. Under usual circumstances the court hears arguments for only one hour on each case, although exceptions are made. Even if the Supreme Court hears a case, it does not necessarily offer a new ruling. The court may let the decision of the lower court stand, or it may remand it to a lower court for review. In order to be heard by the Supreme Court, a case must involve a constitutional question, such as due process, equal protection, or free speech.

HISTORY AND DEVELOPMENT

Major Historic Trends

Services to persons with disabilities have undergone systematic shifts on several dimensions. These dimensions are interrelated; rarely has progress in one area proceeded without progress in several others.

One such dimension can be called "availability of services." In this dimension, services have progressed from a position of exclusion to one of inclusion. In spite of the growing acceptance of nation-wide public education, it was not until the 1870s that significant numbers of special education classes were available. Although in the 1890s most cities had some type of special education services (Scheerenberger, 1983), they were often inadequate and limited to students with mild disabilities.

On an "entitlement of services" dimension, services shifted from being a matter of charity to one of right. In the 1970s, the Center on Human Policy under the leadership of Burton Blatt published a poster that stated, "You gave us your dimes . . . now give us our rights." This poster was meant to convey the change from charity to rights

that was brought about by the passage of several laws that clearly entitled people with handicaps to services. These laws are reviewed later in this chapter.

A third dimension pertains to the "location of services." When people with disabilities were excluded from formal services, their needs were met informally, often inadequately, by the family. As services became a matter of charity, they usually were in inadequate facilities, such as previously condemned buildings or church basements. As public education for students with disabilities became a right, more services moved into regular schools and other traditional educational settings. Many of these schools needed architectural modification to assure access of students with physical handicaps.

In summary, there has been a distinct trend from segregated, isolated services to more integrated programs. This trend involves (a) academic integration, such as special classes located in regular schools, and (b) social integration, as students in those classes participate in various activities within the schools. In different communities, these trends have occurred (or are still occurring) at disparate rates. In the Madison, Wisconsin schools, for example, there have been no segregated special education schools for several years. In Ohio and New York, however, many segregated schools exist where social and educational integration is all but impossible. (For a more extensive discussion of the development of educational integration, see Chapter 8).

Legal Access to Services

The evolution of legal access to services, particularly special education, must be interpreted in terms of a changing social and political climate. Ferguson, Ferguson, and Bogdan (1987) have identified three factors. First, compulsory education laws brought together, for the first time, students with a variety of skills and backgrounds. Second, the development of intelligence tests and eugenic theories provided scientific objectivity for understanding differences among students. The third trend is the emergence of social Darwinism and the assumed efficacy of special classes. As Scheerenberger (1983) points out, in 1934 there were 85,000 students labelled mentally retarded in special classes across the country. The vast majority of these students would be considered mildly handicapped by today's standards. Students with severe handicaps did not win the right to education until recently.

Early Court Cases

At the turn of the 20th century, court cases were decided in a manner that pitted the rights of the "exceptional student" in opposition to the rights of the mass of other students. In the context of the relatively new concept of national public education, students who were seen as disrupting that process could be excluded from schooling. The following two cases represent this phenomenon.

In *Watson v. City of Cambridge* (1883), the court ruled that a student could be excluded from public school if he or she exhibited "disorderly conduct or imbecility." At this time there were few special classes for students to be referred to, and no intelligence tests as they are known today. The school was not expected to meet the needs of the student, rather the student was expected to conform to the program being offered.

In *Beattie v. State Board of Education* (1919), the Wisconsin Supreme Court ruled that the Beatties' child could be excluded from school. By today's standards, we might think of a child so severely handicapped that the schools would say he could not be educated. The Beattie child was not excluded because he exhibited behaviors that were dangerous to himself or others. Evidently he was able to keep up with the course work as well. What was the reason for the courts to approve of the exclusion of this child? Because of his cerebral palsy (apparently quite mild), the court maintained that he produced a "nauseating effect on the teachers and school children and . . . required an undue portion of the teacher's time."

Court Cases Affecting Current Practices

Although *Brown v. Board of Education* (1954) was brought to the United States Supreme Court in response to racial segregation, the decision has deeply affected the way advocates have approached the issue of segregation in special educational services. In this decision, the court made several points:

1. Education is essential for any person to advance in society,
2. Education must be offered to all on an equal basis,
3. Segregation of students on the basis of race is unconstitutional,
4. Separate services are intrinsically unequal.

Thus, advocates for the educational integration of disabled students have argued that integrated education is essential for advancement of students with disabilities in society; the principle of equal access to education includes the right to have special educational services provided in nonsegregated settings; and special education services offered in segregated settings are, by their very nature, inferior.

In *Diana v. State Board of Education* (1970), the plaintiffs charged that the California educational system had overrepresented Mexican-American students in special education classes. They claimed that this overrepresentation was due to the use of standardized intelligence tests that were culturally biased and given only in English to students who did not speak English. The court decision included the following assertions: intelligence tests must be given in the student's natural language, or with an interpreter; all Mexican and Chinese-American students in special education classes were to be retested using new testing procedures; and the state must assume responsibility for improving standardization problems inherent in current testing procedures (Haring, 1982).

The court set forth in *Pennsylvania Association for Retarded Citizens v. The Commonwealth of Pennsylvania* (1971) a series of principles that have been viewed as the precursor to the development of PL 94-142. The court stated that in the past, children with disabilities had been systematically denied access to public education, and that all children, regardless of their level of handicap, could benefit from public education. In addition, under the Bill of Rights all children are entitled to a free appropriate public education on a basis equal to the education provided to others, and this right includes the right to education in the "least restrictive setting." Finally, the court asserted that parents, as guardians for their children, have a right to due process protection regarding the classification and placement of their sons and daughters (Biklen, 1981).

Constitutional Arguments Affecting Persons with Handicaps

Payne and Patton (1982) have noted several of the most common constitutional arguments that have been applied to court cases regarding persons with disabilities.

1. All persons must be provided *equal protection* under the law (14th Amendment). This argument has been used in the fight for equal access to educational services.
2. Under *substantive due process* (5th and 14th Amendments), any legislation must be reasonably related to a legitimate legislative objective, such as the right to appropriate classification.
3. *Procedural due process* (5th and 14th Amendments) requires that if the government restricts the liberty of an individual (such as in an institutional placement), procedural fairness must be guaranteed. This argument has been used in "right to treatment" cases.
4. *Freedom from cruel and unusual punishment* (8th Amendment) has been applied in arguments on the right to receive or refuse treatment and in attempts to limit the use of aversive behavior management procedures.
5. *Freedom from slavery and involuntary servitude* (13th Amendment) protects individuals from performing work against

their will. This argument has been used to outlaw the practice of institutional peonage, a procedure whereby institutional residents are required to perform labor to maintain the institution.

It is important to remember that every citizen with a handicap is a citizen first and thus is entitled to the full protection of the law under the Bill of Rights; the United States Constitution; and all federal, state, and local statutes.

MAJOR CURRENT LAWS

The Rehabilitation Act of 1973 PL 93-112).

As can be seen in Appendix 11-1, rehabilitation services first began with services to veterans in 1918 and then expanded to the civilian population in 1920. This act supercedes all previous vocational rehabilitation acts and, including subsequent amendments from PL 98-221, contains provisions for a variety of services and rights. The seven major sections of the act, which are referred to in legislation as "titles," are:

Title I.   Vocational Rehabilitation Services
Title II. Research
Title III. Supplementary Services and Facilities
Title IV. National Council on the Handicapped
Title V.   Miscellaneous
Title VI. Employment Opportunities for Handicapped Individuals
Title VII. Comprehensive Services for Independent Living

Under Section 7(B) this act, the term "handicapped individual" is defined as "any individual who (i) has a physical or mental impairment which substantially limits one or more of such person's major life activities, (ii) has a record of such an impairment, or (iii) is regarded as having such an impairment" (Sec.7(A)). In addition, the act defines a severe handicap as a "disability which requires multiple services over an extended period of time and results from amputation, blindness, cancer, cerebral palsy, cystic fibrosis, deafness, heart disease, hemiplegia, mental retardation, mental illness, multiple sclerosis, muscular dystrophy, neurological disorders (including stroke and epilepsy), paraplegia, quadriplegia and other spinal cord conditions, renal failure, respiratory or pulmonary dysfunction, and any other disability described by the Secretary in regulations he shall prescribe." (Sec. 7 (13))

The term "Secretary" here refers to the Secretary of the Department of Health and Human Services.

The Rehabilitation Act authorizes the development of state-wide, long-term plans to meet the rehabilitation needs of handicapped persons and specifies that persons deemed to be "severely handicapped" are to be given first priority in preparation for gainful employment. This proviso represented a distinct change in policy. Prior to this act, the common practice in many rehabilitation programs was to serve the most mildly handicapped persons first, in an effort to help the greatest number of people. Unfortunately, this meant that the people who were most in need in any given community often received no services at all. Thus, for the first time even persons with severe handicaps could be prepared for gainful employment. An additional provision called for the initiation and expansion of services to selected groups of persons, such as those who had been institutionalized or who had been either unserved or underserved in the past. Title I requires that each person who receives rehabilitation services must have an "individualized, written rehabilitation program."

Perhaps the most far-reaching provision of the act is under Title V, Section 504, entitled "nondiscrimination under federal grants and programs:"

No otherwise qualified handicapped individual in the United States, as defined in section 7(7), shall, solely by reason of his handicap, be excluded from the participation in, be denied the benefits of, or be subjected to discrimination under any program or activity receiving Federal financial assistance or under any program or activity conducted by any Executive agency or by the United States Postal Service. (Sec. 504)

This statement is strengthened by Section 505 "remedies and attorneys' fees," which specifies that the Civil Rights Act of 1964 may be applied to persons who have been discriminated against in employment and allows courts to award recovery of attorneys' fees as part of the remedy set forth. Other programs are provided funding as described below.

1. *Projects with industry programs* offer handicapped individuals training and employment in realistic work settings to prepare them for long-term competitive employment.
2. *Centers for independent living* offer a variety of services to support handicapped persons, under the proviso that "handicapped individuals will be substantially involved in policy direction and management of such centers, and will be employed by such centers."
3. An *Architectural and Transportation Barriers Compliance Board* is empowered to study and make recommendations concerning transportation accessibility and compliance under the Architectural Barriers Act of 1968.

The act also created the National Institute of Handicapped Research, the National Council on the Handicapped, and the Helen Keller National Center.

The Developmental Disabilities Assistance and Bill of Rights Act

Also known as PL 98-527, this act is the most recent of a series of amendments to Section 2, Title I of the 1963 Mental Retardation Facilities and Community Mental Health Centers Construction Act (PL 88-164). First, in 1970, Congress passed the Developmental Disabilities Services and Facilities Construction amendments which represented the first Congressional effort to specify provisions for persons designated as being developmentally disabled.

These amendments offered the first legal definition of developmental disability, which included persons with mental retardation, cerebral palsy, epilepsy, and other neurological conditions. The amendments specified that the disability must be manifested prior to the age of 18 and present a substantial handicap.

In 1975, further changes were made by the passage of the Developmentally Disabled Assistance and Bill of Rights Act (PL 94-103), in which the definition of developmental disability was expanded to include autism and dyslexia. However, dyslexia was not automatically considered a developmental disability; it had to be a result of another developmental disability or related condition.

Additional amendments passed, the Rehabilitation, Comprehensive Services, and Developmental Disabilities Amendments of 1978 PL 95-602 which dramatically changed the definition of developmental disabilities. In the 8 years before these amendments, developmental disabilities were defined on the basis of categories. One was required to fit into a specific category (mental retardation, cerebral palsy, epilepsy, etc.) in order to be considered developmentally disabled. This categorical approach dominated the field of special education. In the 1978 amendments, in light of criticisms from parents and professionals, Congress offered a new, functional definition of developmental disability and extended the time for onset of the disability to prior to age 22. A final set of amendments was passed in the Developmental Disabilities Act of 1984 (PL 98-527), under which a developmental disability presently is defined as:

a severe chronic disability of a person which (a) is attributable to a mental or physical impairment or combination of mental and physical impairments; (b) is manifested before the person attains age 22; (c) is likely to continue indefinitely; (d) results in substantial functional limitations in three or more of the following areas of major life activity: (i) self-care, (ii) receptive and expressive language, (iii) learning, (iv) mobility, (v) self-direction, (vi) capacity for independent living, and

(vii) economic self-sufficiency; and (e) reflects the person's need for a combination and sequence of special, interdisciplinary, or generic care, treatment, or other services which are of lifelong or extended duration and are individually planned and coordinated. (Sec. 102(7))

This functional approach to defining disability has received much support from professionals, parents, and those with disabilities.

The many versions of the Developmental Disabilities Act constituted a major restructuring in the definition of disabilities, first by creating a cluster of disabilities known as "developmental," and then by changing to a more functional definition. There are, however, several other provisions of the original act and amendments that continue to be important today.

State Planning Councils

Each state is required to have a state developmental disabilities planning council appointed by the governor. These so-called "DD councils" must have representatives from the various state agencies. In addition, one-half of the councils are composed of "disability-related individuals," that is, people with disabilities and their parents, siblings, or other immediate family members. Specifically, at least one-sixth of the members of the council must be disabled, and another sixth must be the immediate relatives or guardians of people with developmental impairments. At least one of the members must be the immediate relative or guardian of a person with a developmental disability who currently resides in an institution. The balance of the membership is open to all members of the public.

State Plans

Each state is required to submit a plan to address the unmet needs of persons with developmental disabilities. The act sets forth four areas of priority. The state plan must focus on at least one and not more than two of these priorities: (a) alternative community living arrangements to help maintain residential options; (b) assistance to young children to overcome the handicapping effects of developmental disabilities; (c) employment-related activities to further independence and productivity; and (d) case management services to aid in obtaining the range of help needed.

The state plan must also contain a variety of assurances regarding quality. Services provided under the state plan must conform to all existing regulations, any buildings used must be in compliance with the Architectural Barriers Act of 1968, the services must be provided in an individualized manner, and the human rights of all persons served in the programs must be protected.

Protection and Advocacy Systems

Each state is required to establish a system to protect and advocate the rights of persons with developmental disabilities. In order to minimize conflict of interest, this system must not be affiliated with any state agency that provides services to persons with developmental disabilities.

University-Affiliated Facilities

This provision of the act calls for the development of a series of facilities, affiliated with universities across the country, to provide interdisciplinary training for individuals who are preparing to work with developmentally disabled persons and their parents. At the present time, some 36 university-affiliated facilities are authorized under this law.

Rights of Persons with Developmental Disabilities

The 1975 amendments, entitled the Developmentally Disabled Assistance and Bill of Rights Act (PL 94-103), set forth specific rights of persons with developmental disabilities, including appropriate treatment, services designed to maximize individual potential, and services in settings that are least restrictive of personal liberty. These rights were not found by the Supreme Court to have the force of law; however, they provide guidelines for appropriate service systems.

The Education of the Handicapped Act

Legislation regarding the education of handicapped students has been significantly altered over the past several decades. The act given the most credit for reshaping special education services in this country is the Education for All Handicapped Children Act of 1975 (PL 94-142). This was a revolutionary piece of legislation, but it is also important to take previous legislation into account. In fact, PL 94-142 constitutes a series of amendments to an earlier law, the Education of the Handicapped Act of 1970 (PL 91-230). That act, known as the EHA, defined handicapped children as:

> mentally retarded, hard of hearing, deaf, speech or language impaired, visually handicapped, seriously emotionally disturbed, orthopedically impaired, or other health impaired, or children with specific learning disabilities, who by reason thereof require special education and related services. (Sec. 602(1))

PL 91-230 represented the first recognition of learning disability as a separate category and offered a lengthy definition in Section 602. This category, known as a "specific learning disability," was distinguished from other disabilities that affect learning (e.g., mental retardation) but which are not "learning disabilities" as such.

The act also created the Bureau for the Education and Training of the Handicapped within the United States Office of Education and made available for the first time substantial amounts of money for projects affecting handicapped students. These projects included the creation of centers to serve deaf-blind children, research to meet the full range of special educational needs of students, training for professionals and other staff engaged in educational programs, dissemination of information and materials about effective special education practices, creation of the National Center on Educational Media and Materials for the Handicapped, and funding of special programs for children with specific learning disabilities.

The Education for All Handicapped Children Act of 1975 (PL 94-142)

This act was passed to amend and expand several of the provisions of the earlier EHA. In 1984, further amendments were made to PL 94-142 and the original Education for Handicapped Children Act, in the form of PL 98-199.

PL 94-142 listed several Congressional findings as indications of the need for new legislation regarding the education of handicapped children:

1. There were over 8 million handicapped children in the United States, and the needs of these children were not being fully met. Fully one-half of all handicapped children were not receiving appropriate services to enable them an equal educational opportunity.
2. More than 1 million handicapped children were excluded entirely from public education and from the benefit of experiencing the public educational process with their peers.
3. Because of the lack of services, many families, at their own expense, had to transport their children great distances to obtain even minimal services.

In order to remedy these concerns, the bill states:

> It is the purpose of this Act to assure that all handicapped children have available to them . . . a free appropriate public education which emphasizes special educational and related services designed to meet their unique needs, to assure the rights of handicapped children and their parents are protected, to assist states and localities to provide for the education of all handicapped children, and to assess and assure the effectiveness of efforts to educate handicapped children. (Sec. 601(c)).

Special Education and Related Services

Under the provisions of this act, "special education" may include specially designed classroom instruction, physical education, home-based instruction, and instruction in hospitals. "Related services" may include transportation, speech pathology and audi-ology, psychological services, physical and occupational therapy, recreation, counseling, and medical services for evaluation and diagnostic purposes.

Individualized Education Program (IEP)

The act also requires that students receive a written statement of their educational needs, and how those needs are to be met. Children who have been previously underserved are to become the states' top priority, followed by those with the most severe disabilities.

Least Restrictive Environment

Schools are required to educate children in what has come to be known as the "least restrictive environment" (LRE), although this phrase does not appear in the actual statute, but is a part of the *regulations*. The popularization of this term points out the power of regulations in addition to legislation. Handicapped students are to be educated to the greatest degree possible, in settings with other children who are not handicapped.

Due Process

Handicapped children and their parents have new and strengthened rights of due process. That is, before any actions are taken with a child who is handicapped, or suspected of having a handicap, the parents must be provided in writing, in their native language, a full explanation of their rights of due process; a description of the action that the school proposes to take, and why such action is warranted; and a description of any tests or other information that were used to come to this recommendation. There are five elements to due process:

1. Reasonable notice of any impending or proposed changes in services,
2. The right to a hearing before an impartial hearing officer,
3. The right to gather evidence, present a defense, and have the support of lawyers and advocates,
4. A written statement of the proceedings and conclusions the school must produce after a hearing,

5. The right of the student, parents, or school district to appeal against the decision of a hearing.

Priorities

Under this legislation, two priorities are stipulated. The first priority for expenditure and services are handicapped children who are not currently receiving an education. The second priority is to serve, within each category of disability, the most severely handicapped students who are not receiving an adequate education.

Financing

PL 94-142 is an excellent example of the difference between authorization and appropriation of funds. This act authorizes funds to be spent on special education; however, once authorized, these funds must be appropriated by Congress. Particularly in recent years of budget cuts, it is possible that reduced appropriations could diminish the power of the act.

CONCLUSION

Legal and legislative initiatives have changed in conjunction with practical applications and philosophical developments over the years. Services to people with disabilities have evolved slowly over the last century, with the rate of change accelerating as a result of the passage of several pieces of federal legislation in the 1970s. In recent decades, legislation has guaranteed a variety of rights for persons with disabilities.

For the rest of this century, activity probably will focus less on the delineation of new rights and more on the use of legislation and litigation to make existing rights into realities. The threats to these rights today come from budget cuts and Supreme Court decisions that may, in a few years, eradicate several decades of legal progress.

A decade ago, in September of 1977, the President's Committee on Mental Retardation called the first national conference on mentally retarded citizens and the law. The 250 attorneys, advocates, and professionals who attended that conference developed a description of the current legal status of persons with mental retardation and other disabilities, as well as a set of conclusions and recommendations (President's Committee on Mental Retardation and National Association for Retarded Citizens, 1977). It is surprising (and a bit depressing) to note that a decade later, many of the issues remain the same.

The conference participants stated that there was a need for people with disabilities to have more substantial levels of personal income, without a loss of eligibility for various entitlement programs. This need continues today.

The participants also stated that there was a need to divert Title XIX funds away from institutional settings and into the development of community-based settings. Since 1977, such legislation has been introduced in community and family living amendments. However, there are still many hurdles between the introduction of this needed bill and the passage of a legislative landmark that would provide the "residential equivalent" of PL 94-142.

Finally, the participants stated the need for legislation to authorize the Justice Department to initiate litigation where there is cause to believe that disabled persons in institutions are being deprived of their constitutional rights. Today that legal authority exists, but the department has been criticized by some members of Congress and other advocates for failing to use its power.

One additional statement from the participants of the conference continues to hold true:

> While litigation and legislation have been potent forces in achieving social change, these strategies must be viewed as two of several means available to effectuate change on behalf of the mentally retarded and developmentally disabled citizens. However, the time is right to utilize these processes as a part of a broader social change process — one more closely integrated with other efforts. Real change is, in large part, dependent upon our ability to change social attitudes, and educate the public regarding our goals. (p. 21)

REFERENCES

Abeson, A. (1976). Litigation. In Weintraub, F. J., Abeson, A., Ballard, J., & LaVor, M. L. (Eds.), *Public policy and the education of exceptional children.* (pp. 240–258). Reston, VA: Council for Exceptional Children.

Beattie v. State Board of Education, 169 Wisc. 231, 172 N.W. 153 (1919).

Biklen, D. (1981). *The least restrictive environment: Its application to education.* Syracuse, NY: Special Education Resource Center, Syracuse University.

Brown v. Board of Education, 347 U.S. 483 (1954).

Developmental Disabilities Assistance and Bill of Rights Act of 1975, PL 94-103.

Developmental Disabilities and Bill of Rights Act of 1984, PL 98-527.

Developmental Disabilities Services and Facilities Construction Amendments of 1970, PL 91-517.

Diana v. State Board of Education, Civil Action No. C70 37RFP(N.D.Cal.January 7, 1970 and June 18, 1973).

Education for All Handicapped Children Act of 1975, PL 94-14.

Education of All Handicapped Children Act, 1975, PL 94-142.

Education of the Handicapped Act of, 1970, PL 91-230.

Ferguson, D. l; Ferguson, P. M., & Bogdan, R. (1987). If mainstreaming is the answer, what is the question? In V. Richardson-Koeler (Ed.) *Educators handbook: A research perspective* (pp. 394–419). NY: Longman.

Haring, N. G. (Ed.). (1982). *Exceptional children and youth.* Columbus, OH: Charles E. Merrill.

Mental Retardation Facilities and Community Mental Health Centers Construction Act of 1963, PL 88-164.

Mental Retardation Facilities and Community Mental Health Centers Construction Act of 1965, PL 89-105.

Payne, J. S., & Patton, J. R. (1981). *Mental Retardation.* Columbus, OH: Charles E. Merrill.

Pennsylvania Association for Retarded Citizens v. the Commonwealth of Pennsylvania, 334F. Supp. 1257 (E.D. Pa., 1971).

President's Committee on Mental Retardation and National Association for Retarded Citizens. (1977). *The future of legal services for mentally retarded persons.* Washington, DC: President's Committee on Mental Retardation.

Scheerenberger, R. C. (1983). *A history of mental retardation.* Baltimore, MD: Paul H. Brookes.

Taylor, S. J., & Biklen, D. (1980). *Understanding the law: An advocate's guide to the law and developmental disabilities.* Syracuse, NY: Human Policy Press.

Vocational Rehabilitation Act, 1973, PL 93-112.

Watson v. City of Cambridge, 1883 157 Mass. 561, 32 N.E. 864.

Table 1
Appendix 11-1: A Chronology of Federal Legislation Affecting Persons with Disabilities

Date	Title
1827	An Act to provide for the location of the two townships of land reserved for a seminary of learning in the territory of Florida, and to complete the location of the grant to the Deaf and Dumb Asylum of Kentucky
1855	An Act to establish in the District of Columbia a government hospital for the insane
1857	An Act to establish the Columbian Institute for the Deaf and Dumb
1879	An Act to promote the education of the blind
1898	An Act regulating postage on letters written by the blind
1904	An Act to promote the circulation of reading matter among the blind
1918	Vocational Rehabilitation Act (for discharged military personnel)
1920	An Act to provide for promotion of vocational rehabilitation of persons disabled in industry of otherwise and their return to civil employment
1921	An Act to establish a Veteran's Bureau and to improve the facilities and services of such bureau and further to amend and modify the War Risk Insurance Act
1924	World War Veteran's Act of 1924
1927	An Act to amend paragraph (1) of Section 22 of the Interstate Commerce Act by providing for the carrying of a blind person, with a guide, for one fare
1931	An Act to provide books for the adult blind
1935	Social Security Act
1936	To authorize the operation of stands in federal buildings by blind persons, to enlarge the economic opportunities of the blind, and for other purposes
1937	To provide special rates of postage on matter for the blind

Date	*Title*
1938	To create a Committee on Purchases of Blind-made Products and for other purposes—Wagner-O'Day Act of 1938
1941	To permit seeing eye dogs to enter government buildings when accompanied by their blind masters, and for other purposes
1943	To amend Title I of Public Law Number 2, 73rd Congress, March 30, 1933, and the Veterans Regulation to provide for rehabilitation of disabled veterans, and for other purposes
1943	Vocational Rehabilitation Act Amendments of 1943
1948	To amend the Civil Service Act to remove certain discrimination with respect to the appointment of persons having any physical handicap to positions in the classified civil service
1954	To authorize cooperative research in education
1954	Vocational Rehabilitation Amendments of 1954
1956	To amend the Interstate Commerce Act in order to authorize common carriers and such attendants at the usual fare charged for one person
1958	To provide in the Department of HEW a loan service of captioned films for the deaf
1958	To encourage expansion of teaching in the education of mentally retarded children through grants to institutions of higher learning and to state educational agencies
1961	To make available to children who are handicapped by deafness the specially trained teachers of the deaf
1962	To provide for the production and distribution of education and training films for use by deaf persons, and for other purposes
1962	To establish in the Library of Congress a library of musical scores and other instructional materials to further educational, vocational, and cultural opportunities in the field of music for blind persons
1962	To amend the Public Health Service Act to provide for the establishment of an Institute of Child Health & Human Development
1963	Mental Retardation Facilities & Community Mental Health Centers Construction Act of 1963
1965	National Technical Institute for the Deaf Act
1965	Mental Retardation Facilities & Community Mental Health Centers Constructions Act of 1965
1966	Model Secondary School for the Deaf Act
1967	Mental Health Amendments of 1967
1967	Vocational Rehabilitation Amendments of 1967
1967	Mental Retardation Amendments of 1967
1968	Vocational Rehabilitation Amendments of 1968
1968	Elimination of Architectural Barriers to Physically Handicapped
1968	Handicapped Children's Early Education Assistance Act
1968	Health Services and Facilities Amendments of 1968
1968	Vocational Education Amendments of 1968
1969	To provide for a National Center on Educational Media and Materials for the Handicapped and for other purposes
1970	To insure that certain federally constructed facilities be constructed so as to be accessible to the physically handicapped
1970	To provide grants for construction of community mental health centers
1970	To revise certain procedures for handling mentally retarded persons in the Forest Haven Institution in the District of Columbia
1970	Developmental Disabilities Services and Facilities Construction Amendments of 1970
1970	Occupational Safety and Health Act of 1970
1970	Housing and Urban Development Act of 1970
1971	Wagner-O'Day Amendments
1971	Intermediate Care Amendments of 1971
1972	Free or reduced-rate transportation for attendants for the blind
1972	Education Amendments of 1972
1972	Maternal and Child Health Amendments
1972	Rights of the blind and other physically handicapped in the District of Columbia
1973	Older Americans Comprehensive Services Amendments of 1973

Date	Title
1973	Maternal and Child Health Amendments
1973	Committee for Purchase of Products and Services of the Blind and Other Handicapped
1973	Rehabilitation Amendments of 1973
1973	Domestic Volunteer Services Act of 1973
1973	Lead-based Paint Poisoning Prevention Amendments
1974	Supplemental Security Income Benefits
1974	General Education Amendments
1974	National School Lunch & Child Nutrition Act of 1974
1974	National Mass Transportation Assistance Act of 1974
1974	Rehabilitation Act Amendments of 1974
1975	National Arthritis Act of 1974
1975	National Health Planning & Resources Development Act of 1974
1975	Education for All Handicapped Children Act

Note. From *Public Policy and the Education of Exceptional Children* by F. J. Weintraub, A. Abeson, J. Ballard and M. L. Lavor (Eds.), 1980. Reston, VA: Copyright 1976 by the Council for Exceptional Children. Adapted by permission.

Table 2. Glossary of Legal Terms

Abstention doctrine: the princple that federal courts will not hear a case if it can be decided by state courts on the basis of state law alone.

Act: a law passed by a legislature; synonym for statute.

Amicus curiae (pl. amici): "friend of the court." This term refers to a third party — a person or organization — who, while having no direct legal interest in the outcome of a lawsuit, submits briefs and, on occasion, evidence to a court in support of a position.

Appeal: an application to a higher court to reverse, modify, or change the ruling of a lower court. An appeal is usually based on the lower court's interpretation of the law or on the manner in which it conducted a case.

Bill: a proposed statute, not yet law.

Brief: a lawyer's written summary of the law and/or facts involved in a particular case.

Capacity: the legal ability to sue or be sued, based on a person's presumed ability to exercise his or her rights.

Cause of action: the legal damage or injury on which a lawsuit is based. There must be a cause of action, or legal "wrong" for a court to consider a case.

Class action: Most lawsuits are individual actions. A class action is a lawsuit brought by one or more persons on their own behalf and on behalf of all persons in similar circumstances ("similarly situated"). A court's ruling in a class action suit applies to all members of the "class."

Common law: the body of law derived from historical usage, as opposed to statutory (written) law.

Complaint: a formal legal document submitted to a court by one or more persons (the plaintiffs) aledges their rights have been violated and demands that the defendants take certain corrective action (relief).

Consent (informed): an intelligent, knowing, and voluntary agreement by someone to a given activity or procedure, such as a medical operation, a scientific experiment, or a commercial contract. The person must be capable of understanding the circumstances and factors surrounding a particular consent decision, information relevant to the decision must be forthrightly and intelligibly provided to the person; and the person must be free to give or withhold consent voluntarily.

Consent agreement (consent judgment or consent decree): a court-ratified and enforced agreement between opposing parties that resolves the consented issues in a lawsuit. A consent agreement, reached after the initiation of a lawsuit, carries the same weight as any other court order because it is ratified by a court.

Constitutional right: a right guaranteed by the United States Constitution or by the constitution of the state in which a person resides.

Discovery: the method of obtaining information possessed by the opposing party in the lawsuit. There are several types of discovery: depositions to obtain oral testimony and interrogatories to obtain written answers to specific questions, requests for documents or materials, requests for mental or physical examinations, and requests for admissions (i.e., that the opposing party admit the truth of certain statements or objective facts).

Due process: a right guaranteed under the 5th and 14th Amendments to the United States Constitution. Substantive due process refers to all citizens' fundamental rights to life, liberty, and property. Procedural due process refers to the fairness of procedures involved in any action that deprives people of their rights.

Equal protection: a right guaranteed by the 14th Amendment that states all citizens are entitled to equal protection under the law; that is, to be free from discrimination in the exercise of rights, except where the state demonstrates a rational basis or compelling interest for apparently unequal treatment.

Evidence: documentation or oral evidence submitted to a court in support of the position of one of the opposing parties to a suit.

Exhaustion of administrative remedies: the doctrine that a person must attempt to resolve issues administratively before filing a lawsuit.

Finding of fact: a determination of the facts in the case, made by a judge or jury. Finding of fact is distinct from a conclusion of law, which only a judge can make.

Guardian: an individual who has the legal authority to make decisions on behalf of another.

Habeas corpus: an order (writ of *habeas corpus*) issued by a court to release a person from unlawful confinement.

Injunctive relief: an order from a court that requires or prohibits the performance of specific acts, in order to remedy the violation of legally protected rights.

Jurisdiction: the authority of a court to hear and decide a suit.

Money damages: court-awarded financial payment for injuries suffered by one party due to the action or inaction of another.

Motion: a request to the court in the context of a specific case to take some action relating to the case.

Opinion: a judge's statement of the reasons for a decision.

Order: a judge's statement.

Ordinance: a local law; that is, a city, town, or county law.

PL (Public Law): the designation of a federal law. The numbers following "PL" refer respectively to the session of Congress during which the law was passed and the order in which the law was passed in that session. For example, PL 94-142 was the 142nd law passed during the 94th Congress.

Party: the plaintiff or defendant in a lawsuit.

Petitioner: the party appealing a court's decision to a higher court. The term is a synonym for appellant. It may also be used to identify the plaintiff in certain courts or types of cases.

Plaintiff: the party who brings a lawsuit, alleging a violation of rights.

Pleadings: the documents submitted to a court in the pretrial stage of litigation. The term is used broadly to refer to the plaintiff's initial complaint, the defendant's answer, and the plaintiff's reply to the answer, and it is sometimes used more narrowly to refer to the plaintiff's complaint.

Precedent: a prior court decision in a relevant case, cited in the interpretation of a law or constitutional provision.

Preliminary injunction: a form of injunctive relief. A preliminary injunction is a temporary order to prevent a party from taking certain actions pending the court's final decision.

Private cause of action: an individual's ability to seek relief from a court for the violation of a statutory or constitutional right (see standing).

Relief: the remedy to some legal wrong or violation of one's rights. Plaintiffs seek from the court certain types of injunctive relief against the defendants, such as declaratory relief (in which the court confirms the rights of the plaintiffs), writs of *habeas corpus* (release), or money damages.

Remand: an order by a higher court returning a case to a lower court for further action consistent with the higher court's decision.

Respondent: the winning party at the trial level in a case that has been appealed.

Review: a reexamination of a court's decision by that same court or by an appeals court.

Sovereign immunity: the legal doctrine that protects the state and federal governments from certain kinds of suits in certain courts, on the general theory that the government ("sovereign") should be free to exercise its authority within reasonable limits.

Special master: a person appointed by a court to monitor, implement, or supervise the implementation of the court's order, or to provide reports to a court prior to a decision.

Standing: the requirement that a plaintiff be an injured party or one in danger of being injured. In other words, a plaintiff must have a direct interest in a suit in addition to a cause of action. Parents or guardians have standing to sue on behalf of their wards.

Statute: a law passed by a state or federal legislature; synonym for "act."

Statute of limitations: a statute that specifies the period of time within which a lawsuit must be brought after an alleged violation of rights. A person loses his or her right to sue after the time period has elapsed.

Stay: a court order postponing the enforcement of a court ruling pending further legal action, such as an appeal to a higher court.

Summary judgment: a judge's ruling on the law in a case where the judge holds that the facts are not in dispute.

Temporary restraining order: a form of emergency injunctive relief, issued (often without a hearing) to preserve the status quo for a brief period pending a full hearing before the court. A party must show that immediate and irreparable harm will result if the order is not issued. For longer-term relief before the court's final decision, a preliminary injunction is necessary.

Tort: a civil wrong for which a private individual may recover money damages. False imprisonment and invasion of privacy are examples of torts.

Verdict: a judge's or jury's decision on a matter submitted in a lawsuit.

Writ of *certiorari*: a request to the United States Supreme Court to review a lower court's ruling. The Supreme Court usually will only hear cases it considers to involve a constitutional question such as due process, free speech, or equal protection.

Note. From *Understanding the Law: An Advocate's Guide to the Law and Developmental Disabilities* by S. J. Taylor and D. Biklen, 1980. Syracuse, NY: Human Policy Press. Copyright 1980 by Human Policy Press. Adapted by permission.

PART III

Specific Disabilities

CHAPTER 12

Childhood Asthma

Thomas L. Creer, Richard J. Marion and Deborah L. Harm

Purcell and Weiss (1970) noted that, historically, asthma has traveled a winding path from being considered a symptom of the central nervous system, to being an immunological disorder, to being "a symptom whose interpretation depends on the particular spectacles through which one is peering" (p. 597). This statement is still true, although the number of spectacles has decreased in recent years and they are primarily worn by immunologists, physiologists, biochemists, and other biological scientists. Three developments illustrate this trend. The first was the discovery by Ishizawka and Ishizawka (1967) of human IgE, the immunoglobulin thought responsible for 95% of allergic reactions, including allergy-triggered asthma. Williams (1982) succinctly describes the role of IgE both in asthma and in attempts to control the disorder:

> Inhaled or ingested antigen bridges IgE antibodies, coating the surface of mast cells, perhaps within the airway lumen, to cause mediator release. Cromolyn prevents this reaction by stabilizing the membrane of the mast cell. Stimulation of intracellular c-AMP by adrenergic drugs, and indirectly by theophylline, inhibits the release of mediators. These drugs also act directly on smooth muscle in the airways to reduce bronchoconstriction. The mediators released from mast cells, notably histamine, produce bronchoconstriction to a variety of inhaled agents and local phenomena, such as the heat exchange induced by exercise, to cause reflex bronchoconstriction via the cholinergic arc. This is blocked by anticholinergic drugs, which also inhibit mediator release from mast cells. (p. 24)

Such immunological factors are thought responsible for the asthma suffered by a large proportion of asthmatic patients, particularly children and young adults (Pearlman, 1984).

A second trend has been the implication of exercise or physical exertion in precipitating asthma (e.g., Chen & Horton, 1977; Deal, McFadden, Ingram, Strauss & Jaeger, 1979). Evidence suggests the development and severity of airway obstruction are due to the degree of airway coolness that takes place during exertion (McFadden, 1984). Airway coolness, in turn, is an immediate

177

function of the exchange of air within the airways. Most asthmatic children (80–90%) show increased bronchial sensitivity to exercise (Price, 1984).

A final trend concerns research on families of molecular chemicals that appear especially effective in increasing vascular permeability and producing bronchoconstriction. Research showed that inhalation of prostaglandin D_2, the most abundant prostanoid generated by human lung mast cells, led to bronchoconstriction in both normal and asthmatic subjects (Hardy, Robinson, Tattersfield & Holgate, 1984). Considering the decrease in pulmonary functioning that occurred with the asthmatic subjects, Hardy and his colleagues concluded that prostaglandin D_2 may be involved in the pathogenesis of bronchoconstriction in allergic asthma. There is also evidence that prostaglandins of the F-series are potent bronchoconstrictors, especially where abnormal levels of the compounds in tissues may occur in some asthmatic patients after aspirin ingestion or prostaglandin infusion for obstetrical purposes (deShazo & Salvaggio, 1984). Evidence also has linked bronchoconstriction to another family of bronchoconstrictors, the leukotrienes C, D, and E (more generally known as the reacting substance of anaphylaxis, or SRS-A). An investigation by Griffin et al. (1983) demonstrated that airflow reduction caused by inhalation of leukotriene D was not only more prolonged (44 minutes) than with inhalation of histamine (20 minutes), a chemical commonly used to challenge asthmatic patients, but was on the average 140 times more potent a bronchoconstrictor than histamine. The significance of this finding was summarized by Weissmann (1983):

> Perhaps an analogy can be drawn with the exploration of the New World: The colonists exploring the leukotrienes have laid out the eastern landscape from Plymouth to Savannah; we confidently await reports of the broad Mississippi, the awesome Rockies, and in due time, the blue Pacific. (p. 455)

Three conclusions emerge from the above discussion. First, the evidence is overwhelmingly clear that asthma is a physical disorder. Despite opinions dating back to antiquity that the disorder is neurological or psychological in origin, there are no data to support such a contention (Creer, 1982; Pearlman, 1984). As noted, above current medications are based upon immunological and biochemical research; the cure for the disorder, whenever the goal is attained, will rest upon this same foundation. Second, the recognition that asthma is a physical disorder has greatly enhanced the role behavioral scientists can play in assisting asthmatic patients. Thus, instead of searching for a nonexistent psychological cure for the disorder — a pursuit that heretofore has dominated the attention of many behavioral scientists (Creer, in press; Purcell & Weiss, 1970; Renne & Creer, 1985) — psychologists can focus their efforts on assisting asthmatic patients to acquire skills for preventing attacks, such as learning to comply with medication instructions, or to ameliorate ongoing episodes, such as practicing self-management techniques (Creer, 1978, 1979, in press; Creer, Harm, & Marion, in press). Finally, the brief description of recent developments in asthma management illustrates the complexity of the disorder and this feature becomes more apparent in examining its characteristics.

DESCRIPTION

Asthma has been known through history; descriptions of the disorder are found in the writings of Hippocrates (McFadden & Stevens, 1983), although Areataeus and Galen in the Christian Era are credited with presenting the first detailed discussions. However, despite other accurate narratives on the disorder, including those made by Moses Maimonides in the 12th century and Sir John Floyer late in the 17th century, it has proven almost impossible to define operationally. Two reasons for this difficulty are noted by Creer, Harm, and Marion (in press). First, while the functional definition of asthma proposed in 1959 has been widely accepted, the degree of reversibility required to confirm a diagnosis of asthma has not been determined (Fletcher & Pride,

1984). Thus, although it is agreed that airway obstruction must be reversed, the precise degree of reversibility is debatable. Second, it has proven impossible to define asthma so as to exclude all other types of respiratory disorders. One study team concluded after considerable deliberation that its definition would include approximately 25% of patients with chronic bronchitis (Porter & Birch, 1971).

Despite difficulties in arriving at a precise and exclusionary definition of asthma, it may be characterized as an intermittent, variable, and reversible airway obstruction (Chai, 1975).

Intermittent Nature

Asthma attacks suffered by most patients occur on an intermittent basis. The frequency of asthmatic episodes varies among patients, and for any given patient. Thus, a patient may experience a number of attacks over a brief period of time, but then remain free of episodes over weeks, months, or even years.

The frequency of attacks experienced by a patient over time is a function of the stimuli that trigger the attacks (Creer, in press). Many patients, particularly youngsters, suffer asthma only during certain seasons; airborne allergens in the environment are the chief culprit. Children may suffer occasional attacks during other periods of the year, particularly if a viral infection is already present; overall, however, attacks are endemic to a given season. In their authoritative review of childhood asthma, Siegel, Katz, and Rachelefsky (1983) reported that regardless of where youngsters reside, asthma attacks generally occur more often and are more severe in the fall. While the reasons for this finding are unclear, explanations suggested by Siegel and his colleagues include an increased frequency of viral infections, temperature and humidity changes, increased air pollution, and greater exposure to house dust.

Other children are less fortunate; they have what is called perennial or intrinsic asthma, in that they are apt to experience asthma during all seasons of the year. There must be some reversibility of the condition in order for the diagnosis of asthma to be confirmed, but many youngsters with perennial asthma experience symptoms almost daily that range from a sensation of tightness in the chest to mild wheezing. The primary reason patients experience perennial asthma is heightened airway responsiveness. As described by Pearlman (1984), "The lower airways behave as if they were hyperirritable, over-responsive to various chemical mediators of physiologic and inflammatory processes and to a large number of unrelated stimuli, many of which have the capacity to activate or release these substances" (p. 460). In contrast to those with seasonal asthma, youngsters with perennial asthma are more responsive to an array of attack precipitants, such as viral infections, allergens, exercise, cold air, chemicals, and environmental factors. Thus, while exposure to the same stimuli will fail either to trigger an attack in a child with seasonal asthma or to precipitate an occasional mild asthmatic episode, it may induce what seems an endless series of attacks in the youngster with perennial asthma.

To further complicate the intermittent nature of asthma, it is impossible to make a differential diagnosis of either perennial (intrinsic) or seasonal (extrinsic) asthma. These are not mutually exclusive categories, a fact that has hampered research (e.g., Clark, 1977; Creer, 1979). The fact that a child with perennial asthma may experience more attacks during a particular season and a youngster with seasonal asthma may experience more virus-induced attacks during a given year has a number of ramifications for researchers (Renne & Creer, 1985). It was a factor leading Clark (1977) to advise, "Patients should wherever possible be used as their own controls, and comparisons between subjects should be kept to a minimum" (p. 226).

Variable Nature

Williams (1980) suggests that asthma has eluded a precise definition because it is an extremely variable condition. Variability refers to fluctuations in the severity of both attacks and the condition itself. Attacks can range from a mild wheeze resulting from a nonbacterial respiratory infection to fatal occlusion of the airways, predominantly by mucus plugs. Williams points out that although conventional definitions of variable or reversible airway obstruction are sufficiently broad to embrace all patients afflicted with the condition, they necessarily overlap with other forms of obstructive pulmonary disease.

Attack severity varies among patients, and within the same patient. At one end of the continuum there are asthmatic children who occasionally suffer mild wheezing. For these youngsters, asthma is little more than a nuisance; they may experience some unpleasantness during attacks, but the condition does not ordinarily interfere with their daily lives (Creer, 1983). At the other end of the continuum, Jones (1976), has described children whose asthma is characterized more by persistent respiratory debilitation than by discrete attacks (although some reversibility should occur if the diagnosis of asthma is confirmed). At this extreme, asthma can become a prepotent consideration in dictating the lifestyle of patients and their families (Creer, 1983).

Because of the variable nature of asthma, there is no standard way of classifying a given attack as mild, moderate, or severe, or patients as having mild, moderate, or severe symptoms. A number of schemes have been suggested — usually based upon the potency, dosage, and schedule of medications taken by patients to control their asthma — but none has found widespread acceptance (Creer, 1982). Another major problem is the difficulty in assessing both asthma and any treatment developed for its alleviation. The problems are well described by Clark (1977):

The benchmark of asthma is its variability, and this in itself makes any assessment of treatment most difficult. Trials are usually undertaken in patients who are in a stable state to minimize this problem, but this state is uncharacteristic of the majority of patients who will be requiring the treatment under test and ignores long-term fluctuations in severity. Variability

may itself lead to difficulties in assessing the response to treatment, particularly when symptoms are present at night. A combination of diary cards and regular measurements of the peak expiratory flow rate has simplified the problem caused by short-term variability, but has not excluded them. The problems of assessing variability is compounded by the fact that any measurement of lung obstruction may not reflect all the variable changes in lung function. (p. 225)

Reversible Nature

The airway obstruction that characterizes asthma reverses either spontaneously or with adequate treatment. The reversible component in resistance to airflow is the *sine qua non* of asthma (McFadden, 1980); it differentiates the condition from other respiratory disorders, such as emphysema, where no reversibility of the physical impairment is possible.

The reversible nature of asthma presents a number of problems to medical and behavioral scientists (Creer, in press; Creer & Winder, 1986; Renne & Creer, 1985). Asthma is at best a relative condition; although the attacks of many children may completely remit, there are youngsters in whom the degree of remission is far less clear. A study by Loren and co-workers (1978), for example, found that many asthmatic children had reduced airflow that was irreversible with intensive treatment, including the administration of corticosteroids. This study brings into question the criterion of reversibility as a characteristic of asthma if there are indeed patients who, despite fulfilling all other criteria demanded for diagnosis, fail to show reversibility of their symptoms. Only future research, coupled with ongoing refinement of the diagnostic criteria now employed, will eventually clarify the matter.

The spontaneous remission of asthma also adds a degree of uncertainty regarding treatment outcome (Creer, Harm, & Marion, in press; Renne & Creer, 1985). Simply put, how do we know if the treatment resulted in any observable changes that may have occurred? An aim is to provide answers under tightly controlled conditions in which a functional relationship can be established between the application of the treatment procedure and the remission of the asthmatic symptoms (Creer, 1978). Even under these types of conditions, however, there is uncertainty. As noted by Clark (1977), "The response to treatment appears to be influenced by factors independent of the treatment given" (p. 225). The matter of spontaneous remission of asthma becomes more complex when considering attacks that occur in the day-to-day lives of patients. As Creer (1979) pointed out, there are a number of studies in the literature in which spontaneous remission cannot be ruled out as an explanation for the treatment outcome observed. The variability of spontaneous remission defies control even in the best-designed study.

Epidemiology

In her excellent review, Smith (1983) complained:

> For asthma, allergic rhinitis, and eczema, examining epidemilogical and natural history information is like looking at a collection of jigsaw puzzle pieces that may or may not belong to a single puzzle. Much of the available data are incomplete or are difficult to compare because of differences in definition and methods. (p. 771)

The enigma is reflected in surveys on the prevalence of childhood asthma. The American Lung Association (1975) noted that separate surveys have estimated that from 5 to 15% of American children suffer asthma. Such a difference would involve millions of children. As pointed out by Creer (1979) this variance makes it difficult to establish health care policy for the disorder in the United States. Estimating the prevalence of asthma is further complicated by analyzing data gathered from worldwide surveys. Smith (1983) listed a number of studies in which 0 to 20% of the children sampled reportedly suffered asthma. Smith concluded that data regarding the prevalence of asthma in children

are more valid than those gathered from adults, as half of the adult population may be misdiagnosed as having chronic bronchitis instead of asthma.

Smith (1983) summarized several interesting epidemiological findings regarding childhood asthma. She noted that the high prevalence rate of the disorder is similar in England, Australia, Scotland, New Zealand, and the United States. Asthma is rare among children from New Guinea and West Africa and also uncommon among American Indians and Eskimos. However, there are areas where childhood asthma, once considered unknown or rare, is on the increase. The best example is provided by a survey conducted on an atoll in the Maldives that is used as a base by the Royal Air Force. Whereas the disorder was rare in the past, 20% of the children under age 15 were diagnosed as asthmatic in 1979. Smith (1983) concluded that if such large increases are not accounted for by differences in methodology or definition, environmental factors must be targeted as the cause of such changes.

Two other important topics in epidemiology concern morbidity and mortality.

Morbidity

The morbidity of childhood asthma is commonly measured by three indices: activity restriction, hospital admissions, and school absenteeism. Leaving the last topic for a later section, the present discussion will review activity restriction and hospital admissions.

1. *Activity restriction.* It was recently noted that epidemiologists and pediatricians in the United States were concerned about a growing number of youngsters afflicted with childhood illness, including asthma. Indeed, surveys conducted by the National Center for Health Statistics reveal such a trend. In a survey of selected health characteristics conducted in 1958, for example, the number of youngsters estimated to suffer a chronic illness was 1.7% (Linder et al., 1959). By 1981, the number of youngsters suffering from chronic illness had more than doubled to 3.8% (*Vital and Health Statistics*, 1983). Methodological differences may account for a small percent of this

change — the survey in 1958 sampled children 15 years and younger, and the survey in 1981 sampled those 17 years and younger — but alone do not account for the doubling of chronic diseases in the United States. If anything, better sampling methodology would reduce this variance. It is likely instead that more chronically ill children, formerly doomed to die at an early age, are living longer. This theory would not be true of asthma, but certainly is the case with another childhood respiratory disorder, cystic fibrosis. Environmental factors also may influence the prevalence of chronic disorders. For example, exposure of mothers to toxic agents during pregnancy may affect their offspring (Clark, Gosnell, Abramson, & Leslie, 1983). And, as Smith (1983) pointed out earlier, environmental factors certainly must be considered a factor in the growing incidence of childhood asthma.

2. *Hospitalization data.* Dorland Davis (1972), former director of the National Institue of Allergy and Infectious Diseases, presented data that indicated there were 134,000 patient discharges with a diagnosis of asthma or hay fever in 1968. The average hospital stay was 8.3 days; the estimated hospitalization cost totaled 62 million dollars. However, the data did not distinguish between children and adults, or between asthma and hay fever. A more recent study fills in gaps in the previous data. The Hospital Discharge Survey (HDS), conducted annually by the National Center for Health Statistics, reflects a national stratified sample of all discharges from nonfederal hospitals. Mullally, Grauman, Evans, and Kaslow (1985) examined all hospital discharges for children less than 15 years of age from 1965 until 1982. Discharge data ($\pm$ SE) in thousands and hospital rates per 100,000 children, during a period when asthma nosology remained constant, are:

	1965	1978
White	21.7 ± 1/46	35.7 ± 3.89
Nonwhite	6.8 ± 0.9/85	25.5 ± 2.8/309

Mullally and his colleagues note that for the years studied, asthma was more prevalent in males and during the months of September to November; it was less prevalent in New England and the West Coast. In this significant study, they concluded that hospitalizations for asthma among children significantly increased during 1965 to 1982, especially among the nonwhite population.

Russo (1985) recently cited findings for other physical disorders regarding hospital admissions among children in the Boston area for 1882 and 1982. In 1882, the leading cause of hospital admissions was rickets; a century later in 1982, the leading cause was asthma.

Mortality

Generally, the greatest impact of asthma is reflected in morbidity rather than mortality data. The death rate from asthma in the United States gradually decreased in the period surveyed by Davis (1972) and Karetzky (1975). In children up to the age of 19 years, the number of deaths in Canada ranged from 12 in 1972 to 23 in 1976 (Collins-Williams, Zalesky, Battu, & Chambers, 1981). A total of 127 Canadian youngsters succumbed to asthma in the years between 1971 and 1977.

Recently, Sly (1984) reported an increase in deaths from childhood asthma in the United States. He noted that deaths of asthmatic children younger than 15 years were 54 in 1977, 60 in 1978, 63 in 1979, and 90 in 1980. Furthermore, the death rate among children 10 to 14 years of age increased from 0.1 to 0.3 per 100,000. There was no geographic pattern to this increase, but death rates did increase more sharply for blacks than for whites.

Data from the National Center for Health Statistics showed that in 1982, the last year surveyed, 104 children under 15 years of age died from asthma (*Advance report of final mortality statistics*, 1982). The death rate among blacks (2.3 per 100,000) was almost double that reported for whites (1.2 per 100,000), but no breakdown was provided according to age.

While there has been a reported increase in deaths due to asthma, few reasons are offered to account for such a finding. A revision of the code used to classify deaths accounts for some but not all of the results (Sly, 1984). Strunk, Wolfson, Labrecque, and Mrazek (1984) suggested that psychological factors were prominent in the deaths of 21 former residents of a treatment facility for asthma between 1973 and 1982. However, Creer (1985) has pointed out that these findings not only were endemic to that particular facility, but seemingly resulted because the patients did not practice self-management skills to control their condition.

DEVELOPMENTAL ISSUES

The clinical picture of children with asthma varies markedly at different age levels, due to the physical and psychological changes taking place during normal development. Medical and behavioral scientists must remain sensitive to this dynamic interaction between developmental changes and childhood asthma. At the same time, youngsters with asthma must learn to cope with a disease process that changes as a result of their development.

Sex Ratio

A preponderance of boys develop asthma. Typically the ratio of boys to girls has been estimated to be 2:1; however, epidemiological reports have varied from as high as 4:1 to as low as 3:2 (Siegel et al., 1983). As asthmatic children mature and approach adulthood, the sex ratio becomes equal. For reasons not clearly understood, the development of asthma symptoms in many girls is delayed until they reach their teens or early twenties and then tends to be quite severe (Smith, 1983). Women may also experience an onset of asthma or a resurgence of symptoms during and subsequent to pregnancy. Although there is speculation that hormonal factors may be involved in the observed sex ratio variation of children with asthma at different ages, the relationship is far from clear (Siegel et al., 1983).

Age of Onset

Asthma may occur at any age. Typically, it occurs prior to the age of 5, the likelihood of developing asthma during adolescence without any prior symptomology, especially for males, is low. When children under the age of 2 develop asthmatic symptoms, physicians are reluctant to diagnose asthma, but label the disease process as bronchiolitis (Pearlman, 1984). Infants who manifest bronchiolitis tend to develop chronic intractable asthma during childhood and young adulthood.

Genetic Factors

Although there is little doubt that asthma has a familial component, specific genetic factors are not understood (Rees, 1984). A child is at increased risk for developing asthma if either parent has a history of asthma. However, the development of asthma is thought to depend on the interaction between the child's predisposition (i.e. genetics) and the environment. Consequently, some children may have a predisposition or inherited sensitivity to asthma but never develop symptoms because of their particular environment; others in the same environment, however, may become symptomatic. The specific environmental factors that lead to asthma are ambiguous. Despite this uncertainty, many families, on the recommendation of their physician, have relocated to various parts of the country in a search to find an environment that would reduce the severity of their child's asthma. Unfortunately, such a move may only bring about a temporary reduction in asthma severity and for some, asthma symptoms may worsen over time due to the exposure to new environmental allergens (Creer, 1979).

When asthma occurs with allergic rhinitis and eczema, genetic factors are better understood. There is evidence that these children have an inherited tendency toward sensitization. The skin, nasal passages, and airways are hypersensitive and therefore overreact to specific allergens. The presence of extrinsic asthma is quite high in children with allergy and eczema. Furthermore, the likelihood that asthma symptoms will remit for an extended period of time is low. Extrinsic asthma is evident in 55% to 60% of children who have a positive family history for eczema. This strong relationship is further supported by the finding that where eczema is uncommon, asthma is also rare (Smith, 1983). For children with allergic rhinitis, skin tests are usually conducted to detect specific allergies. A common misconception is that if a child reacts to administered allergens, asthma must also be present. Many children, in fact, have positive skin tests for a wide range of allergens prior to the development of asthma. Thus, the detection of specific allergies cannot be considered a sufficient condition for the development of asthma.

Genetic factors play a complex role in the development of asthma. Inheritance is clearly polygenic and multifactorial. No matter what the inheritance pattern is, researchers investigating the genetic factors of asthma must first clearly define asthma and then reliably classify it into a discrete and meaningful nosology.

Growing Out of Asthma

As children with asthma physically mature, many will no longer be symptomatic. This phenomenon is commonly referred to as "growing out of asthma." Although no solid evidence exists for the reason a particular child's asthma remits over time, there is speculation that the increased physical size of the bronchioles accounts for the child's improved condition (Siegel et al., 1983). Most children with mild asthma experience an improvement in their condition as they reach their teen years and may become totally asymtomatic. Unfortunately, however, growing out of asthma during adolescence may mean "growing into asthma" once again in later adulthood.

For children who experience severe asthma, the chance of remission is decreased. Rees (1984) reported approximately 20% of children with severe asthma become symptom-free by the age of 21; asthma for another 20% is substantially improved. Asthma does not improve over time for all children, however; approximately 15% experience worsening symptoms.

The notion of growing out of asthma has been challenged recently. Pearlman (1984) contends that growing out of asthma may be the exception rather than the rule. Asthmatic patients may always have some degree of airway obstruction, and over time the severity of the obstruction will become more variable. This is consistent with the finding that asthmatics may have up to a 50% reduction in airway flow and not perceive any breathlessness or other symptoms (Rubinfield & Pain, 1976). Thus, children who outgrow asthma are likely to become increasingly insensitive to airway obstruction rather than experience any major biologic or immunologic change that results in the disappearance of asthma.

Physical and Psychological Development

The child with asthma may experience both physical and psychological complications throughout development. These complications may result from the disorder itself or from the side effects of medication. With early detection of asthma, most of the complications frequently can be reversed, minimized, or altogether avoided. The most common developmental complications that will be reviewed here are physical deformities, physical growth, irreversible lung damage and other medical complications, and psychological and personality changes.

Most asthmatic children escape permanent physical deformities due to asthma. Chest deformities may result with severe asthma in infancy and childhood, before the bony thorax has been fully calcified and fixed. The chest deformity often mimics the thorax deformity seen in patients with rickets. Thus the term "pseudorickets" has been coined to describe this complication in childhood asthma (Siegel et al., 1983). Chest deformities can be avoided with early medical intervention; even if not treated early, however, chest deformities rarely lead to further complications.

The physical growth of children with asthma is frequently normal. When asthma is severe, however, various complications of physical maturation occur. For example, the onset of puberty is often delayed in children with severe intractable asthma

(Rees, 1984), and/or the child's linear growth is suppressed (Siegel et al., 1983). Although little is understood about the relationship between asthma and lack of growth, it is clear that asthma medications, specifically corticosteroids, dramatically affect growth (Morris, 1983). For example, the frequent use of high-dose steroids leads to the characteristic symptoms of cushinoid syndrome.

Irreversible lung damage is uncommon in children with asthma as they develop. Unfortunately, some asthmatics have permanent damage and show emphysema-like symptoms later in life (Siegel et al., 1983). Other medical complications are infection and status asthmaticus, or steadily worsening asthma.

Infections are probably the most common complication among children with asthma. The relationship of infection to asthma is obscure because of the difficulty in determining whether the infection triggers the asthma or whether the asthma triggers the infection. If the former occurs, young children are at a higher risk for frequent asthma, due to the fact that they tend to experience more infection.

Status asthmaticus is a complication of asthma in which a child develops severe airway obstruction that does not respond well to treatment. The younger the child, the faster this airway obstruction can occur (Fireman, 1983). Most deaths of children with asthma are a result of status asthmaticus (Siegel et al., 1983).

Psychological and personality changes are frequently reported by asthmatic children as well as their parents. Asthmatic children must not only learn to cope with a chronic physical disorder, but they must learn to tolerate a disorder that can limit their activity at any given time. Among parents who completed a checklist of potential problems faced by their asthmatic child, over 40% acknowledged that asthma was the focus of their child's life. Furthermore, approximately 37% of the children were viewed as depressed as a consequence of having asthma, and 49% of the youngsters reportedly experienced significant anger over their disorder (Creer, Marion, & Creer, 1983). An important research ques-

tion yet to be answered is how the developmental age of a child with asthma differentially affects behavior and personality.

Related to the issue of psychological changes is the suggestion that asthmatic children may suffer from neuropsychological deficits due to periods of decreased oxygen levels or hypoxemia. Using the Halstead-Reitan neuropsychological test battery with asthmatic children, Dunleavy and Baada (1980) found 35% of the youngsters tested were neurologically impaired, with deficits primarily manifested in visualizing and remembering spatial configurations, incidental memory, and planning and executing visual and tactile motor tasks. These findings have been challenged in a well-designed study investigating the role of medications, especially corticosteroids, in producing the same neurological deficits (Suess & Chai, 1981). Irrespective of whether it is asthma per se or the medication that produces neurological deficits, more research is needed on the topic.

EDUCATIONAL ISSUES

Asthmatic children encounter two major types of academic problems. The first results from their high rate of absenteeism. Data on days lost from school represent one of the more reliable and valid dependent measures of childhood asthma (Creer & Winder, 1986), although the effect of this variable on academic performance is far from clear. The second problem arises from allergies and/or medications taken to control the disorder. While both of these variables appear to interact with academic performance, their exact role is complex and uncertain.

School Absenteeism

In 1963, Schiffer and Hunt reported that asthma was the leading cause of school absenteeism in youngsters and accounted for nearly one-fourth of days lost from school because of chronic illness. The magnitude of absenteeism reflected by this study is staggering but somewhat meaningless, because the comparison was made to other chronic disorders The information is also dated.

A more relevant comparison of days lost from school by asthmatic children is obtained by examining several recent demographic surveys on childhood asthma and school attendance. Such surveys, conducted in different regions of the nation, indicated that 17.3 days were lost from school in Texas (Parcel & Nader, 1977), 26 in New York (Freudenberg et al., 1980), 13 in Ohio (Winder & Jurenec, 1984), 17.5 in Colorado (Creer et al., 1985), and 16.2 in Iowa (Humphries, Weinberger, Vaughan, & Ekwo, 1985). The mean number of days absent in these studies was 18; based on the typical 180-day school year, it suggests that, on the average, asthmatic youngsters were absent 10% of the time. This finding can be compared with data showing that for 1980, the average number of days lost from school was 5.3 per pupil (*Vital and Health Statistics*, 1982).

Their high rate of absenteeism creates a number of problems for asthmatic youngsters. In interviews with parents, Freudenberg and co-workers (1980) reported that 40% thought their youngsters encountered school problems ranging from missed work to difficulties with teachers, Creer et al. (1983) found that 53% of the parents of 78 consecutive admissions to the National Jewish Hospital in Denver for the year 1979–1980 also reported their asthmatic youngsters encountered similar academic problems. In both studies, excessive absenteeism was cited by the parents as a primary factor contributing to children's school problems.

Besides academically falling behind nonasthmatic peers in school, two other problems have been related to days lost from school because of asthma. First, there is the pattern of absenteeism. In a study conducted in Great Britain, Douglas and Ross (1965) administered a battery of intelligence and achievement tests to 3,372 children. Results indicated absenteeism impaired a child's ability to perform in the classroom. Equally important was the finding that frequent, brief absences were more harmful to the child's academic performance than occasional, long periods lost

from school. As noted by Creer and Yoches (1971), the former pattern is more typical of the asthmatic child who is frequently absent from school during certain seasons of the year. Second, Creer and Yoches speculated on other problems produced by excessive absenteeism. Not only did many of the asthmatic children they observed lack social skills necessary for success in the school, but a number displayed deficiencies in attention skills required to complete class assignments.

Allergies and/or Medications

The role of allergies and/or medications taken for their control is more obscure than that of excessive absenteeism in producing academic difficulties for asthmatic children.

The attacks of many asthmatic children are triggered by allergies, and there have been suggestions that allergies can cause learning problems. Szanton and Szanton (1962) contended that children with hearing losses resulting from allergies affecting the middle ear are sometimes considered immature, dull, mentally defective, or emotionally disturbed. These investigators further suggested that an intermittent hearing loss generated by allergies produces a higher incidence of articulation and vocal quality disorders, many of which are overlooked because an audiological analysis is conducted at times when the child is free from allergies. Other evidence in support of allergies causing learning disabilities was presented by Baker and Baker (1980). In an analysis of 80 students with diagnosed allergies who were 8 years and older, it was found that almost 50% manifested articulation or vocal quality errors. The authors concluded that allergic rhinitis is associated with hearing loss and articulation errors, and vocal quality disorders, especially hoarseness accompanied by a breathy voice, often is associated with bronchial asthma.

A more thorough examination of the role of allergies and school performance was reported by McLoughlin and his colleagues (1983). In interviewing parents of 400 children, they found no significant difference between allergic and nonallergic children in terms of academic and language performance, memory, diagnosis of being handicapped, or behavior problems. Only eustachian tube dysfunctions were significantly related to academic and behavior problems. Thus, McLoughlin and his co-workers questioned possible interactions between allergies and learning problems.

A final area of research is concerned with how medications taken to control allergies and particularly asthma affect academic performance. A few studies have reported that these drugs negatively influence academic performance. McLoughlin and his colleagues, for example, found that theophylline, probably the most commonly prescribed asthma medication, was significantly correlated with inattentiveness, hyperactivity, irritability, drowsiness, and withdrawn behavior. Furthermore, this relationship increased the longer a child had been taking theophylline-based drugs, according to parents' accounts. Furakawa and associates (1984) also reported learning and behavior problems associated with theophylline. Although they only investigated six children taking the medication, they reported that theophylline negatively affected the children's performance on the WISC-R, the name-writing test of the Halstead-Reitan neuropsychological battery, and other diagnostic tests assessing reading skills, visual-motor skills, fact retention, and concentration. Another medication taken by the subjects in this double-blind study — cromolyn sodium — had no effect upon the youngsters' performance.

McLoughlin and his co-workers (1983) did not find that beta agonist compounds, another commonly prescribed medication for asthma, had any reported effect upon the children in their survey. However, Creer (1979) presented data illustrating that the introduction of one of these drugs, terbutaline, produced an increase in socially inappropriate behaviors in youngsters receiving the medication, in comparison to those who did not receive it. Finally, as noted in the last section, the work of Suess and Chai (1981) indicates that corticosteroids, the most potent medication prescribed for the control of asthma, affects academic performance.

DIAGNOSIS AND ASSESSMENT

Despite the lack of a completely satisfactory definition of asthma, accuracy of the diagnosis has recently been improved (Creer, 1982). Progress has come from two sources: first, physicians and medical personnel can apply a wide array of sophisticated laboratory procedures to the child suspected of having the disorder (Chai, 1975; Cohen, 1985; Hargreave, Ramsdale, Sterk, & Juniper, 1985); second, concerted efforts have recently been made to standardize criteria used to confirm the diagnosis of asthma (Chai et al., 1975; Eggleston et al., 1979), as well as abnormal lung functioning in children (Taussig, Chernick, Wood, Farrell & Mellins, 1980).

While the initial two steps in diagnosing any illness or disorder are obtaining a comprehensive history and conducting a complete physical examination of the patient, the diagnosis of asthma should not be based solely on the history and symptoms. Skepticism about relying solely upon symptoms presented by a patient to make the diagnosis of asthma is supported by several findings reported in the literature. Goodall (1958) and Fry (1961) followed a total of 2,523 children for 10 to 20 year periods; only 16 to 22% of these children had a history of wheezing, and only 5 to 10% were ultimately diagnosed as having asthma. Pratter, Hingston, and Irwin (1983) examined 34 patients who experienced wheezing, on the basis of which 62% were diagnosed as having asthma. However, clinical testing with a methacholine challenge showed that only 35% of the patients exhibited hyperreactive airways consistent with asthma. Other reports suggest that certain physical signs traditionally assumed to be symptomatic of asthma actually do not indicate the disorder. Rather, these symptoms appear as learned responses acquired in certain social situations (Renne & Creer, 1985). Examples of such symptoms include sneezing (Kushner, 1968), coughing (Alexander et al., 1973), and wheezing (Christopher et al.,

1983; Downing, Braman, Fox, & Carrao, 1982; Rodenstein, Francis, & Stanescu, 1983). Thus, a child should never be diagnosed as having asthma on the basis of symptoms alone; diagnosis of the disorder must be confirmed by laboratory tests.

In order to confirm the diagnosis of asthma, Miller and Kazemi (1983) suggest that three criteria must be demonstrated: functional abnormality of the bronchial smooth muscle, partial or complete reversibility of the physiological abnormality, and chronicity and intermittency of asthma attacks.

Functional Abnormality of Bronchial Smooth Muscle

Abnormality of the bronchial smooth muscle can be demonstrated and assessed by a series of physical challenges. Asthma can be triggered by a variety of stimuli, including irritants, allergens, infections, cold air, exercise, aspirin and related substances, and emotional reactions (Reed & Townley, 1978). Three common physical tests used to assess abnormality of the bronchial smooth muscle include bronchial challenge with allergens, exercise, and bronchial challenge using drugs (histamine and methacholine) to provoke an asthma attack.

Bronchial challenge using allergens consists of having patients inhale minute amounts of stimuli thought to provoke smooth muscle abnormality and, hence, airway obstruction. Common stimuli used in such challenges include extracts taken from grass or tree pollens. Skin tests may be done prior to bronchial challenge tests in order to determine specific stimuli likely to induce an asthma attack. This process usually involves pricking the child's skin with a needle containing a minute amount of the stimulus and then observing the skin for a positive reaction (wheal or flare) around the puncture site. Confirmation of functional abnormality of bronchial smooth muscle following bronchial challenge is determined on the basis of the child's pulmonary function tests. The major instrument used to assess respiratory functions is the spirometer, which provides a graphic record of forced expiration.

The patient takes the deepest breath possible, holds the air for a moment, and, pursing his or her lips around the mouthpiece of the instrument, blows out all the air as quickly and forcefully as possible. Since the performance is effort-dependent, the examiner must make certain the patient complies with instructions; outcome data gathered with such instruments is clearly a function of instructions provided to a patient (Harm, Marion,Kotses, & Creer, 1984). If there is a decrease of 20% or more in the child's pulmonary functions, the child may be diagnosed as having asthma.

As might be expected, patients thought to experience exercise-induced asthma (EIA) can be challenged either by having them exercise in a prescribed manner (Cropp, 1979; Eggleston et al., 1979) or by exposing them to cold air (Deal, McFadden, Ingraham, Breslin, & Jaeger, 1980; McLaughlin & Dozor, 1983). A decrease of 20% or more in the child's pulmonary functions as a result of this activity may indicate a diagnosis of asthma.

Finally, in questionable cases children can be challenged by having them inhale histamine or methacholine. Several reports have presented data on establishing criteria for histamine (e.g., Cockcroft & Berscheid, 1982) and methacholine (Chai et al., 1975; Rosenthal, 1979), although introduction of both stimuli in this manner is still regarded as experimental (Scoggin & Petty, 1982).

Partial or Complete Reversibility of Physiological Abnormality

Once a decrease in the child's pulmonary functioning has been demonstrated, reversibility can be established in the physician's office by at least 20% improvement using bronchodilator treatment. As noted in discussing reversibility, however, it is difficult to obtain with some children. The question of intermittency of attacks also was discussed earlier in describing characteristics of asthma.

TREATMENT AND MANAGEMENT

Medical Treatment

As described earlier, one of the major characteristics of asthma is its extreme variability. Hence, treatment must be continuously evaluated and tailored to the needs of the individual child. In addition to the most obvious treatment, that is, having children avoid stimuli known to precipitate their asthma attacks, medical treatment of asthma falls into two other categories.

The first category of treatment is immunotherapy, which is the process of desensitizing the child to allergens with injections of progressively increasing amounts of the allergen over a relatively long period of time. Although this form of treatment has been shown to be effective for some asthmatic children, it is not widely employed, in part because its effectiveness is limited primarily to specific airborne allergens (Siegel et al., 1983).

The second category of medical treatment is pharmacological therapy. Generally, the first drug prescribed is theophylline, an oral bronchodilator that reduces the frequency and severity of bronchospasm. If asthma is not adequately controlled by theophylline, a beta-adrenergic agent such as metaproterenol, terbutaline, or albuterol may be introduced. In addition to these oral preparations, there are a number of beta-adrenergic inhalants available that can often be administered when the child experiences severe systemic side effects from medications taken orally. Children whose asthma does not respond to theophylline or beta-adrenergic agents, or who experience significant side effects from these medications, may benefit from cromolyn sodium. Cromolyn prevents the release of chemical mediators induced by allergen and nonallergen stimuli. Finally, if the child continues to experience episodes of severe asthma, corticosteroids can be administered. Because of potentially serious side effects resulting from adrenal suppression that may accompany corticosteroid therapy, it should not be used unless all other forms of treatment have failed.

Psychological Factors

A variety of self-regulation strategies have been employed to control asthma. Self-regulation strategies are based upon two approaches: regulation of psychological variables that may be related to asthma, and regulation of physiological variables directly related to the disorder. Psychological variables linked to bronchoconstriction in asthmatic patients primarily include stress, anxiety, and tension (e.g., Luparello, Lyons, Bleecker, & McFadden, 1968). Attempts to control such psychological variables generally include some form of relaxation training alone, relaxation assisted by biofeedback, or relaxation incorporated in systematic desensitization procedures. Theoretically, increasing one's ability to relax eliminates some conditions contributing to bronchoconstriction and, therefore, may be helpful either in rendering an attack less likely or in attenuating asthma symptoms.

Physiological activity related to asthma may be manipulated directly. Biofeedback procedures are invariably employed to assist the individual in bringing physiological activity under control. In such procedures, the patient is instructed to control an electronic signal, which represents an analog of the physiological activity. Biofeedback training has been employed in an attempt to control a wide variety of physiological variables related to asthma, including electromyographic (EMG) training for facial muscle tension (e.g., Kotses, Glaus, Crawford, Edwards, & Scherr, 1976), respiratory flow/volume training (e.g., Danker, Miklich, Pratt, & Creer, 1975), and airways resistance training (e.g., Feldman, 1976). Comprehensive reviews of the empirical findings concerning these self-regulation strategies are available (Creer & Kotses, 1983; Kotses & Glaus, 1981).

For the most part, both psychological and physiological self-regulation procedures appear to benefit asthmatic individuals. The benefits these procedures provide are most readily apparent in terms of improvement in respiratory function measures. However, such improvements are relatively modest when compared with those effected by pharmacological agents (Miklich et al., 1977). In the management of asthma, self-regulation procedures should not be employed exclusive of other therapies. On the other hand, neither should pharmacological treatments be relied on solely, as they present serious problems of drug availability, misuse, and negative side effects. A management approach that balances the use of pharmacological therapy with self-regulation procedures may minimize treatment requirements of both types and thereby maximize overall treatment effectiveness.

Finally, a number of comprehensive self-management programs for asthma, particularly for childhood asthma, have recently been developed (Creer & Winder, 1986). Information concerning these programs is available in a conference summary published by the National Institute of Allergy and Infectious Diseases (1981) and in a review article by Thoreson and Kirmil-Gray (1983). The basic rationale for these programs is that self-management provides the person with skills to assume responsibility for controlling his or her affliction (Creer et al., 1985).

There are two major components common to self-management programs (Creer, in press): education about asthma, and training in self-management skills. First, individuals are provided with information about the mechanics of breathing and respiratory changes that occur during an attack, possible triggers of attacks, and diagnostic procedures used to confirm asthma. In addition, patients and their families learn about pharmacological therapies, that is how different medications act to control asthma and potential side effects of the various drugs. Second, patients and their families are taught specific self-management skills: self-monitoring, self-recording, information processing, decision making, and self-instruction. In self-monitoring, participants learn to observe behavioral (tiredness, irritability), and physical (e.g., wheezing, tightness in the chest) changes that occur in relation to their asthma, as well as medication usage and events or other factors that trigger asthma. Self-recording requires participants to keep written records of the occurrence and severity of attacks, medication compliance, peak flow measures, and precipitating factors. By monitoring and recording information related to their

asthma, participants learn to analyze this information, determine whether a potential problem might require action, and evaluate the problem with respect to possible solutions. Then patients, along with their physicians, select the most appropriate solution from among these choices (decision making). Self-instruction refers to statements made by patients themselves to prompt, direct, or maintain behavior (O'Leary & Dubey, 1979) in the event of an attack.

CURRENT RESEARCH

Medically, research on asthma continues to center around the topics of standardizing diagnostic procedures and testing potential treatments, particularly medications. The result will be operationalized standards applied on a wide basis to diagnose asthma, and a continuation of the trend observed during the past 15 years of developing and marketing more effective medications to treat asthma. Perhaps the most exciting area for asthma research is the investigation of mediators that may be linked to pathological changes in asthma (Kaliner, 1985). Mediators being investigated in this respect, particularly leukotrienes and other lipic mediators, were noted at the beginning of the chapter. It can be anticipated that world-wide investigations into the immunological and biochemical basis for asthma will continue in the future.

On the behavioral side, research will continue into three areas (Creer, 1979): identifying antecedents of asthma and how they may be controlled, to some extent, by patients; developing techniques to assist patients and their families to manage behaviors occurring concurrently with attacks; and reducing harmful consequences of the disorder. The development and implementation of self-management programs for childhood asthma has greatly enhanced this trend. In addition, the abandonment of the psychosomatic model in favor of a scheme proposed by Reed and Townley (1978) that relies upon the identification of precipitating stimuli, physical factors linking the stimuli to responses, and the physiological responses themselves — essentially an S-O-R model so familiar to behavioral scientists — should create a synthesis between medical and behavioral research that cannot help but produce increased benefit to those with childhood asthma. This synthesis is already observed with medical and behavioral scientists using identical dependent variables for their research, ranging from use of blood theophylline levels (Baum & Creer, 1985) to collecting morbidity data related to asthma (Hindi-Alexander & Cropp, 1984). It is hoped that this integration of medical and behavioral research will provide knowledge to solve many of the problems posed by asthma.

SUMMARY

In this chapter, we reviewed various aspects of childhood asthma. While we emphasized the complexity of the disorder — certainly there are more questions about it than there are answers — we fervently hope behavioral scientists will not be deterred from either conducting investigations on childhood asthma or working with patients afflicted with the disorder. Asthma is responsible for a large amount of morbidity data gathered with respect to chronic disorders, particularly hospitalizations and school absenteeism, which in itself makes it worthy of attention by behavioral scientists. Beyond this demand, however, is the challenge that arises simply because there is so much we need to know about asthma. As Creer (1979) has concluded, the extent to which we assist patients with the disorder will eventually be limited only by the horizons of our concern and imagination.

REFERENCES

Advance report of final mortality statistics, 1982. (1984). *NCHS Monthly Vital Statistics Report, 33,* 1–43.

Alexander, A. B., Chai, H., Creer, T. L., Miklich, D. R., Renne, C. M., & Cardoso, R. (1973). The elimination of chronic cough by response suppression shaping. *Journal of Behavior Therapy and Experimental Psychiatry, 4,* 75–80.

American Lung Association. (1975). *Introduction to lung diseases (6th ed.).* New York: American Lung Association.

Baker, B. M., & Baker, C. D. (1980). Difficulties generated by allergies. *Journal of School Health, 50,* 583–585.

Baum, D., & Creer, T. L. (1986). Medication compliance in children with asthma. *Journal of Asthma, 23,* 49–59.

Chai, H. (1975). Management of severe chronic perennial asthma in children. *Advances in Asthma and Allergy, 2,* 1–12.

Chai, H., Farr, R. S., Froehlich, L. A., Mathison, D. A., McLean, J. A., Rosenthal, R. R., Sheffer, A. L., Spector, S. L., & Townley, R. G. (1975). Standardization of bronchial inhalation challenge procedure. *Journal of Allergy and Clinical Immunology, 56,* 323–327.

Chen, W. Y., & Horton, D. J. (1977). Heat and water loss from the airways and exercise-induced asthma. *Respiration, 34,* 305–313.

Children's Disability Days, United States, 1980. (1983). *Vital and Health Statistics.* (Series 10, No. 143, DHHS Publication No. PHS 83-1571). Washington, DC: U.S. Government Printing Office.

Christopher, K. L., Wood, R. P., Eckert, R. C., Blager, F. B., Raney, R. A., & Sourada, J. F. (1983). Vocal-cord dysfunction presenting as asthma. *New England Journal of Medicine, 308,* 1566–1570.

Clark, M., Gosnell, M., Abramson, P., & Leslie, C. (1983, August 1). The rise in childhood illness. *Newsweek,* pp. 47–48.

Clark, T. J. H. (1977). Definition of asthma for clinical trials. Cited in J. E. Stark & J. V. Collins, Methods in clinical trials in asthma. Proceedings of a British Thoracic and Tuberculosis Association Meeting. *British Journal of Diseases of the Chest, 71,* 225–226.

Cockcroft, D. W., & Berscheid, B. A. (1982). Standardization of inhalation provocation tests: Dose vs. concentration of histamine. *Chest, 82,* 572–575.

Cohen, S. H. (1985). Clinical evaluation: Allergy and immunology. *Chest, 87,* 265–305.

Collins-Williams, C., Zalesky, C., Battu, K., & Chambers, M. T. (1981). Death from asthma. *Canadian Medical Association Journal, 125,* 341–345.

Creer, T. L. (1978). Asthma: Psychologic aspects and management. In E. Middleton, Jr., C. E. Reed & E. F. Ellis (Eds.), *Allergy: Principles and practice* (pp. 796–811). St. Louis, MO: C. V. Mosby.

Creer, T. L. (1979). *Asthma therapy: A behavioral health care system for respiratory disorders.* New York: Springer.

Creer, T. L. (1982). Asthma. *Journal of Consulting and Clinical Psychology, 50*, 912–921.

Creer, T. L. (1983). Respiratory disorders. In T. G. Burish & L. A. Bradley (Eds.), *Coping with chronic diseases: Research & applications* (pp. 316–336). New York: Academic Press.

Creer, T. L. (1985). Reflections on residential treatment centers for childhood asthma. *Pediatrics of Japan, 26*, 951–956.

Creer, T. L. (in press). Asthma. In W. Linden (Ed.), *Biological barriers in behavioral medicine.* New York: Plenum.

Creer, T. L., Backial, M., Burns, K. L., Leung, P., Marion, R. J., Miklich, D. R., Taplin, P. S., & Ullman, S. (1985). *The self-management of childhood asthma.* Manuscript submitted for publication.

Creer, T. L., Harm, D. L., & Marion, R. J. (in press). Childhood asthma. In D. K. Routh (Ed.), *Handbook of pediatric psychology.* New York: Guilford.

Creer, T. L., & Kotses, H. (1983). Asthma: Psychologic aspects and management. In E. Middleton, Jr., C. E. Reed & E. F. Ellis (Eds.), *Allergy: Principles & practice* (2nd ed., pp. 1015–1036). St. Louis, MO: C. V. Mosby.

Creer, T. L., Marion, R. J., & Creer, P. P. (1983). The asthma problem behavior checklist: Parental perceptions of the behavior of asthmatic children. *Journal of Asthma, 20*, 97–104.

Creer, T. L., & Winder, J. A. (1986). Asthma. In K. A. Holroyd & T. L. Creer (Eds.), *Self-management in health psychology and behavioral medicine* (pp. 269–303). Orlando, FL: Academic Press.

Creer, T. L., & Yoches, C. (1971). The modification of an inappropriate behavioral pattern in asthmatic children. *Journal of Chronic Diseases, 24*, 507–513.

Cropp, G. J. A. (1979). The exercise bronchoprovocation test: Standardization of procedures and evaluation of response. *Journal of Allergy and Clinical Immunology, 64*, 627–633.

Current estimates from the National Health Interview Survey, United States, 1980. (1982). *Vital and Health Statistics* (Series 10, No. 141, DHHS Publication No. PHS 83-1569). Washington, DC: U.S. Government Printing Office.

Danker, P. S., Miklich, D. R., Pratt, C., & Creer, T. L. (1975). An unsuccessful attempt to instrumentally condition peak expiratory flow rates in asthmatic children. *Journal of Psychosomatic Research, 19*, 209–213.

Davis, D. J. (1972). NIAID initiatives in allergy research. *Journal of Allergy and Clinical Immunology, 49*, 323–328.

Deal, E. C., Jr., McFadden, E. R., Jr., Ingram, R. H., Jr., Breslin, F. J., & Jaeger, J. J. (1980). Airway responsiveness to cold air and hyperpnea in normal subjects and those with hay fever and asthma. *American Review of Respiratory Diseases, 121*, 621–628.

Deal, E. C., McFadden, E. R., Jr., Ingram, R. H., Jr., Strauss, R. H., & Jaegar, J. J. (1979). Role of respiratory heat exchange in production of exercise-induced asthma. *Journal of Applied Physiology, 46*, 467–475.

de-Shazo, R. D., & Salvaggio, J. E. (1984). Immunology. *Journal of the American Medical Association, 252*, 2198–2201.

Douglas, J. W. B., & Ross, J. M. (1965). The effects of absence on primary school performance. *British Journal of Educational Psychology, 35*, 28–40.

Downing, E. T., Braman, S. S., Fox, M. J., & Corrao, W. M. (1982). Factitious asthma: Physiological approach to diagnosis. *Journal of the American Medical Association, 248*, 2878–2880.

Dunleavy, R. A., & Baada, L. E. (1980). Neuropsychological correlates of severe asthma in children 9–14 years old. *Journal of Consulting and Clinical Psychology, 48*, 214–219.

Eggleston, P. A., Rosenthal, R. R., Anderson, S. A., Anderton, S. A., Anderton, R., Bierman, C. W., Bleecker, E. R., Chai, H., Cropp, G. J. A., Johnson, J. D., Konig, P., Morse, J., Smith, L. J., Summers, R. J., & Trautlein, J. J. (1979). Guidelines for the methodology of exercise challenge testing of asthmatics. *Journal of Allergy and Clinical Immunology, 64*, 642–645.

Feldman, G. M. (1976). The effect of biofeedback training on respiratory resistance of asthmatic children. *Psychosomatic Medicine, 38*, 27–34.

Fireman, P. (1983). Status asthmaticus in children. In E. Middleton, Jr., C. E. Reed, & E. F. Ellis (Eds.), *Allergy: Principles and practice* (2nd ed, pp. 997–1002). St. Louis, MO: C. V. Mosby.

Fletcher, C. M., & Pride, N. B. (1984). Definitions of emphysema, chronic bronchitis, asthma, and airflow obstruction: 25 years on from the CIBA symposium. *Thorax, 39*, 81–85.

Freudenberg, N., Feldman, C. H., Clark, N. M., Millman, E. J., Valle, I., & Wasilewski, Y. (1980). The impact of bronchial asthma on school attendance and performance. *Journal of School Health, 50*, 522–526.

Fry, J. (1961). *The catarrhal child.* London: Butterworth.

Furakawa, C. T., Shapiro, G. G., DuHamel, T., Weimer, L., Pierson, W. E., & Bierman, C. W. (1984, March 17). Learning and behavior problems associated with theophylline therapy. *Lancet*, 621.

Goodall, J. F. (1958). Wheezy children. *Journal of the Royal College of Practitioners, 1*, 51–61.

Griffin, M., Weiss, J. W., Leitch, A. G., McFadden, E. R., Jr., Corey, E. J., Austen, K. F., & Drazen, J. M. (1983). Effects of leukotriene-D on the airways in asthma. *New England Journal of Medicine, 30*, 436–439.

Hardy, C. C., Robinson, C., Tattersfield, E., & Holgate, S. T. (1984). The bronchoconstrictor effect of inhaled prostaglandin D_2 in normal and asthmatic men. *New England Journal of Medicine, 311*, 209–213.

Hargreave, F. E., Ramsdale, E. H., Sterk, P. J., & Juniper, E. F. (1985). Advances in the use of inhalation provocation tests in clinical evaluation. *Chest, 87*, 325–355.

Harm, D. L., Marion, R. J., Kotses, H., & Creer, T. L. (1984). Effect of subject effort on pulmonary functions measures. *Journal of Asthma, 21*, 295–298.

Hindi-Alexander, M. C., & Cropp, G. J. A. (1984). Evaluation of a family asthma program. *Journal of Allergy and Clinical Immunology, 74*, 505–510.

Humphries, T., Weinberger, M., Vaughan, L., & Ekwo, E. (1985). Demographic and clinical characteristics of childhood asthma. *Journal of Allergy and Clinical Immunology, 75*, 197.

Ishizawka, K., & Ishizawka, T. (1967). Identification of IgE antibodies as a carrier of reaginic activity. *Journal of Immunology, 99*, 1187–1198.

Jones, R. S. (1976). *Asthma in children.* Acton, MA: Publishing Sciences Group.

Kaliner, M. (1985). Mast cell mediators and asthma. *Chest, 87*, 25–55.

Karetzky, M. S. (1975). Asthma mortality: An analysis of one year's experience, review of the literature and assessment of current modes of treatment. *Medicine, 54*, 471–484.

Kotses, H., & Glaus, K. D. (1981). Applications of biofeedback to the treatment of asthma: A critical review. *Biofeedback and Self-Regulation, 6*, 573–593.

Kotses, H., Glaus, K. D., Crawford, P. L., Edwards, J. E., & Scherr, M. S. (1976). Operant reduction of frontalis EMG activity in the treatment of asthma in children. *Journal of Psychosomatic Research, 20*, 453–459.

Kushner, M. (1968). The operant control of intractable sneezing. In C. D. Spielberger, R. Fox & B. Masterton (Eds.), *Contributions to general psychology: Selected readings for introductory psychology* (pp. 410–412). New York: Ronald Press.

Linder, F. E., Woolsey, T. D., Waterhouse, A. M., Simmons, W. R., Sagen, O. K., Lawrence, P. S., & Cunningham, M. R. (1959). *Children and youth: Selected health statistics, United States, July 1957–June 1958.* (USPHS Publication No. 584-C1). Washington, DC: U.S. Department of Health, Education and Welfare.

Loren, M. L., Leung, P. K., Cooley, R. L., Chai, H., Bell, T. D., & Buck, V. M. (1978). Irreversibility of obstructive changes in severe asthma in children. *Chest, 74*, 126–129.

Luparello, T., Lyons, H. A., Bleecker, E. R., & McFadden, E. R., Jr. (1968). Influences of suggestion on airway reactivity in asthmatic subjects. *Psychosomatic Medicine, 30*, 819–825.

McFadden, E. R., Jr. (1980). Asthma: Pathophysiology. *Seminars in Respiratory Medicine, 1*, 297–303.

McFadden, E. R., Jr. (1984). Pathogenesis of asthma. *Journal of Allergy and Clinical Immunology, 73*, 413–424.

McFadden, E. R., Jr., & Stevens, J. B. (1983). A history of asthma. In E. Middleton, Jr., C. E. Reed & E. F. Ellis (Eds.), *Allergy: Principles and practice* (2nd ed., pp. 805–809). St. Louis, MO: C. V. Mosby.

McLaughlin, F. J., & Dozor, A. J. (1983). Cold air inhalation challenge in the diagnosis of asthma in children. *Pediatrics, 72*, 503–509.

McLoughlin, J., Nall, M., Isaacs, B., Petrosko, J., Karibo, J., & Lindsey, B. (1983). The relationship of allergies and allergy treatment to school performance and student behavior. *Annals of Allergy, 51*, 506–510.

Miller, L. G., & Kazemi, H. (1983). *Manual of clinical pulmonary medicine.* New York: McGraw-Hill.

Morris, H. G. (1983). Pharmacology of corticosteroids in asthma. In E. Middleton, Jr., C. E. Reed & E. F. Ellis (Eds.), *Allergy: Principles and practice* (2nd ed., pp. 593–612). St. Louis, MO: C. V. Mosby.

Mullally, D. I., Grauman, J. S., Evans, R., & Kaslow, R. A. (1985). Hospitalizations of children for asthma in the U.S.: 1965–1982. *Journal of Allergy and Clinical Immunology, 75*, 197.

National Institute of Allergy and Infectious Diseases. (1981). *Self-management educational programs for childhood asthma: II. Manuscripts.* Bethesda, MD: National Institute of Allergy and Infectious Diseases.

O'Leary, S. G., & Dubey, D. R. (1979). Applications of self-control procedures by children: A review. *Journal of Applied Behavior Analysis, 12*, 449–465.

Parcel, G. S., & Nader, P. R. (1977). Evaluation of a pilot school-health-education program for asthmatic children. *Journal of School Health, 47*, 453–456.

Pearlman, D. S. (1984). Bronchial asthma: A perspective from childhood to adulthood. *Amer-*

ican Journal of Diseases of Children, 138, 459–466.

Porter, R., & Birch, J. (Eds.). (1971). Report of the working group on the definition of asthma. Identification of asthma. London: Churchill Livingston.

Pratter, M. R., Hingston, D. M., & Irwin, R. S. (1983). Diagnosis of bronchial asthma by clinical evaluation: An unreliable method. Chest, 84, 42–47.

Price, J. (1984). Asthma in children: Diagnosis. British Medical Journal, 288, 1666–1668.

Purcell, K., & Weiss, J. H. (1970). Asthma. In C. C. Costello (Ed.), Symptoms of psychopathology (pp. 597–623). New York: Wiley.

Reed, C. E., & Townley, R. G. (1978). Asthma: Classification and pathogenesis. In E. Middleton, Jr., C. E. Reed & E. F. Ellis (Eds.), Allergy: Principles and practice (pp. 659–677). St. Louis, MO: C. V. Mosby.

Rees, J. (1984). ABC of asthma: Clinical course. British Medical Journal, 288, 1441–1442.

Renne, C. M., & Creer, T. L. (1985). Asthmatic children and their families. In M. L. Wolraich & D. K. Routh (Eds.), Advances in developmental and behavioral pediatrics (pp. 41–81). Grenwich, CT: Jai Press.

Rodenstein, D. O., Francis, C., & Stanescu, D. C. (1983). Emotional laryngeal wheezing: A new syndrome. American Review of Respiratory Diseases, 127, 354–356.

Rosenthal, R. R. (Ed.) (1979). Workshop procedures on bronchoprovocation techniques for the evaluation of asthma. Journal of Allergy and Clinical Immunology, 64, 561–692.

Rubinfeld, A. R., & Pain, M. C. F. (1976, April 24). Perception of asthma. Lancet, 882–884.

Russo, D. (1985). Clinical training in behavioral health psychology. Behavior Therapist, 8, 43–46.

Schiffer, C. G., & Hunt, E. P. (1963). Illness among children. (Children's Bureau Publication No. 405). Washington, DC: U.S. Government Printing Office.

Scoggin, C. H., & Petty, T. L. (1982). Clinical strategies in adult asthma. Philadelphia: Lea & Febiger.

Siegel, S. C., Katz, R. M., & Rachelefsky, G. S. (1983). Asthma in infancy and childhood. In E. Middleton, Jr., C. E. Reed & E. F. Ellis (Eds.), Allergy: Principles and practice. (2nd ed., pp. 863–900). St. Louis, MO: C. V. Mosby.

Sly, R. M. (1984). Increase in deaths from asthma in the United States. Annals of Allergy, 52, 230.

Smith, J. M. (1983). Epidemiology and natural history of asthma, allergic rhinitis, and atopic dermatitis (eczema). In E. Middleton, Jr., C. E. Reed & E. F. Ellis (Eds.), Allergy: Principles and practice (2nd ed., pp. 771–803). St. Louis, MO: C. V. Mosby.

Strunk, R. C., Wolfson, G. S., Labrecque, J. F., & Mrazak, D. (1984). Predictors of a fatal outcome in childhood asthma: Part 2. Journal of Allergy and Clinical Immunology, 73, 122.

Suess, W. M., & Chai, H. (1981). Neuropsychological correlates of asthma: Brain damage or drug effects? Journal of Consulting and Clinical Psychology, 49, 135–136.

Szanton, V. L., & Szanton, W. C. (1962). Allergic paracusis: New allergic syndrome. New York Journal of Medicine, 62, 3112–3115.

Taussig, L. M., Chernick, V., Wood, R., Farrell, P., & Mellins, R. B. (1980). Standardization of lung function testing in children. Journal of Pediatrics, 97, 668–676.

Thoreson, C. E., & Kirmil-Gray, K. (1983). Self-management psychology and the treatment of childhood asthma: Part 2. Journal of Allergy and Clinical Immunology, 72, 596–606.

Weissmann, G. (1983). The eicosanoids of asthma. New England Journal of Medicine, 308, 454–456.

Williams, M. H., Jr. (1980). Clinical features. Seminars in Respiratory Medicine, 1, 304–314.

Williams, M. H., Jr. (1982). Essentials of pulmonary medicine. Philadelphia: Saunders.

Winder, J. A., & Jurenec, G. S. (1984). Targeting asthmatics in need of asthma education programs (AEP). Annals of Allergy, 52, 224.

CHAPTER 13

Autism

V. Mark Durand and Edward G. Carr

He seems to be self-satisfied. He has no apparent affection when petted. He does not observe the fact that anyone comes or goes, and never seems glad to see father or mother or any playmate. He seems almost to draw into his shell and live within himself. (Kanner, 1943; p. 218)

The enigma of autism has intrigued and disturbed us for over 40 years. Almost since the first description of the syndrome by Leo Kanner in 1943, parents, care-givers, and others have wondered why individuals with autism display such severe social deficiencies, fail to learn to communicate adequately, and sometimes act in bizarre and frightening ways. In the years following Kanner's initial description, numerous investigations of autism were conducted to answer these questions. Many approaches were taken to study autism, including psychoanalytic (Bettelheim, 1967), ethological (Tinbergen & Tinbergen, 1972), cognitive (Hermelin & O'Connor, 1970), biological (Rimland, 1964), and behavioral (Ferster, 1961). Yet, more often questions rather than answers emerge from this work. Issues such as the identification of individuals with autism and what causes them to be autistic remain controversial.

More than 1,100 autism-related publications appeared during the 1970s alone (DeMyer, Hingtgen, & Jackson, 1981). Despite the extent and diversity of research on autism, certain themes have emerged from this work that are useful to those who work or live with people with autism. Therefore, this chapter presents an overview of current knowledge in the field, including discussion of relevant developmental and educational issues. Finally, recent trends in assessment and treatment are highlighted, future directions for this research are suggested.

DESCRIPTION OF AUTISM

Kanner (1943) first identified autism as distinctly different from other psychotic disorders, based on the development of social relationships. Children with schizophrenia were described as withdrawing from previous social relationships, but children with autism were seen as never having been able to establish these relationships. Various criteria for autism have since been offered by a number of investigators, creating significant confusion. In fact, Kanner's own definitions have varied over the years and included as few as two defining characteristics (Eisenberg & Kanner, 1956) and as many as 10 (Kanner, 1943). Some resolution to this confusion, however, may be at hand. The third edition of the American Psychiatric Association's (1980) *Diagnostic and Statistical Manual (DSM-III)* for the first time includes infantile autism as a disorder of childhood. Its criteria for this disorder closely resemble those put forth by Rutter (1978) in his review of related research. It is anticipated that some of the previous disagreement about the definition of autism will be resolved with *DSM-III*'s adoption of these diagnostic criteria.

Six diagnostic criteria are established in *DSM-III* (1980) for classifying Infantile Autism.

(1) Onset before 30 months of age.
(2) Pervasive lack of responsiveness to other people.
(3) Gross deficits in language development.
(4) Peculiar speech patterns if speech is present, such as immediate and delayed echolalia, metaphorical language, and pronominal reversal.
(5) Bizarre responses to the environment, for example, resistance to change and peculiar interest in or attachments to animate or inanimate objects.
(6) Absence of delusions, hallucinations, loosening of associations, and incoherence as exhibited in schizophrenia.

An important consideration in assessing these criteria is their reliability and validity. Initial reliability data appear to be quite good. Adequate diagnostic reliability has been demonstrated with an expert diagnosis of infantile autism (Cantwell, Russell, Mattison, & Will, 1979). Similarly, there appears to be very high interrater agreement for this *DSM-III* diagnosis (Mattison, Cantwell, Russell, & Will, 1979). Thus, it seems that *DSM-III*'s addition of more objective behavioral criteria for diagnosing autism has resulted in a high degree of reliability.

However, the validity of the diagnosis of autism is questionable. A diagnosis should be useful on several dimensions. It should theoretically provide differential information on etiology, treatment, and prognosis, as well as provide a tool for communication among researchers. Except for the last criterion, the diagnosis of infantile autism does not, at present, provide useful information. Relatively little is gained by diagnosing a child as autistic. As we discuss in more detail later in this chapter, there is no treatment recommended for a child diagnosed with autism that is different, say, from a treatment recommended for a child diagnosed with schizophrenia. It should be noted that several clinicians suggest that there may be important subgroups of autism, such as biological (Rimland, 1971) and behavioral (Lovaas, Ackerman, & Taubman, 1983). These efforts may ultimately prove valuable in further defining the syndrome, as well as improving our efforts at helping these persons live a more normal life.

EPIDEMIOLOGY

Autism is a relatively rare disorder that has been estimated to occur in approximately 2 to 5 births per 10,000 (Lotter, 1966; Treffert, 1970). However, due to a lack of agreement about the definition of autism, previous research on prevalence often involved the study of children with quite different characteristics. A recent study by Gillberg (1984) used Rutter's (1978) criteria for autism, which are similar to the criteria in *DMS-III* and therefore in keeping with the definition adopted in this chapter. The children surveyed in this study were born in an urban area of Sweden over a 15-year period (1962–1976). It was found that the average incidence for infantile autism during this time was 2.0 per 10,000 children. This rate corresponds to the lower range of the estimates that have been reported in other studies and therefore suggests that *DSM-III*'s definition of autism is somewhat narrower than the definitions used by other investigators. Specifically, the criterion that the disorder is manifested before the age of 30 months eliminates some children included by other investigators (Lotter, 1966; Wing & Gould, 1979).

DEVELOPMENTAL ISSUES

There is a lore that surrounds children with autism. Descriptions of these children typically include a variety of deficits and idiosyncracies that presumably characterize them as different from other children. Yet, recent evidence suggests that some of the observed differences in these children may be indicative of developmental delay rather than symptomatic of autism. It may be that our relative ignorance of normal development has led to spurious conclusions about autism. Data from the child development literature may shed some light on the nature of the autistic syndrome.

One observation made of children with autism is that they apparently lack self-awareness (Bettelheim, 1967; Goldfarb, 1963; Mahler, 1952). For example, the failure to appropriately use the personal pronouns "I" and "me" has been linked to a lack of self-concept (Despert, 1971). Recent work, however, indicates that some of these children do show at least a rudimentary self-concept; namely, visual self-recognition (Dawson & McKissick, 1984; Ferrari & Mathews, 1983; Neuman & Hill, 1978; Spiker & Ricks, 1984). Spiker and Ricks (1984) found that most of the children in their study could recognize their own image in a mirror and that this ability was correlated with the presence of communicative speech. Thus, few of the mute children with autism showed evidence of self-recognition, and most of the children with some speech did display this ability. This finding parallels the occurrence of self-recognition in normally developing children (i.e., between 18 and 24 months). In other words, children with autism seem to have self-recognition abilities equal to their mental-age-matched peers.

Attachment is another area of development that is thought to be disrupted in children with autism (Rutter, 1978). These children are described as not forming significant social ties with other people. Kanner characterized autism as the failure to develop social relationships. Some have even suggested that all therapeutic efforts should be directed toward developing attachments between these children and their mothers (Tinbergen & Tinbergen, 1983). Recent empirical evidence, however, points to the existence of beginning stages of attachment between children with autism and their mothers. Sigman and Ungerer (1984) studied the social behavior of a group of these children. The authors observed that the children sought proximity to their mothers following a 2-minute separation, and they chose proximity to their mothers over proximity to a stranger. Thus, it appears that children with autism are capable of forming attachments to specific caretakers and that some children may acquire this ability over time.

A number of other characteristics of autism may not differ in form from behaviors displayed by young normal children or children with other developmental disabilities. Stimulus overselectivity (responding to a restricted number of relevant components in a stimulus presentation) was once thought of as possibly limited to autism (Lovaas, Schreibman, Koegel, & Rehm, 1971). Subsequent work pointed to similar deficits in young normal children and children with retardation (Schover & Newsom, 1976; Wilhelm & Lovaas, 1976). Echolalia (repetition of a word or phrase spoken by another person) is a defining characteristic of autism as outlined by *DSM-III*; however, this pattern of speech seems to be part of normally developing language skills in most young children (Nakanishi & Owada, 1973; Ricks & Wing, 1975). Even a response as bizarre as self-injurious behaviour is seen in milder forms among infants (de Lissovoy, 1961).

These and other developmental data may help to further define the syndrome of autism. In other words, this information may help us differentiate characteristics that are symptomatic of autism from those that are simply indicative of developmental delay. More important, however, this knowledge may assist in remediation efforts. Using language as an example, Carr (in 1985) has recently argued that developmental information from the area of psycholinguistics may provide guidelines concerning the content of curriculum items for language training. Psycholinguists have collected detailed information about normal language development, which may be useful in suggesting appropriate tasks. Behavioral workers have documented successful teaching *procedures* (Hart & Risley, 1980; Lovaas, 1977); however, guidelines for selecting appropriate curriculum *content* may usefully be derived from developmental data.

Problems exhibited by individuals with autism may be treated by combining developmental guidelines with behavioural techniques. For example, Charlop (1983) patterned the treatment of autistic echolalia after normal children's use of this behavior. She found that by using these guidelines, echolalic children improved their performances on receptive labeling tasks. Researchers in autism are advised to consider normal child development data for possible integration in their work.

EDUCATIONAL ISSUES

In 1795, Itard (1962) used special education techniques to treat the autistic behaviors of a boy found in the wilderness. Today, structured education is the treatment of choice for children with autism (DeMyer et al., 1981; Rutter, 1968; Schopler, Brehm, Kinsbourne, & Reichler, 1971). Intensive skills training for behavioural deficits and behaviour management techniques for behavioral excesses (Lovaas, Koegel, Simmons, & Long, 1973) are the prevalent intervention strategies in use for the treatment of children with autism.

However, one issue that has received some recent attention and is related to the education of lower-functioning children is whether all children are educable (Kaufman, 1981). The traditional behavioral stance has always been that anyone, no matter how severely impaired, can learn. Therefore, as long as an appropriate teaching environment is set up, any child can be educated (Bricker, 1970). A similar philosophy serves as the basis for Public Law 94-142, which calls for free and appropriate education to be provided for all children

regardless of their handicap. Yet, arguments against the educability of all children have recently been articulated.

Specifically, it is argued that some individuals with profound retardation (including those with autism) may be so impaired that little is gained by extensive educational efforts (Ellis, 1979). It is suggested that by continuing intrusive, unsuccessful training educators, may be guilty of harrassment and denying these individuals the "right to be left alone" (Ellis, 1979). Opponents of this position argue that there is no way to be sure that a given individual is unteachable unless training is attempted and fails (Baer, 1981). Even then, the potential range of teaching procedures is so vast that it is problematic to conclude a person is untrainable.

There is no easy solution to this issue. We have personally observed situations that would support both cases. For example, we once witnessed a child forcibly prompted to put on his pants during "self-help skills training" after three years of unsuccessful efforts. We have also seen children lose skills they once had because the institutional environment they were in no longer challenged their capabilities. An optimistic (behavioral) approach to this issue, which focuses on improving the teaching technology, may be the most constructive course to take. Encouraging innovation in training procedures (along with some common sense) is in the best interest of the children and may ultimately make these arguments moot.

A second issue that is becoming increasingly important for the parents of individuals with autism is "aging out." PL 94-142, which so positively influenced the education of all children with handicaps, provides educational services for individuals up to 21 years of age. At the age of 22, states are no longer required to provide these services. Thus, each year a number of persons with autism "ageout" of these services; that is, they reach an age beyond which services are available. Who, then, is responsible for their lifelong care? Fortunately, some states (e.g., Massachusetts) are beginning to provide continuing services for those who turn 22. This is a trend that it is hoped more states will follow.

ASSESSMENT

We have chosen to categorize assessment procedures into three areas; medical, traditional psychological, and behavioral assessment. Medical assessment includes techniques that are designed to measure biological aspects of individuals (e.g., serotonin levels, presence of rubella). Traditional psychological assessment assumes that certain patterns in the way people behave (e.g., cognitive, social, academic) are stable, and individual measures of these behaviors can be compared to group norms. Behavioral assessment seeks to measure overt behaviors (e.g., rocking, echolalia) and their environmental determinants. These approaches are substantially different methodologically and conceptually and are therefore discussed separately.

Assessing individuals with autism is important for a variety of reasons. For example, making placement decisions for appropriate special education programs is usually the first reason why children with autism are exposed to assessment procedures. Treatment monitoring and selection are additional goals for assessment. Because of the importance of placement and treatment in the habilitation of individuals with autism, these functions of assessment procedures will be highlighted in the discussion to follow. The three assessment approaches (i.e., medical, traditional psychological, and behavioral) each will be evaluated with respect to how they contribute to these activities.

Medical Assessment

Medical assessment research includes investigations of biochemical abnormalities (Ritvo, Rabin, Yuwiler, Freeman, & Geller, 1978), neurophysiological disorders (Rosenbloom et al., 1984), and disease conditions as they relate to infantile autism. A majority of the medical research has assumed that autism is a disorder with a single cause (Rutter, 1978). Yet, numerous medical conditions have been associated with autism, including congenital rubella (Chess, Korn, & Fernandez, 1971), hypsarrhythmia (Taft & Cohen, 1971), tuberose sclerosis (Lotter, 1974), and cytomegalovirus (Stubbs, Ash, & Williams, 1984). Similarly, a number of biochemical and structural deficits have been identified in children with autism (e.g., Ritvo et al., 1978). However, the general consensus from medical assessment research is that although these children do differ from normal children on a variety of dimensions, there is significant variability within the group with autism (Ornitz, 1978). Thus, no single medical sign or signs have to date been useful in differentiating children with autism from others.

Medical assessment has been useful for a variety of research activities. For example, two recent twin studies point to a genetic basis for autism. Folstein and Rutter (1977) found a concordance rate of 36% for autism between monozygotic twins (4 of 11). Using the recent *DSM-III* definition of autism, Ritvo, Freeman, Mason-Brothers, Mo, and Ritvo (1985) found a concordance rate of 95.7% in monozygotic twins (22 of 23) and 23.5% in dizygotic twins (4 of 17). These studies strongly suggest that autism has a genetic origin, and the Ritvo study points to an autosomal recessive inheritance model. These ambitious investigations are offering a first look at the possible etiology of infantile autism.

Additionally, medical information is useful for communicating possible limiting conditions in some children (e.g., presence of seizures). However, the utility of medical assessment for placement and/or treatments decisions has not been demonstrated. For these types of information we must turn to traditional psychological and behavioral assessment.

Traditional Psychological Assessment

The assessment of children with autism with traditional psychological tests has been carried out routinely for only a relatively short time. Up to about 20 years ago, these children were generally considered untestable (Alpern, 1967). However, with the introduction of standardized modifications of traditional tests (Sattler, 1982), along with a behavioral technology for improving compliance, more children with autism have been introduced to psychological assessment. It is safe to assume that in the future every child with autism will participate in some form of traditional psychological assessment.

Traditional psychological tests are instruments that rely on norms to measure differences between individuals (Anastasi, 1968). Specifically, they include measures of academic achievement (e.g., Peabody Individual Achievement Test), intellectual functioning (e.g., Wechsler Intelligence Scale for Children—Revised), and social development (e.g., Vineland Adaptive Behavior Scales). Using these tests, global comparisons can be made between children with autism and children without handicaps.

Estimates of intelligence from standardized tests yield the following generalizations about these children. Children with autism receive scores at both ends of the intellectual continuum. However, the majority fall in the retarded range of intelligence (IQ below 70), with only a very small percentage scoring average or above average on these tests (DeMyer et al., 1974; Gillberg, 1984). These measures of intelligence have been used to determine prognosis. Greater increases in IQ scores have been observed in higher-functioning rather than lower-functioning children with autism following intensive training efforts (DeMyer, 1976). IQ scores for these children predict academic achievement and later adjustment as an adult (DeMyer et al., 1973; Rutter & Lockyer, 1967). Thus, a child with a low IQ score has a poor prognosis for improvement. These findings should be viewed cautiously, however. The follow-up studies cited were conducted on individuals who did not receive the type of intensive behavioral interventions in use today. For example, research with young children with autism suggests that early intervention may be particularly successful (Nordquist & Wahler, 1973; Wolf, Risley, & Mees, 1964), and their prognosis may be more optimistic than previously suggested (Lovaas, 1987). Therefore, conclusions about current predictions of prognosis should be made carefully.

Mothers and fathers of children with autism have been characterized as perfectionistic, cold, and aloof (Kanner, 1949), and from higher socioeconomic backgrounds (Allen, DeMyer, Norton, Pontius, & Yang, 1971; Cox, Rutter, Newman, & Bartak, 1975) and having higher IQs than the general population (Kanner, 1943). Recent evidence suggests that the parents of individuals with autism do not differ from parents of children without handicaps on a variety of personality measures (Koegel, Schreibman, O'Neill, & Burke, 1983; McAdoo & DeMyer, 1978).

A study by Wing (1980) indicates that previous observations of different socioeconomic status (SES) and IQs may have suffered from selection bias. In her sample, no SES differences were found among the parents of groups of children with autism, schizophrenia, and mental retardation. However, higher SES fathers of children with autism were more likely to seek out clinical services and to become members of the National Association for Autistic Children. Thus, previous studies surveying clinics and/or national associations may inadvertently have been biased toward higher SES families. Since higher SES is related to higher IQ, they may also have selected parents with higher IQs. It appears that parents of children with autism may not differ with regard to personality measures, SES, or IQ from parents of normal children or of those with other handicapping conditions.

Perhaps the two most prevalent uses of traditional assessment devices are for research and placement. Recall that intelligence tests have been used in determining prognosis of children with autism. Those who fall within the lower ranges of intellectual functioning appear to be less successful academically and socially later in life (DeMyer et al., 1973; Rutter & Lockyer, 1967). Special education placements are based primarily on the results of these tests (Powers & Handleman, 1984). Thus, information about academic, cognitive, and social functioning is used to place children in settings based on their mental age. What is lacking, however, is evidence that these procedures do in fact result in useful placement decisions. For example, would placing children in educational environments based on their chronological age be more or less beneficial to these children? The validity of using these devices to make placement decisions has not been systematically addressed.

Traditional psychological tests have also had limited impact on the treatment process (Keogh, 1972). Global measures of academic, cognitive, and social functioning may be useful for long-term monitoring of treatment outcome. However, these tests have not been demonstrated to have "treatment validity" (Nelson & Hayes, 1979); in other words, they have not contributed to the process of deciding among specific treatments (e.g., Hoy & Retish, 1984). Assessment devices that point to treatment approaches are sorely needed for intervention with individuals with autism (Durand, 1982b). Behavioral assessment has been suggested as an alternative or adjunct to traditional psychological assessment specifically directed at treatment design.

Behavioral Assessment

Behavioral assessment involves the identification of target behaviors and their controlling variables. The techniques that fall under the general rubric of behavioral assessment include behavioral observations (Johnson & Bolstad, 1973), checklists (e.g., the Autism Screening Instrument for Educational Planning; Krug, Arick, & Almond, 1980), and task analysis (Gold, 1976). Behavioral assessment differs from traditional psychological assessment on at least two dimensions.

First, behavioral assessment focuses on individualized (idiographic) assessment rather than on global (nomothetic) measures of functioning (Nelson & Hayes, 1979). For example, traditional academic achievement testing might place a child's reading on a first-grade level. A behavioral assessment would involve identifying the specific skills (e.g., knows all letters of the alphabet) and deficits (e.g., engages in occasional hand flapping) exhibited by the child that contribute to current levels of functioning.

Second, traditional psychological assessment typically assumes that what is being measured is stable across environments. Behavior on these tests is interpreted as a *sign* of intraorganismic variables (e.g., "personality," "intelligence") (Goldfried & Kent, 1972), and is thus unvarying across settings and assessors. Behavioral assessment, on the other hand, does not adopt this "trait" approach. Behavior is seen as being influenced by both environmental and organismic variables (Mischel, 1968), and is a *sample* of responding in a particular assessment situation (Goldfried & Kent, 1972).

The potential for applying behavioral assessment to placement decisions is promising. As we have discussed, formal psychological testing is typically used to make placement decisions in traditional special education settings. However, informal observations made by administrators and school psychologists are also involved in these judgments (Koegel & Rincover, 1974). Factors such as a child's social and communicative abilities as well as "manageability" are taken into consideration when decisions for placement are made (Newsom & Rincover, 1979). However, behavioral assessment has not formally addressed the issue of appropriate placement of children. Although behavioral assessment as an approach (identification of behavioral excesses and deficits and their controlling variables) may be valuable in making these decisions, specific procedures for this purpose do not exist. No behavioral assessment devices have been documented as useful for the placement of autistic children.

Behavioral assessment should play a major role in treatment. And, without a doubt, it is the *sine qua non* of treatment monitoring. Most clinical outcome studies on autistic behaviors reply on behavioral assessment procedures (e.g., observational data). Moreover, these procedures are ideal for the constant monitoring of programming needed for the successful treatment of individuals with autism. However, treatment validity is lacking. Few behavioral techniques exist for guiding treatment decisions. With respect to providing guidelines for selecting specific treatments, behavioral assessment is a promise that has not been kept.

Future Directions in Assessment

We have been particularly critical of all three types of assessment procedures, and, we feel, for good reason. Adequate psychometrics alone, for example, do not guarantee useful assessment techniques. Placing students in classrooms on the basis of their IQ scores assumes that this grouping is most beneficial for the children. This assumption has yet to be tested. Assessment techniques are needed to point to placement decisions that, in turn, have been demonstrated to result in the acquisition of the greatest number of skills for students. Similarly, reinforcement surveys must point to specific reinforcers for children that have been demonstrated to result in more efficient learning for these children. Finally, procedures that have been demonstrated to help clinicians pick successful interventions for problem behaviors are necessary. The validity of assessment techniques for persons with autism needs to be assessed on the basic of the outcomes these techniques produce.

Related to the above concerns, contemporary work in assessment of problem behavior (e.g., self-injurious behavior, aggression) has begun to address the issue of outcome-based validation. A Motivation Assessment Scale (MAS) has been designed to assess the role of social (e.g., adult attention) and nonsocial (e.g., sensory feedback) factors in the maintenance of such behaviors (Durand & Crimmins, in press). Preliminary data have shown the MAS to be capable of reliably predicting how children will behave in a variety of settings. For example, the MAS can predict if a particular child will engage in substantially more self-injury when presented with a difficult task. This information has been shown to be useful in selecting nonaversive treatments (Carr & Durand, 1985).

Additionally, recent work in sign language training has led to the development of a test that predicts treatment outcome. It appears that some children acquire receptive speech following simultaneous communication training (i.e., the combination of signs with speech), while others do not (e.g., Bonvillian & Nelson, 1976; Carr & Dores, 1981; Miller & Miller, 1973). To explore this finding further, Carr and colleagues (Carr & Dores, 1981; Carr, Pridal, & Dores, 1984) developed a test to predict which children would acquire receptive speech following simultaneous communication training. The test, which assesses children's verbal imitation skills, has demonstrated that children who have good verbal imitation skills acquire receptive speech as well as receptive signing following simultaneous communication training. In contrast, children who have poor verbal imitation skills do not acquire receptive speech. The test is therefore helpful in predicting the outcome of sign language training for children. Future work in assessment should address other areas of behavioral functioning, in order to develop techniques that will produce desirable outcomes for persons with autism.

TREATMENT

Despite 40 years of research on the nature and cause of autism, a "cure" is not currently available. While pockets of optimism exist (e.g., Tinbergen & Tinbergen, 1983), there is no empirical evidence that any treatment or treatments can reliably lead individuals with autism to a normal life. As we have noted in this chapter, autism is the result of a number of biochemical and cognitive deficits. Therefore, it seems unlikely that any one treatment will be completely successful in curing the problem.

In the past, treatment efforts have included such therapeutic approaches as encouraging "ego development" in individuals with autism (Bettelheim, 1967; Kugelmass, 1970). However, treatments based on dynamic theories have had little impact on the lives of people with autism

(Kanner & Eisenberg, 1955). More successful efforts have focused on the specific deficits and excesses displayed by these persons. Identifying excesses and deficits as targets for intervention had its origin in the pioneering work of Ferster (Ferster, 1961; Ferster & DeMyer, 1961, 1962) and Lovaas (Lovaas, Berberich, Perloff, & Schaeffer, 1966; Lovaas, Freitag, Gold, & Kassorla, 1965). These and subsequent investigators have focused on the treatment of certain categories of behaviors that have been identified as important targets for remediation. Emphasis has been placed on behaviors such as language, socialization skills, and the behavioral excesses typically exhibited by individuals with autism (e.g., psychotic speech, self-injurious behavior, tantrums, aggression, and repetitive stereotyped behavior). There has been a move away from the treatment of autism as a unitary entity to the remediation of the various behavior disorders manifested by these persons. In this section we review relevant treatment research.

Language

One defining characteristic of individuals with autism involves a gross deficit in language development. About half of the persons diagnosed as autistic are mute (Lovaas, 1977) and never acquire useful speech (Rutter, 1978). Of those with some speech, much of it is unrecognizable or bizarre in nature (Lovaas et al., 1983). Language deficits can be seen as pivotal to the problems experienced by persons with autism, since they are correlated with an unfavorable prognosis (Lotter, 1978; Rutter, 1968) and may contribute to problems in socialization. The remediation of language deficits therefore has received much attention.

An important first step in teaching language to children with autism was taken by Lovaas and colleagues in the mid-1960s (e.g., Lovaas et at., 1966; Lovaas, Freitas, Nelson, & Whalen, 1967). Using the basic behavioral procedures of shaping and discrimination training, these workers produced verbal imitation in previously mute children. Once these children

acquired verbal imitation skills, subsequent training in more complex forms was facilitated. Later investigations demonstrated success in teaching children to produce labels (Lovaas, 1977), sentences (Garcia, Guess, & Byrnes, 1973; Stevens-Long & Rasmussen, 1974), adjectival inflections (Baer & Guess, 1971), and plurals (Guess, Sailor, Rutherford, & Baer, 1968), along with various other language forms (Carr, 1981). A number of training packages has since been published to assist individuals in teaching speech to persons with autism (Guess, Sailor, & Baer, 1978; Kent, 1974; Lovaas, 1977).

This apparent success in teaching language has not been achieved in all children with autism. Some children make limited progress despite intensive behavioral intervention (Mack, Webster, & Gokcen, 1980). For them, recent work has focused on alternatives to vocal speech (Carr, 1979; Guess, 1980; Sailor et al., 1980). Almost all of the controlled research on these alternatives has been with the use of sign language (Carr, 1982). Sign language research has shown that low-functioning children with autism can be taught to use signs to label (Carr et al., 1978) and to make spontaneous requests of adults (Carr & Kologinsky, 1983). Moreover, for children with some verbal skills (i.e., verbal imitation), simultaneous communication training (using both signs and speech) can facilitate acquisition of receptive speech (Carr & Dores, 1981; Remington & Clarke, 1983). Sign language training may be an alternative for those children who have not benefited from speech training.

In addition to occasionally failing to teach speech to children, behavioral procedures have been criticized for not producing language that is used by children outside of the training setting (Harris, 1975). In response to this criticism, behavioral researchers have recently employed additional procedures in order to promote generalization. One of these procedures, multiple exemplar training, involves teaching language in a variety of settings, across a number of tasks, by more than one teacher (Baer, 1981; Carr, 1980; Stokes & Baer, 1977). This type of training has resulted in generalization of both verbal (e.g., Handleman, 1979) and signing skills (Carr & Kologinsky, 1983).

A final criticism of behavioral work in language has been that children do not readily use their new language skills to communicate spontaneously with others (Carr, 1985; Lovaas et al., 1973). For example, a child might be taught to respond to the phrase "What do you want?" with the word "soda." However, he or she would probably not spontaneously and appropriately request soda without the prompt. A recent trend in language training research addresses this issue of language use. Specifically, Hart and Risley (1980) have developed a set of "incidental teaching" procedures that have helped language-delayed children to communicate with others more spontaneously. Incidental teaching occurs in the natural context (e.g., in the kitchen, at a shopping mall) and with a variety of relevant persons (e.g., teacher, parents, peers). Teaching episodes are initiated by the child and are encouraged through reinforcers related to the topic of discussion (i.e., "natural" reinforcers). It has been suggested that these procedures be tried with children with autism in order to increase their spontaneity (Carr, 1985). Some initial success has been made in teaching spontaneous signing (Carr & Kologinsky, 1983). A suggested direction for future language research is the development and demonstration of successful teaching procedures for producing spontaneity.

Socialization

Disruption in the development of social relationships is a distinctive feature of autism. In fact, what is most striking to a first-time observer is that persons with autism appear to treat other people with no more deference than, say, a piece of furniture. Despite this devastating impairment, relatively few studies have addressed the treatment of social deficits in persons with autism.

In order to increase the social repertoire of children with autism, research has focused on the manipulation of reinforcement contingencies to develop beginning social skills. One skill that has been introduced to these children is social play. Cooperative play with peers and appropriate manipulation of toys are rarely observed in children with autism (Lovaas et al., 1973). In one study, Romanczyk, Diament, Goren, Trunell, and Harris (1975) used shaping and social and tangible reinforcement to encourage social play (i.e., manipulation of a toy simultaneously with another child) among children with autism. They found that they could increase the incidence of social play among these children and that fading out adult involvement increased effectiveness following intervention. It appears that simple social skills (e.g., attention to others, manipulating toys with others) can be taught to children with autism (Hingtgen, Sanders, & DeMyer, 1965; Hingtgen & Trost, 1966; Lovaas et al., 1973).

Several other studies have used non-handicapped peers as treatment agents. Ragland, Kerr, and Strain (1978) used an age-matched peer to increase social interactions among three children with autism. The peer trainer was successful in increasing the frequency of a variety of rudimentary social behaviors in these children (e.g., touching, hugs, sharing toys). However, both this and a subsequent study (Strain, Kerr, & Ragland, 1979) were unsuccessful in producing social responses that were produced in settings other than the training setting, or with persons other than the trainer. Gaylord-Ross, Haring, Breen, and Pitts-Conway (1984) employed a variation of multiple exemplar training (i.e., using a number of peer trainers) and found that their subjects generalized trained social responses to other nonhandicapped peers. These studies suggest that a number of social behaviors can be taught to persons with autism and that training may be carried out with the use of peers.

Although all of these investigations succeeded in teaching children to engage in social behaviors, interpretation of these results should be viewed with caution. What has yet to be demonstrated is that significant others view these behavioral increases as important. In other words, some measure of the social validity (Wolf, 1978) of the effects of social skills training is needed. For example, are nonhandicapped peers more likely to accept children with autism following social skills training? This issue is particularly important in light of recent findings with learning disabled children. Social skills training with these mildly impaired children does not always result in increased acceptance by classmates (Berler, Gross, & Drabman, 1982). Thus, it seems likely that special efforts may be necessary to produce important changes in the social repertoire of more severely handicapped children, such as those with autism.

One approach to insuring the social acceptability of treatment outcome is appropriate selection of responses as targets for training. For example, hugging may not be appropriate as a first response to teach adolescents who interact with other high school students. Selection of appropriate targets for treatment should probably involve persons likely to interact with the trainees. These "significant others" may be able to identify the behaviors needed to be accepted by a particular social group. Future research in this area should address the issue of social validity of both the effects and targets of social skills training. This emphasis is necessary in order to demonstrate clinically significant results from efforts to improve these children's socialization skills.

Problem Behavior

In addition to the deficits in language and socialization displayed by persons with autism, these individuals frequently engage in psychotic speech, seriously disruptive behavior (i.e., aggression, self-injury, tantrums), and repetitive stereotyped behaviors (e.g., rocking, hand flapping). The treatment of these problem behaviors has received considerable attention, in part because of their tendency to interfere with other habilitation efforts (Carr, Newsom, & Binkoff, 1976, 1980; Durand, 1982a; Koegel & Covert, 1972).

Psychotic Speech

Peculiar speech patterns are included as one of *DSM-III*'s criteria for infantile autism. Under this heading are a variety of psychotic speech disorders, including echolalia (i.e., repeating all or part of what another person has said) and bizarre speech (i.e., saying words or phrases that are intelligible but unrelated to the ongoing social context). These behavior patterns are clearly stigmatizing and may interfere with educational efforts (Durand & Crimmins, 1987).

As with socialization skills, relatively little work has been carried out on the psychotic speech of persons with autism. However, some research has looked at the function of psychotic speech. Several studies (Carr, Schreibman, & Lovaas, 1975; Schreibman & Carr, 1978) have suggested that immediate echolalia may be a function of a lack of verbal comprehension. Thus, some children may repeat questions for which they do not have an answer. It has also been suggested that some bizarre speech may be maintained by its auditory consequences (Lovaas, Varni, Koegel, & Lorsch, 1977). Finally, bizarre speech has also been found to serve to terminate academic demands (Durand & Crimmins, 1987). It appears to be a behavior that is maintained in children through a variety of reinforcers (e.g., sensory consequences, escape from demands).

Initial reductions in psychotic speech have been achieved through the reinforcement of incompatible behaviors (Carr et al., 1975; Risley & Wolf, 1967; Wolf et al., 1964). For example, Varni, Russo, and Cataldo (1978) greatly reduced the bizarre speech of one boy by interacting with him when he spoke appropriately about a task and turning away when he engaged in bizarre speech. Schreibman and Carr (1978) taught two children an appropriate, nonecholalic phrase ("I don't know") as a response to a set of previously echoed questions. They found that, in general, echolalia was reduced in these children. Durand and Crimmins (1987) taught their subject to respond to difficult task demands with the phrase, "Help me." Bizaare speech was greatly reduced following this training and at a 6-month follow-up. Teaching children appropriate verbal alternatives to psychotic speech appears to be a successful intervention strategy. However, outcome studies are needed to document generalization and maintenance of these treatment successes in great numbers of individuals.

Disruptive Behavior

Aggression, tantrums, and self-injurious behavior are observed in as many as 70% of persons with autism (Jacobson, 1982). These problem behaviors occupy an inordinate amount of staff time allotted to the care and treatment of these individuals. Disruptive behavior also presents a major obstacle to the habilitation and appropriate placement of persons in the community (Intagliata & Willer, 1982). Because of these concerns, and the threat of physical harm to clients and their care-givers, a large body of research has focused on this problem.

Although usually discussed separately, aggression, tantrums, and self-injury may be usefully conceptualized together. In recent reviews of research on disruptive behavior, it has been pointed out that these forms (e.g., hitting others, screaming, hand-biting) may share common functions (Carr, 1977; Carr & Durand, 1985; Durand & Carr, 1985). For example, self-injurious behavior has been found to be maintained by social attention (Carr & McDowell, 1980; Lovaas & Simmons, 1969), escape from task demands (Carr et al., 1976; Durand, 1982b), tangible consequences (Durand & Carr, 1985; Edelson, Taubman, & Lovaas, 1983), and sensory consequences (Durand, 1982b; Rincover & Devany, 1982). Analogously, aggression and tantrums also have been documented to be maintained by these social and nonsocial influences (Carr & Durand, 1985; Durand, 1984). While aggression, tantrums, and self-injury may differ in topography (i.e., form), they do appear to be maintained by similar consequences (i.e., functions) and therefore, will be considered together in this section.

Noncontingent restraint and pharmacological treatments are commonly used interventions for seriously disruptive behavior (Durand, 1982a). However, the effectiveness of these treatments for disruptive behavior among persons with autism awaits convincing documentation. It is generally accepted that behavioral interventions are the treatments of choice for aggression, tantrums, and self-injury (Favell, Azrin et al., 1982; Harris & Ersner-Hershfield, 1978). Initial attempts at reducing disruptive behavior typically involve reinforcing behaviors that are incompatible (Evans & Meyer, 1985). Variations of this procedure have been labeled differential reinforcement of other behavior (DRO) or differential reinforcement of incompatible behavior (DRI). For example, Lovass and colleagues (Lovaas et al., 1965) found that reinforcing a number of musically related responses (hand-clapping, singing) in a 9-year-old girl resulted in a reduction in her self-injurious head-banging and arm-banging. Unfortunately, clinically significant suppression of seriously disruptive behavior has not generally been achieved through DRO/DRI procedures alone (e.g., Herbert et al., 1973). Because of this, reinforcing incompatible behaviors has typically been part of a treatment regime that also includes some negative consequence for disruptive behavior (Harris & Ersner-Hershfield, 1978).

Among some of the consequences for disruptive behavior that have been successfully combined with DRO/DRI procedures are extinction (Pinkston, Reese, LeBlanc, & Baer, 1973), timeout (Repp & Deitz, 1974), overcorrection (Azrin & Powers, 1975), and contingent electric shock (Lovaas & Simmons, 1969). It is generally agreed that, when properly applied, these procedures are effective in initially reducing seriously disruptive behavior among persons with autism (Carr, 1977; Durand & Carr, 1985; Harris & Ersner-Hershfield, 1978). However, certain caveats are in order.

The first caution in interpreting these investigations involves the debate over the use of aversive consequences (e.g., electric shock) with persons with handicaps. Some argue for their judicious application (e.g., Carr & Lovaas, 1982), and others call for the end of their use (Association for Persons with Severe Handicaps, 1981). In addition, generalization and maintenance of the reductions obtained by these procedures have been limited. Intervention is usually required in each environment in which the disruptive behavior is exhibited (Lovaas et al., 1973).

A new direction in the treatment of behaviors such as aggression, tantrums, and self-injury has been the development of functional communication training (FCT) (Carr & Durand, 1985; Durand & Carr, 1985). FCT involves training the child to substitute appropriate verbal alternatives for problem behavior. For example, if a child's aggression is motivated by adult attention, treatment would involve training the child to verbally recruit adult attention in a more appropriate manner (e.g., by asking the teacher a question such as, "Am I doing good work?"). Thus, FCT involves substituting a different form of the behavior (e.g., a verbal phrase rather than aggression) that serves the same function (e.g., getting attention). FCT has been effective in greatly reducing disruptive behavior among persons with autism (Carr & Durand, 1985), and these gains have been shown to be maintained in new environments (Durand & Carr, 1983). It is recommended that future work focus on identifying responses that can serve as alternatives to severely disruptive behavior.

Stereotyped Behavior

Behavior that is highly consistent and repetitive and that has no apparent adaptive function has been variously labeled "stereotyped" or "self-stimulatory" (Baumeister & Forehand, 1973). These behaviors are observed in a variety of forms, including rocking, hand-flapping, body posturing, and hand-gazing. Up to two-thirds of the persons living in institutions exhibit these behaviors (Berkson & Davenport, 1962), and they have been found to interfere with attention and learning (Koegel & Covert, 1972). A number of theories as to why individuals engage in stereotyped behaviors has been presented (Baumeister & Forehand, 1973; Berkson, 1983), but the most widely accepted view holds that these behaviors are maintained

by their sensory consequences (e.g., vestibular, visual). Thus, behaviors such as body rocking and hand-flapping may continue to be performed because their sensory feedback is reinforcing (Rincover, 1978). Although these behaviors may initially be maintained by sensory consequences, they also may acquire social functions similar to some psychotic speech and disruptive behavior through interactions with parents, teachers, and others (Durand & Carr, in press).

Treatment of sterotyped behavior parallels that of disruptive behavior (Schrader, Shaull, & Elmore, 1983). The most widely used and successful form of intervention involves reinforcing incompatible behavior (DRO/DRI) in combination with such consequences as timeout (e.g., Pendergrass, 1972), overcorrection (e.g., Foxx & Azrin, 1973), and physical restraint (Azrin & Wesolowski, 1980). An additional form of intervention, "sensory extinction," capitalizes on the notion that these behaviors frequently are maintained by their sensory consequences (Rincover, 1978; Rincover, Cook, Peoples, & Packard, 1979). Sensory extinction removes or masks these sensory consequences. In one example, a child's stereotyped behavior involved spinning plates on a table. The auditory feedback that resulted from plate spinning was removed by carpeting the surface of the table. Plate spinning was reduced to near-zero levels. Subsequent work has documented initial success in using sensory extinction in the treatment of stereotyped behavior (Rincover et al., 1979).

A recent development in the treatment of stereotyped behavior is the use of FCT. Recall that some stereotyped behaviors may acquire social functions analogous to other problem behaviors (e.g., escape from task demands). Durand and Carr (in press) treated the escape-motivated hand-flapping and rocking of two children with autism by teaching them to ask appropriately for assistance on their tasks. For such *socially motivated* behaviors, FCT (i.e., asking for help) resulted in significant reductions in these behaviors. Future work should involve assessing the motivating variables for stereotyped behaviors (e.g., sensory consequences, escape) and using this information to design appropriate treatments (e.g., sensory extinction, FCT).

Additional Treatment Research

In addition to language, socialization, and problem behavior, behavioral work has focused on intervention with other behaviors exhibited by persons with autism. Successful outcomes have been achieved in the treatment of self-toileting (Birnbrauer, 1976), self-feeding (Leath & Flourney, 1970), compliance (Lovaas et al., 1973), and cognitive deficits (Schreibman, Koegel, & Craig, 1977). Additionally, researchers have explored the use of peers (Gaylord-Ross et al., 1984), parents (Lovaas, 1978), and siblings (Schreibman, O'Neill, & Koegel, 1983) as treatment agents. Moreover, alternative treatment environments have been used to facilitate treatment success and generalization. These alternatives include group homes (Lovaas et al., 1983) and integrated school settings (Strain, 1983).

It is appropriate to end this section on treatment by describing some exciting new work being conducted with young children with autism. Lovaas (1987) treated two groups of children with autism. One group received intensive behavioral treatment (40 hours or more of one-to-one treatment per week), and another group received less intensive behavioral treatment (10 hours or less of one-to-one treatment per week). Children under 3½ years old were accepted into the program. The project began in 1970, and the progress of these two groups of children has been followed since this time. In brief, the group that received intensive behavioral treatment at this early age had a 50% recovery rate, with another 40% making substantial improvements. Readers should be cautioned that these data are preliminary in nature, but they do suggest a more optimistic attitude toward the prognosis for young children with autism.

SUMMARY

In this chapter we have described recent work and thinking about the nature and care of persons with autism. Definitional issues, epidemiology, developmental implications, and educational issues have been explored. Assessment techniques are sorely needed to help guide care-givers in the placement and treatment of persons with autism. Finally, behavioral approaches to the treatment of specific excesses and deficits have been very successful in making dramatic improvements in the behavior of these individuals. However, generalization and maintenance of these treatment gains are typically not demonstrated. Through the dedication of a number of creative and persistent researchers, the prognosis for persons with autism appears brighter than it was 10 or 20 years ago (DeMyer et al., 1973; Rutter & Lockyer, 1967). It is anticipated that advances in both assessment and treatment techniques will continue to improve the lives of these individuals.

REFERENCES

Allen, J., DeMyer, M., Norton, J., Pontius, W., & Yang, G. (1971). Intellectuality in parents of psychotic, subnormal, and normal children. *Journal of Autism and Childhood Schizophrenia, 1*, 311–326.

Alpern, G. D. (1967). Measurement of "untestable" autistic children. *Journal of Abnormal Psychology, 72*, 478–486.

American Psychiatric Association (1980). *Diagnostic and statistical manual of mental disorders* (3rd ed.). Washington, DC: American Psychiatric Association.

Anastasi, A. (1968). *Psychological testing* (3rd ed.). New York: Macmillan.

The Association for Persons with Severe Handicaps (1981, November). Resolution on intrusive interventions. *TASH Newsletter, 7*, 1–2.

Azrin, N. H., & Powers, M. A. (1975). Eliminating classroom disturbances of emotionally disturbed children by positive practice procedures. *Behavior Therapy, 6*, 525–534.

Azrin, N. H., & Wesolowski, M. D. (1980). A reinforcement plus interruption method of eliminating behavioral stereotypy of profoundly retarded persons. *Behavior Research and Therapy, 18*, 113–119.

Baer, D. M. (1981). A hung jury and a Scottish verdict: "Not proven." *Analysis and Intervention in Developmental Disabilities, 1*, 91–97.

Baer, D. M., & Guess, D. (1971). Receptive training of adjectival inflections in mental retardates. *Journal of Applied Behavior Analysis, 4,* 129–139.

Baumeister, A. A., & Forehand, R. (1973). Stereotyped acts. In N. R. Ellis (Ed.), *International review of research in mental retardation: Vol. 6* (pp. 55–96). New York: Academic Press.

Berkson, G. (1983). Repetitive stereotyped behaviors. *American Journal of Mental Deficiency, 88,* 239–246.

Berkson, G., & Davenport, R. K. (1962). Stereotyped movements of mental defectives: I. Initial survey. *American Journal of Mental Deficiency, 66,* 849–852.

Berler, E. S., Gross, A. M., & Drabman, R. S. (1982). Social skills training with children: Proceed with caution. *Journal of Applied Behavior Analysis, 15,* 41–53.

Bettelheim, B. (1967). *The empty fortress.* New York: Free Press.

Birnbrauer, J. S. (1976). Mental retardation. In H. Leitenberg (Ed.), *Handbook of behavior modification and behavior therapy* (pp. 361–404). Englewood Cliffs, NJ: Prentice-Hall.

Bonvillian, J. D. & Nelson, K. E. (1976). Sign language acquisition in a mute autistic boy. *Journal of Speech and Hearing Disorders, 41,* 339–347.

Bricker, W. A. (1970). Identifying and modifying behavioral deficits. *American Journal of Mental Deficiency, 75,* 16–21.

Cantwell, D. P., Russell, A. T., Mattison, R., & Will, L. (1979). A comparison of *DSM-II* and *DSM-III* in the diagnosis of childhood psychiatric disorders: I. Agreement with expected diagnosis. *Archives of General Psychiatry, 36,* 1208–1213.

Carr, E. G. (1977). The motivation of self-injurious behavior: A review of some hypotheses. *Psychological Bulletin, 84,* 800–816.

Carr, E. G. (1979). Teaching autistic children to use sign language: Some research issues. *Journal of Autism and Developmental Disorders, 9,* 345–359.

Carr, E. G. (1980). Generalization of treatment effects following educational intervention with autistic children and youth. In B. Wilcox and A. Thompson (Eds.), *Critical issues in educating autistic children and youth* (pp. 118–134). Washington, DC: Office of Special Education.

Carr, E. G. (1981). Language acquisition in developmentally disabled children: Preface to the symposium. *Analysis and Intervention in Developmental Disabilities, 1,* 241–243.

Carr, E. G. (1982). Sign language acquisition: Clinical and theoretical aspects. In R. L. Koegel, A. Rincover, & A. L. Egel (Eds.), *Edu-cating and understanding autistic children* (pp. 142–157). San Diego: College-Hill Press.

Carr, E. G. (1985). Behavioral approaches to language and communication. In E. Schopler and G. Mesibov (Eds.), *Current issues in autism: Volume III. Communication problems in autism* (pp. 37–57). New York: Plenum.

Carr, E. G., Binkoff, J. A., Kologinsky, E., & Eddy, M. (1978). Acquisition of sign language by autistic children: I. Expressive labeling. *Journal of Applied Behavior Analysis, 11,* 489–501.

Carr, E. G., & Dores, P. A. (1981). Patterns of language acquisition following simultaneous communication with autistic children. *Analysis and Intervention in Developmental Disabilities, 1,* 347–361.

Carr, E. G., & Durand, V. M. (1985). The social-communicative basis of severe behavior problems in children. In S. Reiss and R. Bootzin (Eds.), *Theoretical issues in behavior therapy* (pp. 219–254). New York: Academic Press.

Carr, E. G., & Kologinsky, E. (1983). Acquisition of sign language by autistic children: II. Spontaneity and generalization effects. *Journal of Applied Behavior Analysis, 16,* 297–314.

Carr, E. G., & Lovaas, O. I. (1982). Contingent electric shock as a treatment for severe behavior problems. In S. Axelrod and J. Apsche (Eds.), *Punishment: Its effects on human behavior* (pp. 221–245). New York: Academic Press.

Carr, E. G., & McDowell, J. J. (1980). Social control of self-injurious behavior of organic etiology. *Behavior Therapy, 11,* 402–409.

Carr, E. G., Newsom, C. D., & Binkoff, J. A. (1976). Stimulus control of self-destructive behavior in a psychotic child. *Journal of Abnormal Child Psychology, 4,* 139–153.

Carr, E. G., Newsom, C. D., & Birkoff, J. A. (1980). Escape as a factor in the aggressive behavior of two retarded children. *Journal of Applied Behavior Analysis, 13,* 101–118.

Carr, E. G., Pridal, C., & Dores, P. A. (1984). Speech versus sign comprehension in autistic children: Analysis and prediction. *Journal of Experimental Child Psychology, 37,* 587–597.

Carr, E. G., Schreibman, L., & Lovaas, O. I. (1975). Control of echolalic speech in psychotic children. *Journal of Abnormal Child Psychology, 3,* 331–351.

Charlop, M. H. (1983). The effects of echolalia on acquisition and generalization of receptive labeling in autistic children. *Journal of Applied Behavior Analysis, 16,* 111–126.

Chess, S., Korn, S. J., & Fernandez, P. B. (1971). *Psychiatric disorders of children with congenital rubella.* New York: Brunner/Mazel.

Cox, A., Rutter, M., Newman, S., & Bartak, L. (1975). A comparative study of infantile autism and specific developmental receptive language disorder: II. Parental characteristics. *British Journal of Psychiatry, 126,* 146–159.

Dawson, G., & McKissick, F. C. (1984). Self-recognition in autistic children. *Journal of Autism and Developmental Disorders, 14,* 383–394.

de Lissovoy, V. (1961). Head banging in early childhood. *Child Development, 33,* 43–56.

DeMyer, M. K. (1976). Motor, perceptual-motor and intellectual disabilities of autistic children. In L. Wing (Ed.), *Early childhood autism* (2nd ed.,) (pp. 169–193). Oxford: Pergamon.

DeMyer, M. K., Barton, S., Alpern, G. D., Kimberlin, C., Allen, J., & Steele, R. (1974). The measured intelligence of autistic children. *Journal of Autism and Childhood Schizophrenia, 4,* 42–60.

DeMyer, M. K., Barton, S., DeMyer, W. E., Norton, J. A., Allen, J., & Steele, R. (1973). Prognosis in autism: A follow-up study. *Journal of Autism and Childhood Schizophrenia, 3,* 199–246.

DeMyer, M. K., Hingtgen, J. N., & Jackson, R. K. (1981). Infantile autism reviewed: A decade of research. *Schizophrenia Bulletin, 7,* 388–450.

Despert, J. L. (1971). Reflections on early infantile autism. *Journal of Autism and Childhood Schizophrenia, 1,* 363–367.

Durand, V. M. (1982a). A behavioral/pharmacological intervention for the treatment of severe self-injurious behaviour. *Journal of Autism and Developmental Disorders, 12,* 243–251.

Durand, V. M. (1982b). Analysis and intervention of self-injurious behavior. *Journal of the Association for the Severely Handicapped, 7,* 44–53.

Durand, V. M. (1984). *Attention-getting problem behavior: Analysis and intervention.* Unpublished doctoral dissertation, SUNY, Stony Brook, NY.

Durand, V. M., & Carr, E. G. (in press). Social influences on "self-stimulatory behavior: Analysis and treatment application. *Journal of Applied Behavior Analysis.*

Durand, V. M., & Carr, E. G. (1985). Self-injurious behavior: Motivating conditions and guidelines for treatment. *School Psychology Review. 14,* 171–176.

Durand, V. M., & Crimmins, D. B. (1987). Assessment and treatment of psychotic speech in an autistic child. *Journal of Autism and Developmental Disorders, 17,* 17–28.

Durand, V. M., & Crimmins, D. B. (in press). Identifying the variables maintaining self-injurious behavior. *Journal of Autism and Developmental Disorders.*

Edelson, S. M., Taubman, M. T., & Lovaas, O. I. (1983). Some social contexts of self-destructive behavior. *Journal of Abnormal Child Psychology, 11,* 299–312.

Eisenberg, L., & Kanner, L. (1956). Early infantile autism 1943–1955. *American Journal of Orthopsychiatry, 26,* 556–566.

Ellis, N. R. (1979). The Partlow case: A reply to Dr. Roos. *Law and Psychology Review, 5,* 15–49.

Evans, I. M., & Meyer, L. H. (1985). *An educative approach to behavior problems: A practical decision model for interventions with severely handicapped learners.* Baltimore: Paul H. Brookes.

Favell, J. E., Azrin, N. H., Baumeister, A. A., Carr, E. G., Dorsey, M. F., Forehand, R., Foxx, R. M., Lovaas, O. I., Rincover, A., Risley, T. R., Romanczyk, R. G., Russo, D. C., Schroeder, S. R., & Solnick, J. V. (1982). Treatment of self-injurious behavior. *Behavior Therapy, 13,* 529–554.

Favell, J. E., McGimsey, J. F., & Schell, R. M. (1982). Treatment of self-injury by providing alternate sensory activities. *Analysis and Intervention in Developmental Disabilities, 2,* 83–104.

Ferrari, M., & Mathews, W. S. (1983). Self-recognition deficits in autism: Syndrome-specific or general developmental delay. *Journal of Autism and Developmental Disorders, 13,* 317–324.

Ferster, C. B. (1961). Positive reinforcement and behavioral deficits of autistic children. *Child Development, 32,* 437–456.

Ferster, C. B., & DeMyer, M. K. (1961). The development of performance in autistic children in an automatically controlled environment. *Journal of Chronic Diseases, 13,* 312–345.

Ferster, C. B., & DeMyer, M. K. (1962). A method for the experimental analysis of the behavior of autistic children. *American Journal of Orthopsychiatry, 32,* 89–98.

Folstein, S., & Rutter, M. (1977). Infantile autism: A genetic study of 21 twin pairs. *Journal of Child Psychology and Psychiatry, 18,* 297–321.

Foxx, R. M., & Azrin, N. H. (1973). The elimination of autistic self-stimulatory behavior by overcorrection. *Journal of Applied Behavior Analysis, 6,* 1–14.

Garcia, E., Guess, D., & Byrnes, J. (1973). Development of syntax in a retarded girl using imitation, reinforcement, and modelling. *Journal of Applied Behavior Analysis, 6,* 299–310.

Gaylord-Ross, R. J., Haring, T. G., Breen, C., & Pitts-Conway, V. (1984). The training and generalization of social interaction skills with autistic youth. *Journal of Applied Behavior Analysis, 17,* 229–247.

Gillberg, C. (1984). Infantile autism and other childhood psychoses in a Swedish urban region: Epidemiological aspects. *Journal of Child Psychology and Psychiatry, 25,* 35–43.

Gold, M. W. (1976). Task analysis of a complex assembly task by the retarded child. *Exceptional Children, 43,* 78–84.

Goldfarb, W. (1963). Self-awareness in schizophrenic children. *Archives of General Psychiatry, 8,* 63–76.

Goldfried, M. R., & Kent, R. N. (1972). Traditional versus behavioral personality assessment: A comparison of methodological and theoretical assumptions. *Psychological Bulletin, 77,* 409–420.

Guess, D. (1980). Methods in communication instruction for severely handicapped persons. In W. Sailor, B. Wilcox, & L. Brown (Eds.), *Methods of instruction for severely handicapped students* (pp. 195–225). Baltimore: Paul H. Brookes.

Guess, D., Sailor, W., & Baer, D. M. (1978). *Functional speech and language training for the severely handicapped.* Lawrence, KS: H & H Enterprises.

Guess, D., Sailor, W., Rutherford, G., & Baer, D. M. (1968). An experimental analysis of linguistic development: The productive use of the plural morpheme. *Journal of Applied Behavior Analysis, 1,* 297–306.

Handleman, J. S. (1979). Generalization by autistic-type children of verbal responses across settings. *Journal of Applied Behavior Analysis, 12,* 273–282.

Harris, S. L. (1975). Teaching language to nonverbal children—with emphasis on problems of generalization. *Psychological Bulletin, 82,* 565–580.

Harris, S. L., & Ersner-Hershfield, R. (1978). Behavioral suppression of seriously disruptive behavior in psychotic and retarded patients: A review of punishment and its alternatives. *Psychological Bulletin, 85,* 1352–1375.

Hart, B., & Risley, T. R. (1980). In vivo language intervention: Unanticipated general effects. *Journal of Applied Behavior Analysis, 13,* 407–432.

Herbert, E. W., Pinkston, E. M., Hayden, M. L., Sajwaj, T. E., Pinkston, S., Cordua, S. G., & Jackson, C. (1973). Adverse effects of differential parental attention. *Journal of Applied Behavior Analysis, 6,* 15–30.

Hermelin, B., & O'Connor, N. (1970). *Psychological experiments with autistic children.* Oxford: Pergamon.

Hingtgen, J. N., Sanders, B. J., & DeMyer, M. K. (1965). Shaping cooperative responses in early childhood schizophrenics. In L. Ullmann & L. Krasner (Eds.), *Case studies in behavior modification* (pp. 130–138). New York: Holt, Rinehart & Winston.

Hingtgen, J. N., & Trost, F. C. (1966). Shaping cooperative responses in early childhood schizophrenics: II. Reinforcement of mutual physical contact and vocal responses. In R. Ulrich, T. Stachnik & J. Mabry (Eds.), *Control of human behavior* (pp. 110–114). Glenview, IL: Scott, Foresman.

Hoy, M. P., & Retish, P. M. (1984). A comparison of two types of assessment reports. *Exceptional Children, 51,* 225–229.

Intagliata, J., & Willer, B. (1982). Reinstitutionalization of mentally retarded persons successfully placed into family care and group homes. *American Journal of Mental Deficiency, 87,* 34–39.

Itard, J. G. (1962). *The wild boy of Aveyron.* New York: Appleton-Century-Crofts.

Jacobson, J. W. (1982). Problem behavior and psychiatric impairment within a developmentally disabled population: I. Behavior frequency. *Applied Research in Mental Retardation, 3,* 121–139.

Johnson, S. M., & Bolstad, O. D. (1973). Methodological issues in naturalistic observations: Some problems and solutions for field research. In L. A. Hamerlynck, L. C. Handy, & E. J. Mash (Eds.), *Behavior change: Methodology, concepts, and practice* (pp. 7–67). Champaign, IL: Research Press.

Kanner, L. (1943). Autistic disturbances of affective contact. *Nervous Child, 2,* 217–250.

Kanner, L. (1949). Problems of nosology and psychodynamics of early infantile autism. *American Journal of Orthopsychiatry, 19,* 416–426.

Kanner, L., & Eisenberg, L. (1955). Notes on the follow-up studies of autistic children. In P. Hoch & J. Zubin (Eds.), *Psychopathology of childhood* (pp. 227–239). New York: Grune & Stratton.

Kaufman, J. M. (Ed.). (1981). Are all children educable? [Special issue]. *Analysis and Intervention in Developmental Disabilities, 1*(1).

Kent, L. R. (1974). *Language acquisition program for the retarded or multiply impaired.* Champaign, IL: Research Press.

Keogh, B. K. (1972). Psychological evaluation of exceptional children: Old hangups and new directions. *Journal of School Psychology, 10,* 141–145.

Koegel, R. L., & Covert, A. (1972). The relationship of self-stimulation to learning in autistic children. *Journal of Applied Behavior Analysis, 5,* 381–387.

Koegel, R. L., Schreibman, L., O'Neill, R. E., & Burke, J. C. (1983). The personality and family interaction characteristics of parents of autistic children. *Journal of Consulting and Clinical Psychology, 51,* 683–692.

Krug, D. A., Arick, J. R., & Almond, P. J. (1980). *Autism screening instrument for educational planning.* (ASIEP) Portland, OR: ASIEP Education Co.

Kugelmass, N. I. (1970). *The autistic child.* Springfield, IL: Charles C. Thomas.

Leath, J. R., & Flourney, R. L. (1970). Three year follow-up of an intensive habit-training program. *Mental Retardation, 8,* 32–34.

Lotter, V. (1966). Epidemiology of autistic conditions in young children: I. Prevalence. *Social Psychiatry, 1,* 124–137.

Lotter, V. (1974). Factors related to outcome in autistic children. *Journal of Autism and Childhood Schizophrenia, 4,* 263–277.

Lotter, V. (1978). Follow-up studies. In M. Rutter & E. Schopler (Eds.), *Autism: A reappraisal of concepts and treatment* (pp. 475–495). New York: Plenum.

Lovaas, O. I. (1977). *The autistic child: Language development through behavior modification.* New York: Irvington.

Lovaas, O. I. (1978). Parents as therapists. In M. Rutter and E. Schopler (Eds.), *Autism: A reappraisal of concepts and treatment* (pp. 369–378). New York: Plenum.

Lovaas, O. I. (1987). Behavioral treatment and normal educational and intellectual functioning in young autistic children. *Journal of Consulting and Clinical Psychology, 55,* 3–9.

Lovaas, O. I., Ackerman, A. B., & Taubman, M. T. (1983). An overview of behavioral treatment of autistic persons. In M. Rosenbaum, C. M. Franks, & Y. Jaffe (Eds.), *Perspectives on behavior therapy in the eighties* (pp. 287–308). New York: Springer.

Lovaas, O. I., Berberich, J. P., Perloff, B. F., & Schaeffer, B. (1966). Acquisition of imitative speech by schizophrenic children. *Science, 151,* 705–707.

Lovaas, O. I., Freitag, G., Gold, V. J., & Kassorla, I. C. (1965). Experimental studies in childhood schizophrenia: Analysis of self-destructive behavior. *Journal of Experimental Child Psychology, 2,* 67–84.

Lovaas, O. I., Freitas, L., Nelson, K., & Whalen, C. (1967). The establishment of imitation and its use for the development of complex behavior in schizophrenic children. *Behavior Research and Therapy, 5,* 171–181.

Lovaas, O. I., Koegel, R., Simmons, J. Q., & Stevens, J. (1973). Some generalization and follow-up measures on autistic children in behavior therapy. *Journal of Applied Behavior Analysis, 6,* 131–166.

Lovaas, O. I., Schreibman, L., Koegel, R., & Rehm, R. (1971). Selective responding by autistic children to multiple sensory input. *Journal of Abnormal Psychology, 77,* 211–222.

Lovaas, O. I., & Simmons, J. Q. (1969). Manipulation of self-destruction in three retarded children. *Journal of Applied Behavior Analysis, 2,* 143–157.

Lovaas, O. I., Varni, J. W., Koegel, R. L., & Lorsch, N. (1977). Some observations on the nonextinguishability of children's speech. *Child Development, 48,* 1121–1127.

Mack, J. E., Webster, C. D., & Gokcen, I. (1980). Where are they now and how are they faring? Follow-up of 51 severely handicapped speech-deficient children, four years after an operant-based program. In C. D. Webster, M. M. Konstantareas, J. Oxman, & J. E. Mack (Eds.), *Autism: New directions in research and education* (pp. 93–106). New York: Pergamon.

Mahler, M. (1052). On childhood psychosis and schizophrenia: Autistic and symbiotic infantile psychosis. *Psychoanalytic Study of the Child, 7,* 286–305.

Mattison, R., Cantwell, D. P., Russell, A. T., & Will, L. (1979). A comparison of *DSM-II* and *DSM-III* in the diagnosis of childhood psychiatric disorders: II. Interrater agreement. *Archives of General Psychiatry, 36,* 1217–1222.

McAdoo, W. G., & DeMyer, M. K. (1978). Research related to family factors in autism. *Journal of Pediatric Psychology, 2,* 162–166.

Miller, A., & Miller, E. E. (1973). Cognitive-developmental training with elevated boards and sign language. *Journal of Autism and Childhood Schizophrenia, 3,* 65–85.

Mischel, W. (1968). *Personality and assessment.* New York: Wiley.

Nakanishi, Y., & Owada, K. (1973). Echoic utterances of children between the ages of 1 and 3 years. *Journal of Verbal Learning and Verbal Behavior, 12,* 658–663.

Nelson, R. O., & Hayes, S. C. (1979). Some current dimensions of behavioral assessment. *Behavioral Assessment, 1,* 1–16.

Neuman, C. J., & Hill, S. D. (1978). Self-recognition and stimulus preference in autistic children. *Developmental Psychobiology, 11,* 571–578.

Newsom, C. D., & Rincover, A. (1979). Behavioral assessment of autistic children. In E. J. Mash & L. G. Terdal (Eds.), *Behavioral assessment of childhood disorders* (pp. 397–439). New York: Guilford.

Nordquist, V. M., & Wahler, R. G. (1973). Naturalistic treatment of an autistic child. *Journal of Applied Behavior Analysis, 6,* 79–87.

Ornitz, E. M. (1978). Biological homogeneity or heterogeneity? In M. Rutter & E. Schopler (Eds.), *Autism: A reappraisal of concepts and treatment* (pp. 243–250). New York: Plenum.

Pendergrass, V. E. (1972). Timeout from positive reinforcement following persistent, highrate behavior in retardates. *Journal of Applied Behavior Analysis, 5,* 85–91.

Pinkston, E. M., Reese, N. M., LeBlanc, J. M., & Baer, D. M. (1973). Independent control of a preschool child's aggression and peer interaction by contingent teacher attention. *Journal of Applied Behavior Analysis, 6,* 115–124.

Powers, M. D., & Handleman, J. S. (1984). *Behavioral assessment of severe developmental disabilities.* Rockville, MD: Aspen.

Public Law 94-142. (1977). *Federal Register* (Part IV). Washington, DC: U.S. Government printing office, August 23, 1977.

Ragland, E. U., Kerr, M. M., & Strain, P. S. (1978). Behavior of withdrawn autistic children: Effects of peer social initiations. *Behavior Modification, 2,* 565–578.

Remington, B., & Clarke, S. (1983). Acquisition of expressive signing by autistic children: An evaluation of the relative effects of simultaneous communication and sign-alone training. *Journal of Applied Behavior Analysis, 16,* 315–328.

Repp, A. C., & Deitz, S. M. (1974). Reducing aggressive and self-injurious behavior of institutionalized retarded children through reinforcement of other behavior. *Journal of Applied Behavior Analysis, 7,* 313–325.

Ricks, D. M., & Wing, L. (1975). Language, communication, and the use of symbols in normal and autistic children. *Journal of Autism and Childhood Schizophrenia, 5,* 191–221.

Rimland, B. (1964). *Infantile autism.* New York: Appleton-Century-Crofts.

Rimland, B. (1971). The differentiation of childhood psychoses: An analysis of checklists for 2,218 psychotic children. *Journal of Autism and Childhood Schizophrenia, 1,* 161–174.

Rincover, A. (1978). Sensory extinction: A procedure for eliminating self-stimulatory behavior in developmentally disabled children. *Journal of Abnormal Child Psychology, 6,* 299–310.

Rincover, A., Cook, A. R., Peoples, A., & Packard, D. (1979). Sensory extinction and sensory reinforcement principles for programming multiple adaptive behavior change. *Journal of Applied Behavior Analysis, 12,* 221–233.

Rincover, A., & Devany, J. (1982). The application of sensory extinction procedures to self-injury. *Analysis and Intervention in Developmental Disabilities, 2,* 67–81.

Risley, T., Wolf, M. (1967). Establishing functional speech in echolalic children. *Behavior Research and Therapy, 5,* 73–88.

Ritvo, E. R., Freeman, B. J., Mason-Brothers, A., Mo, A., & Ritvo, A. M. (1985). Concordance for the syndrome of autism in 40 pairs of afflicted twins. *American Journal of Psychiatry, 142,* 74–77.

Ritvo, E. R., Rabin, K., Yuwiler, A., Freeman, B. J., & Geller, E. (1978). Biochemical and hemotologic studies: A critical review. In M. Rutter & E. Schopler (Eds.), *Autism: A reappraisal of concepts and treatment* (pp. 163–183). New York: Plenum.

Romanczyk, R. G., Diament, C., Goren, E. R., Trunell, G., & Harris, S. L. (1975). Increasing isolate and social play in severely disturbed children: Intervention and postintervention effectiveness. *Journal of Autism and Childhood Schizophrenia, 5,* 57–70.

Rosenbloom, S., Campbell, M., George, A. E., Kricheff, I. I., Taleporos, E., Anderson, L., Rueben, R. N., & Korein, J. (1984). High resolution CT scanning in infantile autism: A quantitative approach. *Journal of the American Academy of Child Psychiatry, 23,* 72–77.

Rutter, M. (1968). Concepts of autism: A review of research. *Journal of Child Psychology and Psychiatry, 9,* 1–25.

Rutter, M. (1978). Diagnosis and definition of childhood autism. *Journal of Autism and Childhood Schizophrenia, 8,* 139–161.

Rutter, M., & Lockyer, V. (1967). A 5–15 year follow-up study of infantile psychosis: I. Description of sample. *British Journal of Psychiatry, 113,* 1169–1182.

Sailor, W., Guess, D., Goetz, L., Schuler, A., Utley, B., & Baldwin, M. (1980). Language and severely handicapped persons: Deciding what to teach to whom. In W. Sailor, B. Wilcox, & L. Brown (Eds.), *Methods of instruction for severely handicapped students* (pp. 71–105). Baltimore: Paul H. Brookes.

Sattler, J. M. (1982). *Assessment of children's intelligence and specific abilities* (2nd ed.). Boston: Allyn Bacon.

Schopler, E., Brehm, S., Kinsbourne, M., & Reichler, R. J. (1971). Effect of treatment structure on development in autistic children. *Archives of General Psychiatry*, 24, 415–421.

Schover, L. R., & Newsom, C. D. (1976). Overselectivity, developmental level, and overtraining in autistic and normal children. *Journal of Abnormal Child Psychology*, 4, 289–298.

Schrader, C., Shaull, J., & Elmore, B. (1983). Behavioral treatment of self-stimulation in the developmentally disabled: A methodological review. *Behavior Modification*, 7, 267–294.

Schreibman, L., & Carr, E. G. (1978). Elimination of echolalic responding to questions through the training of a generalized verbal response. *Journal of Applied Behavior Analysis*, 11, 453–463.

Schreibman, L., Koegel, R. L., & Craig, M. S. (1977). Reducing stimulus overselectivity in autistic children. *Journal of Abnormal Child Psychology*, 5, 425–436.

Schreibman, L., O'Neill, R. E., & Koegel, R. L. (1983). Behavioral training for siblings of autistic children. *Journal of Applied Behavior Analysis*, 16, 129–138.

Sigman, M., & Ungerer, J. A. (1984). Attachment behaviors in autistic children. *Journal of Autism and Developmental Disorders*, 14, 231–244.

Spiker, D., & Ricks, M. (1984). Visual self-recognition in autistic children: Developmental relationships. *Child Development*, 55, 214–225.

Stevens-Long, J., & Rasmussen, M. (1974). The acquisition of simple and compound sentence structure in an autistic child. *Journal of Applied Behavior Analysis*, 7, 473–479.

Stokes, T. F., & Baer, D. M. (1977). An implicit technology of generalization. *Journal of Applied Behavior Analysis*, 10, 349–367.

Strain, P. S. (1983). Generalization of autistic children's social behavior change: Effects of developmentally integrated and segregated settings. *Analysis and Intervention in Developmental Disabilities*, 3, 23–34.

Strain, P. S., Kerr, M. M., & Ragland, E. U. (1979). Effects of peer-mediated social initiations and prompting reinforcement procedures on the social behavior of autistic children. *Journal of Autism and Developmental Disorders*, 9, 41–54.

Stubbs, E. G., Ash, E., & Williams, C. P. S. (1984). Autism and congenital cytomegalovirus. *Journal of Autism and Developmental Disorders*, 14, 183–189.

Taft, L. T., & Cohen, H. J. (1971). Hypsarrhythmia and infantile autism: A clinical report. *Jornal of Autism and Childhood Schizophrenia*, 1, 327–336.

Tinbergen, E. A., & Tinbergen, N. (1972). *Early childhood autism: An ethological approach*. Berlin: Paul Parey.

Tinbergen, N., & Tinbergen, E. A. (1983). *Autistic children: New hope for a cure*. Winchester, MA: Allen & Unwin.

Treffert, D. (1970). Epidemiology of infantile autism. *Archives of General Psychiatry*, 22, 431–438.

Varni, J. W., Russo, D. C., & Cataldo, M.. F. (1978). Assessment and modification of delusional speech in an 11-year-old child: A comparative analysis of behavior therapy and stimulant drug effects. *Journal of Behavior Therapy and Experimental Psychiatry*, 9, 377–380.

Wilhelm, H., & Lovaas, O. I. (1976). Stimulus overselectivity: A common feature in autism and mental retardation. *American Journal of Mental Deficiency*, 81, 227–241.

Wing, L. (1980). Childhood autism and social class: A question of selection? *British Journal of Psychiatry*, 137, 410–417.

Wing, L., & Gould, J. (1979). Severe impairments of social interaction and associated abnormalities in children: Epidemiology and classification. *Journal of Autism and Developmental Disorders*, 9, 11–29.

Wolf, M. M. (1978). Social validity: The case for subjective measurement or how applied behavior analysis is finding its heart. *Journal of Applied Behavior Analysis*, 11, 203–214.

Wolf, M. M., Risley, T. R., & Mees, H. (1964). Application of operant conditioning procedures to the behavior problems of an autistic child. *Behavior Research and Therapy*, 1, 305–312.

CHAPTER 14

Cerebral Palsy

Michael A. Alexander and Roberta E. Bauer

The child with cerebral palsy is superficially classified by the type of motor involvement. Yet, each child represents a unique grouping of problems ranging from additional central nervous system defects to a host of psychosocial issues. Interventions in these children for the related and often more important nonmotor problems are covered elsewhere in this book. This chapter will cover many of the motor issues, but the authors wish to stress that motor interventions, be they therapy, drugs, or surgery, should always be considered in the context of the entire child.

DESCRIPTION OF THE DISORDER

Cerebral palsy occurs in 1 to 2 per 1,000 live births. Life expectancy is normal and the estimated living American population is 400,000 (Taft, 1984).

Cerebral palsy is a nonprogressive disorder of motion and posture due to brain insult or injury occurring in the period of early brain growth (prenatal up to 5 years) (Vining, Accardo, Rubenstein, Farrell, & Roisen, 1976). The diagnosis implies and, in fact, demands that progressive dis-

orders, such as neoplastic processses, hydrocephalus, and degenerative diseases have been excluded. The differential diagnosis includes mental retardation, myopathies/neuropathies, spinal abnormalities, involuntary movement disorders, arthrogryposis, and inherited syndromes, such as familial spastic diplegia, hereditary ataxia, and hereditary microcephally (Vining et al., 1976). Cases of cerebral palsy are divided into the following types:

1. Pyramidal (spastic),
2. Extra pyramidal (rigid, athetoid, or ataxic),
3. Mixed and, rarely,
4. Atonic.

Cerebral palsy can also be further described by the characterization of the limbs involved:

1. Diplegia (both lower extremities and arms to lesser extent),
2. Hemiplegia (an ipsilateral arm and leg),
3. Quadriplegia (all four limbs), and
4. Triplegia (one arm better than the other three limbs).

Spastic diplegia is often associated with prematurity, whether or not there is associated intraventicular hemorrhage. Athetosis is associated with kernicterus and the more severe quadriplegia with hypoxia or congenital infections.

DEVELOPMENTAL ISSUES

Gross motor, self-care, language, cognitive, and social/emotional milestones may be delayed in the chronology of their acquisition, or may be affected qualitatively by motor control problems. Family dynamics and parenting behaviors at different stages in the cerebral palsy child's development may also be affected. Choices of types of treatment modalities are affected by the child's stage of development.

Gross Motor Problems

Failure to achieve head control, independent sitting, and independent ambulation by crawling or walking are often the clinical features that first alert clinicians to the possibility of a neuromuscular problem. Delay in sitting up has the immediate implication of limiting the child's ability to use his or her hands to explore the environment. This diminishes his or her opportunity for cognitive stimulation unless interventions are made.

Prognostically, if children are unable to sit up independently by 4 years of age, it is unlikely that they will ever ambulate independently with or without crutches. Further, if there is no sitting by 4 years of age and no evidence of the persistence of three primitive reflexes present, there is no possibility for ambulation (Bleck, 1975; Molnar & Gordon, 1976), Yet, overall, the prognosis for ambulation in children with cerebral palsy is good. The severity of motor involvement obviously determines the length of delay of functional acquisition. In general, hemiplegics can be expected to walk between age 2 and 3 years. Mild diplegics may only be delayed by a few months. However, the quality of their early walking may be altered, with prolonged toe walking and persistence of the guarding position in the arms for a longer

period of time. When it is appreciated that independent mobility is likely to be delayed well beyond the usual chronologic age of acquisition, consideration of adaptive equipment such as scooter boards, wheelchairs, or walkers should be suggested to allow the child the perceptual experiences of moving through space. Allowing children the independence to choose what they want to see and where they want to go is a further reason for providing a mobility aid (Alexander, 1985).

Self-Care Problems

Self-care milestone delays may first be manifested by feeding difficulties. Pseudobulbar involvement may present in the newborn period as a poor suck with frequent choking. These difficulties may persist as problems are encountered with increasing the food textures. In normal development, the tongue thrust is usually diminished sufficiently by 4 to 6 months of age to allow the introduction of solid foods and cereals. In children with oral pharyngeal involvement, tongue thrust, as well as hypersensitivity of the oral cavity, may necessitate major therapeutic interventions. These interventions include positioning, adapted spoons, and very careful introduction of solid foods texture to accomplish this milestone.

In the more mildly affected children, oral pharyngeal involvement may manifest only as persistence of drooling beyond the expected 12 to 18 months in unaffected children. Although drooling is unlikely to be seen as a significant disability in the preschool years; if persistent, it becomes a major cosmetic as well as social interaction deterrent in the adolescent years. Good correction of drooling can be obtained from surgical intervention (Morgan, Hansen, Wills, & Hoopes, 1981).

Self-feeding, normally expected between 10 to 15 months of age, may be delayed or precluded by the child's upper extremity involvement. Early intervention consists of showing families positions that will diminish reflex influences and encourage hand/mouth activities. At later ages, adaptive equipment (e.g. spoons with special handles, rocker bottom knives, plates with suction cups to hold them to the table) may be suggested by occupational therapists to allow children to be independent in feeding commensurate with their cognitive abilities, despite their motor disabilities.

Delays in dressing and undressing milestones are affected by the different kinds of motor problems. The first is in the hemiparetic, in whom there is frequently sensory neglect of the limb. This neglect obligates the child to learn to clothe the paretic limb first and then use the more functional extremity to continue dressing. Second, spastic muscles or decreased range of motion (due to contracted joints) and diminished purposeful control make it all but impossible for the child to support him- or herself in space and pull an article of clothing over his or her feet or buttocks. Finally, lack of fine motor coordination to accomplish the rather high-level skills of zippering, snapping, and buttoning may prolong a child's dependence on caregivers beyond the usual 4 to 5 years.

A number of contributors may delay independence in personal hygiene and toilet training. These include independent dressing skills and spasticity of adductors, with resultant poor balance and fear of falling. Sensory input from the bladder or rectal sphincters must be counteracted to allow physiological relaxation needed for elimination. Constipation and obstipation are problems in severely involved patients. When a child is approaching adolescence and becoming increasingly sensitive to the need for privacy, therapeutic interventions such as surgery for release of adductor tightness or pharmacological interventions to decrease spasticity may be needed to facilitate self-care and toileting. For the severely involved spastic who often may be of normal cognitive ability, dressing and personal hygiene goals deserve major therapeutic attention. The attainment of independence will have a major impact on the sense of self-worth for these patients.

Language Problems

Postural and motor deficits of cerebral palsy may be completely compatible with normal language development. With extra-pyramidal or with pseudobulbar involvement, however, dysarthria and/or verbal apraxia may inhibit expressive language development. Classic Wernicke's or Broca's aphasias are not seen in the hemiplegic child. The same untoward conditions in the pre- or perinatal period that lead to damage of the motor control areas of the brain may also affect cortical areas later responsible for receptive or expressive language development.

Sensorineural hearing loss is an associated condition in many cerebral palsy children (Taft, 1984). Some studies cite as high as 25% of patients with extrapyramidal involvement as having sensorineural hearing loss; those involved with spastic cerebral palsy may be deaf in approximately 7% of cases (Hopkins, Bice, & Callan, 1954; Taft, 1984). These possibilities put the preschooler with cerebral palsy at high risk for delayed language development.

The attendant social and emotional sequelae of expressive language delays, as well as the cognitive implications of receptive delays, are well-described and not unique to cerebral palsy children. What is unique are the constraints that motor involvement of the upper extremities may place on interventions and strategies for the expressively impaired child. Signing, or the use of an augmentative communication system, require varying amounts of motor facility. The decision regarding the best system requires input from occupational therapists and psychologists for dexterity and cognitive abilities, respectively. Hopes for eventual verbal language and intensive therapy toward that goal need to be weighed against the value of alternative communication systems (e.g. computers) in providing children some method of expressing their needs and establishing social interaction at any level with those around them.

Cognitive Problems

Piagetian Theory

The effects of motor impairment on cognitive development are interesting to consider. The traditional Piagetian theory of intellectual development suggests that more complex schema are developed in the sensori-motor period by the infant's opportunity to observe the effects of his or her motor activity on the environment. The infant's ability to move back and forth from an area where he or she can visually appreciate an object to an area where he or she can no longer see it might at least give infants additional practice in experiencing the notion that objects are permanent. The opportunity to see an object from a different orientation or to manipulate it may allow children to develop a mental concept of what the part of an object that they cannot see looks like in space. This same idea may follow for developing linguistic concepts of spacial relationships. The opportunity to kinetically experience *behind, in front of, on top of,* and *through* might aid in understanding these concepts.

One basis for early intervention and stimulation programs with motorically involved children has been an attempt to simulate normal experiences through stimulating motor activities to compensate for the loss of mobility in the hope of allowing the normal development of intellect. Evidence from studies of the cognitive development of phocomelic children as a result of thalidomide exposure suggests that normal cognitive development is possible despite the lack of motor opportunities to initiate these experiences (Bennett, Chandler, Robinson, & Sells, 1981; Crothers & Paine, 1957).

Although it appears that appropriate cognitive development is possible independent of motor activity, few would argue that experiences gained from motor activity, mobility, and spatial exploration of objects facilitate normal intellectual development. Depending on the degree of motor involvement in cerebral palsyed children, the opportunities for these kinds of motor activities in the first 2 years of life are quantitatively diminished and qualitatively altered. Diminished motor activity, coupled with the "at riskness" of their central nervous systems from additional CNS insults, place these children at double risk for cognitive impairment.

Medical Complications

Associated medical complications, such as poor nutrition, related seizures, and potential sedative effects of the anticonvulsants used for seizures and sensory deficits (hearing and/or visual) combine to make cerebral palsy children at extremely high risk for cognitive impairment. Studies vary in estimates of the frequency of mental retardation associated with cerebral palsy. The range is from 50 to 70%. These data, however, have inherent problems due to the difficulty in using instruments standardized for nonphysically handicapped populations to assess motor-impaired children.

In general, the motor deficits, perceptual deficits, dysarthria, increased tendency to fatigue, and frequently associated intentional weaknesses common to cerebral palsy children negatively affect their performances on cognitive assessment tools. Measurement devices that help sort out areas of strength and weakness, rather than formulate a single score or age level, are more helpful to clinicians in planning rehabilitation or educational strategies. A number of specialized psychometric measures for use with handicapped children are available. Some of these include:

1. The Columbia Mental Maturity Scale,
2. The Leiter International Performance Scales,
3. Raven's Progressive Matrices,
4. Pictorial Test of Intelligence,
5. The Merrill-Palmer Scale of Mental Tests, and
6. The Hiskey Nebraska Test of Learning Aptitudes.

Each of these attempts to describe cognitive strengths, omitting the biases of either motor responses or expressive language difficulties. But in omitting these modalities of response, each also limits the range of abilities described by the measure. Clinicians are reminded, however, that in describing intellectual aptitudes, an experienced psychologist can use these other tools to help answer specific questions. The more standard Stanford–Binet, Wechsler Intelligence Scale for Children—

Revised, and Wechsler—Preschool and Primary Scale of Intelligence may still be helpful in obtaining information because the real world does not alter the testing situation to take handicapping conditions into account. For these reasons, the standardized assessments may indeed have some predictive value concerning which children are likely to succeed in a traditional educational setting as opposed to one with additional specialized resources.

IQ Assessments

The predictive value of early IQ assessments in cerebral palsy children has been examined. Similar to early assessments in other populations, children scoring less than 50 or over 90 on initial IQ testing had high correlations with these scores on retesting. In the borderline 51–89 range, however, poor predictability for scores 14 years later was found (Klapper & Birch, 1967). Klapper and Birch suggest that when borderline scores improve, a possible explanation for the initial low scores may be the emphasis placed on sensori-motor skills in early infant testing. When scores worsen, the early relative strengths in verbal fluency and auditory word skills that served cerebral palsy children well in their early years may not prove as helpful at older ages when advanced skills in abstract thinking are required. Further, as would be expected in the motor-impaired, descriptions of the performance of cerebral palsy children in general show higher verbal abilities than performance abilities; this is particularly striking for those children with IQs in the average range.

Learning Disabilities

Beyond mental retardation per se, learning disabilities have been described in cerebral palsy children with a greater than expected frequency. The most widely documented problem is in the area of visual perception. Cerebral palsy children have been said to have a forced responsiveness to background stimuli, particularly in the area of figure-ground discrimination. Difficulties relating parts to a total configuration give these children difficulty with copying the Bender designs or completing block-design tasks.

Much energy has been directed to research evaluating therapies to remediate these perceptual problems. With regard to the figure-ground difficulties, using learning materials in color appears to help children focus on and discriminate the desired stimulus. (Cruickshank, Bise, Walen & Lynch, 1965).

Although formal perceptual-motor testing or sensory integration therapies can be demonstrated to improve the particular skill for which they are used, efficacy in generalizing to academic skills has not been documented to a significant extent to warrant recommendation of these therapies for learning disabilities in cerebral palsy or other populations (Ayers, 1979).

Attention Deficit Disorder

In the cerebral palsy population, as in other central nervous system deficit groups, attention deficits occur with greater than expected frequencies. The same educational strategies of a highly structured program are indicated for this population. Pharmacological interventions with methylphenidate hydrochloride or dextroamphetamine may not be appropriate for children with seizure disorders because either of these medications has the potential of lowering seizure threshold. Strategies employing verbal mediation training to remediate impulsive as opposed to reflective learning and behavioral style may also be helpful adjuncts to the education of children with these problems.

A significant component in the management of cerebral palsy children's cognitive difficulties is educating the child's family as to the support systems available due to Public Law 94-142. Appropriate educational programming that includes input from physical, occupational, and speech therapists is available to handicapped children who are 3 years old and up. It is worth noting at this point that families may benefit from counselling for their expectations regarding the intensity of therapy received in the school setting. Overall, the goals of educational placement are academic achievement and adequate socialization. If major rehabilitation goals are indicated, it may be more appropriate to arrange for additional therapy time outside the school, or a temporary placement at a rehabilitation center, rather than interfere with a satisfactory school placement.

Social/Emotional Problems

The effect of cerebral palsy on social and emotional milestones is significant. Any disability affects parental and societal expectations, but in cerebral palsy, the motor impairment creates unique patterns.

Infants and Young Children

Newborn children with central nervous system insult may be hyperirritable and classical "noncuddly" babies. On the other end of the spectrum is the severely damaged, lethargic and nearly unresponsive child. Both types of infants provide less positive feedback to nurturing attempts by their caretakers and are at high risk for bonding interactional problems with their parent. Recently, there have been indications of increased incidence of child abuse and neglect in the cerebral palsy population both as a cause of and a result of their motor impairments.

Difficulties achieving skills that allow imitation of motor actions, as well as hypertonicity that is exacerbated by a variety of temperature, sound, or excitement stimuli, make cues from cerebral palsy babies harder to read for parents. This makes it difficult for the child's family to predictively meet his or her needs and thus impedes the establishment of a basic trust in the young infant.

Again, problems with the achievement of independent mobility make cerebral palsy children functionally unable to initiate separation from their parents, and the individuation process expected early in the second year of life is delayed. Children's failure to gain competence in mastery over their own body and their own self-care further restricts separation. The impact on the individual identity of a child who never has the opportunity to control his or her own environment or be self-sufficient is apparent.

Delays in ambulation, self-care, and communication skills are compounded when they prevent the normally increasing interaction with peers that occurs in the preschool. The kinds of play cerebral palsy children can share with peers needs to be actively encouraged to allow cerebral palsy children to experience the turn-taking, cooperative interactions, and role playing that are the social milestones of the preschool age. Special care needs to be taken to ensure that the feedback for appropriate or inappropriate behavior be the same for these children as it is for any others, even if the level of activity may need to be adapted to accommodate the child's disabilities. Preschool teachers, peers, and parents may need additional encouragement to enforce rules of behavior.

An issue of equal significance in the preschool years is support of the child's developing body concept. In making decisions regarding the timing of surgical interventions, clinicians need to bear in mind the threat of such procedures to the child's perception of body wholeness balanced against the advantage of "getting this over with" before school.

In the early school years, when writing, cutting, increasing speed of copying, and gross motor activities are the focus of school activities, the weaknesses of the cerebral palsy child are likely to cause even the midly affected child to be as divergent from his peers as he or she will ever be. Special attention directed at finding compensatory verbal and social strengths and educating the young child to his or her abilities in these areas are needed to support developing self-esteem and self-concept. The gross motor "klutz" last chosen for the second grade soccer team is vulnerable to thinking of peers' rejection as an indictment of his or her self-worth rather than seeing his of her weakness in sports as a minor part of the greater whole.

Adolescence

As school years progress, difficulties in communication and self-care assume greater weight. As adolescence approaches, awareness of body differences causes new problems with acceptance of orthotic devices. Functionally insignificant joint contractures and gait abnormalities that assume new importance to the patient deserve the clinician's empathetic consideration. At this age, handling issues related to sexual functioning, as well as finalizing realistic expectations regarding the extent of disability on the patient's prospects for employability and independence, are major focuses of therapeutic interventions. A repeat discussion with the adolescent of his or her motor difficulties, their causes, and their lack of an inheritable tendency is important.

As with any adolescent, an initial period of time with professionals away from parents may need to be encouraged by the health professional to support both the patient's and the parents' perceptions of the child as an independent emotional entity. Throughout the developmental period, clinicians working with children with cerebral palsy or other disabilities walk a fine line between suggesting therapeutic interventions to change the child's functional ability and accepting the child as he or she is with the disability as a part of who he or she is as a person.

Clinicians are reminded that patients born with disabling conditions have never known themselves in any other way. Paradoxically, therapists' goals of improved cosmesis of gait or physical posturing of upper extremities through activities that do not actually add function to the child's repertoire may be strongly resisted by the child. Attempts to improve the child give a mixed message; the child perceives part of him or herself as not being accepted and vents his or her feelings against the well-meaning therapist or parent. A broader extension of this phenomena may contribute to children rejecting therapy in general. Cooperation is enhanced by letting the child set therapy goals as early as possible. To further enhance the likelihood of a productive therapeutic relationship, professionals need to convey appreciation of the child's worth regardless of physical abilities.

THERAPEUTIC INTERVENTIONS

Therapeutic programs are believed to offer means of providing the necessary education and positive support to a family to help them understand and cope with their child's disability. Proponents of early referral (Arens, Molteno, Magasiner, & Clark, 1983) point out that mothers' group meetings are helpful. Training the parents to perform range of motion and proper positioning techniques (e.g., guaranteeing that the child is appropriately seated and transported safely), and educating them in skin care and other medical problems, and fostering play are all very useful in assisting the mother and other family members to cope and manage the child's disability (Haskins, Finkelstein & Stedmon, 1978). The psychosocial stimulation and early educational experiences for the child have been shown to improve cognitive and social skills (Widmayer & Field, 1981).

Cerebral palsy presents as a difficulty in controlling motor units and inhibiting abnormal reflexes. Techniques to enhance relaxation and isolate individual motor units have been shown to improve manual tasks in cerebral palsy patients when they perform isolated motor tasks (Ortega, 1978). Clinically, it appears that there is not enough carryover to functional tasks. Therapy that is efficacious in helping patients learn stabilization and work in the upright position (Jones, 1967) may not translate into significant functional gains, but may facilitate specific tasks. Gross, Eridy, and Drabman (1982) showed that involving parents as principal therapists resulted in substantial gains in range of motion and use of a particular target limb skill.

Physical Therapy, Biofeedback, and Patterning

Physical therapy has been shown to improve function when used with orthoses and braces or post-surgically (Mathias, 1967). Physical therapists, when using equipment to substitute for function or restraining limbs, such as walkers, wheelchairs, and crutches, enhance optimal functional capability (Alexander, 1985).

Biofeedback has been effective in training children to acquire better proprioceptive information on placement of body parts (e.g., foot flat at mid-stance in the gait cycle) (Conrad & Bleck, 1980). Seeger and

Caudrey (1983), working with a group of children to get the foot flat on the floor, found that there was initial improvement when using a heel switch buzzer. However, gains were not maintained 18–24 months after training. This often has been the case in our own clinical experience with biofeedback. More research is needed to study the lack of treatment durability.

Patterning is the imposition of primitive motor patterns on a brain-injured child seeking to mimic the evolution of advanced motor patterns. It includes particular attention to stimulating the left hemisphere and not the right. These patterns are imposed for hours on end by both family and volunteers. Patterning (Doman Delacato therapy) was examined in an excellent and well-controlled study by Sparrow and Zigler (1978), who found no benefit of patterning for seriously mentally retarded children when using surrogate grandparents. Clinicians have noted deleterious effects (e.g., divorce, behavior problems in siblings) on families of such intense interventions.

Neurodevelopmental Therapy

Neurodevelopmental therapy (NDT) helps the child approximate normal neuromotor maturation and function through the inhibition of primitive reflexes and facilitation of more mature motor responses. It incorporates attention to cognition and works toward allowing the child to at least experience the feeling of normal movement. Anecdotally, many people are impressed with NDT. However, there is a wealth of data that questions its claims of eliminating abnormal reflexes and developing mature motor patterns (Marquis, 1979). Sommerfeld, Fraser, Hensinger, and Beresford (1981) randomly assigned children ages 3 to 22 years to a NDT therapist or to an aide who performed range of motion and functional activities. No differences were evident in the appearance of mature developmental reflexes, improvement in gross motor, or increases in range of motion, although both groups improved in functional skills.

Another study (Wright & Nicholson, 1973) of 47 children under age 6 showed that NDT therapy had no effect on ankle dorsiflexion or abduction of hips, or diminished retention of primitive reflexes. Additional controlled investigations clearly are needed.

Efficacy of Therapies

The use of single-subject methodology has potential utility (see Martin & Epstein, 1976) and the need for objectivization continues (Holt, 1973). Therapists argue that some therapy must be carried out, and that to do nothing is unethical. However, ineffective therapy wastes time, money, and hope. Investigators examining the efficacy of these treatment interventions are extremely concerned that the therapeutic demands placed on the family may precipitate other psychological crises that make it harder for the family to care for the child (Parette, Holder, & Sears, 1984; Perry, Jones, & Thomas, 1981).

Lunberg (1978) found that the physical work capacity of a cerebral palsy population was 50% of that of a corresponding non-handicapped group. He believed that their poor performance was due to their constant hypertonia, involuntary movements, and the need to stabilize segments of their body to partake of voluntary movements. Researchers must pay attention to working with scoring systems for gross motor capability as developed by Reimers (1972). Further, they must determine which primitive reflexes are predictive of ultimate gross motor capability (Bleck, 1975). They also will need to control for associated mental retardation. Shapiro, Accardo, and Capute (1979) found that mental retardation alone delays onset of walking an average of 30 months. Associated neurologic problems can delay walking even further.

Therefore, until the natural history of children with cerebral palsy is understood in terms of reflex activity, energy demands, and particular reflex patterns, it will be very difficult to develop meaningful data on the efficacy of therapies in changing neuromotor control.

Drug Therapy

Pharmacological agents are still used in cerebral palsy. Diazepam can reduce tone, particularly in children with severe retention of primitive reflexes. Dantrolene sodium is known to block calcium ions at the sarcoplasmic reticulum and seems to weaken spastic muscles by decreasing their force of contraction. The drug should be used cautiously, with liver function monitoring, as it can cause hepatotoxicity. Both drugs seem to help most in the severely involved and should be closely monitored.

EQUIPMENT AND POSITIONING DEVICES

The usefulness of devices to facilitate adequate standing (Ivery, McDaniel, Perkins, Robler, & Ruiz, 1981) and walkers that permit movement through space (Mylers, 1983) is well-documented in the literature. A recent technological enhancement in the management of cerebral palsy children has been the advent of inhibitory casting or boots. The boot encloses the foot and ankle, and through positioning and pressure on appropriate sites on the foot inhibits certain tonic reflex movements. This decreases hypertonicity and improves gait (Duncan & Mott, 1983). In a study of 9 children (Sussman & Cusick, 1979), the short leg cast decreased tone, increased stability, and allowed improved and increased mobility in the children. When coupled with other orthoses and elastic straps (Alexander, 1985; Nuzzo, 1980) these devices can significantly improve motoric capability by providing additional stabilization for blocking extraneous movement.

An area of increased research and development is the appropriate seating of children who are either nonambulatory or seldom ambulate appropriately. Seating breaks up patterns of abnormal reflex tone and provides an interface that permits even the most severely deformed child to be transported comfortably and safely (Alexander, 1985; Rang, Doriglas, Bennet, & Kovenska, 1981). In the severe cerebral palsy child, seating has been shown to be efficacious because it supports the thoracic and lumbar spine, it decreases spastic reflexes, distributes sitting pressure, and stabilizes the hips by resisting the hip adductors (Carlson & Winter, 1978).

SURGICAL INTERVENTIONS

Lower Extremities and Hip

The lower extremities are benefited by a number of operations. Early lengthening of the heel cord and transfer of the posterior tibial tendon (Green, Griffen, & Shiavl, 1983; Lee & Bleck, 1980) can eliminate walking on toes (equinus) and the tendency of the foot to turn in (inversion or varus). Surgeries to control interval rotation of the leg, when coupled with kinetic electromyography, can correct toeing in (Ray & Ehrlich, 1979; Samilson, 1981a; Steel, 1980).

Nonambulatory children are at risk for hip dislocation. Early soft-tissue releases can keep the hip in its socket (Koffman, 1981; Reimers, 1980; Wheeler & Weinstein, 1984). Hip dislocation occurs in 28% of all cases with cerebral palsy (Samilson, 1981b). Procedures for the frankly dislocated hip are less than satisfactory (Koffman, 1981). Salvage procedures for the adult hip should be avoided unless the patient has normal intelligence or is an athetoid (Moreau, Drummond, Rogala, Ashworth, & Porter, 1979).

Spinal Curvature

Nonambulatory children are at greater risk for developing spinal curvature scoliosis. Seven percent of ambulatory children with cerebral palsy and 80% of the severe bed-care patients develop curves severe enough to warrant surgery (Samilson, 1981a). Spinal orthoses are used in curves that measure 40 degrees or less. The purpose is to halt or slow down progression of the curve. Once curves have progressed beyond 60 degrees, they will continue to progress after puberty. Surgery is a viable option now that techniques for internal fixation exist. Goals of surgery are to prevent curve progression, relieve back pain, and improve sitting balance (Stanitski, Michili, Hall, & Rosenthal, 1982). On the average, surgery can be expected to correct 41% of a curve (Stanitski et al., 1982).

Brain Stimulators

The advent of implantable cardiac pacemakers has led to the technology for implantable brain stimulators. Stimulators placed over the vermis of the cerebellum are said to significantly improve function in cerebral palsy patients. Claims for improved capabilities include spasticity, behavior, psychometric, speech and functional status, and respiratory strength (Cooper, Riklan, Amin, Waltz, & Cullinan, 1976; Miyasaka, Hoffman, & Froese, 1978). These studies have been criticized for not using impartial observers (Bucy, 1980). Many of these cases receive extensive post-operative physical therapy. In these instances, the surgery was credited, when, in fact, pre-operative therapy would yield the same results without surgery (Alexander, Piedmont, Fletcher, King, & Miller, 1977). Other investigations show that once the unit is in, children do well whether the unit is on or off and that this effect may be due to placebo influence (Alexander et al., 1977; Gahn, Russman, Cerciello, Fiorentino, & McGrath, 1981). Finally, although some researchers can substantiate some changes in tone and reflexes, they see no significant functional outcome and believe the benefits are not worth the risk (Ivan & Ventureyra, 1982a, 1982b). The most recent site of stimulation is the spinal cord, where there are claims of improving cerebral palsy markedly in 32% of cases and moderately in 41% (Waltz, 1982; Waltz & Davis, 1983). The superiority of spinal stimulation over cerebellar stimulation has yet to be determined.

TECHNOLOGY

An exciting area of work is the use of powered chairs in younger cerebal palsy children. Butler, Okamoto, and McKay (1983) showed that power chairs could be provided to children who developmentally were in the 20–39 month age range and that these children were able to master the power chair in 2–12 hours of training. Technology, when provided to a capable child, dramatically changes his or her life. Computers represent another potentially beneficial prospect for improving function. Off-the-shelf computer technology can dramatically alter life-styles of the more severely disabled (Fawcus, 1983). Computers lend themselves to language, speech production, and environmental control. In addition, they assist via sensory enhancement, manipulation, information amplication, recreation, education, and mobility interfaces (Vanderheiden, 1982, 1983). In the synthetic production of speech, using short pictorial codes, coupled with two- and three-key strokes on a computer, allows systems such as MINISPEAK to let the child express his or her feelings in-depth (Baker, 1982). Most importantly, the disabled feel less socially isolated and more articulate and free from the paralyzed psyche (Shane, 1983).

SUMMARY

Cerebral palsy children and their families present a constellation of problems requiring constant attention. When surgery, therapies, and technology are interposed to compensate for specific functional deficits or problems, the results are often dramatic. To date, interventions to "remold the brain" have no scientific validity. All interventions should have a goal that is set for a time frame and uses an effective assessment instrument or endpoint to document reaching the expected outcome. The admonition "Don't just sit there! Do something!" has no role in the management of cerebral palsy.

REFERENCES

Alexander, M. A. (1985). Orthotics, adapted seating, and assistive devices. In G. E. Molnar (Ed.), *Pediatric rehabilitation*. Baltimore: Williams & Wilkins. (pp. 158–175).

Alexander, M. A., Piedmont, A., Fletcher, P. W., King, W. M., & Miller, C. A. (1977). Cerebellar pacemaker evaluation using audio-visual assistance. *Archives of Physical Medicine and Rehabilitation, 58,* 513–154.

Arens, L. J., Molteno, C. D., Magasiner, V., & Clark, C. (1983). Early referral in cerebral palsy. *South African Medical Journal, 63,* 676.

Ayers, J. (1979). *Sensory integration and learning disorders*. Los Angeles: Western Psychological Services.

Baker, B. (1982). Minispeak. *BYTE, 7,* 186–196.

Bennett, F. C., Chandler, L., Robinson, N., & Sells, C. (1981). Spastic diplegia in premature infants. *American Journal Diseases of Children, 135,* 732–737.

Bleck, E. E. (1975). Locomotor prognosis in cerebral palsy. *Developmental Medicine and Child Neurology, 17,* 18–25.

Bucy, P. C. (1980). Cerebellar stimulation. *Surgical Neurology, 13,* 124.

Butler, C., Okamoto, G. A., & McKay, T. M. (1983). Powered mobility for very young disabled children. *Developmental Medicine and Child Neurology, 25,* 466–471.

Carlson, J. M., & Winter, R. (1978). The "Gillette" sitting support orthosis for nonambulatory children with severe cerebral palsy or advanced muscular dystrophy. *Minnesota Medicine, 8,* 469–473.

Conrad, L., & Bleck, E. E. (1980). Augmented auditory feedback in the treatment of equinus gait in children. *Developmental Medicine and Child Neurology, 22,* 713–718.

Cooper, I. S., Riklan, M., Amin, I., Waltz, J. M., & Cullinan, T. (1976). Chronic cerebellar stimulation in cerebral palsy. *Neurology, 29,* 744–753.

Crothers, B., & Paine, R. (1957). *The national history of cerebral palsy*. Cambridge, MA: Harvard University Press.

Cruickshank, W., Bise, H., Walen, N., & Lynch, K. (1965). *Perception in cerebral palsy studies in figure background relationships* (2nd ed.). Syracuse, NY: Syracuse University Press.

Duncan, W. R., & Mott, D. H. (1983). Foot reflexes and the use of the "inhibitive cast." *Foot and Ankle, 4,* 145–149.

Fawcus, R. (1983). Aids to communication: A British perspective. *Rehabilitation World, 7,* 23–25.

Gahn, N. H., Russman, B. S., Cerciello, R. L., Fiorentino, M. R., & McGrath, D. M. (1981). Chronic cerebellar stimulation for cerebral palsy: A double blind study. *Neurology, 31,* 87–90.

Green, N. E., Griffen, P. P., & Shiavi, R. (1983). Split posterior tibial-tendon transfer in spastic cerebral palsy. *Journal of Bone and Joint Surgery, 65A,* 748–754.

Gross, A. M., Eridy, C., & Drabman, R. S. (1982). Training parents to be physical therapists with their physically handicapped child. *Behavior Modification, 5,* 321–327.

Haskins, R., Finkelstein, N. W., & Stedman, D. J. (1978). Infant-stimulation programs and their effects. *Pediatric Annals, 7,* 99–128.

Holt, K. S. (1973). Letter to editor. *Developmental Medicine and Child Neurology, 15,* 537–538.

Hopkins, T., Bice, H., & Callan, K. (1954). *Evaluation and education of the cerebral palsied child* (Vol. 9). Washington, DC: International Council for Exceptional Children.

Ivan, L. P., & Ventureyra, E. C. G. (1982a). Chronic cerebellar stimulation in cerebral palsy. *Child's Brain, 9,* 121–125.

Ivan, L. P., & Ventureyra, E. C. G. (1982b). Chronic cerebellar stimulation in cerebral palsy, applied. *Neurophysical, 45,* 51–54.

Ivery, A., McDaniel, C., Perkins, S., Robler, D., & Ruiz, J. (1981). Supine stander for severely handicapped child. *Physical Therapy, 61,* 525–526.

Jones, A. M. (1967). The traditional method of treatment of the cerebral palsied child. *American Journal of Physical Medicine, 46,* 1024–1031.

Klapper, M., & Birch, E. (1967). A fourteen-year follow-up study of cerebral palsy: Intellectual change and stability. *American Journal of Orthopsychiatry, 37,* 540–547.

Koffman, M. (1981). Proximal femoral resection or total hip replacement in severely disabled cerebral spastic patients. *Orthopedic Clinics of North America, 12,* 91–100.

Lee, C. L., & Bleck, E. E. (1980). Surgical correction of equinus deformity in cerebral palsy. *Developmental Medicine and Child Neurology, 22,* 287–292.

Lundberg, A. (1978). Maximal aerobic capacity of young people with spastic cerebral palsy. *Developmental Medicine and Child Neurology, 20,* 205–210.

Marquis, P. (1979). Therapies for cerebral palsy. *American Family Physician, 19,* 101–105.

Martin, J. E., & Epstein, L. H. (1976). Evaluating treatment effectiveness in cerebral palsy single-subject designs. *Physical Therapy, 56,* 285–294.

Mathias, A. (1967). Physical therapy in relation to orthopedic surgery. *Physical Therapy, 47,* 473–482.

Miyasaka, K., Hoffman, H. J., & Froese, A. B. (1978). The influence of chronic cerebellar stimulation on respiratory muscle coordination in a patient with cerebral palsy. *Neurosurgery, 2,* 262–265.

Molnar, G. E., & Gordon, S. W. (1976). Cerebral palsy: Predictive value of collective clinical signs for early prognostication of motor function. *Archives of Physical Medicine and Rehabilitation, 57,* 153.

Moreau, M., Drummond, D. S., Rogala, E., Ashworth, A., & Porter, T. (1979). Natural history of the discolated hip in spastic cerebral palsy. *Developmental Medicine and Child Neurology, 21,* 749–753.

Morgan, R. F., Hansen, F. C., Wills, J. H., & Hoopes, J. E. (1981). The treatment of drooling in the child with cerebral palsy. *Maryland State Medical Journal, 30,* 79–80.

Mylers, J. W. (1983). A specialized walking frame for children with cerebral palsy. *Journal of Pediatric Orthopedics, 3,* 620–621.

Nuzzo, R. M. (1980). Dynamic bracing: Elastics for patients with cerebral palsy, muscular dystrophy and myelodysplasia. *Clinical Orthopedics and Related Research, 148,* 263–273.

Ortega, D. F. (1978). Relaxation exercise with cerebral palsied adults showing spasticity. *Journal of Applied Behavior Analysis, 11,* 447–451.

Parette, H. P., Holder, L. F., & Sears, J. D. (1984). Correlates of therapeutic progress by infants with cerebral palsy and motor delay. *Perceptual and Motor Skills, 58,* 159–163.

Perry, J., Jones, M. H., & Thomas, L. (1981). Functional evaluation of rolfing in cerebral palsy. *Developmental Medicine and Child Neurology, 23,* 717–729.

Rang, M., Doriglas, G., Bennet, G. C., & Kovenska, J. (1981). Seating for children with cerebral palsy. *Journal of Pediatric Orthopedics, 1,* 279–287.

Ray, R. L., & Ehrlich, M. G. (1979). Lateral hamstring transfer and gait improvement in the cerebral palsy patient. *Journal of Bone and Joint Surgery, 61A,* 719–723.

Reimers, J. (1972). A scoring system for the evaluation of ambulation in cerebral palsied patients. *Developmental Medicine and Child Neurology, 14,* 332–335.

Reimers, J. (1980). The stability of the hip in children. *Acta Orthopedica Scandinavica, 184* (Suppl.), 5–99.

Samilson, R. L. (1981a). Current concepts of surgical management of deformities of the lower extremities in cerebral palsy. *Clinical Orthopedics and Related Research, 158,* 99–107.

Samilson, R. L. (1981b). Orthopedic surgery of the hips and spine in retarded cerebral palsy patients. *Orthopedic Clinics North America, 12,* 83–90.

Seeger, B. R., & Caudrey, D. J. (1983). Biofeedback therapy to achieve symmetrical gait in children with hemiplegic cerebral palsy: Long-term efficacy. *Archives of Physical Medicine and Rehabilitation, 64,* 160–162.

Shane, H. (Chairman). (1983). Nonspeech communication. A position statement. *Rehabilitation World, 7,* 40–43.

Shapiro, B. K., Accardo, P. J., & Caputo, A. J. (1979). Factors affecting walking in profoundly retarded population. *Developmental Medicine and Child Neurology, 21,* 369–373.

Sommerfeld, D., Fraser, B. A., Hensinger, R. N., & Beresford, C. V. (1981). Evaluation of physical therapy service for severely mentally impaired students with cerebral palsy. *Physical Therapy, 61,* 338–344.

Sparrow, S., & Zigler, E. (1978). Evaluation of patterning treatment for the retarded. *Pediatrics, 62,* 137–150.

Stanitski, C. L., Michill, L. J., Hall, J. E., & Rosenthal, R. K. (1982). Surgical correction of spinal deformity in cerebral palsy. *Spine, 7,* 563–569.

Steel, H. H. (1980). Gluteus medius and minimus insertion advancement for correction of internal rotation gait in spastic cerebral palsy. *Journal of Bone and Joint Surgery, 62A,* 919–927.

Sussman, M. D., & Cusik, B. (1979). Preliminary report: The role of short leg, tone-reducing casts as an adjunct physical therapy of patients with cerebral palsy. *Johns Hopkins Medical Journal, 145,* 112–114.

Taft, L. (1984). Cerebral palsy. *Pediatrics in Review, 6,* 35–45.

Vanderheiden, G. (1982). Computers can play a dual role for disabled individuals. *BYTE, 7,* 136–144.

Vanderheiden, G. (1983). Nonconversation communication technology needs of individuals with handicaps. *Rehabilitation World, 7,* 8–12.

Vining, E., Accardo, P. J., Rubenstein, J. E., Farrell, S. E., & Roizen, N. J. (1976). Cerebral palsy: A pediatric developmentalist's point of view. *American Journal of Diseases Children, 130,* 643–649.

Waltz, J. M. (1982). Computerized percutaneous multi-level spinal cord stimulation in motor disorders. *Applied Neurophysiology, 45,* 73–92.

Waltz, J. M., & Davis, J. A. (1983). Cervical cord stimulation in the treatment of athetosis and dystonia. *Advances in Neurology, 37,* 225–237.

Wheeler, M. E., & Weinstein, S. L. (1984). Adductor, tenotomy-obdurator neurectomy. *Journal of Pediatric Orthopedics, 48,* 51.

Widmayer, S. J., & Field, T. M. (1981). Effects of Brazelton demonstrations for mothers on the development of preterm infants. *Pediatrics, 67,* 711–714.

Wright, T., & Nicholson, J. (1973). Physiotherapy for the spastic child and evaluation. *Developmental Medicine and Child Neurology, 15,* 146–163.

CHAPTER 15

Chronic Pain

Francis J. Keefe and Karen M. Gil

Chronic pain is one of the most common disabling conditions that physicians treat. Only too typical is the case of a 38-year-old carpenter who had low-back pain radiating into the right leg for 2 years. He has had two operations on his lower back and has seen many specialists, all of whom agree that further surgery is not likely to help. Although narcotic medication has been prescribed, he takes it only when pain is intolerable for fear that he may become too dependent on it. He is unable to actively participate in the care of his three children or engage in his usual recreational and social activities. He spends most of his day resting in bed or a recliner. It is difficult for him to walk, and he takes his meals standing because sitting for even brief periods of time increases his pain. This man has tried to return to his job several times but he was unable to do the required work. He has problems sleeping because of pain, and he feels depressed and irritable. His wife is supportive, but she is unsure what to do to help him.

Conventional medical and surgical approaches rarely benefit chronic pain patients such as the one described. Indeed, most patients can be characterized as failures of extensive medical and surgical therapy (Urban, 1982). To a great extent, traditional medical approaches to the treatment of chronic pain are inadequate because they are based on a somatosensory model of pain (Turk & Flor, 1984). In this model, pain is conceptualized as a sensory event, and the pain experience is assumed to be proportional to the peripheral damage. Traditional medical and surgical treatments focused on repairing the damage directly. Recently, biomedical scientists have made significant advances in the understanding of chronic pain in areas such as the study of endogenous opiates and mapping of pain pathways, as well as the development of animal models of chronic pain. Innovative neuroaugmentation and neurodestructive procedures have also been developed. Although these might represent interesting and potentially important advances, they are currently useful for only a selected group of patients. Readers interested in a more detailed review of these areas of research should consult Nashold and Bullitt, (1981), Nashold and Friedman (1972), and Urban

(1982). There remains a large group of patients who are not likely to benefit from these procedures.

Many patients have significant behavioral and psychological problems that compound management of their pain conditions. There is growing recognition that these factors determine how patients respond to persistent pain (Keefe, Brown, Scott, & Ziesat, 1982). For example, evidence exists that personality variables, such as depression, tendency to deny emotional distress, and preoccupation with physical complaints, as well as social factors, such as entering the work force at an early age, limited formal education, and doing manual labor, promote the chronicity of pain complaints (Weisenberg, 1977). Patients may also inadvertently learn maladaptive forms of coping that prevent them from returning to previous levels of functioning.

The purpose of this chapter is to review the current status of research in the field of chronic pain. The contributions of psychological and behavioral concepts to the understanding and management of pain conditions will be emphasized throughout.

DESCRIPTION OF THE DISORDER

Pain has been defined by the International Association for the Study of Pain (IASP) as "an unpleasant sensory and emotional experience associated with (actual or potential) tissue damage or described in terms of tissue damage". (IASP Subcommittee on Taxonomy, 1979, p. 250). Chronic pain is typically used to describe pain that is nonmalignant in etiology and that persists for 6 months or longer (Keefe & Brown, 1982).

Chronic pain may result from a wide variety of conditions. Bonica (1977a) has classified these into four categories according to the mechanism believed to be responsible for the pain: (a) peripheral, (b) peripheral-central, (c) central, and (d) psychological.

Peripheral Mechanisms

A major mechanism of chronic pain is persistent nociceptive (underlying tissue damage) input due to injury or disease. Diseases such as arthritis, ulcerative colitis, angina, and some types of cancer pain produce biochemical, mechanical, or thermal stimuli that activate pain receptors in the periphery. These receptors then carry repetitive signals along the pain pathway, thereby generating a chronic pain state.

Peripheral-Central Mechanisms

Some pain conditions are believed to be due to dysfunction in both the peripheral and central portions of the somatosensory system. An initial injury, for example, may result in a vicious cycle in which a reflex response to the injury causes an abnormal change in tissue, which in turn increases nociceptive input. In the case when the sympathetic nervous system responds reflexively in a hyperactive manner, muscle spasms may be produced that lead to vasospasm, liberation of pain-producing substances, and in turn, sensitization of nociceptors to previously nonnoxious stimuli. Thus, the patient's sympathetic response to a peripheral injury may result in chronic pain.

Other diseases may affect nerve fibers in such a way that pain signals that would normally be inhibited are more likely to be experienced as a result of the disease. It is known, for example, that large fibers in peripheral nerves serve to inhibit pain signals transmitted by small fibers. Diseases that reduce the number and function of active large fibers, such as postherpetic neuralgia and diabetes, or exposure to toxic substances may produce chronic pain through this mechanism.

Another peripheral-central mechanism of chronic pain is denervation-hypersensitivity. Patients who have undergone limb amputation have a decrease in the normal sensory input from that damaged area. As a result, abnormal firing in the somatosensory system can occur proximal to the nerve injury. This repetitive abnormal firing is believed to cause the phantom pain sensations. It is also believed to be the mechanism responsible for pain dysesthesias, parasthesias associated with peripheral nerve injuries, and surgical lesions of rhizotomies and cordotomies.

Central Mechanisms

Patients with spinal cord injuries, thalamic lesions, or cortical trauma often experience diffuse burning pain. The precise mechanisms of this "central pain" are unknown, but available evidence suggests that a reduction of descending inhibitory influences or a loss of sensory inputs can produce severe and persistent pain.

Psychological and Behavioral Mechanisms

Psychological mechanisms can both cause and modify chronic pain. One of the most common is the psychophysiological mechanism. Patients who have stress-related pain, such as temporomandibular joint pain, show definite physiological changes that produce pain. For example, increased muscle activity may lead to vasoconstriction, with the subsequent release of pain-producing substances and increase in muscle tension that in turn increases pain. This mechanism is considered responsible for coronary artery disease, muscle tension headache, and migraine headache.

Psychogenic pain is believed to occur in specific personality types, and it is characterized by conflicts over unmet dependency needs and external realities. Chronic pain complaints are also often seen in specific psychiatric diagnostic subgroups, such as patients suffering from depression, hysteria, and dementia psychosis.

In certain patients, an operant conditioning mechanism may exert a significant effect on pain complaints and pain behavior. Patients may learn to adopt a chronic pain life-style because it is highly reinforcing. For example, certain patients may find that avoidance of unwanted responsibilities at home or work, solicitous attention from a spouse or family members, disability payments, or an opportunity to recline is very rewarding. As a result, they may continue to focus on complaints and exhibit a great deal of pain behavior long after the normal healing time for tissue damage. This mechanism is believed to be important in many chronic pain syndromes, particularly in chronic low-back pain patients.

EPIDEMIOLOGICAL ASPECTS OF CHRONIC PAIN

Chronic pain is a major national health problem. Bonica (1980) estimates that about 86 million people in the United States have some type of chronic pain, with 35 million chronic headache sufferers, 18 million back pain patients, and 1 million cancer patients with pain. Millions of others suffer with abdominal pain, and central pain, neuropathies, and other chronic pain conditions.

Several factors make it difficult to precisely pinpoint the extent of chronic pain. *First*, there are numerous pathological conditions that result in chronic pain. Although statistics on incidence of disease may be kept, the precise nature of the complaints are usually not recorded. *Second*, epidemiological factors that may affect pain complaints in one disorder (e.g., gender, weight) may not influence pain symptoms in another disorder. These factors may, therefore, go unreported. *Third*, it is only recently that pain symptoms, per se, have become a topic of research interest.

An indirect way to examine chronic pain epidemiology is to consider data from national surveys of a representative population sample. The National Health Survey (National Health Survey, 1973) conducted nationwide in 1970 provides data on chronic conditions reported as causing limitation of activity and severe disability. Although data on the incidence and severity of pain were not collected, conditions often associated with chronic pain complaints were among the most frequent causes of activity limitation. The leading causes of activity limitation and severe disability for all age groups were heart conditions (which affected 15.5% of the population). Arthritis and rheumatism was the second most frequent cause (14.1%), followed by impairments of the back and spine (6.9%), and impairments of the lower extremities and hips (6.7%). Pain is likely to be a chief complaint in at least three of the four (arthritis, impairments of the back, spine, and lower extremities). It is also a frequent complaint in heart conditions. For individuals under age 45, impairments of the back and spine were the most frequent cause of activity limitation, affecting 10.6% of the population. Moreover, the magnitude of the problem appears to be growing. The NIH Household Survey found that from 1969 to 1976 the prevalence of impairments of the back and spine increased 50%, whereas its incidence increased 20% (Vital and Health Statistics, 1979).

The cost of chronic pain in terms of disability payments, financial compensation, medical costs, and days lost from work is staggering. Estimates suggest that 2½ million Americans are permanently disabled by chronic low-back pain at an annual cost to society of over $1 billion. Low-back problems rank among the leading discharge diagnoses for hospital visits (Pheasant, 1977).

Although it is beyond the scope of the present chapter to consider a wide variety of epidemiological factors affecting a range of chronic pain conditions, we can focus on low-back pain because this disorder is extremely common and has been studied from an epidemiological perspective. Several recent reviews of this literature are available (Andersson, 1981; Kelsey & White, 1980; Steinberg. 1982). These data indicate that demographic factors such as age and gender are very important. Low-back pain problems typically onset by age 25. Low-back pain is most frequently a complaint of individuals between the ages of 50 and 59. The prevalence of disk generation is known to increase with age. However, admissions for disk surgery most frequently occur in the 30–39 age range. Osteoarthritic changes in the spine that occur with age are extremely common and account for a very high percentage of back pain complaints in the elderly (Sarkin, 1977). Although data on the effects of gender on low-back complaints are inconsistent, surveys suggest that males are more likely to present for surgical treatment and evaluation. In populations of patients treated in chronic pain programs, women are typically a majority.

Occupational factors have also been found to be important. Severe back pain was found to occur in 109.6% of workers doing heavy industrial work (e.g., construction, food handling), whereas 6.8% of light-industry workers and sedentary workers reported having severe back pain (Hult, 1954). Research has examined the relative risk for chronic pain complaints posed by different types of work, such as construction, which produces severe stresses on the trunk (Stubbs, 1981), jobs that involve prolonged sitting at a desk or driving (Kelsey & White, 1980), and nursing, which involves frequent lifting of patients (Dehlin, Hedenrud, & Horal, 1976). Innovative programs designed to prevent the onset of pain in such workers are also being investigated.

A variety of medical and social-environmental factors have also been examined by epidemiologists (Andersson, 1981; Kelsey & White, 1980). Although disk herniation is commonly considered to be invariably associated with low-back pain, research shows that pain complaints are not associated routinely with evidence of disk degeneration. However, severe disk degeneration involving several disks is closely associated with pain. Pain complaints and orthopedic conditions, such as spondylolisthesis and osteoporosis, are closely related. Research evidence suggests that both a failure to exercise (with subsequent weakening of the low-back and abdominal musculature) and participation in sports that involve quick repetitive twisting motions (e.g., golf, baseball, bowling) are associated with the development of low-back pain complaints. Although social factors, such as going to work at an early age, limited formal education, and limited income, are not necessarily associated with the onset of low-back pain complaints, they have been found to place patients at risk for chronic pain complaints.

DEVELOPMENTAL ISSUES

Psychological and behavioral approaches to the analysis of pain problems are based on one common assumption: responses to pain are learned and are subject to change as the patient has more experience with pain. Thus, one might expect different responses to pain when it is present for a matter of days or weeks than if pain is present over months. The course of learning is generally slow, and patients, family members, and health-care professionals are often unaware of the gradual development of maladaptive habit patterns.

In this section we consider three stages often seen in clinical patients who are dealing with persistent pain. Although we link these stages to a particular time course, the reader should be aware that an individual patient's progress may vary.

Acute Pain Stage (0–6 months)

In the early stages of dealing with pain, patients show a constellation of responses that are usually quite adaptive. Consider the following case: Mrs. Smith is a 32-year-old mother whose car was hit from behind while stopped at a busy city intersection. In the accident, her head was jerked back violently and she then was thrown forward and restrained by her seatbelt. She has noticed increasingly severe pain in her upper shoulders and neck. She was worried that the pain would continue to increase and become intolerable. As a result of the pain, she sought help in a local emergency room. She was advised to wear a cervical collar, to take minor analgesics and muscle relaxants as needed, and to rest in bed. Her husband was quite concerned and has taken time off from work so that he may help with childcare and household responsibilities. The Smiths have been told that the pain is due to muscle spasm and that it would go away in a few days. Although they are anxious, they have confidence in their doctor.

Responses to acute pain are often quite adaptive and the product of an extensive learning history. These responses can be elicited in an involuntary fashion or by voluntary actions taken by the individual to minimize and reduce pain. Reactions to acute pain can be conceptualized as occurring in three response systems: (a) the subjective, (b) the behavioral, and (c) the psychophysiological.

Subjective responses include both cognitive and affective reactions to pain. Anxiety is the predominant affective response of acute pain patients. It serves an important functional purpose, motivating the patient to seek health care. Although patients may be anxious, generally, they cognitively evaluate their pain at this stage as controllable through their own efforts or medical intervention. This belief is shared and reinforced by those around them. Acute pain is viewed as a warning signal that something is wrong. The expectation of the patient and family is that the underlying cause will be discovered and a cure effected.

Behavioral responses to acute pain include reducing activity, avoiding pain-inducing movements, seeking health care and complying with prescribed regimens, and talking about pain. These behaviors are all quite overt and serve to signal the fact that pain is being experienced to those around the patient. Spouse and family members may respond quite rapidly to body postures and facial expressions indicative of pain to demonstrate their concern and make the patient comfortable. In the acute stage, both the display of pain behavior and the social and environmental response to this behavior are socially acceptable.

Acute pain is characterized not only by local changes due to tissue pathology but also by psychophysiological reactions dependent on higher nervous system activity. Muscle spasm may be a localized response to an injury; generalized muscle tension with excessive guarding and protective reactions often reflects the patient's anxiety about performing movements that they have learned will increase pain. This generalized tension may be evident in muscle contraction, headaches, bruxism, and altered body posture. Autonomic arousal involving substantial increases in heart rate, respiration, skin resistance, and blood pressure may also occur during episodes of severe pain.

For most patients, an effective medical treatment is found, with a result that they recover and no longer experience pain. For these patients, the characteristic responses previously described can be thought of as quite adaptive. For some patients, however, pain persists, and the response patterns evident in this acute stage can become maladaptive.

Pre-Chronic Stage (6–12 months)

Mr. Jones injured his lower back 6 months ago while lifting on the job. He has had constant pain since his injury, but his diagnostic tests have all been negative and surgery is not indicated. Mr. Jones has been told that he needs to live with pain. He has tried to ignore the pain and return to work but finds he is unable to carry on with his responsibilities on the job. He takes oxycodone (Percodan) when he needs to, but he worries that his boss may find out and not let him continue at work. Although he feels good on some days, on other days, he needs to go to bed as soon as he gets home. He finds he is worrying more about the pain and about whether he will be able to continue to work, pay his bills, and support his family. Mr. Jones is finding it increasingly difficult to concentrate and becomes tired much more easily. He no longer socializes with his wife or friends. He is trying to fight his pain and present a brave face to others but finds that at times he is so irritable that it is impossible to control his temper. His wife is very concerned and tries to help by keeping the two boys away from their father.

As pain persists beyond several months, patients may enter a pre-chronic stage in which certain pain behavior patterns become habits. As with Mr. Jones, patients at this point typically attempt to return to their former activities. Patients who are able to do so in a gradual fashion or whose former life-style was fairly inactive are often successful. Other patients may be either unwilling because of psychological reasons or unable because of financial need or limited educational background to return in a gradual fashion to their prior functional status. These patients typically experience flare-ups of pain because of exacerbation of underlying tissue pathology. Their response to these flare-ups may be critical to the learning process. Patients

who become quite anxious or depressed and subsequently take to bed for several days and increase pain medications substantially may find these habits quite reinforcing. As a result, they may be much more likely to respond to subsequent pain increases in a similar manner. On a cognitive level, they may become convinced that they are unable to do activities. They may also become sensitized to simple daily activities that they are actually capable of doing. Patients with passive-dependent personalities may also find this situation highly reinforcing. Of course, these changes do not occur in a vacuum. The response of spouse and family members may be critical. A highly anxious or solicitous spouse may reinforce inactivity and demand that the patient take medication. Patients may also find that their temporary disability payments and workmen's compensation are beginning to run out. This creates added stress and increases the patient's desire to return to work. When the requirements of work are such that the patient is unable to handle the work load however, the pain may be increased, and pain behavior patterns may become more entrenched as a result.

Chronic Pain Stage (12 months or longer)

Mrs. Long has suffered with pain for 5 years. Whereas the pain initially was in the back, she now has complaints of pain in the neck, shoulder, and head. She has had many surgical procedures on her back, but her pain remains unchanged. Her doctors tell her that they are unsure what is causing her pain. Some have even suggested that her pain may be "in your head". Her request for disability payments has been denied, and she has retained a lawyer to fight this decision. When talking about her pain, she looks quite uncomfortable and grimaces, rubs the painful area, and sighs frequently. However, at other times, she appears to be quite comfortable and moves rather easily. She reports that she reclines 90% of the day and that she gets out of the recliner only to eat and use the bathroom. Yet, physical therapy evaluation indicates that she has normal strength in most muscles, suggesting that she is more active than she reports. She takes pain medication daily and goes to the emergency room for pain shots about twice each month when pain becomes intolerable. She has problems sleeping and claims that she only gets 3 to 4 hours of sleep each night. She cries easily and describes herself as depressed and discouraged. Her husband is confused. At times, he is very understanding and supportive, whereas at other times, he is quite angry because he isn't quite sure that she is in as much pain as she says.

There are many patients who fit the description of Mrs. Long. These patients have entered a chronic pain stage in which evidence for underlying tissue damage is minimal, yet pain and pain behavior patterns persist. In these patients, solicitous attention from spouse or family, avoidance of unwanted work or home responsibilities, and financial compensation may function as powerful positive reinforcers for pain behavior. Clearly, as patients become more chronic, there are more opportunities for them to learn that pain behaviors result in these rewards. It is important to point out, however, that although these consequences may be rewarding, the life-style they support can be a very limited and depressing one. Depression is common in chronic pain patients and is usually due to a substantial decrease in the number and range of reinforcing daily activities. It is important to note that the behavior patterns characteristic of this type of chronic pain patient develop so gradually over time that patients and their family are usually not aware of what has happened.

Comment

Although the developmental prospective just outlined is appealing, it has several major problems. *First*, patients may not progress through stages in a uniform fashion. Some patients reach the chronic pain stage rapidly (in a matter of weeks or months). Others continue to demonstrate a prechronic pain pattern after years of continuous pain. *Second*, patients whose pain is not continuous may show a quite different pattern, with distinct changes in behaviour and function only during acute flare-ups. Of course, these responses are also subject to conditioning influences. *Third*, there are many patients with chronic pain, who do show evidence of underlying tissue pathology and whose behavior is quite consistent. These patients do not fit an operant pattern such as that just described. However, they may show a pattern consistent with respondent pain as described by Fordyce (1976). *Fourth*, each recurrence of pain may be more severe and more long-lasting. *Fifth*, patients' early learning experiences with pain or illness, as well as models of pain in their family and social environment, may affect the development and learning of many of the behaviors previously described.

Although there are problems with the developmental prospective, the basic point of this section needs to be emphasized. That is, that patients having persistent pain can learn maladaptive reactions that serve to perpetuate their difficulties in managing pain.

EDUCATIONAL ISSUES

There has been relatively little attention directed to educational issues in the area of chronic pain. Three areas certainly need to be considered: (a) education of health-care professionals, (b) education of the patient, and (c) education of the public.

Bonica (1980) has identified the serious lack of information and training available to health professionals who are likely to treat pain patients. Although health-care personnel are typically taught to manage acute pain problems, there is no organized teaching of management strategies useful for chronic pain patients. Medications effective in the management of acute pain (e.g., narcotics) are often inappropriate in the treatment of chronic pain. The behavioral and psychological problems of the chronic pain patient may go undetected when these patients are treated primarily from a medical perspective. Sources of information on chronic pain in journals and books are extremely limited. Bonica

(1978), for example, reviewed each of the major texts used to train physicians about cancer and found that less than 20 pages out of 5,500 pages in these texts were devoted to the management of pain. The movement towards pain clinics and pain management teams represents an important step towards improving the education of physicians in understanding and managing chronic pain. Students at many teaching hospitals rotate through these clinics on a routine basis, thereby exposing them to a great deal more information about chronic pain management than what has been provided in medical training. As Bonica (1980) points out, however, much more needs to be accomplished with respect to medical education. For example, more journals, such as *Pain*, that cross the multitude of specialized disciplines to consider the broad spectrum of research on pain need to be formed. Research conferences and more postgraduate medical education programs need to be provided as well.

The status of educational materials specifically designed for patients with pain is poor. Although numerous books on the market promise patients that they can cure themselves of chronic pain complaints ranging from headaches to arthritis, only a few have a solid grounding in research and clinical practice, such as James W. Lance's *Headache—Understanding and Alleviation* and Nelson Hendler's and Judith Fenton's *Coping with Chronic Pain*. Both of these books provide accurate descriptions of the basis of their respected pain topics in language that can be readily understood by the lay individual. Both indicate the value of comprehensive treatment approaches. From a psychological perspective, they are also well-written. Both assiduously avoid promising quick cures and underscore the necessity for the patient to view their problem as a chronic problem that will need their ongoing attention. These books also deal in a direct fashion with the psychological and behavioral aspects of persistent pain. Although it is unlikely that patients could use these successfully on their own, we have found them to be a valuable adjunct to our treatment programs. Patients who read about principles of pain

management in these books seem to more readily accept suggestions for treatment and comply better with recommendations. Isolation is a major problem in patients with pain. We often find that in reading these books, the patient feels much less odd and alone. Family members have responded favorably to the books, finding that they give a more detailed background for understanding the problem than has been provided by health-care personnel in the past. There is a definite need for books of this sort.

Other educational approaches to the patient and family also need to be explored. One interesting example is the *Pain Chronicle*, a newsletter formed by patients who had previously participated in our inpatient pain management program. The newsletter is edited by several former patients and is published bimonthly. It contains practical tips on overcoming obstacles, such as taking a major airline flight, going on extended car rides, or going out for dinner or a movie. The program's physical therapist and a biofeedback technician provide brief articles designed to help reinforce patients' understanding of treatment principles. Patients also describe new ways of using recreation time. The newsletter provides an important ongoing link to the program and to other patients.

Until recently, there has been almost no information on chronic pain in the general press. Articles are beginning to appear on a regular basis in weekly periodicals such as *Time* (Wallis, 1984; June 11) and the major national newspapers such as *The New York Times*, *U.S.A. Today*, and *The Los Angeles Times*. Coverage is increasingly being given to patients treated in multidisciplinary pain management programs and to research presented at national and international pain conferences. Despite the heightened news coverage of persistent pain problems, most of the public continues to view pain primarily as an acute problem that will spontaneously remit with the appropriate medical intervention. This perception is a major obstacle towards community and social acceptance of many procedures used in the behavioral management of patients with severe and chronic pain.

ASSESSMENT AND TREATMENT

Medical and Surgical Approaches to Pain

The conventional medical approach to pain evaluation is based on the assumption that pain is a symptom of an underlying somatic problem. The intensity of pain, as well as its location, quality, and temporal characteristics, are viewed as useful indicators for diagnosis. Additional diagnostic tests, such as electromyography, myelography, and computerized tomography (CT) scans, are often used to more precisely identify underlying tissue damage responsible for pain. Treatment procedures are aimed at removing the somatic cause for pain.

Given that pain symptoms are probably the most common reason that patients present for treatment of any disease or injury, it would be impossible to review all of these treatments. However, for those disorders where chronic pain is most likely to occur, a typical treatment sequence can be identified. Initial treatments are typically conservative. For example, in the management of arthritic patients, anti-inflammatory agents, minor analgesics, and rest are often prescribed. For patients having low-back pain, a period of 2 to 3 weeks of strict bedrest, followed by gradual ambulation, is often suggested. In the vast majority of cases, these conservative measures are successful in resolving pain complaints.

When pain persists, however, narcotic medications are typically prescribed. Psychotropic medications may also be used to assist with sleep, anxiety, and depression. Long-term use of narcotics is prohibited because of side effects, such as habituation, constipation, and addiction.

When conservative measures fail or if there is evidence of progressive neurological symptoms, surgical approaches are commonly employed. In the case of lumbar disk disease, surgery involves performing a hemilaminectomy and removing lumbar disk material that is herniated. This procedure is extremely common, particularly in the United States. Estimates suggest that over 200,000 disks per year are excised surgically. Although studies suggest that 60 to 80% of lumbar disk disease patients respond to surgery, follow-up on these studies is very short. Long-term follow-up studies conducted at the Massachusetts General Hospital and Karolinska Institute show that only 22 to 31% of patients get complete and permanent relief of pain following lumbar disk surgery (Barr, 1951).

In the low-back pain population, as well as in other surgical populations, there remains a large group of patients who continue to have pain and functional limitations following surgery. These patients present repeatedly for evaluation. However, relatively few are candidates for additional surgery. Success rates for reoperative lumbar disk disease procedures, for example, are quite low. Further, most surgeons are becoming more conservative about recommending additional surgery. For the past two decades, a number of neurosurgical procedures specifically designed for alleviation of chronic pain have been developed. These include dorsal rhizotomies, sympathectomies, neurectomies, stereotaxic procedures, and the dorsal root entry zone lesion procedure. Unlike initial surgical approaches, which focus on removal of the underlying pathology responsible for pain, these specialized neurosurgical approaches are designed to inhibit or destroy neural pain pathways. These procedures do appear to help some patients greatly; however, they are useful only in carefully selected individuals. In addition, they have significant side effects. Consequently they are typically considered as a last resort for pain control. These procedures are sometimes very effective for a short period, but may fail to relieve pain for longer time intervals. Thus, they are appropriate for patients who have pain secondary to terminal diseases.

Multidisciplinary Approaches to Pain Management

Probably the most significant clinical advance in the management of persistent pain is the development of multidisciplinary treatment programs. Bonica (1977b) has summarized the development of the multidisciplinary approach to pain. He maintains that this development is based on one overriding principle: The problems of chronic pain are complex; therefore, treatments need to be directed at multiple parts of the problem. Pain clinics and pain management programs are now located in most major medical centers in this country and are increasingly being offered in community hospitals and other settings. In these programs, a staff consisting of anesthesiologists, neurosurgeons, orthopedists, psychologists, psychiatrists, physical and occupational therapists, and nurses evaluate and treat each patient. For most patients, multiple treatment techniques are used. Although conservative methods are typically employed, surgical techniques are used in many programs in combination with other pain-control procedures. Treatment may be offered on either an in-patient or out-patient basis. Alternatively, they may be initiated on an in-patient basis, with subsequent follow-up and maintenance while the patient is living outside the hospital.

A detailed description of the multidisciplinary approach to chronic pain management is provided in several recent book chapters and reviews (Follick, Zitter, & Ahern, 1983; Keefe, 1982; Keefe, Gil, & Rose, 1986; Turk, 1983). We will consider in detail behavioral and psychological techniques used in these programs.

Self-Control Procedures

Many patients responding with persistent pain have the resources to learn behavioral methods to regulate their pain and pain behavior. Assessment of the patient's behavioral status often reveals that he or she is making active attempts to cope. For example, a patient may continue to work, attempt to avoid narcotic intake, and remain active in home and community settings. These patients may benefit from training programs that teach them to directly control behavioral, cognitive, and physiological patterns that contribute to their pain. Training may be provided in one or more of the following areas: relax-

ation, exercise, biofeedback to control abnormal and inappropriate muscle activity, assertion, and self-directed physical exercise programs.

Self-Control of Activity Patterns. One set of behavior therapy techniques is designed to teach patients to recognize and modify activity patterns that exacerbate their pain. Self-monitoring is typically used to assess the portion of time spent sitting, standing or walking, and reclining and to evaluate concomitant changes in pain intensity. A diary format similar to that described by Fordyce (1976) is widely used. Two common problems seen in these diaries are overactivity and underactivity. The first is evident when patients continue to engage in activity they find uncomfortable (e.g., sitting) until their pain intensity increases to the point that they need to stop. When this pattern is repeated frequently, the patient learns to fear even simple daily activities they are capable of. Moreover, they begin to avoid doing these and related activities. Other patients spend the vast majority of their day in a reclining position and have extremely limited tolerance for time up and out of bed. A third common problem evident in these diaries is addiction to medication. Patients who wake routinely through the night to take medication may well need a detoxification program. Diary records may be kept during the first few days of an in-patient admission or for several weeks on an out-patient basis. Most clinicians view these diaries as essential in preparing the patient for learning to regulate their own activity patterns.

Once baseline data have been gathered, this information can be used to determine a treatment program. Typically, treatment focuses on teaching patients to work to a pre-set criterion rather than to pain tolerance, with the ultimate goal of returning them to high levels of physical functioning. One treatment method that we find useful is to help patients plan out an activity–rest schedule for their day. Based on baseline data, each hour of the waking day is divided into an activity period during which the patient is up and out of the reclining position, and a rest period in which the patient is reclining and relaxing. The target-activity level each hour is set initially at slightly lower than the patient's estimated pain tolerance and then is slightly increased each day. The rest period is correspondingly decreased. Patients who are overactive typically find that it is extremely difficult for them to exert this degree of control over their behavior. For these patients, every effort is made to help them realize the potentially reinforcing effects of rest. Rest periods are initially set at a minimum, and the patient is encouraged to engage in other pleasant activities simultaneously. One of the most impressive aspects of these self-control programs is the degree to which patients find that they relieve pain, fatigue, and muscle tension. Improvements in these areas are detected by the patients quite readily, and these improvements serve to reinforce compliance with the program. Similar principles underlie physical exercise programs commonly used in chronic pain management.

A second treatment procedure used to modify daily behavior patterns is activity scheduling (Lewinsohn, 1975). In this procedure, patients are asked to identify specific activities and events that are potentially reinforcing for them. The pleasant-event schedule (MacPhillamy & Lewinsohn, 1971) or the reinforcement survey schedule (Cautela & Kastenbaum, 1967) is typically used to help patients select these reinforcing activities. Activity schedules that consist of events and activities that patients judge to be pleasant are then constructed for each patient. At the end of each day, patients record how many of these activities they have engaged in. In addition, a mood rating using one of the forms of the Depression Adjective Checklist (Lubin, 1965) is administered. By examining correlations between mood ratings and pleasant events, it is possible to identify those activities that are most likely to improve mood. Patients are encouraged to attempt to increase the frequency of pleasant activities on a daily basis. The validity of such schedules has been examined and self-reports of the frequency of pleasant activity have correlated well with ratings made by both peers and independent observers (MacPhillamy & Lewinsohn, 1973).

This approach to increasing activity has many advantages in the management of chronic pain patients. *First*, it places the therapy focus on a positive and constructive area, thus deflecting attention from physical symptoms and pain complaints. *Second*, the systematic record-keeping helps patients to be more objective about progress rather than relying on their own impressions, which are often negative and distorted. *Third*, it teaches the individual patient to recognize important daily activities that they may be engaging in that they indeed enjoy.

Self-Control of Cognitive and Affective Responses. Cognitive-behavioral therapy techniques are drawing increasing attention in the treatment of a wide variety of conditions. The area of pain management is no exception. Turk (1983) has been active in the development and evaluation of cognitive techniques specifically designed for pain control. Many of these techniques overlap with other methods described in this chapter. Three important sets of techniques that are uniquely cognitive are (a) patient education, (b) distraction, imagery, and reinterpretation, and (c) cognitive re-structuring.

Chronic pain patients often present with a poor understanding of what is causing their pain and uncertainty about the future of their pain. As a result, many have irrational fears and worries or are convinced that only surgical treatment or invasive procedures are likely to help them in any way. One of the most effective behavior therapy techniques is to provide the patient with a more appropriate and realistic set of thoughts or cognitions about their pain. Typically, patients are told that their pain is real and that they can expect the pain to persist indefinitely. They are told that they need to learn ways to manage the pain rather than to expect a complete cure of their condition. Patients are also provided with explanations as to why various behavior-change procedures such as those discussed are likely to benefit them.

Education of the patient is done best by all members of the treatment team. Consistency across team members promotes acceptance by the patient and enhances his or her motivation to comply with treatment instructions. For many patients, this information considerably relieves anxiety and fosters a more optimistic outlook. Other patients initially may become more depressed when faced with the reality of the permanence of their condition. Although these patients may be resistant to treatment, many show marked improvement in their depression as they begin to participate in a program.

One way to alter patients' reactions to pain is to focus their attention away from the experience of pain. This is the primary approach used in hypnosis. More recently, diversion techniques have come to be used in awake patients and grouped under the term "cognitive strategies." Three methods are commonly used. The *first*, distraction, involves teaching the patient to focus on distracting features of the environment, such as counting ceiling tiles, or focusing their attention on a favorite picture or on a task (e.g., completion of a difficult puzzle). Mental distraction techniques, including counting backwards, reviewing lyrics to a favorite song, etc., are also used. Patients are encouraged to use imagery, such as imagining themselves reclining on a warm beach or sitting in the woods by a pleasant brook. *Second*, reinterpretation methods involve having the patient attempt to alter the pain so as to make it feel like some other sensation, for example, numbness or cold. Finally, guided imagery techniques may also be helpful, especially with children. Guided imagery involves having patients imagine certain scenarios (e.g., they are a football hero hurt in a game and have to undergo a period of pain in order to make the final touchdown). Patients typically find one or more of these cognitive strategies useful, and with practice, they become more effective at using them. Fordyce (personal communication, 1982) has described these methods as "fire extinguishers" useful in managing flare-ups of pain but unlikely to be helpful in managing constant daily pain that is lower in intensity.

Depressed chronic pain patients are prone to cognitive errors such as overgeneralization, excessive feelings of responsibility for negative events, and catastrophizing. Cognitive-behavioral therapy methods such as those developed by Ellis (1979) and Beck (1976) are useful in helping patients analyze and defeat irrational beliefs. Patients are taught to challenge these beliefs using a process of logical reasoning and then to replace irrational beliefs with more realistic thoughts and self-statements. Several authors (Khatami & Rush, 1978) report excellent results in applying this approach to chronic pain patients.

Self-Control of Physiological Responses. Biofeedback and relaxation training procedures are used to help chronic pain patients achieve control over certain physiological reactions. Biofeedback has been used in two major ways. *First*, in some patients, biofeedback can be employed to enhance control over a specific physiological response, such as muscle tension or regional blood flow. Control over these responses is believed to directly alter the physiological cause of pain. An illustration of this approach are the biofeedback procedures used for chronic headache sufferers. For example, muscle contraction headache patients have been helped by providing them with electromyographic biofeedback for muscles of the face, scalp, and neck. When patients learn to decrease excessive muscle activity in these ares, headache pain is diminished. A variety of other chronic pain conditions have been treated with this specific biofeedback approach (see Table 15-1). A review of research on this method indicates that most of these disorders are of a more acute or intermittent nature. Further they have clear physiological references that can be measured noninvasively.

The second major way that biofeedback is used is to assist a process of general relaxation. This type of relaxation training can be effective for several reasons. *First*, patients often react to increased pain with heightened muscle tension and arousal. These responses in turn can increase pain. *Second*, biofeedback-assisted relaxation can

Table 15-1. Examples of Chronic Pain Conditions, Their Underlying Physiological Reactions, and Biofeedback Procedures Used to treat Them

CHRONIC PAIN CONDITION	PHYSIOLOGICAL REACTION	BIOFEEDBACK PROCEDURE
Muscle contraction headache	Increased muscle activity: frontalis, cervical, trapezius muscles	EMG feedback
Low-back pain	Inappropriate use of paraspinal muscles	EMG feedback
Temperomandibular joint pain	Increased muscle activity: masseter muscles	EMG feedback
Migraine headaches	Increased cranial artery blood flow	Temperature feedback
Raynaud's disease	Decreased digital blood flow	Temperature feedback
Angina pectoris	Decreased coronary artery blood flow	Heart rate feedback; Blood pressure feedback
Pain secondary to amputation	Muscle spasms in stump muscles	EMG feedback

alter pain behavior by teaching patients to move in a more relaxed and confident manner. Patients who learn this skill communicate fewer signals to other individuals that they are experiencing pain. Thus, they are probably less likely to become involved in operant pain patterns (see next section). *Third*, patients often avoid simple daily activities that they are capable of, such as sitting, walking up or down stairs, or standing for prolonged periods of time, because they associate pain, anxiety, and fear with these activities. Once patients learn to relax, they can apply this skill in these previously avoided situations. Relaxation provides an incompatible response useful in reducing anxiety and fear. Finally, relaxation can assist patients in making their rest time more efficient and helping reduce insomnia.

The typical sequence of training in biofeedback and relaxation is as follows. Initially, baseline levels of physiological responses are obtained in a laboratory setting. These may be taken either while the patient is at rest or involved in dynamic activities that tend to increase pain (e.g., walking, rotational movements, flexion extension). Patients whose pain is stress-related may be evaluated physiologically during experimental stresses, such as mental arithmetic, cold pressor, or while imaging unpleasant, imaginary scenes. Patients are also encouraged to keep daily records of pain, tension, and/or activity to help estab-

lish the relationship between these parameters. Following baseline, a goal-setting session is typically scheduled to outline the rationale and describe the treatment process. Patients are then trained in progressive relaxation, abbreviated progressive relaxation, meditation, or similar procedures. This intervention is useful even when the primary target is a specific physiological one. This is due to research that indicates that reductions in generalized arousal and tension facilitate training of specific autonomic and central nervous system responses. Biofeedback from a target physiologic response is then provided as the patient attempts to relax. In the laboratory setting, feedback in the form of an audio signal, such as a beeping tone that goes up and down in pitch as the physiologic response changes, or a visual signal, such as a needle on a meter, is provided. Next steps are taken to facilitate transfer of acquired skills from laboratory to other environments. In our laboratory, we provide patients with a relaxation audiotape and instruct them to practice with this twice a day. We also give them a packet of adhesive-backed 1 cm "dots" and encourage them to place these in the environment to use as prompts. Each time the patient sees a dot, they are instructed to engage in a "mini-practice" procedure in which they briefly scan their mulsculature and relax excessively tense muscles. *Third*, portable biofeedback devices are used to train patients in those daily situations that they find produce anxiety or increase their pain.

Operant Conditioning Methods

The hallmark of the operant conditioning approach to chronic pain is the notion that over time patients may learn maladaptive reactions to pain because these reactions have very reinforcing consequences for them. Thus, pain behavior patterns that initially occurred in response to underlying tissue pathology can eventually come under the control of positive reinforcers, such as attention from spouse, avoidance of unwanted work or home responsibilities, compensation or disability payments, or narcotics. Evidence that pain behaviors are excessive in light of physical findings or that pain behaviors are inconsistent in the presence of different individuals may lead one to consider an operant conceptualization.

Treatment techniques based on this model involve control of the important environmental consequences for pain. Patients are typically admitted to a specialized facility where access to medication and attention of staff is tightly controlled. During the first few days of admission, patients are allowed to take medication on an as needed basis and to vary their activity as they wish. Observations by staff of pain behaviors, such as reclining, body posturing, or painful facial expressions, can help pinpoint more precisely the nature of the problem. For example, patients may show a dramatic increase in pain behavior when visited by family or by consulting physicians. At other times, however, they may exhibit little or no pain behavior. In this situation, pain behavior is considered to be under stimulus control, with family or physician serving as discriminative cues eliciting pain behavior. Patients may have a long history of being reinforced by these individuals and thus tend to display pain more in their presence.

Another common pattern is for patients to wait to take pain medication until pain becomes quite severe. They then often request more medication than is prescribed. This pattern suggests that pain medication may be highly reinforcing.

Patients in this pattern often become heavily dependent on medications and require a detoxification program. Some patients are extremely inactive, spending virtually their entire day in bed. Nevertheless, we have often observed them to be quite adept at eliciting attention from other patients and staff members. These individuals may bring the patient their meal or provide them with special favors, such as massages or trying their shoes. Some patients are heavily involved in the "paraphernalia of pain". That is, they use canes, walkers, braces, heating pads, hot packs, recliners, and other special equipment that send clear signals to those around them that they are experiencing severe pain.

Two major treatment techniques can be used to modify abnormal pain behavior patterns. *First*, pain medications can be delivered on a time-contingent rather than pain-contingent basis. Typically, medications are masked in a pain cocktail consisting of a dose of narcotics in a cherry-syrup or coke-syrup base. This is delivered at regular intervals, usually every 4 hours, and the patient is required to take it regardless of pain level. The amount of active medication is gradually reduced so that eventually the cocktail consists only of the syrup base. A *second* major method is social reinforcement by staff. Patients are given copious attention when they engage in well behaviors, such as exercise, walking, involving themselves in recreational activities, smiling, or interacting appropriately. When patients exhibit pain behaviors, attention is withheld or given on a minimal basis. Patients soon learn these contingencies, and dramatic reductions in pain behavior are achieved in a short span of time. To improve maintenance, patients' families also are involved in the program and are taught to attend to well behavior and provide less attention for pain behavior. Patients' reliance on "pain paraphernalia" can be reduced by having them gradually wean themselves away from dependence on these aids.

It is important to note that operant conditioning techniques entail the consent and cooperation of the patient. Procedures such as the pain cocktail and social reinforcement are explained to the patient in a frank and forthright manner. Unless the patient agrees, these programs fail. Even though operant conditioning techniques can be quite powerful, they are ineffective unless the patient is a willing participant.

CURRENT RESEARCH

Over the past 15 years, there has been a significant increase in research in the area of chronic pain. In this section, we concentrate on three important areas of research relevant to the behavioral and psychological approaches to chronic pain. These are behavioral assessment research, behavioral treatment studies, and extensions of behavioral techniques to new populations.

Behavioral Assessment Research

The development of behavioral assessment methods for chronic pain is important for several reasons. *First*, these methods can provide a more objective evaluation of pain than is possible through global clinical ratings and impressions. *Second*, behavioral assessment techniques aid in the identification of social and environmental events that may serve to control pain behavior patterns. *Third*, these methods can provide a database to aid physicians in making a rational decision about the efficacy of the patient's current medical treatment and likelihood of response to specialized pain management treatment. *Finally*, behavioral assessment strategies can help patients gain a better understanding and more realistic appraisal of their own adaptations to chronic pain.

Behavioral observation techniques have recently been developed to record specific pain behavior patterns, such as activity level (Sanders, 1980), medication intake (Ready, Sarkis, & Turner, 1982), and motor pain behaviors (e.g., body posturing, painful facial expressions) (Keefe & Block, 1982). These observation methods are a significant advance over early self-monitoring approaches such as the daily activity diary (Fordyce, 1976). In self-monitoring, the patient keeps a daily record of activities

and pain behavior. However, these records may be affected by negative distortions on the part of the patient (Sanders, 1980) and motivational problems (Kremer, Block, & Gaylor, 1981). Sanders (1980) has described an electromechanical device that can be used to automatically record time spent in the standing or walking position. A modified form of this "uptime monitor" has also been reported by Follick, Ahern, Laser-Wolston, Adams, and Molloy (1985). Keefe and Block (1982) discuss a standardized observational procedure that can be used to sample the behavior of low-back pain patients during a series of standard activities consisting of sitting, standing, walking, and reclining. Cinciripini and Floreen (1982) have extended the use of observation procedures to recording patient behavior on a pain unit.

Observational methods for recording pain and pain behavior also have been employed during medical examinations. Waddell, McCulloch, Kimmel, and Venner (1980) found that patients who displayed excessive reactions to physical examinations were much less likely to be considered candidates for invasive diagnostic tests or surgical intervention. Keefe, Wilkins, and Cook (1984) reported that pain patients were more likely to exhibit pain behaviors while moving during physical examination. Also, the total pain behavior observed was related to physical findings recorded during the examination.

Psychophysical approaches for measuring pain perception also are receiving increased investigative attention. These new procedures are important for two reasons. *First*, like the McGill Pain Questionnaire (Melzack & Torgerson, 1971), they attempt to measure multiple dimensions of the pain experience. *Second*, they promise to provide more reliable and valid methods for evaluating and recording self-reports of pain. Two research groups have been especially active: one under the direction of Bernard Tursky, (Tursky, Jamner, & Friedman, 1982) and the other at the National Institutes of Health under the direction of Richard Gracely (Gracely, McGrath, & Dubner, 1978). These researchers have used advanced psychophysical methods, such as cross-modality matching, magnitude estimation, and scaling procedures, to develop and evaluate pain word descriptors. Their work has shown that two dimensions of the pain experience can be reliably measured with these descriptors: affective and intensity. They are now applying these methods to various clinical disorders.

Considerable attention recently has been directed to strategies that patients report using to cope with, reduce, or minimize their pain. It is believed that maladaptive coping strategies may play a role in the maintenance of chronic pain. Pain coping strategies are typically evaluated through unstructured interviews. Investigators have been interested in developing more objective ways to evaluate patients' use of a wide range of cognitive and behavioral strategies. In our laboratory, we constructed a pain-coping strategies questionnaire that appears to be internally reliable and enables one to assess the extent to which patients use each of six different cognitive strategies (diverting attention, reinterpretation of pain sensations, ignoring pain sensations, coping self-statements, catastrophizing, and praying or hoping), and two behavioral strategies (increasing activity level and increasing pain behaviors). Results of two studies (Rosenstiel, 1982; Rosenstiel & Keefe, 1983) indicate that the type of coping strategy patients use has an impact on measures of adjustment. Similar measures are being designed by other investigators. These have the potential of greatly expanding our knowledge about coping strategies and their efficacy. Ultimately, questionnaires of this sort may be used prior to treatment to identify specific maladaptive coping strategies that may be modified with behavioral treatment.

Behavioral Treatment Studies

A survey of current research on the behavioral treatment of chronic pain reveals a definite lack of controlled outcome research. The reasons for this have been articulated elsewhere (Keefe, 1982) and include the following: (a) the ethical problem of placing patients in no-treatment control conditions, (b) the difficulty of controlling the impact of simultaneous treatments that patients may be receiving, and (c) the need to assess outcome over extended time periods. Despite these difficulties, several innovative studies examining the effectiveness of specific behavioral and psychological treatment approaches have been carried out in the past several years.

Although biofeedback is used extensively in the treatment of chronic pain, it is typically used as an adjunct to a general pain management program. Wolf, Nacht, and Kelly (1982) employed an A–B–A–B design to test the efficacy of biofeedback alone in the management of mechanical low-back pain. Over the course of the investigations multiple evaluations of lumbar paraspinal musculature were performed during dynamic and static activities. When the patient was provided with feedback, significant reductions in pain and improvements in appropriate use of the low-back musculature were obtained. When feedback was withdrawn, performance deteriorated, and pain level increased.

Cognitive-behavioral interventions for chronic pain have also been the subject of controlled studies. Turner (1982) compared a cognitive-behavioral treatment package to progressive relaxation and a waiting-list control group. Patients in both the cognitive-behavioral and relaxation conditions showed improvements. However, those receiving cognitive-behavioral training rated themselves as more improved in ability to tolerate pain and engage in normal activities, and considered themselves as making more progress towards meeting treatment goals.

The operant perspective on pain emphasizes the role that spouse and family members may play in the maintenance as well as modification of pain behavior patterns. In several recent studies, there has been an attempt to evaluate the effect that training spouses in behavioral techniques has in modifying pain behavior patterns. Block (1981) evaluated a spouse-training approach as part of an in-patient pain management program. Spouses were trained to minimize their attention given to pain behavior and reward and praise patients for increases in well behavior. The efficacy of training appeared to vary as a function of marital satisfaction. Only in those couples in which satisfaction was low were significant gains obtained. Even in these marriages, however, spouses had great difficulty in complying with treatment instructions to ignore pain behavior.

Applications to Varied Pain Populations

Behavioral assessment and treatment techniques used for patients with intractable pain are now being extended to a variety of clinical disorders where pain is a feature. Ultimately, we might expect behavioral methods to make their greatest impact when they are used in primary care settings with common disorders, such as arthritis, headache, or for the management of pain in children. Investigators have begun to extend these techniques to a number of populations. For example, Achterberg-Lawlis (1982) has examined the utility of biofeedback and relaxation methods for management of stiffness and pain in rheumatoid arthritic patients. Bradley, et al. (1984) also have tested the usefulness of behavioral techniques with this population. In our own research laboratory, we have begun to use behavioral methods to evaluate pain in head and neck cancer patients (Keefe, Brantley, & Manuel, 1986). Structured interviews and standardized behavioral sampling techniques appear to be promising methods. Our research indicates that pain measures taken prior to treatment are predictive of patients' pain status post-treatment irrespective of medical status factors, such as site of cancer and stage of disease. Some interesting work also is being conducted in the pediatric area with children who face repeated painful medical procedures. Susan Jay and others (Jay, Ozolins, & Elliot, 1983) have developed a number of treatment strategies for management of pain in children who are undergoing bone marrow aspirations. These techniques also have been applied with burn victims (Elliot & Olson, 1983;

Kelley, Jarvie, Middlebrook, McNeer, & Drabman, 1984).

SUMMARY

This chapter reviews the status of behavioral approaches to the assessment and management of chronic pain. Although this is a relatively new clinical and research area, it has generated a considerable amount of interest. The available research suggests that behavioral methods can be beneficial in the overall management of patients suffering from chronic pain. Although chronic pain is a symptom, it cuts across a diverse group of clinical disorders. Certain treatment techniques appear to be helpful for many of these. These include operant conditioning procedures, relaxation training, and cognitive-behavioral therapy methods. Specialized treatment programs for chronic pain are being developed at many major medical centers; most of these incorporate strategies we have described. The quality of research in this area, however, needs to be improved. Initial efforts are primarily descriptive and consist of a consecutive series of patients treated with a particular approach. The development of objective assessment techniques to record pain and pain behavior discussed in this chapter can assist greatly in future research efforts.

Patients with intractable pain are a difficult group to treat and often require a multidisciplinary approach. Even with the best efforts, many fail to make progress. The fact that behavioral techniques have shown any efficacy with this population is indeed impressive. It is our hope that these methods are not restricted solely to these populations in the future. Patients who have common and often age-related pain conditions such as osteoarthritis may benefit from strategies that to date have been used almost exclusively for those suffering with chronic pain. Early intervention may prevent the development of psychological and behavioral problems that contribute to and magnify the suffering experienced by chronic pain patients. If the promise of behavioral techniques for pain management is to be realized, these methods should not be restricted to those with the most difficult and intractable pain problems.

REFERENCES

Achterberg-Lawlis, J. (1982). The psychological dimensions of arthritis. *Journal of Clinical and Consulting Psychology, 50,* 984–992.

Andersson, G. B. (1981). Epidemiologic aspects on low-back pain in industry. *Spine, 6,* 53–60.

Barr, J. S. (1951). Low back and sciatic pain. *Journal of Bone and Joint Surgery, 33,* 633–649.

Beck, A. T. (1976). *Cognitive therapy and emotional disorders.* New York: International Universities Press.

Block, A. R. (1981) *A technique for assessing overt responses of the spouse toward the chronic pain patient.* Unpublished manuscript, Duke University Medical Center, Durham, NC.

Bonica, J. J. (1977a). Neurophysiologic and pathologic aspects of acute and chronic pain. *Archives of Surgery, 112,* 750–761.

Bonica, J. J. (1977b). Basic principles in managing chronic pain. *Archives of Surgery, 112,* 783–788.

Bonica, J. J. (1978). Cancer pain: A major national health problem. *Cancer Nursing Journal, 4,* 313–316.

Bonica, J. J. (1980). Pain research and therapy: Past and current status and future needs. In L. Ng & J. J. Bonica (Eds.), *Pain, discomfort, and humanitarian care,* (pp. 1–46). New York: Elsevier.

Bradley, L. A., Turner, R. A., Young, L. D. Aqudelo, C. A., Anderson, K. O., & McDaniel, L. K. (1984, September). *Effects of cognitive behavioral therapy on pain behavior of rheumatoid arthritis patients.* Paper presented at the Fourth World Congress on Pain, Seattle, WA.

Cautela, J. R., & Kastenbaum, R. A. (1967). A reinforcement survey schedule for use in therapy, training, and research. *Psychological Reports, 20,* 1115–1130.

Cinciripini, P. M., & Floreen, A. (1982). An evaluation of a behavioral program for chronic pain. *Journal of Behavioral Medicine, 5,* 375–389.

Dehlin, O., Hedenrud, B., & Horal, J. (1976). Back symptoms in nursing aides in a geriatric hospital. *Scandinavian Journal of Rehabilitation Medicine, 8,* 47–53.

Elliot, C. H., & Olson, R. A. (1983). The management of children's behavioral distress in response to painful medical treatment for burn injuries. *Behaviour Therapy and Research, 21,* 675–683.

Ellis, A. (1979). *Theoretical and empirical foundations of rational-emotive therapy.* Monterey, CA: Brooks/Cole.

Follick, M. J., Ahern, D. K., Laser-Wolston, N., Adams, A. E., & Molloy, A. J. (1985). An electronical recording device for the measurement of "uptime" or "downtime" in chronic pain patients. *Archives of Physical Medicine and Rehabilitation, 66,* 75–79.

Follick, M. J., Zitter, R. E., & Ahern, D. K. (1983). In E. B. Foa & P. Emmelkamp (Eds.), *Failures in behavior therapy* (pp. 311–334). New York: Wiley.

Fordyce, W. E. (1976). *Behavioral methods for chronic pain and illness.* St. Louis, MO: Mosby.

Gracely, R. H., McGrath, P., & Dubner, R. (1978). Validity and sensitivity of ratio scales of sensory and affective verbal pain descriptors: Manipulation of affect by Diazepam. *Pain, 5,* 19–29.

Hendler, N., & Fenton, J. A. 1979. *Coping with chronic pain.* New York: Clarkson N. Potter, Inc.

Hult, L. (1954). Cervical, dorsal, and lumbar spinal syndromes. *Acta Orthopaedica Scandinavica 17* (Suppl.), 7–102.

International Association for the Study of Pain, Subcommittee on Taxonomy. (1979). Pain terms: A list of definitions and notes on usage. *Pain, 6,* 249–252.

Jay, S. M., Ozolins, M., & Elliot, C. H. (1983). Assessment of children's distress during painful medical procedures. *Health Psychology, 2,* 133–147.

Keefe, F. J. (1982). Behavioral assessment and treatment of chronic pain: Current status and future directions. *Journal of Clinical and Consulting Psychology, 50,* 896–911.

Keefe, F. J., & Block, A. R. (1982). Development of an observation method for assessing pain behavior in chronic low back pain patients. *Behavior Therapy, 13,* 363–375.

Keefe, F. J., Brantle, A., & Manual, G. S. (1986). Pain and the head and neck cancer patient: In E. N. Myers, I. Barofsky and J. W. Yates (Eds.), *Rehabilitation and treatment of head and neck cancer.* (NIH Publication No. 86-2762) U.S. Department of Health and Human Services.

Keefe, F. J., & Brown, C. J. (1982). Behavioral treatment of chronic pain syndromes. In P. A. Boudewyns & F. J. Keefe (Eds.), *Behavioral medicine in general medical practice* (pp. 19–41). Menlo Park, CA: Addison-Wesley.

Keefe, F. J., Brown, C., Scott, D. S., & Ziesat, H. (1982). Behavioral assessment of chronic pain. In F. J. Keefe & J. A. Blumenthal (Eds.), *Assessment strategies in behavioral medicine* (pp. 321–350). New York: Grune & Stratton.

Keefe, F. J., Gil, K. M., & Rose, S. (1986). Multidisciplinary approaches to the management of chronic pain. *Clinical Psychology Review, 6,* 87–113.

Keefe, F. J., Wilkins, R. H., & Cook, W. A. (1984). Direct observation of pain behaviors in low back pain patients during physical examination. *Pain, 20,* 59–68.

Kelley, M. L., Jarvie, G. J., Middlebrook, J. L., McNeer, M. F., & Drabman, R. S. (1984). Decreasing burned children's pain behavior: Impacting the trauma of hydrotherapy. *Journal of Applied Behavior Analysis, 17,* 147–158.

Kelsey, J. L., & White, A. A. (1980). Epidemiology and impact of low back pain. *Spine, 5,* 133–142.

Khatami, M., & Rush, A. J. (1978). A pilot study of the treatment of outpatients with chronic pain: Symptom control, stimulus control, and social system intervention. *Pain, 5,* 163–172.

Kremer, E., Block, A., & Gaylor, M. (1981). Behavioral approaches to chronic pain: The inaccuracy of patient self-report measures. *Archives of Physical Medicine and Rehabilitation, 62,* 188–191.

Lance, J. W. (1975). *Headache — Understanding alleviation.* New York: Scribner's.

Lewinsohn, P. M. (1975). The behavioral study and treatment of depression. In M. Hersen, R. M. Eisler, & P. M. Miller (Eds.), *Progress in behavior modification* (Vol. 1, pp. 19–64). New York: Academic Press.

Lubin, B. (1965). Adjective checklists for the measurement of depression. *Archives of General Psychiatry, 12,* 57–62.

MacPhillamy, D. J., & Lewinsohn, P. M. (1971). *The pleasant events schedule.* Dr. Peter Lewinsohn, Department of Psychology, University of Oregon, Straub Hall, Eugene, Oregon 97403-1227.

MacPhillamy, D. J., & Lewinsohn, P. M. (1973). *A scale for the measurement of positive reinforcement.* Dr. Peter Lewinsohn, Department of Psychology, University of Oregon, Straub Hall, Eugene, Oregon 97403-1227.

Melzack, R., & Torgerson, W. S. (1971). On the language of pain. *Anesthesiology, 34,* 50–59.

Nashold, B. S., & Bullitt, E. (1981). Dorsal root entry zone lesions to control central pain in paraplegics. *Journal of Neuorsurgery, 55,* 414–419.

Nashold, B. S., & Friedman, H. (1972). Dorsal column stimulation for pain. A preliminary report on thirty patients. *Journal of Neurosurgery, 36,* 590–597.

National Health Survey (1973). Limitation of Activity Due to Chronic Conditions. (DHEW Publication No. (HSM) 73-1506) Rockville, MD: U.S. Department of Health, Education and Welfare.

Pheasant, H. C. (1977). Backache — its nature, incidence, and cost. *Western Journal of Medicine, 126,* 330–332.

Ready, L. B., Sarkis, E., & Turner, J. A. (1982). Self-reported vs. actual use of medications in chronic pain patients. *Pain, 12,* 285–294.

Rosenstiel, A. K. (1982, March). *The effect of coping strategies on the relief of pain following surgical intervention for lower back pain.* Paper presented at the meeting of the Society of Behavioral Medicine, Chicago.

Rosenstiel, A. K., & Keefe, F. J. (1983). The use of coping strategies in chronic low back pain patients: Relationship to patient characteristics and current adjustment. *Pain, 17,* 33–44.

Sanders, S. (1980). Toward a practical instrument system for the automatic measurement of "uptime" in chronic pain patients. *Pain, 9,* 103–109.

Sarkin, T. L. (1977). Backache in the aged. *South African Medical Journal, 51,* 418–420.

Steinberg, C. G. (1982). Epidemiology of low back pain. In M. Stanton-Hicks & R. Boas (Eds.), *Chronic low back pain* (pp. 1–13). New York: Raven.

Stubbs, D. A. (1981. Trunk stresses in construction and other industrial workers. *Spine, 6,* 83–89.

Turk, D. C. (1983). *Pain and behavioral medicine: A cognitive-behavioral perspective.* New York: Guildford.

Turk, D. C., & Flor, H. (1984). Etiological theories and treatments for chronic low back pain: II. Psychological models and interventions. *Pain, 19,* 209–233.

Turner, J. A. (1982). Comparison of progressive relaxation training and cognitive-behavioral therapy for chronic low back pain. *Journal of Clinical and Consulting Psychology, 50,* 757–765.

Tursky, B., Jamner, J., & Friedman, R. (1982). The Pain Perception Profile: A psychophysical approach to the assessment of pain report. *Behavior Therapy, 13,* 376–394.

Urban, B. J. (1982). Therapeutic aspects in chronic pain: Modulation of nociception, alleviation of suffering, and behavioral analysis. *Behavior Therapy, 13,* 430–437.

U.S. Department of Health, Education, and Welfare. (1979). *Vital and health statistics: Limitation of activity due to chronic conditions.* United States Series 10-No. 111. Washington, DC: U.S. Government Printing Office.

Waddell, G., McCulloch, J. A., Kimmel, E., & Venner, R. M. (1980). Nonorganic physical signs in low back pain. *Spine, 5,* 117–125.

Wallis, C. (1984, June 11). Unlocking pain's secrets. *Time*, pp. 58–66.

Weisenberg, M. (1977) Pain and pain control. *Psychological Bulletin, 84,* 1008–1014.

Wolf, S. L., Nacht, M., & Kelly, J. L. (1982). EMG feedback training during dynamic movement for low back pain patients. *Behavior Therapy, 13,* 395–406.

CHAPTER 16

Epilepsy

Bruce P. Hermann, Bindu T. Desai and Steven Whitman

Epilepsy, one of the oldest known disorders, was studied and discussed in some detail by Hippocrates and his colleagues over 2,000 years ago. Physicians of that era were fascinated by the mysteries of epilepsy—what caused it, why were there so many and such strange physical manifestations, how could it be treated, and so on. Although these questions are better understood today, and although epilepsy is studied in a more scientific way, much of the mystery remains. We still do not know the cause of a large proportion of the cases of epilepsy; we still often do not know which manifestation of epilepsy will be produced under which circumstances, and treatment for epilepsy is ineffective for about one third of all cases.

In addition to these medical mysteries, epilepsy has long been surrounded by social confusion and stigmatization. Two thousand years ago, it was believed that seizures were the work of either God or the devil (Temkin, 1971). One hundred years ago, Cesare Lombroso, an Italian physician, declared epilepsy to be the essence of the "criminal man" and founded the school of criminal anthropology based upon such

notions (Lombroso-Ferrero, 1911/1972). In addition, because it was believed that epilepsy was inherited (and assumed that it was a negative condition, related to idiocy and criminality), people with epilepsy were subjected to the multiple eugenic schemes that spread throughout this country at the beginning of the 20th century (Chase, 1977). In fact, as of 1971, nine states still had laws calling for the sterilization of people with epilepsy (Schneider & Conrad, 1983).

Such medical mysteries and social confusion help shape the world of people with epilepsy, and it is within this world that our knowledge about this disorder is acquired. As such, our knowledge is limited in many ways. For example, because of the stigma and resulting discrimination surrounding epilepsy, people with the disorder often prefer that others not know of their condition. Additionally, it is often hard to diagnose epilepsy because medical histories and electrophysiological tests are not always good markers. As a result of these social and medical limitations, it is often difficult to determine the prevalence of epilepsy, the extent to which it is inherited, and many other aspects of central importance.

Many of these problems, both medical and social, stem from the fact that epilepsy is located in the brain. It is for this reason that some of the most interesting and important questions arise. For example, many researchers believe that patients with epilepsy suffer a disproportionate amount of psychopathology. The cause of this psychopathology is a major issue. If it is biological, stemming from misfiring neurons, then understanding this process will help us understand the relationship between the mind and the brain. If, on the other hand, the cause of psychopathology in people with epilepsy is a social issue, such as stigmatization, then this will help us understand the relationship between the individual and society. This opposition is, of course, an aspect of the several-hundred-year-old nature–nurture controversy.

The constellation of all of these factors makes epilepsy a fascinating disorder to study. The fact that epilepsy is one of the commonest neurological problems, affecting over 2 million people in the United States, makes it an important disorder to study. We hope, in this chapter, to convey not only the current state of knowledge about epilepsy, but also some of the larger medical and social aspects involved in its understanding. We begin by describing epilepsy in some detail. This is followed by a summary of the epidemiology of the disorder that will emphasize what is known and what is unknown. We next discuss the developmental issues and then present a review of medical and psychological assessment and treatment. Finally, we review current research and perspectives about epilepsy, again from both a medical and psychological point of view.

DESCRIPTION OF THE DISORDER

Seizures can be a *symptom* of many underlying diseases, but epilepsy per se is defined as a condition where two or more seizures occur unrelated to an acute provocation such as meningitis, drug withdrawal, or withdrawal from alcohol. An epileptic seizure results from sudden, excessive rapid firing of nerve cells, and produces a change in the individual's awareness of the environment or loss of consciousness and uncontrollable body movements.

Generalized Tonic-Clonic Seizure

Many *types* of seizures exist (see Table 16-1). The most common type is called generalized tonic–clonic or *grand mal*. These seizures are associated in most people's minds with the words "convulsion" or "fits." The seizure may begin with essentially no warning or may begin with an "aura" or warning that informs the individual that he or she is about to have a seizure. Depending on the specific electroencephalogram (EEG) pattern, as well as the clinical features of the attack, tonic-clonic seizures can be classified as either primary generalized (e.g., warning-less attack, corticoreticular EEG pattern) or partial with secondary generalization (e.g., aura preceding seizure, focal epileptiform discharges). The aura may be a strange smell, a flash of light, or a funny taste in the mouth. Within seconds, the individual loses consciousness, falls, and becomes very stiff (the tonic phase). A few seconds later there is jerking of the limbs (the clonic phase), the eyeballs roll up, the individual has frothing at the mouth, and may bite his or her tongue and lose urine. In about a minute the jerking stops and the person falls asleep for 1 to 3 hours (the postictal phase). Sometimes this phase consists of headache, confusion, or fatigue. Suggested first aid for such a seizure includes laying the individual flat on the ground, turning the head to one side, and waiting for a minute or two. The seizure will generally stop in this time. During the seizure, the person is unaware of what is going on. After the seizure is over, the individual will generally be confused, will not recall what was said during the seizure, nor will he or she remember what happened during the seizure. Most people who have these seizures tend to have only one at a time. It is a medical emergency, however, when there are a

Table 16-1. Classification of Seizures

Partial Seizures

A. Simple Partial (consciousness not impaired)
1. With motor signs (Jacksonian)
2. With somatosensory and special sensory signs
3. With automatic signs
4. With psychic symptoms

B. Complex Partial (consciousness impaired)
1. Simple partial onset followed by impaired consciousness
2. Impaired consciousness at onset

C. Secondarily Generalized (partial onset evolving to generalized tonic–clonic seizures)

Generalized Seizures

A. Absence (petit mal)
B. Myoclonic
C. Tonic–clonic (grand mal)
D. Clonic
E. Tonic
F. Atonic (drop attacks)

---

flurry of seizures, and the person should be admitted to a hospital. Such a condition is known as *status epilepticus*, which fortunately is uncommon.

Absence Seizure

Another type of seizure is the *absence* or *petit mal* seizure. An absence is a brief stare that lasts for about 10 seconds, during which the individual has fluttering of the eyelids and/or lip smacking (Penry, Porter, & Dreifuss, 1975). These seizures, which often begin in early childhood, have the ability to disrupt an individual's life, as they can occur over 100 times a day. The child may get into trouble at home or school if the seizures are mistaken for lack of attention or absent-mindedness. The absence and the primary generalized tonic–clonic seizures are classified as *generalized* seizures because they initially involve both hemispheres of the brain, thereby resulting in impairment of consciousness. Other types of generalized seizures include *infantile spasms*, which begin in the first year of life. These seizures are brief and consist of flexion of the lower half of the body and

the head, with the arms extended giving the appearance of paying obeisance—hence the name "salaam seizures." Infantile spasms form a part of the triad known as West's syndrome. The other two features of this syndrome are mental retardation and a distinctly abnormal EEG pattern known as hypsarrhythmia.

Partial Seizures

Seizures are also classified into a category called *partial seizures* because these seizures occur in only a part of the brain (Commission on Classification and Terminology of the International League Against Epilepsy, 1981). They may or may not impair consciousness. Those seizures where consciousness is not impaired throughout the seizure are called *simple* partial seizures, whereas seizures with impairment of consciousness are called *complex* partial seizures.

Simple partial seizures may consist of the jerking of one arm or leg (partial motor seizures), tingling and numbness on one side of the body (partial sensory seizures), or the perception of flashes of light or strange smells and tastes (partial seizures with special sensory symptoms).

Complex partial seizures are the single most common type found in adults. They usually occur when there is abnormal nerve cell activity in a part of the brian known as the temporal lobes. These lobes, for reasons yet unknown, are more susceptible to seizures than other parts of the brain. The temporal lobes are, among other things, the nerve centers for recognizing smell and taste. They also control our ability to speak, hear, and remember. When a seizure begins in one of the temporal lobes, it causes a change in a person's behavior. A strange look may appear on the face. The person stares for a few seconds, turns his or her head to one side, and then begins to have *automatisms*, which are movements of the body over which the person has no control. An individual may smack his or her lips, chew, rub hands, and walk about aimlessly. This typically occurs for a minute or two before the individual gradually regains awareness of the surroundings.

Finally, some individuals may experience tonic–clonic seizures that result from the generalized spread of epileptiform activity from a well-defined focus in one cerebral hemisphere. These are called partial seizures with secondary generalization. It is important to differentiate these attacks from primary generalized tonic-clonic seizures (even though the attacks look the same, i.e., grand mal) because different medications may be particularly effective for the different types.

A special type of seizure known as *febrile seizures* (Nelson & Ellenberg, 1981) occurs in little children when they have a fever. This causes some parents much anxiety, which is misplaced, because a febrile seizure does not mean that the child will grow up to have epilepsy. The implications of these seizures are discussed in detail in the section on developmental issues.

MEDICAL ASSESSMENT

Physicians who deal with epilepsy first try to decide what type of seizure a person has and then try to find a cause for it. The physician attempts to clarify as many details as possible about what happens during a seizure. The following are questions a physician might ask:

1. Is there a warning or an aura?
2. What kind of aura is it?
3. Is there a strange smell, a funny taste, a tingling feeling in one hand?
4. Does the person lose consciousness?
5. Does he or she fall?
6. Has anyone seen the person have a seizure?
7. What did he/she notice?
8. Is the tongue bitten?
9. Is there loss of urine?
10. Do the limbs jerk?
11. Does the person appear dazed?
12. Does he or she move about as if in a trance?
13. How long does the seizure last?
14. Does the person fall asleep after the seizure or complain of a headache and muscle fatigue?

By putting together a description of what happens during a seizure, the physician decides whether the person has epilepsy and, if so, what type. Sometimes, however, the description is not clear and special investigations may help to confirm whether a person does have epilepsy. These special investigations include an EEG and a computerized tomographic (CT) scan of the brain. In a few epilepsy centers, patients are studied by a technique known as videotelemetry and positron emission tomography (PET) scan.

An EEG records the electrical activity of different areas of the brain and can reveal the site, called the epileptic focus, where the seizure begins (see Figure 16-1). The EEG shows an epileptic pattern when it exposes an abnormality generally seen with seizures. Sometimes, as in primary generalized tonic–clonic and absence seizures, the epileptic pattern is produced by all areas of the brain (see Figure 16-2).

A CT brain scan gives a simulated picture of a particular area of the brain by measuring differences in density. For instance, bone, which is dense, shows up as an opacity on the developed film, whereas cerebro-

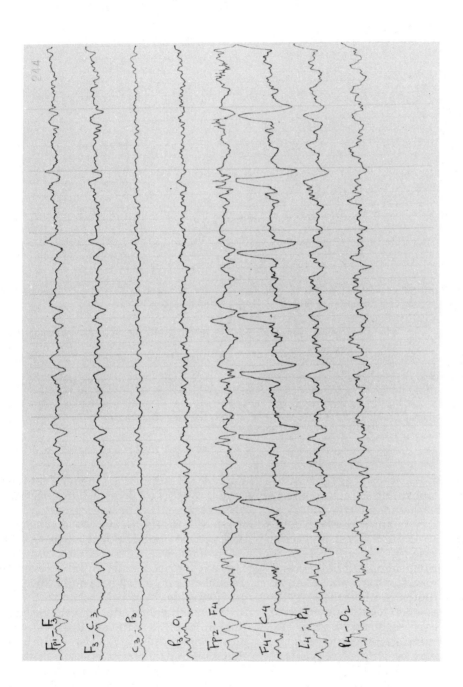

Figure 16-1. EEG tracing showing normal activity in the upper part that records from the left side of the brain. Compare with the lower half, which shows abnormal epileptic activity coming from the right side of the brain. The abnormal activity is most pronounced in the line marked F4-C4.

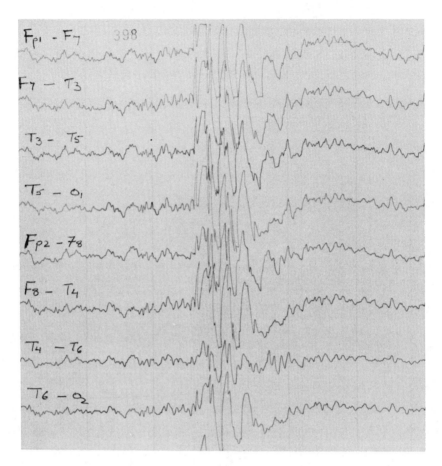

Figure 16-2. EEG tracing showing a "burst" of epleptiform activity affecting all areas of the brain. Compare with Figure 16-1

spinal fluid (CSF), which is virtually similar to water, shows up as a lucency. In epilepsy, CT brain scans may reveal lesions such as tumors, cysts, and scars of old injuries. Figure 16-3 is the CT scan of a brain tumor that caused a 35-year-old man to have secondarily generalized tonic–clonic seizures. CT brain scans are more likely to show a brain lesion in older people with partial seizures when nearly one fourth of such individuals may have a structural lesion of the brain detected on the scan.

Videotelemetry uses closed-circuit television and continuous EEG recording and is generally available only in special epilepsy centers. Videotelemetry, which enables physicians to study precisely what happens during a seizure, has clarified the

sequence of events in absence and complex partial seizures. Videotelemetry is used to observe patients with severe epilepsy who may need surgery to control their seizures. An accurate seizure-type diagnosis is reached when seizures recorded on videotape are analyzed in detail. It may even be possible to pinpoint what part of the brain is responsible.

PET scanners, developed very recently (Engel, 1982), measure how different parts of the brain use energy. A part of the brain that is injured for any reason is likely to use less energy than a normal brain. An example of the usefulness of a PET scan would be for a person who has seizures that begin on the left side of the brain. When he or she is not having seizures, the left side

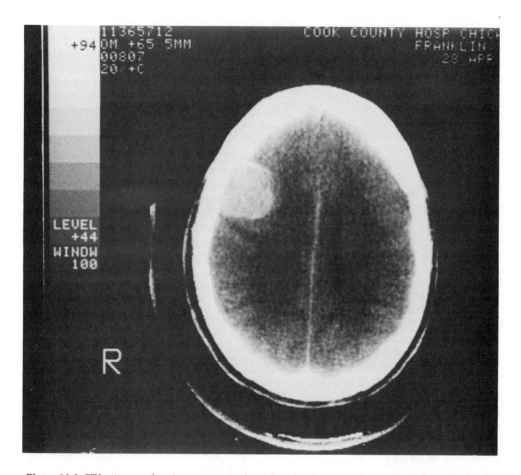

Figure 16-3. CT brain scan showing a tumor on the right side of the brain. Compare with normal left side.

uses less energy than the normal right side, which PET scan will reveal. The left side will appear pale on the scan as compared to the right. During a seizure, the left side uses *more* energy than the right and shows what is called a discrete zone of hypermetabolism.

CAUSES OF EPILEPSY

Despite common belief, current knowledge suggests that epilepsy is not inherited. With present methods of investigation, a cause can be attributed in about 40% of all cases. The major known causes of epilepsy are described below.

Perinatal factors include lack of or diminished oxygen supply (anoxia) during labor and delivery and birth trauma leading to hemorrhage in the brain or in its covering membranes (the arachnoid and dura). Ammon's Horn sclerosis, a lesion in the temporal lobe, results from anoxia suffered by the fetus during protracted labor, and is believed to be responsible for many of the cases of complex partial seizures.

Head injury is a relatively common cause of epilepsy. Seizures that follow head injury are of two types: *early* seizures occurring in the first 7 days after a head injury and *late* seizures that occur *after* the 7 days. Only late seizures are considered to be epileptic. Late seizures occur in half of the patients who sustain an injury where an object such as shrapnel actually penetrates the substance of the brain (Jennett, 1975). In nonpenetrating, or blunt, head injury, the likelihood of developing epilepsy depends upon the injury's severity. Epilepsy develops in about 10% of patients who have prolonged coma, bleeding into the brain, or a skull fracture (Annegers et al., 1980). Children, however, have a higher rate of post-traumatic epilepsy, even with minor head injury (Jennett, 1975; Desai et al., 1983a).

Other causes of epilepsy include *tumors*, which are more likely to cause seizures in adults than in children. Tumors that destroy the gray matter of the brain also have a greater chance of causing seizures than tumors that occur in other parts of the brain. Infections of the brain (encephalitis) or its covering (meningitis) cause seizures in the acute phase; epilepsy may follow as a sequela, especially in children.

Infection with a parasite (the cyst of a tapeworm) is a frequent cause of seizures in people from Latin America (McCormick, Zee, & Heiden, 1982). Seizures can also occur because of a *cluster of abnormal blood vessels* in a part of the brain (an arteriovenous malformation) or from a *stroke*.

The brain is made up of billions of nerve cells called neurons. Neurons are highly active cells that receive signals or stimuli from inside and outside the body and react to these stimuli by electrical as well as chemical means. Normal neuronal activity is responsible for our ability to move, think, remember, react, and so forth. A seizure represents abnormal neuronal activity. Individual neurons become hyperexcitable and affect neighboring neurons. This group of neurons is then said to become excitable in *synchrony*. The exact mechanism leading to a seizure is as yet unknown, although we do understand the changes that occur in the electrical response of individual neurons as well as in the levels of neurotransmitters or chemical messengers between neurons. A further discussion of cellular mechanisms leading to a seizure is presented in the medical research section of this chapter.

EPIDEMIOLOGY

The many medical and social complexities of epilepsy make it difficult to gain a firm grasp on its epidemiologic features. For examples, epilepsy does not require registration, as do several infectious diseases, some chronic diseases, and birth and death. Furthermore, it is well-known that some people with epilepsy do not seek medical attention for their disorder. Finally, because of the stigma attached to epilepsy, many people will not tell researchers that they have the disorder. It is obvious how such complexities would impact on our knowledge about epilepsy's prevalence, the number of years it persists, and even its vocational and psychological correlates. Delineating the epidemiology of epilepsy, which is essential, is also difficult but not impossible. It is necessary to keep in mind, however, how these complexities limit our abilities to generalize our findings.

Definitions

In most epidemiological studies, *epilepsy* is defined as consisting of at least two seizures (see the section on Description of the Disorder) that occur any time during a person's life and that are not directly provoked by metabolic causes (Hauser & Kurland, 1975). Such metabolic causes include fever, brain infections, head trauma, drugs, and alcohol withdrawal. The "direct provocation" is difficult to determine and the definition of "direct" varies. For example, how long after alcohol withdrawal must a seizure occur in order to be unprovoked? There seems to be no agreement on this interval and it remains a clinical determination. On the other hand, it is generally agreed that the interval after head injury is 7 days. Thus, a seizure occurring within 7 days of a head injury is regarded as being provoked and is called an *early seizure* (Jennett, 1975; Desai et al., 1983a,b). A seizure occurring more than 7 days after a head injury is defined as unprovoked and is part of epilepsy. Finally, if a person has not had a seizure for at least 5 years and has not been on antiepileptic medications, he or she is said to have *inactive epilepsy* (Hauser & Kurland, 1975). Such cases are generally not included in prevalence determinations unless concepts such as "lifetime prevalence" are under consideration.

This review of the basic components of a definition of epilepsy facilitates the following discussion of the epidemiology in this field. Information about the incidence and prevalence of epilepsy is presented, relevant demographic differentials are discussed, and one very illuminating study in this area is summarized. Finally, mortality in epilepsy is discussed.

Incidence and Prevalence

The *incidence* of a condition is defined as the number of new cases that develop in a given time period, divided by the population at risk. In studies of epilepsy, incidence is usually expressed in cases per 100,000 population. The *prevalence* of a condition is defined as the number of cases that exist in a given time period, divided by the population at risk. In studies of epilepsy, prevalence is usually expressed in cases per 1,000 population.

There have been many studies of the prevalence of epilepsy—about 50 in all—from all parts of the world, about half of these have included incidence data as well. (See Zielinski, 1982, for a recent, comprehensive, and critical review of many of these studies.) As one would expect, and fear, definitions and case-finding techniques vary widely. The problem with such a situation is that it then becomes impossible to determine if varying results are produced by methodological differences or if they reflect real differences among populations.

And the results of these studies do indeed vary. For example, incidence rates range from a low of 11 (per 100,000 population) in Norway (Krohn, 1961) to a high of 70 in southeastern England (Pond, Bidwell, & Stein, 1960). Prevalence rates vary similarly, ranging from 1.5 (per 1,000) in Niigata City, Japan (Sato, 1964), to 5.4 in Rochester, Minnesota (Hauser & Kurland, 1975), to 19.5 in Bogata, Colombia (Gomez, Arciniegas, & Torres, 1978), to 24.2 in the

Illinois prison system (Whitman et al., 1984).

Generally speaking, the prevalence rate equals the incidence rate multiplied by the average duration of a disorder. Thus, we would expect that if epilepsy has similar duration in all communities, the prevalence-to-incidence ratios would be constant from community to community, even though there is great variation in prevalence and incidence rates among communities. Unfortunately, when one compares prevalence-to-incidence ratios, substantial variation persists. For example, the ratio was calculated by us to be 6.7 (prevalence = 4.2/1,000, incidence = 63/100,000) in England and Wales (Crombie, Pinsent & Watts, 1960), 11.3 (prevalence = 5.4, incidence = 48) in Rochester, Minnesota (Hauser & Kurland, 1975), and 21.0 (prevalence = 4.2, incidence = 20) in Warsaw, Poland (Zielinski, 1974a). Such large differences almost certainly could not be caused by variation in duration among communities, nor by other factors such as differential mortality rates. Instead, these ratios suggest that not only does methodology and the impact of sampling bias vary from study to study, but that they also vary within studies that determine both incidence and prevalence.

Demographic Differentials

An interesting observation about the epidemiology of epilepsy is that despite the very substantial variation in incidence and prevalence findings across studies, the direction of demographic differentials remains consistent. For example, virtually all studies of incidence and all studies of prevalence have found males to be at greater risk than females for epilepsy. This fact is consistent with the fact that males are about twice as likely as females to sustain head injuries (Whitman, Coonley-Hoganson, & Desai, 1984; Frankowski, Anneggers & Whitman, 1985).

It is also the case that every study that has investigated age-specific incidence rates has found the highest rates in the young, usually in the first 10 years of life. Most studies then detect gradually decreasing incidence rates with age. However, Hauser and Kurland (1975) found that rates in Rochester started to rise at about age 60.

Finally, every study in the United States that has investigated the race and class correlates of epilepsy have found poor people and black people to be at greater risk (Whitman, Coleman, Berg, King & Desai, 1980). The methodologies of most of these earlier studies were weak, with one exception (Shamansky & Glaser, 1979). Recently, however, more methodologically sound studies in a prison system (Whitman et al., 1984) and in the Bronx (Hauser, Tabaddor, Factor, & Finer, 1984) have provided more substantial evidence in support of this association between poverty and epilepsy. Preliminary results from a door-to-door survey of epilepsy in the Watts community of Los Angeles are also consistent with this association (Lampert et al., 1984).

A Special Study

We would like to summarize an epidemiological study of epilepsy that demonstrates and solves the methodological difficulties we have been alluding to throughout this discussion. In 1969, Janusz Zielinski (1974a) reviewed all the records of medical and social services in the city of Warsaw to determine the number of cases of epilepsy known by these sources. Such cases generated a prevalence of active epilepsy of 4.2 (per 1,000 population). He then implemented a random 0.5% door-to-door survey of the city, backed up by appropriate neurological exam. This survey generated a prevalence of active epilepsy of 7.8, almost twice the rate known to all medical sources in the city. Virtually all of the known cases (91%) had been on antiepilepsy medication at some point in their lives and 77% were currently on medication. However, in the door-to-door survey, these figures fell to 57% and 35%, respectively. Furthermore, those not attending medical services had the more benign forms of epilepsy and were doing much better in their day-to-day lives.

Zielinski's remarkable study confirms two major conclusions. First, any survey of medical sources, even the most thorough, will miss a large proportion of people with epilepsy. Second, medical and social studies of *patients with epilepsy* carried out at medical centers and/or social service facilities are going to be about those most seriously afflicted with the disorder and will thus produce substantially and negatively distorted images of the lives of *people with epilepsy*.

Mortality

People with epilepsy are at greater risk of death than the general population. Factors that are specific to epilepsy and that sometimes cause death are status epilepticus (see the sections on Generalized Tonic–Clonic Seizure and Treatment of Status Epilepticus) and accidents that can occur during a seizure (e.g., drowning, falling from a high place). In addition, it is likely that the chronic effects of seizures and drugs taken over many years also place the individual at greater risk of death.

A sound study of mortality in patients with epilepsy has been carried out by Hauser, Annegers, and Elveback (1980) in Rochester, Minnesota. They found that patients with epilepsy had a risk of dying that was about twice that of other people living in the "West Northcentral" part of the United States. The risk varied somewhat according to sex, etiology of epilepsy, type of epilepsy, and so on. Zielinski (1974b) found similar dynamics in his study of epilepsy in Warsaw.

Two caveats must be noted. First, all of the methodological problems previously discussed are, of course, relevant here because one can only know mortality rates among people with epilepsy if one knows who has epilepsy. Second, it is important to understand that many of the social factors that afflict people with epilepsy are known to impact negatively upon the health of the general population. These include unemployment, diminished social support, discrimination, and poverty. It would thus seem reasonable that the additional mortality risk faced by people with epilepsy is caused not only by biological factors but by social factors as well.

Conclusion

The methodological problems inherent in this field make generalizing difficult. Nonetheless, we would like to offer a few summary statements about the epidemiology of epilepsy. To date, there has been only one population-based U.S. study that included all age groups (Hauser & Kurland, 1975). As this is being written, a second study of this nature is being completed (Lampert et al., 1984).

Hauser and Kurland found a prevalence of about 6/1,000 in Rochester, Minnesota. However, they were able to include only cases registered in medical facilities. Furthermore, Rochester is a middle-class, professional community (Hauser & Kurland, 1975). Zielinski (1974a) found that when cases not known to medical facilities were included, the prevalence rose by 86% (from 4.2 to 7.8%). If the same situation were to prevail in Rochester, this would produce a prevalence rate of 11.2, or just over 1%. It is probably reasonable to view this as a general estimate for middle-class communities in the United States.

Higher prevalence rates of epilepsy will certainly exist in poorer communities, but it is not yet possible to know how much higher these rates might be. Diverse clues from two studies (Hauser, Tabaddor, Factor, & Finer, 1984; Whitman et al., 1984) suggest that rates might be as much as 100% higher, somewhat above 2%.

MEDICAL TREATMENT

Because epilepsy is a symptom, treatment depends, first, on the underlying cause. Patients with epilepsy secondary to a brain tumor have to be treated primarily for the tumor. If, however, an obvious surgically correctable lesion is not present, treatment proceeds along medical lines. The mainstay of medical treatment is drugs. These antiepileptic drugs (AEDs) either prevent groups of neurons from discharging in hypersynchrony or prevent spread of discharge. An ideal drug would be one that prevents or stops all seizures, does not sedate the patient, is free of side effects, and has no cumulative side effects.

As such a drug does not exist, the physician has to balance the gains obtained by using a particular drug against its side effects. Principles governing the use of AEDs include choosing a well-known drug before trying out less well-known ones and starting with only one drug and raising its dose close to where it may result in toxicity before deciding that the drug is ineffective in seizure control. Drugs must be administered with an understanding of how they act, how they are broken up by the body into various products or metabolites, how long a dose remains in the bloodstream, and how quickly the drug achieves a stable level in the blood (steady state). AEDs should always be discontinued gradually, as an abrupt stoppage of medicine may result in status epilepticus. Table 16-2 summarizes clinically relevant properties of commonly used antiepileptic drugs. We will briefly review important side effects of these drugs. For a detailed account of these drugs, the interested reader is referred to three excellent reviews (Glaser, Penry, & Woodbury, 1980; Penry, & Newmark, 1979; Woodbury, Penry, & Pippenge, 1982).

Side Effects of Commonly Used Drugs

Carbamazepine (Tegretol) is an ideal drug for children with generalized tonic–clonic seizures or partial seizures, as it does not create the behavioral problems associated with phenobarbital, nor does it have unpleasant side effects on the skin such as coarsening of the facial features and hirsutism. *Phenobarbital* is inexpensive and is effective in preventing recurrence of febrile seizures if given continuously so that adequate blood levels of the drug are maintained (Nelson & Ellenberg, 1981). Its main side effects are sedation and drowsiness. It also may cause paradoxical excitement in children and suppress rapid eye movement (REM) sleep, the stage of sleep where dreams occur. Also some patients may suffer a severe sleep disturbance when the drug is discontinued and a REM rebound occurs. Sedation may create many difficulties for the patient, especially when the drug is first begun. Sedation and loss of

Table 16-2. Properties of Commonly Used Anti-Epileptic Drugs

Drug	Average daily dose in mg	Optimal plasma levels mcg/ (ml)	% of drug that is protein bound	Half-life in hours	Unwanted side effects and toxicity	Efficacy of drug in terms of seizure types
Carbamazepine	1,200	4–8	70	12 ± 3	Vertigo, diplopia, ataxia, blood dyscrasias	Generalized tonic-clonic seizures and all types of partial seizures
Ethosuximide	1,000	40–100	0	30 ± 6	Anorexia, headache, lethargy, hiccups, leucoperia	Absences, Absence status
Phenobarbital	90	15–40	40–50	96 ± 12	Sleepiness, paradoxical excitement in children, rash	Generalized tonic-clonic seizures and all types of partial seizures
Primidone*	750	5–15	0–50	12 ± 6	Sedation, nausea, ataxia	Generalized tonic-clonic seizures and all types of partial seizures
Phenytoin	300	10–20	90	24 ± 12	Ataxia, drowsiness, gum hypertrophy, skin rash	Generalized tonic-clonic seizures and all types of partial seizures
Valproic acid	1,500	40–100	90	12 ± 6	Nausea, vomiting, cramps, weight gain, hepatic toxicity	Absences, Myoclonic, Atonic seizures, Generalized tonic-clonic seizures

* Phenobarbital is derived from primidone

concentration are not always related to the dose of phenobarbital that is given, although the sedative effect does decrease with chronic use. Lack of concentration and the inability to perform fine and skilled movements may persist however, even with chronic use. Many physicians thus prefer carbamazepine to phenobarbital.

Phenytoin (Dilantin) is an excellent drug for generalized tonic-clonic and all types of partial seizures. It is also the drug of choice for the treatment of major motor status epilepticus. However, phenytoin can cause trouble with balance and walking (ataxia) when blood levels of the drug are high. This is an indication for decreasing the dose. Chronic phenytoin therapy may lead

to coarsening of the facial features and hirsutism, which are especially distressing in younger patients. It causes overgrowth of gum tissue (gum hypertrophy), which can be kept to a minimum by meticulous oral hygiene.

Valproic acid (Depakene), a relatively new AED, is very useful in the treatment of absences and atonic seizures (drop attacks). It helps in the treatment of generalized tonic–clonic seizures but is of little value in treating partial seizures. As valproic acid may (rarely) cause severe and even fatal liver disease, blood tests that check liver function have to be done frequently when the drug is first started. The drug should be discontinued if these tests become abnormal. Side effects of valproic acid include weight gain and loss of hair. Sedation and ataxia may also occur but are generally due to concomitant use of other AEDs such as phenobarbital or phenytoin. Tremor of the hands, stupor, and problems with the functions of the pancreatic gland have also been noted with valproic acid.

Use of Antiepileptic Drugs in Pregnancy

The treatment of a pregnant woman with epilepsy poses a dilemma. As maternal seizure activity can produce fetal distress, prevention of any seizures is desirable. However, prescribing AEDs to the epileptic mother is associated with a two- to three-fold increase in the incidence of congenital malformations in the newborn compared to infants of mothers not on AEDs (Pedley & Goldensohn, 1982). Because most studies show increased seizure frequency in over one third of pregnant women with epilepsy, AEDs are continued during pregnancy (Dalessio, 1985). There are two major exceptions to this statement. One is trimethadione (Tridione), a drug used for absences, which is not prescribed in pregnancy because of its known higher risk for congenital malformations. The second, valproic acid, is not used unless absolutely necessary, because of recent reports that suggest an association between valproic acid and deformities of the vertebral column and spinal cord (Gomez, 1981). Aside from these two drugs, there is no proof that one drug is safer than another, and, indeed, there is very little evidence for a specific drug-related syndrome (Janz et al., 1982).

The risk of congenital malformation is increased by the use of two or more drugs. As a general rule, one attempts to maintain satisfactory seizure control in pregnancy with a single drug given in the lowest possible dose. Congenital malformations seen with the use of AEDs in pregnancy include cleft lip and palate (chelio-palatoschisis), facial deformities, abnormalities of the fingers and toes, and developmental disturbances. The interested reader is referred to Dalessio's recent review (1985) and to the monograph, *Epilepsy, Pregnancy, and the Child* (Janz et al., 1982) for a detailed analysis of this complex issue. Further studies are necessary before the dilemma of maternal seizure control versus congenital malformation can be satisfactorily resolved. The recommendations in our brief discussion outline presently accepted medical practice.

Treatment of a Single Seizure

A single seizure is likely to recur in 10% of patients in the first year, 21% by 2 years and 27% by 3 years (Hauser & McRoberts, 1982). AEDs may be withheld until a second seizure occurs, especially in patients where there is no obvious cause for the seizure and the EEG is normal, as the taking of AEDs does not affect the rate of recurrence after a single seizure.

Treatment of Status Epilepticus

Status epilepticus is a neurologic emergency that requires prompt attention. Permanent brain damage can occur if the status lasts for more than 1 hour. The aim of treatment is therefore to try to stop the status as soon as possible, preferably within 30 minutes, to prevent recurrence of seizures, to maintain adequate oxygen supply to the body, to keep the blood pressure within the normal range, and to correct any disturbance in the body's metabolism or electrolyte content that may have led to status.

A patient with status is treated in intensive medical care units, as a close watch of various parameters such as blood oxygen content, blood pressure, and so forth, is necessary. Drugs such as phenytoin and phenobarbital are given intravenously to control seizure activity. A protocol for treating status (Delgado-Escueta, Wasterlain, Treiman, & Porta, 1982) is now generally followed in all major hospitals in the country. The interested reader is referred to it for further details.

Discontinuation of AEDs

The question of when to discontinue AEDs remains a matter of some controversy. In order to discontinue AEDs without exposing the patient to a risk of having further seizures, the physician has to know the natural history of the epilepsy. Because of the many different diseases and many seizure types, the prognosis for epilepsy varies greatly from individual to individual. The likelihood that seizures will persist for many years depends on several factors, including the age at which seizures first began, the type, number occurring in the first 2 years after onset, and whether or not a family member has epilepsy. Persons with generalized seizures have a higher rate of remission (80%) than those with partial ones (65%) 20 years after the onset of epilepsy (Annegers, Hauser, & Elveback, 1979). Epilepsy of unknown cause is more likely to remit than symptomatic epilepsy. Presently, we cannot predict the natural history of epilepsy in a given individual.

However, many physicians advise discontinuing AEDs if the patient has been seizure-free for 2 to 5 years. The shorter period of 2 years is applied to children, the longer one of 5 years for adults, although there is no specific information that favors one over the other. Some physicians insist that the EEG be normal before drug therapy is discontinued. About one third of all patients with epilepsy are in this category. The discontinuation of AEDs is advisable if further seizures are unlikely, as long-term use of AEDs is associated with adverse effects on reading skills, memory concentration, skin, liver, and connective tissue (Pedley & Goldensohn, 1982). Discontinuation of AEDs is associated with a risk of relapse; some 10% of such patients have a seizure recurrence in the following decade (Chadwick, 1984).

Further studies are needed to clarify whether drugs can be safely stopped in 2, 3, or 5 years, whether EEG recordings should feature in the decision to stop AEDs, and whether AEDs themselves increase the chances for remission. For an in-depth discussion of this issue, Chadwick's (1984) chapter entitled "When Can Anticonvulsant Drugs be Stopped?" is highly recommended.

Surgical Therapy

Surgical therapy may be indicated in a small proportion of patients with partial seizures: those whose seizures remain uncontrolled after an adequate trial with appropriate AEDs. The criteria for patient selection vary, but patients with clearly defined complex partial seizures that consistently begin from one part of the temporal lobe are likely to benefit from surgery (Glaser, 1980). The surgery consists of removal of a part of the temporal lobe (temporal lobectomy). Patients who are considered to be possible candidates for temporal lobectomy should be referred to special centers that have surgeons with wide experience in this procedure. In such centers of repute, benefits are said to occur in more than three fourths of those operated upon (Rasmussen, 1983b). Besides temporal lobectomy, other surgical procedures that have sometimes been used include sectioning of the band of fibers that connects both hemispheres of the brain (central commissurotomy) (Gates, Leppik, Yap, & Gumnit, 1984; Wilson, 1978) and removal of the hemisphere itself (hemispherectomy) (Rasmussen, 1983a). The interested reader is referred to the literature for a fuller account of the use of surgery in epilepsy (Engel, 1982; Purpura, Penry, & Walter, 1975; Wilson, Reeves, & Gazzaniga, 1982).

CURRENT MEDICAL RESEARCH

Research has focused on techniques that lead to more accurate diagnosis, such as videotelemetry and PET scanning, newer drugs, precise monitoring of blood levels of drugs and their metabolites, and further understanding of the basic mechanisms of a seizure. As the uses of videotelemetry and PET scanning have been reviewed in an earlier section, we shall now discuss the use of blood levels when using drugs, new drugs, and the research into basic mechanisms at the cellular level.

AED levels have been used for the past two decades to better correlate drug usage with control of seizures. AED levels have helped to pinpoint whether the drug achieves sufficient concentration in the blood, which may be low because of inadequate absorption or an increased rate of drug breakdown. If two AEDs are given, they may interact, leading to unusually high or low levels of one drug. Occasionally the patient may not comply with a prescribed drug regimen, which leads to very low drug levels (Desai, Riley, Porter & Perny, 1978). Recent research focuses on measuring "free" levels of AEDs. About 90% of the total dose of any AED is bound to protein in the blood; this is the inactive form of the drug. The 10% that is free or unbound is the *active* portion of the drug, or that part of the drug that actually exerts an antiepileptic effect on the neuron. In some instances, it is important to know whether the free level of the drug has increased. Generally, measurement of the blood level measures the total amount of drug, both free and inactive. The free fraction can increase without the total levels being changed. The patient may have signs of toxicity that are puzzling to the physician, as the blood levels are in the normal or therapeutic range. Knowing the free level by itself is then very useful, for it reveals what has been going on. This increase in free levels is especially important when two drugs such as phenytoin and valproic acid are used together.

Newer drugs are constantly being sought, and drug trials conducted, as no presently available AED is ideal in providing excellent seizure control without side effects or sedation. Seizure occurrence may be related to increased electrical activity or to changes in levels of chemical messengers (neurotransmitters) used by neurons. A new drug, gamma-vinyl-GABA (GVG) blocks the breakdown of GABA (gamma-amino-butyric acid). GABA is an *inhibitory* neurotransmitter. That is, it serves to dampen messages sent by neurons to one another. GVG acts by increasing GABA levels and thereby increasing inhibition in neurons. Preliminary trials on GVG show that the drug may be useful, especially in the treatment of complex partial seizures (Browne et al., 1983). Extensive trials with this drug are under way in the United States and Europe.

Research into basic seizure mechanisms has focused on the sequence of events at the cellular level that initiate and result in seiz-

ures. Thin slices of a part of the guinea pig brain—the hippocampus—have been studied in the laboratory, as well as slices of excised epileptogenic gray matter of humans (Prince, Connors, & Benardo, 1983). These studies show that before a seizure occurs a group of neurons fire in hypersynchrony. These neurons show a change in the normal balance between calcium and sodium currents flowing into the cell and potassium currents flowing outside the cell. They generate a larger than normal signal to neighboring groups of neurons. If these "epileptic" or "pacemaker" neurons are able to recruit sufficient numbers of neighboring neurons, the abnormal electrical activity spreads through the brain and results in a seizure (Ward, 1983). Presently, the role of calcium ions as well as that of neurotransmitters and neuropeptides is under active investigation.

DEVELOPMENTAL ISSUES

Although 80% of women with seizures have normal children, there is a slightly greater risk that women who are on AEDs during the pregnancy will have infants who have a smaller head size, slower body growth, or mental retardation (Helge, 1982; Nelson & Ellenberg, 1982).

Neonatal Seizures

Neonatal seizures that occur in the first month of life. Bergman, Painter, Hirsch, Crumrine & David (1983) have reported that seizures tend to be more common in very premature infants (22.7% of those at gestational age of 31 weeks or less had seizures), than in those born at 32 to 36 weeks gestation (1.6%) and those born at 37 weeks gestation or more (0.16%). About 85% of the very premature infants died, compared to 57% of those born at 32 to 36 weeks and 17% for full-term infants. The outcome in premature infants who survived was not different from full-term babies. When the infants were evaluated about 3 years later, 2% were normal or had minor abnormalities that caused no disability, 20% were moderately disabled, 23% were severely disabled, and 5% were dead. A poor outcome appeared more likely if the infant had many seizures, and if seizures began after the first 7 days of life.

Febrile Seizures

Patients with febrile seizures have a 3 to 6 times greater risk of developing epilepsy compared to the general population. The risk is greater if the patient had an initial prolonged febrile seizure lasting more than 30 minutes, preexisting brain damage, or a family history of epilepsy. When none of these features is present, the risk is about 1.3% (Nelson & Ellenberg, 1978). No long-term psychological impairment is associated with febrile seizures.

Age at Onset of Seizures and Development

It had been suggested that children who have seizures early in life have a poorer outcome in terms of mental retardation and neurological abnormalities. A recent study (Ellenberg, Hirtz, & Nelson, 1984) of 52,360 children, 75% of whom were followed for 7 years, demonstrated that children with neurological or developmental abnormalities assessed in the first year of life did not have their first seizue earlier than children without abnormality. However, outcome was significantly worse in these children: 81% had epilepsy, mental retardation, cerebral palsy, or a combination of these, compared to 65% of those who were normal on early examination. Also, 3 out of 4 of these 110 children had epilepsy only. Early age of seizure onset did not have a poor prognosis with regard to intellectual function, cerebral palsy, and epilepsy.

Intelligence and Epilepsy

A prospective study of the IQ scores of 72 children and 45 siblings reported that there was no appreciable difference between the epileptic and nonepileptic children on initial testing and on follow-up 4 years later (Bourgeois, Prensky, Palkes, Talent & Busch, 1983). Eleven percent of the epileptic patients had a persistent decrease in IQ of 10 points or more. These patients had a higher incidence of AED blood levels in the toxic range, and their epilepsy was more difficult to control. Drug toxicity, especially related to phenobarbital, was a better predictor of decrease in IQ than was seizure control. These findings suggest that, at least in younger children, total seizure control should not be achieved if the price to be paid is repeated episodes of toxicity with AEDs.

PSYCHOLOGICAL ASSESSMENT

This section discusses two aspects of the psychological evaluation of the epileptic child: cognitive assessment and behavioral assessment. Each is an important consideration in the evaluation and treatment of the individual with epilepsy.

Cognitive Evaluation

People with epilepsy by definition suffer from a neurological disorder, and it is well known that neurological dysfunction can result in a compromise of higher cortical functioning. Because even subtle disturbances in neuropsychological ability can have significant effects on the individual's ability to function successfully in several important life roles, it is important to determine the pattern of cognitive strengths and weaknesses that exist in a given patient so that such a pattern can be taken into consideration in rehabilitation, vocational planning, educational counseling, and so on. In children with epilepsy, assessment is even more crucial, as they are in the process of acquiring skills and information that will serve as the basis for future learning and development. It is also imperative to define the nature and extent of deficits that might compromise children's educational progress and achievement so that they can obtain the special services to which they are entitled under PL 94-142.

Another reason for careful assessment is that several factors related to the disorder and its treatment (seizure control, seizure type, number of medications, and medication type) have been found to affect the quality and speed of cognitive processing. Hence, it is important to obtain a baseline picture of the child's cognitive function so that changes in the adequacy of higher cortical functioning can be objectively identified and steps can be taken to remediate the factors responsible for any identified deficits.

Finally, it is important to note that when referring to cognitive assessment, we do not mean to imply simply IQ testing. Rather, a more comprehensive picture of the child's capabilities needs to be obtained. Such a picture includes functions such as verbal and nonverbal short-term memory, sensori-motor functions, receptive and expressive language function, and visual-spatial skills, to name only a few.

We will briefly overview one of the assessment procedures we have used to evaluate cognitive function in children with epilepsy. This will give the reader a sense of the type of evaluation that we are advocating. Following this we will overview a few select seizure-related variables to demonstrate how cognitive functions may be affected by factors related to the child's epilepsy.

Luria–Nebraska Neuropsychological Battery—Children's Revision (LNNB-CR) (Golden, 1981)

This is at the current time an *experimental* downward extension of the adult version of the Luria–Nebraska Battery, which was designed for children aged 8 through 12 but which is not yet recommended for widespread clinical use. This particular battery was initially selected for use by our group because it permitted the evaluation of a wide range of adaptive abilities in a reasonable period of time and, as will be shown, it seems to have significant discriminatory ability.

The battery in its current form is comprised of 149 items grouped into 11 summary scales similar to those on the adult LNNB: Motor, Rhythm, Tactile, Visual, Receptive Speech, Expressive Language, Writing, Reading, Arithmetic, Memory, and Intelligence. The item grouping was conducted largely within the conceptual framework outlined by Luria (1973, 1980)

and later by Christensen (1975) and was designed to provide a global picture of major classes of neuropsychological abilities. Each item on the scales is intended to tap a basic skill area, thus providing the examiner with a comprehensive and detailed assessment of a variety of functions.

Performance on each item is reported as a scaled score (0, 1, 2) according to normative data derived from 120 children without evidence of neurological or psychiatric illness. Scaled scores are adjusted for age when appropriate. A scale score of 0 indicates that an individual's performance was equal to or less than 1 standard deviation below the mean; a scale score of 1 is indicative of performance between one and two standard deviations below the mean; and a scale score of 2 indicates performance greater than two standard deviations below the mean.

The composition and function of each summary scale can be described briefly as follows:

Motor. This scale is designed to measure basic fine motor speed, coordination, imitation of movement, and simple construction praxis.

Rhythm. This evaluates the child's ability to make simple tonal discriminations, to maintain a melodic pattern vocally, to count auditorily presented tones, and to reproduce simple rhythmic patterns.

Tactile. This scale taps finger localization, two-point discrimination, pinprick and pressure sensation, movement detection, graphesthesia, and stereognostic skills in both the right and left hands.

Visual. Items on this scale are designed to measure simple visual recognition from pictures, identification of pictures presented in an indistinct fashion or in an overlapping array, and use of spatial relationships.

Receptive Speech. This assesses the child's ability to decipher phonemes, to recognize individual words, to follow simple commands, and to understand more complex grammatical structures.

Expressive Language. A scale that evaluates the child's ability to correctly repeat simple words and sentences presented orally and visually, to use automatized speech, to name objects from visual and oral descriptions, and to speak in response to several stimuli.

Writing. This scale is comprised of items that test the ability to analyze letter sequences, to spell, copy, write from dictation, and to perform automatized writing tasks.

Reading. The scale attempts to measure letter recognition, sound synthesis, nonsense syllable reading, and word, sentence, and paragraph reading.

Arithmetic. Items are designed to evaluate number recognition and writing, number comparison, and simple mathematical processes.

Memory. This scale evaluates verbal and nonverbal short-term memory with and without interference.

Intelligence. This scale includes items similar to those on the Picture Arrangement, Picture Completion, Vocabulary, Comprehension, Arithmetic, and Similarity scales of the Wechsler Intelligence Scale for Children—Revised (WISC-R) appropriate for this age range. Other items measure the ability of the child to make simple generalizations and basic deductions.

The results of several validity studies have been reported in detail by Gustavson et al. (1984). In summary, those studies have been found to be effective in discriminating brain-damaged children from those who are neurologically intact. The test also has been found to measure a number of fundamental skills related to, but independent of, intelligence and achievement.

We will now briefly examine the effects of two seizure-related variables on neuropsychological function in a sample of 74 epileptic children attending our clinics.

First, what are the effects of the child's seizure type on the adequacy of higher cognitive functioning? When we compared children with complex partial seizures (CPS) (*N* = 30) to those with primary generalized epilepsies (GE) (*N* = 34), the CPS group performed better on 10 of the 11 LNNB scales (Table 16-3); three of these differences were statistically significant (Writing, Arithmetic, Intelligence). The group of children with primary generalized epilepsies could be divided further into those suffering from absence attacks (*N* = 13) and those with tonic–clonic spells (*N* = 8). The children with absence attacks performed better on 10 of the 11 scales relative to the tonic–clonic children. So, in summary, there appear to be some overall differences in the adequacy of neuropsychological functioning when children are classified according to their diagnosed seizure type.

Second, what effect does the age at seizure onset have? To answer this question, we regressed each scale on age at onset, treating duration as a covariate, for each seizure type. Table 16-4 presents the significant relationships. Age at onset was significantly related to five scales in the CPS group and five scales in the GE group—with reading and mathematics being significantly related to age at onset in both groups.

The point of this very brief exposition is to demonstrate that some seizure-related variables have demonstrable effects on neuropsychological function and that a delineation of the pattern of cognitive strengths and weaknesses should be an intrinsic part of the multidisciplinary evaluation of the child with epilepsy. For a much fuller exposition and review of the literature, the interested reader is referred to Dikmen (1980) and Dodrill (1981, 1982). We hope this brief review demonstrated the information that can be derived from an evaluation of the child's cognitive function.

Finally, not only is it important to assess each child, it is very often of great value to reassess the child periodically, as changes in the clinical state and/or treatment of the child may take place. Consider the case of a

Table 16-3. Average LNNB Scale Scores for Children with Complex Partial Epilepsy and with Generalized Epilepsy

Scale	Complex Partial Epilepsy ($N = 30$)	Generalized Epilepsy ($N = 34$)	Significance Level
Motor	46.4	49.6	
Rhythm	54.3	55.1	
Tactile	55.7	55.3	
Visual	54.9	55.5	
Receptive speech	65.6	64.7	
Expressive speech	53.6	58.3	
Writing	54.6	63.5	0.04
Reading	56.3	62.9	
Mathematics	59.4	70.2	0.03
Memory	59.7	61.6	
Intelligence	57.6	64.2	0.05
Scales > 60	3.3	4.8	
Scales > 70	1.9	2.9	

Table 16-4. LNNB Scales Significantly Related ($P \le 0.10$) to Age at Onset with Duration of Seizures Used as Covariate, by Seizure Type

	Significance Level	
Scale	Complex Partial Epilepsy ($N = 30$)	Generalized Epilepsy ($N = 34$)
Motor	—	—
Rhythm	—	0.10
Tactile	0.06	—
Visual	—	—
Receptive speech	—	0.04
Expressive speech	0.01	—
Writing	—	0.01
Reading	0.01	0.06
Mathematics	0.07	0.03
Memory	0.01	—
Intelligence	—	0.01
Scales > 60	0.02	0.05
Scales > 70	0.02	0.02

child who presented to us at age 8 with poorly controlled complex partial seizures. At initial evaluation, he was taking phenytoin (Dilantin). His Verbal, Performance and Full Scale WISC-R IQ scores were 100, 119, and 111, respectively. Primidone (Mysoline) was then added to his treatment regimen and the seizures were brought under good control. However, the parents and the school noticed a slow but significant deterioration in his academic performance at school and a decline in his alertness and cognitive capacity. He was retested 1 year later and was indeed found to have lost some intellectual capacity: his Verbal, Performance, and Full Scale IQ scores were now 96, 96, and 96. The primidone was then discontinued and replaced by carbamazepine (Tegretol) (he was still receiving Dilantin). Seizure control continued to be good but now there were reports of increased alertness and improved performance at school. Retesting 1 year later showed IQ levels compared to those obtained at intake 3 years earlier—Verbal, Performance, and Full Scale IQ scores were 103, 114, and 109, respectively.

In summary, not only is assessment of the child with epilepsy an essential venture, but continued monitoring of his or her intellectual state can be a valuable enterprise.

We do not mean to advocate the use of any particular battery or test. However, we do mean to advocate the process—that is, comprehensive evaluation of the child's cognitive status and academic progress.

Behavioral Assessment

The issue of behavioral change and psychopathology in individuals with epilepsy has been an area of considerable interest to neurologists, psychiatrists, and psychologists for quite some time. One reason for this interest has been the belief that careful study of individuals with psychopathology and epilepsy in general, or specific seizure types in particular, would lead to an understanding of the biological determinants of psychopathology. A second reason for this interest in epilepsy–psychopathology relationships has been the belief that behavioral problems are overrepresented among individuals with epilepsy, thereby presenting a significant clinical problem. A considerable literature exists regarding the epilepsy–psychopathology link, and reviews of this literature abound. In this chapter we cannot discuss at length the numerous substantive theoretical and technical issues. To that end, we refer the reader to available reviews and analyses of the literature (Hermann & Whitman, 1984; Lishman, 1978; Stevens, 1975). For the purpose of this chapter, we prefer to provide the reader with a general conceptual orientation to the problem of psychopathology in epilepsy. This will help to put the many

known or suspected etiological factors into a more comprehensive format that will also facilitate approaches to assessment, treatment, and prevention.

To that end, first consider Table 16-5, which provides a listing of the many variables that are either known or suspected as being among the precursors of psychopathology in epilepsy. These variables have been classified into three overall categories: neuroepilepsy factors, psychosocial factors, and medication factors. Within the neuroepilepsy and psychosocial categories we have tried to further subdivide the variables, whereas for medication factors we have followed the categories suggested by Reynolds (1981).

Although many investigators and authors have hypothesized that behavior problems are a result of the interplay of these three factor groupings, an empirical evaluation and assessment of this multietiological perspective is completely lacking.

Some trends in the literature make evident the potential usefulness of this approach. For instance, depression in epilepsy has been found or postulated to be primarily the result of psychosocial variables such as locus of control (Matthews & Barabas, in press), the patient's fear of seizures (Mittan, 1986), the stigma and discrimination associated with epilepsy (Arntson, Droge, Norton, & Murray, 1986), parents' attitudes toward their child's epilepsy and their subsequent differential treatment of the child (Hartledge & Green, 1972, Long & Moore, 1979), and other factors. Further, certain drugs, particularly the barbituates, have been posited to contribute to the etiology of depression in epilepsy.

On the other hand, the psychoses sometimes seen in patients with epilepsy have been thought to be largely a function of neuroepilepsy factors such as seizure type (Trimble, 1983), laterality of the epileptiform activity (Flor-Henry, 1969; Sherwin, Peron-Magnan, Bancaud, Bonis, & Talairach, 1982), seizure control (Jensen & Larsen, 1979; Kristensen & Sindrup, 1979), etiology of the epilepsy (Kristensen & Sindrup, 1979) and several other neuroepilepsy factors. Further, both psychosocial

Table 16-5. High-Risk Variables for Psychopathology in Epilepsy, Grouped According to Hypothesis

Neuroepilepsy	Psychosocial	Medication
a Age at onset	a Fear of seizures	a Number of medications
b Seizure control	b Perceived stigma	b Serum level
c Duration of seizures	c Perceived discrimination	c Medication type
d Seizure type	d Adjustment to epilepsy	d Folic acid level
e Multiple seizure types	e Locus of control	
f Etiology	f Life-event changes	
g Type of aura	g Social support	
h Neuropsychological status	h Socioeconomic status	
	i Childhood home environment	

(Wolf, Thorbecke, & Even, 1986) and medication (Reynolds, 1981) factors have been thought to contribute.

Again, it is important to note that although there have been hypotheses as to the relative etiological loading of specific behavioral problems, there have been no direct empirical tests to confirm the relative importance of neuroepilepsy, psychosocial variables, and medication ones.

However, in the assessment of the etiology of psychopathology in children with epilepsy, these three groups of factors need to be assessed in the context of a multidisciplinary perspective so that some sense of the causative factors can be gleaned. As can be easily seen in this conceptual approach, the treatment steps taken will depend on what the specific etiologic factors are perceived to be.

SUMMARY

We have attempted to present the reader with an overview of epilepsy based upon the most current information. We have also suggested that epilepsy is a complicated disorder and that gaps in our knowledge exist. Optimal medical and psychological treatment is limited by these gaps. It is thus most likely the case that involving the person with epilepsy in his or her treatment is even more important than usual. Such involvement would facilitate decisions about available choices.

Finally, it is essential to understand that the social dimensions of the lives of people with epilepsy are important. Regarding epilepsy as only a biological condition to be treated with certain antiepilepsy drugs is an approach that will fail more often than it will succeed. The misfiring neurons that generate seizures are located in the brain of an individual, that individual is located in a society. The biochemistry, the individual's personality, and the structure of society are all involved in shaping the life of that person. A full understanding of the synergistic relationships that exist among these factors will improve the lives of people with epilepsy.

Acknowledgement—Steven Whitman's research is supported by the Epilepsy in the Urban Environment Research Project.

REFERENCES

Annegers, J. F., Grabow, J. D., Groover, R. V., Laws, E. R., Elveback, L. R., & Kurland, L. T. (1980). Seizures after head trauma: A population study. *Neurology, 30,* 683–689.

Annegers, J. F., Hauser, W. A., & Elveback, L. R. (1979). Remission of seizures and relapse in patients with epilepsy. *Epilepsia, 20,* 729–737.

Arntson, P., Droge, D., Norton, R., & Murray, E. (1906). The perceived psychosocial consequences of having epilepsy. In B. P. Hermann & S. Whitman (Eds.), *The social dimensions of psychopathology in epilepsy* (pp. 143–161). New York: Oxford University Press.

Bergman, I., Painter, M. J., Hirsch, R. P., Crumrine, P. K., David, R. (1983). Outcome in neonates with convulsions treated in an intensive care unit. *Annals of Neurology, 14,* 642–647.

Bourgeois, B. F., Prensky, A. L., Palkes, H. S., Talent, B. K., & Busch, S. G. (1983). Intelligence in epilepsy: A prospective study in children. *Annals of Neurology, 14,* 438–444.

Browne, T. R., Mattson, R. H., Napoliello, M. J., Perry, J. K., Smith, D. B., Treiman, D. M., Wilder, B. J. (1983). *Multicenter single-blind study of gamma-vinyl-GABA for refractory complex partial seizures.* Paper presented at the meeting of the 15th Epilepsy International Symposium, Washington, DC.

Chadwick, D. (1984). When can anticonvulsant drugs be stopped? In C. Warlow & J. Garfield (Eds.), *Dilemmas in the management of the neurological patient* (pp. 133–143). Edinburgh: Churchill Livingstone.

Chase, A. (1977). *The legacy of Malthus: The social costs of the new scientific racism.* New York: Knopf.

Christensen, A. L. (1975). *Luria's neuropsychological investigation.* New York: Spectrum.

Commission on Classification and Terminology of the International League Against Epilepsy (1981). Proposal for revised clinical and electroencephalographic classification of epileptic seizures. *Epilepsia, 22,* 489–501.

Crombie, D. L., Cross, K. W., Fry, J., Pinsent, J. F. H., & Watts, C. A. H., (1960). A survey of the epilepsies in general practice. A report by the Research Committee of the College of General Practitioners. *British Medical Journal, 2,* 416–422.

Dalessio, D. J. (1985). Seizure disorders and pregnancy. *New England Journal of Medicine, 312,* 559–563.

Delgado-Escueta, A. V., Wasterlain, C., Treiman, D. M., Porta, R. J. (1982). Management of status epilepticus. *New England Journal of Medicine, 306,* 1337–1340.

Desai, B. T., Riley, T. L., Porter, R. J., Penny, J. K. (1978). Active noncompliance as a cause of uncontrolled seizures. *Epilepsia, 14,* 447–452.

Desai, B., Whitman, S., Coonley-Hoganson, R., Coleman, T., Gabriel, G., & Dell, J. (1983a). Seizures and civilian head injuries. *Epilepsia, 24,* 289–296.

Desai, B., Whitman, S., Coonley-Hoganson, R., Coleman, T., Gabriel, G. & Dell, J. (1983b). Seizures in relation to head injury. *Annals of Emergency Medicine, 12,* 543–546.

Dikmen, S. (1980). Neuropsychological aspects of epilepsy. In B. P. Hermann (Ed.), *A multi-disciplinary handbook of epilepsy* (pp. 36–73). Springfield, IL: Charles C Thomas.

Dodrill, C. B. (1981). Neuropsychology of epilepsy. In S. B. Filskov & T. J. Boll (Eds.), *Handbook of clinical neuropsychology* (pp. 366–395). New York: Wiley.

Dodrill, C. B. (1982). Neuropsychology. In J. Laidlaw & A. Richens (Eds.), *A textbook of epilepsy* (2nd ed., pp. 282–291). Edinburgh: Churchill Livingstone.

Ellenberg, J. H., Hirtz, D. G., Nelson, K. B. (1984). Age at onset of seizures in young children. *Annals of Neurology, 15,* 127–134.

Engel, J. (1982). Recent developments in the diagnosis and therapy of epilepsy. *Annals of Internal Medicine, 97,* 554–598.

Flor-Henry, P. (1969). Psychosis and temporal lobe epilepsy: A controlled investigation. *Epilepsia, 10,* 363–395.

Frankowski, R. F., Annegers, J. F., & Whitman, S. (1985). The descriptive epidemiology of head trauma in the United States. In D. P. Becker & Poulishoct, J. T. (Eds.), *Central nervous system trauma: Status report.* National Institute of Health, pp. 33–43.

Gates, J. R., Leppik, I. E., Yap, J., Gumnit, R. J. (1984). Corpus callosotomy: Clinical and electroencephalographic effects. *Epilepsia, 25,* 308–316.

Glaser, G. H. (1980). Treatment of intractable temporal lobe-limbic epilepsy (complex partial seizures) by temporal lobectomy. *Annals of Neurology, 18,* 455–459.

Glaser, G. H., Penry, J. K., & Woodbury, D. M. (1980). Antiepileptic drugs—mechanisms of action. *Advances in neurology: Vol. 27.* New York: Raven.

Golden, C. J. (1981). The Luria-Nebraska children's battery: Theory and initial formulation. In G. Hynd & J. Obrzut (Eds.), *Neuropsychological assessment and the school-age child: Issues and procedures.* New York: Grune & Stratton.

Gomez, J. G., Arciniegas, E., & Torres, J. (1978). Prevalence of epilepsy in Bogota, Colombia. *Neurology, 28,* 90.

Gomez, M. R. (1981). Possible teratogenicity of valproic acid. *Journal of Pediatrics, 98,* 508–509.

Gustavson, J. L., Golden, C. J., Wilkening, G. N., Hermann, B. P., Plaisted, J. R., & MacInnes, W. D. (1984). The Luria–Nebraska Neuropsychological battery—childrens' revision: Validation with brain-damaged and normal children. *Journal of Psychoeducational Assessment.*

Hartlage, L. C., & Green, J. B. (1972). The relation of parental attitudes to academic and social achievement in epileptic children. *Epilepsia,* *13,* 21–26.

Hauser, W. A., Anderson, E., Loewenson, R. B., & McRoberts, S. M. (1982). Seizure recurrence after a first unprovoked seizure. *New England Journal of Medicine, 307,* 522–528.

Hauser, W. A., Annegers, J. F., & Elveback, L. R. (1980). Mortality in patients with epilepsy. *Epilepsia, 21,* 399–412.

Hauser, W. A., & Kurland, L. T. (1975). The epidemiology of epilepsy in Rochester, Minnesota, 1935–1967. *Epilepsia, 16,* 1.

Hauser, W. A., Tabaddor, K., Factor, P. R., & Finer, C. (1984). Seizures and head injury in an urban community. *Neurology, 34,* 746–751.

Helge, H. (1982). Physical, mental and social development including diseases: Review of the literature. In D. Janz, M. Dam, & A. Richens (Eds.), *Epilepsy, pregnancy and the child* (pp. 391–395). New York: Raven.

Hermann, B. P., & Whitman, S. (1984). Behavioral and personality correlates of epilepsy: A review, methodological critique, and conceptual model. *Psychological Bulletin, 95,* 451–497.

Janz, D., Dam, M., Richens, A., Bossi, L., Helge, H., Schmidt, D. (1982). In D. Janz, M. Dam, & A. Richens (Eds.), *Epilepsy, pregnancy and the child.* New York: Raven.

Jennett, W. B. (1975). *Epilepsy after non-missile head injuries* (2nd ed.). London: Heinemann.

Jensen, I., & Larsen, J. K. (1979). Psychoses in drug resistant temporal lobe epilepsy. *Journal of Neurology, Neurosurgery, and Psychiatry, 42,* 948–954.

Kristensen, O., & Sindrup, E. H. (1979). Psychomotor epilepsy and psychosis: III. Social and psychological correlates. *Acta Neurologica Scandinavica, 59,* 1–9.

Krohn, W. (1961). A study of epilepsy in northern Norway, its frequency and character. *Acta Psychiatrica Scandinavica, 36* (Suppl. 150), 215–225.

Lampert, D. I., Locke, G. E., Hauser, W. A., Wheeler, N., Whitman, S., Civen, R., Jaurez, G., & Lurd, G. (1984) *Prevalence of epilepsy in an urban minority population.* Paper presented at the American Epilepsy Society, San Francisco, CA.

Lishman, W. A. (1978). *Organic psychiatry: The psychological consequences of cerebral disorder.* Oxford: Blackwell Scientific.

Lombroso-Ferrero, G. (1972). *Criminal man according to the classification of Cesare Lombroso.* Montclair, NJ: Patterson Smith. (Originally published 1911)

Long, C. G., & Moore, J. R. (1979). Parental expectations for their epileptic children.

Journal of Child Psychology and Psychiatry, 20, 299–312.

Luria, A. R. (1973). *The working brain.* New York: Basic Books.

Luria, A. R. (1980). *Higher cortical functions in man* (2nd ed.). New York: Basic Books.

Matthews, W. S., & Barabas, G. (1986). Perceptions of control among children with epilepsy. In B. P. Hermann & S. Whitman (Eds.), *The social dimensions of psychopathology in epilepsy.* (pp. 162–182). New York: Oxford University Press.

McCormick, G. F., Zee, C. S., & Heiden, J. (1982). Cysticercosis cerebri. *Archives of Neurology, 39,* 534–539.

Mittan, R. J. (1986). Fear of seizures. In B. P. Hermann & S. Whitman (Eds.), *The social dimensions of psychopathology in epilepsy.* pp. 90–121). New York: Oxford University Press.

Nelson, K. B., & Ellenberg, J. H. (1978). Prognosis in children with febrile seizures. *Pediatrics, 61,* 720–727.

Nelson, K. B., & Ellenberg, J. H. (1981). *Febrile seizures.* New York: Raven.

Nelson, K. B., & Ellenberg, J. H. (1982). Maternal seizure disorder, outcome of pregnancy, and neurologic abnormalities in the children. *Neurology, 32,* 1247–1254.

Pedley, T. A., & Goldensohn, E. S. (1982). Epilepsy: Changing concepts and approaches. In S. H. Appel (Ed.), *Current neurology* (Vol. 4, pp. 225–240). New York: Wiley.

Penry, J. K., & Newmark, M. E. (1979). The use of antiepileptic drugs. *Annals of Internal Medicine, 90,* 207–218.

Penry, J. K., Porter, R. J., & Dreifuss, F. E. (1975). Simultaneous recording of absence seizures with videotape and electroencephalography. A study of 374 seizures in 48 patients. *Brain, 98,* 427–440.

Pond, D. A., Bidwell, B. H., & Stein, L. (1960). A survey of epilepsy in fourteen general practices: I. Demographic and medical data. *Psychiatria, Neurologia, Neurochirurgia, 63,* 217.

Prince, D. A., Connors, B. W., & Benardo, L. S. (1983). Mechanisms underlying interictal transitions. In A. V. Delgado-Escueta, C. G. Wasterlain, D. M. Treiman, & R. J. Porter (Eds.), *Advances in neurology: Vol. 34* (pp. 177–187). New York: Raven.

Purpura, D. P., Penry, J. K., & Walter, R. D. (1975). Neurosurgical management of the epilepsies. *Advances in neurology: Vol. 8.* New York: Raven.

Rasmussen, T. B. (1983a). Hemispherectomy for seizures revisited. *Canadian Journal of Neurological Science, 10,* 71–78.

Rasmussen, T. B. (1983b). Surgical treatment of complex partial seizures: Results, lessons and problems. *Epilepsia, 24,* (Suppl), S65–S76.

Reynolds, E. H. (1981). Biological factors in psychological disorders associated with epilepsy. In E. H. Reynolds & M. R. Trimble (Eds.), *Psychiatry and epilepsy* (pp. 264–290). Edinburgh: Churchill Livingstone.

Sato, S. (1964). An epidemiologic and clinicostatistical study of epilepsy in Niigata City: Epidemiologic study. *Clinical Neurology, 4,* 413.

Schneider, J. W., & Conrad, P. (1983). *Having epilepsy: The experience and control of illness.* Philadelphia: Temple University Press.

Shamansky, S., & Glaser, G. (1979). Socioeconomic characteristics of childhood seizure disorders in the New Haven area: An epidemiologic study. *Epilepsia, 20,* 457–474.

Sherwin, I., Peron-Magnan, P., Bancaud, J., Bonis, A., & Talairach, J. (1982). Prevalence of psychosis in epilepsy as a function of the laterality of the epileptogenic lesion. *Archives of Neurology, 39,* 621–625.

Stevens, J. R. (1975). Interictal clinical manifestations of complex partial seizures. In J. K. Penry & D. D. Daly (Eds.), *Advances in neurology: Vol. 11* (pp. 85–1212). New York: Raven.

Temkin, O. (1971). *The falling sickness: A history of epilepsy from the Greeks to the beginnings of modern neurology* (2nd ed.). Baltimore, MD: Johns Hopkins University Press.

Trimble, M. R. (1983). Personality disturbances in epilepsy. *Neurology, 33,* 1332–1334.

Ward, A. A. (1983). Physiological basis of chronic epilepsy and mechanisms of spread. In A. V. Delgado-Escueta, C. G. Wasterlain, D. M. Treiman, & R. J. Porter (Eds.), *Advances in neurology; Vol. 34* (pp. 189–197). New York: Raven.

Whitman, S., Coleman, T., Berg, B., King, L., &

Desai, B. T. (1980). Epidemiological insights into the socioeconomic correlates of epilepsy. In B. Hermann (Ed.), *A multidisciplinary handbook of epilepsy* (pp. 243–271). Springfield, IL: Charles C Thomas.

Whitman, S., Coleman, T., Patmon, C., Desai, B. T., Cohen, R., & King, L. (1984). Epilepsy in prison: Elevated prevalence and no relationship to violence. *Neurology, 34,* 775–782.

Whitman, S., Coonley-Hoganson, R., & Desai, B. (1984). Comparative head trauma experiences in two socioeconomically different Chicago-area communities: A population study. *American Journal of Epidemiology, 119,* 570–580.

Wilson, D. H., Reeves, A. G., & Gazzaniga, M. S. (1978). Division of the corpus collosum for uncontrollable epilepsy. *Neurology, 28,* 649–653.

Wilson, D. H., Reeves, A. G., & Gazzaniga, M. S. (1982). "Central" commissurotomy for intractable generalized epilepsy: Series two. *Neurology, 32,* 687–697.

Wolf, P., Thorbecke, R., & Even, W. (1986). Social aspects of psychosis in patients with epilepsy. In B. P. Hermann & S. Whitman (Eds.), *The social dimensions of psychopathology in epilepsy* (pp. 269–283). New York: Oxford University Press.

Woodbury, D. M., Penry, J. K., & Pippenge, C. E. (1982). *Antiepileptic drugs.* New York: Raven.

Zielinski, J. J. (1974a). *Epidemiology and medical-social problems of epilepsy in Warsaw.* Warsaw: Psychoneurological Institute.

Zielinski, J. J. (1974b). Epilepsy and mortality rate and causes of death. *Epilepsia, 15,* 191–201.

Zielinski, J. J. (1982). Epidemiology. In J. Laidlaw & A. Richens (Eds.), *A textbook of epilepsy* (pp. 16–33). Edinburgh: Churchill Livingstone.

CHAPTER 17

Hearing Impairment

Laszlo K. Stein

Man's need to communicate with his fellow man is possibly his greatest uniquely human need. The sense of hearing, the primary means by which infants develop language and speech, serves as the basis for human communication, with its attendant social and intellectual interaction, throughout an individual's life. Impairment of hearing, whether it be congenital deafness, acquired loss through illness, or the gradual loss of hearing in later years, results not only in the primary handicap of impaired communication but also the companion handicap of the social stigma imposed on the hearing impaired by hearing people.

Curiosity about persons labeled "deaf and dumb" and the attitudes of society toward them can be traced back to ancient and medieval times. For centuries, not only the public but the eminent scientists of the day held the deaf to be fools who were incapable of learning and possessed of evil. [The interested reader is referred to Flint (1979) for a concise review of the history of education for the hearing impaired.] Only relatively recently were some of these misconceptions gradually eliminated; but

many remain: witness the unfortunate terms *deaf and dumb* and *deaf-mute* that still persist in the popular press. Fortunately, the past two decades have been marked by a remarkable explosion of medical and technological advances in the fields of otology and audiology and by enlightened interest in the educational and sociological betterment of persons with hearing loss.

The introduction of potent antibiotics and the development of microsurgical techniques have significantly reduced hearing loss through control of serious infections and the restoration of middle ear function. Advances in electronics (transistor and microchip technology) and the resultant improvement in amplification, as well as the miniaturization of components, have enabled many more hearing impaired persons to obtain effective help from hearing aids. Significant interest in the plight of deaf children by such diverse fields as psychology, psychiatry, linguistics, and sociology has radically changed traditionally held views on the education and habilitation of children born deaf. Finally, the growing demands by handicapped citizens, including the deaf, for equal rights and opportunities has done much to reduce the lack of understanding and the insecurity bred of ignorance that often characterizes the hearing public's attitude toward the deaf.

This chapter highlights current knowledge available from the diverse professional fields involved in the study and treatment of hearing impairment. When possible, the chapter also attempts to integrate the various and often differing opinions, approaches, and techniques advanced in aiding this segment of the disabled population.

DESCRIPTION OF THE DISORDER

Basic Terms

The word *deaf* is still mistakenly used by some lay and professional persons to mean both partial and total loss of hearing. More accurately, if the term deaf is to be used, it should be reserved to identify the individual with a total or near-total loss of hearing, with impairment so severe that he or she has little or no usable hearing even with amplification. In the educational or social sense, the term *deaf* is often used to identify that segment of the hearing impaired population who find it difficult or impossible in many areas to function in the hearing world. Social clubs for the deaf, theatres of the deaf, and educational facilities, ranging from the preschool level to residential schools to colleges exclusively for the deaf, are part of the deaf culture. Most, but not all, profoundly hearing impaired persons lost their hearing before the onset of speech (the prelingually deaf) and many, but again not all, communicate using sign language.

The terms *hearing impairment, hard-of-hearing, hearing disability,* and *hearing handicap* generally convey different meanings for medical, educational, clinical, and medico-legal purposes. Impairment in the medical sense implies some deviation from normal, usually poorer performance or function. Hard-of-hearing is commonly used by educators to distinguish between a

deaf student and a student with a lesser degree of impairment, whose residual hearing allows good use of wearable amplification and who requires some level of special or supplementary services to develop effective oral communication. The disadvantage imposed by a hearing loss on a person's ability to communicate is generally referred to as a handicap. Hearing disability, in contrast, is most often associated with determination of the percentage of hearing loss for purposes of compensation.

Many scales and descriptive labels have been proposed to designate degree of hearing impairment or loss. Very early it became aparent that a simple ratio value similar to that used for labeling visual acuity did not take into account all the various factors that may play a role in determining a person's total degree of hearing impairment. Several different percentages of hearing handicap classifications have been proposed for medico-legal purposes, but again, the rationale and methods for calculating such percentages have come under severe criticism. Probably the most widely accepted classification systems employ adjective descriptors. Table 17-1 lists the average level of hearing using pure tone audiometry at 500, 1,000, and 2,000 Hz (Hertz, in honor of Heinrich Hertz, is now preferred to denote frequency in cycles per second [cps]) in the better ear and the presumed degree of impairment. This system of classifying degree of hearing impairment on the basis of a three-frequency average of pure tone thresholds, although preferred for clinical use, has some acknowledged limitations. Basically, it does not take into account the individual's ability to understand speech, even when the level of the speech is raised sufficiently through amplification to theoretically overcome the loss of sensitivity for pure tones. One of the principal problems associated with sensorineural hearing loss (irreversible hearing loss due to damage to the end organ of hearing, the cochlea) is a reduced ability to understand speech. Speech recognition ability may be directly related to the pattern of the pure tone loss, but in many cases, poor or reduced speech recognition ability may be a sequela of a

Table 17-1 Average hearing level for the frequencies 500, 1,000, and 2,000 Hz and the presumed degree of hearing impairment

AVERAGE HEARING LEVEL IN dB FOR 500, 1,000, AND 2,000 Hz (1969 ANSI)	PRESUMED DEGREE OF HEARING IMPAIRMENT
0–15	Normal hearing
16–25	Slight hearing loss
26–40	Mild hearing loss (Level where amplification may be needed to understand speech)
41–55	Moderate hearing loss
56–70	Moderately severe hearing loss
71–90	Severe hearing loss
91+	Profound hearing loss (Level where even amplified speech may not be understood)

particular type of hearing loss. Additional factors that increase the degree of handicap beyond that predicted by the pure tone average are poor tolerance for loud sounds, abnormal growth in loudness of sound, and distortion of sound.

Figure 17-1 shows a standard audiogram used to record the results of pure tone audiometry by air conduction (via earphones) and bone conduction (direct stimulation of the cochlea through vibration of the skull), the results of speech audiometry (speech recognition thresholds and speech recognition or discrimination testing), and data from other frequently employed diagnostic test procedures. Although a young otologically normal adult is capable of hearing sounds from the very low pitch of 20 Hz to high tones approximating 20,000 Hz, the human ear is most sensitive in the 500 to 5,000 Hz range. The range of frequencies most important for the understanding of speech extends roughly from 400 to 3,000 Hz. Speech, and certainly music, contain frequencies below 400 Hz and above 3,000 Hz, but they are not necessary for near perfect intelligibility or understanding of conversational speech. This is illustrated by the fact that telephones transmit a frequency range of sound only slightly greater, from roughly 270 to 3,500 Hz. This range could be reduced even further without affecting the intelligibility of speech; however, recognition of the caller's voice would suffer. Superimposed on the audio-

gram for illustrative purposes is the approximate distribution of the frequency and intensity of the sounds of conversational speech at a distance of approximately 1 meter. This range contains almost all the frequency elements that distinguish the vowels and most consonants. Important to remember is that the consonant sounds of speech are the most important for understanding and that any significant loss of hearing for frequencies above 1,000 to 1,500 Hz dramatically reduces intelligibility of single words.

Zero hearing level, or normal threshold, for pure tones as shown on the audiogram is based on surveys of young otologically normal adults. Normal hearing, however, is a range that extends 10–15 decibel (dB) above and below the zero line. The hearing level (HL) scale in decibels shown on the ordinate of the audiogram is for standardization and calibration purposes related to the physical measure of sound in sound pressure level (SPL).

Because decibel (abbreviated dB with a capital B in honor of Alexander Graham Bell and never pluralized) is so frequently used in relation to hearing loss or in reference to environmental noise, it is important to remember that it refers to a logarithmic scale that deals in ratios. It was adopted in acoustics and engineering to deal with an unwieldy range of values. To illustrate, for acoustic pressures, the standard reference level is 0.0002 dynes per square centi-

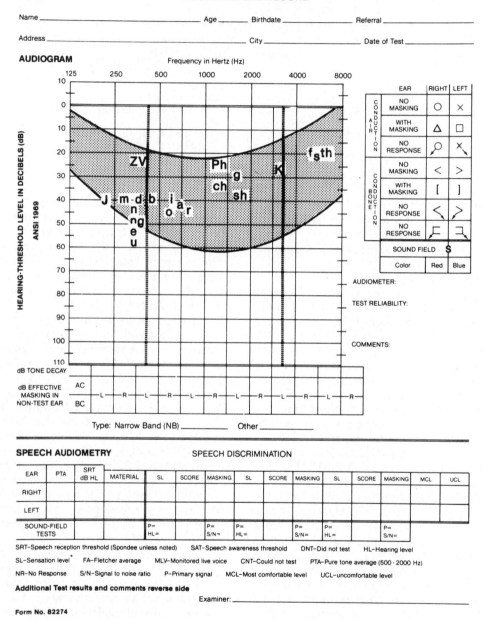

Figure 17-1. Standard audiogram for recording the results of pure tone air conduction and bone conduction testing, speech test scores, and other audiometric test data. Superimposed on the audiogram for illustrative purposes are the average range of intensity of faint to loud speech at a distance of 1 meter from the listener and the frequency spectrum of common speech sounds.

meter (0 dB SPL), close to the intensity of the faintest mid-frequency sound heard by a young otologically normal listener. A sound pressure level of 140 dB, loud enough to be painful, however, exerts a pressure that is 10 million times as great. Thus, the need for a ratio scale to express in convenient numbers a tenfold increase in acoustic pressure as 20 dB, a hundredfold increase as 40 dB, etc. This same ratio principal applies when we talk about loudness, the psychological attribute of acoustic pressure. On the logarithmic decibel scale of an audiogram, a mid-frequency sound that is increased by 10 dB sounds about twice as loud. Thus, if a pure tone is made more intense or raised from 20 dB to 50 dB, it sounds 2 × 2 × 2 or 8 times as loud. The reader interested in a more detailed description of the acoustics of sound and speech is referred to Davis and Silverman (1970) and Durrant and Lovrinic (1981).

Types of Hearing Disorders

The physiological complexity of the hearing mechanism may be appreciated by considering the ear as a transducer converting sound waves into mechanical energy, then into fluid energy, and finally into electrical energy in the form of nerve impulses. This unique feat is accomplished by the three main parts of the ear: (a) the outer and middle ear mechanism, (b) the inner ear or cochlea, and (c) the central auditory system of the central nervous system (Figure 17-2).

A disorder involving the outer or middle ear mechanism, the mechanical portion of the system, results in what is termed a *conductive* hearing loss. Failure of the eardrum (tympanic membrane) or the ossicles of the middle ear cavity (Figure 17-2) to effectively convert sound waves into mechanical energy can reduce hearing sensitivity up to 60 dB. Sound louder than 60 dB can bypass the mechanical transmission system because its force is great enough to stimulate the cochlea through vibration of the skull. The second major type of hearing loss is termed a *sensorineural* condition (often but incorrectly called nerve deafness) and stems from damage to the cochlea or audi-

tory (eighth) cranial nerve. A sensorineural hearing loss, in contrast to a conductive condition, is generally irreversible and can cause hearing loss ranging from a minor reduction in threshold for certain frequencies to total loss of sensitivity (deafness). Involvement of the central auditory mechanism, beyond the level of the eighth nerve and its first synapse at the level of the brainstem, usually does not result in a true loss of hearing sensitivity, but rather, in various forms of auditory processing problems. Because our focus here is on hearing loss, we will restrict our discussion to conductive and sensorineural types of hearing impairment.

Conductive Hearing Loss

Table 17-2 lists the principal known causes of conductive hearing impairment. The two major forms of conductive disorders that affect children are congenital malformation involving the outer ear (pinna or auricle), ear canal, or structures of the middle ear, and infection of the middle ear space. A congenital malformation or absence (microtia or atresia) of the auricle or pinna is more a cosmetic problem than a hearing one. It is, however, very likely to be associated with closure of the ear canal and malformation of the structures of the middle ear, in which case a severe hearing loss may be present. If the inner ear or cochlea is unaffected, the hearing loss will be conductive and not exceed 60 dB, and the probability very good for normal or near-normal hearing with wearable amplification that delivers sound to the cochlea via bone conduction rather than by the conventional air conduction route. Cosmetic surgery to rebuild or reshape an atretic pinna is a definite possibility. Restoration of usable hearing through surgery in the case of an atretic ear canal is occasionally successful if the blockage is caused by soft tissue, rather than bone, and if middle ear structures are intact.

Impacted earwax (cerumen) and inflammation of the external ear canal (external otitis, dermatitis) may cause irritation and, if chronic, require medical treatment. It is important to remember that these conditions can affect the comfortable and satis-

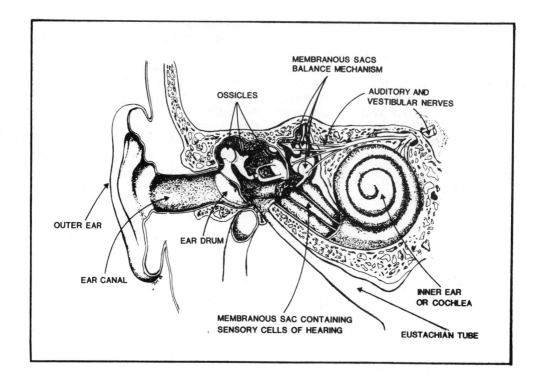

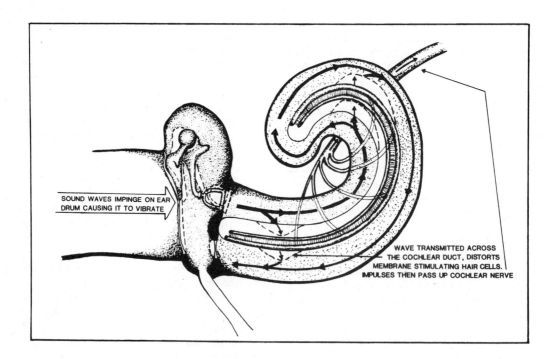

Figure 17-2. (see Opposite)

Table 17-2. Principal Causes of Hearing Impairment

CONDUCTIVE TYPE	SENSORINEURAL TYPE
Congenital or Prelingual Malformations of the external ear and canal Middle ear malformations	
	Congenital or Prelingual Genetic or Hereditary Prenatal, Perinatal, and Postnatal Rubella Cytomagalovirus (CMV) Toxemia, diabetes, other systematic maternal illness Toxoplasmosis Syphilis Maternal alcoholism Hypoxia (asphyxia) Low birthweight or prematurity Ototoxic drugs (Aminoglycosides) Traumatic delivery Hyperbilirubenemia (Kernicteris) Bacterial meningitis
Acquired or Postlingual Otitis media (acute, chronic, serious) Cholesteatoma Otosclerosis Ossicular discontinuity due to trauma	
	Acquired or Postlingual Labyrinthian concussion or fracture Ototoxic drugs (Aminoglycosides) Meniere's disease Acute viral or bacterial labyrinthitis Sudden idiopathic hearing loss Noise induced/acoustic trauma Acoustic neuroma (eighth nerve) Presbycusis

Figure 17-2. The human hearing mechanism. Shown are the outer ear (pinna), the ear canal (the external auditory meatus), the eardrum (tympanic membrane), the middle ear cavity with the middle ear bones (ossicles), the balance mechanism (vestibular system), the inner ear (cochlea), and the auditory and vestibular nerves (eighth cranial nerve).

The eardrum separates the ear canal from the middle ear cavity. Sound waves transmitted along the ear canal impinge on the eardrum, causing minute vibrations that are transmitted to the three middle ear bones. These bones, suspended within the middle ear cavity, form a connecting system with the eardrum and transfer energy to the fluid-filled inner ear. The last bone of the ossicular chain, the stapes, fits into a tiny opening, the oval window, in one wall of the middle ear cavity. The rocking motion of the stapes creates pressure waves in the fluid of the inner ear. Sound waves impinging on the relatively large surface of the eardrum are transformed into mechanical energy delivered through the ossicles to the smaller footplate of the stapes. The difference in the relative areas of the eardrum and oval window increases the pressure of vibrations by a ratio of about 10 to 1.

The inner ear or cochlea, shaped like a snail shell, consists of a series of spiral chambers or spaces within the skull's sponge-like temporal bone. Another series of chambers form the balance or vestibular system. Extending from the inside of the spiral is a horizontal partition consisting of a bony ridge, a ligament, and a thin membrane (the basilar membrane), thus separating the spiral into upper (scala vestibuli) and lower (scala tympani) portions. These spaces are filled with fluid (the perilymph). The vibrations of the stapes at the oval window are transmitted in the perilymph upward in the scala vestibuli. Within the space of the scala vestibuli and separated from the scala tympani by the basilar membrane is the membranous cochlear duct. The cochlear duct contains endolymphatic fluid and is continuous with the vestibular system, the semicircular canals. Within the cochlear duct and superimposed on the basilar membrane is the organ of Corti. Composed of a complex assortment of cells, including well-defined rows of hair cells arranged to transmit different frequencies, the organ of Corti is the sensory end organ of hearing.

Fluid motion in the scala vestibuli caused by the vibration of the stapes in the oval window exerts motion on the basilar membrane and movement of the hair cells of the organ of Corti. This mechanical or fluid action is transformed by movement of the hair cells into electrical energy that stimulates the fibers of the auditory portion of eighth nerve. These nerve potentials are transmitted via the eighth nerve to the auditory central nervous system in the brain stem, the thalamus, and, ultimately, to the auditory cortex, where sound is perceived.

factory use of a hearing aid, especially in children.

The most common cause of conductive hearing loss in childhood is an inflammatory and infectious disorder of the middle ear and mastoid. *Otitis media* is a bacterial or viral infection of the mucous membrane lining of the Eustachian tube, middle ear, and occasionally, the sponge-like spaces of the temporal bone. When accompanied by the production of liquid that accumulates in the middle ear space and restricts or dampens movement of tympanic membrane, frequently causing hearing loss, it is called otitis media with effusion (OME). Uncomplicated otitis media is usually treated with varying degrees of effectiveness by orally administered antibiotics and decongestant medications. Chronic otitis media with effusion (COME), as the name implies, is a long-term (from 12 weeks onward) or recurrent infection of the middle ear and may require surgery. The procedure, known as myringotomy, involves an incision made in the tympanic membrane to drain the effusion, ventilate the middle ear space to promote healing, and restore hearing to a normal level. A small tube may be inserted to facilitate ventilation. Untreated, chronic, or secretory otitis media, in addition to pain and considerable discomfort, can result in a chronic hearing loss of mild to moderate degree, and in the extreme, a spread of the infection to the mastoid, cochlea, or cranial cavity. Otologists and audiologists are now recognizing that the mild to moderate hearing loss caused by chronic otitis media can have a marked effect on the development of speech and language skills of the young child. In some instances, wearable amplification may be recommended as a adjunct to medical treatment.

In addition, there are numerous other, but relatively rare, abnormalities of the middle ear that can cause hearing impairment. These include penetrating wounds, tumors or cysts such as cholesteatoma, and fracture of the temporal bone. By far the most important causes of conductive hearing loss in adults are dysfunction of the Eustachian tube and infections of the middle ear and a hereditary disease of the bony capsule surrounding the inner ear known as *otosclerosis*. In otosclerosis, the normally hard bony capsule is invaded by softer bone, which eventually hardens and becomes sclerotic. In the process, the new bone fixes the stapes firmly in the oval window and reduces or prevents transmission of vibrations by the middle ear bones to the fluid of the inner ear. In a way, this is similar to some forms of arthritis that limit movements of finger or knee joints. Otosclerosis generally begins in youth and progresses gradually over years, causing increasing loss of hearing. In its simplest form, otosclerosis can cause a moderate to severe loss of hearing (60 to 70 dB), and because the loss is principally conductive, a hearing aid can provide good results. Initially, surgery to free the fixed stapes (the stapes mobilization operation) often reulted in good restoration of hearing; however, the frequent problem of reankylosis of the stapes led to the development of the stapedectomy procedure. By replacing the stapes with a prosthesis (vein graft, or polyethylene or wire strut), the problem of ankylosis was largely overcome and the chance of restoring hearing permanently improved considerably.

Additional surgical procedures for reconstruction of the conductive mechanism include myringoplasty (grafting a perforation of the eardrum) and tympanoplasty (replacement of the ossicular chain).

Sensorineural Hearing Loss

Sensorineural hearing loss may be congenital or acquired. Congenital denotes present at birth, a condition sometimes difficult to prove, but in terms of language and speech development, there is no real difference between the child whose loss was present at birth or whose loss occurred during the first 3 years of life (the prespeech or prelingual period). Each will fail to develop language and speech normally; and therefore, in the habilitative sense, it is more appropriate to speak of hearing impairment occurring prelingually or postlingually.

Prelingual Hearing Impairment. Causes of prelingual hearing impairment are numerous and varied but can be classified under three main headings: genetic disorders, of which there are many types; maternal infection; and a long list of prenatal, perinatal, and postnatal states or conditions.

Hereditary deafness is believed to account for 35 to 50% of childhood deafness (Konigsmark & Gorlin, 1976). Because of the importance of inheritance in the etiology of childhood deafness, it is important to identify the principal ways genetic deficits can be inherited. All hereditary material, in the form of deoxyribonucleic acid (DNA) is carried as genes on the chromosomes. Each human body cell contains 23 pairs of chromosomes: 22 pairs are termed *autosomes* and the remaining pair are *sex chromosomes* (two X chromosomes constituting a female, and one X and one Y, a male). The number of genes distributed throughout the 46 chromosomes of the human cell is estimated to aproximate 100,000. Abnormalities may occur during cell division, producing an individual with a chromosomal defect. The most common autosomal chromosomal defect is Down syndrome, characterized by a pattern of multiple anomalies that often includes hearing loss. Although imperfectly understood, we do know that there are several genetic and environmental factors that predispose to the formation of chromosomal aberrations: late maternal age, autoimmune disease, and exposure to radiation. Examination under light microscopy of single cells, such as those in amniotic fluid obtained early in the pregnancy (amniocentesis), is enabling clinical cytogeneticists to identify and classify increasing numbers of chromosomal defects. These advances have important implications for genetic counseling.

Defects involving single genes, unfortunately, cannot be detected through currently available cytogenetic laboratory techniques, and determination of whether the etiology of the disease is truly familial must be made through a careful history of the family pedigree. Often, but not always, diagrammatic construction of a family history of the occurrence of prelingual hearing loss can be helpful in establishing whether the trait is dominant, recessive, or sex-linked.

Autosomal dominant inheritance refers to an alteration of DNA in a particular gene of a corresponding pair of chromosomes. The presence of one abnormal gene and one normal gene (heterozygote state) means there is a 50% chance of an affected individual passing the gene on to an offspring. Dominantly inherited disorders generally are milder and may arise as a spontaneous mutation or secondary to receiving the gene from either parent. In contrast, *autosomal recessive inheritance* is a condition where an individual must receive two abnormal genes (homozygous state). There is a 25% chance of two carrier parents, often asymptomatic, producing an affected child, a 50% chance their children will be carriers like themselves, and a 25% chance of a genetically normal child. Consanguinity, the marriage of two unaffected people with recent common ancestors, such as cousins, for example, increases the chances each may have the same recessive gene inherited from those common and possibly unaffected ancestors. *Sex-linked* or *X-linked inheritance* refers to single gene inheritance in which the genetic change is on one of the X chromosomes. Because males have only one X chromosome, they are usually affected more severely. The pattern of inheritance is from female to male. There is a 50% chance that the carrier female with two X chromosomes, one with the affected gene, will produce an affected male and a 50% chance of an unaffected but carrier female.

It is estimated that 10–20% of all profound prelingual deafness is autosomal dominant, about 20–40% due to autosomal recessive inheritance, and 1–3% sex-linked (Konigsmark, 1972). The probability that deaf parents with a recessive pattern of deafness will have deaf children is only slightly greater because the chances are small that two deaf persons will have the same genetic deafness. If two normal hearing persons happen to be carriers of the same recessive gene, theoretically there is a 25% chance their offspring would be affected; however, if the parents are affected by the same recessive type of deafness, all the offspring will be affected.

Associated anomolies occur in about one third of all children with inherited deafness. Konigsmark (1976) lists approximately 70 types of syndromes that include deafness. Many observable dysmorphic syndromes, such as facial or skeletal dysplasia, malformation, or skin disorders, may also be characterized by conductive or sensorineural hearing loss.

The second major factor that places infants at higher risk for hearing loss are a group of infectious diseases often referred to as the *TORCH* complex: TO for toxoplasmosis, R for rubella, C for cytomegalic inclusion disease, and H for herpes. Sometimes the O will refer for others (mumps, syphilis, *streptococcus*, enterovirus, hepatitus B virus, etc.). *Maternal rubella* during the first trimester of the pregnancy, once a major cause of hearing loss, blindness, deafness and blindness, and psychomotor retardation, is now declining as a result of an effective vaccine. *Cytomegalovirus* (CMV) is a common virus that is harmless to most people. Most children and adults who contract a CMV infection have no symptoms and may be unaware they have come in contact with the virus. A member of the herpes group of viruses, CMV poses the greatest risk to the developing fetus of a woman who contracts the virus for the first time during her pregnancy. The virus is passed across the placenta to the unborn child and may interfere with development of the central nervous system, causing mental retardation and/or hearing loss. It is estimated that about 1 in 100 babies born in the United States has CMV infection, and, of these, 10–15% will develop disabilities that include hearing loss, low IQ, and learning problems. About 1 in 1,000 babies will have a more severe form of the disease characterized by mental retardation or deafness.

The third major class of pre- and perinatal factors that places neonates at risk for hearing loss includes a variety of conditions or states: *prematurity*, low birthweight (birthweight less than 1,500 gm), *apnea* or *asphyxia* (hypoxia), *aminoglycoside ototoxicity*, and *hyperbilirubinemia*. With the low-birthweight, premature, or difficult delivery baby, absence of respiration at birth (apnea) or an asphyxic episode can produce hypoxemia (deficient oxygenation of the blood), causing pathological changes in the cochlea or auditory brainstem.

Aminoglycosides are a group of antibiotics derived from various species of streptomyces. Included is streptomycin, which proved so effective in the treatment of tuberculosis. Others are kanamycin, genamicin, tobianycin, amikacins, and metimicin. Although the therapeutic value of aminoglycosides is unquestioned in the treatment of serious infections, their toxic side effects on vestibular and cochlear function constantly raises the question of risk versus benefit. This is especially true for low-birthweight infants, many of whom receive at least one course and often multiple courses of aminoglycoside therapy. Although the risk with newborns appears small (often it is difficult to implicate aminoglycoside therapy as a single cause when other factors associated with hearing loss such as apnea, hypoxia, meningitis, etc., are present), the potential toxic effects should be of concern, and efforts should be continued to develop accurate therapeutic guidelines.

Hyperbilirubinemia, an elevated bilirubin level in blood plasma, is a hemolytic fetal or neonatal disorder often caused by the incompatibility of the Rh or ABO factors of maternal and fetal blood. High levels of bilirubin (a by-product formed when the spleen fragments dead red blood cells) in the blood can cause jaundice (yellow staining of the skin) and kernicterus, the deposition of blood pigment in the brain. Clinical manifestations of the condition include cerebral palsy, dental enamel dysplasia, and hearing impairment. Exchange transfusion and keeping the bilirubin level below a critical level through phototherapy — exposure to blue light — offer the best protection against development of neurological or auditory sequelae.

Bacterial meningitis is the leading reported cause of acquired deafness in infants and young children. According to recent surveys, fully 37% of all specified postnatal causes of hearing loss among students enrolled in programs for the hearing impaired in the United States is attributed to meningitis (Gentile & Rambin, 1973;

Schildroth, 1982). Although advances in antimicrobial therapy have reduced mortality, among long-term sequelae, hearing loss is one of the most common problems. Occurring primarily in children under 3 years of age and most frequently in infants under 1 year of age, the incidence of sensorineural hearing loss following meningitis has been reported to vary between 10 and 20% (Ozdamar, Kraus, & Stein, 1983). Isolated instances of improvement in hearing after recovery from meningitis have been reported but, in general, the hearing loss of variable degree is permanent. Because of the high risk of hearing loss, every case of bacterial meningitis, particularly when the type of pathogen is hemophilus influenza or *pneumococcal*, should be tested for possible hearing loss before discharge home from the hospital.

According to the 1970–1971 Annual Survey of Hearing Impaired Children and Youth on the reported causes of hearing loss, a specified cause was reported for 56% of the students, cause could not be determined for 27%, and cause was not reported for 16% (Gentile & Rambin, 1973). Although some of the estimated 25–30% of congenital deafness listed in surveys as cause unknown may in fact be due to an unrecognized autosomal recessive factor. At the present time, the etiology of hearing loss in significant numbers of children remains a mystery. In addition to the concern such negative findings pose for parents, the delay in early identification of hearing loss poses a serious problem because of the absence of any risk factors that would alert the pediatrician to possible hearing loss and the fact that the majority of these seemingly well babies are cared for in well-baby nurseries, where hearing screening is not generally routine. The awareness of the parent and the sensitivity of the child's physician remain the crucial factors for identification of hearing loss in these children.

Postlingual Hearing Impairment. Three of the major known causes of hearing loss with onset in adulthood are: Meniere's disease, noise-induced loss, and the hearing loss that classically appears in the elderly (*presbycusis*).

Meniere's disease, first described in 1861, is characterized by hearing loss, vertiginous attacks (dizziness), and tinnitus (ringing or buzzing in the ear). The hearing loss is sensorineural, often fluctuating in severity and usually progressive. In addition to the handicap imposed by the hearing loss and tinnitus, which may be unilateral or bilateral, the patient with Meniere's disease experiences often incapacitating episodes of vertigo that may be accompanied by nausea and vomiting. The pathology of the disease is distention of the endolymphatic system (*endolymphatic hydrops*) of the cochlear and vestibular mechanism (balance mechanism). Diagnosis is often by exclusion of other diseases such as acoustic neuroma or vestibular neuritis. In a small percentage of patients, a specific etiology such as allergy or hypometabolic state can be determined, but in the majority, there is no apparent cause. Medical treatment begins conservatively with the use of vasodilators or other medications to control symptoms. The use of a hearing aid may also be recommended. In those instances where symptoms cannot be adequately controlled by medication or spontaneous prolonged remission has not occurred and symptoms become disabling, surgery to relieve the endolymphatic hydrops or to section the eighth nerve may be recommended.

Noise-induced hearing loss due to exposure to excessive levels of noise in the environment or work place is a major public health problem. Federal, state, and local governments are actively involved in setting safe standards for noise levels and exposures in the work environment, enforcing regulations for providing ear protection for workers, and compensating workers for disabling hearing loss attributable to noise exposure. In addition, the problem of excessive noise levels or what may be perceived as excessive, for example, in neighborhoods adjacent to or in the vicinity of airports, have become environmental and quality of life issues.

There are two principal forms of noise-induced hearing loss: loss that develops gradually after years of exposure to excessive levels of steady or fluctuating broad spectrum noise, and loss, often termed *acoustic trauma*, the results from exposure to intense but brief or impulse-type noise (explosion, gunfire, etc.). Exposure to steady-state or brief noise can produce both temporary and permanent changes in hearing as well as tinnitus and a variety of physiological and psychological changes.

The single most characteristic sign of noise-induced hearing loss or acoustic trauma is a loss of sensitivity in the 4,000 Hz region. A single brief exposure may only produce a temporary shift in threshold, but with prolonged or repeated exposure, the loss at 4,000 Hz becomes greater and the higher frequencies become affected more and more. There is always greater hearing loss at the higher frequencies than at the lower ones. It is believed that the main reason why hearing in the 4,000 Hz range is affected most, even by low frequency noise, is that the ear canal resonates or amplifies 3,000 Hz sounds, and therefore, more energy will be transmitted to the cochlea at this and higher frequencies. The differential diagnosis of noise-induced hearing loss from other possible causes of high-frequency hearing loss (prebycusis, hereditary progressive sensorineural loss, ototoxic drugs, etc.) involves not only thorough otologic and audiologic examination but also a careful history and comparison of past findings (audiograms if they are available) with current results.

The establishment of safe levels of noise exposure has been the subject of extensive study and debate for many years. The acoustic intensity or level of noise as measured by a sound level meter can be expressed in decibels. As examples, normal conversational speech and the volume of television audio or stereo music in the home normally would fall in the 67–75 dBA range (dBA for the A weighted scale of a sound level meter). In comparison, a chainsaw at 110 dBA or heavy construction equipment at 120 dBA may be uncomfortably loud and potentially injurious if exposure is prolonged or repetitive. Determination of what is hazardous noise exposure is a function of acoustic intensity or noise level, duration of exposure, whether the noise is steady or intermittent,

and the spectrum of the noise. To illustrate the difficulty of formulating a single decibel level that would universally serve as a standard for safety, if exposure at 85 dBA to a steady-state noise for an uninterrupted 8 hours was determined as potentially hazardous to hearing, a noise that fluctuated in intensity or one that was intermittent would deliver less energy to the ear and therefore, in theory, the 85 dBA level could be raised or the 8-hour duration lengthened to equal the same energy as the original standard. Conversely, exposure for 4 hours at 90 dBA is believed to be equivalent to the 85 dBA 8-hour standard. The Occupational Safety and Health Administration (OSHA) has devised standards and regulations that include recommendations for the use of ear protection devices (earplugs or sound isolation muffs), the monitoring of the hearing of workers, and the reduction of high levels of noise through acoustical design changes. For certain industries, compromise between strictly auditory factors and economic issues may influence the formulation of these standards and regulations. Excellent reviews of noise and noise-induced hearing loss are provided by Kryter (1970), Lipscomb (1979), and Ward (1984).

Presbycusis, literally old-age hearing, affects an estimated 40% of the elderly. Approximately 6 to 7 million Americans age 65 years and older are believed to have trouble hearing in one or both ears, and with the gradual aging of the American population, the number of Americans with hearing loss is expected to increase.

Presbycusis is characterized by a gradual loss of high-frequency hearing, usually beginning in the fifth and sixth decades of life. Accompanying the gradual loss for high frequency pure tones is typically a reduction in speech recognition ability. Not only is the sensitivity for sound affected, but speech becomes less clear even when made louder: the characteristic, "Don't shout, I can hear you, I just can't understand you" response of an affected elderly person.

The pathophysiology of presbycusis is imperfectly understood. Histopathological studies have implicated cochlear atrophy (the loss of hair cells of the basal end of the organ of Corti) and secondary loss of cochlear nerve fibers to explain high-frequency hearing loss and reduced speech recognition ability. The terms *peripheral* and *central presbycusis* have been coined to differentiate speech recognition performance that is proportional to the loss of pure tone sensitivity from speech recognition performance that is disproportionately poorer. Confounding the question of presbycusis is the fact that aging is a highly individual matter. Some "young" 80-year-olds may show no signs of hearing impairment, whereas some in their 50s may already be experiencing difficulties. Added are such factors as history of exposure to noise, general health, and cognitive and emotional status.

Treatment is generally limited to the use of hearing aids and counseling. Successful use of a hearing aid or aids is again a highly individual matter. Patients with clinical signs of central presbycusis may not do as well with amplication as those with uncomplicated loss of hearing sensitivity. Motivation to remain active and to participate in social activities plays an important part in the rehabilitation process.

PREVALENCE OF HEARING IMPAIRMENT

Hearing loss is frequently described as the nation's number one handicapping disability, affecting more Americans than can-

cer, heart disease, tuberculosis, blindness, multiple sclerosis, venereal disease, and kidney disease combined. Some 15.2–17.4 million Americans are said to experience difficulty in hearing or understanding speech. This estimate, which includes all degrees of hearing difficulty from significant bilateral hearing loss to tinnitus without accompanying hearing deficiency, is based on data gathered primarily by survey interviews or by direct audiometric examinations.

Among recent studies using the interview technique is the National Health Interview Survey (HIS), conducted annually by the federal government (Reis, 1982). Shown in Table 17-3 is the steady progressive growth in the prevalence rate of hearing impairment in one or both ears with increasing age. For the 75-year-old and over population, it is estimated that nearly 40% will have some degree of hearing impairment.

A second widely quoted interview study, the National Census of the Deaf Population conducted in 1971 (Schein & Delk, 1974), concentrated primarily on the deaf population: those with significant bilateral impairment and those who lost hearing prelingually (before age 3) and prevocationally (before age 19). The 0.100 or 1 per 1,000 prevalence rate reported for prelingual deafness in the civilian noninstitutionalized population (Table 17-4) is identical to the frequently reported 1 per 1,000 incidence figure for the occurrence of deaf-

Table 17-3. Prevalence rates of hearing impairment, per 100 persons, in the civilian, noninstitutionalized population of the United States. Rates are based on 1977 interview data

AGE GROUP IN YEARS	NUMBER	PREVALENCE RATE (%)
<5	96,034	0.63
5–14	592,595	1.63
15–24	922,012	2.32
25–34	1,380,760	4.29
35–44	1,344,130	5.82
45–54	2,269,974	9.79
55–64	3,095,322	15.35
65–74	3,430,852	24.10
75+	3,087,095	38.55
All	16,218,774	7.64

Table 17-4. Prevalence of hearing impairment, as reported in interviews, in the civilian, noninstitutionalized population of the United States, by degree and age at onset

DEGREE	AGE AT ONSET	PERCENT OF TOTAL U.S. POPULATION	NUMBER*
All hearing impairment	All	6.603	15,250,883
Significant bilateral impairment	All	3.236	7,474,157
Deafness	All	0.873	2,016,359
	Prevocational**	0.203	468,867
	Prelingual***	0.100	230,969

*Based on 1982 Census bureau population estimates
**Prior to 19 years
***Prior to 3 years

ness in the general newborn population as found by various infant hearing screening surveys. The validity of the 1 per 1,000 prevalence rate for prelingual deafness is further supported by the fact that by actual count, the number of children in deaf classrooms is very close to the figure that would be predicted by taking the 0.1% prevalence rate and applying it to the general school population. For example, Illinois in 1983 had 2,341 students enrolled in classrooms for the deaf and a general school population of 2,283, 740: 0.1% of 2,283,740 would predict 2,283 deaf students.

Estimates of the prevalence of prevocational deafness and significant deafness with onset at any age include individuals who rely on sign language as their primary means of communication, as well as those who have effective aural/oral communication skills. Some of the prevocationally deaf may not always requre special classroom placement or special services such as vocational rehabilitation. All, however, due to the severity of their hearing loss, experience in varying degrees limitations in communication that can fairly or unfairly restrict their access to educational employment, and social opportunities.

DIAGNOSIS AND ASSESSMENT

The diagnosis of the underlying cause of hearing loss, and determination of the severity of the loss and the functional disability produced by the loss are dependent on careful otological, audiological, and related medical testing. The first goal of the otological and audiological examinations is to determine whether a medically or surgically treatable or correctable condition exists.

The evaluation of the patient with complaint of hearing impairment should begin with a carefully taken history, a general survey of the health of the person, and an otoscopic examination. Ear wax (cerumen) and debris may have to be removed so that the tympanic membrane can be visualized through an otoscope and the mobility of the tympanic membrane determined by a pneumatic otoscope. These direct examinations can reveal perforation of the drum, inflammation, and fluid in the middle ear space. The otoscopic examination is vital in the evaluation of both adults and children, even when sensorineural hearing loss is suspected. In addition, the nasopharynx should be carefully examined.

Tests

Audiological examination with the adult or the child old enough to voluntarily respond begins with pure tone audiometry. Pure tones, sounds at specified frequencies, are delivered via earphones at calibrated intensities to the patient who signals whether the signal is heard. The results of bone conduction testing, where the signal is transmitted directly to the skull via a vibrator, is compared to air conduction results. Equal air conduction and bone conduction thresholds when both are depressed suggest a sensorineural loss. The converse, when bone conduction thresholds are better than air conduction thresholds, suggests a conductive-type loss, for example, dysfunction of the middle ear mechanism. The configuration of the air conduction audiogram — flat, sloping, or notched — and the relationship between air and bone conduction thresholds provide valuable diagnostic information concerning posssible etiology and severity of the hearing loss.

The second test considered essential in the diagnosis and assessment of hearing loss is speech audiometry. Because the individual's ability to hear and understand speech is essential to communication, determination of the level at which speech can be recognized, how well speech materials can be understood when loud enough to theoretically overcome a moderate or severe loss, and at what level of intensity speech becomes uncomfortable to the listener are important questions for both diagnosis and the estimation of how much help can be expected from rehabilitative measures. Speech materials consisting of spondaic words (equal stress on each syllable), phonetically balanced (PB) word lists, and a variety of sentence tests have been developed to obtain speech recognition thresholds and speech recognition scores under earphones or via loudspeakers in a sound field. Speech audiometry is particularly useful in the assessment of central auditory processing problems and has been extensively employed in the selection of hearing aids.

In addition to pure tone and speech audiometry, the field of audiology over the past 20 years has developed a wide variety of special diagnostic or site lesion tests. These include self-recording threshold (Bekesy) audiometry, tests of recruitment for Meniere's or cochlear disease, tone decay tests for retrocochlear lesions, tests for functional hearing loss or malingering, and competing message tests for central auditory processing problems. Edited texts by Jerger (1973), Rose (1978), Rintelman (1979), and Northern (1984) contain excellent reviews of specialized audiological test procedures.

Infants and patients untestable by conventional audiometry (the multiply handicapped, mentally retarded, etc.) pose a particularly difficult problem in identifying hearing loss. Because they cannot voluntarily respond, methods have been devised to measure involuntary physiological or neurophysiological responses to auditory stimuli. The startle reflex of the infant (Moro's reflex, auralpalpebral reflex, etc.) to a loud sound, typically a hand clap or the dropping of a wastebasket, has been used for years by both parent and pediatrician to "test" baby's hearing. This method was somewhat formalized by introduction of calibrated electronic noise makers. But the reliability of the observer's judgment as to the presence or absence of a response was often notoriously poor, especially if the observer was inexperienced.

The past 10 years have been marked by important methodological advances in infant hearing screening and the early confirmation of hearing loss. Language stimulation activities therefore now can be initiated during the critical early language learning period. In 1982, the Joint Committee on Infant Hearing issued a position statement recommending that the hearing of infants who manifest any of the risk criteria shown in Table 17-5 should be screened optimally by 3 months of age, but no later than 6 months of age (Joint Committee on Infant Hearing, 1982). Introduction of automated screening devices that record neonatal motor activity coincident with an auditory signal (the Crib-o-gram and the Auditory Response Cradle) and the auditory brainstem response (ABR) test provided the technology to effectively screen hearing in newborns. Using sensors incorporated within a crib or molded bed, the Crib-o-gram and the Auditory Response Cradle automatically record bodily movements or changes in respiration when a loud sound is presented to the infant. Microprocessor technology has replaced the subjective examiner in deciding whether the infant's response or lack of response is correlated with a calibrated sound.

Auditory brainstem response (ABR), or as it is sometimes called, brainstem auditory evoked response (BAER) or brainstem

Table 17-5. Factors identifying infants at risk of hearing impairment

Family history of childhood hearing impairment

Congenital perinatal infection (e.g., eytomegalovirus, rubella, herpes, toxoplasmosis, syphilis)

Anatomic malformations involving the head or neck (e.g., dysmorphic appearance, including syndromal and nonsyndromal abnormalities, overt or submucous cleft palate, morphologic abnormalities of the pinna)

Birthweight <1500 g

Hyperbilirubinemia at a level exceeding indications for exchange transfusion.

Bacterial meningitis, especially *Haemophilus influenzae*

Severe asphyxia, which may include infants with Apgar scores of 0–3 or who fail to institute spontaneous respiration within 10 minutes, and those with hypotonia persisting to 2 hours of age.

evoked response (BSER), is an electrophysiological test that records changes in the electrical activity of the brainstem in response to sound. Through electrodes attached to the scalp of the infant, electrical activity of the brain is recorded in a manner similar to the electroencephalograph (EEG). Added is a small average response computer to electronically sum changes in the electrical potential of the brain evoked by sound and to reduce or cancel generally irregular or random background electrical activity. Interpretaion of the ABR record is based on the amount of time, measured in milliseconds, required for the generation of electrical discharges in the various area of the central auditory nervous system following activation of the eardrum by the test signal. The only requirement of the infant or child being tested is to lie quietly, preferably asleep, either naturally or with the help of a mild sedative. For comprehensive reviews of the principles, methodology, and clinical application of auditory brainstem response, the interested reader is referred to Jacobson (1985), to Swigart (1986) for reviews on neonatal hearing screening, and to Northern and Downs (1984) for comprehensive coverage of hearing in children.

HABILITATION AND REHABILITATION

The medical treatment of hearing loss and the possible restoration of hearing through surgery, primarily for conductive-type losses, as well as medical management of some of the accompanying symptoms of sensorineural loss, have been referred to in preceding sections. In the following sections, discusssion will center on the use of wearable amplification for irreversible hearing loss, therapy and educational management of hearing impaired children, and the additional handicapping conditions often associated with hearing impairment.

Hearing Aids

Since the introduction of the first vacuum-tube hearing aid in the early 1920s, advances in the manufacture of amplification devices for the hearing impaired have followed technological breakthroughs in the fields of electronics and miniaturization. Development of the transistor and microchip technology enabled manufacturers to progressively reduce the size of hearing aids from desk top models to body-worn units to aids that fit entirely within the ear canal. User vanity, most often attributed to the size and conspicuousness of an aid, was the principal reason why large numbers of hearing impaired persons refused to avail themselves of the benefits of amplification. Although vanity (the hearing aid, as reading glasses, is often a symbol of aging) still remains a problem, research and development aimed at improving performance and the subsequent help a hearing aid can provide are now assuming increasing importance.

Contemporary hearing aids, regardless of type or size, consist essentially of a miniature microphone (input transducer), amplifier, and speaker (output transducer). Three basic types are available: the body aid, the behind-the-ear or ear-level type (an eyeglass-aid incorporated in the temple bar of eyeglasses is essentially the same as a behind-the-ear aid), and the in-the-ear type, which includes canal and all-in-the ear models. The body-type aid is now used mainly with young children, individuals with very special amplification needs, or persons who cannot physically manage smaller aids. In 1984, body aids comprised less than 2% of all hearing aid sales. The behind-the-ear aid is coupled to a separate earmold custom-made to fit the ear canal of the user. In contrast, the all-in-the-ear aid incorporates the case for the aid and the earmold into one unit, part or most of which fits into the ear canal. Behind-the-ear aids and all-in-the ear models now account for approximately 36 and 60%, respectively, of all hearing aids sold. The popularity of the all-in-the-ear types has increased dramatically since 1975, due largely to improved electroacoustic performance, particularly for mild and moderate losses, and their obvious cosmetic advantage.

The major performance parameters of a hearing aid are acoustical gain and frequency response. Acoustical gain is simply the difference between acoustical input at the microphone and the acoustical output at the speaker. As an example, an acoustical input of 60 dB SPL (approximately the level of conversational speech at a distance of 1 meter) to an aid with a gain of 50 dB yields an acoustical output at the receiver of 110 dB SPL. Acoustical gain of hearing aids can range from 20 to 80 dB. For hearing losses of mild degree, hearing aids with mild gain would be selected; for moderate loss, moderate gain aids, etc. The acoustical gain is different at different frequencies and can be modified in a variety of ways.

The frequency response of a hearing aid is limited in comparison to stereo systems, due mostly to the very small components used. In general, a hearing aid amplifies frequencies from 500 Hz to, at maximum, 4,000 or 5,000 Hz; however, the frequency response is not uniform throughout this range. Peak amplification generally occurs in the 1,000 to 3,000 Hz range. Various tone control settings and modifications of the resonance characteristics of the earmold can tailor the frequency response to emphasize low or high frequencies and the slope of the frequency response curve to compensate in part for the configuration of the pure tone loss. In addition to a volume control and either an internally adjustable or fixed tone setting, many contemporary hearing aids have automatic gain control to limit maximum output to protect against loud sounds and a telephone coil to allow the aid to be used with a telephone.

Approximately 35% of hearing aid sales in 1984 were binaural fittings (an aid fitted to each ear). The advantages of binaural amplification, even when the loss in the two ears is not identical, are increased directional hearing ability and greater separation of the primary signal from background sound. Many audiologists now routinely recommend infants be provided a behind-the-ear aid for each ear.

Nearly 60% of all hearing aids sold in 1984 were to individuals over 65 years of age, another indication of the continuing "graying of America." The 40- to 65-year age bracket was next highest, accounting for over 25% of all hearing aid sales, whereas sales to persons 18 years and under amounted to less than 7%.

Researchers, both within the industry and the fields of electronics and speech and hearing science, are making steady progress in reducing the size and improving the performance of hearing aids. Current efforts are centering on development of a digital signal processing hearing aid that utilizes computer technology to process the sound, selectively filter unwanted background noise while amplifying and passing the speech signal, and electronically suppressing acoustic feedback caused by acoustic leakage at the earmold.

Cochlear Implant

Probably the most dramatic and publicized recent development in devices to enable the profoundly deaf to obtain "hearing" has been the cochlear implant. In many patients with profound sensorineural hearing loss, the hair cells of the cochlea may be absent or functionally impaired, whereas the auditory, or eighth, nerve may be more or less intact. In 1957, Djourna and Eyries (1957) reported that electrical stimulation of the auditory nerve by the direct application of an electrode implanted into the cochlea induced a sensation of hearing in a profoundly deaf patient. Interest in this phenomenon and the inducement of hearing sensations in profoundly deaf individuals by electrical stimulation increased rapidly largely through the pioneering efforts of House and Urban (1973), Simmons (1966), Michelson (1971), and their colleagues.

In the strict sense, the cochlear implant is not a new type of hearing aid, but rather, an electrical stimulator that replaces the activity of the cochlea by exciting the auditory nerve fibers. A cochlear implant system, and there are now several different types being manufactured, consists essentially of a microphone and a speech processor unit that converts sound into coded electrical currents or signals, a transmitter that sends these signals through the skin to a receiver implanted under the skin behind the ear, and one or multiple electrodes implanted either within the vicinity of the round window, inserted directly into the scala tympani of the cochlea, or directly into the auditory nerve fibers.

At the current state of development, the amount of hearing a person obtains from cochlear implant is quite limited, although claims differ widely. The prosodic features of speech, such as the timing pattern of utterances, intonation, and word stress, are effectively transmitted and perceived, phonetic and other sound elements less well; the implantee's ability to recognize words, understand sentences, or conduct conversations can vary widely. This apparent variability in speech performance among implantees, even when similar cochlear implant systems are used, is thought to be more related to the cognitive or perceptual processing style of the individual than to differences among the systems. What is fairly clear is that the ideal candidate for cochlear implant is the well-educated person who developed speech and language in a natural way but who suddenly lost all hearing, due to lifesaving but ototoxic antibiotics, for example, and is now motivated to use the unfamiliar cues, however minimal, provided by the cochlear implant to monitor his/her environment and augment lip reading skills (Millar, Tong, & Clark, 1984). Adults, postlingually deafened are the primary candidates for implantation at most centers, but implants have been done on pre- and postlingually deafened children.

Further development and improvements may be expected with the cochlear implant. The external speech processor and the signal processing strategy for the transfer of acoustic information to controlled electrical currents are the key elements. The possibility that the cochlear implant or similar device eventually will enable the prelingually or congenitally deaf child to learn a new set of electrically stimulated auditory inputs and use new perceptual stategies to communicate effectively is exciting and not unrealistic to contemplate.

THERAPY AND EDUCATION FOR HEARING IMPAIRED CHILDREN

Quite possibly, no area of special education has been subjected to as much difference of expert opinion and controversy as the field of deaf education and its various philosophies or methods. Essentially, the question reduces to differences of opinion among the advocates of the oral, manual, and total communication philosophies of deaf education and the significant variations of these three major categories. Although the roots of the methodologies of deaf education can be traced back to the late 1700s and early 1800s when a French priest, L'abbé de L'Epée, developed a "natural language of gestures" to teach deaf pupils and to such distinguished names as Thomas Hopkins Gallaudet and Alexander Graham Bell, we can only briefly highlight the major methodologies and again refer the reader to Flint (1979) for a concise historical review.

Oral Methods of Deaf Education

Oral or aural/verbal methods of deaf education emphasize training audition and lip reading and exclude any use of natural gestures or manual communication (sign language). Major emphasis is placed on auditory stimulation through early and concentrated training using hearing aids. At the preschool level, much of the training is done at home, often, for example, following the home study course offered by the John Tracy Clinic in Los Angeles. A variation of the oral method is the "unisensory" or "acoupedic" approach, where attention is focused entirely on audition and no attempt is made to teach lipreading. Described as applicable to the young child, the method depends on early identification, early amplification, total exposure to oral language, and extraordinary dedication by the parent (Pollack, 1970).

In contrast, the multisensory method, used with older children, includes with auditory training, motorkinesthic training in speech production, and the reading and writing of orthographic forms of English. Proponents of these methods argue that orally trained children can succeed in a hearing society. The appesal to parents is obvious. Also obvious is the fact that the children who do best in oral programs are those with adequate residual hearing, normal or superior intelligence, no additional handicapping conditions, and parents with strong resources. It cannot be denied that there have been and will continue to be outstanding successes with oral methods, but the fundamental assumption of the advocates of oralism that every deaf child first should be given the opportunity to communicate using speech has been subjected to severe criticism.

Arguments against oralism and its variants include reports that profoundly deaf children, whose residual hearing is limited to the frequencies 250 and 500 Hz, are probably responding to tactual stimulation and possess no real sense of hearing. Also, because many sounds and words look alike at the lips (homophenous words such as bat and mat) or are not visible (sounds made at the back of the throat such as k and g), lip-reading is too ambiguous and difficult to master for the congenitally deaf. At best, lipreading, or as it is sometimes called, speech reading, is a supplement or aid for the hard-of-hearing. The most passionate arguments have centered on the failure of large numbers, sometimes claimed to be the majority, of deaf children to achieve even rudimentary language and communication skills. Frequently cited in support is a survey of the results of standardized achievement tests with 19,000 deaf and hard-of-hearing children in the United States. One of the most telling findings was that the highest average score in paragraph meanings, which represents language comprehension, obtained by the 19-year-old hearing impaired pupils was equivalent only to a fourth-grade reading level (Reis, 1973).

Manual Deaf Education

The first school for the deaf in the United States, the American School for the Deaf in Hartford, Connecticut, was established in 1817 as a result of Thomas Hart Gallaudet's interest in the system of sign language taught by L'Epée and later his pupil, L'Abbé Sicard, in Paris. In the United States, L'Epée's system gradually fused with the natural gestures used in America to form American Sign Language or "Ameslan." American Sign Language has been described as an independent language that incorporates through repeated use and understanding natural gestures that then become formalized signs. Although supplemented by finger spelling, Ameslan does not necessarily follow acceptable English syntax, is somewhat concrete, and is limited in the expression of abstract concepts. Despite these acknowledged shortcomings, proponents argue that the sign or manual system enables deaf children to develop language skills and, therefore, an education, that it is the preferred method of communication for the majority of deaf adults, and that with the advent of certification of interpreters for the deaf (National Registry of Interpreters for the Deaf [RID]) and their increasing use in courts of law, hospitals, and on the television, the stigma or strangeness associated with sign language in the past is lessening.

Total Communication

Although combined or simultaneous methods that used speech, lipreading, hearing aids, fingerspelling, and sign language had been introduced earlier, in the 1970s, a philosophy of teaching emerged that is termed total communication. Defined as a philosophy that uses every and all means to develop language and communication in the deaf child, it encourages use of natural gestures, Ameslan, fingerspelling, hearing aids and auditory training, and speech, all simultaneously. After initial resistance by special education programs that traditionally started all children in oral methods and later transferred those children found not doing well into manually oriented programs, total communication was rapidly adopted by most programs throughout the country. In part, this revolutionary change was in response to the criticism that by keeping deaf children in oral-type programs and waiting until they failed at 8 or 10 years of age, language learning was being denied during the critical period when children are biologically programmed for language learning (Lenneberg, 1967). Just as language stimulation and a healthy parent–child relationship in terms of communication is crucial for the experientially deprived child, so it is for the deaf child, the argument went. Those in favor of manual communication readily accepted total communication because it did not compromise their position. Opponents expressed concern, with some justification as it later turned out, that in actual practice the inherent difficulty in emphasizing all modes of communication simultaneously might favor manual communication, the easier and quicker of the methods to learn. In addition, the requirement that parents learn sign language, in a real sense acknowledgement that their deaf child was different, was seen as a potential area of concern.

Many educators view the emergence of total communication as encouraging, if for no other reason than its emphasis on any means that works to develop language and communication may reduce the dogma and adversarialness that has marked the education of the deaf child for almost 150 years. years. Less stress on the "method" and more emphasis on the detection and diagnosis of hearing loss during infancy, support for the research and development necessary for technological breakthroughs for improvement in amplification and speech processing devices, new approaches to language learning, and finally, progressive advances in teacher preparation, should be the goals of everyone concerned about the welfare of deaf children. Those programs that emphasize other approaches should not be isolated, but rather, viewed as possible resources for the development of techniques that could strengthen all programs.

ADDITIONAL HANDICAPPING CONDITIONS

Additional handicapping conditions or secondary problems are estimated to occur in 30% of the deaf school-age population. Most frequently reported are mental retardation, perceptual or learning disorders, emotional/behavioral problems, and visual impairment.

Mental retardation may be classified as either a primary or secondary problem, depending largely on severity and educational placement required. Deaf classrooms for the educable mentally handicapped are part of most large special education systems. Estimates of the incidence of hearing loss among the most severely mentally retarded vary considerably, ranging from 8% to as high as 40% (Lloyd & Reid, 1967; Reynolds & Reynolds, 1979). Even among defined subpopulations, there is little agreement regarding either the incidence or nature of hearing impairment. In Down syndrome populations, for example, estimates of the occurrence of conductive loss, a medically treatable condition, range from 22 to 41%, sensorineural loss ranges from 9 to 17% (Brooks, Wooley, & Kanjilal, 1972). Contributing to the difficulty of obtaining generalizable data on hearing loss among the mentally retarded are the high numbers reported as "untestable" or "difficult to test" by conventional behavioral audiometry. Again, figures vary, rising from 24% of all institutionalized mentally retarded as untestable by behavioral audiometry to a high of 97% as untestable for the most mentally retarded categories. A recently completed 4½ year study, using auditory brainstem response (ABR) testing with 122 profoundly mentally retarded children from a single residential facility, found that: (a) 32% of this population showed, by ABR, a hearing loss (12% conductive loss and 20% sensorineural loss), (b) of the 15% with bilateral sensorineural loss, 7% had losses in the mild to moderate loss range and 8% in the severe to profound range, and (c) that six of nine children fitted with a hearing aid accepted the aid and displayed positive behavioral or attentional changes, despite their severe mental retardation (Stein et al., 1987). The availability of ABR now makes it possible to identify hearing loss in the severely mentally retarded, the necessary first step in providing the otologic and audiologic care that far too often this population has not received.

Perceptual or *learning disabilities* beyond that directly attributable to hearing impairment are increasingly recognized but still poorly understood. The hard-of-hearing child may demonstrate many of the same auditory processing problems that characterize a hearing learning-disabled child, whereas visual perceptual or processing difficulties present in the deaf child may seriously interfere with acquisition of sign language or reading skills. In each instance, the child is doubly penalized and will require special help from instruction that incorporates knowledge of both hearing impairment and learning disabilities.

A number of studies since 1968 have documented the high prevalence rate of *emotional* or *behavioral problems* among deaf school-age children. Graham and Rutter (1968) found a 15.4% rate of psychiatric disorder among deaf children. Vernon (1969) reported psychological testing indicated 22.5% of a residential school population were emotionally disturbed. Meadow and Schlesinger (1971) indicated 31.2% of surveyed deaf children were emotionally disturbed, 11.6% of whom were severely disturbed. And Freeman, Malkin, and Hastings (1975), through a large-scale survey, found 22.6% of deaf children judged as having a psychiatric disorder of moderate to severe degree. These figures indicate that, in comparison to the general school population, nearly 5 times as many deaf children show signs of emotional disturbance. Among deaf students, the incidence of emotional disturbance is higher among boys and those with additional handicaps.

Some of the more commonly listed symptoms of disturbance shown by deaf children are:

1. Chronic depression,
2. Low frustration tolerance,
3. Overdependence and compliance,
4. Lack of flexibility,
5. Few social contacts,
6. Unusual withdrawal,
7. Attention-getting behavior,
8. Nervous habits,
9. Inappropriate laughter or silliness, and
10. Aggressiveness and potential danger to others.

On the surface, some of the symptoms may not appear to be serious; however, when chronic they may be signs of an underlying pathology that, for example, may limit the development of satisfactory interpersonal relationships, the process responsible for the internalization of rage and control of impulsivity. The adult equivalent of these symptoms can be quite serious.

The two most common factors in the environment of deaf children that can account for their emotional or behavioral differences are the lag in language development and its effect on family communication and socialization, and the psychological response of parents to the diagnosis of hearing impairment. Rainer, Altshuler, and Kallman (1963) and Grinker (1969) emphasized the significance of parental response when they noted that many of the mental health problems of the deaf adult can be traced to deficiencies in early parent–child relationships, unrealistic expectations by parents, and the inability of parents to cope in a healthy manner with the fact that their growing child is different from hearing children and to a certain extent will always be different. The ideal early intervention program must include early diagnosis, comprehensive medical services, a productive strategy for development of language and communication, and psychotherapeutic counseling for parents to help them achieve a satisfactory emotional adjustment to the birth of a hearing-impaired child (Stein & Jabaley, 1981).

Among adult hearing impaired individuals, the psychological or psychiatric consequences of hearing loss may be many and varied. The effect of hearing loss on an elderly person may be isolation, whereas the effect of congenital deafness may be severe enough to require psychiatric hospitalization. Rodda (1974) estimated a 10% incidence of psychosis or borderline problems in the deaf population he studied. Although the incidence of schizophrenia among the deaf is no higher than among the hearing, serious behavioral problems in the deaf population, such as impulsivity, aggressiveness, and antisocial behavior are placed as high as 20–25% (Grinker, 1969; Rainer et al., 1963). These figures refer only to more disturbed deaf adults and do not include those whose emotional disability, although less severe, may have prevented or impaired social or vocational functioning.

The first mental health project for the deaf began in 1955 and led to the establishment of the country's first outpatient mental health clinic that utilized manual or sign language as an aid in diagnosis and treatment (Rainer et al., 1963). Others soon entered the field, with the following among the first programs: St. Elizabeth's Hospital, Washington, DC; the David T. Siegel Institute, Michael Reese Hospital, Chicago, IL; and the University of California at San Francisco Center on Deafness, San Francisco, CA. Today more than half the states have either specialized inpatient or outpatient mental health services for deaf persons. Comprehensive reviews of the psychiatric, psychological, and psychosocial aspects of deafness and the research and practice of counseling deaf people are contained in edited texts by Stein, Mindel, and Jabaley (1981) and Anderson and Watson (1985).

The *deaf–blind* are a special category of handicapped children and adults. As a result of the impact of the 1963–1965 rubella epidemic, believed responsible for an estimated 3,000 deaf-blind births, Regional Centers for Services to Deaf-Blind Children were established by federal and state agencies. The physical and developmental characteristics of 101 deaf-blind children were described by Stein, Palmer, and Weinberg (1982). Approximately one half had major signs of neurologic problems (abnormal head size, abnormal EEG, neuromuscular disorders). A severe hearing handicap was twice as common as a severe visual disability and three quarters of these children were significantly retarded in language and general development. The estimate of the number who, as adults, might become fairly independent in terms of daily skills and vocational effort was virtually zero; most, if not all, would probably require supervised care for the rest of their lives. With the exception of maternal rubella, the major causes of deaf-blindness have not been eradicated, and earlier and better diagnosis and educational programming may improve the prognosis for babies born suspected deaf-blind. The crucial importance of providing timely and comprehensive diagnostic services is underscored by the results of a study that tested, by ABR, 82 severely developmentally delayed infants and children suspected of being both deaf and blind (Stein, Ozdamar, & Schnabel, 1981). Fully 34, or 43%, of the 82 suspected deaf-blind children had ABR thresholds within the normal hearing range and therefore, technically not deaf as the term is normally defined. Earlier use of ABR in adequately equipped and staffed hospital centers may help separate the truly deaf from those with a functioning peripheral auditory mechanism so that appropriate educational management can be initiated.

SUMMARY

Hearing impairment, the nation's number one handicapping disability, affects some 15.2 to 17.4 million Americans. Most seriously affected are the congenitally or prelingually deafened, whose primary handicap of impaired communication may severely retard educational and vocational achievement. But even those with relatively mild losses can experience isolation and alienation.

Medical and technological advances in the fields of otology and audiology and enlightened interest in the educational and sociological betterment of persons with hearing loss over the past 20 years have had a significant effect. However, many important questions in terms of the pretreatment, habilitation, and rehabilitation of hearing loss remain. The next decade promises that even greater advances will be made, particularly in technology that could enable even the most severely hearing impaired to communicate effectively in a hearing world.

REFERENCES

Anderson, G. B., & Watson, D. (Eds.) (1985). *Counseling deaf people: Research and practice.* Fayetteville: Arkansas Rehabilitation, Research and Training Center on Deafness and Hearing Impairment: University of Arkansas.

Brooks, D. N., Wooley, H., & Kanjilal, G. C. (1972). Hearing loss and middle ear disorders in patients with Down's syndrome. *Journal of Mental Deficiency and Research, 16,* 21–29.

Davis, H., & Silverman, S. R. (1970). *Hearing and deafness* (3rd ed.). New York: Holt, Rinehart & Winston.

Djourno, A., & Eyries, C. (1957). Prosthèse auditive par excitation électrique à distance du nerf sensoriel à l'aide d'un bobinage inclus à demeure. *Press Medicale, 35,* 14–17.

Durrant, J. D., & Lovrinic, J. H. (1981). *Basis of hearing science.* Baltimore: Williams & Wilkins.

Freeman, R. F., Malkin, S. F., & Hastings, J. O. (1975). Psychological problems of deaf children and their families: A comparative study. *American Annals of the Deaf, 120,* 391–345.

Flint, R. W. (1979). History of education for the hearing impaired. In L. J. Bradford & W. G. Hardy (Eds.), *Hearing and hearing impairment* (pp. 19–37). New York: Grune & Stratton.

Gentile, A., & Rambin, J. B. (1973). *Reported causes of hearing loss for hearing impaired students, United States: 1970–1971.* Washington, DC: Office of Demographic Studies, Gallaudet College.

Graham, P., & Rutter, M. (1968). Organic brain dysfunction and child psychiatric disorder. *British Medical Journal, 3,* 695–700.

Grinker, R. R. (Ed.). (1969). *Psychiatric diagnosis, therapy, and research on the psychotic deaf.* Washington, DC: Social Rehabilitation Service, Department of Health, Education and Welfare.

House, W. F., & Urban, J. (1973). Long-term results of electrode implantation and electronic stimulation of the cochlea of man. *Annals of Otology, Rhinology, and Laryngology, 82,* 504–510.

Jacobson, J. T. (Ed.) (1985). *The auditory brainstem response.* San Diego: College-Hill.

Jerger, J. (Ed.). (1973). *Modern developments in audiology.* New York: Academic.

Joint Committee on Infant Hearing. (1982). Position statement. *Journal of Pediatrics, 70,* 496.

Konigsmark, B. W. (1972). Genetic hearing loss with no associated abnormalities: A review. *Journal of Speech and Hearing Disorders, 37,* 89–99.

Konigsmark, B. W., & Gorlin, R. J. (1976). *Genetic and metabolic deafness.* Philadelphia: Saunders.

Kryter, K. D. (1970). *The effects of noise on man.* New York: Academic.

Lenneberg, F. H. (1967). *Biological foundations of language.* New York: John Wiley & Sons.

Lipscomb, D. (1979). Noise and society. In L. J. Bradford & W. G. Hardy (Eds.), *Hearing and hearing impairment* (pp. 515–530). New York: Grune & Stratton.

Lloyd, L. J., & Reid, M. J. (1967). The incidence of hearing impairment in an institutionalized mentally retarded population. *American Journal of Mental Deficiency, 71,* 746–763.

Meadow, K. P., & Schlesinger, H. S. (1971). The prevalence of behavioral problems in a population of deaf school children. *American Annals of the Deaf, 116,* 346–348.

Michelson, R. P. (1971). Electrical stimulation of the human cochlea. *Archives of Otolaryngology, 93,* 317–323.

Millar, J. B., Tong, Y. C., & Clark, G. M. (1984). Speech processing for cochlear implant prostheses. *Journal of Speech and Hearing Research, 27,* 280–296.

Northern, J. L. (Ed.). (1984). *Hearing disorders* (2nd ed.). Boston: Little, Brown.

Northern, J. L., & Downs, M. R. (1984). *Hearing in children*. Baltimore: Academic Press.

Özdamar, Ö., Kraus, N., & Stein, L. (1983). Auditory responses in infants with bacterial meningitis; I. Audiological evaluation. *Archives of Otolaryngology, 109,* 13–18.

Pollack, D. (1970). *Educational audiology for the limited hearing infant.* Springfield, IL: Charles C. Thomas.

Rainer, J. D., Altshuler, K. Z., & Kallman, F. J. (Eds.). (1963). *Family and mental health problems in a deaf population* (2nd ed.). Springfield, IL: Charles C. Thomas.

Reis, P. (1973). *Academic and achievement test results of a national testing program for hearing impaired students.* Office of Demographic Studies. Washington, DC: Gallaudet College.

Reis, P. W. (1982). Hearing ability of persons by sociodemographic and health characteristics: United States. In *Vital and health statistics.* Series 10, No. 140. DHHS Pub No. PHS 82–1568. Public Health Service. Washington, DC: U.S. Government Printing Office.

Reynolds, W. M., & Reynolds, S. (1979). Prevalance of speech and hearing impairment of non-institutionalized mentally retarded adults. *American Journal of Mental Deficiency, 84,* 62–66.

Rintelman, W. F. (Ed.) (1979). *Hearing assessment.* Baltimore: University Park.

Rodda, M. (1974). Behavioral disorders in deaf clients. *Journal of the Rehabilitation of the Deaf, 7,* 1–13.

Rose, D. E. (Ed.). (1978). *Audiological assessment* (2nd ed.). Englewood Cliffs, NJ: Prentice-Hall.

Schein, J. D., & Delk, M. C. (1974). *The deaf population of the United States.* Silver Spring, MD: National Association of the Deaf.

Schildroth, A. N. (1982). *Annual survey of hearing impaired children and youth, 1980–81.* Washington DC: The Gallaudet Research Institute, Center for Assessment and Demographic Studies, Gallaudet College.

Simons, F. B. (1966). Electrical stimulation of the auditory nerve in man. *Archives of Otolaryngology, 84,* 24–76.

Stein, L., & Jabaley, T. (1981). Early identification and parent counselling. In L. Stein, G. Mindel, & T. Jabaley (Eds.), *Deafness and mental health.* New York: Grune & Stratton.

Stein, L., Kraus, N., Özdamar, Ö., Cartee, C., Jabaley, T., Jeantet, C., & Reed, N. (1987). Hearing loss is an institutionalized mentally retarded population. Identification by auditory brainstem response. *Archives of Otolaryngology, 113,* 32–35.

Stein, L., Mindel G., & Jabaley, T. (Eds.) (1981). *Deafness and mental health.* New York: Grune & Stratton.

Stein, L., Palmer, P., & Weinberg, B. (1982). Characteristics of a young deaf-blind population. *American Annals of the Deaf, 127,* 828–837.

Stein, L., Özdamar, Ö., & Schnabel, M. (1981). Auditory brainstem responses with suspected deaf-blind children. *Ear and Hearing, 2,* 30–40.

Swigart, E. T. (Ed.). (1986). *Neonatal hearing screening.* San Diego: College-Hill.

Vernon, M. (1969). *Multipli handicapped deaf children: Medical, educational, and psychological considerations.* (CEC Research Monograph.) Washington, DC: Council for Exceptional Children.

Ward, W. D. (1984). Noise-induced hearing loss. In J. L. Northern (Ed.), *Hearing disorders* (2nd ed., pp. 143–152). Boston: Little, Brown.

CHAPTER 18

Hyperactivity and Attention Deficit Disorders

Mark D. Rapport

Hyperactivity, or more recently, attention deficit disorder (ADD) with hyperactivity (American Psychiatric Association, 1980) is one of the most serious and enigmatic developmental disabilities of childhood for which there is no known cure. Over 2,500 articles (Ross & Ross, 1982) have appeared on the subject, dating back to the earliest descriptions of the disorder in the 1860s (Still, 1902). Prevalence estimates suggest it occurs in 3 to 5% of the school-age population (Barkley, 1981), or approximately one child in every classroom (O'Leary, 1980), and accounts for up to 30% of referrals to child psychological and pediatric clinics in the United States (Safer & Allen, 1976).

Several myths have been perpetuated regarding the course and treatment of the disorder (see review by Whalen & Henker, 1980) with perhaps the most serious one being that ADD children eventually outgrow (i.e., developmentally mature) their problems. Long-term follow-up studies of 1 (Quinn & Rapoport, 1975), 2 (Riddle & Rapoport, 1976), 3 (Weiss, Kruger, Danielson, & Elman, 1975), 5 (Minde et al., 1971), and 10 (Hechtman, Weiss, Finklestein, Werner, & Benn, 1976) years, however, have not substantiated these claims. As adolescents, ADD children continue to evince distractability, emotional immaturity, poor goal maintenance, deficits in rule-governed behavior, impulsivity, and inferior results on academic and cognitive tests (Weiss & Hechtman, 1979). Consequently, findings of low self-esteem, educational underachievement, and depression place these children at risk for adult psychopathy (see review by Wender, Reimherr, & Wood, 1981).

Of further dismay are the recent findings reported by Satterfield and his colleagues (1982), who prospectively followed 110 hyperactive and 88 prematched normal-control boys from early childhood through adolescence. Institutionalization rates for the hyperactive boys were more than 19 times higher, and rates of serious and multiple criminal offenses up to 26 and 28 times higher, respectively, compared to normal controls. This suggests a strong relationship between childhood hyperactivity, juvenile delinquency, and institutionalization.

Due to the rather pessimistic outcome associated with the disorder, researchers have begun to investigate related and possibly contributing areas, such as causal attributions (Bugental, Whalen, & Henker, 1977; Whalen & Henker, 1976), risk factors (Firestone & Prabhu, 1983; Waldrop & Goering, 1971), diet variables (Feingold, 1976), environmental factors (Jacob, O'Leary, & Rosenblad, 1978), specific setting characteristics (Whalen et al., 1978), social skills (Pelham, O'Bryan, & Paluchowski, 1978), stimulus governance (Lesnik-Oberstein, van der Vlugt, Hoencamp, Juffermans, & Cohen, 1978), brain abnormalities (Carparulo et al., 1981), the differential effects of reinforcement and punishment schedules (Cunningham & Knights, 1978; Douglas & Parry, 1983; Firestone & Douglas, 1975), physiological correlates (Delamater & Lahey, 1983), family interactions (Tallmadge & Barkley, 1983), frustration tolerance (Rapport, Tucker, Du Paul, Merlo, & Stoner, 1986), distractibility (Radosh & Gittelman, 1981), and attentional deployment strategies (Goldberg & Konstantareas, 1981).

In a similar vein, several investigations, known collectively as the "relative efficacy studies" (Gadow, 1984), have examined the most popular treatments for attention deficit disorder, including various forms of behavior, drug (primarily the psychostimulants and more recently, imipramine and desipramine), and cognitive therapies.

The present chapter will review and summarize many of these studies in an attempt to provide the reader with an accurate description of the disorder, an overview of epidemiological findings, and a discussion of relevant developmental and educational issues. For those charged with diagnosing and caring for ADD children, the chapter section covering assessment and treatment may be most germane. Finally, in keeping with tradition, a section on current and future research is offered, followed by a chapter summary.

DESCRIPTION OF THE DISORDER

Core Components

Historically, researchers and clinicians stressed the overt fidgetiness, restlessness, and gross motor overactivity of the disorder (Chess, 1960; Wender, 1971; Werry, 1968; Werry & Sprague, 1970) which were thought to diminish in most children as they approached adolescence. A conceptual shift regarding the core features of ADD children has subsequently redirected this emphasis to diagnostically more relevant and pervasive behavior problems, such as deficits in impulse control (Brown & Sleator, 1979; Rapport, DuPaul, Stoner, Birmingham, & Masse, 1985), attention (Douglas, 1972), problem solving (Douglas, 1980), and rule-governed behavior (Barkley, 1981; 1982).

This shift in diagnostic emphasis occurred largely as a result of Douglas's work (1972), which suggested that the primary deficiency of ADD children was in their ability to "stop, look, and listen", (i.e., to sustain attention and inhibit impulsive responding in response to situational demands), and long-term follow-up studies showing continued difficulties in these areas (as well as others), despite a maturational reduction in overactivity per se (Weiss, Hechtman, & Perlman, 1978).

As a result, the latest addition of the *Diagnostic and Statistical Manual of Mental Disorders (DSM-III;* American Psychiatric Association, 1980) has replaced the label "hyperactivity" or "hyperkinetic reaction of childhood" with *attention deficit disorder* (ADD) *with hyperactivity* (see Table 18-1). The *DSM-III* further distinguishes between ADD with and without associated hyperactivity (referring here to the historical components of excessive activity and fidgetiness); however, there is minimal evidence or reason to substantiate the differential diagnosis to date (King & Young, 1982).

Two additional sets of diagnostic criteria that have been elaborated in recent years may serve to delineate and further clarify the nature of ADD children. The first is a result of Loney's (1980) extensive work,

Table 18-1. Diagnostic Criteria for Attention Deficit Disorder with Hyperactivity

---

The child displays, for his or her mental and chronological age, signs of developmentally inappropriate inattention, impulsivity, and hyperactivity. The signs must be reported by adults in the child's environment, such as parents and teachers. Because the symptoms are typically variable, they may not be observed directly by the clinician. When the reports of teachers and parents conflict, primary consideration should be given to the teacher reports because of greater familiarity with age-appropriate norms. Symptoms typically worsen in situations that require self-application, as in the classroom. Signs of the disorder may be absent when the child is in a new or a one-to-one situation.

The number of symptoms specified is for children between the ages of 8 and 10, the peak age for referral. In younger children, more severe forms of the symptoms and a greater number of symptoms are usually present. The opposite is true of older children.

A.   *Inattention.* At least three of the following symptoms:
   (1)   often fails to finish things he or she starts
   (2)   often doesn't seem to listen
   (3)   easily distracted
   (4)   has difficulty concentrating on schoolwork or other tasks requiring sustained attention
   (5)   has difficulty sticking to a play activity

B.   *Impulsivity.* At least three of the following symptoms:
   (1)   often acts before thinking
   (2)   shifts excessively from one activity to another
   (3)   has difficulty organizing work (this not being due to cognitive impairment)
   (4)   needs a lot of supervision
   (5)   frequently calls out in class
   (6)   has difficulty awaiting turn in games or group situations

C.   *Hyperactivity.* At least two of the following symptoms:
   (1)   runs about or climbs on things excessively
   (2)   has difficulty sitting still or fidgets excessively
   (3)   has difficulty staying seated
   (4)   moves about excessively during sleep
   (5)   is always "on the go" or acts as if "driven by a motor"
D.   Onset before the age of 7
E.   Duration of at least 6 months
F.   Not due to schizophrenia, affective disorder, or severe or profound mental retardation

---

Note: From the *Diagnostic and Statistical Manual of Mental Disorders,* 3rd ed., by the American Psychiatric Association, 1980, Washington, DC: Author.

suggesting a poorer adolescent outcome in ADD children presenting with a history of conduct disturbance or aggressive behavior. Thus, a diagnosis of ADD with or without aggressiveness may prove beneficial, especially in treatment planning. The second set of criteria were developed by Barkley (1982) and tend to be more rigorous yet easier to apply than those of the *DSM-III*, as they provide specific guidelines regarding normative criteria, onset, and duration of symptoms. He defines attention deficit disorder as:

a developmental disorder of attention, impulse control, and rule-governed

behavior (compliance, self-control, and problem solving) that arises early in development, is significantly chronic and pervasive in nature, and is not attributable to mental retardation, deafness, gross neurologic impairment or severe emotional disturbance (i.e., psychosis or autism.) p.89.

The most notable improvement of Barkley's (1982) criteria over those provided in the *DSM-III* (1980) is not so much in the definition as the operationalization of diagnostic criteria (see Table 18-2). These and other criteria will be discussed more fully in the assessment section (see also Barkley, 1982, for a detailed discussion).

Table 18-2. Barkley's (1982) Criteria for Defining Hyperactivity in Children

1.	Parent and/or teacher complaints of poor attention span, impulsivity, restlessness, and inability to restrict behavior as a situation demands.
2.	These complaints of behavior must place the child 2 standard deviations above the mean for his age group relative to children of similar chronological or mental age as determined by a well-standardized behavior rating scale of parent or teacher opinion.
3.	The parents must report that the child's behavior has been problematic since 5 years of age (up to 5 years, 11 months).
4.	The chronicity or duration of symptoms as reported by parent or teacher must be at least 1 year for children 6 years of age or younger.
5.	The pervasiveness of the behavior problems is determined by the extent to which the symptoms occur in more than one situation. Using the Home Situations Questionnaire for parent, or the School Situations Questionnaire for teachers, the child must be rated as a problem in at least 50% of the settings on either scale.
6.	The child must have an intellectual estimate of at least 70 or higher on a well-standardized measure of intelligence, or his or her symptoms as measured in Number 2 are compared against children of similar mental age.
7.	The child cannot display symptoms of autism or psychosis, as defined in the *DSM-III*, or show evidence of blindness, deafness, severe language delay, or gross neurologic disease.

Note: Criteria are adapted from "Guidelines for defining hyperactivity in children (Attention Deficit Disorder with Hyperactivity)" by R. Barkley, 1982, in B. Lahey & A. Kazdin (Eds.), *Advances in Child Clinical Psychology*, Vol 5, New York: Plenum. Copyright 1982 by Plenum Press. Reprinted with permission.

The core components of the disorder (inattention, impulsivity, and hyperactivity) have been extensively documented in both laboratory and field settings. The inattention component is typically characterized by a short attention span, an inability to maintain and selectively attend to relevant stimuli (Busby & Broughton, 1983; Douglas & Peters, 1979), and distractibility (Bremer & Stern, 1976). There is still disagreement, however, as to whether these children are more distractible or actually seek external stimulation (Douglas & Peters, 1979).

Problems with impulse control are evidenced by an inability to delay responding under appropriate circumstances (Gordon, 1979; Ross & Ross, 1976), failure to consider alternatives to or consequences of one's behavior (Douglas, 1972), deficient delay of gratification skills (Rapport et al., 1986, poor self-control (Douglas, 1980; Hinshaw, Henker, & Whalen, 1984a; Rosenbaum & Baker, 1984), difficulties in regulating behavior in accordance with situational demands (Routh, 1980), and deficiences in learning rule-governed (vs. contingency-governed) behavior (Barkley, 1981, 1982).

Although the exhibition of more overt bodily activity as compared to normal children was once considered the distinguishing characteristic of ADD children, there has been continuing controversy and debate regarding this. In general, objective and reliable measurements of motor activity in this population have yielded inconsistent result (Barkley, 1977) owing to differences in types of activity monitored (e.g., wrist movements vs. quadrant changes), specific setting characteristics (e.g., laboratory vs. classroom), types of measurements employed (e.g., rating scales vs. stabilimetric cushions), source differences (e.g., parents vs. teachers), and length of observations. In perhaps the most rigorous study to date, Porrino et al. (1983) monitored the activity level of 12 hyperactive and 12 matched control children *continuously* (i.e., 24 hours per day) over a 1-week period across settings (home and school) using a recently developed solid-state acceleration-sensitive device. Hyperactives generally exhibited higher levels of motor activity regardless of the time of day (e.g., even during sleep), and most notably during structured school activities.

Secondary Problem Behaviors

In addition to the core components just described, ADD children typically exhibit a wide range of complimentary and secondary problem behaviors. For example, they are typically characterized as less compliant to requests (Campbell, 1975), attention-seeking (Tallmadge & Barkley, 1983), more talkative (Copeland, 1979; Whalen et al., 1978), easily frustrated (Freibergs & Douglas, 1969; Rapport et al., 1986, unusually sensitive to rewards (Parry & Douglas, 1983) and loss of rewards (Douglas & Parry, 1983), and deficient in social skills (King & Young, 1982). They also frequently experience difficulties with peer relationships (King & Young, 1981; Klein & Young, 1979; Milich, Landau, Kilby, & Whitten, 1982; Pelham & Bender, 1982).

Of particular interest are the relationship problems observed between ADD children and their parents. Early investigators frequently attributed the conduct problems of ADD children to faulty parenting. Consequently, several investigations have directly examined the interactions of ADD and normal children with their respective parents. The findings thus far clearly indicate that ADD children are less compliant and more attention-seeking, and also exhibit negative and competing behaviors significantly more often compared to normal parent-child dyads. As a result, the mothers of ADD children issue commands more frequently, are more negative, and provide greater amounts of structure, supervision, and assistance (Tallmadge & Barkley, 1983). Interestingly, ADD children tend to misbehave less in the presence of their fathers. This is most likely due to the rapid deployment of upper limit controls in the latter.

Although the directionality of behavioral sequences is difficult to establish in correlational investigations such as those previously described, the evidence from drug treatment studies strongly supports the notion that parents of ADD children are responding to, rather than causing, the problem behaviors (Barkley & Cunningham, 1979; Humphries, Kinsbourne, & Swanson, 1978).

Additional home problems typically reported by parents of ADD children include: difficulties in getting their children to complete chores and homework, poor listening skills, the need for excessive supervision (especially during family outings, shopping trips, and visits with relatives), risk-taking behaviors, and noncompliance to rules and requests despite negative sanctions.

EPIDEMIOLOGICAL FINDINGS

Researchers have speculated as to the etiologic nature of attention deficit disorder (ADD) since its earliest clinical descriptions. Initially, the disorder was attributed to brain injury or neurological insult (Bradley, 1937; Strauss & Lehtinen, 1947), which was probably correct, given the populations studied at the time (e.g., postencephalitic children). Although a small subsample of ADD children present with histories or evidence of brain trauma, the majority clearly do not (Carparulo et al., 1981; Rie & Rie, 1980; Rutter, 1982). Consequently, the label "minimal brain damage" was replaced with *"minimal brain dysfunction"*, as the latter implied an alteration in brain function without specifying location or nature (Wender, 1971).

The evidence of brain dysfunction in ADD children is equivocal and largely based on inferences drawn from investigations involving (a) responsiveness to psychostimulants, (b) specific areas of the brain thought to be responsible for observed behavior, and (c) basal or reactive differences in physiological activity. Most of these studies involved ADD children, but have also relied heavily on laboratory work with lesioned animals.

Responsivity to Psychostimulants

Bradley's (1937) frequently cited "paradoxical" effects of psychostimulants were the basis of the popular and long-standing hypothesis that a central neurophysiological dysfunction involving catecholamine metabolism was responsible for ADD children's behavior. In corroborative work with laboratory animals, for example, the neurophysiological effects of methylphenidate are to facilitate the action of norepinephrine and dopamine by blocking reuptake from the synapse, inhibiting the action of monoamine oxidase (MAO), and facilitating release of catecholamines (Solanto, 1984). Thus, the response to drug treatment may be viewed as an inhibiting effect such that the range of stimuli attended to and behaviors exhibited are constricted, similar to the stereotypic effects observed in animals at high doses of psychostimulants (Robbins & Sahakian, 1979). As a result, some investigators have suggested that a confirmed diagnosis be based on ADD children's responsiveness to medication (Klein & Gittelman-Klein, 1975), which for obvious reasons, is both inappropriate and misleading. For example, the nature and physiological effects of stimulant medication have been found to be similar in both normal and hyperactive children (Rapoport, Buchsbaum, Weingartner, Zahn, & Ludlow, 1980; Rapoport et al., 1978, Wender, Epstein, Kopin, & Gordon, 1971), which argues against the notion of a specific drug interaction with an organic dysfunction in the latter.

Implicated Areas of the Brain

One of the most appealing and parsimonious explanations regarding ADD has been suggested by Wender (1971, 1972). Based on clinical and empirical observations that ADD children exhibit a lessened ability to learn through reinforcement and punishment, he hypothesized that the primary physiological deficits were related to areas of the limbic system (e.g., medial forebrain bundle and hypothalamus) directly involved with reinforcement and to deficient metabolism (or poor modulation) of monoamine neurotransmitters such as serotonin, dopamine, and norepinephrine (which may be inherited). According to this hypothesis, ADD children should demonstrate a unique sensitivity or reaction to rewards and punishment. Several studies have investigated this possibility and demonstrated that ADD children indeed show an unusual sensitivity to rewards (Douglas & Parry, 1983) and loss of rewards (Freibergs & Douglas, 1969; Parry & Douglas, 1983).

Of particular interest is a recent, large-scale study carried out in the People's Republic of China (Yu-cun & Yu-feng, 1984), which reported significantly lower levels of a central norepinephrine (NE) metabolite (MHPG-SO4) in the urine of ADD children, especially those with positive genetic factors in their family history. Thus, there is at least preliminary evidence that the activity of the central NE system of ADD children is reduced compared to normals, and that a genetic-metabolic hypothesis warrants further investigation.

Others have speculated that the primary deficit of ADD children involves attention, which may be due to defective inhibitory processes in the brain. Consequently, an underaroused or poorly modulated reticular activating system (RAS) has been inculpated (Satterfield & Dawson, 1971; Zentall, 1975, but has received limited empirical support (Callaway, Halliday, & Naylor, 1983; Rosenthal & Allen, 1978; Satterfield, Atoian, Brashers, Burleigh, & Dawson, 1974). Similarly, dysfunction of forebrain inhibition (vs. a simple RAS-arousal hypothesis) has been implicated, which is consistent with behavior exhibited by animals with lesions in these areas, ADD children's poor performance on tasks requiring behavioral inhibition (Gordon, 1979; McClure & Gordon, 1984), and the often cited immaturity that characterizes their behavior.

Differences in Physiological Activity/Reactivity

One of the most compelling hypotheses to date holds that ADD children are either physiologically underaroused and/or experience difficulty in modulating arousal when faced with changing environmental stimuli. In general, moderate states of arousal (used here to refer to the quantitative physiological dimension that reflects an individual's capability for processing incoming stimuli) are considered necessary for optimal psychological functioning (Hebb, 1955) and have traditionally been portrayed as an inverted U-shaped (i.e., quadratic) function. Conversely, lower arousal levels have been shown to be insufficient for adequate performance, whereas supraoptimal levels interfere with task execution (Bindra, 1959; Yerkes & Dodson, 1908). A similar U-type relationship also has been demonstrated between arousal and attention (Kahneman, 1973).

Initial speculation regarding this hypothesis was based on observed patterns of EEG underarousal in ADD children (Hastings & Barkley, 1978). However, research has not yielded autonomic or electroencephelogram (EEG) variables that consistently differentiate these children from normals (Solanto, 1984). Yet, other investigators have presented evidence of poorly modulated arousal levels (as opposed to basal differences) when faced with task demands (Firestone & Douglas, 1975), lower electrodermal responsiveness to stimuli as compared to normals (Cohen & Douglas, 1972; Zahn, Abate, Little, & Wender, 1975), reduced cardiac orienting responses (Porges, Walter, Korb, & Sprague, 1975; Sroufe, Sonies, West, & Wright, 1973; Zahn et al., 1975), and an unusual inclination by ADD children to seek stimulation (Douglas, 1974; Douglas & Peters, 1979; Zentall & Zentall, 1976). Conversely, reducing stimulation appears to have little or no effect on their behavior, or in some cases, increases their activity levels (Cruickshank, Bentzen, Ratzeburg, & Tannhauser, 1961), especially when having to repeat a task.

Other Factors

A plethora of other factors have been associated with ADD, including inadequate environmental stimulation (Tizard, 1968), environmental constraints such as crowding (McNamara, 1972), lack of attention by proximate adults (Gewirtz, Bauer, & Roth, 1958), minor physical anomalies (Rapoport & Quinn, 1975), hereditary mechanisms (Cantwell, 1972, 1975; Stewart, Cummings, Singer, & deBlois, 1981), chemical toxins such as lead poisoning (Millar, Schroeder, Mushak, & Boone, 1981), an atypical interaction between temperament, environment, and care-givers (Whalen & Henker, 1980), and diet (Feingold, 1976) or food colorings (Rose, 1978). Interestingly, the latter two variables have received a disproportionate amount of publicity, owing to their simplistic and intuitive appeal, despite a clear lack of empirical support (Conners, 1980; Mattes & Gittelman, 1981).

Due to the range and diversity of factors associated with ADD, many have come to view the disorder as a final commom pathway by which a variety of toxic, congenital, and environmental influences are expressed (Rapoport & Quinn, 1975). Unfortunately, the usefulness of corollaries or "marker variables" as explanations of behavior is limiting and adumbrates the need for investigations that focus on establishing functional relationships. At present, one may comfortably take the position that the nature of the underlying deficits in ADD children remains poorly understood.

DEVELOPMENTAL ISSUES

The developmental course of an attention deficit disorder has received considerable attention over the past decade in an effort to better understand and identify children at risk. As stated earlier, professionals initially considered hyperactivity a disorder limited to childhood, which subsided or disappeared during adolescence. Clearly, this is not the case with many (and probably most) ADD children and is reflected in the latest edition of the *Diagnostic and Stastistical Manual.* The *DSM-III* (1980) describes three characteristic courses of the disorder: (a) a persistence of all symptomatology into adulthood, (b) a continuance of the primary symptoms (inattention and impulsivity) into adulthood, with an abatement of the overactivity component as the child nears adolescence (residual type), and (c) a disappearance of all symptoms at puberty. The relative frequency of these courses is unknown, nor are they supported by empirical evidence.

Infancy and Early Childhood

Many parents of ADD children present with positive histories of pre-, pari-, and postnatal complications that may place their children at risk. The most commonly described ones include difficulties with pregnancy, maternal smoking, ingestion of prescribed drugs to avert miscarriage, obstetrical complications during delivery, jaundice at birth, low birthweight, and the presence of minor physical anomalies (see review by Firestone & Prabhu, 1983).

During the post- or neonatal period, complaints of difficult temperament are common. Problems related to feeding, such as colic, specific food preferences, and milk allergies, are frequently described by parents, as well as irritable mood and abnormal sleep patterns (Barkley, 1981). It is important to note, however, that not all ADD children present with all or even some of these difficulties and that many parents are poor historians and have no basis by which to draw comparisons regarding normal child development.

More commonly, parents experience their first glimpse of what is in store for them as the child becomes mobile. Aside from a generally higher activity level per se, ADD children are typically described as always on the go, into everything, energetic, fearless, and out of the crib and playpen at an early age. Consequently, they are more prone to accidental poisonings, accidents, and general mischief (although usually in search of stimulation or out of curiosity as opposed to malicious intent). In response, parents must maintain a constant vigil and take precautions such as fencing off safety areas. They generally spend much of their time chasing or cleaning up after their child, narrowly avoiding near-misses, and saying "No"! Many parents report a more stable sleep pattern at this age, yet when asked what their child's bed looks like in the morning, generally reply "a mess".

Other problems commonly reported during the first 5 years of development include frequent colds, upper respiratory tract infections, ear infections, excessive demands for attention, increased aggressiveness, immature interactions with siblings and other children, and difficulty playing alone (The "Mom, what can I do now"? phrase becomes overused by age 5). It is worth noting that although ADD children are typically more troublesome and require more supervision, they do have their "good" days and are frequently described by parents and caregivers as cute,

impish, sensitive, and as having robust personalities.

Middle Childhood

Between the ages of 6 and 12 years, ADD children continue to demonstrate difficulties with peer relationships, impulsivity (poor self-control), inadequate delay skills (easily frustrated), and listening to and complying with parental requests. These deficiencies are exacerbated as they enter school, and if the child has not been referred for treatment previously, he or she most certainly will be forthright (due to most teachers' familiarity with age-appropriate norms and the demands for sustained attention in school settings). In many cases, however, the child will be excused as "immature" by well-meaning but misinformed school personnel, and held back or marginally passed into the next grade with the hope that she or he will "mature" over the summer months.

Adolescence

As noted earlier, the adolescent outcome for many ADD children is characterized by delinquency or antisocial behavior, alcohol abuse, poor peer relationships (they tend to establish friendships with children who also seek a high level of environmental stimulation), continued underachievement in school, emotional immaturity, and an impulsive response style. Fidgetiness has usually replaced the excessive motor activity by adolescence (Shaffer & Greenhill, 1979), but continued difficulties in paying attention remain (Weiss, 1975).

Adulthood

Several long-term studies are now available regarding the outcome (Weiss & Hechtman, 1979) and treatment (Wender, et al., 1981) of ADD children as adults, the interested reader is referred to these sources for more extensive reviews. As young adults, ADD persons generally gain some control over their impulsivity, with a resulting decrease in delinquency, and are able to adjust surprisingly well to occupational settings. Conversely, many problems remain, such as low self-esteem (Mann & Greenspan, 1976), an increased frequency of psychopathy (Borland & Heckman, 1976), alcoholism (Tarter, McBride, Buonpane, & Schneider, 1977), and labile mood (Shelley & Riester, 1972).

Comprehensive reviews regarding the developmental course and adult outcome of ADD children are available from several sources (Ross & Ross, 1976; Shaffer & Greenhill, 1979; Weiss, 1975; Weiss & Hechtman, 1979; Weiss et al., 1978).

EDUCATIONAL ISSUES

There is consensus among professionals that the direct and indirect effects of educational experiences (or a lack thereof) have a profound influence on a child's development and adult life. The school environment sets the stage for the development of social skills, academic competence, self-esteem, and adult–child relationships, to name a few. It is a setting in which children can be excited about or turned-off to learning. Hence, it becomes an especially critical and realistic concern for those involved in educating and treating ADD children.

The voluminous literature to date attests to the difficulties ADD children experience in educational settings, wherein their greatest behavioral deficits (sustaining attention and impulsivity) are challenged on a daily basis. Not surprisingly, these children have more failing grades, experience a disproportionately higher number of grade-level retentions, are frequently placed in special education classrooms (Cantwell & Satterfield, 1978; Minde et al., 1971), and generally underachieve (Lambert & Sandoval, 1980), despite their intellectual abilities. Their school behavior typically results in poor peer relationships (Pelham & Bender, 1982), rejection by classmates (Milich et al., 1982), low self-esteem (Campbell, Endman, & Bernfield, 1977; Mendelson, Johnson, & Stewart, 1971), and frequent referrals to authorities. Of further concern are the relatively recent findings that 50% (Lambert & Sandoval, 1980) to 80%

(Safer & Allen, 1976) of ADD children experience some type of learning disability. The empirical relationship between these two diagnoses has been addressed in several studies (Anderson, Halcomb, & Doyle, 1973; Delamater, Lahey, & Drake, 1981; Doyle, Anderson, & Halcomb, 1976).

The classroom behavior of ADD children is typically characterized by inattention, a failure to complete assignments on a consistent basis, difficulty following directions, motor restlessness, variability of mood, carelessness in completing academic work, difficulty staying seated, a proclivity to pester other children, and disruptive behavior (Rapport, 1983). These behaviors generally reflect the underlying deficits of ADD children: impulsivity and the inability to sustain attention.

The design and implementation of school-based treatment protocols over the past decade initially focused on reducing excessive motor movement (Doubros & Daniels, 1966), disruptiveness (O'Leary, Pelham, Rosenbaum, & Price, 1976), and out-of-seat behavior (Twardosz & Sajwaj, 1972). Many investigators found, however, that simply reducing or eliminating problem behaviors was insufficient for successful school functioning, that is, the programs fell under the "dead man rule", (Dr. Ogden Linsley is credited with originating this rule, which purports that if a "dead man" can successfully fulfill the imposed contingencies, then the program is of limited value — it doesn't teach adaptive behavior). Consequently, two areas of research inquiry developed.

The first area involves the identification of critical treatment parameters that are directly related to school functioning (see review by Rapport, 1983). For example, investigators have found that certain types of within-task stimulation (Radosh & Gittelman, 1981; Zentall, Zentall, & Booth, 1978), such as appealing distractors on a child's paper, tend to interfere with ADD's children's academic performance. Similarly, the use of mild, negative feedback (Cunningham & Knights, 1978; Firestone & Douglas, 1977) provided on a contingent (Douglas & Parry, 1983) and frequent basis

(Freibergs & Douglas, 1969) is a more effective scheduling strategy. When applications are extended to the school environment, it is important to target academic completion and accuracy rates as opposed to social deportment (Ferritor, Buckholdt, Hamblin, & Smith, 1972; Rapport, 1983), and to allow self-pacing in completing assignments (Whalen et al., 1978, Whalen & Henker, 1980). Interestingly, the use of positive reinforcement and material rewards has been found to promote erratic and impulsive responding in many ADD children (Penney, 1967; Penney & Lupton, 1961; Witte & Grossman, 1971).

The second area of inquiry has focused on the development of school-based intervention strategies. The majority of work in this area has involved comparing individual to group contingencies (Rapport, Murphy, & Bailey, 1980); investigating the effects of teacher attention and reprimands (Rosen, O'Leary, Joyce, Conway, & Pfiffner, 1984); and increasing academic productivity via token delivery (Ayllon, Layman, & Kandel, 1975; Ayllon & Roberts, 1974; Robinson, Newby, & Ganzel, 1981), response cost (Rapport, Murphy, & Bailey, 1982), or teacher/parent management techniques (O'Leary & Pelham, 1978).

When one combines the available knowledge from the two areas of inquiry, the basis for a school-based, empirical treatment approach emerges. After completing a thorough diagnostic work-up (see Assessment section), the child's curriculum should be carefully scrutinized to insure that he or she is working on an appropriate level. Curricula materials should be devoid of highly salient stimuli (e.g., colored stars), broken-up into short assignments to minimize frustration, and preferably arranged using the Premack Principle (i.e., less interesting assignments followed by highly interesting ones in an alternating sequence). Instructions should be written (when possible) and limited to one assignment area (vs. multiple instructions). Once the child demonstrates an understanding of the assignment, she or he should be set on-task and allowed a reasonable amount of time to complete the work, with short breaks interspersed at regular intervals

(depending on the child's age and level of assignment difficulty). A feedback system that minimizes interruptions, provides immediate negative (albeit mild) consequences for academic nonproductivity, requires minimal teacher involvement (e.g., response cost; see Rapport et al., 1982), and circumvents the possibility of a no-win situation (i.e., the child should not be able to beat the system by losing all points or tokens) should be formally introduced to the child. It is important that the child participate in this process and in the selection of potential reinforcers. In the past, I have had the most success with "earnables," which involve structured free time and normally scheduled activities (e.g., working on a special project. A teacher should avoid buying the child out with edibles and material rewards (which soon lose their effectiveness or become too costly), and establish a firm time period(s) for reinforcement delivery that is not too distant from the work period (i.e., avoid home-based or after-school consequences when possible — these children are impulsive and have inadequate delay skills!). If possible, establish a reasonable relationship between what the child is working on and how he or she might use this skill in the near future (i.e., experiential learning strategy).

Two additional recommendations involve extracurricular assistance. Because many of these children attend special remedial classes, it is important to adjust the regular classroom assignments accordingly. I have seen several of these children come back from special tutorials and be required to complete their full set of academic class work or face being behind (a frustrating situation even for "normal" children). Summer tutoring is strongly encouraged to maintain previous academic gains, but should be limited to an hour or two, 3 days per week.

The question of whether psychostimulant medication helps the ADD child function better in school is a matter of considerable debate (see review by Gadow, 1984). The answer largely depends on how the medication is prescribed (slowly titrated vs. fixed-dose), whether the child is a "favorable responder," the dosage schedule used (low vs. high), which dependent variables are targeted for evaluative purposes (social behavior vs. academic performance vs. achievement test scores), and the degree/complexity of the child's problems. The use of medication alone and in combination with behavioral interventions will be discussed in the Treatment section of this chapter.

ASSESSMENT

The diagnosis and assessment of an attention deficit disorder is a multifaceted process. It is incumbent upon the clinician to fully understand and appreciate the complexity involved in this process, due to the potential misuse of treatments such as central nervous system (CNS) stimulants and response cost.

Fortunately, the literature is replete with instruments and interview formats specifically developed for diagnosing and assessing ADD children. Several excellent texts have also been devoted to this subject (Barkley, 1981, 1982; Mash & Terdal, 1981; Trites, 1979; Whalen & Henker, 1980). Depicted in Table 18.3 are the most widely used diagnostic instruments, the primary area that they assess, and their respective sources. Obtaining these instruments is a relatively easy process and will provide the clinician with relevant cutoff scores, age-appropriate norms, and specific guidelines for usage.

In addition to the diagnostic and assessment instruments described in Table 18-3, an independent evaluation of the child's school functioning is highly valuable. In general, rates of on-task behavior, percentage of academic work completed, and assignment accuracy should be collected over a 2-week time span (Rapport et al., 1982). This information will prove valuable in treatment planning (e.g., does the child require an in-class treatment program?) and outcome assessment. In evaluating over 60 ADD-H children during the past 3 years, we have found that their "normal" control classmates are typically on-task an average of 75 to 85% of the time, and complete 80% or more of their academic assign-

ments on a daily basis. The importance of these observations will become apparent in the treatment section.

The clinician also will need to rule out childhood disorders that are similar to ADD-H, such as overanxious disorder, separation anxiety, conduct disorder, adjustment disorder with anxious mood, pervasive developmental disorders, oppositional disorder, and Tourette's syndrome. Where appropriate, multiple diagnosis should be made.

TREATMENT

CNS stimulants are the most widely used and best-studied treatments for ADD-H, due to their cost efficiency and demonstrated effects on sustained attention (Rapport, DuPaul, Stoner, & Jones, 1986; Sykes, Douglas, & Morgenstern, 1973), activity level (Porrino et al., 1983), academic performance (Rapport et al., 1980, 1982; 1985), impulsivity (Brown & Sleator, 1979; Rapport, DuPaul, Stoner, Birmingham, & Masse, 1985), parent–child relationships (Barkley, Karlsson, Strzelecki, & Murphy, 1984), social behavior (Hinshaw et al., 1984a), information processing (Reid & Borkowski, 1984), and classroom deportment (Conners & Taylor, 1980). According to a recent survey of medication trends in the United States (Safer & Krager, 1983), approximately 2.6% of public elementary school children are prescribed medication for hyperactivity, with methylphenidate (Ritalin) being the most widely used (91% of the cases).

Not surprisingly, there has been considerable controversy and debate regarding the long-term clinical efficacy and use of CNS stimulants with ADD children. For example, some authors have presented the issue in moralistic terms (Box, 1978; Schrag & Divoky, 1975) or as a choice between "pills and skills" (O'Leary, 1980). Arguments of this type make for entertaining cocktail conversation, but obfuscate the need for well-controlled empirical investigations. Most informed professionals would agree that psychostimulants have been overprescribed and/or inadequately monitored in the past; however, the misuse

Table 18-3. Diagnostic Instruments and Primary Area of Assessment

NAME OF INSTRUMENT	AREA OF ASSESSMENT AND SOURCE
1. *Diagnostic and Statistical Manual of Mental Disorders (DSM-III)*	Diagnostic criteria for ADD and ADD-H (American Psychiatric Association, 1980). Clinician ratings.
2. SNAP Rating Scale	Incorporates the *DSM-III* diagnostic criteria in a rating scale format (Swanson, Nolan, & Pelham, 1981). Clinician, teacher, or parent ratings.
3. Werry-Weiss-Peters Activity Scale	Assesses the child's behavior in the familial and surrounding environment (Routh, Schroeder, & O'Tuama, 1974). Parent ratings.
4. Barkley's Home Situations Questionnaire	Assesses the occurrence and severity of the child's behavior at home (Barkley, 1981). Parent ratings.
5. Conners Parent and Teacher Rating Scales	Useful for diagnosis and assessing treatment outcome. Yields factor groupings (Goyette, Conners, & Ulrich, 1978). Parent and teacher ratings.
6. Abbreviated Conners Teacher Rating Scale (ACTRS)	Shortened version of Number 5 above. Useful in screening and assessing treatment outcome (Werry, Sprague, & Cohen, 1975). Teacher ratings.
7. ADD-H: Comprehensive Teacher Rating Scale (ACTeRS)	A recently developed rating scale for diagnosis and treatment monitoring — emphasis on attention (Ullmann, Sleator, & Sprague, in press). Teacher ratings.
8. Personality Inventory for Children (PIC)	Provides a comprehensive personality profile. Four scales distinguish ADD children from other clinical groups: adjustment, hyperactivity, delinquency, and social skills (Lachar, 1982). Parent ratings.
9. Teacher's Self-Control Rating Scale (TSCRS) and Children's Perceived Self-Control Scale (CPSCS)	Both rating scales are useful in assessing children's self-control and perceived competency (Humphrey, 1982). Teacher and child ratings.
10. Parent and Child Interview Formats and Developmental History	Provides specific guidelines for conducting interviews and obtaining a thorough developmental history (Barkley, 1981, 1982; Mash & Terdal, 1981). Clinician use.
11. The Gordon Diagnostic System (GDS) a. Continuous Performance (Vigilance) Task b. Delay Task	A recently developed, empirically based diagnostic instrument that measures attention and impulsivity (Gordon, 1979). Clinician use.
12. Matching Familiar Figures Test	Assesses children's cognitive style in approaching tasks: reflectivity-impulsivity (Kagan, Rosman, Day, Aîbert, & Phillips, 1964). Clinician use.
13. Response Class Matrix	Assesses the interactions and reciprocal influences between the child and his/her parent (Mash, Terdal, & Anderson, 1973). Independent raters.
14. Classroom Observation Code	A recently validated coding system for differentiating ADD from normal children in classroom settings (Abikoff, Gittelman, & Klein, 1980). Independent raters.

of a treatment does not negate its potential value (i.e., *abusus non tollit usum*) (Rapport, 1984).

Over the past several years, two broadly defined areas of empirical research have emerged regarding psychopharmacological treatment. These are pediatric/behavioral psychopharmacology and clinical efficacy studies. The pediatric/behavioral pharmacology area primarily has addressed questions regarding factors that contribute to drug efficacy and action. For example, we have recently found that a child's rate of behavior in a drug-free state contributes to drug efficacy (i.e., the effects are rate-dependent; Rapport, DuPaul, & Smith, 1985; Rapport & DuPaul, 1986). Drug effectiveness also depends on (a) whether a child shows a "favorable response" to medication (Rapport, Stoner, DuPaul, Birmingham, & Tudar, 1985), (b) which behavior is targeted for assessment, that is, behavioral specificity (Rapport et al., 1985; Sprague & Sleator, 1977), and (c) each child's unique responsivity to the drug (Rapport, DuPaul, Stoner, & Jones 1985). Further, a child's body weight appears to have little or nothing to do with drug responsiveness (Rapport & DuPaul, 1986). Thus, clinicians will need to carefully monitor children who are prescribed psychostimulant medication by incorporating several outcome measures (e.g., classroom on-task behavior, academic completion rates and accuracy, social/peer relationship ratings, treatment emergent effect scales) during controlled clinical drug trials.

The most recent clinical efficacy studies have focused on designing new treatments or combining psychostimulant and behavioral treatments as a result of (a) the multifaceted problems that frequently accompany ADD-H (Barkley, 1981, 1983), (b) the relatively poor long-term outcome associated with drug treatment alone (Satterfield et al., 1982), and (c) the equivocal effects of psychostimulants on academic performance (Gadow, 1983). It is worth mentioning that the diminutive effects of stimulant therapy typically cited in long-term outcome studies are tentative at best. For example, there are few, if any, metho-

dologically rigorous studies on long-term outcome (Pelham, 1983); most have been retrospective in nature and are plagued with shortcomings, such as poor medication compliance, high attrition rates, lack of medication continuance, disregard for individual responsivity or responder status, lack of appropriate control groups, and poorly defined groups of children. In addition, children's dosages were ubiquitously determined by ratings of improved social behavior, whereas outcome was based on cognitive and academic measures. We now know, however, that these behaviors are optimized at widely discrepant dosage levels (Rapport, Stoner, DuPaul, Birmingham & Tucker, 1985; Rapport, DuPaul, Stoner, Jones, 1986; Sprague & Sleator, 1977) and largely depend on a given's child's idiosyncratic response and drug-free rate of behavior (Rapport & DuPaul, 1986).

Nevertheless, several of the recent clinical efficacy studies have shown encouraging results by combining psychostimulant treatment with various forms of behavior therapy. For example, the combination of methylphenidate and a cognitive-behavioral intervention has been shown to positively affect ADD children's social behavior (Hinshaw et al., 1984b); however, medication adds little to this intervention when applied to self-control (Hinshaw et al., 1984a). The most positive outcomes associated with a combined treatment approach have focused on ADD children's school performance and/or behavior (see review by Rapport, 1983). In general, various forms of behavior therapy (e.g., home-based reinforcement programs, token systems, parent/teacher management training), combined with methylphenidate, have produced clinical improvement in children's attention and work completion rates (Pelham, Schnedler, Bologna, & Contreras, 1980), social deportment (Gittelman-Klein et al., 1976), emotional adjustment, and academic performance (Firestone, Kelly, Goodman, & Davey, 1981).

The choice as to which treatment(s) to use depends on the child's presenting problems (e.g., school difficulties, poor self-control, aggressiveness, inadequate social skills) and the likely impact of these problems on everyday functioning (i.e., severity). For some ADD-H children, a moderate dose of medication will sufficiently improve attention and school functioning if properly prescribed and titrated. For others (and probably the majority), several different therapeutic interventions will be required, either additively or collectively. A thorough assessment and familiarity with empirically based treatment techniques will prepare the clinician to make these decisions. It should be remembered, however, that there are no cures for ADD-H. Once treatment is removed, the child typically reverts back to his or her previous response style. Thus, other factors, such as the likelihood of treatment compliance, continuance, cooperation, and follow-up, play a critical role in treatment planning.

CURRENT RESEARCH AND FUTURE DIRECTIONS

The present trends in ADD-H research are to establish effective treatment protocols and to better understand the underlying mechanisms that contribute to successful treatment outcome. The focus on treatment is primarily a result of the poor long-term outcome associated with the disorder and recognition by professionals that a monolithic approach cannot adequately address the multifaceted problems exhibited by these children. Thus, researchers are beginning to examine the efficacy of behavioral-cognitive approaches in treating ADD-H children's self-control (Hinshaw et al., 1984a; Rosenbaum & Baker, 1984) and interpersonal difficulties (Hinshaw et al., 1984b).

Similarly, several studies have recently been completed regarding the effects of methylphenidate on ADD-H children's curiosity behavior (Fiedler & Ullman, 1983), parent–child interactions (Barkley et al., 1984), information processing (Reid & Borkowski, 1984), learning (Rapport, Stoner, DuPaul, Birmingham & Tucker, 1985; Stephens, Pelham, & Skinner, 1984),

personality dimensions (Rapport & Siviski, 1983), and impulsivity (Rapport, DuPaul, Stoner, Birmingham & Masse 1985).

Other studies regarding the management of ADD-H children in school (Rosen et al., 1984) and familial environments (Dubey, O'Leary, & Kaufman, 1983), the effects of reinforcement on reaction time (Douglas & Parry, 1983) and concept identification (Parry & Douglas, 1983), and deficient problem-solving abilities (Tant & Douglas, 1982) have yielded promising results.

Finally, several studies currently are underway that examine the contribution of a child's basal physiological activity (Law of Initial Value), pre-drug rate of behavior (rate dependency), and clinic-based test (performance to medication responsivity) as well as the effects of CNS stimulants on search strategies and learned information. Newly developed educational delivery systems, such as computerized instruction, are also being explored as alternative teaching strategies for ADD-H children.

SUMMARY

Attention deficit disorder with hyperactivity appears to be a polythetic (as opposed to monothetic) phenotypic category (i.e., one in which members having the greatest number of shared characteristics [clinical features] are grouped together). Thus, no single characteristic is essential or sufficient for group membership and ADD children should present with behaviors that covary, yet are different from normals and other diagnostic groups of children at a greater than chance occurrence. Multivariate personality research has been plagued with methodological difficulties in identifying core characteristics of ADD, due to differences in source factors and the variability ADD children exhibit across settings. For example, parents may not be as familiar with age-appropriate norms in comparison to teachers (Ross & Pelham, 1981). Also, ADD children do not consistently exhibit the full range of problem behaviors in a physician's office (Sleator & Ullmann, 1981). When source variables are controlled for, however, the evidence of an independent, polythetic ADD syndrome is relatively convincing (Trites & Laprade, 1983).

From a sociobiological approach, ADD children may represent the biological link to our ancestral hunters. It is interesting to speculate that these individuals would have had short attention spans, an ability to cope with highly stimulating and changing environments, and a readiness to act both quickly (impulsively) and aggressively. The continuance of these characteristics in the gene pool would undoubtedly have survival value until recent times. The world as we know it today, however, requires an individual to "stop, look, and listen."

REFERENCES

Abikoff, H., Gittelman, R., & Klein, D. F. (1980). Classroom observation code for hyperactive children: A replication of validity. *Journal of Consulting and Clinical Psychology, 48,* 555–565.

American Psychiatric Association. (1980). *Diagnostic and statistical manual of mental disorders* (3rd ed.). Washington, DC: Author.

Anderson, R. P., Halcomb, C. G., & Doyle, R. B. (1973). The measurement of attentional deficits. *Exceptional Children, 39,* 543–549.

Ayllon, T., Layman, D., & Kandel, H. J. (1975). A behavioral-educational alternative to drug control of hyperactive children. *Journal of Applied Behavior Analysis, 8,* 137–146.

Ayllon, T., & Roberts, M. D. (1974). Eliminating discipline problems by strengthening academic performance. *Journal of Applied Behavior Analysis, 7,* 71–76.

Barkley, R. (1977). A review of stimulant drug research with hyperactive children. *Journal of Child Psychology and Psychiatry, 18,* 137–165.

Barkley, R. (1981). *Hyperactive children: A handbook for diagnosis and treatment.* New York: Guildford.

Barkley, R. A. (1982). Specific guidelines for defining hyperactivity in children (attention deficit disorder with hyperactivity). In B. Lahey & A. Kazdin (Eds.), *Advances in clinical child psychology* (Vol. 5, pp. 137–180). New York: Plenum.

Barkley, R. A. (1983). Hyperactivity. In R. J. Morris & T. R. Kratochwill (Eds.), *The practice of child therapy.* (pp. 87–112) Elmsford, NY: Pergamon.

Barkley, R., & Cunningham, C. (1979). The effects of Ritalin on the mother-child inter-actions of hyperactive children. *Archives of General Psychiatry, 36,* 201–208.

Barkley, R. A., Karlsson, J., Strzelecki, E., & Murphy, J. V. (1984). Effects of age and ritalin dosage on the mother-child interactions of hyperactive children. *Journal of Consulting and Clinical Psychology, 52,* 750–758.

Bindra, D. (1959). *Motivation, a systematic reinterpretation.* New York: Ronald.

Borland, B. L., & Heckman, H. K. (1976). Hyperactive boys and their brothers: A 25-year follow-up study. *Archives of General Psychiatry, 33,* 669–675.

Box, S. (1978, Summer). Hyperactivity: The scandalous silence. *American Educator,* pp. 22–24.

Bradley, C. (1937). The behavior of children receiving benzedrine. *American Journal of Psychiatry, 94,* 577–585.

Bremer, D. A., & Stern, J. A. (1976). Attention and distractability during reading in hyperactive boys. *Journal of Abnormal Child Psychology, 4,* 381–387.

Brown, R. T., & Sleator, E. K. (1979). Methylphenidate in hyperkinetic children: Differences in dose effects on impulsive behavior. *Pediatrics, 64,* 408–411.

Bugental, D. B., Whalen, C., & Henker, B. (1977). Causal attributions of hyperactive children and motivational assumptions of two behavior change approaches: Evidence for an interactionist position. *Child Development, 48,* 874–884.

Busby, K. A., & Broughton, R. J. (1983). Waking ultradian rhythms of performance and motility in hyperkinetic and normal children. *Journal of Abnormal Child Psychology, 11,* 431–442.

Callaway, E., Halliday, R., & Naylor, H. (1983). Hyperactive children's event-related potentials fail to support underarousal and maturational lag theories. *Archives of General Psychiatry, 40,* 1243–1248.

Campbell, S. (1975). Mother-child interaction: A comparison of hyperactive, learning disabled and normal boys. *American Journal of Orthopsychiatry, 45,* 51–57.

Campbell, S. B., Endman, M., & Bernfeld, G. A. (1977). A three-year follow-up of hyperactive pre-schoolers into elementary school. *Journal of Child Psychology and Psychiatry, 18,* 239–249.

Cantwell, D. (1972). Psychiatric illness in the families of hyperactive children. *Archives of General Psychiatry, 27,* 414–417.

Cantwell, D., (1975). *The hyperactive child — Diagnosis, management, current research.* New York: Spectrum.

Cantwell, D. P., & Satterfield, J. H. (1978). The prevalence of academic underachievement in hyperactive children. *Journal of Pediatric Psychology, 3*, 168–171.

Carparulo, B. K., Cohen, D. J., Rothman, S. L., Young, J. G., Katz, J. D., Shaywitz, S. E., & Shaywitz, B. A. (1981). Computed tomographic brain scanning in children with developmental neuropsychiatric disorders. *Journal of the American Academy of Child Psychiatry, 20*, 338–357.

Chess, S. (1960). Diagnosis and treatment of the hyperactive child. *New York Journal of Medicine, 60*, 2379–2385.

Cohen, N. J., & Douglas, V.I. (1972). Characteristics of the orienting response in hyperactive and normal children. *Psychophysiology, 9*, 238–245.

Conners, C. K. (1980). *Food additives and hyperactive children.* New York: Plenum.

Conners, C. K., & Taylor, E. (1980). Pemoline, methylphenidate, and placebo in children with minimal brain dysfunction. *Archives of General Psychiatry, 37*, 922–930.

Copeland, A. P. (1979). Types of private speech produced by hyperactive and nonhyperactive boys. *Journal of Abnormal Child Psychology, 7*, 169–177.

Cruickshank, W. M., Bentzen, F. A., Ratzeburg, F. H., & Tannhauser, M. T. (1961). *A teaching method of brain-injured and hyperactive children* Syracuse, NY: Syracuse University Press.

Cunningham, S. J., & Knights, R. M. (1978). The performance of hyperactive and normal boys under differing reward and punishment schedules. *Journal of Pediatric Psychology, 3*, 195–201.

Delamatar, A. M., & Lahey, B. B. (1983). Physiological correlates of conduct problems and anxiety in hyperactive and learning-disabled children. *Journal of Abnormal Child Psychology, 11*, 85–100.

Delamater, A. M., Lahey, B. B., & Drake, L. (1981). Toward an empirical subclassification of "learning disabilities": A psychophysiological comparison of "hyperactive" and "nonhyperactive" subgroups. *Journal of Abnormal Child Psychology, 9*, 65–77.

Doubros, S. G., & Daniels, G. J. (1966). An experimental approach to the reduction of overactive behavior. *Behaviour Research and Therapy, 4*, 251–258.

Douglas, V. (1972). Stop, look, and listen: The problem of sustained attention and impulse control in hyperactive and normal children. *Canadian Journal of Behavioural Science, 4*, 159–182.

Douglas, V. I. (1974). Sustained attention and impulse control: Implications for the handicapped child. In J. A. Swets & L. L. Elliott (Eds.), *Psychology and the handicapped child* (pp. 149–168). Washington, DC: U.S. Office of Education.

Douglas, V. I. (1980). Treatment and training approaches to hyperactivity: Establishing internal or external control. In C. Whalen & B. Henker (Eds.), *Hyperactive children: The social ecology of identification and treatment.* (pp. 283–317). New York: Academic.

Douglas, V. I., & Parry, P. A. (1983). Effects of reward on delayed reaction time task performance of hyperactive children. *Journal of Abnormal Child Psychology, 11*, 313–326.

Douglas, V., & Peters, K. (1979). Toward a clearer definition of the attentional deficit in hyperactive children. In G. Hale & M. Lewis (Eds.), *Attention and the development of cognitive skills.* (pp. 173–247) New York: Plenum.

Doyle, R. B., Anderson, R. P., & Halcomb, C. G. (1976). Attention deficits and the effects of visual distraction. *Journal of Learning Disabilities, 9*, 59–65.

Dubey, D. R. O'Leary, S. G., & Kaufman, K. F. (1983). Training parents of hyperactive children in child management: A comparative outcome study. *Journal of Abnormal Child Psychology, 11*, 229–246.

Feingold, B. F. (1976). Hyperkinesis and learning disabilities linked to the ingestion of artificial food colors and flavours. *Journal of Learning Disabilities, 9*, 551–559.

Ferritor, D. E., Buckholdt, D., Hamblin, R. L., & Smith, L. (1972). The noneffects of contingent reinforcement for attending behavior on work accomplished. *Journal of Applied Behavior Analysis, 5*, 7–17.

Fiedler, N. L. & Ullman, D. G. (1983). The effects of stimulant drugs on curiosity behaviors of hyperactive boys. *Journal of Abnormal Child Psychology, 11*, 193–206.

Firestone, P., & Douglas, V. (1975). The effects of reward and punishment on reaction times and autonomic activity in hyperactive and normal children. *Journal of Abnormal Child Psychology, 3*, 201–216.

Firestone, P., & Douglas, V. I. (1977). The effects of verbal and material rewards and punishers on the performance of impulsive and reflective children. *Child Study Journal, 7*, 71–78.

Firestone, P., Kelly, M. J., Goodman, J. T., & Davey, J. (1981). Differential effects of parent training and stimulant medication with hyperactives. *American Academy of Child Psychiatry, 20*, 135–147.

Firestone, P., & Prabhu, A. N. (1983). Minor physical anomalies and obstetrical complications: Their relationship to hyperactive, psychoneurotic, and normal children and their families. *Journal of Abnormal Child Psychology, 11,* 207–216.

Freibergs, V., & Douglas, V. I. (1969). Concept learning in hyperactive and normal children. *Journal of Abnormal Child Psychology, 74,* 388–395.

Gadow, K. D. (1983). Effects of stimulant drugs on academic performance in hyperactive and learning disabled children. *Journal of Learning Disabilities, 16,* 290–299.

Gasow, K. D. (1984). *Relative efficacy of pharmacological, behavioral, and combination treatments for enhancing academic performance.* Manuscript submitted for publication.

Gewirtz, J., Bauer, M., & Roth, C. (1958). A note on the similar effects of low social availability of an adult and brief social deprivation on young children's behavior. *Child Development, 29,* 149–152.

Gittelman-Klein, R., Klein, D. F., Abikoff, H., Katz, S., Gloisten, A. C., & Kates, W. (1976). Relative efficacy of methylphenidate and behavior modification in hyperactive children: An interim report. *Journal of Abnormal Child Psychology, 4,* 361–379.

Goldberg, J. O., & Konstantareas, M. M. (1981). Vigilance in hyperactive and normal children on a self-paced operant task. *Journal of Child Psychology and Psychiatry, 22,* 55–63.

Gordon, M. (1979). The assessment of impulsivity and mediating behaviors in hyperactive and nonhyperactive boys. *Journal of Abnormal Psychology, 7,* 317–326.

Goyette, C. H., Conners, C. K., & Ulrich, R. F. (1978). Normative data on the revised Conners Parent and Teacher Rating Scales. *Journal of Abnormal Child Psychology, 6,* 221–236.

Hastings, J. E., & Barkley, R. A. (1978). A review of psychophsiological research with hyperkinetic children. *Journal of Abnormal Child Psychology, 6,* 311–324.

Hebb, D. O. (1955). Drives and the CNS (conceptual nervous system). *Psychological Review, 62,* 413–448.

Hechtman, L., Weiss, G., Finklestein, J., Werner, A., & Benn, R. (1976). Hyperactives as young adults: Preliminary report. *Canadian Medical Journal, 115,* 625–630.

Hinshaw, S. P., Henker, B., & Whalen, C. K. (1984a). Self-control in hyperactive boys in anger-inducing situations: Effects of cognitive-behavioral training and of methylphenidate. *Journal of Abnormal Child Psychology, 12,* 55–77.

Hinshaw, S. P., Henker, B., & Whalen, C. K. (1984b). Cognitive-behavioral and pharmacologic interventions for hyperactive boys: Comparative and combined effects. *Journal of Consulting and Clinical Psychology, 52,* 739–749.

Humphrey, L. L. (1982). Children's and teachers' perspectives on children's self-control: The development of two rating scales. *Journal of Consulting and Clinical Psychology, 50,* 624–633.

Humphries, T., Kinsbourne, M., & Swanson, J. (1978). Stimulant effects on cooperation and social interaction between hyperactive children and their mothers. *Journal of Child Psychology and Psychiatry and Allied Disciplines, 19,* 13–32.

Jacob, R. G., O'Leary, K. D., & Rosenblad, C. (1978). Formal and informal classroom settings: Effects on hyperactivity. *Journal of Abnormal Child Psychology, 6,* 47–59.

Kagan, J., Rosman, B. L., Day, D., Albert, J., & Phillips, W. (1964). Information processing in the child: Significance of analytic and reflective attitudes. *Psychological Monographs, 78,* (1, Whole No. 578).

Kahneman, D. (1973). *Attention and effort.* Englewood Cliffs, NJ: Prentice-Hall.

King, C. A., & Young, R. D. (1981). Peer popularity and peer communication patterns: Hyperactive versus active but normal boys. *Journal of Abnormal Child Psychology, 9,* 465–482.

King, C., & Young, R. D. (1982). Attentional deficits with and without hyperactivity: Teacher and peer perceptions. *Journal of Abnormal Child Psychology, 10,* 483–496.

Klein, D. F., & Gittelman-Klein, R. (1975). Problems in the diagnosis of minimal brain dysfunction and the hyperkinetic syndrome. *International Journal of Mental Health, 4,* 45–60.

Klein, A. R., & Young, R. D. (1979). Hyperactive boys in their classroom: Assessment of teacher and peer perceptions, interactions, and classroom behaviors. *Journal of Abnormal Child Psychology, 7,* 425–442.

Lachar, D. (1982). *Personality Inventory for Children (PIC). Revised format manual supplement.* Los Angeles: Western Psychological Services.

Lambert, N., & Sandoval, J. (1980). The prevalence of learning disabilities in a sample of children considered hyperactive. *Journal of Abnormal Child Psychology, 8,* 33–50.

Lesnik-Oberstein, M., van der Vlugt, H., Hoencamp, E. Juffermans, D., & Cohen, L. (1978). Stimulus-governance and the hyperkinetic syndrome. *Journal of Abnormal Child Psychology, 6,* 407–412.

Loney, J. (1980). Childhood hyperactivity. In R. H. Woody (Ed.), *Encyclopedia of clinical assessment, 1,* 265–285. New York: Jossey-Bass.

Mann, H. B., & Greenspan, S. I. (1976). The identification and treatment of adult brain dysfunction. *American Journal of Psychiatry, 133,* 1013–1017.

Mash, E. J. & Terdal, L. G. (Eds.). (1981). *Behavioral assessment of childhood disorders.* New York: Guildford.

Mash, E. J., Terdal, L. G., & Anderson, K. (1973). The response class matrix: A procedure for recording parent-child interactions. *Journal of Consulting and Clinical Psychology, 40,* 163–164.

Mattes, J. A., & Gittelman, R. (1981). Effects of artificial food colorings in children with hyperactive symptoms. *Archives of General Psychiatry, 38,* 714–718.

McClure, F. D., & Gordon, M. (1984). Performance of disturbed hyperactive and nonhyperactive children on an objective measure of hyperactivity. *Journal of Abnormal Child Psychology, 12,* 561–572.

McNamara, J. J. (1972). Hyperactivity in the apartment-bound child *Clinical Pediatrics, 11,* 371–372.

Mendelson, W., Johnson, N., & Stewart, M.A. (1971). Hyperactive children as teenagers: A follow-up study. *Journal of Nervous and Mental Diseases, 153,* 273–279.

Milar, C., Schroeder, S., Mushak, P., & Boone, L. (1981). Failure to find hyperactivity in preschool children with moderately elevated lead burden. *Journal of Pediatric Psychology, 6,* 85–96.

Milich, R., Landau, S., Kilby, G., & Whitten, P. (1982). Preschool peer perceptions of the behavior of hyperactive and aggressive children. *Journal of Abnormal Child Psychology, 10,* 497–510.

Minde, K., Lewin, D., Weiss, G., Lavigueur, H., Douglas, V., & Sykes, E. (1971). The hyperactive child in elementary school: A 5-year, controlled follow-up. *Exceptional Children, 38,* 215–221.

O'Leary, K. D. (1980). Pills or skills for hyperactive children. *Journal of Applied Behavior Analysis, 13,* 191–204.

O'leary, S. G., & Pelham, W. E. (1978). Behavior therapy and withdrawal of stimulant medication in hyperactive children. *Pediatrics, 61,* 211–217.

O'Leary, K. D., Pelham, W. E., Rosenbaum, A., & Price, G. H. (1976). Behavioral treatment of hyperkinetic children. *Clinical Pediatrics, 15,* 510–515.

Parry, P. A., & Douglas, V. I. (1983). Effects of reinforcement on concept identification in hyperactive children. *Journal of Abnormal Child Psychology, 11,* 327–340.

Pelham, W. E. (1983). The effects of psychostimulants on academic achievement in hyperactive and learning-disabled children. *Thalamus, 3,* 1–49.

Pelham, W. E., & Bender, M. E. (1982). Peer relationships in hyperactive children: Description and treatment. In K. Gadow & I. Bialer (Eds.), *Advances in learning and behavioral disabilities* (Vol. 1, pp. 365–436). Greenwich, CT: JAI Press.

Pelham, W. E., O'Brian, B., & Paluchowski, C. (1978, November). *Social-skills training with hyperactive children: A preliminary evaluation of a coaching procedure and a reward system.* Paper presented at the annual meeting of the Association for the Advancement of Behavior Therapy, Chicago, Ill.

Pelham, W. E., Schnedler, R. W., Bologna, N. D., & Contreras, J. A. (1980). Behavioral and stimulant treatment of hyperactive children: A therapy study with methylphenidate probes in a within-subject design. *Journal of Applied Behavior Analysis, 13,* 221–236.

Penney, R. K. (1967). Effects of reward and punishment on children's orientation and discrimination learning. *Journal of Experimental Psychology, 75,* 140.

Penney, R. K., & Lupton, A. A. (1971). Children's discrimination learning as a function of reward and punishment. *Journal of Comparative Physiological Psychology, 54,* 449.

Porges, S. W., Walter, G. F., Korb, R. J., & Sprague, R. I. (1975). The influence of methylphenidate on heart rate and behavioral measures of attention in hyperactive children. *Child Development, 46,* 727–733.

Porrino, L. J., Rapoport, J. L., Behar, D., Sceery, W., Ismond, D. R., & Benney, W. E. (1983). A naturalistic assessment of the motor activity of hyperactive boys. *Archives of General Psychiatry, 40,* 681–687.

Quinn, P., & Rapoport, J. (1975). One-year follow-up of hyperactive boys treated with imiprimine and methylphenidate. *American Journal of Psychiatry, 132,* 241–245.

Radosh, A., & Gittelman, R. (1981). The effect of appealing distractors on the performance of hyperactive children. *Journal of Abnormal Child Psychology, 9,* 179–189.

Rapoport, J. L., Buchsbaum, M., Weingartner, H., Zahn, T. P., & Ludlow, C. (1980). Dextroamphetamine: Cognitive and behavioral effects in normal and hyperactive boys and normal men. *Archives of General Psychiatry, 37*, 933–943.

Rapoport, J. L., Buchsbaum, M. S., Zahn, T. P., Weingartner, H., Ludlow, C., & Mikkelsen, E. J. (1978). Dextroamphetamine: Cognitive and behavioral effects in normal prepubertal boys. *Science, 199*, 560–563.

Rapoport, J., & Quinn, P. (1975). Minor physical anomalies (stigmata) and early developmental deviation: A major biologic sub-group of "hyperactive children." *International Journal of Mental health, 4*, 29–44.

Rapport, M. D. (1983). Attention deficit disorder with hyperactivity: Critical treatment parameters and their application in applied outcome research. In M. Hersen, R. Eisler, & P. Miller (Eds.), *Progress in behavior modification* (pp. 219–298), New York: Academic.

Rapport, M. D. (1984). Hyperactivity and stimulant treatment: Abusus non tollit usum. *Behavior Therapist, 7*, 133–134.

Rapport, M. D., & DuPaul, G. J. (1986). Hyperactivity and methylphenidate: Rate-dependent effects on attention. *International Clinical Psychopharmacology, 1*, 45–52.

Rapport, M. D., DuPaul, G. J., & Smith, N. F. (1985). Rate-dependency and hyperactivity: Methylphenidate effects on operant responding. *Pharmacology, Biochemistry & Behavior, 23*, 77–83.

Rapport, M. D. DuPaul, G. J., Stoner, G., Birmingham, B., & Masse, G. (1985). Attention deficit disorder with hyperactivity: Differential effects of methylphenidate on impulsivity. *Pediatrics, 76*, 938–943.

Rapport, M. D., DuPaul, G. J., Stoner, G., & Jones, J. T. (1986). Comparing classroom and clinic measures of attention deficit disorder: Differential, idiosyncratic, and dose-response effects of methylphenidate. *Journal of Consulting and Clinical Psychology, 54*, 334–341.

Rapport, M. D., Murphy, A., & Bailey, J. S. (1980). The effects of a response cost treatment tactic on hyperactive children. *Journal of School Psychology, 18*, 98–111.

Rapport, M. D., Murphy, A., & Bailey, J. S. (1982). Ritalin versus response cost in the control of hyperactive children: A within subject comparison. *Journal of Applied Behavior Analysis, 15*, 205–216.

Rapport, M. D., & Siviski, R. (1983, December). *The effects of psychostimulant treatment on personality dimensions in attention deficit disorder children.* Paper presented at the meeting of the World Congress on Behavior Therapy, Washington, DC.

Rapport, M. D., Stoner, G., DuPaul, G. J., Birmingham, B. K., & Tucker, S. 1985). Methylphenidate in hyperactive children: Differential effects of dose on academic, learning, and social behavior. *Journal of Abnormal Child Psychology, 13*, 227–244.

Rapport, M. D., Tucker, S. B., DuPaul, G. J., Merlo, M., & Stoner, G. (1986). Hyperactivity and frustration: The influence of control over and size of rewards in delaying gratification. *Journal of Abnormal Child Psychology, 14*, 191–204.

Reid, M. K., & Borkowski, J. G. (1984). Effects of methyphenidate (ritalin) on information processing in hyperactive children. *Journal of Abnormal Child Psychology, 12*, 169–186.

Riddle, D., & Rapoport, J. (1976). A 2-year follow-up of 72 hyperactive boys. *Journal of Nervous and Mental Disease, 162*, 126–134.

Rie, H., & Rie, E. (Eds.). (1980). *Handbook of minimal brain dysfunction: A critical review.* New York: Wiley.

Robbins, T. W., & Sahakian, B. J. (1979). "Paradoxical" effects of psychomotor stimulant drugs in hyperactive children from the standpoint of behavioural pharmacology. *Neuropharmacology, 18*, 931–950.

Robinson, P. W., Newby, T. J., & Ganzell, J. L. (1981). A token system for a class of underachieving hyperactive children. *Journal of Applied Behavior Analysis, 14*, 307–315.

Rose, R. L. (1978). The functional relationship between artificial food colors and hyperactivity. *Journal of Applied Behavior Analysis, 11*, 439–446.

Rosen, L. A., O'Leary, S. G., Joyce, S. A., Conway, G., & Pfiffner, L. J. (1984). The importance of prudent negative consequences for maintaining the appropriate behavior of hyperactive students. *Journal of Abnormal Child Psychology, 12*, 581–604.

Rosenbaum, M., & Baker, E. (1984). Self-control behavior in hyperactive and nonhyperactive children. *Journal of Abnormal Child Psychology, 12*, 303–318.

Rosenthal, R. H., & Allen, T. W. (1978). An examination of attention, arousal, and learning dysfunctions of hyperkinetic children. *Psychological Bulletin, 85*, 689–715.

Ross, A. O., & Pelham, W. E. (1981). Child psychopathology. *Annual Review in Psychology, 32*, 278–342.

Ross, D. M., & Ross, S. A. (1976). *Hyperactivity: Research, theory, action,* New York: McGraw-Hill.

Ross, D. M., & Ross, S. A. (1982). *Hyperactivity: Current issues, research, and theory* (2nd ed.). New York: Wiley.

Routh, D. K. (1980). Developmental and social aspects of hyperactivity. In C. K. Whalen & B.

Henker (Eds.), *Hyperactive children: The social ecology of identification and treatment.* New York: Academic.

Routh, D. K., Schroeder, C. S., & O'Tuama, L. (1974). Development of activity level in children. *Developmental Psychology, 10,* 163–168.

Rutter, M. (1982). Syndromes attributed to "minimal brain dysfunction" in childhood. *American Journal of Psychiatry, 139,* 21–33.

Safer, D., & Allen, R. (1976). *Hyperactive children: Diagnosis and management.* Baltimore, MD: University Park Press.

Safer, D. J. & Krager, J. M. (1983). Trends in medication treatment of hyperactive school children. *Clinical Pediatrics, 22,* 500–504.

Satterfield, J. H., Atoian, G. E., Brashers, G. C., Burleigh, A. C., & Dawson, M.E. (1974). Electrodermal studies of minimal brain dysfunction children. In *Symposium on the clinical use of stimulant drugs in children* (pp. 87–95). Amsterdam: Excerpta Medica.

Satterfield, J. H., & Dawson, M. E. (1971). Electrodermal correlates of hyperactivity in children. *Psychophysiology, 8,* 191–197.

Satterfield, J. H., Hoppe, C. M., & Schell, A. M. (1982). A prospective study of delinquency in 110 adolescent boys with attention deficit disorder and 88 normal adolescent boys. *American Journal of Psychiatry, 139,* 795–798.

Schrag, P., & Divoky, D. (1975). *The myth of the hyperactive child and others means of child control.* New York: Pantheon.

Shaffer, D., & Greenhill, L. (1979). A critical note on the predictive validity of "the hyperkinetic syndrome." *Journal of Child Psychology and Psychiatry, 20,* 61–72.

Shelly, E. M., & Riester, F. D. (1972). Syndrome of MBD in young adults. *Disabled Nervous Systems, 33,* 335–339.

Sleator, E. K. & Ullmann, R. K. (1981). Can the physician diagnose hyperactivity in the office? *Pediatrics 67,* 13–17.

Solanto, M. V. (1984). Neuropharmacological basis of stimulant drug action in attention deficit disorder with hyperactivity: A review and synthesis. *Psychological Bulletin, 95,* 387–409.

Sprague, R. L., & Sleator, E. K. (1977). Methylphenidate in hyperkinetic children: Differences in dose effects on learning and social behavior. *Science, 198,* 1274–1276.

Sroufe, L. A., Sonies, W. D., West, W. D., & Wright, F. S. (1973). Anticipatory heart-rate deceleration and reaction time in children with and without referral for learning disability. *Child Development, 44,* 267–275.

Stephens, R. S., Pelham, W. E., & Skinner, R. (1984). State-dependent and main effects of methylphenidate and pemoline on paired-associate learning and spelling in hyperactive children. *Journal of Consulting and Clinical Psychology, 52,* 104–113.

Stewart, M., Cummings, C., Singer, S., deBlois, C. (1981). The overlap between hyperactive and unsocialized aggressive children. *Journal of Child Psychology and Psychiatry, 22,* 35–46.

Still, G. F. (1902). Some abnormal physical conditions in children. *Lancet, 1,* 1077–1082.

Strauss, A. A., & Lehtinen, L. E. (1947). *Psychopathology and education of the brain-injured child.* New York: Grune & Stratton.

Swanson, J., Nolan, W., & Pelham, W. (1981, August). *The SNAP rating scale for the diagnosis of the attention deficit disorder.* Paper presented at the meeting of the American Psychological Association, Los Angeles.

Sykes, D. H., Douglas, V. I., & Morgenstern, G. (1973). Sustained attention in hyperactive children. *Journal of Child Psychology and Psychiatry, 14,* 213–220.

Tallmadge, J., & Barkley, R. A. (1983). The interactions of hyperactive and normal boys with their fathers and mothers. *Journal of Abnormal Child Psychology, 11,* 565–580.

Tant, J. L., & Douglas, V. I. (1982). Problem solving in hyperactive, normal, and reading-disabled boys. *Journal of Abnormal Child Psychology, 10,* 285–306.

Tarter, R. E., McBride, H., Buonpane, N. & Schneider, D. V. (1977). Differentiation of alcoholics: Childhood history of minimal brain dysfunction, family history, and drinking pattern. *Archives of General Psychiatry, 34,* 761–768.

Tizard, B. (1968). Observations of overactive imbecile children in uncontrolled environments. *American Journal of Mental Deficiency, 72,* 540–547.

Trites, R. L. (Ed.). (1979). *Hyperactivity in children: Etiology, measurement, and treatment implications.* Baltimore, MD: University Park Press.

Trites, R. L., & Laprade, K. (1983). Evidence for an independent syndrome of hyperactivity. *Journal of Child Psychology and Psychiatry, 24,* 573–586.

Twardosz, S., & Sajwaj, T. (1972). Multiple effects of a procedure to increase sitting in a hyperactive retarded boy. *Journal of Applied Behavior Analysis, 5,* 73–78.

Ullmann, R. K., Sleator, E. K., & Sprague, R. L. (in press). A new rating scale for diagnosis and monitoring of ADD children. *Psychopharmacology Bulletin.*

Waldrop, M. F., & Goering, J. D. (1971). Hyperactivity and minor physical anomalies in elementary school children. *American Journal of Orthopsychiatry, 4,* 602–607.

Weiss, G. (1975). The natural history of hyperactivity in childhood and treatment with stimulant medication at different ages. *International Journal of Mental Health, 4,* 213–226.

Weiss, G., & Hechtman, L. (1979). The hyperactive child syndrome. *Science, 205,* 1348–1354.

Weiss, G., Hechtman, L., & Perlman, T. (1978). Hyperactives as young adults: School, employer, and self-rating scales obtained during ten-year follow-up evaluation. *American Journal of Orthopsychiatry, 48,* 438–445.

Weiss, G., Kruger, E., Danielson, N., & Elman, M. (1975). Effects of long-term treatment of hyperactive children with methylphenidate. *Canadian Medical Association Journal, 112,* 159–165.

Wender, P. (1971). *Minimal brain dysfunction in children.* New York: Wiley.

Wender, P. H. (1972). The minimal brain dysfunction syndrome in children *Journal of Nervous and Mental Disease, 155,* 55–71.

Wender, P. H., Epstein, R. S., Kopin, I. J., & Gordon, E. K. (1971). Urinary monoamine metabolites in children with minimal brain dysfunction. *American Journal of Psychiatry, 121,* 1411–1415.

Wender, P. H., Reimherr, F. W., & Wood, D. R. (1981). Attention deficit disorder (minimal brain dysfunction) in adults: A replication study of diagnosis and drug treatment. *Archives of General Psychiatry, 38,* 449–456.

Werry, J. (1968). Developmental hyperactivity. *Pediatrics Clinics of North America, 19,* 9–16.

Werry, J., & Sprague, R. (1970). Hyperactivity. In C. Costello (Ed.), *Symptoms of psychopathology* (pp. 397–417). New York: Wiley.

Werry, J., Sprague, R., & Cohen, M. (1975). Teacher Rating Scale for use in drug studies with children — an empirical study. *Journal of Abnormal Child Psychology, 3,* 217–229.

Whalen, C. K., Collins, B. E., Henker, B., Alkus, S. R., Adams, D., & Stapp, J. (1978). Behavior observations of hyperactive children and methylphenidate (Ritalin) effects in systematically structured classroom environments: Now you see them, now you don't. *Journal of Pediatric Psychology, 3,* 177–187.

Whalen, C. K., & Henker, B. (1976). Psychostimulants and children: A review and analysis. *Psychological Bulletin, 83,* 1113–1130.

Whalen, C. K., & Henker, B. (Eds.). (1980). *Hyperactive children: The social ecology of identification and treatment.* New York: Academic.

Witte, K. L., & Grossman, E. E. (1971). The effects of reward and punishment upon children's attention, motivation and discrimination learning. *Child Development, 42,* 499–504.

Yerkes, R. M., & Dodson, J. D. (1908). The relation of strength of stimulus to rapidity of habit formation. *Journal of Comparative Neurology, 18,* 459–482.

Yu-cun, S., & Yu-feng, W. (1984). Urinary 3-methoxy-4-hydroxphenylglycol sulfate excretion in seventy-three schoolchildren with minimal brain dysfunction syndrome. *Biological Psychiatry, 19,* 861–870.

Zahn, T. P., Abate, F., Little, B., & Wender, P. (1975). MBD, stimulant drugs and Ans activity. *Archives of General Psychiatry, 32,* 381–387.

Zentall, S. (1975). Optimal stimulation as theoretical basis of hyperactivity. *American Journal of Orthopsychiatry, 45,* 549–561.

Zentall, S., & Zentall, T. R. (1976). Activity and task performance of hyperactive children as a function of environmental stimulation. *Journal of Consulting and Clinical Psychology, 44,* 693–697.

Zentall, S. S., Zentall, T. R., & Booth, M. E. (1978). Within-task stimulation: Effects on activity and spelling performance in hyperactive and normal children. *Journal of Educational Research, 71,* 223–230.

CHAPTER 19

Learning Disabilities

Ronald E. Reeve and James M. Kauffman

Among the developmental disorders, learning disabilities is the most controversial and the least understood. Paradoxes abound. Although it is generally accepted that the disorder has a basis in central nervous system dysfunction, no reliable medical procedure exists for diagnosing the condition. Identifying individuals with learning disabilities is conceded by all involved to be an extraordinarily difficult and complex process, yet over 1,000 people *per day* in the United States alone are newly and officially labeled as learning disabled. "Experts" abound, but the likelihood of agreement among any two of them with regard to appropriate diagnosis and treatment is quite small. For these reasons, some have suggested that the whole concept of learning disabilities is of dubious validity (e.g., Algozzine & Yssledyke, 1983; Ysseldyke, Algozzine, & Epps, 1983; Ysseldyke et al., 1983). Although the majority of professionals working in this field are somewhat less pessimistic about the current status and future prospects of this category of exceptionality, there clearly is less consensus than confusion about learning disabilities.

BRIEF HISTORY

Learning disabilities (or LD) is an umbrella term referring to a condition that is assumed to underlie difficulties in acquiring basic academic skills (i.e., reading, writing, spelling, arithmetic calculating, etc.) in the absence of any other explanation for the problem. Many other common terms are subsumed under LD. For example, *dyslexia* often is used to mean learning disabilities, specifically in the area of reading; *dyscalculia* means a deficiency in the ability to perform arithmetic calculations. Almost every form of academic function has its own term to designate *dys*function.

Reading problems were the first to be recognized in the professional literature, and that remains the most prominent subtype of LD, probably comprising the major deficit for two-thirds of all LD children (Schroeder, Schroeder, & Davine, 1978). Hinshelwood (1896, 1911) and Morgan (1896) offered early descriptions and analyses of the disorder, which they called "word blindness." Hinshelwood believed that the problem resulted from defects in the part of the brain that is responsible for visual memory. His perspective foreshadowed much of the theory, research, and practice in LD over the next 80 years, in that he assumed a neurological basis for the disorder, emphasized the role of visual perception and visual memory in reading, and suggested that a systematic step-by-step teaching method was essential to overcome the disorder.

It is possible to conceptualize the early development of the field of LD as following two different, though frequently intersecting paths. One was focused primarily on visual perceptual and visual motor functioning, whereas the other was concerned primarily with language processes.

Visual Perception and Perceptual-motor functioning

Although Hinshelwood's work was a precursor to this line of inquiry, it had relatively little direct impact on the field. Kurt Goldstein's (1939) did, however. Goldstein studied soldiers who had suffered brain injuries during World War I. He identified a "syndrome" of behaviors that characterized many of these men, including concreteness of thought, perseveration, figure-background confusion, forced responsiveness to stimuli (distractibility), meticulosity, and catastrophic reaction (i.e., emotional outbursts).

Two German scientists who emigrated to the United States in the 1930s, Alfred Strauss and Heinz Werner, were central figures in developing this line of inquiry, both through their own research and through the impact they had on the young professionals (e.g., Cruickshank, Kirk, Kephart) who trained with them at the Wayne County Training School near Detroit. Strauss and Werner were quite interested in determining whether or not the syndrome of behaviors identified by Goldstein in brain-damaged adults also was characteristic of children with brain injuries. The Wayne County Training School primarily served mentally retarded children. Strauss and Werner identified two groups of subjects from that pool: one consisting of children who appeared to

have experienced some type of brain damage (*exogenous*) and the other made up of familial mentally retarded children with no apparent brain insult (*endogenous*). Extensive studies indicated that these brain-damaged mentally retarded children were qualitatively different from the familial group, and that their behaviors were similar in most ways to Goldstein's brain-damaged soldiers (Strauss & Kephart, 1955; Strauss & Lehtinen, 1947).

The next major step occurred when Cruickshank determined, through studies of children who had definite brain damage but were not mentally retarded (a cerebral palsy group), that many of the same behaviors existed in children who had normal intelligence and brain impairments. Cruickshank noted the problems these children had with visual figure–ground confusion and perceptual-motor skills, but such behaviors as hyperactivity and distractibility also appeared to be present (Cruickshank, Bice, & Wallen, 1957).

To this point, then, a link had been established between brain damage and various aberrant behaviors, including hyperactivity, attention problems, visual perceptual and visual motor deficits, and difficulties in controlling emotions. A major conceptual leap followed. Cruickshank and a group of colleagues (Cruickshank, Bentzen, Ratzeburg, & Tannhauser, 1961) collaborated in a project in Montgomery County, Maryland, during the late 1950s. Their subjects were a group of children whose behaviors were so troublesome to school personnel that they had been excluded or were in danger of being excluded from school. Based on extensive psychological and perceptual-motor testing, these children were considered to be hyperactive and perceptually impaired. Because their behaviors were very similar to those of children who clearly had brain damage, Cruickshank and his colleagues *assumed* that they were brain damaged. The project used many of the teaching techniques originally suggested by Strauss, Werner, Lehtinen, and others at Wayne County, including severely reduced environmental stimuli, heavily structured teaching, and an emphasis on development of visual-perceptual skills.

The "brain damage" believed to underlie these children's school learning and behavior problems usually could not be verified by medical evaluations, presumably because the diagnostic procedures available to physicians were too crude to detect the subtle neurological malfunctions involved. As a result, it became common to refer to such children as having *minimal brain damage* (MBD), minimal cerebral dysfunction, or a condition connoted by a similar term. The key point is this: The diagnosis of brain injury was made on the basis of the *behaviors*, typically including visual-perceptual and visual-motor problems, hyperactivity, and distractibility, accompanied by difficulties in learning; the neurological basis was inferred.

This line of research and theory, associating children's learning problems with brain impairments primarily affecting visual-perceptual, visual-motor, and attentional processes, had and continues to have enormous impact on the field. In addition to Strauss, Werner, Lehtinen, and Cruickshank, other prominent pioneers who can be identified with this perspective include Marianne Frostig and Newell Kephart.

Language Development

The central role of language in higher order learning has long been recognized. It follows, then, that disorders in language functions, whether resulting from brain trauma or generalized developmental disability of unknown origin, will interfere with learning.

Although not as widely publicized as visual-perceptual and perceptual-motor types of LD, language-based learning disabilities were recognized relatively earlier. In the 1860s Broca identified the left frontal lobe of the brain as the expressive speech center by performing autopsies on two men who had lost the ability to speak (*acquired expressive aphasics*). Later work by Wernicke, Jackson, and Head further clarified the brain–behavior relationships critical to speech and language (C. R. Smith, 1983). These individuals focused on the effects of brain damage. Eisenson (1954) extended this earlier work to children, differentiating between acquired aphasia and developmental aphasia (poor language development), which he believed could result either from brain damage or from slow or uneven neurological maturation. Eisenson also noted that children with language disturbances frequently evinced behaviors such as attention problems, perseveration, and emotional lability—a very similar cluster to that originally noted in children by Strauss and Werner.

Osgood (1957), Wepman (Wepman, Jones, Bock, & Van Pelt, 1960), Myklebust (1954), and Kirk (Kirk & Kirk, 1971) developed models of normal language development based on information processing theory. These models, then, were applied to understanding, differentially diagnosing, and devising clinic and classroom intervention strategies for developing children's language skills.

Myklebust viewed reading and writing as the highest levels of language ability, dependent on the efficient functioning of all lower-level language functions (e.g., internal language, speech, etc.). Thus, he directly linked language problems to learning disabilities in reading and written expression. Kirk was a leader, particularly in assessment and school remediation techniques — he developed the Illinois Test of Psycholinguistic Abilities (ITPA), based on Osgood's communication model (Kirk, McCarthy, & Kirk, 1961), to pinpoint strengths and weaknesses in children's information processing channels. This profile then was used to design educational programs to remediate the underlying weaknesses.

After 1960

By the early 1960s, then, a "new" type of handicapping condition was becoming widely recognized. Terminology was problematic, mostly emphasizing the disorder's presumed neurological basis (e.g., brain injured, minimal brain dysfunction, etc.) Clements (1966) identified 38 terms used to designate children exhibiting such disorders. Despite the confusion resulting from so many different labels, however, thousands of parents and teachers recognized their children in the behavioral descriptions accompanying whatever term was used. In 1964, the Association for Children with Learning Disabilities (ACLD) was formed. The ACLD chose the term *learning disabilities* partly in response to its use by Kirk in addressing a convention of parents in 1963. Kirk had suggested that many of the other terms were medically oriented, and therefore outside the areas of expertise of parents, teachers, and psychologists. However, he also expressed concern about establishing a new category of exceptionality (Kirk, 1976). Nonetheless, the parents chose to use learning disabilities in the title of their organization. Professionals followed the lead of parents when they formed the Division for Children with Learning Disabilities (DCLD: now CLD) within the Council for Exceptional Children (CEC) in 1968. LD thus became widely accepted.

Formal federal recognition of LD began in 1966, when the National Advisory Committee on Handicapped Children (authorized under the Elementary and Secondary Education Amendments of 1966—PL 89-750) was formed. The advisory committee defined learning disabilities and proposed that Congress deal with the problem through legislation. Funds for research, teacher training, and demonstration projects in LD were authorized in 1970 (U.S. Office of Education, 1970). By 1975, 45 states had created LD categories for state support of special education services (Gillespie, Miller, & Fielder, 1975). Only after the Education for All Handicapped Children Act (PL 94-142) was passed in 1975 were special education services federally mandated. Thus, the present day concept of learning disabilities, which has its roots in the 1800s, is a relatively new phenomenon. For more comprehensive histories of LD, see Hallahan and Cruickshank (1973), Kavale and Forness (1985) and Wiederholt (1974).

CURRENT DEFINITION

The definition included in PL 94-142 is a slight modification of the one proposed by the National Advisory Committee on Handicapped Children in 1967. It reads as follows:

> "Specific learning disability" means a disorder in one or more of the basic psychological processes involved in understanding or in using language, spoken or written, which may manifest itself in an imperfect ability to listen, think, speak, read, write, spell, or to do mathematical calculations. The term includes such conditions as perceptual handicaps, brain injury, minimal brain dysfunction, dyslexia, and developmental aphasia. The term does not include children who have learning problems which are primarily the result of visual, hearing, or motor handicaps, of mental retardation, of emotional disturbance, or of environmental, cultural, or economic disadvantage.

Viewed along with the "Rules and Regulations" accompanying its issuance (see *Federal Register*, December 29, 1977, 42, 62083), this definition has three major components that are included in most other LD definitions: (a) The individual's information processing efficiency is disordered, presumably the result of unspecified neurological difficulties; (b) ability to perform academic tasks is impaired such that school achievement is below expected levels based on intellectual aptitude; and (c) the problem is not caused by sensory deficits (i.e., difficulties with visual and auditory acuity) or by any other physical, social, or emotional factor.

The biggest criticisms of the PL 94-142 definition, beyond the obvious awkwardness and imprecision of the terminology (e.g., "imperfect ability," "psychological processes"), center on its definition by exclusion. LD seems to be what is left if a person is *not* learning and *nothing else* seems to be wrong. However, no competing definition has emerged as clearly superior (see Hallahan & Bryan, 1981; Kavale & Forness, in press; Kneedler & Hallahan, 1983).

EPIDEMIOLOGY

The actual incidence of learning disabilities in the United States is unknown. The number of students identified as LD has become so large that some professionals and federal officials speak of a "cap" on identification to check what they believe are abuses of special education services (i.e., they feel that many students with mild learning difficulties are being inappropriately identified as LD; Sontag, Button, & Hagerty, 1982). This situation is the direct result of the imprecision of the definition, the paucity of reliable and valid assessment techniques, relative newness of the field, and lack of large-scale epidemiological studies. Consequently, LD "experts" estimate that anywhere from 0 to 80% of the population is learning disabled (Tucker, Stevens, & Ysseldyke, 1983). Most authorities, however, concur that a 1–3% incidence is an appropriate "guestimate."

Reasonably accurate data are available about the number of *identified* school-age LD children, because yearly child counts, required under PL 94-142, are compiled in Washington, DC, based on information provided by each state. The numbers in the LD category have increased at a nearly unbelievable rate in the past few years. In the 5 years between 1976 and 1981, approximately 168,000 new cases per year were identified as LD. Currently, about 4% of the school age population in the United States is labeled LD, making LD the largest category of exceptionality included under PL 94-142. The prevalence of LD is considerably higher than the prevalence of speech impairment and mental retardation, the second and third most common handicaps (U.S. Department of Education, 1984).

Though the data may not be reliable, they strongly suggest that LD prevalence is much higher among persons 6–21 years of age than among other age groups. This is largely an artifact of two factors. First, the category is so new that relatively few people were labeled as LD until 5 to 10 years ago, and the official labeling agency usually is the school. Thus, people who have not been in school for the past 5 to 10 years are not likely ever to have been identified. Second, because LD is very difficult to diagnose at pre-school ages (and because most children are not in formal school settings prior to age 5 or so), few young children are labeled LD.

Boys more often are identified as LD than are girls. The reported ratio ranges from approximately 2:1 to 6:1 (Coleman & Sandhu, 1967; Rubin & Balow, 1971). At this point, it is not clear whether this sex difference in rates of identification is more physiologically based (e.g., males are more vulnerable to birth injury and/or mature more slowly) or socially based (boys who fail in school act out more, drawing attention to themselves and thus are referred more often).

Regarding intelligence, results of several large-scale studies (e.g., Kirk & Elkins, 1975; Norman & Zigmond, 1980; Shepard, Smith, & Vojir, 1983) concur that the average measured IQ of identified LD children is in the low to middle 90s. No consistent SES or racial factors in LD indidence have emerged in the research literature, although concerns have been expressed that blacks may be underrepresented among the LD population, as they are overrepresented among the mentally retarded (U.S. Office of Education, 1981). The fear is that a bias operates to make LD a white, middle class version of mental retardation.

ETIOLOGY

Some children who have experienced educationally barren home environments during their developmental years, or who have had the misfortune of being subjected to poor teaching during their early schooling, may be considered LD and placed in special programs. Most authorities, however, disagree with this practice. The federal definition specifically excludes from the LD category those whose "... learning problems ... are primarily the result of ... environmental, cultural, or economic disadvantage"; and the "Rules and Regulations" (*Federal Register*, December 29, 1977, 42, 65083) go on to state that the achievement/aptitude discrepancy is to be considered as indicative of LD when the child has been "... provided with learning experiences appropriate for the child's age and ability levels."

The most prominent view is that learning disabilities reflect an inefficiency in the information processing system within the individual. Obviously, a learning problem can be greatly exacerbated by unfortunate environmental conditions at home, school, or elsewhere; the severity of the handicap also can be ameliorated, one would hope, by appropriate environmental conditions, such as effective educational interventions. However, the basis for the disorder itself generally is believed to be *within* the individual; that is, something is amiss in the complex "wiring" system involved in the individual's ability to take in, make sense of, and output (through speaking, writing, etc.) relevant stimuli.

Several etiological factors in learning difficulties have been identified. These are discussed very briefly next. What is *not* known is the extent to which any one or more of these can account for a particular LD *individual's* problems.

Brain Injury

The oldest of causal explanations for learning problems—injury to the brain— may occur prior to, during, or after birth (Pasamanick & Knobloch, 1973). Colletti (1979), for example, reports that 9–12% of all surviving newborns show signs of intracranial hemorrhages at birth. After the neonatal period, accidents, brain tumors, high fevers, childhood diseases, etc., are so common that perhaps 20% of all children have suffered a serious insult to the brain by the time they are 6 years old (Colletti, 1979). Both the site and the severity of the damage are important in determining the extent to which a brain injury interferes with learning, if at all.

Heredity

Like most other abilities and disabilities, learning efficiency and learning problems run in families (Owen, Adams, Forrest, Stolz, & Fisher, 1971; Silver, 1971). Parents and siblings of LDs are much more likely to have learning problems than are relatives of non-LDs. Twin studies provide strong indications that these learning difficulties somehow are genetically transmitted (e.g., Hallgren, 1950). One popular notion is that many learning disabilities result from a maturational lag in the development of skills important for academic success. Children encountering tasks for which they are not developmentally prepared will fail, become frustrated, and develop inappropriate learning strategies. According to proponents of this view, the problem would not have occurred if the child simply had been allowed to mature further before being expected to perform school tasks (Abrams, 1968; Kinsbourne & Caplan, 1979). These differences in maturational clocks are assumed to be genetically based.

Biochemical Irregularities

For learning to occur, stimuli must reach the brain and be processed there. Electrochemical impulses carry the stimuli along the organism's neurological pathways. If the balance of chemicals is off, the flow of information into and out of the brain is altered: The learning efficiency and other behaviors of the individual will be affected.

The clearest indications of the relationship between biochemical abnormalities and learning problems have come from studies of drug effects on children with hyperactivity and attentional disorders (see Chapter 18, this volume). Psychostimulant drugs; for example, methylphenidate (Ritalin) and pemoline (Cylert), result in improved behavior in 60–90% of hyperactive children (Whalen & Henker, 1976). Current theory is that this improvement occurs because the drugs release chemicals that inhibit neurotransmissions, allowing children to screen out irrelevant stimuli and therefore to focus attention on one stimulus at a time (Kinsbourne & Caplan, 1979).

The biochemistry of learning is a relatively new field. In addition to the effects of psychostimulant drugs on behavior, interest also is focusing on such topics as vitamin deficiencies, sugar excesses, and thyroid disorders.

Other Causes

A number of other etiological factors are known to have potential for disrupting the normal acquisition of academic skills. Generally, these can be seen as subsets of one or more of the above (brain injury, heredity, biochemical abnormality), in that they are assumed to result from or to cause one or more of these broader classes of difficulties.

Malnutrition and severe sensory deprivation during early development are known to affect the brain and subsequent learning (Cravioto & DeLicardie, 1975). More recently, some evidence linking chemicals in certain foods with cognitive and behavioral problems has been reported, although research is inconclusive (Swanson & Kinsbourne, 1980). Individuals with allergies to specific foods, which result in a variety of toxic reactions (e.g., hives, headaches), appear to be quite common, and may affect ability to learn during the period shortly after ingestion. Perhaps 60–80% of individuals are allergic to one or more foods (Mayron, 1979).

Lead poisoning (Walzer & Richmond, 1973), carbon monoxide inhalation (Beard & Wertheim, 1967), mercury contamination (Wedig, 1974), and a host of other environmental toxins also affect learning, with the degree of impairment determined by the degree and duration of exposure, as well as the developmental level of the child.

DEVELOPMENTAL ISSUES

Until about 1975, learning disabilities seemed to be primarily a phenomenon of elementary-school-age children. Few preschool or secondary school programs existed. "Conventional Wisdom" purported that, with regard to LD accompanied by hyperactivity and attention disorders, children "grew out of" the problem by adolescence. Many professionals believed that, with adequate intervention, LD could be cured much as though it were a case of strep throat that would respond to antibiotics. Very little was known about or done for the adult with learning disabilities.

Recently, greater attention has been directed to the nature of LD across the life span of affected individuals. It now is clear that one does not grow out of LD, nor is it a disease that can be cured. However, it does manifest itself somewhat differently at each developmental stage, at least in part due to the variety of demands made by society on individuals at various stages of their lives. These differences affect both *diagnosis* and *intervention*. The most neglected developmental stages remain the preschool, adolescent, and adult years.

Preschool Years

One of the classic methods of determining LD is to look for uneven patterns of strength and weakness within an individual. However, normal cognitive, affective, and psychomotor development during the first 6 years of life does not occur in steady progression, but rather in a series of fits and starts, bursts, and plateaus. Imbalances among skills are the norm. Thus, this criterion is not very useful for LD diagnosis with very young children. Most tests used with preschool children also lack adequate reliability. Further, the *learning* in learning disability typically refers to school types of learning — reading, math, etc. Because it is not expected that preschoolers will attempt these tasks, finding a discrepancy between aptitude and achievement is not possible. These issues make diagnosis of LD prior to age 6 a very chancy proposition. At this stage, professionals are actually predicting learning problems rather than identifying them. Accuracy of this prediction is enhanced if the child's delays are relatively more severe, if the child's age is close to school entrance age, and if the assessment items resemble school tasks (Bower, 1978; Kinsbourne & Caplan, 1979).

Given the difficulties inherent in accurately diagnosing LD before school age, professionals frequently choose to withhold attaching the label for fear of stigmatizing the child and hence lowering the expectations (e.g., Keogh & Becker, 1973). However, PL 94-142 requires labeling children as having some type of handicap in return for federal reimbursement, which results in a quandary for school personnel.

Remediation at this age generally consists of attempts to improve whatever "preacademic" skills seem weak. Given the central role of language in learning, much attention typically is focused on developing speech discrimination, verbal labeling, conceptual thinking, and other speech and language functions. Children whose motor skills are delayed likewise may benefit from intensive practice in structured gross and/or fine motor tasks, and those who have difficulty sitting still may have their attentional skills improved by being taught to point with their fingers to direct their eyes or to use verbal mediation to talk their way through tasks.

Adolescent and Adult Years

By the time youngsters have been in school for enough years to be considered to be at a secondary level, it is a relatively easy matter to determine whether or not they have a severe discrepancy between their aptitude and their achievement. However, determining whether that discrepancy is due to an underlying learning disability rather than emotional disorders, poor teaching, or some other cause may be even more difficult than during younger years. This is because the few existing tests of psychological processing (e.g., the Beery, the ITPA), weak as they may be psychometrically for younger children, are not at all appropriate for older youngsters or adults. They frequently lack norms beyond elementary school ages. Further, LD children, as they mature, compensate such that their "processing" problems manifest themselves in a more subtle manor (Deshler, 1978).

Programming efforts for LD adolescents and adults are relatively new and thus lack external validation. Generally, they focus on continued development of basic academic skills (reading, writing, and mathematics). Often, some specialized help in content areas is essential if the individual is in high school or college. For example, because so much reading is required to keep up in history, literature, and similar courses, a tutor may be employed to read the material. Tests in content areas may need to be given orally to LD students who have reading and/or writing disabilities to assess their acquisition of knowledge.

Career education and vocational training become critical in secondary school. Whether or not to attempt college is one issue for the adolescent or young adult with LD. Over 100 colleges now offer specially adapted educational programs for the learning disabled, and a wide range of other postsecondary educational options (technical schools, night programs, etc.) exist. However, without guidance and support, many LD high school graduates will not attempt further schooling. Choices must be made in the light of specific areas of disability. For example, certainly it would be disastrous for a youngster with severe visuo-spatial deficits to attempt to become a draftsman or an engineer, regardless of how understanding the instructors might be.

Adolescents and adults likewise face emotional and social hurdles. Persistent social skill deficits interfere with friendship patterns, dating, job acquisition, and general life satisfaction. Years of academic failure lead to generalized low self-confidence and unwillingness to face new challenges, especially if these involve further training or education (Polloway, Smith, & Patton, 1984).

On the positive side, severe learning disabilities now are recognized as a handicapping condition for adults (Section 504, The Rehabilitation Act of 1973; PL 93-112). As a result, discrimination in admission to college or in employment is prohibited by any agency or other program receiving any kind of federal assistance, as long as the individual is otherwise qualified. Federally funded vocational rehabilitation programs gradually have geared up to assist LD adults in training for and finding appropriate jobs.

ASSESSMENT

Two different functions of assessment must be recognized. The first is for the purpose of arriving at a diagnosis, that is for determining whether or not a given individual is, in fact, learning disabled. The second is to aid in planning appropriate psychoeducational interventions for those who are considered to be LD. Although some portion of the information acquired in the diagnostic process may be applicable to the design of the intervention, the overlap between assessments in current practice typically is small (Thurlow & Ysseldyke, 1982).

Diagnosis

The process of arriving at a diagnosis begins when someone (parents, teachers, or even the individual of concern) brings the individual to the attention of a professional or group of professionals, (a referral is made). Because PL 94-142 includes LD among the handicapping conditions, the rest of the process of diagnosis and treatment is subject to the provisions of the law, if the referred person is within the age range covered by the law (the federal law requires that individual states serve those from 3-21; some states include even younger and older people). For those who are outside the age band included under federal and state laws, the diagnosis of LD is typically left to agencies such as mental health centers, departments of health, and departments of vocational rehabilitation or to private practitioners such as psychologists or physicians. In these situations, the assessment process is extraordinarily varied, with the choice of instruments and other procedures dependent on the training and theoretical orientation of the professional involved.

Tests

When an individual is suspected of having a learning disability and she or he falls within the purview of PL 94-142, the process is considerably more uniform. Most school systems have a "screening" procedure built into their special education eligibility system. The referral (whether initiated by a parent, teacher, or professional) goes to a screening committee. If the members believe there is reason to suspect that a handicap exists, and after parental permission is granted, the referred person may be given standardized achievement tests as well as a quick test of "intelligence" (e.g., the Slosson Intelligence Test or the Peabody Picture Vocabularly Test). Typically, a special education teacher will do this screening testings. Observations of the student in classroom settings also are made. If indications of a learning disability (or other handicapping condition) are seen, a full evaluation ensues. Required components include a medical examination (to look for sensory and other health factors that may explain the problems in school), an evaluation of the child's social functioning and home environment, an educational assessment, and a psychological evaluation. The academic achievement testing done at the screening level may suffice for the educational component.

The psychological assessment typically is of central importance. It serves a dual purpose: (a) to establish the level of "aptitude" against which actual school performance is compared (to determine whether the "severe discrepancy" required by law exists), and (b) to determine whether or not evidence exists of "disorders in one or more of the basic psychological processes . . ." With school-aged children and adolescents, the most commonly administered test is the Wechsler Intelligence Scale for Children–Revised (WISC-R) (Wechsler, 1974). The WISC-R includes 12 "subtests" divided into verbal and performance scales. These are combined to yield a "Full Scale IQ" score, which generally is considered to be the most reliable and valid estimate of ability to learn that is presently available. Psychologists typically look beyond the full scale score to seek hints of psychological processing problems. For example, the next level of analysis of the obtained WISC-R scores involves an examination of how the referred person performed on clusters of subtests requiring verbal versus nonverbal versus attention/concentration skills. As an example, if scores on the performance scale, which requires visual-perceptual and visual-motor abilities, were markedly lower than other parts of the WISC-R, a hypothesis of information processing deficits in these areas would be made. Further testing of visual perceptual organization skills usually would be conducted to evaluate the accuracy of this hypothesis. The psychologist might administer the Bender Gestalt Test (Koppitz, 1963), the Developmental Test of Visual Motor Integration (Beery, 1967), the Motor-Free Visual Perception Test (Colarusso & Hammill, 1972), or some similar instrument to evaluate hypotheses about problems in visual perceptual or visual motor functioning.

Interestingly, given the historical dominance of the viewpoint that *visual perceptual* disabilities point to learning disabilities, relatively few identified LD individuals show this pattern of deficits. In fact, studies indicate that the most common WISC-R pattern of low scores for LDs is on the group of subtests that are most sensitive to attention problems (i.e., the Freedom from Distractibility Factor — Arithmetic, Digit Span, and Coding). In groups of identified LD children, the *highest* scores tend to be on spatial-perceptual tasks (Block Design, Object Assembly, Picture Completion) (Smith, Coleman, Dokecki, & Davis, 1977).

Another common practice is to evaluate the amount of "scatter" among the individual subtests. Traditional clinical wisdom indicates that an uneven profile of subtest scores reflects developmental imbalance in the development of psychological processing skills, and thus is suggestive of the presence of a learning disability. Two cautions are important. First, normal individuals often show considerable scatter — the average difference between highest and lowest subtest scores is 7 (Kaufman, 1976); second, among groups of identified LD children and adolescents, scatter has not been found to be substantially greater than for normals (Kavale & Forness, 1984). In recent years, several other tests of cognitive ability, such as the Woodcock-Johnson (1977) and the Kaufman Assessment Battery for Children (Kaufman & Kaufman, 1983), have been published. They apparently are used extensively in some localities, but the WISC-R remains the most commonly used test in the United States for assessing intellectual ability.

Documenting psychological processing disorders has proven to be an illusory goal. This is so both because of the diversity of theoretical perspectives on how information is processed by humans and because the tests available to measure these processes generally lack satisfactory psychometric properties (i.e., their reliabilities tend to be too low to be useful in making individual diagnoses) (Salvia & Ysseldyke, 1981). Good tests for such psychological processes as attention, visual and auditory perception, short-term and long-term auditory and visual memory, etc., are not available.

Aptitude–Achievement Discrepancy Procedures

Despite the difficulties inherent in trying to pin down possible psychological processing disorders, the number of people identified as LD continues to rise dramatically. Several large-scale studies indicate that a major proportion of those identified do not show evidence of being behind their expectancy level academically; there is no evidence of the "severe discrepancy" between aptitude and achievement required by law (e.g., Norman & Zigmond, 1980; Shepard, Smith, & Vojir, 1983). Perhaps those identified as LD showed some evidence of processing problems, so they were diagnosed as LD without consideration of a discrepancy notion. Or perhaps the diagnostic criteria for inclusion in this category are so nebulous that many children who are experiencing school difficulties simply because they are not very intelligent are labeled as LD to obtain additional help for them. Whatever the reasons, these factors have forced a shift in the focus of diagnostic assessment away from process considerations and much more toward the descrepancy notion. Several states (e.g., Iowa) have adopted quantitative aptitude/achievement discrepancy procedures for use in LD eligibility decisions, with the goal of making diagnosis of LD more objective (and less frequent).

Two major types of these aptitude-achievement discrepancy procedures can be delineated — arithmetic and statistical. *Arithmetic* procedures typically involve the calculation of expected achievement by using a formula that is computationally some sort of ratio of age, IQ, and/or grade level. The Harris (1975) formula, which appeared in the draft versions of the federal "Rules and Regulations" for PL 94-142 but later was withdrawn, and the Myklebust (1967) formula are the best known of these. *Statistical* procedures are based on normal curve notions. They include simple subtraction of standard scores for achievement from IQ scores (e.g., 15 or more points difference might be considered a severe discrepancy), as well as more sophisticated comparisons that build in corrections for varying tests reliabilities, the correlations between the IQ and achievement measures, and/or the regression to the mean phenomenon (e.g., Cone & Wilson, 1981).

Although these quantitative procedures may help to make the process more objective by focusing LD eligibility considerations on data rather than clinical judgments, they share major conceptual and practical problems when used rigidly. The most critical problem is the assumption that intelligence *tests* accurately measure intelligence (and hence aptitude) for LD individuals. If a referred person has a learning disability that affects his or her visual perceptual skills, or ability to pay attention, or language processing skills, then certainly the IQ obtained on a test will be lowered to the extent that the test used requires those abilities. The aptitude estimate for that individual will be spuriously low, making it less likely that a discrepancy will be identified. The quantitative procedures, at best, do nothing except document that a person is underachieving, not that he or she is LD. Other possible causes of underachievement (e.g., lack of adequate schooling, emotional problems) must be considered before the LD diagnosis is appropriate.

Eligibility Determination

Under PL 94-142, once the component assessments (medical, educational, psychological, social) are completed, school personnel from various disciplines who comprise the special education Eligibility Committee meet together to consider the information acquired and to determine whether or not the individual is learning disabled. Once a decision is made to classify a person as LD, an "Individualized Education Program" (IEP) must be formulated to indicate very specific goals and objectives for the LD student. At this point, it often becomes necessary to do further assessment to learn what specific academic skills have been acquired and what must be taught. It is unfortunate that the great volume of information obtained during the eligibility determination process usually has so little direct application to designing educational interventions. Alternative models that would pull together these two purposes of assessment are only now beginning to appear (Howell, Kaplan, & Serapaglia, 1980; Smith, 1980).

EDUCATIONAL ISSUES

Many of the major issues in educating children with learning disabilities parallel those for any category of developmentally disabled children. The demands of PL 94-142 and the rules and regulations attendant thereto, for example, apply with full effect to the learning disabled. Thus, education in the "least restrictive" environment, development of individualized education plans, provision of related services, and parent involvement in the child's education have been major items of concern. Very recently, as previously noted, the secondary and postsecondary education and vocational opportunities of LD adolescents and young adults have become focal issues (Hallahan, Kauffman, & Lloyd, 1985; Mangrum & Strichart, 1984; Smith, 1981)

Mode of Education

Currently, most LD students are educated in regular classes and resource rooms (U.S. Department of Education, 1984). That is, they spend most of their school day in regular classes with their nonidentified classmates, going to a special resource teacher for tutoring or instruction in small groups in the academic subjects in which they are having the most difficulty. This widely preferred mode of special education is defended as appropriate and least restrictive (in accordance with federal law) for nearly all LD students. It is not, however, without its critics, who argue that the "least restrictive" education is not necessarily the least segregated setting (Cruickshank, 1977) and that concern about restrictiveness has taken precedence over educational effectiveness (Morse, 1984).

Theoretical Models

Contemporary teachers and trainers of practitioners must select their assumptions about the nature of the problem and techniques for approaching learning disabilities from an array of divergent theoretical explanations. Theoretical models guiding the work of researcherss and practitioners can be clustered into five major groups: process, cognitive, behavioral, direct instruction, and holistic. These theories are not peculiar to LD but are, rather, general theories of instruction that apply to students with all types of developmental disabilities.

Process Model

Historically, *process training* has dominated the field of learning disabilities (Hallahan & Cruickshank, 1973; Hallahan & Kauffman, 1976). The assumption underlying this approach is that LD students have deficits in their abilities to perceive and interpret stimuli, that is that psychological or central processing problems are the essence of learning disabilities. A student may have a reading disability, for example, because of an inability to perceive and integrate (process) visual information.

Intervention, therefore, would include training in the process of visual perception before reading tasks are presented. Process training may include training in visual perception, auditory perception, motor learning, or any combination of these processes that are assumed to underlie academic performance.

The assumption underlying process training — that academic instruction will be fruitless until basic processing problems are remediated — has been hotly attacked and defended (e.g., Gersten & Carnine,

1984, 1985; Hammill & Larsen, 1974; Kavale, 1981, 1985). Our opinion is that the weight of evidence is on the side of those who argue that academic disabilities are most effectively remediated by a direct attack on academic skill deficits; the case for perceptual process training does not rest on reliable empirical data.

Cognitive Model

The recent surge of interest and research in *cognitive* psychology has influenced many researchers' and clinicians' views of the nature of learning disabilities. LD is conceptualized by some as a *thinking* disability, an inability to apply cognitive strategies to problem solving. Deficits in listening, comprehension, memory, and self-instruction strategies (any or all of the thinking-about-thinking skills now referred to as metacognition) are assumed to be the underlying problem in a variety of developmental disabilities, including LD (see Hallahan, 1980; Rooney & Hallahan, 1985). Consequently, educational intervention based on cognitive theory includes a variety of procedures designed to teach metacognitive strategies, including self-monitoring, self-recording, and self-instruction (Hallahan, Hall, Ianna, Kneedler, Lloyd, Loper, & Reeve, 1983; Hallahan, Lloyd, Kauffman, & Loper, 1983). Although research regarding the use of cognitive strategies by LD students has been promising, the approach has not received uncritical acceptance (S. G. O'Leary, 1980), nor can it now be said to have fulfilled its promise of a key to unlock the abilities of all students with academic problems or to produce in LD students a pervasive, generalized ability to solve academic problems (Meichenbaum, 1980).

Behavioral Model

Educational interventions in LD based on *behavioral* psychology rely primarily on precise definition of target skills and reinforcement of successive approximations of correct performance. The underlying assumptions are that academic tasks and social skills can be analyzed into logical components and are effectively taught through presentation of appropriate stimuli and consequences (see Haring, Lovitt, Eaton, & Hansen, 1978; Lovitt, 1975, 1982). Although considerable research evidence supports the efficacy of a behavioral approach to many learning problems (Hallahan & Kauffman, 1976; Lovitt, 1981, 1982; Wallace & Kauffman, 1978), behaviorism has been criticized as inadequate for explaining and guiding children's learning and learning disabilities (Astman, 1984; Neal, 1984).

Direct Instruction Model

Direct instruction is based on a logical analysis of the concept to be taught rather than an analysis of the characteristics of the learner (Engelmann & Carnine, 1982). A basic assumption is that rarely is learning or failure to learn peculiar to an individual; rather, it is a function of the examples of concepts that are presented. When a student fails to learn, it is almost certainly because the teacher has not presented educational tasks in a sequence that removes the possibility of the student's learning an erroneous concept. Normal students learn from instruction that is not carefully planned or executed with great precision, but LD students do not learn unless they are instructed more precisely and unambiguously. At this time, research appears to support the contention that highly structured, directive teaching based on logical analyses of tasks rather than the characteristics of individuals or groups of students is the most productive approach to learning problems, including those problems called learning disabilities (Lloyd, 1984; Lloyd & Carnine, 1981). This conclusion is not, however, universally shared among special educators (Brown, 1985; Heshusius, 1984; Poplin, 1984).

Holistic Model

A holistic perspective on learning disabilities has recently been suggested (Heshusius, 1984; McNutt, 1984; Neal, 1984; Poplin, 1984). Holism in education apparently represents a rough analogue of holistic medicine. It is an attempt to react educationally to the phenomenological "whole" of learning disabled persons. An assumption underlying the holistic movement in learning disabilities is that a variety of theoretical perspectives may be useful in teaching and learning, but that the reductionist approach of any one theory is inadequate. Holism is an attempt to view learning disabilities in highly phenomenological terms rather than merely as a problem of segmenting learning problems into objectively assessed components that are related to school-defined deficits in the individual.

TREATMENT

Treatments for learning disabilities have as their ultimate objectives the resolution of learning difficulties and related psychological or medical problems. We have already described the diversity of approaches to education, all of which are direct attempts to overcome the academic aspects of learning disabilities by offering more effective instruction. Noneducational treatments include a variety of medical and psychological interventions intended to facilitate academic learning and/or treat the social-emotional dimensions of LD student's problems. Medical treatment includes interventions such as medication or dietary control at known or presumed physiological substrates of the problem. Psychological treatment includes psychotherapies designed to address known or suspected social-emotional concomitants of learning disabilities.

Medical Treatment

Medical treatment of learning disability typically centers on concern for two prominent behavioral features of the disorder: hyperactivity and attention deficit. Because these are dealt with in Chapter 18, we will not comment further here, except to note the importance of teachers' observations of classroom behavior and academic performance in assessing the effects of medication (see also Gadow, 1981; Kauffman & Hallahan, 1979; K. D. O'Leary, 1980; Sprague & Ullmann, 1981).

Psychological Treatment

The professionals who deal with learning disabilities have reached a consensus that social and emotional problems are very frequent concomitants of academic disabilities or school failure (Hallahan & Bryan, 1981; Hallahan et al., 1985; Smith, 1981). Consensus is not found, however, regarding the causal relationship between social-emotional disorders and LD. The predominant opinion today appears to be that although learning disabilities sometimes are the result of severe and protracted psychological disorder, psychological disorder is more often the eventual outcome of chronic inability to achieve academically at a level commensurate with the expectations of parents, teachers, peers, and self.

Psychological treatment ranges from traditional therapies based on the notion that problems in learning are caused by unresolved intrapsychic conflicts (e.g., Bettelheim, 1961, 1970) to cognitive and behavior therapies in which disordered behavior, both social and academic, is addressed as a learning problem (e.g., Hallahan, Hall, et al., 1983; Hallahan, Lloyd et al., 1983; Schumaker, Deshler, Alley, & Warner, 1983). Our opinion is that the majority of evidence supports the efficacy of a direct behavioral approach to psychological treatment of the social and emotional problems associated with academic difficulties. Because the psychological concomitants of learning disability are so diverse, including as they do the full range of disorders from social withdrawal and depression to conduct disorder and delinquency, full discussion of psychological treatment is beyond the scope of this chapter. Readers will find the volumes by Morris and Kratochwill (1983) and Ollendick and Hersen (1983) useful resources.

CURRENT RESEARCH

As is common in new areas of educational, psychological, or medical inquiry, much of the early research in LD was clinical in nature, focusing on identified LD children and typically failing to attend to subject selection criteria, to use control groups, or otherwise to adhere to careful research procedures (Kavale & Nye, 1981). Thus, many of the generally accepted tenets regarding LD were not based on methodical research. During the 1970s many studies concentrated on refuting or confirming assumptions regarding what LD is or how to treat it. Among the major findings of that period were that processing disorders could not be reliably assessed with current neuropsychological or psychoeducational techniques, and that trying to remediate presumed process deficits did not appear to result in academic gains (e.g., Hammill & Larsen, 1974). Behaviorists stepped into this apparent void in LD theory and practice, suggesting that the underlying cause was irrelevent; school failure itself is the behavior of concern. The resulting behaviorally oriented focus on breaking the teaching-learning process down into discrete units (task analysis), monitoring each stage of skill acquisition (direct daily measurement), etc., has been a critical step forward for the field.

Current research in LD is ongoing in a number of provocative areas. Much of this was spearheaded by the federally funded LD Research Institutes supported at five universities from 1977 to 1983 (Kneedler & Hallahan, 1983). Several representative research areas are mentioned briefly in the following paragraphs.

Academic Strategies

It has become clear that many LD children do not acquire efficient strategies for handling academic tasks in the automatic way normal children do; thus, they do not profit from conventional instruction. However, they can be taught task-appropriate strategies that, when used, will improve their cognitive and academic performance (Hallahan, 1980; Hallahan, Hall et al., 1983; Hallahan, Lloyd et al., 1983).

Among the simplest and most effective of these strategies is *self-monitoring* (Hallahan, Lloyd, & Stroller, 1982). This technique uses the principles of cognitive-behavior modification (Meichenbaum, 1977), a relatively new perspective in psychology that recognizes the link between observable behaviors and what goes on in the mind. Hallahan et al. demonstrated that off-task LD children could be taught to keep track of and alter their own behavior, increasing their attention and academic productivity. The general notion has numerous potential applications in improving both the social behavior and the school performance of LD children.

Social Skills

The same subtle problems that interfere with an LD student's ability to acquire reading, writing, or arithmetic skills in the same way as most people do also appear to interfere frequently with their perception of social cues. A great deal of interest recently has focused on social skill deficits of the LD person. Both diagnosis and treatment of social inadequacies are becoming major research thrusts (Bryan, Pearl, Donahue, Bryan, & Pflaum, 1983).

Adolescent and Adult Issues

The last few years have seen a burst of interest in what happens to LD students as they mature (Schumaker et al., 1983). Because the first formal programs for LD children were begun only about 30 years ago, few individuals older than 40 can be identified for study. However, emerging longitudinal research strongly indicates that LD is a developmental disorder with life-long impact (see Hechtman & Weiss, 1983; Polloway et al., 1984; Vogel, 1982).

Related, more specific research centers on clarifying the link between LD and juvenile delinquency (JD) and later criminal behavior. This became an area of interest when JD specialists noted that many adjudicated adolescents could not read and had experienced other academic difficulties. Concern was expressed that LD led directly to JD, perhaps LD children became frustrated and angry over their inability to keep up in school and thus turned to antisocial acts. Large-scale research projects have clarified the relationship. It appears that no causal link between LD and JD exists, although more delinquents than nondelinquents have experienced school failure (Dunivant, 1982).

Neuropsychology

Earliest conceptions of the etiology of LD were that some type of brain abnormality was at the root of the disorder. As it became clear during the period of the 1950s–1970s that existing assessment techniques were not able to verify neurological problems in most instances, the field moved toward less medical, more behavioral assessment techniques. In the mean time, substantial advances in neuropsychological theory and assessment have occurred. Now a major renewal of interest is being seen in brain–behavior relations in general, and in the educational and psychological implications of unusual brain function in particular (e.g., Hynd, 1981). This promises to be a heavily researched area for years to come.

SUMMARY

The field of learning disabilities is connected historically to work with brain-damaged adults and children for whom the brain injury was inferred from behavior. Consequently, current definitions of LD carry an assumption that the learning disorders of the identified population have their origin in neurological dysfunction, whether of not direct evidence of such dysfunction can be found. The definition under which PL 94-142 is administered includes three major components: (a) information processing in areas related to academic performance is inefficient, presumably due to neurological dysfunction; (b) academic performance lags significantly behind intellectual aptitude; and (c) learning difficulty is not caused be sensory, physical, social, or emotional factors.

Epidemiological information regarding LD is limited because of the vagueness and uncertainty of the definition of the disorder. Nevertheless, professional consensus is that 1–3% of the school population is affected. Currently, about 4% of the school-age population is identified as LD. Boys outnumber girls by a ratio of 2:1 to

6:1. The causes of LD are mostly unknown in the individual case, although a variety of etiologies are suspected and, occasionally, pinpointed for the individual: brain injury, malnutrition, food toxins, lead and other environmental chemicals, heredity, and a host of other biochemical factors.

LD is now recognized as a developmental disorder with impact over the life span. However, most cases are diagnosed during the years of school attendance. Identification during preschool years and following secondary school attendance presents particular problems because of the heavy emphasis on school-based learning in the definition and the unavailability of psychometric norms for groups younger or older than typical public school age. Assessment of the disorder requires testing to estimate intellectual aptitude (usually with the WISC-R) and ability to perform in specific academic skill areas. Such testing does not assess information processing or psychological process deficits directly; moreover, the size of the aptitude-achievement discrepancy required for identification of a student as LD is an open question, one for which criteria vary widely among the psychologists and educators who apply diagnostic standards.

Most LD students are educated in resource rooms, arrangements under which they spend a significant portion of the school day integrated with their non-handicapped peers. Educators choose from a variety of theoretical models of instruction in approaching remedial tasks, including psychological process, cognitive, behavioral, direct instruction, and holistic models. Little research support is found for a psychological process approach.

Medical treatment of the disorder typically involves prescription of psychoactive drugs to control hyperactivity and disorders of attention. When psychoactive drugs are prescribed, it is essential that the effects be carefully monitored by parents and teachers. Psychological treatment ranges from traditional psychoanalytic therapy to behavior therapy. Evidence weighs in favor of a direct, behavioral approach to treatment of the social and emotional problems associated with school failure.

Current areas of research include academic strategy training, remediation of social skill deficits, neuropsychological aspects of learning difficulties, and issues in the management of LD in adolescents and adults. Research related to definition and identification of LD is needed for progress in understanding this most controversial of the developmental disorders.

REFERENCES

Abrams, A. L. (1968). Delayed and irregular maturation versus minimal brain injury. Recommendations for a change in current nomenclature. *Clinical Pediatrics, 7,* 344–349.

Algozzine, B., & Ysseldyke, J. (1983). Learning disabilities as a subset of school failure: The oversophistication of a concept. *Exceptional Children, 50,* 242–246.

Astman, J. A. (1984). Special education as a moral enterprise. *Learning Disability Quarterly, 7,* 299–308.

Beard, R. R., & Wertheim, G. A. (1967). Behavioral impairment associated with small doses of carbon monoxide. *American Journal of Public Health, 57,* 2012–2022.

Beery, K. E. (1967). *Developmental test of visual-motor integration: Administration and scoring manual.* Chicago: Follett.

Bettelheim, B. (1961). The decision to fail. *The School Review, 69,* 389–412.

Bettelheim, B. (1970). Listening to children. In P. A. Gallagher & L. L. Edwards (Eds.), *Educating emotionally disturbed children: theory to practice* (pp. 36–53). [Monograph] Lawrence: University of Kansas, Department of Special Education.

Bower, E. M. (Ed.) (1978). Early screening programs. *American Journal of Orthopsychiatry, 48,* 1–186.

Brown, V. L. (1985). Two perspectives on Engelmann and Carnine's *Theory of Instruction.* [Review of *Theory of instruction: Principles and applications.*] *Remedial and Special Education, 56,* 58–59.

Bryan, T. H., Pearl, R., Donahue, M., Bryan, J., & Pflaum, S. (1983). The Chicago Institute for the Study of Learning Disabilities. *Exceptional Education Quarterly, 4*(1), 1–22.

Clements, S. D. (1966). *Minimal brain dysfunction in children: Terminology and identification.* (U.S. Department of Health, Education, and Welfare, NINDB Monograph No. 3). Washington, DC: U.S. Government Printing Office.

Colarusso, R. P., & Hammill, D. D. (1972). *Motorfree visual perception test*. San Rafael, CA: Academic Therapy Publications.

Coleman, J. C., & Sandhu, M. (1967). A descriptive relational study of 364 children referred to a university clinic for learning disorders. *Psychological Reports, 20,* 1091–1105.

Colletti, L. F. (1979). Relationship between pregnancy and birth complications and the later development of learning disabilities. *Journal of Learning Disabilities, 12,* 659–663.

Cone, T. E., & Wilson, L. R. (1981). Quantifying a severe discrepancy: A critical analysis. *Learning Disability Quarterly, 4,* 359–371.

Cravioto, J., & DeLicardie, E. R. (1975). Environmental and nutritional deprivation in children with learning disabilities. In W. M. Cruickshank & D. P. Hallahan (Eds.), *Perceptual and learning disabilities in children, Vol 2: Research and theory* (pp. 3–102). Syracuse, NY: Syracuse University Press.

Cruickshank, W. M. (1977). Guest editorial. *Journal of Learning Disabilities, 10,* 193–194.

Cruickshank, W. M., Bice, H. V., & Wallen, N. E. (1957). *Perception and cerebral palsy*. Syracuse, NY: Syracuse University Press.

Cruickshank, W. M., Bentzen, F. A., Ratzeburg, F. H., & Tannhauser, M. T. (1961). *A teaching method for brain-injured and hyperactive children*. Syracuse, NY: Syracuse University Press.

Deshler, D. D. (1978). Psychoeducational aspects of learning disabled adolescents. In L. Mann, L. Goodman, & J. L. Weiderholt (Eds.), *Teaching the learning disabled adolescent*. Boston: Houghton Mifflin.

Dunivant, N. (1982). *The relationship between learning disabilities and juvenile delinquency: Brief summary of research findings*. Williamsburg, VA: National Center for State Courts. (National Institute for Juvenile Justice and Delinquency Prevention, Office of Juvenile Justice and Delinquency Prevention, U.S. Department of Justice Grant No. 78-JN—AX—0028).

Eisenson, J. (1954). *Examining for aphasia*. New York: The Psychological Corporation.

Engelmann, S., & Carnine, D. (1982). *Theory of instruction: Principles and applications*. New York: Irvington.

Gadow, K. D. (1981). Effects of stimulant drugs on attention and cognitive deficits. *Exceptional Education Quarterly, 2,* 83–93.

Gersten, R., & Carnine, D. (1984). Auditory-perceptual skills and reading: A response to Kavale's meta-analysis. *Remedial and Special Education, 5,* 16–191.

Gersten, R., & Carnine, D. (1985). Two ships crossing in the night. *Remedial and Special Education, 6,* 46–47.

Gillespie, P. H., Miller, T. L., & Fielder, V. C. (1975). Legislative definitions of learning disabilities: Roadblocks to effective service. *Journal of Learning Disabilities, 8,* 660–666.

Goldstein, K. (1939). *The organism*. New York: American Book.

Hallahan, D. P. (Ed.). (1980). Teaching exceptional children to use cognitive strategies [Topical issue]. *Exceptional Education Quarterly, 1.*

Hallahan, D. P., & Bryan, T. H. (1981). Learning disabilities. In J. M. Kauffman & D. P. Hallahan (Eds.), *Handbook of special education* (pp. 141–164). Englewood Cliffs, NJ: Prentice-Hall.

Hallahan, D. P., & Cruickshank, W. M. (1973). *Psychoeducational foundations of learning disabilities*. Englewood Cliffs, NJ: Prentice-Hall.

Hallahan, D. P., Hall, R. J., Ianna, S. O., Kneedler, R. D., Lloyd, J. W., Loper, A. B., & Reeve, R. E. (1983). Summary of research findings at the University of Virginia Learning Disabilities Research Institute. *Exceptional Education Quarterly, 4,* 95–114.

Hallahan, D. P., & Kauffman, J. M. (1976). *Introduction to learning disabilities: A psychobehavioral approach*. Englewood Cliffs, NJ: Prentice-Hall.

Hallahan, D. P., Kauffman, J. M., & Lloyd, J. W. (1985). *Introduction to learning disabilities* (2nd ed.). Englewood Cliffs, NJ: Prentice-Hall.

Hallahan, D. P., Lloyd, J. W., Kauffman, J. M., & Loper, A. B. (1983). Academic problems. In R. J. Morris & T. R. Kratochwill (Eds.), *The practice of child therapy* (pp. 113–141). Elmsford, NY: Pergamon.

Hallahan, D. P., Lloyd, J. W., & Stoller, L. (1982). *Improving attention with self monitoring: A manual for teachers*. Charlottesville, Va.: University of Virginia Learning Disabilities Research Institute.

Hallgren, B. (1950). Specific dyslexia: A clinical and genetic study. *Acta Psychiatrica et Neurologica Scandinavica (Suppl.), 65,* 1–287.

Hammill, D. D., & Larsen, S. (1974). The effectiveness of psycholinguistic training. *Exceptional Children, 41,* 5–14.

Haring, N. G., Lovitt, T. C., Eaton, M. D., & Hansen, C. (1978). *The fourth R: Research in the classroom*. Columbus, OH: Merrill.

Harris, A. (1975). *How to increase reading ability: A guide to developmental and remedial methods* (6th edition). New York: McKay.

Hechtman, L., & Weiss, G. (1983). Long-term outcome of hyperactive children. *American Journal of Orthopsychiatry, 53,* 532–541.

Heshusius, L. (1984). Why would they and I want to do it? A phenomenological-theoretical view of special education. *Learning Disability Quarterly, 7,* 363–368.

Hinshelwood, J. A. (1896). A case of dyslexia: A peculiar form of word-blindness. *Lancet, 2,* 1451–1454.

Hinshelwood, J. A. (1911). *Congenital word blindness.* London: H. K. Lewis & Co.

Howell, K. W., Kaplan, J. S., & Serapaglia, T. (1980). *Diagnosing basic skills: A handbook for deciding what to teach.* Columbus, OH: Merrill.

Hynd, G. W. (Ed.) (1981). Neuropsychology in the schools [Special issue]. *The School Psychology Review, 10.*

Kauffman, J. M., & Hallahan, D. P. (1979). Learning disability and hyperactivity (with comments on minimal brain dysfunction). In B. B. Lahey & A. E. Kazdin (Eds.), *Advances in clinical child psychology: Vol. 2* (pp. 71–105). New York: Plenum.

Kaufman, A. S. (1976). A new approach to the interpretation of test scatter on the WISC-R. *Journal of Learning Disabilities, 9,* 160–168.

Kaufman, A. S., & Kaufman, N. L. (1983). *Kaufman Assessment Battery for Children.* Circle Pines, MN: American Guidance.

Kavale, K. A. (1981). The relationship between auditory perceptual skills and reading disability: A meta-analysis. *Journal of Learning Disabilities, 14,* 539–546.

Kavale, K. A. (1985). Auditory perceptual skills and reading: A rejoinder to Gersten and Carnine about what Kavale did. *Remedial and Special Education, 6,* 43–45.

Kavale, K. A., & Forness, S. R. (1984). A meta-analysis of the validity of Wechsler Scale profiles and recategorizations: Patterns or parodies. *Learning Disability Quarterly, 7,* 136–156.

Kavale, K. A., & Forness, S. R. (1985). Learning disability and the history of science: Paradigm or paradox? *Remedial and Special Education, 6,* 12–23.

Kavale, K. A., & Nye, C. (1981). Research definitions of learning disabilities: A survey of the literature. *Learning Disability Quarterly, 4,* 383–388.

Keogh, B. K., & Becker, L. D. (1973). Early detection of learning problems: Questions, cautions, and guidelines. *Exceptional Children, 40,* 5–11.

Kinsbourne, M., & Caplan, P. (1979). *Children's learning and attention problems.* Boston: Little, Brown.

Kirk, S. A. (1976). Samuel A. Kirk. In J. M. Kauffman & D. P. Hallahan (Eds.), *Teaching children with learning disabilities: Personal perspectives* (pp. 238–269). Columbus, OH: Merrill.

Kirk, S. A., & Elkins, J. (1975). Characteristics of children enrolled in child service demonstration centers. *Journal of Learning Disabilities, 8,* 630–637.

Kirk, S. A., & Kirk, W. D. (1971). *Psycholinguistic learning disabilities: Diagnosis and remediation.* Urbana: University of Illinois Press.

Kirk, S. A., McCarthy, J. J., & Kirk, W. D. (1961). *Illinois test of psycholinguistic abilities* (Experimental ed.). Urbana, IL: University of Illinois Press.

Kneedler, R. D., & Hallahan, D. P. (Eds.). (1983). Research in learning disabilities: summaries of the institutes [Topical issue]. *Exceptional Education Quarterly, 4.*

Koppitz, E. M. (1963). *The Bender gestalt test for young children.* New York: Grune & Stratton.

Lloyd, J. W. (1984). How shall we individualize instruction — or should we? *Remedial and Special Education, 5,* 7–15.

Lloyd, J. W., & Carnine, D. (Eds.). (1981). Structured instruction: Effective teaching of essential skills [Topical issue]. *Exceptional Education Quarterly, 2.*

Lovitt, T. C. (1975). Applied behavior analysis and learning disabilities. Part II: Specific research recommendations and suggestions for practitioners. *Journal of Learning Disabilities, 8,* 504–518.

Lovitt, T. C. (1981). Charting academic performances of mildly handicapped youngsters. In J. M. Kauffman & D. P. Hallahan (Eds.), *Handbook of special education* (pp. 393–417). Englewood Cliffs, NJ: Prentice-Hall.

Lovitt, T. C. (1982). *Because of my persistence, I've learned from children.* Columbus, OH: Merrill.

Mangrum, C. T., & Strichart, S. S. (1984). *College and the learning disabled student.* New York: Grune & Stratton.

Mayron, L. W. (1979). Allergy, learning, and behavior problems. *Journal of Learning Disabilities, 12,* 32–42.

McNutt, G. (1984). A holistic approach to language arts instruction in the resource room. *Learning Disability Quarterly, 7,* 315–320.

Meichenbaum, D. (1977). *Cognitive behavior modofication.* New York: Plenum.

Meichenbaum, D. (1980). Cognitive behavior modification with exceptional children: a promise yet unfulfilled. *Exceptional Education Quarterly, 1,* 83–88.

Morgan, W. P. (1896). A cases of congenital word blindness. *British Medical Journal, 2,* 1378.

Morris, R. J., & Kratochwill, T. R. (Eds.) (1983). *The practice of child therapy*. Elmsford, NY: Pergamon.

Morse, W. C. (1984). Personal perspective. In B. Blatt & R. J. Morris (Eds.), *Perspectives in special education: personal orientations* (pp. 101–124). Glenview, IL: Scott, Foresman.

Myklebust, H. R. (1954). *Auditory disorders in children*. New York: Grune & Stratton.

Mykleburst, H. (1967). Learning disabilities: Definition and overview. In H. Myklebust (Ed.), *Progress in learning disabilities* (Vol. 1). New York: Grune & Stratton.

Neal, C. (1984). The holistic teacher. *Learning Disability Quarterly, 7*, 309–313.

Norman, C. A., Jr., & Zigmond, N. (1980). Characteristics of children labeled and served in school systems affiliated with child service demonstration centers. *Journal of Learning Disabilities, 13*, 542–547.

O'Leary, K. D. (1980). Pills or skills for hyperactive children. *Journal of Applied Behavior Analysis, 13*, 191–204.

O'Leary, S. G. (1980). A response to cognitive training. *Exceptional Education Quarterly, 1*, 89–94.

Ollendick, T. H., & Hersen, M. (Eds.) (1983). *Handbook of child psychopathology*. New York: Plenum.

Osgood, C. E. (1957). A behavioristic analysis of perception and language as cognitive phenomena. In J. S. Bruner (Ed.), *Contemporary approaches to cognition*. Cambridge, MA: Harvard University Press.

Owen, F. W., Adams, P. A., Forrest, T., Stolz, L. M., & Fisher, S. (1971). Learning disorders in children: Sibling studies. *Monographs of the Society for Research in Child Development, 36*(4, Serial No. 144).

Pasamanick, P., & Knobloch, H. (1973). The epidemiology of reproductive causality. In S. G. Sapir, & A. C. Nitzburg (Eds.), *Children with learning problems: Reading in a developmental-interaction approach*. New York: Brunner/Mazel.

Polloway, E. A., Smith, J. D., & Patton, J. R. (1984). Learning disabilities: An adult development perspective. *Learning Disability Quarterly, 7*, 179–186.

Poplin, M. S. (1984). Toward an holistic view of persons with learning disabilities. *Learning Disability Quarterly, 7*, 290–294.

Rooney, K. J., & Hallahan, D. P. (1985). Future directions for cognitive behavior modification research: The quest for cognitive change. *Remedial and Special Education, 6*, 46–51.

Rubin, R., & Balow, B. (1971). Learning and behavior disorders: A longitudinal study. *Exceptional Children, 38*, 293–299.

Salvia, J., & Ysseldyke, J. E. (1981). *Assessment in special and remedial education* (2nd ed.). Boston: Houghton Mifflin.

Schroeder, C., Schroeder, S., & Davine, M. (1978). Learning disabilities: Assessment and management of reading problems. In B. Wolman, J. Egan, & A. Ross (Eds.), *Handbook of mental disorders in childhood and adolescence* (pp. 212–237). Englewood Cliffs, NJ: Prentice-Hall.

Schumaker, J. B., Deshler, D. D., Alley, G. R., & Warner, M. M. (1983). Toward the development of an intervention model for learning disabled adolescents: The University of Kansas Institute. *Exceptional Education Quarterly, 4*, 45–74.

Shepard, L. A., Smith, M. L., & Vojir, C. P. (1983). Characteristics of pupils identified as learning disabled. *American Educational Research Journal, 20*, 309–331.

Silver, L. (1971). Familial patterns in children with neurologically based learning disabilities. *Journal of Learning Disabilities, 4*, 349–358.

Smith, C. R. (1980) Assessment alternatives: Nonstandardized procedures. *School Psychology Review, 9*, 46–57.

Smith, C. R. (1983) *Learning disabilities: The interaction of learner, task, and setting*. Boston: Little, Brown.

Smith, D. D. (1981). *Teaching the learning disabled*. Englewood Cliffs, NJ: Prentice-Hall.

Smith, M. D., Coleman, J. M., Dokecki, P. R., & Davis, E. E. (1977). Intellectual characteristics of school labeled learning disabled children. *Exceptional Children, 43*, 352–357.

Sontag, E., Button, J. E., & Hagerty, G. (1982, December). *Quality and leadership in special education personnel preparation*. Paper presented at an invitational meeting for personnel preparation, Office of Special Education Programs, U. S. Department of Education, Washington, DC.

Sprague, R. L., & Ullmann, R. (1981). Psychoactive drugs and child management. In J. M. Kauffman & D. P. Hallahan (Eds.), *Handbook of special education* (pp. 749–766). Englewood Cliffs, NJ: Prentice-Hall.

Strauss, A. A., & Kephart, N. C. (1955). *Psychopathology and education of the brain-injured child, Vol. 2: Progress in theory and clinic*. New York: Grune & Stratton.

Strauss. A. A., Lehtinen, L. E. (1947). *Psychopathology and education of the brain-injured child*. New York: Grune & Stratton.

Swanson, J. M., & Kinsbourne, M. (1980). Food dyes impair performance of hyper active children on a laboratory learning test. *Science, 207,* 1485–1487.

Thurlow, M. L., & Ysseldyke, J. E. (1982). Instructional planning: Information collected by psychologists versus information considered useful by teachers. *Journal of School Psychology, 20,* 3–10.

Tucker, J., Stevens, L. J., & Ysseldyke, J. E. (1983). Learning disabilities: The experts speak out. *Journal of Learning Disabilities, 16,* 6–14.

U.S. Department of Education (1984). *Sixth annual report to Congress on implementation of Public Law 94-142, The Education for All Handicapped Children Act.* Washington, DC: U.S. Government Printing Office.

U.S. Office of Education (1970). *Third annual report of the National Advisory Committee on Handicapped Children.* Washington, DC: U.S. Department of Health, Education and Welfare.

U.S. Office of Education (1981). *Third annual report to Congress on implementation of Public Law 94-142, The Education for All Handicapped Children Act.* Washington, DC: U.S. Government Printing Office.

Vogel, S. A. (1982). On developing LD college programs. *Journal of Learning Disabilities, 15,* 518–528.

Wallace, G., & Kauffman, J. M. (1978). *Teaching children with learning problems* (2nd ed.). Columbus, OH: Merrill.

Walzer, S., & Richmond, J. B. (1973). The epidemiology of learning disorders. *Pediatric Clinics of North America, 20,* 719–736.

Wechsler, D. (1974). Wechsler Intelligence Scale for Children — revised. New York: Psychological Corporation.

Wedig, J. (1974). Early detection of mercurialism. In C. Xintras, B. L. Johnson, & I. deGroot (Eds.), *Behavioral toxicology.* Washington, DC: U.S. Department of Health, Education and Welfare.

Wiedderholt, J. L. (1974). Historical perspectives on the education of the learning disabled. In L. Mann & D. Sabatino (Eds.), *The second review of special education* (pp. 103–152). Philadelphia: JSE Press.

Wepman, J. M., Jones, L. V., Bock, R. D., & Van Pelt, D. (1960). Studies in aphasia: Background and theoretical formulations. *Journal of Speech and Hearing Disorders, 25,* 323–332.

Whalen, C., & Henker, B. (1976). Psychostimulants and children: A review and analysis. *Psychological Bulletin, 83,* 1113–1130.

Woodcock, R. W., & Johnson, M. B. (1977). *Woodcock-Johnson psycho-educational battery.* Hingham, MA: Teaching Resources.

Ysseldyke, J. E., Algozzine, B., & Epps, S. (1983). A logical and empirical analysis of current practice in classifying students as handicapped. *Exceptional Children, 50,* 160–166.

Ysseldyke, J. E., Thurlow, M., Graden, J., Wesson, C., Algozzine, B., & Deno, S. (1981). Generalizations from five years of research on assessment and decision making: The University of Minnesota Institute. *Exceptional Education Quarterly, 4*(1), 75–93.

CHAPTER 20

Mental Retardation in Children

Madalyn E. Tyson and Judith E. Favell

INTRODUCTION

Mental retardation is typically diagnosed during childhood and often remains a serious, pervasive problem with implications that extend through life. There may be considerable impact on the family, as well as on the mentally retarded individual's relationship with others and on the options available to him or her, such as means of earning a living and the ability to live independently.

The last two decades have witnessed massive changes in the field of mental retardation. The options for mentally retarded children are considerably greater than they were 20 years ago. Parents at that time were faced with one major decision to be made regarding their mentally retarded children: whether to institutionalize them or keep them at home. The prevailing orientation was on the child's deficits; that is, the emphasis was on the fact that the child would never learn and would remain dependent on others.

Parents now have a number of support services to help them cope with the reality of providing for a handicapped child. Furthermore, there is a decided emphasis on what the child *can* learn. Even the most basic accomplishments (i.e., progressing from washing one's hands with a verbal prompt as opposed to full physical assistance) is a cause for celebration, because the child is progressing in demonstrating skills to enable him or her to function at a more independent level.

DESCRIPTION OF THE DISORDER

Definitions

There is some degree of consensus on how to define mental retardation (Grossman, 1983), but it is by no means acceptable to all practitioners in the field (i.e., Bijou, 1966; Frankenberger, 1984; Gold, 1980; Kazdin & Straw, 1976; Mercer, 1971; Whitman, Scibak, & Reid, 1983; Zigler, Balla, & Hodapp, 1984). A universally accepted definition has been unfeasible due to the highly relative and culturally determined nature of this disorder (Gearheart & Litton, 1975). The American Association on Mental Deficiency (AAMD) has set forth the most widely endorsed definition currently in use:

Mental retardation refers to significantly subaverage general intellectual functioning resulting in or associated with impairments in adaptive behavior and manifested during the developmental period. (Grossman, 1983, p. 1).

The AAMD definition represents an effort to incorporate several criteria (i.e., a chronological age of up to 18 years for onset, deficits in adaptive behavior, low measured intelligence) that simultaneously must be present before an individual can be diagnosed as mentally retarded. This multidimensional approach to definition is in keeping with other recognized systems, such as the *Diagnostic and Statistical Manual of Mental Disorders*, 3rd edition, (American Psychiatric Association, 1980), and the World Health Organization's *International Classification of Diseases-9 (ICD-9)*, (1978).

The accepted IQ cut-off score of 70, or 2 standard deviations (*SDs*) below the mean, is intended as a general guide, however. A child whose measured IQ is somewhat higher than 70, but with deficits in adaptive behavior, for example, might be diagnosed as mentally retarded. In other words, clinical judgment is relied upon in borderline cases.

One component of the AAMD definition that is most attacked by critics is the inclusion of adaptive behavior. The AAMD (1974) defines adaptive behavior as "the effectiveness of an individual in coping with the natural and social demands of his or her environment." Critics contend that the notion of adaptive behavior is vaguely defined and not reliably measured. Zigler et al. (1984) advocate the sole use of an IQ of at least 2 standard deviations below the mean, along with considerations of etiology. Clausen (1967) had earlier recommended that mental retardation be defined by IQ alone because the determination rests primarily on the basis of IQ.

The debate over the usefulness of considering adaptive behavior in the definition of mental retardation will doubtless continue. However, Spreat, Roszkowski, and Isett (1983) pointed out that definitions of intelligence have proven to be no less problematic to resolve.

Some practitioners have proposed environmentally oriented approaches to definition. Mercer (1971, 1973) viewed mental retardation as an achieved social status rather than a condition inherent in the individual. As such, she recommended that mental retardation be defined sociologically, and thus vary from social system to social system. Gold (1980) also regarded mental retardation as a function of the resources and training capabilities of a society, rather than a focus on biological limitations. He described failure to learn as a deficit of the environment rather than of the individual.

Bijou (1963, 1966) and others (i.e., Kazdin & Straw, 1976; Whitman et al., 1983) do not view the concept of intelligence as being either educationally functional or scientifically valid. A behavioral orientation shifts the focus from mentality to mentally retarded behavior, in the the "retarded individual is one who has a limited repertory of behavior shaped by the events that constitute his history" (Bijou, 1966, p.2). The behavioral approach does not ignore physiological or sociocultural determinants of mentally retarded behavior. Instead, this treatment-oriented approach places relatively greater emphasis on the contingencies that can be rearranged to teach more functional adaptive behavior (Kazdin & Straw, 1976; Sulzer-Azaroff & Mayer, 1977; Whitman et al., 1983).

Despite the proliferation of behavioral approaches with mentally retarded individuals, the term mental retardation is still the accepted designation for these persons. The retention of the term perpetuates a reliance on the mentality of the individuals as being the sole defining feature.

Classification

Subgroupings have been a means of further defining such a heterogeneous group as the mentally retarded. Many persons view classification as necessary to the provision of quality service delivery (i.e., Grossman, 1983; Hobbs, 1975a, 1975b; Warren, 1984), as well as to direct prescription and research efforts.

Classification systems vary across several dimensions. The most commonly used system subdivides the mentally retarded into four levels of functioning, as based on IQ: (a) mild retardation, 50-70, (b) moderate, 35-49, (c) severe, 20-34, and (d) profound, below 20 (American Psychiatric Association, 1980; Grossman, 1983). An alternate classification system has been in use by special educators: educable mentally retarded (EMR), trainable mentally retarded (TMR), and severely and profoundly mentally retarded (SPMR) (MacMillan, 1982). These categories correspond roughly to the previous classification system (e.g., EMR to mild and TMR to moderate). Further, there is sometimes an additional subgrouping of the mildly handicapped group within the academic setting: (a) the EMR, (b) the learning disabled (LD), and (c) the behaviorally disordered (BD).

Often, mentally retarded children have at least one other disability in addition to a primary diagnosis of mental retardation. These individuals display a wide range of disabilities that may or may not be associated with physical handicaps, neurological impairment, behavioral problems, or emotional disturbance (MacMillan, 1982). The 1983 AAMD *Manual* lists the following specific etiological classifications:

1. Infections and intoxications,
2. Trauma or physical agent,
3. Metabolism or physical agent,
4. Gross brain disease (postnatal),
5. Unknown prenatal influence,
6. Chromosomal abnormalities,
7. Other conditions originating in the perinatal period,
8. Following psychiatric disorder,
9. Environmental influences, and
10. Other conditions.

However, the vast number of cases of mental retardation have no known etiology. Baumeister and MacLean (1979) expressed puzzlement that the description of etiology was in depth; yet the AAMD definition did not incorporate medical classification in its formal diagnosis criteria. To date, no reliable behavioral differences between the various etiological groups have been demonstrated (Ellis, 1969).

In regard to etiological considerations, the mentally retarded often are assigned to one of two basic groups: (a) cultural-familial (also referred to as psychosocial disadvantage), in which mental retardation is largely attributed to environmental reasons, and (b) organic, in which one can identify a known organic cause (Zigler, 1967). Some skepticism also exists as to the usefulness of this distinction, given the difficulties in separating biological and psychological causes (Cegelka & Prehm, 1982; MacMillan, 1982). Ellis and Cavelier (1982) have stated that there are currently no reliable diagnostic procedures to sort the mentally retarded into cultural-familial and organic designations.

Baumeister and MacLean (1979) have alternately conceptualized a continuum of bahavioral characteristics, along with an underlying continuum of neurological impairment, as a more accurate account of mental retardation. They emphasized that a host of factors must be taken into account (i.e., type, extent, source, etc., of biological conditions) before any statement of causality of mental retardation can be made.

Without a solidly accepted definition and classification conventions, some practitioners view findings from research and their implications for treatment as having limited usefulness. Taylor (1980) reviewed the use of the AAMD classification system in research published in the *American Journal of Mental Deficiency* and *Mental Retardation* between the years of 1973 and 1979. He specifically looked at descriptions of subjects, tests, and test scores, as well as the correctness of classifications used. Only 28% of the investigators even used the AAMD classification system, whereas a large number of these studies misclassified their subjects when reporting test scores. Frankenberger (1984), in a survey of states' definitions of mental retardation, noted a lack of uniform agreement. Not all states (67%) included adaptive behavior in their definition of mental retardation, despite its being an integral component of the AAMD definition.

The lack of uniform agreement and usage of both definition and classification in mental retardation is of great concern to some individuals, in that service delivery from area to area will vary markedly as a result. Behaviorally oriented practitioners have been unimpressed with this "raging controversy," however. Although the professed intent of definition and classification systems for mentally retarded individuals has been to direct assessment, treatment, and research, this avenue of debate is viewed as unproductive when applied on an individual basis.

PREVALENCE AND INCIDENCE

Related to the definition of mental retardation are estimates of its prevalance and incidence. These terms frequently have been used interchangeably, leading to confusion in the literature (Marozas, May, & Lehman, 1980). The difference between prevalence and incidence has been described in the following manner: prevalence indicates the total number of cases at a given time, whereas incidence refers to the number of new cases in a given period (Morton & Hebel, 1979).

There is currently no direct way to accurately measure the total number of mentally retarded individuals. Obviously, prevalence and incidence estimates vary with the broadness of the definition of mental retardation. Silverstein (1977) used hypothetical data to estimate prevalence rates, with cutting scores of 2, 1½, and 1 SD below the mean. Nationwide prevalence data ranged from as little as 100,000 to approximately 30 million individuals depending on that definition.

Previous estimates have placed the prevalence rate at approximately 6 million individuals, or about 3% of the total population. However, these estimates were based on consideration of IQ alone. Tarjan, Wright, Eyman, and Keeran (1973) disputed this prevalence rate and placed it at approximately 1% or 2 million individuals. Grossman (1983) also agreed that an estimate of about 1% of the population, or an incidence rate of approximately 125,000 births per year, is probably most accurate. He saw little usefulness in national estimates, given the marked variations between communities, the use of single or multiple diagnostic criteria, and current difficulties in identifying causes of mental retardation or age of onset.

Factors

Four factors seem especially relevant in supporting a truer prevalence rate of 1% (Tarjan et al., 1973), because inclusion of these considerations limits the scope of who is designated as mentally retarded. First, not only must a child's IQ score be lower than 70, but he or she also must demonstrate deficits in adaptive behavior. Second, most cases are undetected until well into the school years, when academic failure is noted. Third, many persons are no longer regarded as mentally retarded upon leaving school. Finally, the lower the IQ, the higher the mortality rate, given that life expectancies for lower-functioning individuals are less than for the general population. In partial support for these factors, Baird and Sadovnick (1985) conducted an investigation of both prevalence and incidence of the population of British Columbia. They found the highest prevalence rate for those aged 15 to 29 years. The lowest prevalence rates were for the over age 50 group and those persons from birth up to 4 years of age.

MacMillan (1982) cited a number of factors associated with prevalence rates. In addition to age variations (although artificially inflated due to academic demands), sex variations have also been noted. The number of males labeled as mentally retarded far exceeds females, probably due to sex-linked recessive conditions as well as different expectancies for males in our society. Community, state, social class, and race variations have also been noted. For example, rural areas appear to have a higher prevalence rate than urban environments, and lower socioeconomic status individuals and members of minority groups are represented disproportionally in classes for EMR children.

Some researchers have focused attention on estimates of prevalence and incidence, in the hope of fostering prevention and control of mental retardation. Clarke and Clarke (1977), however, state that prospects for amelioration are not good. Earlier estimates that mental retardation could be reduced 50% by the end of the century is now deemed unlikely. Mild mental retardation, which comprises the majority of cases, poses the greatest dilemma for prevention because so little is yet known concerning causes.

It seems apparent from the available literature that we are not certain how our efforts to treat mental retardation are impacting on the prevalence and incidence of the problem. It may be quite some years before we can ascertain how our current service delivery systems, which have expanded considerably in recent years, are affecting the degree and scope of mental retardation.

DIAGNOSIS AND ASSESSMENT

Diagnosis, derived through a thorough assessment of an individual, is the foundation for developing appropriate treatment. Many severe forms of mental retardation are diagnosed by physicians within a short time after birth (MacMillan & Meyers, 1979). Alternately, MacMillan (1982) estimated that between 70 and 85% of all mental retardation diagnoses are derived from educational personnel when a child is in school. These diagnoses are generally of mild mental retardation, which is difficult to assess earlier, chiefly because of lack of physical signs.

Diagnosis rests on the use of standardized assessment tools, which remain a cornerstone of psychological and educational services for mentally retarded individuals. Behavioral assessment has also become an invaluable adjunct or alternative to more traditional assessment instruments. This direct observational approach has proven exceptionally useful in providing functional prescriptions for treatment and training.

Standarized Assessment

Intelligence Tests

The intellectual functioning of mentally retarded children is usually assessed via the Stanford-Binet Intelligence Scale or one of the Wechsler Scales (WPPSI, WISC-R, or the WAIS-R). These tests can also be used to assess strengths and weaknesses in intellect and to develop remedial approaches (Kaufman, 1979). The Stanford-Binet yields one IQ score, which is computed by dividing the child's derived mental age by the child's chronological age and then multiplying by 100. The Wechsler scales, by contrast, yield a performance IQ, a verbal IQ, and an overall full-scale IQ. Both scales have limited usefulness with nonverbal severely and profoundly handicapped children, because both IQ tests rely heavily on verbal performance. The Slosson Intelligence Test can be used successfully in place of the Wechsler Scales or the Stanford-Binet, in that it can provide accurate IQ scores and mental ages for low-functioning individuals.

Alternative tests have been developed for those individuals who cannot be assessed by traditional means (Anastasi, 1976). The Peabody Picture Vocabulary Test—Revised (PPVT-R) can be administered in 15 minutes or less and measures receptive use of language. This test yields a standard score that can be roughly interpreted as an IQ score. The Leiter International Performance Scale, which was constructed for cross-cultural purposes, has been used for assessing mentally retarded children. It is administered without instructions and also yields an IQ score.

The Kauffman Assessment Battery for Children (K-ABC), recently published in 1983, has been the first scale to rival the WISC-R and the Stanford-Binet in the assessment of mentally retarded children (Kamphaus & Reynolds, 1984). This test focuses on process rather than content of specific tasks. In a recent comparison of the K-ABC with the WISC-R, Naglieri (1985) demonstrated that the K-ABC is a better predictor of academic performance.

In some cases due to extreme physical handicaps, instances when a child is nonverbal, or with a very young child, developmental scales have been employed to at least derive an estimate of mental age or provide a fine-grained assessment of the skills an individual can demonstrate. Chief among these tests are the Bayley Scales of

Infant Development, the Ordinal Scales of Psychological Development, and the Neonatal Behavioral Assessment Scale.

Adaptive Behavior Tests

Along with one or more assessments of intellectual functioning, tests of adaptive behavior are also employed. Of these, the most popular tests are the AAMD's Adaptive Behavior Scale (ABS) and the Vineland Social Maturity Scale. Both are checklists and can be filled in by someone familiar with the child's behavior or by an interview technique, whereby the psychologist interviews a significant other (e.g., direct care staff or parent).

The Vineland had been particularly useful, in that it yields both an age equivalent and a social quotient that can be roughly employed as an intelligence measure. However, the Vineland has been replaced by the Vineland Adaptive Behavior Scales, which provide an adaptive behavior composite score and mental age scores. This may have limited usefulness for profoundly mentally retarded individuals, in that an IQ or social quotient score cannot be attained. In contrast, the Adaptive Behavior Scale has two sections: Part I assesses adaptive behavior via 10 domains. Part II measures maladaptive behavior via 13 domains. The test supplies percentile scores per domain rather than the overall score provided by the Vineland. This attests to the notion that adaptive behavior is composed of a variety of factors and cannot be reduced to one single scaore. Some individuals, however, do total the raw scores to derive a composite score for the ABS (Spreat et al., 1983).

Examiners must be careful even with their use of standardized assessment tools to prevent labels assigned by previous evaluations to alter their expectations of performance. Burdg and Graham (1984), for example, compared examiner's behavior with respect to 40 normal; preschool children who were assigned by sex to four conditions: normal male, normal female, developmentally delayed male, and developmentally delayed female. Results indicated that the label of develop-mentally delayed had a negative impact on test scores and performance ratings.

Behavioral Assessment

An adjunct or alternative approach to standardized assessment devices has been the incorporation of direct observation of actual behavior (Kazdin & Straw, 1976; Sulzer-Azaroff & Mayer, 1977). This approach has been employed successfully to design interventions. Briefly, the components of behavioral assessment begin with selecting an operationally defined response, as well as assessing the antecedent and consequent stimuli associated with that response. Next, a method of observation is employed, such as interval, frequency, or duration recording. Finally, independent observers are used to assess the accuracy of measurement over time. This overall measurement approach is followed during baseline, intervention, and follow-up phases, and can be applied or adapted for observation of a wide range of behaviors.

The most important component of behavioral approaches to assessment is the use of repeated, direct observation (Whitman et al., 1983). This method is superior to traditional assessment tools for guiding interventions because it provides a truer picture of a given individual's behavior over time in the context of real-life circumstances. The "snapshot" approach of norm-based traditional assessment tools often provides little useful information to guide educational planning for mentally retarded children.

A behavioral approach to assessment is closely related to treatment and accountability. This data-based approach, which analyzes the environmental contingencies that impact on behavior, aids the practitioner in determining treatment needs and selecting the type of treatment to employ, as well as in evaluating the effectiveness of the interventions selected. More rigorous adherence to research design in carrying out interventions can also lead to ascertaining important causal relationships that control human behavior.

The proliferation of data-based, effective treatment approaches delineated in the

literature attests to the usefulness and prac-
ticality of a behavioral approach to effective treatment of mentally retarded individuals. However, applied behavioral
analysis is still in its infancy. Much work is
yet needed to extend the application of
behavior analysis to ensure the generalization and long-term maintenance of treatment effects.

APPROACHES

The underlying philosophy in the field
of mental retardation views the individual,
regardless of level of handicap or age, as
being capable of learning. Environmental
stimulation is also viewed as essential for
maximum growth (Cegelka & Prehm,
1982). These orientations hold true regardless of the theoretical base of the
practitioner.

There are, however, some differences in
how practitioners conceptualize how
learning takes place for a given individual.
In applications to the mentally retarded,
the developmental model and the remedial
model have been the two major conceptualizations of how children learn (Guess et al.,
1979). The next section will briefly overview these orientations, as well as the
impact of the medical model on the
handicapped.

Developmental Model

A central tenet of this approach is that
children's development is based on the
readiness to acquire new tasks. Hagen, Barclay, and Schwethelm (1982) viewed the
developmental approach to teaching the
mentally retarded as emphasizing a somewhat passive manner of intervention.
Because the major responsibility for
growth rests "within" the child, it seems
easier to wait until a child has achieved
readiness for a given task before beginning
training.

Much of the current theory and practice
in child development is based on work conducted by Piaget (1964; Piaget & Inhelder,
1969). Although his body of work is too
extensive to review here, a brief description of the major features of Piaget's theory
are in order.

Piaget's Theory of Cognitive Development

This theory postulated that development
is sequential, hierarchical in organization,
irreversible, and universal. Children are
seen as passing through four distinct stages
of growth that are invariant in order: (a)
sensorimotor (birth to 2 years), (b) preoperational (2 to 5 years), (c) concrete operations
(5 to 12 years), and (d) abstract reasoning
(12 to maturity). Kahn (1976, 1977) viewed
many severely mentally retarded children,
and most profoundly mentally retarded
children, as functioning in the sensori-
motor period.

There are three other important aspects
of this theory. Development is viewed as
preceding learning; an individual must
possess various cognitive structures
(*schema*) before learning can take place. The
child is also viewed as an active learner;
environmental interaction is necessary to
bring about change. The notion of *object
permanence*, achieved by the end of the sensorimotor stage, is also a feature stressed by
those who apply this approach to working
with the mentally retarded. Object permanence refers to the ability of a child to be
aware of the presence of an object, whether
it is in view or temporarily out of view.

The Ordinal Scales of Psychological
Development (Uzgiris & Hunt, 1975),
which were devised to measure cognitive
function in normal infants, have also been
used with severely mentally retarded children. Recently, Kahn (1983) showed that
three of the Uzgiris and Hunt scales (i.e.,
vocal imitation, object permanence, and
gestural imitation), along with mental age
and chronological age, could reliably predict performance on four scales (independent functioning, language, self-direction,
and socialization) of the Adaptive Behavior
Scale.

Cognitive Development Models

Two contrasting models of cognitive
development have been proposed: the
developmental model and the *difference or
defect model*. These models are directed at
those mentally retarded children who
would be classified as "cultural-familial" or
mildly mentally retarded. Generally, the

IQ cutoff used in these theories extends down to 50, with those having an IQ below this point considered to function quite differently from the normal population (MacMillan, 1982).

The developmentalists, in their "similar sequence hypothesis," claim that mentally retarded children proceed through the same stages and sequences of cognitive development as nonmentally retarded children, but that they progress at a slower rate and to a more limited upper stage of cognition (Zigler, 1966, 1982). Another tenet, the "similar structure hypothesis," states that the cognitive performance of groups of cultural-familial mentally retarded and nonmentally retarded individuals of equal mental age (MA) will not differ.

Numerous studies, many utilizing Piagetian tasks, have been conducted to support these views (Silverstein, Pearson, Keller, & McLain, 1982; Weisz, Yeates, & Zigler, 1982; Weisz & Zigler, 1979; Woodward, 1979). Weisz and Zigler (1979), in their review of 3 longitudinal and 28 cross-sectional studies, for example, found overwhelming support for the similar sequence hypothesis.

The difference approach, by contrast, assumes that varied IQ levels produce qualitatively poorer performance by mentally retarded persons when matched to the same MA nonmentally retarded persons. The defect model further presumes that learning disabled children are less proficient in acquiring and integrating new information (Hagen et al., (1982). Kahn (1985) recently demonstrated support for the similar sequence hypothesis, but results upheld the defect position.

Critics of the developmental position have claimed that developmentalists explain whatever conclusions they derive as support for their theory (i.e., Ellis & Cavelier, 1982; Milgram, 1973; Spitz, 1983). Ellis and Cavelier (1982), for example, have not noted any compelling evidence for proving or disproving that development occurs in stages or continuously. In addition, they did not view the cultural-familial mentally retarded as necessarily free of neurological impairment.

Spitz (1983) argued that when differences between groups have been found in developmental research, these differences are explained by motivational factors not necessarily supported by the data (i.e., need for approval, high failure expectancy, failure avoidance). He viewed the developmental model as difficult to prove or disprove, given that a position based on proving no differences between groups is akin to proving the null hypothesis — which one can only fail to reject.

Much of the developmental-difference arguments have failed to provide practical information in school settings. Strichart and Gottlieb (1982) cited several reasons: (a) the use of laboratory research tasks that are not relevant in the classroom, (b) manipulation of variables under controlled laboratory conditions, whereas there are uncontrolled variables in the natural environment, (c) use of subjects who are often unrepresentative of the general mentally retarded population, and (d) the lack of equation for other variables, such as social class, educational experience, and central nervous system integrity, that might affect the outcomes.

Behavioral Model

Unlike much developmental research, applied behavior analysis research takes place in the natural environment and holds constant the uncontrolled variation of other variables, while specific independent variables are manipulated to empirically examine their treatment effects. The beginnings of behavioral analysis took place in operant research laboratories with animals, such as pigeons and rats. Applications of behavioral approaches to humans in the early 1960s spawned an entire field of applied research that has evolved from the ongoing behavior analysis work conducted in the laboratory.

Application of behavior analytic techniques to mentally retarded individuals has become the largest endeavor in the field of applied behavior analysis. The range of interventions has covered such topics as: (a) teaching self-help, vocational, leisure, social, gross motor, community survival, and communication skills; (b) ameliorating behavior problems, such as self-injurious behavior, aggression, and tantrums; (c) training staff, parents, and others in the effective use of behavioral procedures; and (d) managing staff. The range of applications within these and other categories has been considerable.

Briefly, the basic unit of analysis, known as the three-term contingency, is the stimulus–response–stimulus. The bulk of the work in the field has focused on the contingent application of reinforcement or punishment consequences for specified response. Relatively little work, by comparison, has been conducted with the antecedent stimuli that set the occasion for responding.

The procedures used to teach new skills typically involve some variation of prompting, shaping, chaining, and reinforcement techniques. Usually, a behavior or part of a behavior is prompted by some means, such as by the teacher modeling a behavior or otherwise cuing the student verbally, gesturally, or physically to perform the response. The student's subsequent response, whether fully correct or an approximation of the intended behavior, is then reinforced. If parts of a behavior are taught in this manner, they are combined into an entire intact skill by some variation of a chaining procedure. Reinforcement and prompting are gradually reduced during and after training, and a maintenance procedure that features intermittent reinforcement for continued demonstration of the skill is generally employed.

Behavioral technology has also been widely applied to the treatment of problem behaviors, such as aggression, self-injury, and tantrums (Favell, 1983; Favell, McGinsey, & Schell, 1982). The techniques employed include analyzing the biological and environmental conditions maintaining the problem, reinforcing alternative adaptive behavior, and arranging consequences that will decrease the probability of the problem behavior occurring.

The literature provides considerable empirical support for the efficacy of these basic procedures (Hersen, Van Hasselt, & Matson, 1983; Whitman et al., 1983).

Applied behavior analysis has been largely responsible for the successful habilitation efforts conducted with mentally retarded children.

Integration of Behavioral and Developmental Approaches

The conceptualizations of how individuals learn have led to some very different applications of work conducted with mentally retarded individuals, as typified by the developmental and behavioral approaches. The developmental approach follows a norm-based model detailing nonhandicapped individuals' sequence of normal development. A behavioral approach, by contrast, is a highly individualized criterion-referenced approach that is concerned with an individual's performance in a given situation and is directed at improving that performance.

The behavioral model also assumes that each child is capable of learning, regardless of level of handicap. This model relies more on the assessment of deficiencies and selecting objectives for training to remediate these deficits. Although acquisition of some skills necessarily comes before others, there is no strict adherence to the steps of normal development. Progress proceeds hierarchically from simple to complex skills. Thus, practitioners might presume that as long as they can objectively task-analyze a skill (i.e., break it down into its component parts), it can be taught (Guess et al., 1978).

Some individuals (i.e., Guess et al., 1979; Holvoet, Guess, Mulligan, & Brown, 1980) advocate integrating remedial and developmental approaches as a means to develop effective instructional sequences. A proposed Functional Curriculum Sequencing (FCS) model combines the logic of both developmental and remedial approaches to skills training by combining both hierarchical and horizontal sequences of component responses. Otherwise stated, the horizontal sets of skills are taught as response classes (as opposed to specific, unitary responses) that could be related either topographically (i.e., by the form of the specific behavior) or functionally (i.e., whether responses provide the same effect on the environment). The vertical building from simple to complex repertoires of behavior would still be followed. This type of teaching could span various domains of skills at one time.

For example, a behavior such as "opening" could be taught as a set of responses across the following domains: (a) vocational: opening envelopes, boxes, jars, containers, (b) self-help: opening doors, toothpaste tubes, (c) leisure: opening a container of blocks, and so on. The benefit of such an approach would be to teach a skill of "opening" via multiple exemplars that would generalize to new situations. The efficacy of such an integration of developmental and behavioral approaches still requires empirical verification.

Medical Model

The medical model had at one time been the reigning approach to mental retardation. With a shift that focuses on the usefulness of environmental contingencies to maximize the learning capabilities of the mentally retarded, the role of the medical model has changed considerably. Ongoing assessment of mentally retarded individuals' health, prevention, research, and the use of pharmacological treatment provide the major roles for health practitioners.

Medical assessment includes a thorough physical examination, laboratory tests, and a health history. Of special interest is the assessment and treatment of any health problems that may affect an individual's performance (Cegelka & Prehm, 1982).

Clarizio and McCoy (1983) cited significant contributions of medical science to treatment of mental retardation, including surgical techniques for correcting hydrocephaly, serum for Rh-negative blood incompatibility, and the vaccines for polio, measles, smallpox, and scarlet fever. Whitman et al. (1983) also recounted the contributions of such prevention strategies as genetic counseling, reduction of conception rates that are high-risk for mentally retarded children, and such diagnostic techniques as amniocentesis.

Some medical research has focused on diet. For pregnant women, nutritional diet is considered crucial for giving birth to a healthy infant (Clarizio & McCoy, 1982). Isaacson and Van Hartesveldt (1978) have discussed diet as an important determinant of brain and body chemistry. However, to date, mixed results have been found. Additives, such as artificial food color, have been demonstrated to be associated with hyperactivity. Weathers (1983) recently investigated the effects of a megadose of multivitamin/mineral supplements on the IQ, vision, and visual-motor integration of Down syndrome children. No differences were found in any of the measures, a finding that seriously called into question earlier research on the benefits of vitamins.

In their review of pharamacological treatment, Isaacson and Van Hartesveldt (1978) describe medical approaches as focusing on the brain dysfunction aspects of mental retardation. They divide treatment into two overall approaches: to promote recovery from brain damage and to ameliorate symptoms of brain damage. The most promising recovery approach is in supplying extra amino acids to the brain via oral or intramuscular injection.

Controlling behavioral symptoms, however, constitutes a more prevalent role for medical intervention. Seizures, which occur frequently in the mentally retarded, are controlled via phenytoin (Dilantin) and barbituates. Amphetamines have been used to decrease hyperactivity. Major tranquilizers of the phenothiazine family, such as chlorpromazine (Thorazine) or thioridazine (Mellaril), are sometimes used in conjunction with a minor tranquilizer such as diazepam (Valium) in an attempt to control aggressive behavior and self-injury. Perhaps the most commonly used drug to control aggression is thioridazine (Singh & Aman, 1981). However, side effects such as reduced responsiveness to surroundings or involuntary motor movements may occur.

Numerous studies have been conducted to ascertain the prevalence and/or the benefits of using psychotropic medication with mentally retarded individuals. In a double-blind placebo controlled study (Singh & Aman, 1981), for example, the investigators measured hyperactivity, bizarre behavior, and self-stimulation under two conditions of thioridazine use: (a) at the individual dosage previously clinically determined as effective, or (b) at a relatively low standardized dose that was half the mean individualized dosage. Results indicated that there were equivalent therapeutic effects with either dose. The major implication of this investigation was that too high a drug dose might be used when not necessary.

Gadow and Kalachnik (1981) summarize concerns in the use of psychotropic and antiepileptic medications for controlling behavior. Studies are often methodologically flawed and clinical practice monitoring may be less than satisfactory. In addition, higher doses of drugs may impair learning and performance. There is considerable concern that drugs might be used as a substitute for training and treatment.

Schalock, Foley, Toulouse, and Stark (1985) have demonstrated in their community-based model of intervention that through the combined use of behavioral interventions, medication, and close monitoring, it is possible to reduce drug use significantly, as well as promote positive behavior change.

ISSUES

Educational

Prior to the passage of The Education for All Handicapped Children Act in 1975 (PL 94-142), severely handicapped children were not typically admitted to public schools. Criteria for admission to TMR classes required that a child be toilet trained, be able to learn in a group situation, and have no behavior problems (Meyers, Zetlin, & Blacher-Dixon, 1981). The schools were prepared to teach only mildly and moderately mentally retarded children, not the severely or profoundly mentally retarded. EMR children were placed in a self-contained special classroom with some integration into the regular educational setting. TMR children were sometimes placed in special classes on the elementary school grounds or in special day schools (MacMillan, 1982).

This scenario is less prevalent, given that the law now mandates a free and appropriate education for even the most severely handicapped, and in the least restrictive environment. PL 94-142 challenges long-held assumptions concerning the capabilities of handicapped persons, as well as our communities' responses to the problems of severe disabilities (Kauffman, 1981). In general, the notion of what education can be has dramatically changed. Basic self-help skills such as toileting, dressing, and eating can now be taught within school settings (Meyers, MacMillan, & Zetlin, 1978).

Briefly, the basic rights of PL 94-142 include: (a) education in the least restrictive setting in an environment as close as possible to that of nonhandicapped individuals, (b) an Individualized Educational Plan (IEP) that includes written programs, objectives, and criteria for accountability, (c) the right to due process (e.g., parental access to records and evaluations), and (d) protection against discriminatory testing during assessment. Other aspects of the law include "zero reject," whereby no child, regardless of severity of handicap, can be denied a free and appropriate education. This means that busing and other auxiliary services must now be provided by local communities with no expense to the parents.

As noted by Hawkins and Hawkins (1981), some individuals would not consider "education" as encompassing the teaching of basic community living skills, which are generally more useful educationally for severely and profoundly mentally retarded children. Education has historically focused on academic skills that were not necessarily functional for the individual. A further complication is that the school setting itself may not be the best suited for either assessing or teaching practical skills. Recommendations include planning relevant IEP's, assessing parental needs and providing parent training, researching the functional relevance of skills, and adapting the school's environment to reflect the home environment. This will help maximize generalization of skills taught in the school environment.

As the outcomes of our teaching approaches are examined, particularly with those who are severely and profoundly handicapped, it is obvious that an array of basic skills can be trained — in self help, socialization, language, and in the reduction of inappropriate behaviors that may interfere with the demonstration of more appropriate functional skills (Whitman & Scibak, 1979). This is due greatly to the proliferation of behavior analysis techniques that have considerably affected educational programming for the mentally retarded. How community attitudes to the increased visibility of mentally retarded children have changed as a result of these efforts remains a topic for continued debate.

Placement Options

MacMillan (1982) has described various treatment options that are now available to mentally retarded children. Resources do vary from community to community; some are able to offer a wider range of services than others. MacMillan and Borthwick (1980) have noted trends away from the diagnosis and placement of mildly mentally retarded children in special programs. They cited a heavier workload for teachers (due to meetings, paperwork, etc.) and fear of litigation unless the most obviously mentally retarded are identified. This latter point is particularly true for minority groups, who are usually disproportionally represented in special educational programs.

Placement options begin with the *regular classroom* with no ancillary services. The benefits are that EMR children are likely to do as well as low-IQ children already in those classes and that it will avoid labeling and discrimination. Several problems may be associated with this type of placement: (a) EMR children might be rejected by nonmentally retarded peers because of behavior, (b) they will be unable to compete favorably, (c) they might receive "social promotions" not based on performance, and (d) the presence of EMR children in the classroom may have a negative impact on the nonmentally retarded. Semmel, Gottlieb, and Robinson (1979) did not find differences in gains as a result of regular or special classes. This finding tends to support the use of the regular classroom, given that they are less costly than special classrooms and provide a more normalized

environment for the mentally retarded child.

A second option is the *regular class with an itinerant teacher or resource room.* This arrangement can have advantages because: (a) it can serve more students, (b) mentally retarded children can be with their nonmentally retarded peers about 50% of time, (c) it is less expensive to operate than special classes, and (d) labeling may be avoided.

A third option, the *special class*, historically was not meant to be exclusionary, but was designed to protect the mentally retarded child from failure and peer rejection. Problems include the following:

1. A large proportion of minority children (Mercer, 1973)
2. Isolation of the mentally retarded child from normal peers
3. Little evidence that grouping helps
4. Possible labeling of children
5. Existence of more flexible arrangements.

Finally, *special schools* may provide more resources than a single school, especially in the case when there are not enough TMR children for a special class in one school district. The disadvantages include: (a) considerable travel, (b) little interaction with normal peers and, most importantly, (c) unnecessary referral of a child simply because the school is there.

Mainstreaming

The first notion of educating the handicapped and nonhandicapped in one educational setting is attributed to Bricker and Bricker (1971). The proportion of handicapped to nonhandicapped children may vary considerably from program to program. Odom and Speltz (1983) advocate the use of the term *integrated special education* to refer to those places that incorporate a high proportion of handicapped children, with the term *mainstreamed* saved solely for those programs that have only a low proportion of handicapped children.

Peck and Cooke (1983) reviewed several studies that employed quasi-experimental designs to compare developmental gains in integrated versus nonintegrated settings. They conclude that mainstreaming is not harmful to either group and may provide developmental benefits for handicapped children.

There has been difficulty with interpreting mainstreaming research, however, given the lack of control groups and random assignment and the differences in interpretation of educational and statistical significance, because even statistically significant result may not be educationally significant. Another difficulty is that data bases used to evaluate mainstreaming tend to rely on IQ and achievement data. Also, the use of large numbers obscures benefits or disadvantages to individual children (Strain & Kerr, 1981). Peck and Cooke (1983) recommend more reliance on matching subjects by developmental age as opposed to chronological age, and the use of measures of interaction and material engagement to provide more interpretable conclusions.

Strain and Kerr (1981) have summarized some of the major findings from attitudinal mainstreaming research. Mental retardation is still viewed as a biological condition associated with severe disability, and the public still views public education for handicapped children unfavorably. Most striking is that the attainment of skills and the display of competent behavior by mentally retarded individuals is not viewed as evidence of general ability.

In addition, regular classroom teachers are less favorable to the mentally retarded than are special education teachers. McEvoy, Nordquist, and Cunningham (1984), demonstrated that although both regular and special educators' attitudes were affected by child characteristics, the regular classroom teachers were affected by the size of the integration ratio of handicapped children.

Thus, despite a wealth of research on mainstreaming efforts, definitive conclusions as to the efficacy of this approach are lacking. However, as Meyers, MacMillan, and Yoshida (1980) pointed out, empirical research may not matter, because the mainstreaming movement may be a result of the policy and resources of local communities.

Early Intervention

The evaluation of the effects of early intervention programs with mentally retarded children parallels some of the same findings and problems that beset evaluation of mainstreaming efforts. White and Casto (1985) reviewed 162 early intervention studies and concluded that little is known as to the efficacy of these attempts. Most of their review focused on disadvantaged and at-risk populations, as little empirical data are available for mentally retarded children. They found a reliance on measures of IQ as opposed to more careful description of program variables, such as age at which the intervention began, long-term effects, parental involvement, and curriculum. They advocate use of random assignment to treatment conditions, verification of the independent variables employed, more appropriate outcome measures, and reliable data collection.

Dunst (1983) has delineated directions that might be useful within early intervention programs. He expressed alarm at the reliance on inanimate objects to form the basis for infant curricula and the relative lack of emphasis on more crucial social affective behaviors. Second, he also identifies the need for further development of parent–infant interaction coaching techniques. Third, he advocates that varying levels of parental involvement be permitted and fourth, that the family as a system be treated instead of the child alone. Finally, he also describes the need for more useful outcome measures than IQs or developmental quotients. He prefers a focus on the child's ability to adapt to progressively more complex demands throughout life as a better measure of the success of early intervention.

In sum, the constellation of treatment services that comprise early intervention have little empirical basis for mentally retarded children. Considerable work remains to evaluate the long-term effects of our treatment delivery systems.

SUMMARY

Mentally retarded children have been the focal point for a proliferation of work conducted during the previous two decades. The wealth of research, treatment strategies, social policy decisions, as well as our ever-expanding constellation of service systems, attest to the concern our society has demonstrated for the welfare of mentally retarded individuals.

It is clear from the literature reviewed, however, that the field of mental retardation as a whole is in its infancy. Such basic questions as: who should be described as mentally retarded, how can mental retardation be prevented, and how do mentally retarded individuals best develop and learn will continue to be subjected to further debate and scrutiny. The answers to these questions are not as yet definitive.

Just what new directions will be undertaken for the treatment and care of mentally retarded persons will depend on the position and resources society will uphold. Our efforts to provide quality services to mentally retarded children have been considerable; how our efforts will be continued still remains uncertain for the challenging years to come.

REFERENCES

American Association on Mental Deficiency. (1974). *Adaptive behavior scale manual.* Washington, DC: Author.

American Psychiatric Association. (1980). *Diagnostic and statistical manual of mental disorders* (3rd ed.). Washington, DC: Author.

Anastasi, A. (1976). *Psychological testing* (4th ed.). New York: Macmillan.

Baird, P. A., & Sadovnick, A. D. (1985). Mental retardation in over half-a-million live births: An epidemiological study. *American Journal of Mental Deficiency, 89,* 323–330.

Baumeister, A. A., & MacLean, W. E. (1979). Brain damage and mental retardation. In N. R. Ellis (Ed.), *Handbook of mental deficiency: Psychological theory and research* (2nd ed., pp. 197–230). Hillsdale, NJ: Erlbaum.

Bijou, S. W. (1963). Theory and research in mental (developmental) retardation. *Psychological Record, 13,* 95–110.

Bijou, S. W. (1966). A functional analysis of retarded development. In N. R. Ellis (Ed.), *International review of research in mental retardation* (Vol. 1, pp. 1–20). New York: Academic.

Bricker, D., & Bricker, W. (1971). Toddler research and intervention project report: Year I. *IMRID Behavioral Science Monograph 20.* Nashville, TN: Institute on Mental Retardation and Intellectual Development, George Peabody College.

Burdg, N. B., & Graham, S. (1984). Effects of sex and label on performance ratings, children's test scores and examiners' verbal behavior. *American Journal of Mental Deficiency, 88,* 422–427.

Cegelka, P. T., & Prehm, H. J. (1982). *Mental retardation: From categories to people.* Columbus, OH: Charles E. Merril.

Clarizio, H. F., & McCoy, G. F. (Eds.). (1983) *Behavior disorders in children* (3rd ed.). New York: Harper & Row.

Clarke, A. D. B., & Clarke, A. M. (1977). Prospects for prevention and ammelioration of mental retardation: A guest editorial. *American Journal of Mental Deficiency, 81,* 523–533.

Clausen, J. A. (1967). Mental deficiency: Development of a concept. *American Journal of Mental Deficiency, 71,* 727–745.

Dunst, C. J. (1983). Emerging trends and advances in early intervention programs. *New Jersey Journal of School Psychology, 2,* 26–40.

Ellis, N. R. (1969). A behavioral research strategy in mental retardation: Defense and critique. *American Journal of Mental Deficiency, 73,* 557–566.

Ellis, N. R., & Cavelier, A. R. (1982). Research perspectives in mental retardation. In E. Zigler & D. Balla (Eds.), *Mental retardation: The developmental-difference controversy* (pp. 121–154). Hillsdale, NJ: Erlbaum.

Favell, J. E. (1983). The management of aggressive behavior. In E. Schopler & G. Mesibov (Eds.), *Autism in adolescents and adults* (pp. 187–222). New York: Plenum.

Favell, J. E., McGimsey, J. F., & Schell, R. M. (1982). Treatment of self-injury by providing alternative sensory activities. *Analysis and Intervention in Developmental Disabilities, 2,* 83–104.

Frankenberger, W. (1984). A survey of state guidelines for identification of mental retardation. *Mental Retardation, 22,* 17–20.

Gadow, K. D., & Kalachnik, J. (1981). Prevalence and pattern of drug treatment for behavior and seizure disorders of TMR students. *American Journal of Mental Deficiency, 85,* 588–595.

Gearheart, B. R., & Litton, F. W. (1975). *Mental retardation: A life cycle approach.* St. Louis, MO: Mosby.

Gold, M. C. (1980). An alternative definition of mental retardation. In M. C. Gold (Ed.), *"Did I say that?" Articles and commentary on the Try Another Way System.* Champaign, IL: Research Press.

Grossman, H. J. (Ed.). (1983). *Classification in mental retardation.* Washington, DC: American Association of Mental Deficiency.

Guess, D., Horner, R. D., Utley, B., Holvoet, J., Maxon, D., Tucker, D., & Warren, S. (1978). A functional curriculum sequencing model for teaching the severely handicapped. *AAESPH Review, 3,* 202–215.

Hagen, J. W., Barclay, C. R., & Schwethelm, B. (1982). Cognitive development of the learning–disabled child. In N. R. Ellis (Ed.), *International review of research in mental retardation* (Vol. 11, pp. 1–41). New York: Academic.

Hawkins, R. P., & Hawkins, K. K. (1981). Education of severely retarded children. *Analysis and Intervention in Developmental Disabilities, 1,* 13–22.

Hersen, M., Van Hasselt, V. B., & Matson, J. L. (1983). *Behavior therapy for the developmentally and physically disabled.* New York: Academic.

Hobbs, N. (1975a). *The future of children.* San Francisco: Jossey-Bass.

Hobbs, N. (ed.). (1975b). *Issues in the classification of children* (Vols. 1, 2). San Francisco: Jossey-Bass.

Holvoet, J., Guess, D., Mulligan, M., & Brown. (1980). The individualized sequencing model (II): A teaching strategy for severely handicapped students. *Journal of the Association for the Severely Handicapped, 5,* 337–351.

Isaacson, R. L., & Van Hartesveldt, C. (1978). The biological basis of an ethic for mental retardation. In N. R. Ellis (Ed.), *International review of research in mental retardation* (Vol. 9, pp. 159–186). New York: Academic.

Kahn, J. V. (1976). The utility of the Uzgiris and Hunt scales of sensorimotor development with severely and profoundly retarded children. *American Journal of Mental Deficiency, 80,* 663–665.

Kahn, J. V. (1977). Cognitive training of severely and profoundly retarded children. In M. A. Thomas (Ed.), *Developing skills in severely and profoundly handicapped children* (pp. 1–3). Reston, VA: The Council for Exceptional Children.

Kahn, J. V. (1983). Sensorimotor period and adaptive behavior development of severely and profoundly mentally retarded children.

American Journal of Mental Deficiency, 88, 69–75.

Kahn, J. V. (1985). Evidence of the similar-structure hypothesis controlling for organicity. *American Journal of Mental Deficiency, 89,* 372–378.

Kamphaus, R. W., & Reynolds, C. R. (1984). Development and structure of the Kaufman Assessment Battery for Children. *The Journal of Special Education, 18,* 213–228.

Kauffman, J. M. (1981). Editor's introduction. *Analysis and Intervention in Developmental Disabilities, 1,* 1–3.

Kaufman, A. S. (1979). *Intelligent testing with the WISC-R.* New York: Wiley.

Kazdin, A. E., & Straw, M. K. (1976). Assessment of behavior of the mentally retarded. In M. Hersen & A. J. Bellack (Eds.), *Behavioral assessment: A practical handbook* (pp. 337–368). Elmsford, NY: Pergamon.

MacMillan, D. L. (1982). *Mental retardation in school and society.* Boston: Little, Brown.

MacMillan, D. L., & Borthwick, S. (1980). The new EMR population: Can they be mainstreamed? *Mental Retardation, 18,* 155–158.

MacMillan, D. L., & Meyers, C. E. (1979). Educational labeling of handicapped learners. In D. C. Berliner (Ed.), *Review of research in education* (pp. 151–194). Washington, DC: American Educational Research Association.

Marozas, D. S., May, D. C., & Lehman, L. C. (1980). Incidence and prevalence: confusion in need of clarification. *Mental Retardation, 18,* 229–230.

McEvoy, M. A., Nordquist, V. M., & Cunningham, J. L. (1984). Regular and special education teachers' judgments about mentally retarded children in an integrated setting *American Journal of Mental Deficiency, 89,* 167–173.

Mercer, J. R. (1971). The meaning of mental retardation. In R. Koch & J. C. Dobson (Eds.), *The mentally retarded child and his family: A multidisciplinary handbook* (pp. 23–46). New York: Brunner/Mazel.

Mercer, J. R. (1973). *Labeling the mentally retarded.* Berkeley: University of California Press.

Meyers, C. E., MacMillan, D. L., & Yoshida, R. K. (1980). Regular class education of EMB students, from efficacy to mainstreaming: A review of issues and research. In J. Gottlieb (Ed.), *Educating mentally retarded persons in the mainstream* (pp. 176–206). Baltimore, MD: University Park Press.

Meyers, C. E., MacMillan, D. L., & Zetlin, A. (1978). Education for all handicapped children. *Pediatric Annals, 7,* 348–356.

Meyers, C. E., Zetlin, A., & Blacher-Dixon, J. (1981). The family as affected by schooling for severely retarded children: An invitation to research. *Journal of Community Psychology, 9,* 306–315.

Milgram, N. A. (1973). Cognition and language in mental retardation: Distinctions and implications. In D. K. Routh (Ed.), *The experimental psychology of mental retardation.* Chicago: Aldine.

Morton, R. F., & Hebel, J. R. (1979). *A study guide to epidemiology and biostatistics.* Baltimore, MD: University Park Press.

Odom, S. L., & Speltz, M. L. (1983). Program variations in preschools for handicapped and nonhandicapped children: Mainstreamed vs. integrated special education. *Analysis and Intervention in Developmental Disabilities, 3,* 89–103.

Peck, C. A., & Cooke, T. P. (1983). Benefits of early childhood mainstreaming. *Analysis and Intervention in Developmental Disabilities, 3,* 1–22.

Peters, L. G. (1980). Concepts of mental deficiency among the Tamang of Nepal. *American Journal of Mental Deficiency, 84,* 352–356.

Piaget, J. (1964). Development and learning. *Journals of Research in Science Teaching, 2,* 176–186.

Piaget, J., & Inhelder, B. (1969). *The psychology of the child.* New York: Basic Books.

Schalock, R. L., Foley, J. W., Toulouse, A., & Stark, J. A. (1985). Medication and programming in controlling the behavior of mentally retarded individuals in community settings. *American Journal of Mental Deficiency, 89,* 503–509.

Semmel, M. I., Gottlieb, J., & Robinson, N. (1979). Mainstreaming: Perspectives on educating handicapped children in the public schools. In D. C. Berliner (Ed.), *Review of research in education* (pp. 223–279). Washington, DC: American Educational Research Association.

Silverstein, A. B. (1977). Note of prevalence. *American Journal of Mental Deficiency, 77,* 380–382.

Silverstein, A. B., Pearson, L. B., Keller, M. H., & McLain, R. R. E. (1982). A test of the similar sequence hypothesis. *American Journal of Mental Deficiency, 86,* 551–553.

Singh, N. N., & Aman, M. G. (1981). Effects of thioridazine dosage on the behavior of severely retarded persons. *American Journal of Mental Deficiency, 85,* 580–587.

Spitz, H. H. (1983). Critique of the developmental position in mental-retardation research. *Journal of Special Education, 17,* 261–294.

Spreat, S., Roszkowski, M. J., & Isett, R. D. (1983). Assessment of adaptive behavior in the mentally retarded. In S. Breuning, J. Matson, & R. Barrett (eds.), *Advances in mental retardation and developmental disabilities* (Vol. 1, pp. 45–95). Greenwich, CT: JAI.

Strain, P. S., & Kerr, M. M. (1981). *Mainstreaming of children in schools: Research and programmatic issues.* New York: Academic.

Strichart, S. S., & Gottlieb, J. (1982). Characteristics of mild mental retardation. In T. L. Miller & E. E. Davis (Eds.), *The mildly handicapped student* (pp. 37–65). New York: Grune & Stratton.

Sulzer-Azaroff, B., & Mayer, G. R. (1977). *Applying behavior analysis procedures with children and youth.* New York: Holt, Rinehart & Winston.

Tarjan, G., Wright, S. W., Eyman, R. K., & Keeran, C. V. (1973). Natural history of mental retardation: Some aspects of epidemiology. *American Journal of Mental Deficiency, 77,* 369–379.

Taylor, R. L. (1980). Use of the AAMD classification system: A review of recent research. *American Journal of Mental Deficiency, 85,* 116–119.

Uzgiris, I., & Hunt, J. McV. (1975). *Assessment in infancy: Ordinal scales of psychological development.* Urbana: University of Illinois Press.

Warren, S. A. (1984). Teaching difficult goals with difficulty. *Mental Retardation, 22,* 109–111.

Weathers, C. (1983). Effects of nutritional supplementation on IQ and certain other variables associated with Down syndrome. *American Association on Mental Deficiency, 88,* 214–217.

Weisz, J. R., Yeates, K. D., & Zigler, E. (1982). Piagetian evidence and the developmental-difference controversy. In E. Zigler & D. Balla (Eds.), *Mental retardation: The developmental-difference controversy* (pp. 213–276). Hillsdale, NJ: Erlbaum.

Weisz, J. R., & Zigler, E. (1979). Cognitive development in retarded and nonretarded persons: Piagetian tests of the similar sequence hypothesis. *Psychological Bulletin, 86,* 831–851.

White, K., & Casto, G. (1985). An integrative review of early intervention efficacy studies with at-risk children: Implications for the handicapped. *Analysis and Intervention in Developmental Disabilities, 5,* 7–31.

Whitman, T., & Scibak, J. (1979). Behavior modification research with the severely and profoundly retarded. In N. R. Ellis (Ed.), *Handbook of mental deficiency* (2nd ed., pp. 289–340). Hillsdale, NJ: Erlbaum.

Whitman, T. L., Scibak, J. W., & Reid, D. H. (1983). *Behavior modification with the severely and profoundly retarded: Research and application.* New York: Academic.

Woodward, W. M. (1979). Piaget's theory and the study of mental retardation. In N. R. Ellis (Ed.), *Handbook of mental deficiency* (2nd ed., pp. 169–195). Hillsdale, NJ: Erlbaum.

World Health Organization. (1977). *Manual of the International Statistical Classification of Diseases, Injuries, and Causes of Death* (9th revision, Vol. 1). Geneva: Author.

Zigler, E. (1966). Mental retardation: Current issues and approaches. In L. W. Hoffman & M. R. Hoffman (Eds.), *Review of child development research* (Vol. 2). New York: Russell Sage.

Zigler, E. (1967). Familial mental retardation: A continuing dilemma. *Science, 155,* 292–298.

Zigler, E. (1982). Developmental versus difference theories of mental retardation and the problem of motivation. In E. Zigler & D. Balla (Eds.), *Mental retardation: The developmental-difference controversy* (pp. 163–188). Hillsdale, NJ: Erlbaum.

Zigler, E., Balla, D., & Hodapp, R. (1984). On the definition and classification of mental retardation. *American Journal of Mental Deficiency, 89,* 215–230.

CHAPTER 21

Mental Retardation in Adults

Johnny L. Matson

INTRODUCTION

Mental retardation has been an area for considerable debate and study in the fields of health, mental health, and special education. Prevention has been a particularly popular area for study, as has academic training, aggressive behavior toward other children, and other related school problems. Obviously, all of these issues revolve primarily around children and their problems. Only recently have adults received attention in the experimental literature that in any way approximates the research developments with mentally retarded children.

This trend to greater emphasis on adults is considered critical due to special problems adults exhibit. For example, vocational skills, some social interpersonal behaviors, shopping, and sewing are among the behavioral areas that are most likely to be considered pertinent to mentally retarded adults when compared to children. Research into these topic areas has been addressed only recently. Similarly, there are problem areas that can be treated across the age spectrum, but they may take on a different character with the adult population. For example, an adult mentally retarded person who is incontinent and is to be treated for this problem may require a habilitative program somewhat different than one employed with a child. Since the condition in the instance of an adult has typically been occurring for a much longer period of time, it is likely to be more resistant to change. For example, if the person does not want to be toilet trained and therefore resists, the strategies needed to deal with such noncooperation (because of the difference in size and strength compared to children) will vary substantially given the potential for disruption.

The focus of this chapter will be on the types of problems that are typically identified with mentally retarded adults and how they are treated. A qualitative difference will hopefully emerge between some areas of assessment and intervention based on chronological age with mentally retarded adults.

DESCRIPTION OF THE DISORDER

The definition of mental retardation is primarily based on behavior rather than physiology. For example, a Down Syndrome person is not diagnosed as mentally retarded (and some are not) based on how marked his or her physical characteristics appear. Rather, performance on age-appropriate behaviors constitutes the determining factor. Thus, definitions of mental retardation have been based on test performance of individuals who are compared to a norm group using the criterion of being two standard deviations below the mean. The American Association on Mental Deficiency (AAMD) has proposed the most frequently used definition, and the American Psychiatric Association (APA), among other professional groups, has adopted it.

Two criteria for arriving at the definition are used. These included a score on a standardized intelligence test such as the Stanford-Binet (see section on Assessment, p. 355) and an adaptive behavior scale using guidelines for the major categories of mental retardation (mild, moderate, severe, and profound) that are proposed in the AAMD's classification manual (Grossman, 1977). Finally, the person must be classified as mentally retarded before the age of 18. It should be pointed out, however, that special education literature uses terms that are roughly equivalent to those just mentioned. They refer to mild as *educable mentally retarded*, moderate as *trainable mentally retarded*, and severe and profoundly mentally retarded are classified together and labeled *severely handicapped*. The four strata of classification of the mentally retarded individual proposed by the AAMD approximately correspond to two, three, four, and more standard deviations below the mean. Persons in the profound range of mental retardation typically are measured on intelligence tests other than the Wechsler Scale or the Stanford-Binet. Tests that measure nonverbal behavior, such as the Bailey, are more commonly used.

EPIDEMIOLOGICAL FINDINGS

In this chapter, epidemiology has been broken down into three major categories: prevalence, incidence, and etiology. Prevalence and incidence will be the first topics of discussion. These two terms differ in that *prevalence* is the number of defined cases at a particular point in time, while *incidence* is the number of persons that have had the condition (Morton & Hebel, 1979). For many problems, this distinction is important, particularly if the condition is of short duration, such as the flu. Just about everyone has had the flu at one time or another, but at a specific point in time, usually only a fraction of the population would be afflicted. This situation does not exist to nearly the same degree with a problem assumed to be irreversible, as is the case with mental retardation. Because of this situation with mentally retarded persons, the numbers for these two concepts (incidence and prevalence) are similar. Therefore, incidence will be reported but not prevalence. It should also be noted that the similarity of incidence and prevalence with mentally retarded adults is even greater than with children, because many cases are not identified until the child is school-aged and because, as noted previously, persons must evince the condition before age 18.

It should be pointed out that the rate of mental retardation, as reflected in incidence and prevalence figures, can fluctuate considerably across cultures and time. This occurs because instruments used to measure the condition and the professional communities' conceptualization of the problem can vary considerably. While some efforts at medically based evaluations of mental retardation have been made, it is still defined primarily as a behavioral phenomenon. That is, as previously noted, the degree to which mental retardation is evinced is determined primarily by each person's performance, whether it is judged by an IQ test or related to adaptive behavior. Medical science has been confined primarily to determining particular types of mental retardation and its etiology or causes.

The first attempt to establish incidence of mentally retarded persons in a systematic fashion was made by the English Royal Commission of 1904. They estimated that 0.46% of the general population was mentally retarded (McMillan, 1982). The figures that are in part used today to reflect incidence result from studies by Goddard (1911) and Terman (1919), both of whom used the Stanford-Binet (with about 3% of the population falling into the mentally retarded group).

There has been a move in recent years, however, to decrease this incidence figure. New definitions, as opposed to any cures, have been primarily responsible for lowering the incidence rates. For example, the AAMD now requires that a person be two, rather than one, standard deviations below the mean on an individual intelligence test. Also, this person must score in the mentally retarded range on an accepted adaptive behavior scale, such as the American Association on Mental Deficiency Adaptive Behavior Scale (Nihira, Foster, Shellhaas, & Leland, 1969). With these new criteria in place, the incidence of mental retardation in the United States is now estimated from between 1% and 3% (Birch, Richardson, Baird, Horobin, & Illsey, 1970; Mercer, 1970, 1973a, b; Tarjan, Wright, Eyman, & Keeran, 1973). Changes in political, social, and other cultural factors are likely to result in further changes regarding definition and incidence in the future.

Another factor that should be briefly mentioned is etiology. In a chapter of this type it would be impossible to go into all the causes of mental retardation, because the nature of the disorder is multifaceted. It can be said with some confidence, however, that milder forms of the disorder are more likely to be due primarily to environmental factors, while profound mental retardation is likely to be due to genetic, biological, and physical factors. Additionally, environmental factors such as intrauterine infection (Thompson & Glasgow, 1980), Rubella (Singer, Rudolph, Rosenberg, Rawls, & Bonsuk, 1967) and asphyxia (Borit & Herndon, 1970; Bormada, Mossy & Shuman, 1979), if they have a major physical effect on the nervous system, can result in mental retardation. This latter group of conditions, therefore, are a combination of environmental, biological, and physiological variables.

The number and type of genetic disorders that can affect normal intellectual growth and development are also numerous. This group of conditions has been divided into three major categories (Abuelo, 1983). These are single gene problems that may be transmitted by dominant recessive or X chromosome-linked genes. Phenylketonuria (PKU) is an example of this condition. Approximately 1% of newborns are affected, and the full range of problems is reviewed in other literature (e.g. McKusick, 1978). The second group of conditions is referred to as multifactorial problems. Spina Bifida, which consists of an opening in the spine, is an example. These problems are believed to be due to a number of gene irregularities that work in combination with the environment. The third type of problem consists of chromosomal disorders such as Down Syndrome. These disorders are generally due to meiotic errors that occur during formation of either the sperm or the egg. As noted previously, only a few examples are possible due to the complexity of this issue. Great strides have been made in identifying problems of this sort, and further developments and improvements in avoiding some forms of mental retardation are likely.

ASSESSMENT

Numerous studies have been conducted and many scales have been developed to assess the mentally retarded. This trend may be due in large part to the emphasis on prevention in the medical profession (Matson & Mulick, 1983) and the emphasis on classification by psychologists. However, despite the many studies conducted to date, research across topic areas has been very uneven. Thus, intelligence tests and adaptive behavior scales have been frequently studied (Meyers, Nihira, & Zetlin, 1979; Sattler, 1974; Wechsler, 1955), but assessment of psychopathology with mentally retarded persons has been understudied (Matson & Frame, 1983). Since entire volumes have been written on assessment of mentally retarded persons (Matson & Breuning, 1983), only a brief overview can be made here. Various examples of assessment methods will be reviewed by topic area.

Standardized Trait Tests

Perhaps the most discussed, and at the same time, the most controversial area of assessment, has been standardized testing. Furthermore, this area has perhaps the longest history of study. The intent of these assessment methods from the outset has been to identify, and therefore provide special care, training, and education for mentally retarded persons. While various approaches have flourished, two major dimensions of assessment, the IQ test and adaptive behavior scales, have become the most common methods.

The IQ test was introduced by Binet and Simon in 1905 (Barrett & Breuning, 1983). The typically used intelligence tests have been standard. These have primarily been the Stanford-Binet (L–M) (Terman & Merrill, 1973) and the Wechsler Scales (Wechsler, 1955). Both of these instruments are administered individually and require approximately 1 to 1½ hours to complete.

The Stanford-Binet has usually proven more useful for evaluating persons with low intelligence (e.g., severe-to-profound mental retardation). However, it is also the case that the lowest functioning persons are untestable with all instruments of this type. (This is not to imply that they are untestable, however.) The subtests of the Stanford-Binet can be classified in several categories including language, memory, conceptual thinking, reasoning, numerical reasoning, visual–motor skills, and social intelligence (Sattler, 1974). Also, the mental age concept was derived primarily from this scale, and has been a common way of describing this handicapped group. The resulting mental age score is then matched against normative data for chronological age and the IQ is thus determined.

The most frequently used measure of intelligence for adults, however, had been the WAIS. It is commonly employed with mild and moderately mentally retarded persons. Lower functioning persons are typically evaluated more accurately with the Stanford-Binet (Barrett & Breuning, 1983). The WAIS also contains subtests that correspond to a number of broadly defined categories that are presumed to reflect major aspects of intellectual development. These include general knowledge, social judgment, numerical reasoning, verbal conceptual thinking, language, auditory memory, nonverbal reasoning, and perceptual organization. The subtests are organized under two major categories, which are verbal and nonverbal. Five subtests comprise each category. As with the Stanford-Binet, a large sample was used for standardization (1,200 subjects).

Other measures of intelligence are also available to meet special needs. For example, to save time, group test administration can be conducted using the Slosson Intelligence Test (Slosson, 1971). This instrument correlates highly with the Stanford-Binet primarily because it was patterned after that scale. It should be cautioned that the Slosson is primarily for screening purposes and therefore should not be used for diagnosis and placement decisions (Barrett & Breuning, 1983).

Another important area of specialty testing involves evaluating severe and profoundly mentally retarded persons. Because of the low level of skills possessed by that group, it is not possible to use the IQ measures just noted, simply because they do not measure severe deficits very well. Thus, to provide meaningful information regarding the adults' abilities, some descriptions of rudimentary developmental skills and behavioral observations are substituted.

Adaptive Behavior

The AAMD formally added the adaptive behavior component to the definition of intelligence in the *Heber*, (1961) and later in the AAMD classification manual (Grossman, 1973, 1977). In addition to broadening the definition of mental retardation by including adaptive behavior and making more conservative classification and placement decisions, this emphasis has resulted in a marked increase in the number and type of adaptive behavior scales. These measures have been reviewed thoroughly in other literature (e.g., Meyers, Nihira, & Zetlin, 1979). Besides providing a more conservative definition of the syndrome, there are several reasons for the increasing emphasis on measures of adaptive behavior.

First, there has been considerable discontent with traditional IQ measures for defining mental retardation. It was felt by many that streetwise behaviors of many mentally retarded persons were not being tapped adequately. Also, many severe and profoundly mentally retarded persons with physical sensory handicaps have been judged untestable with standardized intelligence tests, because items were inappropriate given their range of skills and lack of verbal behavior. Also no normative data existed on these tests for these more handicapped persons. Finally, and of equal importance, is the current emphasis on programming rather than custodial care. Adaptive scales allow for more specific identification of behaviors that can be targeted for treatment. Along these same lines, adaptive behavior measures provide a sensitive means for evaluating program effectiveness.

It would not be possible to review all the measures of adaptive behavior in one brief chapter. Many speciality measures are available, including the Fairview Self-Help Scale (Ross, 1969, 1970), Fairview Language Evaluation Scale (Boroskin, 1971), Fairview Social Skills Scale (Ross & Giampiccolo, 1972), Matson Evaluation of Social Skills with Youngsters (Matson, Helsel, & Rotatori, 1983), Cain–Levine Social Competency Scale (Cain, Levine, & Elzey, 1963), California Preschool Social Competency Scale (Levine, Elzey, & Lewis, 1969) and Social and Prevocational Information Battery (Halpern, Raffeld, Irvin, & Link, 1975), to name a few.

Two adaptive behavior scales that measure a broad range of skills have historically been used most often with mentally retarded persons and are the measures used in evaluating intelligence. These are the Vineland Social Maturity Scale (Vineland) (Doll, 1953) and the AAMD Adaptive Behavior Scale (AAMD–ABS) (Nihira, Foster, Shellhaas, & Leland, 1974). The Vineland has a more unitary trait approach than is evident with the AAMD–ABS. While the Vineland measures general developmental

level, the AAMD–ABS can be used to evaluate several domains, including self-help skills, physical development, communication skills, cognitive functioning, domestic and occupational activities, self-direction, and responsibility and socialization. Until recently, the norms for the Vineland were very outdated, and in 1984 new norms with some revisions were made. Because the AAMD–ABS has both school age and adult versions and is endorsed by the AAMD, it has become the more popular of the two scales.

Behavioral Observations

Adaptive behavior scales are the midpoint between behavioral observations and measures that are strictly trait oriented, such as IQ tests. With intelligence tests, a unitary or several unitary traits are evaluated and, as a result, assessment tends to be somewhat global. Specific operational behaviors are not evaluated. Adaptive behavior scales assess more specific behaviors such as toilet training skills, but the degree to which these scales can be used to evaluate specific behaviors is somewhat limited due to the idiosyncratic nature of the population being evaluated.

Behavioral observation is concerned with discrete observable phenomenon, but few behaviors are assessed, and thus, traits are not considered. A broad range of behaviors of mentally retarded adults have been measured using this method, including toilet training (Foxx & Azrin, 1973; Van Wagenen, Meyerson, Kerr & Mahoney, 1969), self-injury (Griffin, Locke, & Landers, 1975; Sajwaj & Hedges, 1971), aggressive behavior (Harris & Wolchik, 1979; Matson & Stephens, 1978; Iwata & Bailey, 1974; Vukelitch & Hake, 1971), spelling (Matson, Kazdin, & Esveldt-Dawson, 1980), hair pulling (Matson, Stephens, & Smith, 1978), social skills (Matson & Andrasik, 1982a), and depression (Matson, Senatore, Kazdin, & Helsel, 1983).

Behavioral assessment has been reviewed in several other chapters of this book and has been discussed in detail elsewhere as it pertains to mentally retarded persons (Matson & Andrasik, 1982; Matson

& Breuning, 1983). The advantages of this procedure with the mentally retarded adult are that: (a) few scales are available that can measure the range of behaviors on which mentally retarded adults are being trained, particularly in the last few years where the emphasis on adapting in the community has greatly increased; (b) measuring discrete behaviors can be useful in providing the accountability that is necessary with behaviorally oriented training procedures; and (c) behavioral assessment can be very cost efficient since it allows the trainer to assess only behaviors that are directly related to treatment goals rather than a far-reaching number of behaviors, as is the case with most adaptive behavior scales. This method has proven to be the most widely used assessment approach in the literature with mentally retarded adults: a trend that is likely to continue.

TREATMENT

Entire volumes are devoted to the treatment of problem behaviors in mentally retarded persons. Books of this type have only emerged in the last few years and attest to the intensive research efforts that are occurring (see Matson & Andrasik, 1982b; Matson & McCartney, 1981). Given the massive amount of research, it would not be possible to cover all the relevant studies in this chapter. Therefore, only some of the major areas and studies that exemplify the research noted will be reviewed. There are a number of medically related treatments that might also be viewed not as treatment, but as preventive measures. Some of these areas include genetic counseling (Pueschel & Goldstein, 1983) and nutrition (Huber, 1983). A second area that is psychologically based, psychotherapy, will not be covered (Nuffield, 1983). None of these topics fit clearly into the treatment category, and in the case of psychotherapy, the area does not have a strong data base with mentally retarded adults. Thus, the current review will be restricted to psychopharmacology and behavior modification.

Psychopharmacology

Drug research with mentally retarded persons has lagged behind that for persons of normal intelligence. Despite this fact, considerable study has occurred in recent years. The drugs most frequently used by psychiatrists and pediatricians, that are of the most interest to psychologists and special educators, are tranquilizers and anticonvulsants. There have been a number of studies both on the incidence and treatment effects of these agents. The incidence studies have been restricted primarily to mentally retarded adults residing in institutions. However, later studies have been conducted in community settings. Some general conclusions may be drawn from these studies that were conducted with over 3,000 persons both in and outside the institution.

Antipsychotic medications, although employed somewhat more frequently in the community, are used with 40 to 60% of the mentally retarded adults studied (Davis, Cullari & Breuning, in press; Cohen & Sprague, 1977; Hughes, 1977; Lipman, 1970; Sewell & Werry, 1976; Spencer, 1974; Silva, 1979; Tu, 1979). In these same studies, rates of anticonvulsant drug use were in the 50 to 75% range. These studies would suggest that effects and side effects of medications need careful and extensive study. A major problem with the majority of studies that have been conducted to evaluate drug effects have been methodological problems, which plague the bulk of this research (Aman & Singh, 1983). However, even with these reservations, some general comments about treatment effects are in order for some frequently used drugs.

Thiorcidazine (Mellaril®)

Twenty-four studies using Mellaril have been reported and reviewed previously, with only six of these viewed as methodologically adequate (Aman & Singh, 1980). Mellaril has been found to be effective in controlling both aggression and stereotypic behaviors. Very high dosages have proven to result in a number of undesirable side effects without any additional gains with respect to the target responses.

Chlorpromazine (Largactil®, Thorazine®)

Compared to Mellaril, there are less available data on the effectiveness of these drugs with mentally retarded persons. Additionally, recent evidence suggests that Mellaril may be more effective with mentally retarded persons for acting out, stereotypy and other inappropriate behaviors than chlorpromazine (Aman & Singh, 1983). Data are not sufficient to strongly substantiate these claims, however.

Haloperidol (Haldol®, Serenace®)

As with the other drugs previously noted, haloperidol seems to be an effective method of controlling aggressive, stereotyped, and hyperactive behavior (Sprague & Baxley, 1978). It should be cautioned, however, that very little sound data are available to make firm judgments on treatment effectiveness, side effects, and the effects of this agent in relation to the other drugs previously mentioned.

Anticonvulsants

Considerable evidence suggests that anticonvulsants are effective in reducing problems associated with seizures (Aman & Singh, 1983). These drugs are also thought to have antipsychotic properties, and they also allow the general control of aggressive behavior (Aman & Singh, 1983; Kaufmann & Katz-Garris, 1979). This attitude may contribute to the widespread use of this drug with mentally retarded adults, as alluded to earlier in this chapter. A disconcerting aspect of this state of affairs is that much of the research does not support this contention (Conners & Werry, 1979; Stores, 1978). More recently, Tegretol (carbamazepine) has been studied with respect to this phenomenon. Very modest support for Tegretol's effect on these inappropriate behaviors has been noted in a review of the experimental literature (Remschmidt, 1976).

Other drugs have also been studied, but the areas previously discussed constitute the major thrust and the most actively researched areas of drug use and possible abuse with mentally retarded persons. These studies and the others that are available suggest that very little is known about

the effects of such drugs on mentally retarded persons despite widespread use. Future research is therefore needed to provide leads on when and how major tranquilizers and other psychotropic drugs should be used with mentally retarded adults.

BEHAVIOR MODIFICATION

The researchers employing behavior modification strategies have been far more active than professionals in other areas of treatment or assessment with mentally retarded adults. The number of studies with good methodological control are numerous and impressive. Also, the number of problems treated have been far-reaching. Of all the areas that have received attention in the behavior modification literature, research with mentally retarded adults has perhaps the largest and longest number of credits and tradition. This trend goes back to the 1960s and 1970s, when the hard-core group of mentally retarded institutionalized persons were receiving custodial care but little else. At the time, insight-oriented approaches dominated psychology and thus, few psychologists or psychiatrists were interested or felt they had anything to offer this group. The thrust of treatment or the lack of it changed through the pioneering work of a few dedicated professionals. The types of problems approached were basic for survival, and the most rudimentary life adjustment skills were selected for intervention. For example, self-help was one of the first areas studied. Areas that have also been the subject of intensive research include stereotyped behaviors, vocational skills, social skills, toilet training, and communication (Matson & Andrasik, 1982b) Matson & McCartney, 1981; Whitman, Scibak, & Reid, 1983).

Stereotyped Behaviors

Milder forms of this problem which are typically referred to as stereotypies and the more severe version, self-injurious behaviors, have been widely researched. There have not only been a large number of experimental studies, but entire books written primarily on this phenomenon (Hollis & Meyers, 1982; Matson & Frame, in press). A number of very successful treatments have been employed to curb these problems. Rather than try to discuss the various studies, a few examples will be given. Some of the most frequently studied of the self-injurious behaviors are pica (ingestion of non-nutritive substances), scavenging behavior, mouthing of objects, and coporphagy (ingestion of feces). These problems, which are fairly common in mentally retarded adults, have been effectively treated by a number of investigators (Foxx & Martin, 1975; Matson, Stephens & Smith, 1979; Rusch, Close, Hops & Agosta, 1976). It has been suggested that behavior modification may be the most effective procedure to date for these particular forms of self-injury (Schroeder, Schroeder, Rojahn & Mulick, 1981). Another common form of self-injurious behavior is chronic ruminative vomiting, which may be life threatening in some cases. Satiation seems to be an effective treatment for this problem (Kohlenberg, 1970; White & Taylor, 1967). However, the reinforcement of alternative activities has also proven effective (Mulick, Schroeder, & Rojahn, 1977). It should be emphasized that, at this point, a number of behavioral procedures have been of value for a wide range of stereotypies. However, it is difficult to make strong conclusions about the effectiveness of one procedure compared to another given the idiosyncratic nature of the problem and the small number of persons with a particular type of self-injury. Group studies are just not feasible. Thus, a clear treatment of choice is not likely to emerge in the near future. However, it is currently possible to note treatment alternatives that may be effective.

Self-Help Skills

Research on the training of self-help skills with mentally retarded adults has proliferated in the last few years, primarily because such skills are so basic to proper adjustment and adaptation to the normal living environment. Also, the emphasis on normalization (Wolfensberger, 1969) is an excellent example of the social and political pressure that has been evident in many parent and professional groups toward the teaching of just these sorts of skills (Morris & Brown, 1982). Because of this major trend, a broad range of skills have received attention.

One area is self-feeding. Studies have been conducted with respect to both the skills necessary to enhance adaptive behavior and for decreasing inappropriate behaviors that interfere with feeding (Reid, 1983). A number of inappropriate behaviors have been treated, which include throwing food, stealing food, moving from one table to another, yelling, eating with one's hands, mouth-to-plate eating, and eating very rapidly (Albin, 1977; Christian, Holloman, & Lanier, 1973; Favell, McGimsey, & Jones, 1980; Hamilton & Allen, 1967; Henrikson & Doughty, 1967; Martin, McDonald, & Omichinski, 1971).

In addition to trying to improve these problems, a wide range of eating skills have been trained. Two studies which exemplify this range of behaviors will be briefly described. Additionally, it should be pointed out that the training strategies described here are similar to those employed in many of the other studies to be reviewed.

Stimbert, Minor, and McCoy (1977) taught rudimentary eating skills which consisted of limiting training on the use of one utensil (a spoon); the emphasis was on moving food from the plate to the mouth. While praise was given for correct responses, eating errors were treated by manual guidance, restitutional overcorrection, and tray time-out. This latter procedure consisted of pushing the food tray out of the child's reach. The second trainer who sat behind the subject would physically prevent the use of "two-handed" eating or engaging in inappropriate behavior. This training method proved to be highly effective.

More complex skills have also been trained with higher functioning mentally retarded persons. Matson, Ollendick, and Adkins (1980) trained a broad range of behaviors in 40 mentally retarded adults (40 others served as controls). Skills were ordered into five major categories, with a number of behaviors listed under each of these. They were:

ORDERLINESS
- picks up utensils
- appropriate noise level
- appropriate line behavior
- stays seated during meals
- finishes eating before leaving the table
- returns tray and utensils properly

EATING
- chews food before swallowing
- takes small bites
- swallows before next bite
- drinks properly — glass in one hand
- eats at a normal pace (not too fast)

UTENSIL USAGE
- uses spoon appropriately
- uses fork appropriately
- uses knife appropriately
- holds utensils properly

NEATNESS
- eats neatly
- uses napkin
- does not talk with mouth full
- has good posture

TABLE MANNERS
- chews with mouth closed
- elbows off table
- hand in lap
- pushes chair in

Another important area of self-help skill development is self-dressing. These skills are important since they allow the individual greater control over the environment and thus, greatly enhances their independence. Emphasis in early studies was primarily on a few basic skills, such as putting on and taking off a shirt (Minge & Ball, 1967), and as more studies began to appear, an emphasis on training a broader range of skills was noted. Thus, behaviors such as tying shoes and fastening bras were reported by Martin, Keogh, Bird, Jensen and Darbyshire (1971). Other behaviors that have been taught are: putting on and removing pants and shirt (Azrin, Schaeffer,

& Wesolowski, 1976), and color-coordinating outfits (Nutter & Reid, 1978).

A few pertinent studies have also been conducted on a wide range of normalizing skills that enhance independent living and hence, adjustment to the community. While many treatment procedures have been employed, the emphasis in the great majority of them has been the use of reinforcement and verbal and physical prompts. Some of the behaviors that have been trained include money management (Wunderlick, 1972; Borakove & Cuvo, 1976; Lowe & Cuvo, 1976), oral hygiene (Cheney, Kluft, & Levicki, 1974), emergency skills (Matson, 1980), sewing, mending (Saunders, 1978), and mobility.

Pedestrian skills are particularly pertinent for persons in the community given the risk factors involved. One study on this topic was conducted by Matson (1980). Fifteen mentally retarded adults were treated while an additional 15 served as controls. Subjects were from 21 to 55 years of age, and they were in the moderate-to-severe range of mental retardation. The behaviors deemed necessary for appropriate pedestrian skills included walking on the correct side of the street, not bumping into other pedestrians, not staring at others, walking across the street only when the light is green, and crossing the street only at the corner. Trainers who had degrees in psychology or special education worked with five clients at a time. Training was conducted in three separate settings. First, an analogue setting was employed which consisted of a simulated model of two city blocks with intersections, small movable cars, and people. The skills necessary for appropriate pedestrian behavior were then practiced. A second setting consisted of an intersection on hospital grounds with a traffic light that could be changed at will by a trainer. Finally, a downtown area of a small city served for generalization training. A safety monitor was also used and was there to insure that the clients did not make any moves that might be potentially dangerous. The classroom training, which consisted of modeling and performance by the clients using the model of a city intersection, was compared to independence training. The independence training procedure differed from classroom training in several ways. The rationale for the modifications was based on observations of residents who exhibited lack of generalization to the live environment, frequent lack of motivation, and an inability to conceptualize how classroom training pertained to live performance of targeted pedestrian skills. It was hypothesized that additional training components could make the subjects in training more informed and involved in their treatment. The inclusion of these latter training procedures was the rationale for labeling this treatment package as independence training. Additional goals of the procedure were to make the program as socially reinforcing as possible by enlisting the support and encouragement of staff and peers, and to enhance generalization to live situations by providing training that more closely approximated the behavior to be performed in the natural environment.

The first phase of independence training involved teaching the subject to recognize common pedestrian signs. The rationale was that subjects could more accurately demonstrate appropriate pedestrian behavior if they were able to recognize and respond correctly to the appropriate street crossing signals. Subjects were trained to recognize the function of red, green, and yellow lights, and how to identify stops, yields, signal lights, pedestrian crossings, and school crossing signs.

The second phase of independence training consisted of teaching the target behaviors to subjects. The mode of training involved using instruction in the school room for 2 weeks then using training at the mock intersection for the remainder of the treatment period. Training sessions were 30 minutes in length and conducted in groups of three.

A typical session at the mock intersection included the following: (a) walking to the mock intersection; (b) the trainer asking one subject to perform each target behavior; (c) the trainer asking questions about the target behaviors; (d) the trainer correcting the subject by verbal and manual prompts as necessary (prompts to the client to attend to training were also pro-

vided to the other subjects in the group as needed to ensure attendance); (e) the trainer asking the subject to evaluate his/her performance soon after completion; (f) the trainee giving a verbal evaluation of client performance; and (g) subjects who observed the performing subject being asked to make positive statements about the target behaviors exhibited. Then another client was asked by the staff person to perform the target behaviors.

Other skills that can enhance a person's ability to adapt better in the community have also been studied. Some other behaviors that have been effectively modified include shopping (Matson, 1981) and showering skills (Matson, DiLorenzo, & Esveldt-Dawson, 1981). Research in this area has become quite prevalent in recent years, and the results have been very encouraging. It seems likely that research of this type will continue.

Another area related to normalization of mentally retarded persons is social skills. This topic has been heavily researched with mentally retarded adults in recent years and has been reviewed extensively in other literature (e.g., Andrasik & Matson, 1984; Matson & DiLorenzo, 1984). A large body of research has begun to appear that demonstrates the nature and extent of social skill deficiencies in mentally retarded persons. For example, not only are these persons deficient in social skills (McDaniel, 1960), but improved social skills are likely to enhance community adjustment (Bell, 1976; Crawford, Aiello, & Thompson, 1979; Schalock & Harper, 1978, 1979). Also, it has been shown that mentally retarded adults fired from competitive employment are often let go due to interpersonal problems (Greenspan & Shoultz, 1981). Additional social deficiencies are likely to be exacerbated by attitudes of many community members (Raskin, 1979). Based on these data, it is not surprising that interpersonal behaviors have become a major area of investigation.

Studies on social skills have been of two major types: operant conditioning and social learning approaches. The operant studies were the first to appear. For example, Brodsky (1967) studied the correspondence between verbal and non-verbal behavior of two young adults (17 and 25 years of age). These women were reinforced to increase the number of verbal initiations that they made toward others. Treatment proved effective for both persons. Some other social behaviors effectively trained include social greetings by hand-waving (Stokes, Baer & Jackson, 1974), voice-loudness (Jackson & Wallace, 1974), and question asking (Twardosz & Baer, 1973). These behaviors are all prosocial, but many inappropriate behaviors have also been modified. Among the inappropriate responses are talking or grunting out-loud and bizarre laughter (Schultz, Wheman, Renzaglia, & Karan, 1978).

As noted, the early research on social skills training with mentally retarded persons was primarily operant. However, more recently a social skills training approach that emphasizes modeling, instructions, performance feedback, and social reinforcement has become popular. Turner, Hersen, and Bellack (1978) note several reasons why this method might be useful with mentally retarded persons. First, the approach emphasizes training small steps of a few discrete behaviors. Second, modeling has proven to be a well-suited approach for treating these persons. Third, the trainee receives considerable individual attention that is of benefit in stimulating recalcitrant individuals to respond. Fourth, training can become highly reinforcing. And fifth, this approach allows ample opportunity to try new responses under the supervision and guidance of someone well-versed in appropriate responding. A broad range of behaviors have been successfully treated with this method. Responses trained have included frequency of looking at the therapist, content of speech, physical appearance, facial mannerism, posture, affect, overall assertiveness, tone of voice, personal appearance, complying with requests, responding quickly, being cheerful, making positive self-statements, talking clearly, smiling, or giggling, and appropriateness of physical gestures (Matson & Stephens, 1978; Matson & Zeiss, 1978; Matson, Zeiss, Zeiss, & Bowman, 1980).

These data and the research of many others suggest that social skills training can be a very effective way of modifying the social problems of mentally retarded persons.

Vocational Skills

Besides social skills, the other area in the behavior modification literature receiving the most attention in recent years is vocational training. The majority of the research has focused on whether mentally retarded adults can acquire various vocationally related skills. For example, skills that have been trained included the assembly of a cable harness (Hunter & Bellamy, 1976), saw chains (O'Neill & Bellamy, 1978), and increasing production rates (Crosson, 1969; Huddle, 1967; Zimmerman, Overpeck, Eisenberg, & Garlick, 1969). Additional studies have begun to appear that define many jobs that mentally retarded persons can perform that were previously considered outside their capability. Some of these tasks include forms of agricultural work (Jacobs, 1978), jobs as porters (Tomasulo, 1976), clerical jobs, service station attendants, food service jobs in university settings, and upholstery-related jobs. Many of these skills have been taught using behavior modification. It is likely, given current trends, that research of this nature will become increasingly important.

Communication

An area that somewhat overlaps social skills training is communication. In this instance, the person is learning *how* to speak, however rather than *when* to speak. Of course, communication is essential to community adaptation (Meyers, Nihira, & Zetlin, 1979). Additionally, as Salisbury, Wambold, and Walter (1978) rightly point out, there are many ways of communicating in addition to speech. The two primary methods of developing speech have been developmental and behavioral. Both have proven effective in clinical practice (Schiefelbusch, Ruder, & Bricker, 1976).

It should also be pointed out that communication involves both sending and receiving communication; both of these modes are frequently refered to with respect to communication training (Cuvo & Riva, 1980). It should also be emphasized that it is possible for a mentally retarded person to exhibit receptive behaviors independently of expressive behaviors and vice versa (Guess, 1969). The types of training procedures that are used with these skills can vary considerably, but it is not unusual to begin with imitation of motor skills and to work toward verbal behaviors. A typical example of this form of training is described by Matson, Esveldt-Dawson, and O'Donnell (1980). They had a therapist imitate appropriate sounds for words, followed by the child making the same sounds. Approximations of an appropriate response were reinforced, and corrective feedback was provided where appropriate. Also, when an inappropriate sound occurred (as the subject became more accurate in responding), the child was required to write the appropriate word 10 times.

It should be pointed out that teaching speech is a very complex task and one that can be given only a brief review here. It should be noted, however, that some of the behaviors to consider include syntactic development (Garcia, 1974), improvement and expansion of language (Sailor, 1971), and the use of manual signing (Fristoe & Lloyd, 1979). Bliss symbols (McNaughton & Kates, 1974) and the Rebus System (Woodcock, 1965) are two other related approaches. This area is expanding rapidly and taking on a very specialized and complex nature.

SUMMARY AND FUTURE DIRECTIONS

Research with mentally retarded adults until recently has not been a topic generating nearly the activity that is evident with mentally retarded children. Many of the efforts in medication, for example, have been in prevention, and the efforts with special education have largely been focused on school populations. With adults, particularly since the early 1970s, when deinstitutionalization became popular, training studies were primarily with self-help skills and the elimination of maladaptive behaviors, such as aggression. This latter problem, for want of a better solution, was treated primarily with heavy dosages of major tranquilizers. New emphasis on environmentally based methods, particularly behavior modification, has been helpful in curbing the overuse of these drugs.

Many areas previously unstudied have become major topics of research with mentally retarded adults in recent years. The volume of research on social skills and vocation training is perhaps the most striking example of this trend. Special education in particular has begun to put a great deal of attention on life adjustment or survival skills in adults. These are extremely important areas of concentration and they, emphasize the need for education and support of the mentally retarded adult throughout the life span. Unfortunately, mentally retarded senior citizens have not received much attention. With the advent of better medical care, the life span of this group has been expanded considerably. Thus, determining how these persons can be cared for and integrated into the community becomes even more important. The elderly, in general, have been segregated in nursing homes, and many people who were functionally normal in young adulthood are functioning in the mentally retarded range due to senility and various degenerative diseases. What we have learned in treating mentally retarded adults in general may prove important in the care and habilitation of these persons as well.

If the past is any indication, future research in social and vocational skills will gain equal stature with other areas of research with mentally retarded persons. Furthermore, research with adults has proven valuable, and the unique needs of this special population are being recognized. The successes noted in the past suggest further emphasis and development of drug and behaviorally oriented treatments for this group.

REFERENCES

Abuelo, D. N. (1983). Genetic disorders. In J. L. Matson & J. A. Mulick (Eds.), *Handbook of mental retardation*. New York: Pergamon Press.

Albin, J. B. (1977). Some variables influencing the maintenance of acquired self-feeding behavior in profoundly retarded children. *Mental Retardation, 15,* 49–52.

Aman, M. G., & Singh, N. N. (1980). The usefulness of thioridazine for treating childhood disorders: Fact or folklore? *American Journal of Mental Deficiency, 84,* 331–338.

Aman, M. G., & Singh, N. N. (1983). Pharmacological intervention. In J. L. Matson, & J. A. Mulick (Eds.), *Handbook of mental retardation.* New York: Pergamon Press.

Andrasik, F., & Matson, J. L. (1984). Social skills with the mentally retarded. In M. A. Milan & L. L'Abate (Eds.), *Handbook of social skills training and research.* New York: John Wiley & Sons.

Azrin, N. H., Schaeffer, R. M., & Wesolowski, M. D. (1976). A rapid method of teaching profoundly retarded persons to dress by a reinforcement–guidance method. *Mental Retardation, 14,* 29–33.

Barrett, R. P., & Breuning, S. E. (1983). Assessment of intelligence. In J. L. Matson & S. E. Breuning (Eds.)., *Assessing the mentally retarded.* New York: Grune and Stratton.

Bell, N. J. (1976). IQ as a factor in community lifestyle of previously institutionalized retardates. *Mental Retardation, 14,* 29–33.

Birch, H. B., Richardson, S. A., Baird, D., Horobin, G., & Illsey, R. (1970). *Mental subnormality in the community: A clinical and epidemiological study.* Baltimore: Williams & Wilkins.

Borakove, L. S., & Cuvo, A. J. (1976). Facilitative effects of coin displacement on teaching coin summation to mentally retarded adolescents. *American Journal of Mental Deficiency, 81,* 350–356.

Borit, A., & Herndon, R. M. (1970). The fine structure of plaques fibromyeliniques in ulegyria and in stauts marmaratus. *Acta Neuropathologica, 14,* 304–311.

Bormada, M. A., Mossy, J., & Shuman, R. M. (1979). Cerebral infarcts with arterial occlusion in neonates. *Annals of Neurology, 6,* 495–502.

Boroskin, A. (1971). *Fairview language evalution scale: Birth to six years.* Costa Mesa, CA: Fairview State Hospital.

Brodsky, G. (1967). The relationship between verbal and non-verbal behavior change. *Behaviour Research and Therapy, 5,* 183–191.

Cain, L. F., Levine, S., & Elzey, F. F. (1963). *Manual for the Cain-Levine Social Competency Scale.* Palo Alto, CA: Consulting Psychologist Press.

Cheney, H. G., Kluft, G., & Levicki, G. A. (1974). Dental student's educational program for mentally handicapped children. *Mental Retardation, 12,* 54–55.

Christian, W. P., Holloman, S. W., & Lanier, C. L. (1973). An attendant-operated feeding program for severely and profoundly retarded females. *Mental Retardation, 11,* 35–37.

Cohen, M. N., & Sprague, R. L. (1977, March). *Survey of drug usage in two midwestern institutions for the retarded.* Paper presented at the Gatlinburg Conference on Research in Mental Retardation, Gatlinburg, Tennessee.

Connors, C. K., & Werry, J. S. (1979). Pharmacotherapy of psychopathology in children. In H. C. Quay, & J. S. Werry (Eds.), *Psychopathological disorders of children.* New York: John Wiley & Sons.

Crawford, J. L., Aiello, J. R., & Thompson, D. E. (1979). Deinstitutionalization and community placement: Clinical and environmental factors. *Mental Retardation, 17,* 59–63.

Crosson, J. A. (1969). A technique for programming sheltered workshop environments for training severely retarded workers. *American Journal of Mental Deficiency, 73,* 814–818.

Cuvo, A. J., & Riva, M. T. (1980). Generalization and transfer between comprehension and production: A comparison of retarded and nonretarded persons. *Journal of Applied Behavior Analysis, 13* 313–331.

Davis, V. J., Cullari, S., & Breuning, S. E. (in press). Drug use in community foster-group homes. In S. E. Breuning & A. D. Poling (Eds.), *Drugs and mental retardation.* Springfield, IL: Charles C. Thomas.

Doll, E. A. (1953). *Measurement of social competence: A manual for the Vineland Social Maturity Scale.* Minneapolis, MN: Educational Publishers.

Favell, J. E., McGimsey, J. F., & Jones, M. L. (1980). Rapid eating in the retarded: Reduction by nonaversive procedures. *Behavior Modification, 4,* 481–492.

Foxx, R. M., & Martin, E. D. (1975). Treatment of scavenging behavior (coprophagy and pica) by overcorrection. *Behaviour Research and Therapy, 13,* 153–162.

Foxx, R. M., & Azrin, N. H. (1973). *Toilet training the retarded: A rapid program for day and nighttime independent toileting.* Champaign, IL: Research Press.

Fristoe, M., & Lloyd, L. L. (1979). Nonspeech communication. In N. R. Ellis (Ed.), *Handbook of mental deficiency, psychological theory, and research* (2nd ed.). Hillsdale, NJ: Erlbaum.

Garcia, E. (1974). The training and generalization of a conversational speech form in nonverbal retardates. *Journal of Applied Behavior Analysis, 7,* 137–149.

Goddard, H. H. (1911). Two thousand normal children by the Binet measuring scale of intelligence. *Pedagogical Seminary, 18*, 231–258.

Greenspan, S., & Shoultz, B. (1981). Why mentally retarded adults lose their jobs: Social competence as a factor in work adjustment. *Applied Research in Mental Retardation, 2*, 23–38.

Griffin, J. C., Locke, B. J., & Landers, W. (1975). Manipulation of potential punishment parameters in the treatment of self-injury. *Journal of Applied Behavior Analysis, 8*, 458–464.

Grossman, H. (Ed.) (1973). *Manual on terminology and classification in mental retardation.* (Special Publication No. 2.) Washington, DC: American Association on Mental Deficiency.

Grossman, H. (1977). *Manual on terminology and classification in mental retardation.* Washington, DC: American Association on Mental Deficiency.

Guess, D. A. (1969). A functional analysis of receptive language & productive speech: Acquisition of the plural morpheme. *Journal of Applied Behavior Analysis, 2*, 55–64.

Halpern, A., Raffeld, P., Irvin, L. K., & Link, R. (1975). *Examiners manual for the social and prevocational information battery.* Monterey, CA: CIB/McGraw-Hill.

Hamilton, J., & Allen, P. (1967). Ward programming for severely retarded institutionalized residents. *Mental Retardation, 5*, 22–24.

Harris, S. L., & Wolchik, S. A. (1979). Suppression of self-stimulation: Three alternative strategies. *Journal of Applied Behavior Analysis, 12*, 185–198.

Heber, R. (1961). A manual on terminology and classification in mental retardation (2nd ed.). *American Journal of Mental Deficiency* (Monograph supplement).

Henrikson, K., & Doughty, R. (1967). Decelerating undesired mealtime behavior in a group of profoundly retarded boys. *American Journal of Mental Deficiency, 72*, 40–44.

Hollis, J. H., & Meyers, C. E. (Ed.) (1982). *Life-threatening behavior: Analysis and intervention.* Washington, DC: American Association on Mental Deficiency.

Huber, A. M. (1983). Nutrition and mental retardation. In J. L. Matson & J. A. Mulick (Eds.), *Handbook of mental retardation.* New York: Pergamon Press.

Huddle, D. (1967). Work performance of trainable adults as influenced by competition, cooperation, and monetary reward. *American Journal of Mental Deficiency, 72*, 198–211.

Hughes, P. S. (1977). Survey of medication in a subnormality hospital. *British Journal of Mental Subnormality, 23*, 88–94.

Hunter, J., & Bellamy, T. (1976). Cable harness construction for severely retarded adults: A demonstration of a training technique. *AASSPH Review, 1*, 2–13.

Iwata, B. A., & Bailey, J. S. (1974). Reward vs. cost token systems: An analysis of the effects upon students and teacher. *Journal of Applied Behavior Analysis, 7*, 567–576.

Jackson, D. A., & Wallace, R. F. (1974). The modification and generalization of voice loudness in a fifteen-year-old retarded girl. *Journal of Applied Behavior Analysis, 7*, 461–471.

Jacobs, J. W. (1978). Cleaning: Sheltered employment for retarded adults in rural areas. *Mental Retardation, 16*, 118–122.

Kaufman, K. R., & Katz-Garris, L. (1979). Epilepsy, mental retardation, and anticonvulsant therapy. *American Journal of Mental Deficiency, 84*, 256–259.

Kohlenberg, R. (1970). The punishment of persisting vomiting: A case study. *Journal of Applied Behavior Analysis, 3*, 241–245.

Levine, S., Elzey, F. F., & Lewis, M. (1969). *California preschool social competency scale.* Palo Alto, CA: Consulting Psychology Press.

Lipman, R. S. (1970). The use of psychopharmacological agents in residential facilities for the retarded. In F. J. Menolascino (Ed.), *Psychiatric approaches to mental retardation.* New York: Basic Books.

Lowe, M. L., & Cuvo, A. J. (1976). Teaching coin summation to the mentally retarded. *Journal of Applied Behavior Analysis, 9*, 81–87.

Martin, G. L., Keogh, B., Bird, E., Jensen, V., & Darbyshire, M. (1971). Operant conditioning in dressing behavior of severely retarded girls. *Mental Retardation, 9*, 27–31.

Martin, G. L., McDonald, S., Omichinski, M. (1971). An operant analysis of response interactions during meals with severely retarded girls. *American Journal of Mental Deficiency, 76*, 68–75.

Matson, J. L. (1980). A controlled group study of pedestrian skill training for the mentally retarded. *Behaviour Research and Therapy, 18*, 99–106.

Matson, J. L. (1981). Use of independence training to teach shopping skills to midly mentally retarded adults. *American Journal of Mental Deficiency, 86*, 178–183.

Matson, J. L., & Andrasik, F. (1982a). Training leisure time social interaction skills to mildly mentally retarded adults. *American Journal of Mental Deficiency, 86*, 533–542.

Matson, J. L., & Andrasik, F. (1982b). *Treatment issues and innovations in mental retardation.* New York: Plenum Press.

Matson, J. L., & Breuning, S. (1983). *Assessing the mentally retarded.* New York: Grune & Stratton.

Matson, J. L., & DiLorenzo, T. (1984). Mental handicap and organic impairment. In C. R. Hollin & P. Trower (Eds.), *Handbook of social skills training.* Oxford, England: Pergamon Press Ltd.

Matson, J. L., DiLorenzo, T. M., & Esveldt-Dawson, K. (1981). Independence training as a method of enhancing skill acquisition of the mentally retarded. *Behavior Research and Therapy, 19,* 399–405.

Matson, J. L., Esveldt-Dawson, K., & O'Donnell, D. (1980). Overcorrection, modeling and reinforcement procedures for reinstating speech in a mute boy. *Child Behavior Therapy, 1,* 363–371.

Matson, J. L., & Frame, C. (1983). Psychopathology. In J. L. Matson & C. Frame (Eds.), *Assessing the mentally retarded.* New York: Grune & Stratton.

Matson, J. L., & Frame, C. (in press). *Stereotyped movement disorders.* New York: Guilford Press.

Matson, J. L., Helsel, W. J., & Rotatori, A. (1983). Development of a rating scale to measure social skills in children: The Matson Evaluation of Social Skills with Youngsters (MESSY). *Behaviour Research and Therapy, 21,* 335–340.

Matson, J. L., Kazdin, A. E., & Esveldt-Dawson, K. (1980). Training interpersonal skills among mentally retarded and socially dysfunctional children. *Behaviour Research and Therapy, 18,* 419–427.

Matson, J. L., & McCartney, J. R. (1981). *Handbook of behavior modification with the mentally retarded.* New York: Plenum.

Matson, J. L., & Mulick, J. A. (1983). *Handbook of mental retardation.* New York: Pergamon Press.

Matson, J. L., Ollendick, T., & Adkins, J. (1980). A comprehensive dining program for mentally retarded adults. *Behaviour Research and Therapy, 18,* 107–112.

Matson, J. L., Senatore, V., Kazdin, A. E., & Helsel, W. J. (1983). Verbal behaviors in depressed and non-depressed mentally retarded persons. *Applied Research in Mental Retardation, 14,* 79–84.

Matson, J. L., & Stephens, R. (1981). Increasing appropriate behavior of explosive chronic psychiatric patients with a social-skills training package. *Behavior Modification, 2,* 61–76.

Matson, J. L., Stephens, R. M., & Smith, C. (1978). Treatment of self-injurious behavior with overcorrection. *Journal of Mental Deficiency Research, 22,* 175–178.

Matson, J. L., & Zeiss, R. (1979). The buddy system: A method for generalized reduction of inappropriate interpersonal behavior of retarded psychiatric patients. *British Journal of Social and Clinical Psychology, 18,* 401–405.

Matson, J. L., Zeiss, A. M., Zeiss, R. A., & Bowman, W. (1980). A comparison of social skills training and contingent attention to improve behavioral deficits of chronic psychiatric patients. *British Journal of Social and Clinical Psychology, 19,* 57–64.

McDaniel, J. (1960). Group action in the rehabilitation of the mentally retarded. *Group Psychotherapy, 13,* 543.

McKusick, V. (1978). *Mendelian inheritance in man: Catalogs of autosomal dominant, autosomal recessive, and x-lined phenotypes* (5th ed.). Baltimore: The John Hopkins University Press.

McMillan, D. L. (1982). *Mental retardation in school and society.* Boston: Little, Brown and Company.

McNaughton, S., Kates, B. (1974, June). *Visual symbols: Communication system for the prereading physically handicapped child.* Paper presented at the AAMD Conference, Toronto, Canada.

Mercer, J. R. (1970). Sociological perspective on mild mental retardation. In H. C. Haywood (Ed.), *Social-cultural aspects of mental retardation,* pp. 378–391. New York: Appleton-Century-Crofts.

Mercer, J. R. (1973a). *Labeling the mentally retarded.* Berkeley, CA: University of California Press.

Mercer, J. R. (1973b). The myth of 3% prevalence. In R. K. Eyman, C. E. meyers, & G. Tarjan (Ed.), *Socieobehavioral studies in mental retardation.* Washington, DC: Monographs of the American Association on Mental Deficiency.

Meyers, C. E., Nihira, K., & Zetlin, A. (1979). The measurement of adaptive behavior. In N. Ellis (Ed.), *Handbook of mental deficiency: Psychological theory and research.* Hillsdale, NY: Lawrence Erlbaum Associates.

Minge, M. R., & Ball, T. S. (1967). Teaching of self-help skills to profoundly retarded patients. *American Journal of Mental Deficiency, 71,* 864–868.

Morton, B. F., & Hebel, J. R. (1979). *A study guide to epidemiology and biostatistics.* Baltimore: University Park Press.

Mulick, J. A., Schroeder, S. R., & Rojahn, J. A. (1977, March). *A comparison of four procedures for the treatment of chronic ruminative vomiting.* Paper presented at the Gatlinburg Conference on Mental Retardation, Gatlinburg, Tennessee.

Nihira, K., Foster, R., Shellhaas, M., & Leland, H. (1969). *AAMD adaptive behavior scale.* Washington, DC: American Association on Mental Deficiency.

Nihira, K., Foster, R., Shellhaas, M., & Leland, H. (1974). *AAMD adaptive behavior scale public school version.* (Revised by N. Lambert, M. Windmiller, & L. Cole). Washington, DC: American Association on Mental Deficiency.

Nuffield, E. (1983). Psychotherapy. In J. L. Matson, & J. A. Mulick (Eds.), *Handbook of mental retardation.* New York: Pergamon Press.

Nutter, D., & Reid, D. H. (1978). Teaching retarded women a clothing selection skill using community norms. *Journal of Applied Behavior Analysis, 11,* 475–487.

O'Neill, C. T., & Bellamy, G. T. (1978). Evaluation of a procedure for teaching sawchain assembly to severely retarded women. *Mental Retardation, 16,* 37–41.

Pueschel, S., & Goldstein, A. (1983). Genetic counseling. In J. L. Matson & J. A. Mulick (Eds.), *Handbook of mental retardation.* New York: Pergamon Press.

Raskin, J. G. (1979). Criminal behavior of discharged mental patients: A critical appraisal of the research. *Psychological Reports, 44,* 1–27.

Reid, D. H. (1983). Trends and issues in behavioral research on training, feeding, and dressing skills. In J. L. Matson & F. Andrasik (Ed.), *Treatment issues and innovations in mental retardation.* New York: Plenum.

Remschmidt, H. (1976). The psychotropic effect of carbamazephine in non-epileptic patients, with particular reference to problems caused by clinical studies in children with behavioral disorders. In W. Birkmayer (Ed.), *Epileptic seizures, behaviour, pain.* Bern, Switzerland: Hans Huber.

Ross, R. T., (1969). *Fairview self-help scale.* Costa Mesa, CA: Fairview State Hospital.

Ross, R. T. (1970). *Manual for the Fairview self-help scale.* Costa Mesa, CA: Fairview State Hospital.

Ross, R. T., & Giampiccolo, J. S., Jr. (1972). *Fairview social skills scale.* Costa Mesa, CA: Fairview State Hospital.

Rusch, F., Close, D., Hops, H., & Agosta, J. (1976). Overcorrection: Generalization and maintenance. *Journal of Applied Behavior Analysis, 9,* 498.

Sailor, W. (1971). Reinforcement and generalization of productive plural allomorphs in two retarded children. *Journal of Applied Behavior Analysis, 4,* 305–310.

Sajwaj, T., & Hedges, D. (1971). *"Side-effects" of a punishment procedure in an oppositional retarded child.* Paper presented at Western Psychological Association, San Francisco, CA.

Salisbury, C., Wambold, C., & Walter, G. (1978). Manual communication for the severely handicapped: An assessment and instructional strategy. *Education and Training of the Mentally retarded, 13,* 383–397.

Sattler, I. M. (1974). *Assessment of children's intelligence.* Philadelphia: W. B. Saunders.

Saunders, R. M. (1978). Presentability as a goal for work activities clients. *Vocational Education and Work Adjustment Bulletin, 9,* 15–19.

Schalock, R. L., & Harper, R. S. (1978). Placement from community-based mental retardation programs: How well do clients do? *American Journal of Mental Deficiency, 83,* 240–247.

Schalock, R. L., & Harper, R. S. (1979). Training in independent living can be done. *Journal of Rehabilitation Administration, 3,* 128–132.

Schiefelbusch, R. L., Ruder, K., & Bricker, W. (1976). Training strategies for language deficient children: An overview. In N. Haring and R. L. Schiefelbusch (Eds.), *Teaching special children.* New York: McGraw-Hill.

Schroeder, S. R., Schroeder, L. S., Rojahn, J., & Mulick, J. A. (1981). Self-injurious behavior: An analysis of behavior management techniques. In J. L. Matson, & J. R. McCartney (Eds.), *Handbook of behavior modification with the mentally retarded.* New York: Plenum Press.

Sewell, J., & Werry, J. S. (1976). Some studies in an institution for the mentally retarded. *New Zealand Medical Journal, 84,* 317–319.

Shultz, R., Wehman, P., Renzaglia, A., & Karan, D. (1978). Efficacy of contingent social disapproval of inappropriate verbalizations of two severely retarded males. *Behavior Therapy, 9,* 657–662.

Silva, D. A. (1979). The use of medication in a residential institution for mentally retarded persons. *Mental Retardation, 17,* 285–288.

Singer, D. B., Rudolph, A. J., Rosenburg, H. S., Rawls, W. E., & Bonsuk, M. (1967). Pathology of the congenital rubella syndrome. *Journal of Pediatrics, 71,* 665–675.

Slosson, R. L. (1971). *Slosson intelligence test (SIT) for children and adolescents.* East Aurora, NY: Slosson Educational Publications.

Sprague, R. L., & Baxley, G. B. (1978). Drugs for behavior management, with comment on some legal aspects. *Mental Retardation and Developmental Disabilities, 10,* 92–129.

Spencer, D. A. (1974). A survey of the medication in a hospital for the mentally handicapped. *British Journal of Psychiatry*, *124*, 507–508.

Stimbert, V. E., Minor, J. W., & McCoy, J. F. (1977). Intensive feeding training with retarded children. *Behavior Modification*, *1*, 517–529.

Stokes, T. F., Baer, D. M., & Jackson, R. L. (1974). Programming the generalization of a greeting response in four retarded children. *Journal of Applied Behaviour Analysis*, *7*, 599–610.

Stores, G. (1978). Antiepileptics (anticonvulsants). In J. S. Werry (Ed.), *Pediatric psychopharmacology: The use of behavior modifying drugs in children.* New York: Brunner/Mazel.

Tarjan, G., Wright, S. W., Eyman, R. K., & Keeran, C. V. (1973). Natural history of mental retardation: Some aspects of epidemiology. *American Journal of Mental Deficiency*, *77*, 369–379.

Terman, L. M. (1919). *The intelligence of school children.* Boston: Houghton Mifflin.

Terman, L. M. & Merrill, M. A. (1973). *Stanford-Binet Intelligence Scale.* Boston: Houghton Mifflin.

Thompson, J. A., & Glasgow, L. A. (1980). Interauterine viral infection and the cell-mediated immune response. *Neurology*, *30*, 212–215.

Tomasulo, D. J. (1976). An economical approach to the development of a training program for porters. *Mental Retardation*, *14*, 12–13.

Tu, J. (1979). A survey of psychotropic medication in mental retardation facilities. *Journal of Clinical Psychiatry*, *40*, 125–128.

Turner, S., Hersen, M., & Bellack, A. S. (1978). Use of social skills training to teach prosocial behaviors in an organically impaired and retarded patient. *Journal of Behavior Therapy and Experimental Psychiatry*, *9*, 253–258.

Twardosz, S., & Baer, D. M. (1973). Training two severely retarded adolescents to ask questions. *Journal of Applied Behavior Analysis*, *6*, 655–661.

Van Wagenen, R., Meyerson, L., Kerr, W., & Mahoney, K. (1969). Field trails of a new procedure for toilet training. *Journal of Experimental Child Psychology*, *8*, 147–159.

Vukelitch, R., & Hake, D. F. (1971). Reduction of dangerously aggressive behavior in a severely retarded person through a combination of positive reinforcement procedures. *Journal of Applied Behavior*, *4*, 215–225.

Wechsler, D. (1955). *Manual for the Wechsler Adult Intelligence Scale.* New York: Psychological Corporation.

White, J. C., & Taylor, D. J. (1967). Noxious conditioning as a treatment for rumination. *Mental Retardation*, *5*, 30–33.

Whitman, T. L., Scibak, J. W., & Reid, D. H. (1983). *Behavior modification with the severely and profoundly retarded.* New York: Academic Press.

Wolfensberger, W. (1969). The origin and nature of our institutional models. In R. B. Kugel & W. Wolfensberger (Ed.), *Changing patterns in residential services for the mentally retarded.* Washington, DC: U.S. Government Printing Office.

Woodcock, R. W. (1965). *The Rebus reading series.* Nashville, TN: Institute on Mental Retardation and Intellectual Development, George Peabody College for Teachers.

Wunderlick, R. A. (1972). Programmed instruction: Teaching coinage to retarded children. *Mental Retardation*, *10*, 21–23.

Zimmerman, J., Overpeck, C., Eisenberg, H., & Garlick, B. (1969). Operant conditioning in a sheltered workshop. *Rehabilitation Literature*, *30*, 323–334.

CHAPTER 22

Multiply Disabled Children

Verna Hart

The young mother held the baby in her arms and voiced her fears. She had been advised to make an appointment for the baby with yet another doctor. A heart problem at birth had necessitated immediate surgery. An auditory evoked potential hearing test while still in the hospital, a further appointment after the child was released, and a visit to the pediatric ophthalmologist had all confirmed the presence of problems for the baby. Now she was being referred for another examination, this time to a neurologist to verify suspected motor problems and possible mental retardation. She stated that it was hard for her to keep appointments, the news she received was always so gloomy. She also wondered how many other things could possibly be wrong with her baby.

INTRODUCTION

The story is not an unusual one as far as diagnosing multiple disabilities is concerned. The majority of such problems are not diagnosed at birth or even in the newborn period, but continue to be confirmed throughout a period of time. Many of the problems are of a medical nature. There is an attempt to identify and classify those of a genetic or metabolic nature as soon after birth as possible. Doctors and nurses will often run tests on children who act or appear differently than those in the surrounding bassinets. Because genetic and metabolic difficulties can be confirmed through laboratory tests, their presence can be validated at an early age. However, the extent of the educational problems or the eventual development of children with such conditions is unknown because of individual differences.

Once a genetic or metabolic difficulty has been ascertained, physicians who are familiar with sequela of different medical conditions will then be alert to the possibility of the presence of additional problems. For example, infants who have been identified as children with Down Syndrome will be examined carefully to determine possible heart problems, hearing loss or a problem with visual acuity, all conditions that often accompany the genetic abnormality. Information that a mother has been exposed to the rubella virus (3-day measles) during the first 3 months of her pregnancy will also alert the doctor to the possibility of visual, hearing, heart, and mental disabilities.

However, most of the problems that eventually are labeled as multiple disabilities are not identified during the infant's stay in the neonatal unit of the hospital. Unless the eyes are malformed or missing, visual problems may not be readily apparent. Even congenital cataracts are usually not apparent until after the first few days in the hospital and, if the children stay in the newborn nursery for the average number of days, may not appear until after they are taken home. A hearing loss may not be readily evident to the observers. Motor problems may not be obvious at birth and not really noticed until expected developmental motor milestones fail to appear (Lewis & Fox, 1983). Unless the infants have stigmata associated with a syndrome or are grossly malformed, mental retardation can sometimes take years before being diagnosed. Learning disabilities will not appear at birth although the children may show early signs of hyperactivity. Seizures in the newborn period may or may not lead to epilepsy. Although there is evidence to show that autistic children may be different from birth, there is no effort to identify and label children at that period. Even though the extremes of many conditions may be diagnosed relatively early, milder disabilities may not be diagnosed for years: a total loss of vision or hearing or profound retardation will usually be noticed much earlier than will a less severe loss. Thus, children may be born, go home from the hospital and have parents who are unaware that they have even one problem, let alone two or more of them.

Because not all children are located through intitial medical identification and classification, additional means must be used to locate children with disabilities. Developmental screening will sometimes discover problems that were previously not noticed. Children who have been noted to have genetic, infectious or metabolic conditions will be monitored for additional problems. Children who have single disabilities will be watched to see if there are other problems that accompany them. Routine screening of all pediatric patients by pediatricians, nurses and preschool program personnel can often locate other children who have not been previously identified.

Not all multiple disabilities are present before or at birth. While some are prenatal or perinatal in origin, others occur after birth. Early intervention with children who have a single disability has been advocated to prevent additional problems. If a child should be born into a family where the presence of a single condition creates an environment where the parents are unable to deal with the problem or the child, it is not unusual for additional problems of retardation to appear because of lack of stimulation or to have emotional problems arising in the daily interaction among family members.

Thus, multiple disabilities may be present and identified at birth; they may be present at birth but not identified; they may be present at birth but partially identified; or they may result because there was a single condition that, because of environmental factors, became multiple in nature. There is no single definition as to what constitutes the term, *multiple disabilities*, or common characteristics among those who are said to possess them.

DESCRIPTION OF THOSE WITH MULTIPLE DISABILITIES

Those with multiple disabilities severe enough to prevent them from being educated with nonhandicapped peers in the regular classroom or with peers who have single handicapping conditions are educationally termed *multiply handicapped*. However, defining these students is a problem because there is so much variance among the children who are labeled in this manner. For years, children who had cerebral palsy were labeled as multiple disabled. Now these children often are grouped into a separate category with other children who are labeled neurologically impaired. At the present time, the term *multiple handicaps* usually refers to children whose major handicap is not a single disability with minor problems in other areas, but one where a number of problems are so severe that it is impossible to identify one as more handicapping than the other. Even the combined disabilities of deafness and blindness may not place one in the category of multiple handicaps. For example, in 1973 the U.S. Office of Education, Bureau of Education for the Handicapped awarded a contract to report on the severely handicapped. The population definition used for that project included both multiple handicapped and deaf-blind who exhibited other behaviors in addition to being deaf-blind *or* multiply handicapped (Tawney & Demchak, 1984). Currently, deaf-blind may be counted as a separate category or it may be considered a part of multiply handicapped.

The 1963–1965 rubella epidemic had a tremendous impact on the education of multiply impaired children, because attention was brought to them due to the large number of children affected and the severity of their multiple problems. Prior to that epidemic, not enough multihandicapped children had survived the impact of previous viral infectious epidemics to have an impact on the school systems. The advent of antibiotics, life-saving equipment in the neonatal intensive care units and the effectiveness of heart surgery on newborn children all allowed many children to live who previously would have expired shortly after birth. With the excellent care they received, these children soon came to the attention of many medical care providers and educational systems. The multiplicity of problems was overwhelming to most people who worked with them. Never before had such children been part of the educational systems. It was difficult to find staff to work with them and those who were willing were usually poorly prepared to take on such a tremendous responsibility.

The children were at first placed in classes for the visually or auditorially impaired. Then, in 1968, the passage of Public Law 90-247, Part C, which amended Title VI of the Elementary and Secondary Education Act (Elementary and Secondary Education Amendments of 1967, January 2, 1968) provided financial impetus for the provision of programs specifically for deaf-blind children. The definition for eligibility for such programs, set forth in Public Law 91-230, Title VI, Part C, Section 622 (April 13, 1970), states that a child must have auditory and visual handicaps in combination which cause such problems that they cannot properly be accommodated in special education programs solely for the hearing or visually handicapped (McVeigh, 1984).

The passage of Public Law 94-142, the Education of All Handicapped Children Act of 1975, created an even larger diversity among the multiple handicapped school population, because children who had never even been in educational programs were now assured their rightful place in them. The large influx of very severely involved students taxed facilities for dealing with the multihandicapped. Assessment problems and assigning students to programs became difficult because of their diversity. Students with sensory deficits and mild additional handicaps were different in need from those who had two major disabilities, and they in turn were different from the wheelchair-bound motorically involved students who could not speak or write but were normal in intelligence. Yet all of these students may have been labeled multiply handicapped. As noted by Tawney and Demchak (1984), the problem in definition and description persists.

Public Law 94-142 also contributed to earlier educational programming for the multiply handicapped population. Up to its passage, few significantly impaired children were included in intervention programs (Bailey & Bricker, 1984). Because of its mandate that children be educated in the least restrictive environment possible, Public Law 94-142 also allowed placement of severely involved children in residential schools that previously excluded them. Children with a single impairment were no longer served by the residential schools but were placed in their communities with their nonhandicapped peers. This created openings in the residential schools and administrators modified academic and college-oriented programs to accommodate the multiply handicapped (Myths Behind Residential Schools, 1984). However, Williams (1984) notes that a survey of state-operated residential schools for the deaf enrolling 90% of the residential population reported continued to exclude those students who are severely or profoundly multiply handicapped with low mental functioning levels. Such exclusion illustrates the fact that, although there is a continuum of degree of severity for each disability from mild to severe, the degree of impact on individuals is often overlooked and particular students may be excluded by generic labels. In addition, there is a lack of consistency between schools and school systems as to the definition and placement of those with multiple disabilities. Some provide separate classes for them while too often, others assign them to classes for the severely and profoundly retarded, even though their intellect may be above that stipulated for assignment to such classes.

Although students are often classified by their major multiple disabilities, there is great variance in the population. If, for example, we use the term "blind-retarded" to describe a student, there is little to describe the functioning level of that child. The term *blind* can range from legal blindness, in which case there is usually a great deal of remaining useful vision, to low vision, where there is less vision but it is still usable, to total lack of sight. The retardation may range from mild to moderate to severe to profound. Similarly, the term *deaf-blind* may refer to a student who is profoundly deaf and totally blind, hard of hearing and blind, deaf and partially seeing, or hard of hearing and partially seeing. One study of 50 children who had been labeled as deaf and blind showed that 22% of them had hearing sensitivity within the normal range, but had other problems that precluded speech and language development (Bernstein & Roeser, 1972). Thus, there is difficulty in labeling a child because each of the multiple problems usually has a range of functioning attached to it. Much also depends upon the use that the child makes of the remaining intact senses or abilities.

Because of difficulties in classifying, assessing and assigning students with multiple problems, various approaches have been suggested. One which appears to have a lot of potential examines level of func-

tioning rather than concentrating on labels. It groups the students into those who are ambulatory and nonambulatory and then, within each group, looks at their functioning levels. Such grouping allows for the variability in functioning levels as well as in ability to move about in the environment. These groupings are as follows:

Group 1: Nonambulatory
Subgroup A. Lacks all adaptive behavior. Medical state may be fragile.
Subgroup B. Adaptive behavior severely impaired. Does not perform unless supervised.
Subgroup C. Adaptive behavior severely impaired. Performs unsupervised.
Subgroup D. Adaptive behavior moderately impaired. Does not perform unsupervised.
Subgroup E. Adaptive behavior moderately impaired. Performs unsupervised.
Subgroup F. Mental and functioning ability average or above. Does not perform unsupervised.
Subgroup G. Mental and functioning ability average or above. Performs unsupervised.

Group 2: Functionally Ambulatory. May use adaptive equipment or mobility aids but is able to travel independently from one position to another.
Subgroup A. Lacks most adaptive skills.
Subgroup B. Adaptive skills severely impaired. Does not perform unless supervised.
Subgroup C. Adaptive skills severely impaired. Performs unsupervised.
Subgroup D. Adaptive behavior moderately impaired. Does not perform unless supervised.
Subgroup E. Adaptive behavior moderately impaired. Performs unsupervised.
Subgroup F. Mental and functioning ability average or above. Does not perform unless supervised.
Subgroup G. Mental and functioning ability average or above. Performs unsupervised.

Several of these groups may be combined for educational purposes, but such initial grouping more carefully delineates the functioning levels for assessment and placement considerations.

A student with multiple handicaps has more than just a combination of handicaps. When there is more than one problem, there is an interaction that is not additive but multiplicative. In the case of a combination of deafness and blindness, this is particularly true because vision and hearing are distance receptors and their impairment means that the individual will lose those distance receptors and must replace them with the near receptors of touch, taste and smell. Since these are not nearly as effective in providing a complete picture, the information upon which precepts and concepts are formed will be limited and often misleading. How does one tell the height of a house or the look of clouds if the distant receptors are limited? If a person has a single handicapping condition of loss of hearing or loss of vision, the other non-handicapped sense sometimes can be used for information. However, the loss of both senses means that the individual must have contact with an object or individual to get a clear idea of what the parameters are. Since we are unable to touch, taste or smell many objects, the information received will of necessity be limited.

Because there is so much variability among those with multiple disabilities, there can be no descriptors that will apply to all such individuals. However, there are some general statements that can apply to those individuals labeled *multiply handicapped*.

1. The larger the number of associated disabilities that an individual possesses, the less likelihood there is for optimal normalization (Denhoff, 1979).
2. A high incidence of moderate to severe motor impairment is found in this population (Guess, 1978). Early motor abnormalities are used as an indicator of problems in central nervous system integrity (Knobloch, Malone, Ellison, Stevens, & Zdeb, 1982). A lack of such integrity plus other confounding variables results in cognition, motivation and affect all being affected by impaired motor behavior (Molnar, 1982).
3. Mental age is generally more meaningful than chronological age as a descriptor of the children's status (Gordon, 1975).
4. Disabilities, even in combination, will range in severity from mild to moderate and severe, to profound.
5. If the individual was premature, the earlier the prematurity the greater the risk for a combination of developmental disabilities. Small-for-date infants have less of a good prognosis for development than do premature infants (Drillien, 1970).
6. Even though an infant is born with what looks like a combination of severe disabilities, the outcome is not predictable because of plasticity of the brain and infant variability. Such plasticity decreases with maturation of the child's neurological system that is completed in the first decade of life.
7. Language development, cognition and socialization are all interrelated and so intervention must include all areas of development (Wilkinson & Saywitz, 1982).

INCIDENCE OF MULTIPLE DISABILITIES

Children continue to be identified with multiple disabilities. McVeigh (1984) notes that prior to the rubella epidemic of 1964–1965, there were an estimated 140 deaf-blind infants born each year. He states that during that epidemic, the number rose to 2,000 per year and that high numbers remain today because of deaf-blindness caused by genetic anomalies, congenital malformations and infectious disease. Although infant mortality has been reduced, medical science has contributed to an upsurge in multiple birth defects because the lives of more severely involved babies are being saved.

In their study of the varied sequelae of congenital rubella following the 1964 epidemic, Chess, Korn, and Fernandez (1971) reported that in their psychiatric examinations of 243 children, only 118 of them were noted to be normal. They reported a correspondence between psychiatric disorder and physical impairments; as the number of physical handicaps increased, there was more likely to be a display of coexisting behavioral pathology. They also noted a high number of multiple defects in their population: 72 had only one, while 47 children had two, 47 had three, and 27 had four disabilities.

In a study of the rubella sequellae in 330 children at Johns Hopkins University, 60% were noted to have hearing defects, 29% had serious mental deficits, and only 5% had IQ scores of 110 or higher. Small body size, cardiac defects and visual handicaps were also observed. A high proportion of those with normal intelligence, vision and hearing were reported to have academic problems in school consistent with a diagnosis of minimal brain damage (Hardy & Welcher, 1980).

Although any number of biological influences may affect development, there is increasing evidence that nutritional factors both during fetal and early postnatal life may also affect development. There is almost a linear relationship between an infant's birth weight and intellectual functioning measured at 4 and 7 years. Other factors in the environment also must be included because the educational level of the immediate caretakers, the coping ability and the quality of parenting have all been noted to have impact on the developing infants (Hardy & Welcher, 1980). In fact, parents' education or socioeconomic status is the best single predictor of outcome for both normal and risk infants (McCall, 1981). Thus, not only are the initial disabilities important, but many other factors also must be considered in terms of incidence and potential for the child's ultimate functioning.

Prematurity should not be overlooked as a contributor of large numbers of multiply disabled children. Infants are now being saved by new medical instrumentation and techniques. However, the very low birth weight babies may be saved at a cost. While most low birth weight infants show transient abnormal central nervous system signs between 4 and 12 months, these resolve so the infants appear to be maturing normally

(Bax, 1981). In fact, over the last dozen years, the birth weight at which roughly half of the infants survive has dropped from 1300 to 800 grams in well-run perinatal centers. (The figures are not nearly as good in general hospitals where there are no well-equipped neonatal units.) Because cerebral palsy is often associated with premature births, it should be noted that in the 1950s, 60% of infants weighing less than 1500 grams were later diagnosed as cerebral palsied compared with less than 10% today. However, surviving infants with very low birth weights continue to present large numbers of developmental disabilities (Cohen, 1983). Of those weighing less than 750 grams, less than half survive. Of those weighing less than 1000 grams, 50% have intraventricular hemorrhages (IVHs), 10% have retrolental fibroplasia and many have chronic lung disease (Avery, 1982). These later conditions are all relevant to multiple disabilities, because hemorrhages into the brain can cause permanent damage to the tissues and can result in deafness, blindness, cerebral palsy, mental retardation and seizures. While there are different severities in the hemorrhages, the more severely affected children have a high mortality rate and those surviving have a high incidence of handicapping conditions. High levels of oxygen are associated with the IVHs and with retinopathy of prematurity. The latter condition also has varying levels of severity, with the most serious resulting in total blindness. Chronic lung disease may necessitate a child being monitored and on oxygen. Babies are often kept alive for long periods of time, even years, and then suddenly expire, causing extreme anguish to their parents and those who have worked so hard to keep them alive.

It is difficult to tell which infants will survive and which will not. It is also difficult to predict which children will exhibit no abnormalities from those with the most severe learning problems. Many of the disabled children do survive and they present problems to both the health care and educational institutions because of the severity and numbers of their handicaps.

The actual incidence of the various types of multiple handicaps is difficult to ascertain because of the lack of consensus as to what constitutes the classification, as well as the fact that no figures are kept that total all of the combinations that may be present. Healy (1984) reported that 60–70% of all children with cerebral palsy are mentally retarded, 50% have an eye muscle imbalance problem, and refractive errors are almost as common, that their recumbent positions make them more susceptible to middle ear infection which can cause conductive hearing loss, and that there is seizure activity in 35–45%. Wolraich (1984) reports that 60% of the children with spina bifida have significant intellectual and motor handicaps. In their annual report in 1983, the American Printing House for the Blind, an agency funded by Congress to conduct an annual census of all of the blind children in educational programs throughout the country, found approximately 40% of the 44,313 children registered had multiple handicaps (American Printing House for the Blind, 1983). The Office of Demographic Studies at Gallaudet College compiles a similar list of children enrolled in schools and classes for the deaf and noted 8,805 students who were deaf and multihandicapped out of a total of 46,322 students enrolled (American Annals of the Deaf, 1984).

However, none of these students just mentioned will appear in the numbers of multihandicapped children given as incidence figures. Why? Because the information is kept according to the most disabling of the handicaps. Thus, all of the students previously mentioned would be listed under their major handicapping conditions: cerebral palsy, crippling or other health impaired, visually handicapped or hearing handicapped. Only those whose combination of difficulties are felt to be their major problem are counted under the multiply handicapped group. Because of this, the incidence of multiple problems appears low. However, if all of the multiply impaired were enumerated under a single heading, multiple handicaps would appear as a much larger category.

Even the United States Office of Special Education is unable to provide an actual count of the number of multiply impaired because of the differing ways that states report their counts. Some include multiply disabled under specific categories and others count them separately. Deaf-blind students in some states are included with multihandicapped while they are separated in others. The totals of children reported annually are also in doubt. By law, all handicapped children must be served. Thus, the numbers reported should represent all the handicapped children in the country. However, it is a known fact that states differ in the rigor with which they pursue their search for handicapped children and that some do little to seek out children because identifying such children means that the states must then provide educational services to them. The numbers of children from ages 3 to 21 served under Public Law 94-142 and reported in 1984 by the U.S. Department of Education in its Sixth Annual Report to Congress on the Implementation of the Education for All Handicapped Children Act are as follows:

Learning disabled	1,723,759
Speech impaired	1,120,176
Mentally retarded	678,054
Emotionally disturbed	313,876
Other health impaired	48,104
Multihandicapped	50,367
Hard-of-hearing and deaf	49,119
Orthopedically impaired	46,459
Visually handicapped	21,298
Deaf-blind	1,383

DEVELOPMENTAL ISSUES

Because so many children fail to show immediate definitive signs of any type of disability, or because they may demonstrate one and be suspected of others, continuing observation throughout their early years is particularly important. Taft (1981) noted several indicators of motor problems that might be observed as early as the neonatal period or as late as 4 or 5 years of age. His list includes delayed motor milestones, poor sucking, early handedness, early rolling over, asymmetric crawling, persistent drooling, prolonged toe walk, feet turning in or out, and trouble climbing stairs. To this list can be added a persistence of primitive reflexes, tone which is either too high or too low, and heightened reflex reactions. Behavioral factors that have been noted while the infants are still hospitalized as newborns are their limited responses to stress or illness. Although manifested in lethargy, closed eyes or poor feeding, there is an attempt to withdraw or tune out stimuli. Some of the babies do not like to be held. The infants will often become jittery if disturbed. If they cannot escape from the stress, they begin to exhibit overt symptoms (Lubchenco, 1981). In fact, the failure of the children to handle stress is seen by some investigators as the reason for handicapped children's increased vulnerability for behavior disorders (Bax, 1981).

The role of the parents also must be mentioned when considering factors contributing to children's early development. To foster the best type of early environment, Parmalee (1981) emphasizes the necessity of quality in mother–infant interaction and states that this can be accomplished by interpreting the babies' behavior for them, showing them how to handle the babies and praising them for successful efforts. By providing additional social and financial support, Parmalee feels they will be better able to cope with any special problems their child may have. He found that a baby with a mother that is able to sustain good interaction at 1 and 8 months showed enhanced general competence when tested at 9 and 12 months. If there continued to be good interaction at 2 years, the child performed better at 5 years on the Stanford-Binet Intelligence Test. Because Minde (1982) reported that all mothers of ill premature babies showed a uniformly low rate of interaction with their infants, intervention into increasing the mother–child interaction seems particularly important.

Barnard (1981) advocates learning about the context of an infant's life by carefully observing ordinary activities such as feeding and eating. Since feeding is one of the first parenting skills that must be undertaken, and since multihandicapped children are particularly prone to problems in this area, failure makes adjustment to the child even more difficult. Bernard notes that such observations showed mothers working extra hard during the babies' first months to compensate for their children's unresponsiveness and other difficulties. However, toward the children's first birthdays, there is evidence of parental "burnout." Parents who have children with impairments are particularly at risk because of the enormous stresses placed on them and because of the many adjustments required of them. The numbers of contacts with different professionals alone would be overpowering to most parents. A recent survey showed that the average number of professionals serving visually handicapped children was 11, with one parent noting a total of 17 (Moses, 1984). Dealing with professionals is only one of the pressures a parent might feel. Others include extreme reactions to the child, lack of acceptance of the child or of the situation, incomplete mourning, lack of control with its accompanying feelings of helplessness, and economic burdens (Aradine, 1983). In fact, mothers may be so overwhelmed that they are unable to function. Women who have had problems severe enough to require hospitalization are reportedly unable to differentiate between their own and their children's needs (Cohler & Grunebaum, 1982), thus increasing the danger of impaired infant–mother interactions.

The infants themselves also have impact on the interactions between parent and child. Increasing information shows the influence on the mother–child relationship by the infants' temperaments. Although Carey (1982) is quick to point out that a difficult child and a difficult interaction are not necessarily the same, certain temperamental patterns predispose children to behavior problems. He notes that such characteristics as adaptability and persistence might strongly influence the behavior outcome, particularly in terms of successful rehabilitation. Rothbart discusses the "goodness of fit" between the child's temperament and the environment for quality growth of the child. She also relates that the quality of balance between child and caregiver is essential for maximum affective and cognitive development of both child and caregiver (Rothbart & Derryberry, 1982).

Ramey (1979) discusses the model to account for the varying multiple risk factors within and between the children, their families and the environment that has been developed by Ricciuti, with the idea of reducing outcomes despite acknowledged risk conditions. Acknowledging certain of these risk conditions, Ramey (1979) has been able to show, in a longitudinal study, that intervention in the mother–infant interaction reversed the predicted levels of development based on the mothers' initial attitudes and interactional behaviors.

Recognizing that their children have problems is also important. The ability of mothers to estimate the functioning levels of their children showed that those with only, younger and middle children with mild or moderate retardation were better able to predict their levels than were mothers with older or severely and profoundly retarded children (Higgins, 1979). It seems particularly relevant that those mothers who have the most difficulty in recognizing the extent of the problems are those with children who have the greatest impairment. Thus, mothers with multiple disabled children who have additional problems are under a great deal of pressure to meet all of their children's needs plus those of society's expectations.

EDUCATIONAL ISSUES

The children who are multihandicapped present a real challenge to educators, with problems in medical, learning, psychological and social areas. Because of the unique combinations of handicaps that the children may have and the individual manner in which they may react to them, it is difficult to form arbitrary parameters for their education. The children are not alike and individual programming is of essence. This is not to say they should not be taught in groups, because they can learn in such settings. All too often, individualized instruction has meant a one-to-one teacher–pupil relationship and the children fail to learn to interact with their peers.

Not only individualized but systematic instruction is essential for this population. Task analysis is necessary, with the ability to further break down tasks a necessary prerequisite for instructing pupils who are multi-impaired. Levine and Oberklaid (1981) list some areas of dysfunction that characterize such children: selective attention, visual processing, temporal–sequential organization, language, gross and fine motor function, memory, behavioral adaptation and neuromaturation status. Because some children exhibit only a few and others, all of them, blanket statements cannot be made as to which are more relevant. All of the areas must be assessed and considered when educational plans are formed. Friedman (1982), when discussing affective disorders, adds other elements that should be considered when discussing intervention: degree of central nervous or physical impairment, areas of healthy function, relationship to others, tolerance of pain, discomfort and anxiety, conceptualization and communication, developmental phase, personality structure and temperament, frustration tolerance, duration and severity of the problem, family dynamics, and proneness to regression of the child and family.

Educational issues, then, are many and involved, when it comes to teaching such complicated children.

There is no common agreement as to the type of curriculum to be used with multi-handicapped children. Much seems to depend upon the ages of the children. Three theoretical models comprise the major types of curricula currently in use: operant, developmental and ecological (Brinker, 1985). Although the use of task analysis has come from the operant approach and has been incorporated into other types of instructional techniques, pure operant techniques have come under criticism because the theoretical basis assumes increasing or decreasing behaviors already in the children's repertoires. Since many of the children with multiple disabilities have few or no response patterns in many areas of programming, a strict operant model has been difficult to implement. The developmental approach, based on the large body of information that children sequentially pass through stages of development, has been particularly popular for use with young children. Weaknesses in the use of this approach result when the tasks themselves become the objectives, rather than the underlying processes that the children need to proceed on to more advanced levels. Thus, screwing caps on jars becomes the desired goal rather than the reach, grasp, and wrist rotation that are a part of the task and that would allow the children to undertake more complicated tasks.

The ecological model places emphasis on the criteria of ultimate functioning. Since the goal of education is to keep children in the community and help them to become participating members of those communities, emphasis is upon the activities that will allow the students to take part in community situations. A weakness in this model is the lack of principles for selection of the environments in which the individuals can participate, or criteria for evaluation of environments of different communities (Brinker, 1985). Thus, there may be inappropriate objectives when one participates in one community compared to pariticipation in others. For these reasons, it is necessary to consider all the ramifications of the educational issues before choosing an appropriate theoretical basis and curriculum for the students.

The choice of curriculum is not only a factor in educating the students, but also the amount of time spent in direct instruction with multiply disabled children is extremely important. These children, for the most part, do not learn incidentally. Merely exposing them to subjects does not result in their learning the tasks; they must be specifically taught. In fact, it is so important that Fredericks, Anderson, and Baldwin (1979) note in their study of learning tasks accomplished that 78% of the variance was accounted for by the amount of instruction time and percentage of the curriculum materials that were task-analyzed.

A typical types of instructional materials may also play a part in educating certain types of multiply handicapped children. Studying a group of severely/profoundly retarded multiply handicapped deaf-blind children, the use of a black light environment allowed for the removal of all distracting stimuli and for exaggeration of critical features and resulted in significant gains over training under normal light (Potenski, 1983).

Working with a different population of neurologically impaired multiply handicapped preschoolers, Carner and Levy (1980) noted learning strategies that differed from their subjects' nonhandicapped peers: unstated rules were not understood by the multihandicapped, there was little internalization of the problem-solving set, little intrinsic motivation, and solutions tended to be specific, percept-bound and not easily generalized. Like many other authors before them, Carner and Levy also relate that almost constant intervention and structuring was necessary in order for the students to respond in the learning environment.

Thus, it can be seen that there are critical educational issues when dealing with multiply disabled individuals. They do not learn adventitiously, but must be specifically taught. There must be structured, systematic instruction using carefully planned task analysis. A functional curriculum should be developed that is based on the abilities of the individual student involved. Experiences that are missing from their lives should be included, in order for them to successfully exist in their least restrictive environment. However, the great variation between and among the different types of children with multiple disabilities negates one single curriculum that can cover the total population with that diagnosis. With no other group is individualizing, programming and instruction more important than with this one.

ASSESSMENT AND TREATMENT

Three distinct problems lead to difficulty in assessing and treating multiply impaired children. They are difficult to test, there is a lack of appropriate tests with which to assess them, and there is a scarcity of well-trained professionals to evaluate them.

Individual differences between and among the children who are called multiply disabled have already been discussed. These differences make it particularly hard to find instrumentation and methodologies to evaluate them. Although they both would be labeled multihandicapped, a child who is deaf and neurologically involved would be very different to assess from a child who is blind and retarded. Even two individuals who carry the label of *deaf-blind* would be very different to evaluate if one were legally blind and moderately hearing impaired and the other were profoundly deaf and totally blind. One could be tested using residual senses while the other could not. One could supplement touch, taste and smell while the other could not. Thus, there is no single test or even a single battery of tests that is available to assess the children. The combination of disabilities presented by individual children necessitates modifications in test selection because of the needs of those individual children.

Other factors also make the children difficult to test. Most of them have had very aversive experiences because of their medical problems. They often are fearful of new experiences and resist the testing situation. Many have not had the opportunity for normal learning experiences and so cannot respond to even elementary assessment measures. Many also cannot respond to the typical assessment instrument because of their physical, mental or emotional disabilities. For example, children may have to be outfitted with their adaptive equipment and appliances before they can respond. If the evaluators are not familiar with the proper use and limitations of such equipment, the children may not respond, not because they don't know the answers, but because they are physically unable to do so.

The lack of appropriate assessment tools presents very real problems to those assessing the children. Most instruments were normed on a nonhandicapped population and may be very difficult to use with those who are multiply impaired. Even the few tests that have been developed and standardized on a handicapped population have been developed primarily with children who are singularly involved. The need for instrumentation that is valid,

reliable and well-standardized is great. The logistics of developing such a test are almost overwhelming, however, when one considers the low incidence of the population of multiply disabled and the variation among and between those who are affected.

The variance among the children increases the need for a variety of assessment instruments. The multiple problems of the children necessitate instrumentation in many areas. Tools are needed in all areas of development and for varying levels of severity. For example, assessment of elementary self-care subjects such as feeding, toileting, dressing and grooming are needed as well as assessment for sophisticated use of computers and robots that some children might use to accomplish their self-care skills.

Minute steps are also needed in the instruments. Most assessment instruments, even those which have been developed using handicapped populations, demand such increase in sophistication between items at the various age levels that many of the severely involved multiply impaired children are unable to attain the behaviors needed for an increment on those tests. Professionals can work for long periods of time with the children and see improvement. The increments between items on the assessment instruments are too great for such improvement to be noted, however. For this reason, there has been an increasing use of single-subject designs in assessing the children. Although most of the assessment centers on criterion-referenced tasks and lacks a normed group against which to measure the progress of the children, such measures show that the children do make progress when properly taught.

The unique needs of multiply disabled individuals necessitate the use of an assessment team. Because of the variance among the children, team membership may vary with different children. However, a broad-based team should be available for those undertaking the assessment role. A broad spectrum of medical specialists is needed, as are occupational, physical and speech therapists, psychologists, orientation and mobility and low vision specialists, educators, social workers, audiologists, adaptive physical educators, prevocation specialists, and so forth.

Unfortunately, there is a dearth of individuals with training and experience in assessing multiply impaired children. Some professionals have taken particular interest in a type of multiple disability and have specialized in assessment and treatment of that particular problem. There is such a shortage of well-trained people in some of the areas that many children are transported across the country to be seen by the few who are knowledgeable. The lack of well-trained professionals makes it particularly important that the individuals who are assessing the children use a team approach where there is open communication between the various team members during the assessment procedure. All areas of development are able to be covered in this manner. With such communication, education of the team members to various aspects of the children's disabilities also can take place, with a richer background brought to the evaluation of subsequent children. Additional problems that have previously gone undiagnosed in the children may also come to attention during such open communication.

It is also important that those who have developed an expertise in assessing and treating multiply disabled children pass on that information to others. Curriculum in institutions preparing personnel to work on assessment teams should contain the information that has been and is being gathered by those who are working with this population.

CURRENT RESEARCH

Research with the population of multiply disabled children is difficult to carry out because of the nature of the group. The inexactness of the term used to define the population, the different use of the term in various sections of the country, the variance among the group of children who have been termed *multiply disabled*, the small incidence of the group, the grouping of many of the multihandicapped group

into the larger groups of disabilities, the unique combination of disabilities within each individual, and the varying degrees of severity of each of the disabilities all add to the difficulty in designing good research studies with this population. Although small studies continue, they often would be difficult to replicate because the subjects are not well-enough defined.

Well-designed studies are needed. Descriptive studies could help to define the population. Incidence studies using well-defined criteria would help to determine the kinds and severity of problems. Studies are needed as to the best techniques to use in educational settings. Assessment instruments are needed and studies on their effectiveness determined. The prevention of secondary handicaps needs examination. The list could go on. Few researchers are interested in the low-incidence population with such divergence, a group that includes many who are non- or poorly motivated and who often make small growth gains over long periods of time. However, there are small studies that show that these children do respond to intervention. Many make gains that previously were not thought possible. Brilliant minds can be locked behind multiple physical problems.

It is urged that all those who are working with this population disseminate the findings of the work that they are doing. Only through such means will additional information be shared. If not, what is known about this group will be based on the small studies that are sparse in number but that will undoubtedly continue because of the investigators' commitment to this population. Such information will be geared to specific multihandicapped populations but will not generalize to larger populations.

SUMMARY

Children with multiple disabilities present unique challanges to those who work with them. They are difficult to define because of the multiplicity of causation, they are formidable when trying to determine their incidence because of the manner by which they are defined and then enumerated, a challenge to assess and treat, and a joy when they meet or surpass expectations. Because they have not been carefully examined as a distinct entity, much work remains to be carried out with this group. It is a group where the incidence will continue to grow because medical advances are now keeping babies alive and allowing others who would previously have died to survive. Action is needed by all professionals in contact with them to ensure that there is quality in their lives.

REFERENCES

American Annals of the Deaf. (1984). *Annual report, 129* (2), p. 188.

American Printing House for the Blind. (1983). *Annual Report.* Louisville, KY: American Printing House for the Blind.

Aradine, C. (1983). Parents of medically impaired infants. In V. Sasserath & R. Hoekelman (Eds.), *Minimizing high-risk parenting* (pp. 50–55). Somerville, NJ: Johnson & Johnson Baby Products Company.

Avery, G. (1982). *Prematurity: A major health problem.* (Matrix No. 1.) Paper presented at the Research Forum on Children and Youth, Washington, DC, May 18–19, 1981.

Bax, M. (1981). The intimate relationship of health, development, and behavior in the young child. In C. Brown (Ed.). *Infants at risk: Assessment and intervention, an update for health care professionals and parents.* Somerville, NJ: Johnson and Johnson Baby Products Company.

Bailey, E. & Bricker, D. (1984). The efficacy of early intervention for severely handicapped infants and young children. *Topics in Early Childhood Special Education. 4,* 30–51.

Barnard, K. (1981). An ecological approach to parent–child relations. In C. Brown (Ed.), *Infants at risk: Assessment and intervention, an update for health care professionals and parents.* Somerville, NJ: Johnson & Johnson Baby Products Company.

Bernstein, P., & Roeser, R. (1972). Audiological assessment of deaf-blind children. Paper presented at the Annual Meeting of the American Speech and Hearing Association, San Francisco, CA, November 18–21, 1972.

Brinker, R. (1985). Curricula without recipes: A challenge to teachers and a promise to severely mentally retarded students. In D. Bricker & J. Filler (Eds.). *Severe mental retardation: From theory to practice,* (pp. 208–229).

Reston, VA: Division on Mental Retardation, Council for Exceptional Children.

Carey, W. (1982). Clinical appraisal of temperament. In M. Lewis & L. Taft (Eds.). *Developmental disabilities: Theory, assessment, and intervention,* (pp. 371–379). New York: SP Medical & Scientific Books.

Carner, L., & Levy, L. (1980). *Learning strategies of neurologically impaired/multiple handicapped and nonhandicapped preschool children.* Paper presented at the Annual International Convention of the Council for Exceptional Children, Philadelphia, PA.

Chess, S., Korn, S. & Fernandez, P. (1971). *Psychiatric disorders of children with congenital rubella.* New York: Brunner/Mazel.

Cohler, B., & Grunebaum, H. (1982). Children of parents hospitalized for mental illness: II. The evaluation of an intervention program for mentally ill mothers of young children. *Journal of Children in Contemporary Society, 15,* 57–66.

Cohen, S. (1983). Low birthweight. In C. Brown (Ed.), *Childhood learning disabilities and prenatal risk,* (pp. 70–78). Somerville, NJ: Johnson and Johnson Baby Products Company.

Denhoff, E. (1979). *Early signs of organic symptomatology in high-risk infants.* Paper presented at the Training Institute of the Center for Clinical Infant Programs, Washington, DC, December 6, 1979.

Drillien, W. (1970). The small-for-date infant: Etiology and prognosis. *Pediatric Clinics of North America, 17,* 9–24.

Fredericks, B., Anderson, R., & Baldwin, V. (1979). Time related to gains. *AAESPH Review, 4,* 81–95.

Friedman, D. (1982). Developmental disabilities: Intervention strategies in the affective domain. In M. Lewis & L. Taft (Eds.), *Developmental disabilities: Theory, assessment, and intervention,* (pp. 401–408). New York: Spectrum Publications, Inc.

Lewis, M. & Fox, N. (1983). Issues in infant assessment. In C. Brown (Ed.), *Childhood learning disabilities and prenatal risk,* (pp. 78–83). Somerville, NJ: Johnson and Johnson Baby Products Company.

Gordon, R. (1975). *Evaluation of behavioral change: Part 1: Study of multi-handicapped young children.* Final report. Washington, DC: Bureau of Education for the Handicapped (DHEW/OE), Grant No.: OEG-0-72-5386.

Guess, D. (1978). *Review of selected literature: Assessment of motor and sensory/motor skills in severely/multiple handicapped infants and young children.* Lawrence, KS: University of Kansas

Research Institute for the Early Childhood Education of the Handicapped.

Hardy, J., & Welcher, D. (1980). Language development in handicapped children. In A. Reilly (Ed.), *The communication game.* Somerville, NJ: Johnson & Johnson Baby Products Company.

Healy, A. (1984). Cerebral palsy. In J. Blackman (Ed.), *Medical aspects of developmental disabilities in children, birth to three,* (p. 35). Rockville, MD: Aspen Systems Corporation.

Higgins, T. (1979). *Parent awareness of retardation in preschool children.* Paper presented at the 87th Annual Meeting of the American Psychological Association, New York, September 1–5, 1979.

Knobloch, H., Malone, A., Ellison, P., Stevens, F., & Zdeb, M. (1982). Considerations in evaluating changes in outcome for infants weighing less than 1,501 grams. *Pediatrics, 69,* 285–295.

Levine, M. & Oberklaid. (1981). Early description and prediction of developmental dysfunction in preschool children. In M. Lewis & L. Taft (Ed.), *Developmental disabilities: Theory, assessment, and intervention,* (pp. 213–228). New York: SP Medical & Scientific Publishers.

Lubchenco, L. (1981). Gestational age, birth weight, and the high-risk infant. In C. Brown (Ed.), *Infants at risk: Assessment and intervention, an update for health care professionals and parents,* (pp. 12–18). Somerville, NJ: Johnson & Johnson Baby Products Company.

McCall, R. (1981). Predicting developmental outcome: Resume and redirection. In C. Brown (Ed.), *Infants at risk: Assessment and intervention, an update for health care professionals and parents.* Somerville, NJ: Johnson & Johnson Baby Products Company.

McVeigh, V. (1984, July). Services for deaf-blind children and youth — Coming of age? *DVH Quarterly, 4,* 8–12.

Minde, K. (1982). The impact of medical complications on parental behavior in the premature nursery. In M. Klaus & M. Robertson (Eds.), *Birth, interaction and attachment* (pp. 98–104). Somerville, NJ: Johnson & Johnson Baby Products Company.

Molnar, G. (1982). Intervention for physically handicapped children. In M. Lewis & L. Taft (Eds.), *Developmental disabilities: Theory, assessment, and intervention,* (pp. 149–174). New York: SP Medical & Scientific Books.

Moses, E. (1984, Fall). *All in a day's work, Awareness,* p. 1.

Myths behind residential schools. (1984). *The Lantern, 14,* 6–11. Watertown, MA: Perkins School for the Blind.

Parmalee, A. (1981). Early intervention for preterm infants. In C. Brown (Ed.), *Infants at risk: Assessment and intervention, an update for health care professionals and parents,* (pp. 82–89). Somerville, NJ: Johnson & Johnson Baby Products Company.

Potenski, D. (1983). Use of black light in training retarded, multiply handicapped, deaf-blind children. *Journal of Visual Impairment and Blindness, 77,* 347–348.

Ramey, C. (1979). *Maternal characteristics and intellectual development: Implications for parent education to prevent sociocultural mental retardation.* Paper presented at the 87th Annual Meeting of the American Psychological Association, New York, September 1–5, 1979.

Rothbart, M., & Derryberry D. (1982). Theoretical issues in temperament. In M. Lewis, & L. Taft (Eds.), *Developmental disabilities: Theory, assessment, and intervention,* (pp. 383–400). New York: SP Medical & Scientific Books.

Taft, L. (1981). Clinical appraisal of motor functions. In D. Radcliffe (Ed.), *Developmental disabilities in the preschool child,* (pp. 25–27). New York: SP Medical and Scientific Books.

Tawney, J., & Demchak, M. (1984). Severely retarded? Severely handicapped? Multiply handicapped? A definitional analysis. *Topics in Early Childhood Special Education, 4,* 1–18.

Wilkinson, J. & Saywitz, K. (1982). Theoretical bases of language and communication development in preschool children. In M. Lewis and L. Taft (Eds.), *Developmental disabilities: Theory, assessment, and intervention,* (pp. 301–319). New York: SP Medical & Scientific Books.

Williams, P. (1984). Admission policies and practices of state-operated residential schools for the deaf. *Exceptional Children, 50,* 550–551.

Wolraich, M. (1984). Hydrocephalus. In J. Blackman (Ed.), *Medical aspects of developmental disabilities in children birth to three,* (p. 139). Rockville, MD: Aspen Systems Corporation.

CHAPTER 23

Musculoskeletal Disorders

Kenneth Carr Wright and John J. Nicholas

INTRODUCTION

The musculoskeletal system consists of muscles, bones, joints, and connective tissue that hold them together. There are several hundred diseases that affect the muscloskeletal system. In this chapter, we will cover the more common and severe musculoskeletal disabilities. This material will also be of value in treating the more common disorders. Disorders of the musculoskeletal system are a major cause of disability in American today. A study of the effects of disease classified by organ system found that musculoskeletal disease accounted for a moderate number of hospital admissions and very few deaths. Yet, it caused far more limitation of activity than any other disease in an organ system category (Kottke, Lehmann, & Stillwell, 1982). One of the common causes of musculoskeletal disability is amputation of an arm or leg.

AMPUTATIONS

An amputaiton is the complete or partial loss of a limb or other body part. Most amputations result from a surgical pro-

cedure following disease or trauma to a limb; however, a small number are due to congenital defects. The primary treatment for an amputation is the prescription of a prosthesis or artificial limb. The purpose of the prosthesis is to restore the function and appearance of the missing limb as much as possible. It must not be forgotten that no prosthesis is as effective as the limb it replaces. Simply providing a prosthesis is not adequate for gaining maximum function. The amputee must undergo intensive rehabilitation training to reach his/her full potential.

Epidemiological Findings

In 1975, it was estimated that there were 400,000 amputees in the United States, and 43,000 new amputations occurred each year (Kay & Newman, 1975). In children under the age of 10, almost all amputations are due to congenital defects. The epidemiology of these defects is unknown, although in some cases, they may be due to maternal exposure to toxic agents as in the epidemic of limb deficiencies due to thalidomide in the early 1960s. In teenagers, amputations are frequently due to malignancies such as osteogenic sarcoma. Throughout early adulthood, trauma is the most frequent cause of amputation. Industrial injuries are a frequent cause of upper extremity amputations. In the middle aged-to-elderly population, vascular disease becomes the most common cause of amputation.

The majority of amputations involve the lower extremities. The most common level of amputation today is the below-knee amputation (BKA). The next most common level is the above-knee amputation (AKA). In the past, the above-knee amputation was much more frequently performed, but as surgeons have learned of the superior functioning of the BKA, they have used it in place of the AKA whenever possible. Another form of amputation commonly encountered is the Symes, in which the foot and ankle are removed. A portion of the heel is preserved giving these amputees the ability to bear some weight directly on the stump, something other amputees are not able to do. Other lower extremity levels of amputation include the hip disarticulation, where the entire leg and femur are removed from the pelvis, and the hemipelvectomy, in which a portion of the pelvis is removed as well. There are a number of different or partial foot amputations; in general these do not produce major disability. In the upper extremity, the most common operation is the below-elbow amputation (BEA) followed in frequency by the above-elbow amputation (AEA), partial hand, shoulder disarticulation, and wrist disarticulation (Kay & Newman, 1975).

Developmental Issues

In many ways, children adapt to amputations much better than adults. Children who have a congenital amputation do not undergo the grief reactions and alteration of body image that adults undergo. The effect of the amputation on psychological maturation will depend largely on the adjustment of the parents. Accepting, practical parents will facilitate normal psycho-logical development. Parents who are over-protective or rejecting may adversely affect development. Major difficulties in adjustment often occur during the teenage years. At this stage, body image and independence are major concerns, and the adolescent may reject a functional prosthesis because of its appearance.

Prosthetic fitting of children must take into consideration the stage of motor development. Infants with congenital upper extremity amputations should be fitted with a prosthesis between 3 and 6 months of age, at which time, hand functioning is beginning to occur. The childhood lower extremity amputee should be fitted with a prosthesis by 8 to 10 months when standing and cruising occur. Children's prosthetics should be made so that changes to allow for growth can be easily made.

Educational Issues

Most children with amputations are able to manage successfully in a normal school classroom. Adaptive equipment may need to be provided for certain tasks. Sports help build physical and social skills, and should be encouraged within the capabilities of the child. Contact with a vocational rehabilitation counselor in the early high school years is helpful to explore career options and help the student orient his/her educational program towards appropriate career goals.

Assessment and Treatment

Rehabilitative and psychological management of the amputee should ideally begin before the surgical procedure takes place. The amputation should be viewed as a positive step towards regaining function rather than as a failure of medical management. The person confronted with the loss of a limb must undergo and resolve the process of grief if he/she is to adjust to the disability satisfactorily. A number of fears are present, some of which, to the medical professional, may seem quite inappropriate. Psychological adjustment is facilitated by pre-prosthetic counseling. This should include a description of the rehabilitation training process, a simple description of the prosthetic device that will be prescribed, and a prognosis of what type of function will be present. It is often very helpful to have the patient visited by a successfully rehabilitated amputee.

Immediately after amputation surgery, the residual limb (stump) is considerably swollen. In some centers this is treated by an immediate post-op rigid or semi-rigid dressing. If this is not used, the amputee should learn how to wrap the stump with ace bandages to gradually squeeze out the edema fluid. Amputees should also learn a program of exercises to maintain muscle strength and joint range-of-motion in the limb, which would otherwise not be used. In most instances, a period of 1 to 3 months is required before the wound is healed and the swelling reduced to the point that prosthetic fitting can take place. For lower-extremity amputees, training in crutches, walker, or a wheelchair is necessary during this interim period.

When the stump is mature, a prosthesis may be prescribed and fitted. This should take place in a prosthetic clinic staffed by a physiatrist or orthopedic surgeon, physical therapist, and prosthetists. The medical condition, employment, and avocations of the patient must all be taken into consideration. Limitations of space preclude a complete description of all the different types of prosthetic devices available.

We will consider the upper-extremity prosthetics separately from the lower-extremity prosthetics, because the function of these two types of devices is quite different.

The primary goal of lower-extremity prosthetics is to provide optimal ambulation. All lower-extremity prosthetics must include the following: a socket which holds the stump and provides for the transmission of weight from the amputee's body to the prosthesis; suspension which prevents a prosthesis from falling off when it is not in contact with the ground; and a prosthetic foot which comes in contact with the ground. In an AK prosthesis, an artificial knee joint is usually provided so that the amputee's gait will simulate that of an able-bodied person's.

Generally speaking, the longer the stump that is preserved in a lower-extremity amputee, the more function available. Patients with partial foot and Symes amputations have very little disability. BK amputees will have a smooth, natural gait with little, if any, limp. They will be able to go up and down stairs well, but will have difficulty running. Energy expenditure is increased and, therefore, the BK amputee must walk at a slower pace to maintain energy expenditure at a normal rate. Fisher and Gullickson (1978) estimated that the speed of a BK ampute is 36% slower than normal. An AK amputee will have a more noticeable limp than a BK amputee. Going up and down stairs is difficult and running is nearly impossible. Energy consumption is higher than the BK amputee. Fisher and Gullickson (1978) estimated the speed of walking to be 43% slower than normal. The energy costs with hip disarticulation and hemipelvectomy prostheses are even greater. These patients will almost always need crutches or canes for effective ambulation. Bilateral lower-extremity amputation will add considerably to the disability. Ambulation with bilateral BK amputations is feasible. A patient with bilateral AK amputations may be able to walk with normal prostheses for a short distance, but this is rarely practical for everyday mobility, and outpatients especially prefer to use a wheelchair.

Upper-extremity prostheses are designed to assist in the manipulation of objects rather than in walking. Many activities can be performed using only one hand, especially if adapted equipment is used. Therefore, upper-extremity amputees should be seen by an occupational therapist shortly after their amputation for training in one-handed activities. There are currently no upper-extremity prostheses that can provide the fine motor function or sensation of the normal hand. Prosthetic training for the upper-extremity amputee is designed to train the amputee to use the prosthesis to hold or stabilize an object which then can be manipulated with the normal hand. A major exception is in the bilateral upper-extremity amputee. Functional capabilities of the bilateral upper-extremity amputee are much less than the unilateral amputee, and all manipulative activities must be performed with a prosthesis. Although virtually all tasks can be performed with a well-designed prosthesis and appropriate adaptive equipment, the time needed to perform the task may be very long. This is due to the lack of sensation of the prosthesis, as well as the loss of fine manipulation.

Most conventional upper-extremity prostheses consist of a harness, which holds the prosthesis to the shoulders, a socket which fits over the stump, a terminal device for manipulation, and a control system. The terminal device may be either a metal hook or an artificial hand. Artificial hands offer optimum cosmesis, but hooks have superior manipulative capacity. Control systems involve cables reaching from the shoulder harness to the terminal device. By appropriately shrugging the shoulder, the amputee can voluntarily open and close the terminal device, thereby using it to grasp objects. An AE amputee's shrugging in the opposite direction can lock and unlock the elbow joint thereby allowing positioning of the elbow for a given task. Wrist supination and pronation may also be adjusted by manually twisting the prosthetic wrist with the normal hand. Commonly, the most difficult task in upper-extremity prosthetic rehabilitation is learning the precise angle at which to position the wrist before attempting a task.

An alternate control system for the upper-extremity prosthesis is the myoelectric system. In a myoelectric prosthesis, small electrodes on the skin are used to detect the electricity produced by a muscle contraction. This signal is then used to turn a switch on and off. This switch controls an electric motor which powers the prosthesis. Most commonly, the motor is used to open and close the fingers. However, wrist supination and pronation and elbow flexion have also been triggered myoelectrically. Myoelectric prostheses usually require a less bulky suspension system and are more cosmetically acceptable than conventional prostheses. However, they are more prone to mechanical failure, and require frequent recharging of batteries.

They are many times more expensive and respond more slowly than conventional prostheses. With technological advances, these problems are becoming less troublesome. We may expect myoelectric prostheses to assume a greater role in upper extremity prosthetics of the future.

Pain or skin breakdown of the stump is a common problem of prosthetic use. Most times, this is due to a poorly fitted prosthesis and is managed adequately by alteration of the socket. Pain may be due to a neuroma. A neuroma is a tangled mass of nerve endings growing from the severed end of a nerve that was cut during the amputation surgery. These are often quite tender to the touch and may cause exquisite pain. Neuromas may be managed by modification of the prosthesis to avoid pressure on the neuroma. They may also be treated by steroid injection. In severe cases, a surgical procedure may be necessary to remove the neuroma and reposition the cut nerve ending. Phantom pain may also be a problem. All amputees at some time will experience phantom sensation — that is, a "sensation" in the limb that is no longer present. Some individuals will perceive this sensation as painful. This is particularly true if the limb which was amputated was the source of severe pain for a long time prior to the surgery. A number of treatments have been used for phantom pain, but none has been of outstanding value. Most clinicians feel that phantom pain resolves best when the amputee promptly learns to use a well-fitted prosthesis.

Current Research

Many improvements are being made in the design and fabrication of prosthetic devices. New synthetic plastics and metal alloys with improved strength, lightness, and comfort are being used to replace older materials such as wood, leather, and steel. New prosthetic designs include the Seattle foot, a device which allows BK amputees to run more naturally. Improved electronic technology is being used to improve myoelectric devices. One recent interesting project involved the use of an electric motor to control an above-knee prosthetic knee.

RHEUMATOID ARTHRITIS

Description of the Disorder

Rheumatoid arthritis is a disease characterized by chronic inflammation of multiple joints. It is now known that rheumatoid arthritis is an autoimmune disease. In other words, the body erroneously produces antibodies to the body's own tissues. Therefore, the immune system which under ordinary circumstances attacks and destroys germs which have inundated the body, now attacks the body's own tissues. The main site of inflammation in rheumatoid arthritis is in the synovium, or lining of the joints. The synovial cells normally produce synovial fluid that lubricates the joint and remove debris. In rheumatoid arthritis this synovium is swollen with inflamed cells. This enlarged synovium or pannus, produces substances which erode the cartilage, ligaments, and bones surrounding the joint. Therefore, a joint affected by rheumatoid arthritis becomes swollen, warm, and very painful to movement. Weight-bearing on effected joints becomes difficult because of the pain produced (Harris, 1981).

Because of the pain and swelling associated with rheumatoid arthritis, patients tend not to move. This has several adverse effects. The first of these is loss of range-of-motion. If a joint is not moved through the full arc of which it is capable, the connective tissue of the joint capsule will eventually become stiff. When this occurs the patient may be unable to perform many activities that require full range-of-motion, such as bending down to tie one's shoe or washing one's back. In addition, lack of movement causes the muscles surrounding a joint to atrophy, losing their bulk and strength. Such atrophy causes difficulty in performing functions that require muscular strength. These weak muscles are unable to stabilize a joint as well as they did previously, leading to increased mechanical stress and pain on the arthritic joint.

In patients with longstanding rheumatoid arthritis, specific joint deformities may develop. These occur due to stretching of inflamed ligaments and joint capsules, contractures in other joints, and bony erosions. At times, the bones of the joint might actually slip away from each other causing a subluxation.

Characteristically, rheumatoid arthritis affects small joints symmetrically. Joints that are commonly affected earlier include proximal interphalangeal and metacarpalphalangeal joints in the hands and the metatarsalphalangeal joints in the feet. The shoulders, elbows, wrists, hips, and knee joints are also commonly affected. Many tendons and ligaments are also lined with synovium and may become inflamed.

Certain deformities of joints are quite common in longstanding rheumatoid arthritis. In the hands, the metacarpalphalangeal (MCP) or knuckle joints tend to become subluxed downward. The fingers tend to deviate in an ulnar direction (toward the little finger side of the hand). Inflammation and slippage of tendons in the fingers may cause an exaggerated flexion deformity of the proximal interphalangeal (PIP) joint producing the so-called "boutonniere" deformity. Alternatively, there may be exaggerated extension of this joint, leading to the "swan's neck" deformity. Disease of the joints of the thumb may cause it to lose its stability and ability to grasp. In the foot, rheumatoid arthritis patients commonly have flat feet, claw-toed deformities, and pain over the metatarsal heads (balls of the feet). Painful bulges of the synovial capsule may occur in the back of the knee, which is known as a Baker's cyst.

Rheumatoid arthritis may affect organ systems other than the muscloskeletal system. Many patients develop subcutaneous nodules over the elbows and other extensor surfaces, known as rheumatoid nodules. Some patients develop Sjogren's Syndrome, in which one loses the ability to produce tears and saliva. This may result in serious damage to the eye and tooth decay. The kidneys, bronchi, and liver may also function less well. In women, the genitals may not produce normal lubrication during sexual arousal, rendering sexual intercourse painful unless an artificial lubricant is used. Many patients with rheumatoid arthritis develop peripheral neuropathy. This may cause loss of sensation in the hands and feet and increased muscle weakness. It usually is relatively mild. Some patients will develop vasculitis (i.e., inflammation in the walls of the blood vessels). These patients may develop skin ulcers. If the blood vessels leading to nerves are involved, they may have a severe loss in scattered nerves causing a condition known as mononeuritis multiplex. Patients may develop a carpal tunnel syndrome. In this disorder, swelling of the tendon sheaths of the finger flexors pinches the median nerve as it travels through a tight space in the wrist. This may cause pain, loss of sensation, and weakness in the hands, Many patients with rheumatoid arthritis suffer chronic anemia. They may also have fluid in the linings of their lungs, known as plural effusion. These last two conditions are rarely serious, but add to the patient's overall disability.

Rheumatoid arthritis may affect children as well as adults. Juvenile rheumatoid arthritis (JRA) is divided into three types. The first type is known as systemic JRA or Still's Disease. In this disorder, children have arthritis of multiple joints, fever, skin rash, enlarged lymph nodes and spleen, and occasionally myocarditis. Of patients with JRA, 40% will experience polyarticular arthritis without systemic symptoms. The other 40% will have pauciarticular arthritis in which fewer than five joints are involved — usually large joints of the lower extremities. These children are at risk for the development of iridocyclitis, inflammation of the eye which may eventually lead to blindness. They should be seen by an opthalmologist every 3 months for examination with a slit lamp microscope for early detection and treatment (Molnar et al., 1982).

Epidemiological Findings

Rheumatoid arthritis effects between 1 and 2% of the adult population. It is approximately 2½ times more likely to affect women than men. Young women are much more likely than young men to develop rheumatoid arthritis, whereas in the elderly, the incidence is nearly equal. Race does not appear to be a significant factor.

Developmental Issues

In general, the developmental problems of children with juvenile rheumatoid arthritis are similar to those of children with other chronic diseases. Children with inflamed or deformed joints may need to be excused from contact sports and other activities that would produce excessive joint strain.

Assessment and Treatment

Rheumatoid arthritis is a progressive disease characterized by remissions and exacerbations. For this reason, the patient must be periodically reassessed so that treatment can be most effective. Each patient should be thoroughly examined by his physician. This examination should measure the degree of inflammation and effusion in affected joints. The range-of-motion should be measured and any deformities should be noted. Yearly X-rays of affected joints are helpful to follow progression of joint erosions and deformities. Blood tests are helpful to establish the diagnosis of rheumatoid arthritis and to follow its progression. Among these tests are the rheumatoid factor test, which measures an antibody formed primarily in patients with rheumatoid arthritis. Another helpful test is the erythrocyte sedimentation rate. This measures the rate at which red blood cells settle to the bottom of a test tube. Elevated erythrocyte sedimentation rate is a nonspecific indicator of inflammation and can be used to follow exacerbations and remissions. When the diagnosis has not been clearly established, microscopic and chemical analysis of joint fluid withdrawn from the affected joint with a syringe is very helpful. In addition to the tests performed by a physician, the patient should be evaluated by physical and occupational therapists. These evaluations should measure the patient's rate of performance in functional activities such as ambulation, dressing, eating, personal hygiene, and housekeeping. Assessment by psychiatrists, psychologists, or social workers may be indicated if patients and their families are having difficulty adjusting to the disability.

Treatment of the patient with rheumatoid arthritis may involve drugs, physical and occupational therapy, counseling, and surgery. Drugs are used to control inflammation and relieve pain. The most commonly used drugs are aspirin and the other nonsteroidal antiinflammatory drugs (NSAIDs). Aspirin must be taken in much higher doses than usually used for self-medication of headaches and other minor pains. Aspirin is highly effective and the cheapest of the medications. However, it has the common side effect of causing gastrointestinal upset and may promote the development of ulcers. Therefore, in patients unable to tolerate therapeautic levels of aspirin, other NSAIDs are often used. These drugs are highly effective in decreasing pain. None of them seems to affect the development of joint deformities or progression of the disease.

When the NSAIDs are not sufficient to control symptoms, gold and penicillamine may be of value. Gold is usually given by weekly injections. Though it is a highly effective drug, there are serious side effects. It may cause suppression of the bone marrow leading to the failure to produce platelets, white cells or red cells. It may also cause kidney damage. For this reason, patients who are receiving gold should receive weekly urine and blood tests. Skin rashes are also a common problem. Penicillamine produces loss of taste, but this is transient and the sense of taste returns after several months even if the medication is continued. It also causes kidney and bone marrow disease and needs to be followed the same way as gold.

Adreno–cortico–steroid medications are also very helpful in relieving the inflammation of rheumatoid arthritis. They were used widely in the 1950s and 1960s. However, the high rate of side effects has caused physicians to use them much more sparingly today. Side effects include loss of calcium from the bones, obesity of the trunk, worsening of diabetes mellitus, high blood pressure, and impaired resistance to infection. For this reason they are not recommended for prolonged periods of time at high doses. However, they are used much more commonly for local injection into individual joints. Here they may produce a dramatic improvement of symptoms with minimal systemic effects. A joint may be injected three to four times a year without causing damage.

Physical therapy is very helpful in the treatment of pain and functional loss. Heat in the form of hot packs, hydrotherapy, or moistaire cabinets decreases pain and stiffness of the joint. Arthritis in the hands can be conveniently treated by dipping the fingers into a container of melted paraffin and allowing the paraffin to harden on the hands. Actively inflamed joints are also relieved by rest. Preventing movement in a joint leads to rapid decrease in the inflammation and effusion. This can be accomplished by splints or casts, however, their usefulness is limited by their weight and awkwardness. In some patients with severe deformities, the functional splints or braces may relieve pain by transferring weightbearing forces away from the painful joint.

Exercise is very important in the prevention of functional loss. However, excessive exercise or joint use will increase inflammation. Isometric exercises, in which the muscles across the joint contract without moving the joint, can maintain muscle strength without increasing inflammation. Range-of-motion exercises should be performed by moving the joints through a full arc of motion once or twice each day. This will prevent shortening of the muscles and tightening of the joint capsules.

Occupational therapy treatment is aimed at maximizing the patient's performance of his/her everyday activities. Patients with rheumatoid arthritis should be taught joint protection measures. The patient is instructed in the methods of performing tasks that put the least amount of stress on arthritic joints. For example, when removing cookie sheets from the oven, they should be placed on the palm of the upturned hand rather than pinched between the forefinger and thumb. Patients should also be instructed in work simplification. The patient is taught how to perform activities with maximum economy of movements.

All patients with rheumatoid arthritis should receive appropriate counseling. Patients often have misconceptions about their disease. They may feel that it is mandatory that they "keep moving" or that they will stiffen up and lose function. Unnecessary activities such as pacing will actually increase inflammation and joint deformity. Another misconception is that if patients perform their daily activities or job, they do not need special exercises. The movements performed in daily activities do not provide full range-of-motion and strengthening contractions of all the necessary muscles and joints. The patient will suffer much less from the arthritis if exercises are performed diligently while decreasing unnecessary activities.

Patients may also need counseling as to how to deal with the psychological and social effects of their disability. In the past, it was sometimes felt that rheumatoid arthritis affected people with certain personality types. However, it is now felt that recurrent pain and limitation of movement tend to make patients with rheumatoid arthritis angry, frustrated, and depressed. This may have an adverse effect on their relationships with family members and friends. Arthritis may also interfere with sexual activity. This is often seen in women who are unable to spread their legs because of arthritis in the hips. These problems may cause significant marital discord. Counseling on appropriate sexual positions and encouraging a greater communication between partners so that they are able to work out their sexual difficulties is helpful.

Orthopedic Surgery

In patients with severe joint deformities, orthopedic surgical procedures may provide relief. The most commonly performed procedure today is the total joint prosthesis. In this procedure, the diseased joint is surgically cut out and an artificial joint of metal and plastic is implanted in its place. The most commonly used and the most successful total-joint replacement is the hip. Other joints for which replacements are available include the knee, ankle, shoulder and small joints of the hands. These procedures relieve the pain from the affected joint and may increase range-of-motion and functional ability as well. Unfortunately, these artificial joints tend to wear out or loosen with time and are, therefore, more commonly used in older patients who are less likely to wear them out in their remaining life span. The most serious complication is infection of the artificial joint which necessitates operative removal. Other surgical procedures that may be of value include fusion of small joints in the fingers and thumb, resectioning of the metatarsal heads (the balls of the feet) to reduce foot pain, and sophisticated procedures to repair boutenniere and swan's neck deformities.

Current Research

In recent years, many advances have been made in the understanding of the immunology of rheumatoid arthritis. It is conceivable that a cure for rheumatoid arthritis may be developed in the not too distant future. In the meantime, advances are made each year in the pharmacological and surgical treatment. A field which has aroused much interest of late is compliance with treatment programs in rheumatoid arthritis. It is known that only about half of all medications prescribed are taken as ordered. The rate of compliance for treatments such as exercise and splinting is even less. A number of investigators are studying the factors in doctor–patient relationships which affect compliance and are devising strategies to optimize patient follow-through.

DEGENERATIVE JOINT DISEASE

Degenerative joint disease is a type of arthritis affecting primarily the elderly. It is also known as osteoarthritis or osteoarthrosis. Degenerative joint disease

(DJD) is probably the result of cumulative wear and tear on a joint over many years of use. The initial abnormality is a roughening of the cartilage of the joint. Subsequent metabolic changes in the cartilage lead to excessive growth of the underlying bone leading to the development of bone spurs (or osteophytes). With time, the cartilage wears completely away leaving bare bone to rest on bare bone. This causes pain with weight-bearing or use. A number of factors accelerate the development of DJD. These include trauma to the joint, loss of sensation to the joint due to a neurologic condition, and certain metabolic abnormalities such as ochrinosis and chondrocalcinosis.

In contrast to rheumatoid arthritis, there is usually not much inflammation and effusion in joints affected with degenerative joint disease. Only one, or at most, a few joints are involved. Joints commonly affected are the hips, the knees, and the small joints of the fingers and thumbs. The joints of the spine are also frequently affected. Many elderly patients have marked DJD on X-rays of the spine without having any symptoms. If an osteophyte pushes against a nerve root as it leaves the spinal canal, the patient will suffer from a radiculopathy, with pain, sensory loss, and often weakness in the distribution of the nerve root that is affected. In other patients, there may be so many osteophytes that the spinal canal is narrowed, putting pressure on the spinal cord and nerve roots which travel down it (spinal stenosis). When this occurs in the neck, the patient may experience symptoms of spinal cord compression which include weakness, muscle spasticity, abnormalities of bladder and bowel function, and sensory abnormalities. If the lower part of the spine is involved, the patients often experience pain in their legs while walking that is relieved when the patient rests. Since similar symptoms may be caused by poor circulation in the leg (vascular claudication), careful diagnostic studies must often be performed to determine that spinal stenosis is present. In the neck and low back, a surgical procedure will be required to relieve pressure on the neural structures.

Epidemiological Findings

Over 80% of people older than 55 show evidence of DJD on X-ray. However, most of these people will not have symptoms. Obesity is a predisposing factor to DJD of the weight-bearing joints. Cumulative repetitive trauma due to occupational stress also contributes to DJD. Sex or race are not predisposing factors.

Assessment and Treatment

Assessment of the patient with DJD should include a careful physical examination of the involved joints, noting any deformity present and range-of-motion. A functional history should be taken to find out what activities are limited by the joint disease. X-ray examination is essential to determine the extent and nature of the joint disease. Usually these measures are sufficient to make the diagnosis.

Treatment of DJD is similar to that of rheumatoid arthritis, although usually less-extensive measures need to be taken. Nonsteroidal antiinflammatory drugs are commonly used to decrease pain. Injection of steroids into joints is often helpful when only one or two joints are severely involved. Pain with walking and weight-bearing joints of the hip or knee may be greatly relieved by the use of a cane held in the hand opposite to the side of the pain. In obese patients, weight reduction is very helpful, but difficult to achieve. Weak muscles around involved joints should be strengthened, which increases the stability of the joint and often relieves pain. Most patients profit from training in occupational therapy, work simplification and joint protection techniques. When nonsurgical methods fail to provide adequate pain relief, total joint replacement is highly effective, especially in the hip.

Current Research

Current studies are investigating the role of heredity, previous trauma, and overuse of the joint in the development of DJD.

ANKYLOSING SPONDYLITIS

Ankylosing spondylitis is an inflammatory disease affecting primarily the joints of the spine. Ankylosing spondylitis (AS) affects primarily young men, usually in the first through third decades of life. This disease runs in families and most patients with ankylosing spondylitis carry the HLA-B27 genetic marker. The etiology of AS is unknown. Like rheumatoid arthritis, AS is believed to be an autoimmune disease in which the lymphocytes invade the joints and tendons of the body with resulting inflammation and destruction. New bone bridges are formed leading to ankylosis, or fusion of the affected joints. The first joint to be affected is usually the sacroiliac joint. With time, virtually all the joints of the spine become ankylosed (made solid with bone) leading to the characteristic "bamboo spine", seen on X-rays. Disease in the costochondral joints which connect the ribs to the spine leads to ankylosis and loss of the ability to expand the chest with a deep breath. Other joints may be affected, particularly the hips and shoulders.

Patients with AS usually present with pain and stiffness in the low back. As time goes on, they lose range-of-motion of the spine and other affected joints. They often have a characteristic postural deformity with stooped shoulders, flexed head and neck, and flexed hips and knees.

AS may occur as part of other multisystem diseases. These include psoriatic arthritis, Reiter's syndrome, and regional enderitis and ulcerative colitis.

Epidemiological Findings

As noted, AS affects primarily young men. It has been suggested that AS may occur almost as frequently in females as in males with a much milder presentation which is often mistaken for mechanical spine disease. The prevalence of AS has been estimated to be approximately 1% in Caucasians. The prevalence is much higher in American Indians. American blacks have a slightly lower incidence than Caucasians, and orientals have a very low rate of AS (Calin, 1981).

Assessment and Treatment

AS often begins with back pain and stiffness, and the diagnosis may be missed for several years. Evidence of disease of the sacro-iliac joints on X-rays of the pelvis is usually the earliest diagnostic sign. A measurement of HLA-B27 on white blood cells may be of value. However since the majority of people who are HLA-B27-positive do not have AS, it cannot be used as specific evidence of the disease. A number of physical signs are helpful to follow the progression of AS. These include measuring the amount of expansion of the rib cage with a deep inspiration, measuring the distance between fingertips and floor when one is bending over, the distance from wall to occiput when standing erect, and the Shober's test. The Shober's test is a measure of the amount of flexion possible in the lumber spine.

Unfortunately, no current treatment is able to prevent the eventual fusion of the spine. Therefore, treatment is geared towards minimizing pain and deformity. Nonsteroidal antiinflammatory drugs are commonly used. Physical therapy for exercises to maintain good posture will result in the spine eventually fusing into a functional position.

SUMMARY

As we have seen, musculoskeletal disorders cause disability by interfering with normal walking and the ability to manipulate objects. Today, many interventions are available to help these patients function more efficiently. Optimal results are obtained when the pharmacologic, surgical, rehabilitative, and educational measures are approached in a coordinated fashion, tailoring the treatment plan to the individual patient.

REFERENCES

Calin, A. (1981). Ankylosing spondylitis. In W. N. Kelley, E. D. Harris, S. Ruddy, & C. B. Sledge (Eds.), *Textbook of reheumatology* (pp. 1017–1032). Philadelphia, PA: W. B. Saunders.

Fisher, S. V., & Gullickson, G. (1978). Energy costs of ambulation in health and disability. *Archives of Physical Medicine and Rehabilitation,* 59, 124–133.

Harris, E. D. (1981). Rheumatoid arthritis: The clinical spectrum. In W. N. Kelley, E. D. Harris, S. Ruddy, & C. B. Sledge (Eds.), *Textbook of rheumatology* (pp. 928–963). Philadelphia, PA: W. B. Saunders.

Kay, H. W., & Newman, J. D. (1975). Relative incidences of new amputations. *Orthotics and Prosthetics,* 29, 3–16.

Kottke, F. J., Lehmann, J. F., & Stillwell, G. K. (1982). Preface. In F. J. Kottke, J. F. Lehhmann, & G. K. Stillwell (Eds.), *Krusen's handbook of physical medicine and rehabilitation* (p. xii). Philadelphia, PA: W. B. Saunders.

Molnar, G. E., Alexander, M., Badell-Ribera, A., Easton, J. K. M., Eng, G. D., Halpern, D., Matthews, D., & Saturen, P. (1982). Pediatric rehabilitation. In the American Academy of Physical Medicine and Rehabilitation (Eds.), *Medical knowledge self-assessment program in fiscal medication and rehabilitation syllabus* (pp. C-1 to C-26). Chicago, IL: American Academy of Physical Medicine and Rehabilitation.

CHAPTER 24

Language and Communication Disorders

Ann P. Kaiser, Cathy L. Alpert, and Steven F. Warren

INTRODUCTION

Until recently, humans were sometimes distinguished from other species by two characteristics: language and tool use. Both characteristics are indicative of human ability to mediate the environment by acting upon it indirectly. Trees are brought down with axes rather than directly by hands; lunch is selected by a series of verbal requests to a waiter rather than picking out food items in the restaurant's kitchen (although trees can be brought down by hand and lunch is often prepared rather than requested). The ability to act on the environment indirectly adds greatly to the range, efficiency, and flexibility of human behavior. In the case of tool use, tasks that are beyond the strength, perceptual limits, or motor precision of humans can be accomplished easily through the use of specialized tools such as winches, microscopes, or laser beams. Language permits rapid communication of complex information across contexts in which the individ-ual is physically engaged in other tasks (e.g., talking while demonstrating a complex surgical procedure). Tools are employed to act primarily on the physical environment; language is used to mediate the social environment by affecting the behavior of others.

Language use is implicit in adult human behavior. Like other tools in a highly technological culture, language is used so frequently and flexibly by most adults that it is typically noticed only when it fails to function properly. In fact, miscommunications sometimes persist because they are infrequent and unexpected. Recent naturalistic descriptions and experimental studies with dolphins and primates suggest that these characteristics are not unique to humans. However, the extent of use of language and other tools *does* appear to differentiate humans from other species.

In the context of a culture that is both highly linguistic and social, communication disorders may be especially disabling. Language is the primary means by which information is conveyed in social and instructional contexts. Individuals who have difficulty communicating, encoding and decoding meanings in these contexts will be limited seriously in their ability to achieve their goals. Much learning is metalinguistic rather than directly experiential. Language is used to describe events or relationships that are never observed directly. Children with language deficits may be further handicapped by difficulties in learning academic skills because these skills are generally taught through verbal instruction. Also, language is a primary means of social interaction. When this means is impaired, social interaction is constrained. Persons may be limited in their access to normal social interaction, as well as to employment opportunities, if their communication skills are markedly less than the standards of their peers. Even relatively minor speech disorders may seriously impair social conversation and information exchange.

This chapter describes language disabilities and their educational treatments. The descriptions derive from our assumptions about normally developing language and communication. Thus, before describing communications disabilities and their treatment, we briefly describe the nature of language and our assumptions about its forms and functions. A discussion of the theoretical model on which this discussion is based may be found in Rogers-Warren and Warren (1981).

The current view of language and communication is bases on the following assumptions:

1. *Language is social behavior.* The purpose of language is to mediate the behavior of others in the context of social interaction (Skinner, 1957; Halliday, 1970). Mediation of another person's behavior occurs when the listener behaves in accordance with the speaker's message. For example, the speaker mediates the listener's behavior when requests are made, commands are given, comments that draw the listener's attention to some aspect of the environment are made, or when information is sought from the listener, the listener responds accordingly. The functions of

language and other communicative behavior (gesture, written language, signs) are defined by their effects in social interchanges.

2. *Formal language is based in social interaction and arises from the child's early nonverbal communicative interchanges with a primary caregiver* (Tronick, Als, & Adamson, 1979). Children's social interactions are initially nonverbal. Early social turn-taking forms the basis for later verbal conversational turns. Typically, during the first 2 years of life, children progress from participating nonverbally in turn-taking interchanges with their caregivers, to signalling the caregiver by means of directed looking, gesture, vocalization, to using single words, and finally, to using linguistically complete multiword utterances.

3. *Language as a formal and as a functional system is learned.* The most basic processes that underlie language-learning are those common to all learning: discrimination and generalization (Wetherby, 1978; Skinner, 1957). Learning language depends on the ability to perceive, to organize, to associate, and to respond to complex visual and auditory stimuli. Thus, cognitive and perceptual processing skills are essential to language-learning. The efficiency and breadth of learning will be influenced by the skills that the child brings to the social interactions in which language is learned and used. Generative, functional language use depends on the same processes that are critical to initial learning (Rogers-Warren & Warren, 1981).

4. *Elaborated forms of communication are built on simpler forms.* The progression of communication moves from signals (e.g., cries) to the use of signs (e.g. systematic, consistent gesturing to indicate wants), to the use of increasingly complex linguistic forms, to the metalinguistic uses of language (Bruner, 1975). Each step in this progression depends on the child's perceptual, cognitive and social abilities at that point in time. A delay in any aspect of this triad may retard the language learning process (Bloom & Lahey, 1978).

5. *Language learning occurs in an ecosystem.* Because language is a social behavior, learned in social contexts, it is part of a

reciprocal influence pattern between child and caregiver, between learner and teacher. The child's social responsiveness and particular responses to caregiver's attempts to teach language alter the environment and the characteristics of the next interchange in significant ways. Both child and caregiver learn how language will work in their interchanges and both behave on the basis of what they have learned (Kaye & Charney, 1980; Schacter, 1979).

The common theme of these assumptions is the integral nature of social interaction to the development of communication. Social intention or function is primary in communication, however, the form and mode of communication are also essential characteristics of the communication act. Figure 24-1 shows a model of language learning and use which integrates functional and formal aspects of language. Although this model primarily addresses productive language, a similar scheme might be used to illustrate receptive language. Language has both receptive and productive components; the basic processes underlying each component are related but not necessarily iconic to one another.

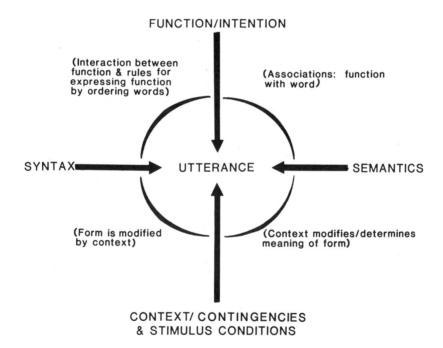

Figure 24-1. A changing vector analysis model of language learning and use

Figure 24-1 suggests that the productive form of communication, an utterance or speech act, is determined by four contributing forces: (a) the speaker's social intention (i.e., the function(s) he/she wishes to accomplish by this act); (b) the interactional context (i.e., social, cultural parameters of the communication context; the speaker's knowledge of the nonlinguistic rules related to these contexts; and the naturalistic contingencies provided by the environment); (c) the speaker's semantic knowledge (i.e. word meanings, conceptual knowledge, knowledge of basic relational meanings that can be expressed by language); and (d) syntactic knowledge (i.e. knowledge of the rules for combining forms to refer to certain events and social intentions). In addition, the precise form of the communicative act will be determined by the mode of communication (speech, sign, symbol) and the competency of the speaker in producing forms using knowledge of that mode. For example, for a speaker to utter a sentence, he/she must have competency in producing the phonological repertoire (consisting of individual sounds, and rules for combining them) of the language which he/she is speaking. Similarly, to carry on conversation in American Sign Language, the conversation must be able to produce the signs that represent individual units of meaning within that system.

The model in Figure 24-1 presupposes strong environmental influences on both learning and performance. That is, all aspects of the communication system may be learned as a result of the contingencies provided for functional communication. The use of elaborated forms develops from the increasingly fine discrimination of intention and environmental contingencies. In this sense, the model is learning-based, although humans clearly bring highly developed perceptual, discriminative, and motor response repertoires to the task of learning. Observational as well as contingency-based learning may play a role in acquisition of both the forms and functions of language.

In this model, language disability may arise from deficits in social interaction, from learning difficulties, or from physiologically based impairments that disrupt the production of the communication mode. Disruption in either the formal (phonological, syntactic) or functional (semantic, pragmatic) aspects of the communications system may result in a serious language disability.

The remainder of this chapter is based on this model and the assumptions regarding the social nature of language. Social communication and the functional use of language will be discussed. Minimal attention will be given to the speech mode and problems associated with speech deficits. Consistent with our assumptions regarding the critical role of the environment in language learning and performance, environmental issues in development and intervention are emphasized.

DESCRIPTION OF LANGUAGE DISORDERS AND EPIDEMIOLOGICAL FINDINGS

Problems in the acquisition and use of language have been associated with most types of developmental disabilities (McCormick, 1984). Descriptions are available, for example, of speech, language, and communication characteristics generally associated with disorders such as autism (Alpert & Rogers-Warren, 1985), cerebral palsy, hearing impairment (Braverman-Callahan & Radziewicz, 1985), and mental retardation (Rosenberg, 1982). Although it is possible to determine, through research and clinical observation, the *general* characteristics of communication disorders associated with particular developmental disabilities, precise predictions of *specific* communication impairment on the basis of disability classification is different for two reasons. First, persons who share a common diagnostic classification rarely comprise a homogeneous group. A range of individual abilities across developmental domains (including communication) is typically found among members of any etiological classification. Second, environmental influences can have a profound effect on the course and extent of communication development and use (cf.

Owens, 1985; Rosenburg, 1982). Because individuals, even those with initially similar skills, experience widely varied environments, the specific characteristics of their communication skills may also vary.

The communication system is complex, consisting of multiple, interrelated components. Disorders in the ability to communicate effectively may be associated primarily with a particular component of the communication system; however, because the components operate interactively, a disorder in one area may affect functioning in other areas. In some persons, all aspects of the system may be disordered. Because communication is a complex process, potential disorders are often multiple, interrelated, and difficult to diagnose separately.

The remainder of this section focuses on three critical dimensions of the communication system — form, content, and use (Bloom & Lahey, 1978). The importance of each of these areas to the communication process is described, examples of disorders associated with each area are discussed, and where appropriate, epidemiological findings related to communication/language disorders are identified.

Disorders Related to Form

The form of language has to do with its surface or structural properties. For example, when speech is the mode of expression, its quality is determined by structural attributes including sound production and the use of morphological and syntactical rules. Fluency and characteristics associated with voice, such as pitch, intensity, intonation, and prosody, also contribute to the quality of form. Speech production problems may have an organic or a functional base. Organic problems arise from physical or neurological impairment; functional problems are related to incorrect learning, discrimination difficulties, and short auditory memory span (McCormick, 1984).

Children with form disorders may have a specific message (i.e., content) to convey and the intention and social skills (i.e.,

pragmatic abilities) necessary for communication, but they have difficulty determining or producing the appropriate forms and/or sequences of forms (i.e., sounds, words, grammatical morphemes) to represent their message. Production problems may be related to (a) deficits in content–form linkages (i.e., either the necessary connections between content and form have not been made or problems exist in matching the appropriate learned form(s) with the content); or (b) difficulties in producing the forms that have been selected to represent the message.

Disorders of articulation (including substitutions, omissions, distortions, and additions) are the most common type of speech production problem (Polloway & Smith, 1982). Articulation disorders are common among the general population and they frequently are associated with developmental disabilities such as hearing impairment (Jensema, Karchmer, & Trybus, 1978). A number of studies have investigated articulation deficiencies of the mentally retarded (Bangs, 1961; Schiefelbusch, 1963; Spradlin, 1963; Wolfensberger, Mein, & O'Connor, 1963). Schlanger (1973) reviewed such studies and concluded that disorders of articulation, voice, and rhythm, including slurred speech, are found among mildly retarded persons (IQs of 50–70), and that the incidence of these problems increases at lower levels of intellectual functioning. Several investigators have reported that among mentally retarded persons, disorders of articulation, voice, and rhythm are more frequently found among persons with Down Syndrome and that Down Syndrome children's articulatory development lags behind the development of other aspects of language performance (Dodd, 1976; Ingram, 1976; Schlanger, 1973). A more recent study by Stoel-Gammon (1980), however, suggests that when Down Syndrome children are compared with MLU-matched (mean length of utterance) nonretarded children on phonological abilities, they "are as good as, if not better than, the normal population" (p. 27). In general, the research in this area suggests that phonological development by mentally retarded individuals is characterized by developmental delay rather than developmental deviance (see also Bartolucci & Pierce, 1977).

Difficulty in using standard syntax and morphology also characterizes many children with language delays and disorders. These children may display regular and irregular errors related to the use of grammatical morphemes (e.g. to indicate tense and number), word order, subject–verb agreement, and particular categories of speech (e.g., prepositions, connectives, and articles) appropriately in spontaneous speech. Studies on the syntactic and morphologic abilities of mildly retarded individuals indicate that development in these domains does not differ qualitatively from development by nonretarded persons (Ingram, 1972; Johnston & Schery, 1976; Lackner, 1968; Naremore & Dever, 1975; Shotick & Blue, 1971; Wheldall, 1976). However, development is slower, and even when retarded and nonretarded individuals are matched for mental age, mentally retarded persons appear to use shorter, less complex sentences than their nonretarded peers (McLeavey, Toomey, & Dempsey, 1982). It has been reported that retarded persons learn and use linguistic rules (Graham & Graham, 1971; McLeavey et al., 1982), but that they tend to rely more on primitive word rules than their language peers (Semmel, 1967). According to McLeavy et al. (1982), mentally retarded persons may depend on early syntactic forms for a longer time, and that while advanced syntactic forms are learned by mildly retarded persons, that they are used less frequently.

Form disorders have been reported among children described as aphasic and learning disabled, as well as children with cerebral palsy and hearing impairments. Children who stutter also display a problem with form. A summary of form disorders generally associated with the diagnostic categories of hearing impairment, cerebral palsy, learning disability, and mental retardation, are presented in Table 24-1

Disorders Related to Content

The content of language has to do with the semantic or meaning dimension of language. Semantic abilities are directly linked to the child's cognitive knowledge about objects, persons, events, and relationships in the world. In order to communicate this knowledge via oral language, the child must learn to "map" what he knows about the world with linguistic forms (i.e., words, phrases, sentences). In normal language development, the content dimension of language is inextricably linked to cognitive development, the ability to express meaning using linguistically appropriate forms, and, as will be discussed, the ability to communicate the message in a socially appropriate manner.

The abilities to use linguistic forms and grammatical rules (and to link them to content), and to use language for purposes of communication (i.e., pragmatic skills), are tied to the child's level of cognitive functioning. Generally, semantic abilities develop at about the same rate as other aspects of the communication system. Problems associated with the content dimension of language have been linked to limited learning about the perceptual and functional characteristics of objects, actions, and/or events and their relations, due to, for example, visual impairment, restrictions on mobility, and attentional and/or perceptual deficits and, with more general deficits in learning abilities. Studies examining semantic development by mentally retarded individuals report evidence of developmental lag, but no qualitative differences between mentally retarded children (Dooley, 1976; Leonard, Cole & Steckol, 1979). Semmel and Herzog (1966) reported, however, that word meanings for the retarded population tend to be more concrete than those of nonretarded persons. Children with mental retardation, visual impairments, learning disabilities, spina bifida, and children classfied as autistic may show delays in semantic development. The nature of the content disorders generally associated with these disability classifications is summarized in Table 24-1.

Table 24-1 Primary language/communication disorders associated with various disability classifications*

DISABILITY CLASSIFICATION	FORM	DISORDER CONTENT	USE
Autistic/ Autistic-like		Problems in semantic functioning have been observed in both productive and receptive language skills. The children are less likely to use a "probable-event strategy" in comprehending linguistic stimuli than are normal children matched on verbal and nonverbal ability (Tager-Flusberg, 1981a). (The probable-event strategy has a cognitive-semantic base and involves application of knowledge about the world to understanding linguistic input.) Infrequent use of the probable-event strategy may reflect deficient conceptual or semantic knowledge to linguistic stimuli. Impared semantic functioning also has been reported in the expressive language of persons with autism. Simmons and Baltaxe (1975) reported a variety of violations in semantic constraints (i.e., the rules governing the occurrence of elements of meaning) in language of high-functioning adolescents.	Poor discourse communication skills as characterized by deficiencies in the use of (a) appropriate strategies to sustain a conversation and (b) semantically appropriate responses to questions (Tager-Flusberg, 1981b). When questions are asked by the autistic individual, he or she often already knows the answers to them (Hurtig, Ensrud, & Tomblin, 1982). Baltaxe (1977) reported impairment in 3 areas of pragmatic functiong by highly verbal adolescents: (a) speaker-hearer role relationships; (b) the rules of conduct governing a dialogue; and (c) differentiating old and new information.
Cerebral Palsy	Dysarthria due to "the inability to coordinate resonation, articulation, and respiration mechanisms" because of "a disturbance in voluntary control over the speech musculature." The children have difficulty speaking "with normal muscular speed, strength, precision, or timing" (McCormick, 1984, p. 91). Speech may be slow and labored (spastic		

Table 24-1 continued

DISABILITY CLASSIFICATION	FORM	DISORDER CONTENT	USE
	children), jerky (athetoid children), or tremorous and quavering (ataxic children).		
Hearing Impaired	Articulation errors (especially related to voiceless stops and fricatives). Voice disorders related to intensity, quality, pitch, and fluency, are also common.		
Learning Disabled	Articulation errors. Fluency problems involving rapid and jerky speech. Inappropriate prosody. Immature grammar and sequencing deficits.	Form–Content linkage problems. Difficulty responding to verbal directions. Vocabulary deficiencies. A subgroup of children show *dysnomia*, an expressive language problem involving problems with word finding and retrieval (Wiig, Lapointe, & Semmel, 1977). These children may substitute nonverbal communication (e.g., gesturing and pointing) for speech. They may substitute "catch-all" words/phrases (e.g., "you know") for language unavailable to them and/or circumlocute (i.e., talk around) the message they are attempting to express.	In ambiguous or socially complex situations, learning disabled children may show deficits in question-asking, initiating verbal interactions, responding to inadequate messages, maintaining a conversation and holding the conversational floor. Learning disabled children also may have difficulty adjusting their speech to the needs of the listener (Bryan, Donahue, & Pearl, 1981).
Mentally Retarded (based on Owens, 1985, p. 185)	*Phonologic:* High incidence of disorders of articulation, voice, and rhythm, including slurred speech. Incidence increases at lower levels of intellectual functioning. Phonological development characterized by developmental delay rather than deviance. *Morphologic:* Qualitatively similar to normal development, but at a slower	Developmental lag, but little difference between semantic functioning of mentally retarded and nonretarded persons. Word meanings are more concrete than those of nonretarded persons.	Language of retarded children (like that of nonretarded children) fulfils functions earlier expressed through gesture. The conversational role of retarded persons tends to be one of nondominance.

Spina Bifida

sequence of sentence development; shorter, less complex sentences; fewer subject elaborations of relative clauses; sentence word order has precedence over word relationships; reliance on more primitive forms.

Children with hydrocephalus associated with myelomeningocele (the most severe type of spina bifida) may display "chatterbox" or "cocktail party" language (Lawrence, 1971; Swisher & Pinkser, 1971). These children converse readily and excessively. They use appropriate syntax and phonological patterns, but the content of their language reflects conceptual weakness and disorganized thought processes. The children appear not to understand what they are saying (Bloom & Lahey, 1978).

Visually Impaired

Visually impaired children may experience delays in semantic development due to restrictions on mobility and a reduced experimental base. Formation of word–concept linkages may be impeded and spontaneous word production may be somewhat delayed. Restrictions on the perception of object and event relations and lack of exposure to attributes and actions may result in delay in production of word combinations.

*Only the *primary* language/communication disorders associated with each disability is presented; hence, information is not included under all column headings listed under *Disorder* for each disability classification.

Disorders Related to Use

In addition to its code or form and semantic (content) base, language has a function. Language, both verbal and nonverbal, is used to affect the environment in particular, intended ways. Pragmatic skill is the ability of speakers to adhere to rules governing the use of language in social contexts (e.g., taking turns; maintaining the topic of conversation; relating new to old information; using listener cues to modify one's; behavior) to achieve desired environmental outcomes (e.g., altering the listener's behavior, beliefs, and/or attitudes) (Bates, 1976). It involves the ability to consider such factors as (a) the desired effect of communication on the environment and (b) the prevailing social and physical conditions for purposes of determining what will be expressed, and how, when, where, and to whom it will be expressed.

Children with pragmatic disorders may have a message to communicate and a demonstrated understanding of a code and rules for using it, but they have difficulty "saying the right thing the right way at the right time . . ." (Ervin-Tripp, 1971, p. 37). Problems with use may take a variety of forms. Children may show disruptions in basic interactional strategies such as looking at the listener's face/eyes during joint interaction, following the listener's gaze to attend to a focal point, and taking turns during reciprocal interactions. Difficulties in talking about contextually relevant topics and maintaining the topic of conversation are also characteristic of use problems. In addition to talking about things that are out of context, pragmatically impaired children may make abrupt shifts in conversational topics and/or "string together ideas tangentially without regard for the listener's perspective" (McCormick, 1984, p. 106). Normal speakers make adjustments in their own behavior, in part, on the basis of particular listener variables. Children with pragmatic disorders, however, may be less able to use such variables (e.g., age, sex, position, presumed knowledge of the listener) for purposes of making modifications in their communicative attempts. Along these same lines, pragmatically impaired children may have problems receiving and/or interpreting the listener's verbal and nonverbal conversational cues, and adjusting their behavior accordingly. Failure to modify unsuccessful communicative attempts, and problems with deixis* and relating new to old information have also been observed in children with use problems. A limited amount of research has dealt with the pragmatic aspects of language functioning in the mentally retarded. Owens and MacDonald (1982) reported that the language of retarded and nonretarded children fulfils functions that were expressed earlier through gestures. Further, the distribution of these functions is similar for both groups when they are matched for language development level. Hayes and Koch (1977), and Bedrosian and Prutting (1978) reported that the conversational role of retarded individuals seems to be one of nondominance. Bedrosian and Prutting found this to be the case even though the mentally retarded subjects displayed the ability to control conversations in ways similar to those of nonretarded adults. Use problems that have been observed in the mentally retarded and in autistic children and children with learning disabilities are summarized in Table 24-1

Summary

Both child abilities and the environment contribute to communication development and to communication disorder. Disruptions can and do occur within specific aspects of the communication system; however, the interrelatedness of components often results in problems in one area affecting other aspects of the system. In addition,

* Deictic categories include person deixis, time deixis, and space deixis. The appropriate use of these categories is dependent upon a shared understanding by the speaker and listener of: (a) the identify of the speaker so that the pronouns *I* and *you* can be used correctly; (b) the relationship of events in time for purposes of adverbial (e.g., now, then) and tense selection; and (c) the proximal contrast in relation to whatever the speaker is making reference (e.g., this, that; here, there).

secondary development problems also may arise as a result of communication disorders. Examples of secondary problems include behavior disorders, fatigue, inattentiveness, academic learning problems, and social isolation. The environment plays a critical role in accentuating or remediating the primary and secondary effects of communication disorders. Characteristics of the environment that facilitate language learning and use will now be explored.

EDUCATIONAL ISSUES

Nearly all persons with developmental disabilities require language intervention to learn functional communication skills. Most intervention occurs in educational or therapeutic clinical settings rather than in a medical context, largely because relatively few speech and language deficits arise from physical anomalies correctable by medical procedures. Even when there is a physical basis for language deficits, such as presence of a cleft palate, individualized instruction in speech and language will be needed in addition to medical treatment.

Because language develops concurrent with other types of learning and is the basis for other learning, intervention is frequently integrated into the child's academic programming. Language intervention is often a long-term undertaking. Programming throughout preschool, primary and secondary education is common when the individual's deficits are severe. Children with mild language disabilities may have intensive intervention during preschool and early primary grades, with less formal supportive instructions continuing as a part of other academic instruction thereafter. In general, the more serious the child's language deficits are, the more intensive and long-term the intervention effort must be. When there are serious cognitive deficits, as in the case of mentally retarded children, language intervention should be linked with instruction in cognitive and conceptual areas. Severely retarded individuals may require continuing intervention throughout the school years and into adulthood to support acqui-

sition and maintenance of a minimal functional repertoire.

Although it is efficient to include language intervention as part of an academic curricula, formal, academic instruction and the normal conditions for language learning are quite dissimilar. The differences in learning conditions may affect the acquisition and use of functional communication skills. Normally, children acquire language in the course of conversational interactions with their caregivers and peers. Formal, structural aspects of the communication system (words, sentences) are learned concurrently with the pragmatic or social aspects of language use. Language learning is integrated with the child's emerging social skills. Language is learned as a functional means of social interaction. New, more specific or complex forms are learned as a means of communicating more effectively. When language is taught in a didactic, instructional context, the functions of language (i.e., the reinforcers for its use) are those typical to instructional settings (e.g., teacher approval) rather than those associated with conversation and normal social interaction (functional control over the environment). The precise instructional procedures needed to establish a basic linguistic repertoire may mitigate against generalization to social interaction. Finally, if instruction overemphasizes form, the student's language learning may be thoroughly dissociated from his emerging social interaction skills.

Ideally, language taught through direct instruction should not differ from naturally acquired language in either form or function. Newly taught forms should be used in conversational contexts to describe the speaker's needs, wants, knowledge and intentions. Newly taught forms should generalize across settings, persons, and events and should be integrated into the child's existing communication repertoire to insure generative, functional use. For normally developing children, generalized and generative social usage emerge without particular attention to the conditions which support language. In training language deficient children, instruction must provide the basis for integrating new language skills with existing social and language skills, or intervention will not fully remediate the child's deficit.

Attention to training new forms must not override efforts to develop functional communication. The training environment must be one in which functional use of language is supported. Language trainers must be conversational and communicatively responsive to the child in order to foster functional, spontaneous communication. Communicatively, training conditions should resemble those provided by caregivers of young language-learning children. Caregivers of normal children are highly responsive to children's communication attempts (Schacter, 1979). Teaching is secondary to communicating with the child. Caregiver speech is communicatively matched to the child's emerging language and progressive in relationship to the child's changing skills (Rogers-Warren, Neilson, & Blair, 1985). Caregivers request and model forms which are slightly more complex than the ones the child is currently using, while still speaking in ways that are simpler and more discriminable than their speech to other adults (Snow & Ferguson, 1977; Hoff-Ginsberg & Shatz, 1982).

Designing an educational environment where many children with different needs are enrolled to provide both systematic instruction and naturalistic support for emerging communication is a challenging task. Teaching functional language requires precise environmental arrangements. Parents, siblings, peers, caregivers, teachers and other significant persons in the child's life, in addition to speech language clinicians and language trainers, may need to be involved in "educational" interventions.

The need for long-term, intensive intervention across a variety of language-use contexts also poses a particular challenge for service delivery. Large numbers of children require training on a daily basis in functional communication contexts. Training must follow precise, individualized plans. Data on performance must be collected and monitored as a basis for adjusting the training program to meet each child's needs. There is a considerable gap between the "ideal" treatment for language deficits and what is typically available in educational settings such as public schools and day treatment centers. How to provide the types of comprehensive intervention necessary to remediate language and communication deficits is a pressing educational issue. Demonstration of effective strategies which insure generalized acquisition of a comprehensive communication repertoire in a cost-efficient manner for large numbers of children are needed.

ASSESSMENT AND TREATMENT ISSUES

In this section, assessment and treatment are discussed in the context of the model of communication presented at the beginning of this chapter. Multiple components of the child's communication system are considered. The social–environmental context of language use is addressed. Child and environmental components of intervention and assessment are closely described. Educational interventions are emphasized because most treatment for language deficits occurs in educational settings with secondary treatment in primary living settings. In keeping with our social perspective on language, the development of functional communication skills is presented as the primary objective of treatment.

Assessing Communication Skills

The purpose of assessment is to *describe* the child's existing language skills and to gather a data base for *prescribing* a set of treatment goals and strategies. There are four basic assessment strategies that are used alone or in combination to diagnose the child's deficits and to develop a prescriptive intervention program. These are: (a) use of standardized tests, (b) observation and language sampling, (c) use of probes or criterion-referenced tests, and (d) gathering reports of the child's language from familiar adults. Each general strategy might be applied to the phonological, lexical, syntactic and semantic domains of the language system and include assessment of both productive and receptive modes. Verbal as well as nonverbal (e.g., signing) language sytems might be evaluated by any of these means. However, careful adaptation would be needed to meaningfully use a standardized test format to evaluate a child's nonvocal communication system. Pragmatic use might be assessed via the last three strategies (observation, probes, and reports) but currently, there are few standardized tests of pragmatic use. Table 24-2 contains examples of each strategy.

In addition to the child's language skills, assessment may target related domains such as cognition and motor development. Assessing the child's ability to learn under various conditions (e.g., individualized, direct instruction; small group instruction, incidentally from teacher in context of other activities) is also important to prescribing a treatment strategy. Assessing the environments in which the child is expected to use language provides important information about environment contributions to the child's deficit and potential support for newly trained language. Environmental assessment is particularly critical for children living in residential treatment facilities where staff–child interaction may be less frequent and qualitatively different from parent–child interactions. Table 24-3 illustrates one approach to environmental assessment.

To make use of the information gathered, during the assessment process, the evaluating professional must integrate information from various sources in order to develop a profile of the child's strengths and weaknesses related to communication. Primary assessment may focus on broadly assessing the child's skills relative to critical developmental milestones in receptive and productive language development across phonological, lexical, syntactic and semantic components. Secondary assessment, often in the form of criterion-referenced tests, provides a more in-depth analysis of a particular aspect of the language system (e.g., syntax) or a particular skill within the domain (e.g., use of color and number adjectives). Where discrepancies occur (e.g., between parent

report and observed pragmatic use), additional assessment may be required. Initial assessment provides a basis for selecting general treatment targets and general strategies; ongoing assessment evaluates changes in the child's special skills and the effectiveness of the chosen treatment strategy. Many developmentally disabled children evidence multiple deficits. Frequently, it is necessary to set priorities among the potential targets for intervention. The selection of priorities depends on several factors, including the child's age and entry skill level, the child's potential for learning a comprehensive linguistic system, the resources available for training, and the evaluating professional's assumptions about the nature of language and primary targets for intervention.

Treatment

The goals of language intervention are (a) to remediate existing deficits in the child's communication repertoire, and (b) to facilitate the child's continued acquisition of new language. To meet the first goal, an intervention program must be designed to expand on the child's functional communicative repertoire. This typically is accomplished by teaching the child specific skills in one or more structural domains (i.e., lexicon, syntax, semantics) and facilitating the child's use of these new skills in social conversational settings. Most developmentally disabled children will require intervention on both the formal and functional aspects of language use. Until recently, the formal or structural components of the communication system have been the primary, and frequently the only, targets for intervention. Increasingly, professionals have begun to recognize that true remediation of communication deficits occurs only when the trained forms have been thoroughly generalized across appropriate social contexts and when these forms have been sufficiently integrated into the child's existing communication system to be used generatively (Warren & Rogers-Warren, 1985). Utilizing teaching strategies known to

Table 24-2 Four Basic Strategies for Assessing Syntactic, Semantic, and Pragmatic Skills

PROCEDURE	DESCRIPTION	SYNTAX	SEMANTICS	PRAGMATICS
Standardized Tests	Contain standardized procedures related to: (a) stimuli and instructions to present in eliciting child responses, and (b) scoring and interpretation of child responses. The standards for interpretation usually are norms based on a representative sample of persons against whom the child is compared. Test norms may be presented as a mean with a measure of variability, such as standard deviation, or as a number expressed in standard score form (z, T, etc.). A child's performance on a test typically is presented as an age-equivalent score of relative standing.	Assessment of Children's Language Comprehension (Foster, Giddan, & Stark, 1972) Carrow Elicited Language Inventory (Carrow, 1974) Clinical Evaluation of Language Functioning (Semmel & Wiig, 1980) Illinois Test of Psycholinguistic Abilities (Kirk, McCarthy, & Kirk, 1968) Preschool Language Scale (Zimmerman, Steiner, & Evatt, 1969) Test for Auditory Comprehension of Language (Carrow, 1973) Test of Early Language Development (Hresko, Reid, & Hammill, 1981)	Boehm Test of Basic Concepts (Boehm, 1971) Clinical Evaluation of Language Functioning (Semmel & Wiig, 1980) Illinois Test of Psycholinguistic Abilities (Kirk, McCarthy, & Kirk, 1968) Preschool Language Scale (Zimmerman, Steiner, & Evatt, 1969) Test for Auditory Comprehension of Language (Carrow, 1973) Test of Early Language Development (Hresko, Reid, & Hammill, 1981)	Let's Talk Inventory for Adolescents (Wiig, 1983)
Criterion-Referenced Tests	Typically designed to assess a child's acquisition of instructionally relevant skills. Skills of interest are identified and task-analyzed in terms of their component responses. An absolute standard of performance (indicating mastery of a skill) is determined and the child's performance on each skill is expressed in percentage form or as a fraction of the	Administer tasks designed to elicit production or test comprehension of particular structures and/or grammatical morphemes or to test knowledge of particular linguistic rules.	Administer tasks designed to assess comprehension and use of semantic relations and/or understanding of nonliteral language.	Administer tasks designed to elicit use of particular pragmatic funtions and to assess pragmatic skills such as turntaking, topic initiation, and maintenance of conversational topic.

Norms for comparison are not required; however, procedures for test administration should be clearly stipulated.

Parent Report	Parents often can provide valuable information about the child's developmental history, language acquisition, and current language and communication skills and strategies. Information from parents may supplement and/or validate findings from assessment procedures (Bloom & Lahey, 1978).	Two common methods for obtaining information from parents are *interviews* and *questionnaires*. Two examples of informant-interview scales are the Verbal Language Development Scale (VLDS) (Mecham, 1971), which provides a rough language-age-equivalent for children below 3 years, and the Receptive-Expressive Emergent Language (REEL) Scale (Bzoch & League, 1971), which seeks information on expressive and receptive language acquisition over the language age period from birth to 3 years.
Direct Observation	Involves the collection and analysis of spontaneous language samples that are representative of the child's typical use of language. Because the conversational partner, the setting, and the stimuli or materials present may affect the child's language, it is advisable to collect samples under several conditions — e.g., with the parent at home; with the teacher or therapist at school; with a peer at home or at school. The sample should be long enough to include instances of the behaviors to be measured; 50 to 100 different utterances is considered adequate for most analyses (Bloom & Lahey, 1978).	Examples of direct observational measures include: Mean Length of Utterance (MLU) Developmental Sentence Analysis (Lee, 1974) Use of grammatical morphemes Types of clause structures used Elements contained in noun and verb phrases Structure of negatives and questions Use complex sentences (James, 1985) Type-Token Ratio (TTR) (Templin, 1957) Types of concrete and relational meanings found in the sample (Miller, 1981) Use of intra- and inter-sentence relations (Bloom & Lahey, 1978; Leonard, Steckol, & Panther, 1983; Miller, 1981; Prutting, 1979) Use of pragmatic functions Pragmatic skills such as turntaking, topic initiation, and topic maintenance

Table 24-2 continued

PROCEDURE	DESCRIPTION	SYNTAX	SEMANTICS	PRAGMATICS
	Language samples can be recorded through audiotaping or videotaping with a good audio microphone. Verbatim transcriptions are developed from the recordings and analyses of verbal behavior are based on the transcriptions. Analyses of nonverbal behavior can be derived from the videotapes or from contextual notes on the situation and the child's nonverbal behaviors.			

Table 24-3 Guidelines for Assessing the Language Environment

1. *What type(s) of child responses are elicited?*
   _____Questions and instructions requiring a verbal response.
   _____Instructions requiring a nonverbal response.
   _____Conversational or commentary requiring no response.

2. *What type(s) of language models are presented?*
   _____Conversation occurs in the language environment, but it is not directed toward the child.
   _____Language is directed toward the child, but it generally is not matched to the child's level of functioning and appears not to serve a teaching purpose.
   _____Language is directed toward the child that is matched to his or her level of functioning. Imitative responses from the child generally are not elicited.
   _____Particular language forms that are appropriate for the child's level of functioning are presented and imitative responses are required.

3. *What kind(s) of consequences are presented for language use?*
   _____Positive feedback for using any language.
   _____Positive feedback for using specific language forms.
   _____No feedback for language usage.
   _____Negative feedback or constraints on language usage.
   _____Natural consequences fro language usage such as _____materials, _____social interaction, _____attention from conversational partner.

4. *What opportunities exist for language usage?*
   _____Obligatory response occasions: questions, demands for verbalization.
   _____Social response occasions: greetings, conversation opportunities.
   _____Functional response occasions: requests for materials, indicating preferences.
   _____Descriptive response occasions: an event and a listener.
   _____Imitative response occasions: prompted or unprompted opp;ortunities to repeat verbal forms modeled in the environment.

5. *Description of nonverbal environment:*
   _____A variety of toys and materials are accessible to the child.
   _____Toys and materials are present but are inaccessible to child.
   _____Few or no toys or materials are available.
   _____Television is watched _____little _____some _____much of the time.
   _____Other _____

---

facilitate generalization to conversational use is critical to successful remediation of language deficits (see Stremel-Campbell & Campbell, 1985, for a review of these strategies).

The second goal, facilitating the child's continued acquisition of language, is a critical outcome of language intervention. However, this goal has seldom been addressed directly in intervention research or clinical treatment. Given the complexity of the communication system and the limited resources available for direct training, it is essential that treatments be designed to support the child's learning of additional language skills without direct intervention. Ideally, intervention should include teaching the child strategies that might allow more efficient learning from the natural environment. One commonly taught strategy is generalized imitation. Generalized imitation may allow a child to learn new language forms by observing and repeating them. While the exact role of imitation in normal language development is still disputed (Owens, 1984), there is evidence from intervention studies with retarded children that imitation is critical to learning even a small set of language structures. Active programming to assist the child in learning other strategies, such as cross-modal transfer, seeking confirmatory input, turn-taking in conversation, and frequent use of language, also may support continued, unprogrammed learning (cf. Rogers-Warren, Warren, & Baer, 1983).

Models of Intervention

Over the last 20 years, two general models of intervention have emerged. The behavioral model of intervention focuses on teaching functional skills in a logical order which does not necessarily follow the normal developmental sequence. The developmental model, as its name implies, is based on the normal developmental progression and teaches language skills in the order they typically appear in normally-developing children. In general, adherents of the behavioral model have argued that when a child deviates substantially from the normal developmental progression, teaching functional skills is a more parsimonious approach to training (Guess, Sailor, & Baer, 1978). Developmentalists, on the other hand, argue that the normally occurring sequence of behaviors is an implicitly functional organization of behavior and intervening consistent with this organization will be optimally effective in furthering language development (Guess et al., 1978). Although initially, behavioral and developmental intervention models could be differentiated by teaching method (with behavioral intervention programs relying primarily on operant teaching procedures and developmental programs using less structured facilitation approaches), this is no longer necessarily true. Direct instruction technology (the use of shaping, fading, reinforcement, and other behavior man-

agement techniques) is used in combination with curricula developed from both behavioral and developmental perspectives.

Direct instruction technology is based on operant conditioning procedures. These procedures have been demonstrated to be effective in teaching the phonological (cf. McReynolds, 1983), the lexical (Lovaas, 1977), morphological (Baer & Guess, 1971), and syntactic (Hester & Hendrickson, 1977) aspects of the language system. Although there are numerous studies demonstrating primary learning of various linguistic forms, recent research describing the longitudinal generalization of newly trained forms (Warren & Rogers-Warren, 1983a; Warren & Kaiser, in press) suggests that such training does not automatically produce generalized use of these forms in conversational contexts. Application of specific generalization-facilitating techniques typically is needed to insure spontaneous use of newly learned forms (Stremel-Campbell & Campbell, 1985). Training which involves multiple exemplars of the forms, indiscriminable contingencies, "loose" stimulus control, and sequential modification across settings or persons is more effective in producing functional use than training that does not incorporate these procedures (Stokes & Baer, 1977; Warren & Rogers-Warren, 1985).

Direction Instruction

Direct instruction has been used primarily in one-to-one sessions conducted outside the child's normal learning settings. In part, the evidence of limited generalization to other contexts may have resulted from the setting as well as the particular procedures. Although didactic teaching is effective in teaching discrete skills to a single child, it is often inefficient given the large numbers of children requiring language intervention. As a result, language teaching in small groups has become increasingly common. Research comparing individual and small group instruction suggests that with careful planning, small group instruction may be equally effective and potentially may facilitate social interaction and incidental learning (Reid & Favell, 1984).

Incidental Teaching

One of the most promising language intervention strategies is incidental teaching (Hart, 1985; Halle, Alpert, & Anderson, 1984). Incidental teaching is a naturalistic intervention procedure which applies operant teaching strategies in the context of everyday social communicative interaction. Linguistic forms are taught in their functional communicative contexts. For example, a child may be incidentally taught to use color adjectives; in the context of an art activity. Incidental teaching is typically child-initiated and the teacher fits the specific content of the teaching episode to fit the child's indicated interest. Child responses in an incidental teaching episode are functionally reinforced by consequences the child specifies. For example, a child may nonverbally indicate that he/she wants a particular toy by reaching for the toy. The teaching adult prompts the child to specify what is wanted. If the child is unable to respond, the adult models an appropriate response for the child to imitate (e.g., "Red truck, please"). The child's prompted response results in the adult providing the requested object. Effective incidental teaching requires careful arrangement of the environment so that the adult controls some of the objects that the child may find reinforcing. In order for incidental teaching to facilitate language development, the intervention must be carefully designed to teach language that is slightly more advanced than the child's current language skills. The same types of assessment and data collection that are essential to effective direct instruction are needed in incidental teaching. There are several advantages of incidental teaching. Forms are taught in their functional contexts and thus, the child has opportunities to acquire and practice new language in the exact settings in which it will be used. Incidental teaching resembles the types of interactions observed between mothers and their normally developing children, while in-corporating the behavioral techniques that have been shown to be effective and often necessary with handicapped learners. Incidental teaching may be an effective means of increasing children's unprogrammed language learning because it sensitizes the child to the naturally occurring language models and demands for language. Leonard (1981) has argued, based on his review of studies of training language-delayed children, that more flexible, naturalistic interventions such as incidental teaching are more likely to produce generalized effects on the child's language repertoire. Experimental analyses of incidental teaching with a range of children has demonstrated that a variety of linguistic forms can be taught successfully (see Warren & Kaiser, in press, for a comprehensive review). Only a few studies have specifically examined the generalized effects of incidental teaching (c.f. Warren, McQuarter & Rogers-Warren, 1984; Rogers-Warren & Warren, 1980), but these studies have produced extremely promising results.

Effective language intervention requires careful assessment and selecting intervention procedures to fit the learning requirements of the child. Severely handicapped children may require intensive individual instruction, especially during the acquisition of their first linguistic forms. Incidental teaching may have particular advantages for handicapped children who have difficulty generalizing newly trained forms or learning the pragmatic aspects of language use (Rogers-Warren & Warren, 1980). Although all settings offer numerous opportunities for incidental teaching, successful application of incidental teaching procedures requires planning and skilled teaching. Thus, both child and environmental factors must be considered in selecting an optimal intervention strategy. Using multiple strategies with a single child is highly recommended if resources permit. Ongoing evaluation of the child's learning and actual use of newly trained language should be the primary criteria for determining if a particular treatment strategy is effective.

Commercially Available Programs

There are currently a number of language intervention programs commercially available. Many of these programs are based on research findings, and for the most part, they prescribe appropriate strategies for language intervention. Because children's needs are varied, no single published program is likely to provide an ideal set of objectives and procedures for any given child. Typically, skilled clinicians tailor their treatment to the child's specific needs and draw on a variety of teaching strategies and curriculum items to design an individualized program. Ongoing data collection and assessment of primary learning and generalization are essential to effective language intervention, regardless of the therapist, intervention model or selection of strategies and target behaviors.

Summary

During the last 20 years, a technology for teaching new linguistic forms to language-deficient children has evolved. Clearly, new language skills can be learned by even the most severely handicapped child using direct instruction technology. The critical issues in language intervention are insuring that the child learns functional skills and generalizes them to the appropriate social communication contexts. There is an increasing emphasis on efficiency in teaching and toward training children in the use of strategies that will permit rapid learning of language that is not directly trained. Language intervention is an imperfect but evolving technology enhanced by skilful clinicians and dependent on empirical research to identify more effective treatment strategies.

CURRENT RESEARCH

Considerable research has focused on the development and treatment of abnormal language during the past 2 decades (cf. Schiefelbusch, 1978; Morehead & Morehead, 1976; Warren & Rogers-Warren, 1985). Research has progressed from simple comparisons between age-matched normal and handicapped children to complex analyses of mother–child interaction patterns and individual differences in language learning. At the same time, research on language remediation has progressed from demonstrations that very specific aspects of the linguistic system (e.g., plurals, Guess, 1969; Sailor, 1971; Welch & Pear, 1980) can be taught to mentally retarded children, to analyses of the generalized effects of comprehensive language intervention (Warren & Rogers-Warren, 1983a).

Handicapped children are truly heterogenous. Even children who are evidencing the same syndrome, such as Down Syndrome are remarkably varied in their language development. Specific prediction of individual developmental outcomes is usually difficult except in cases of profound mental retardation. Individual patterns of development, combined with the complexity of the process of language acquisition, make the empirical analysis of abnormal language development an extraordinarily difficult task. Data-based descriptions of atypical language development have been further hindered by the lack of a comprehensive theory of normal language development. In part, as a result of shifting conceptualizations of the normal process of language acquisition, the existing analyses of atypical development appear somewhat discontinuous. Some aspects of development, such as morphology and syntax, have been thoroughly described for various populations. Other aspects such as pragmatic and semantic development, are less well described. An integrated description of the formal and functional aspects of the communication system is lacking for any single disability group.

Since the general descriptive research findings were presented in an earlier section, the interactional bases of language development, individual differences and predictors of language development, and intervention will be emphasized in this section.

Interactional Bases

A primary question by researchers interested in atypical language development has been, "how do the social interactional environments of handicapped children differ from those of normal children? " The study of the interactional bases of abnormal language development followed the shift toward studying language development in the context of dyadic interaction in the normal child language literature (Rogers-Warren, Warren, & Baer, 1983). A number of studies have examined how early mother-child interaction differs between dyads with normal and handicapped children (e.g., Buim, Rynders & Turnure, 1974; Rondal, 1978; Terdal, Jackson & Garner, 1976). In general, this research has found relatively few differences between mother-child interactions in these type of dyads when normal and handicapped children are carefully matched for developmental level. Mothers in both groups adjust the rate, complexity, prosody, and functions of their language to match their children's language levels. As the child's competence in using and understanding language increases, mothers continue to shift the form of their own language so that it remains slightly more complex than the child's. In this way, mothers model new language. Recent data on mother's naturalistic language teaching suggest that mothers also may shift their tactics for teaching language as the child's skill develops (Moerk, 1977; Rogers-Warren, Blair, & Alpert, 1984).

There are some subtle but potentially important differences in parental interactions with atypical children. For example, Stoneman, Brady, and Abbott (1983) demonstrated that mothers with Down Syndrome children were more directive and their children less responsive. Although mothers of handicapped children may be matching appropriately to their child's behavior, the differences resulting from this adaptive matching to the child's behavior may be important. For example, mothers' increased directiveness in response to handicapped children's lower frequencies of spontaneous speech contributes to a more constrained, less conversational interaction (Maurer, 1985). Mothers of mentally retarded children prompt language much more directly than

mothers of normal children and thus, model a smaller range of lexical forms and linguistic structures (Kaiser & Blair, 1985).

Individual Differences

Research comparing groups of normal and handicapped children is implicitly limited in its ability to account for the heterogenity in handicapped children's language development. Recently, research has begun to focus on the systematic analysis of individual differences within groups of handicapped children. Miller and Chapman (Chapman, 1981; Miller & Chapman, 1984) described individual differences observed in 42 mentally retarded children; seen in a speech clinic. Three different patterns of language performances were identified: (a) delayed productive language relative to cognitive development; (b) delayed comprehension and production; and (c) language comprehension and production equivalent to cognitive level. These three patterns were observed at every cognitive level from late sensorimotor to late preoperational stages. These findings may be important to designing interventions that fit children's learning strategies and developmental patterns.

The systematic analysis of individual child and dyad differences has implications for understanding of language development in both normal and handicapped children and for analyzing and predicting the relative effects of different types of language remediation strategies. For example, analyses of individual differences may be a feasible strategy for isolating the relative effects of nonverbal cognitive abilities and environmental variables on language acquisition. Determining the relative efficacy of different language intervention strategies applied to various profiles of language development may lead to the development of comprehensive language intervention strategies that can be matched to the specific needs and learning characteristics of individual handicapped children.

The effects of individual differences in mother behavior have been analyzed.

Mahoney, Finger, and Powell (in press) studied 60 mother–handicapped child dyads and found three patterns of mother interaction style that related directly to developmental status of the children. They found that mothers who were (relatively) neither highly controlling nor very directive in their routine interactions with their children had children with the highest Bayley scores in their matched group, while mothers; who used many directives and presented many repetitions and incomplete sentences had children with lower scores. Although direction of effects (i.e., does mother behavior influence child functioning or vice versa?) is a concern, Mahoney and Finger's findings suggest that the developmental prognosis for a particular child may be influenced by his/her particular environmental context for language learning.

Intervention

Research on effective language intervention strategies has been conducted for nearly 25 years. Early studies that sought to teach vocabulary or a small set of syntactic forms were very promising (e.g. Baer & Guess, 1971; Wheeler & Salzer, 1970). Well-controlled experiments demonstrated that mentally retarded children could be taught a variety of linguistic skills such as labeling objects (Stephens, Pear, Wray, & Jackson, 1975; Welch & Pear, 1980), use of verb tense markers, and pluralization (e.g., Guess, 1969; Sailor, 1971). Based of these empirical demonstrations, a technology for language intervention has been developed that largely relies on a didactic adult controlled massed-trial instructional approach incorporating behavioral teaching procedures such as imitation and differential reinforcement (cf. Lovaas, 1977; Gray & Ryan, ;1973; Guess, Sailor & Baer, 1978; Stremel & Waryas, 1974).

The primary limitation of this direct-instruction technology appears to be the extent to which it produces both generalization of newly trained skills to appropriate communication situations and general changes in children's communicative competence (Rogers-Warren & Warren, 1980; Costello, 1983). This limitation probably results from two characteristics of the instructional technology. The first is primarily pragmatic. This technology was developed from a research model in which a speech clinician or language trainer worked with a child individually each day for 20–30 minutes or in a small group only once or twice a week outside the classroom for 15–20 minute training session. Low frequency, less intensive training is much less effective in teaching complex language skills to a child with a serious learning problem. There are also inherent features of a didactic training approach that mitigate against generalization of newly trained skills. These include: (a) an emphasis on teaching the structural forms rather than the communicative functions of language; (b) failure to emphasize language use in conversational setting; (c) failure to capture the child's attention and interest and fully capitalize upon these in the training process; (d) difficulty in maintaining an accurate and effective communication match with the child; (e) difficulty in teaching frequent independent language initiations (as opposed to rote responding) in the didactic teaching context.

Although the limitations of didactically based training approaches are apparent, didactic training is an efficient means of establishing an initial skill repertoire in a severely retarded child. Some of the limitations of didactic training encountered in teaching complex functional skills to more mildly handicapped children can be overcome by incorporating procedures known to facilitate generalization. Research has shown that language training that includes the use of multiple exemplars (e.g. Campbell & Stremel-Campbell, 1982; Anderson & Spradlin, 1980), employs examples organized in matrix fashion to illustrate the underlying rules for recombination (e.g., Goldstein, 1985), is structured to promote cross-modal (e.g. receptive to expressive) transfer (e.g. Sidman, 1971; Sidman & Tailby, 1982; Spradlin, Cotter, & Baxley, 1973) and/or employs other generalization facilitating techniques (e.g. Stremel-Campbell & Campbell, 1985) ultimately enhances generalization.

Research also has been conducted on ways to teach language directly in the natural settings of handicapped children using parents and teachers as language trainers and generalization facilitators (Warren & Rogers-Warren, 1985). Naturalistic teaching approaches have obvious appeal because language can be taught by people with handicapped children throughout the day in varied functional contexts, thereby facilitating generalization. One very promising conversational based approach developed by applied behavior analysts is incidental or milieu language teaching (described previously, p. 413). A substantial experimental literature (see review by Hart, 1985) has demonstrated that this approach teaches broadly defined target skills in the natural environment, typically results in the generalization of these skills, and results in general gains in both the formal and functional aspects of language. Furthermore, this approach represents something of a convergence between two perspectives of language remediation —behavioral and developmental (Warren & Rogers-Warren, 1986) and in many respects mimics processes known to be central to normal language acquisition (Hart, 1985).

Although early results of conversationally based language remediation approaches are promising, there are many unanswered research questions: (a) How effective are these techniques with severely retarded children (most research has involved mildly handicapped children)? (b) What range of skills can be taught effectively with these techniques? (c) To what extent can parents be taught to use these techniques effectively? (d) How effective are these techniques compared to didactic training approaches? (e) Do these techniques actually accelerate language development or simply teach children how to use skills already in their repertoires? (f) How can these techniques be used in classrooms that are highly structured for academic learning (to date, these techniques have been used primarily in semi-structured free play situations or at snack times in preschool language programs)? (g) What are the relative effects of conversationally based approaches on children at the same developmental level but evidencing different patterns of delay (e.g., productive delay only vs. productive and receptive delay)?

Summary

Although there has been substantial research on abnormal language development and remediation in the past 2 decades, a full description and explanation of abnormal development is not yet available. An optimal technology for remediating language delays and disorders remains elusive. However, it is now clear that abnormal development has multiple causes and is a heterogeneous condition. Furthermore, a single effective remediation strategy for all language-deficient children is unlikely to be developed. Instead, future efforts must focus on strategies for matching intervention with disorders/delays specific to a child's developmental level, learning characteristics, and everyday language learning environments.

REFERENCES

Alpert, C. L., & Rogers-Warren, A. (1983). *Mothers as incidental language trainers of their language-disordered children.* Paper presented at the Gatlinburg Conference on Mental Retardation, March 1983.

Alpert, C. L., & Rogers-Warren, A. K. (1985). Communication in autistic persons: Characteristics and intervention. In S. F. Warren and A. K. Rogers-Warren (Eds.), *Teaching functional language.* Austin, TX: Pro-Ed.

Anderson, S. R., & Spradlin, J. E. (1970). The generalized effects of productive labeling training involving comment object classes. *Journal of the Association of the Severely Handicapped, 5,* 143–157.

Baer, D. M., & Guess, D. Receptive training of adjectival inflections in mental retardates. *Journal of Applied Behavior Analysis, 4,* 129–139.

Baltaxe, C. A. M. (1977). Pragmatic deficits in the language of autistic adolescents. *Journal of Pediatric Psychology, 2*, 176–180.

Bangs, T. (1961). Evaluating children with language delay. *Journal of Speech and Hearing Disorders, 26*, 6–18.

Bartolucci, G., & Pierce, S. J. (1977). A preliminary comparison of phonological development in autistic, normal, and mentally retarded subjects. *British Journal of Disorders of Communications, 12*, 137–147.

Bates, E. L. (1976). *Language and context: The acquisition of pragmatics.* New York: Academic Press.

Bedrosian, J., & Prutting, C. (1978). Communicative performance of mentally retarded adults in four conversational settings. *Journal of Speech and Hearing, 21*, 79–95.

Bloom, L., & Lahey, M. (1978). *Language development and language disorders.* New York: John Wiley & Sons.

Boehm, A. (1971). *Boehm test of basic concepts.* New York: The Psychological Corporation.

Braverman-Callahan, J., & Radziewicz, C. K. (1985). Hearing-impaired children: Language acquisition and remediation. In D. K. Bernstein and C. Tiegerman (Eds.), *Language and communication disorders in children.* Columbus, OH: Charles E. Merrill.

Bruner, J. S. (1975). The ontogensis of speech acts, *Journal of Child Language, 2*, 1–19.

Bruner, J., Roy, C., & Ratner, N. (1980). The beginnings of requests. In Nelson, K. E. (Ed.), *Children's language,* Vol. 3. New York: Gardner Press.

Bryan, T., Donahue, M., & Pearl, R. (1981). Studies of learning disabled children's pragmatic competence. *Topics in Learning and Language Disabilities, 1*, 29–39.

Buium, N., Rynders, J., & Turnure, J. (1974). Early maternal linguistic environment of normal and Down's syndrome language-learning children. *American Journal of Mental Deficiency, 79a*, 52–58.

Bzoch, K., & League, R. (1971). *The receptive-expressive emergent language scale.* Gainesville, FL: Computer Management Corporation.

Campbell, C. R., & Stremel-Campbell, K. (1982). Programming "loose training" as a strategy to facilitate language generalization. *Journal of Applied Behavior Analysis, 15*, 295–301.

Carrow, E., (1973). *Test of auditory comprehension of language.* Austin, TX: Urban Research Group.

Carrow, E. (1974). *Carrow elicited language inventory.* Austin, TX: Learning Concepts.

Chapman, R. S. and Miller, J. F. (1980). Analyzing language and communication in the child. In R. L. Schiefelbusch (Ed.), *Nonspeech Language and Communication: Analysis and Intervention.* Baltimore: University Park Press.

Costello, J. M. (1983). Generalization across settings: Language intervention with children. In J. Miller, D. Yoder, & R. L. Schiefelbusch (Eds.) *Contemporary issues in language intervention.* Rockville, MD: American Speech-Language-Hearing Association.

Dodd, B. (1976). A comparison of the phonological systems of mental age matched normal, severely subnormal and Down's syndrome children. *British Journal of Disorders of Communications, 11*, 27–42.

Dooley, J. F. (1976). *Language acquisition and Down's syndrome: A study of early semantics and syntax.* Unpublished doctoral dissertation. Harvard University.

Ervin-Tripp, S. (1971a). Social backgrounds and verbal skills. In R. Huxley & E. Ingram (Eds.), *Language acquisition: Models and methods,* New York: Academic Press.

Ervin-Tripp, S. (1971b). Sociolinguistics. In J. Fishman (Ed.), *Advances in the Sociology of Language.* Mouton, The Mague.

Foster, C., Giddan, J., & Stark, J. (1972). *ACLC: Assessment of children's language comprehension.* Palo Alto, CA: Consulting Psychologists Press.

Goldstein, H. (1985). Enhancing language generalization using matrix and stimulus equivalence training. In S. F. Warren & A. K. Rogers-Warren (Eds.), *Teaching functional language.* Baltimore: University Park Press.

Graham, J., & Graham, L. (1971). Language behavior of the mentally retarded: Syntactic characteristics. *American Journal of Mental Deficiency, 73*, 623–629.

Gray, B., & Ryan, B. (1973). *A language program for the nonlanguage child.* Champaign, IL: Research Press.

Guess, D. (1969). A functional analysis of receptive language and productive speech: Acquisition of the plural morpheme. *Journal of Applied Behavior Analysis, 2*, 55–64.

Guess, D., Sailor, W., & Baer, D. M. (1978). *Functional speech and language training for the severely handicapped.* Lawrence, KS: H & H Enterprises, Inc.

Halle, J., Alpert, C. L., & Anderson, S. R. (1984). Natural environment language assessment and intervention with severely impaired preschoolers. *Topics in Early Childhood Special Education, 4*, 35–56.

Halliday, M. A. K. (1970). Language structure and language function. In J. Lyons (Ed.), *New horizons in linguistics*. Harmondsworth: Penguin Books.

Hart, B. (1985). Naturalistic language training strategies. In S. F. Warren & A. Rogers-Warren (Eds.), *Teaching functional language*. Austin, TX: Pro-Ed.

Hayes, C., & Koch, R. (1977). Interpersonal distance behavior of mentally retarded and non-retarded children. *American Journal of Mental Deficiency, 82*, 207–209.

Hester, P., & Hendrickson, J. (1977). Training functional expressive language: The acquisition and generalization of five-element syntactic responses. *Journal of Applied Behavior Analysis, 10*, 316.

Hoff-Ginsberg, E., & Shatz, M. (1982). Linguistic input and the child's acquisition of language. *Psychological Bulletin, 92*(1), 3–26.

Hresko, W., Reid, D., & Hammill, D. (1981). *The test of early language development*. Austin, TX: Pro-Ed.

Hurtig, R., Ensrud, S., & Tomblin, J. B. (1982). The communicative function of question production in autistic children. *Journal of Autism and Developmental Disorders, 12*, 57–69.

Ingram, D. (1972). Transivity in child language. *Language, 47*, 888–910.

Ingram, D. (1976). *Phonological disability in children*. New York: Elsevier.

James, S. (1985). Assessing children with language disorders. In D. K. Bernstein and E. Tiegerman (Eds.), *Language and communication disorders in children*. Columbus, OH: Charles E. Merrill.

Jensema, C., Karchmer, M., & Trybus, R. (1978). *The rated speech intelligibility of hearing impaired children: Basic relationships and a detailed analysis* (Series R, No. 6). Washington, DC: Gallaudet College, Office of Demographic Studies.

Johnston, J., & Schery, T. (1976). The use of grammatical morphemes by children with communication disorders. In D. Morehead & A. Morehead (Eds.), *Normal and deficient child language*. Baltimore: University Park Press.

Kaiser, A. P., & Blair, G. (1985). *Naturalistic contingencies in mothers' intereactions with normal and retarded children*. Paper presented at the annual meeting of American Psychological Association, Los Angeles, CA, August 1985.

Kaiser, A. P., & Blair, G. (In preparation). *Interactional Strategies of Mothers with Normal and Mentally Retarded Children*.

Kaye, K. & Charney, R. (1980). How mothers maintain "dialogue" with two-year olds. In D. Olson (Ed.) *The social foundations of language and thought*. New York: W. W. Norton.

Kirk, S., McCarthy, J., & Kirk, W. (1968). *Illinois test of psycholinguistic ability*. Revised Edition. Urbana, IL: University of Illinois Press.

Lackner, J. (1968). A development study of language behavior in retarded children. *Neuropsychologia, 6*, 301–320.

Lawrence, E. R. (1971). Spina bifida children in school: Preliminary report. *Developmental Medicine and Child Neurology, 25*, 44–46.

Lee, L. (1974). *Developmental Sentence Analysis*. Evanston, IL: Northwestern University Press.

Leonard, L. B. (1981). An invited article facilitating linguistic skills in children with specific impairment. *Applied Psycholinguistics, 1*, 89–118.

Leonard, L. B., Cole, B., & Steckol, K. F. (1979). Lexical usage of retarded children: An examination of informativeness. *American Journal of Mental Deficiency, 84*, 49–54.

Leonard, L., Steckol, K., & Panther, K. (1983). Returning meaning to semantic relations: Some clinical applications. *Journal of Speech and Hearing Disorders, 48*, 25–36.

Lovaas, O. I. (Ed.). (1977). Building the first words and labels. In *The autistic child: Language development through behavior modification*, (pp. 35–55). New York: John Wiley & Sons.

Mahoney, G., Finger, I., & Powell, A. (in press). The relationship of maternal behavioral style to the developmental status of organically impaired mentally retarded infants. *American Journal of Mental Deficiency*.

Maurer, H. (1985). *Context of directions given to young normally developing and down syndrome children: Development over two years*. Unpublished manuscript, Vanderbilt University, Nashville, TN.

McCormick, L. (1984). Perspectives on categorization and intervention. In L. McCormick and R. L. Schiefelbusch (Eds.), *Early language intervention*. Columbus, OH: Charles E. Merrill.

McLeavey, B., Toomey, J., & Dempsey, P. (1982). Nonretarded and mentally retarded children's control over syntactic structures. *American Journal of Mental Deficiency, 86*, 485–494.

McReynolds, L. V. *Generalization in articulation training*. Unpublished manuscript, Speech and language research, Ralph L. Smith Mental Retardation Center, 39th & Rainbow Blvd., Kansas City, KS 66103.

Mecham, M. (1971). *Verbal language development scale [VLDS]*. American Guidance Service.

Miller, J. (1981). *Assessing language production in children: Experimental procedures.* Baltimore: University Park Press.

Miller, J. F., & Chapman, R. S. (1984). Disorder of communication: Investigating the development of language of mentally retarded children, *American Journal of Mental Deficiency, 88,* 936–546.

Miller, J. F. & Chapman, R. S. *An Overview of SALT: Systematic Analysis of Language Transcripts.*

Moerk, E. L. Verbal channel of communication and instructional aspects of verbal interactions. In *Pragmatics and Semantics of Language Development,* (Ch.6, pp. 203–279).

Naremore, R., & Dever, R. (1975). Language performance of educable mentally retarded and normal children at five age levels. *Journal of Speech and Hearing Research, 18,* 82–95.

Owens, R. (1984). *Language development: An introduction.* Columbus, OH: Charles E. Merrill.

Owens, R. (1985). Mental retardation: Difference or delay? In D. K. Bernstein & E. Tiegerman (Eds.), *Language and communication disorders in children.* Columbus, OH: Charles E. Merrill.

Owens, R., & MacDonald, J. (1982). Communicative uses of the early speech of nondelayed and Down syndrome children. *American Journal of Mental Deficiency, 86,* 503–510.

Polloway, E. A., & Smith, J. E. (1982). *Teaching Language Skills to Exceptional Learners.* Denver, CO: Love Publishing Company.

Prutting, C. (1979). Process (/pra/,ses/n) The action of moving forward progressively from one point to another on the way to completion. *Journal of Speech and Hearing Disorders, 44,* 3–30.

Reid, H., & Favell, J. E. (1984). Groups instruction with persons who have severe disabilities: A critical review. *Journal of the Association for Persons with Severe Handicaps, 9* 167–177.

Rogers-Warren, A. K., Blair, G., & Alpert, C. L. (1984). *Language teaching strategies of mothers with normal and handicapped children.* Paper presented at the annual meeting of the American Psychological Association.

Rogers-Warren, A. K., Neilsen, L. M., & Blair, G. (1985). Mothers questions to their language learning children. *Journal of Child Language.*

Rogers-Warren, A., & Warren, S. F. (1980). Mands for verbalization: Facilitating the display of newly taught language. *Behavior Modification, 4,* 361–382.

Rogers-Warren, A. K., & Warren, S. F. (1981). Form and function in language learning and generalization. *Analysis and intervention in developmental disabilities, 1,* 389–405.

Rogers-Warren, A., Warren, S. F., & Bear, D. M. (1983). Interactional bases of language learning. In K. Kernan, M. Begab, & R. Elgerton (Eds.), *Environments and Behavior: The Adaptation of Mentally Retarded Persons.* Baltimore: University Park Press.

Rondal, J. A. (1978). Maternal speech to normal and Down's syndrome children matched for mean length of utterance. In C. E. Meyers (Ed.), *Quality of life in severely and profoundly mentally retarded people: Research for foundations for improvement.* Washington, DC: American Association on Mental Deficiency, 193–264.

Rosenburg, S. (1982). The language of the mentally retarded: Development, processes, and intervention. In S. Rosenberg (Ed.), *Handbook of applied psycholinguistics: Major thrusts of research and theory.* Hillsdale, NJ: Lawrence Erlbaum.

Schacter, F. F. (1979). *Everyday mother talk to toddlers: Early intervention.* New York: Academic Press.

Schiefelbusch, R. (Ed.). (1963). Language studies in mentally retarded children. *Journal of Speech and Hearing Disorders, Monograph Supplement No. 10.*

Schiefelbusch, R. (Ed.) (1978). *Bases of language intervention.* Baltimore: University Park Press.

Schiefelbusch, R. (1980). *Nonspeech Language and Communication: Analysis and Intervention.* University Park Press: Baltimore.

Schlanger, B. B. (1973). *Mental Retardation.* New York: Bobbs-Merrill.

Semmel, M. (1967). Language behavior of mentally retarded and culturally disadvantaged children. In J. Magary & R. McIntyre (Eds.), *Distinguished lectures in special education.* Berkeley: University of California Press.

Semmel, M., & Herzog, B. (1966). The effects of grammatical form class on the recall of Negro and Caucasian educable retarded children. *Studies of Language and Language Behavior, 3,* 1–9.

Semmel, M., & Wiig, E. (1980). *Clinical evaluation of language functioning.* Columbus, OH: Charles E. Merrill.

Shotick, A., & Blue, M. (1971). Influence of CA and IQ levels on structure and amount of spontaneous verbalization. *Psychological Reports, 29,* 275–281.

Sidman, M. (1971). Reading and auditory-visual equivalences. *Journal of Speech and Hearing Research, 14,* 5–17.

Sidman, M., & Tailby, W. (1982). Conditional discrimination vs. matching to sample: An expansion of the teaching paradigm. *Journal of the Experimental Analysis of Behavior, 37*, 5–23.

Simmons, J. Q., & Baltaxe, C. (1975). Language patterns of autistic children who have reached adolescence. *Journal of Autism and Childhood Schizophrenia, 5*, 333–351.

Skinner, B. F. (1957). *Verbal Behavior.* New York: Appleton-Century-Crofts.

Snow, C., & Ferguson, C. (Eds.). (1977). *Talking to children: Language input and acquisition.* Cambridge: Cambridge University Press.

Spradlin, J. (1963). Language and communication of mental defectives. In N. Ellis (Ed.), *Handbook of mental deficiency.* New York: McGraw-Hill.

Spradlin, J. E., Cotter, V. W., & Baxley, N. (1973). Establishing a conditional discrimination without training: A study of transfer with retarded adolescents. *American Journal of Mental Deficiency, 77*, 556–566.

Stephens, C. E., Pear, J. J., Wray, L. D., & Jackson, C. S. (1975). Some effects of reinforcement schedules in teaching picture names to retarded children. *Journal of Applied Behavior Analysis, 7*, 433–447.

Stoel-Gammon, C. (1980). Phonological analysis of four Down's syndrome children. *Applied Psycholinguistics, 1*, 31–48.

Stokes, T. F., & Baer, D. M. (1977). An implicit technology of generalization. *Journal of Applied Behavior Analysis, 10*, 349–367.

Stoneman, C., Brady, G. H., & Abbott, D. (1983). In-home observations of young Down syndrome children with their mothers and fathers. *American Journal of Mental Deficiency, 87*, 591–600.

Stremel-Campbell, K., & Campbell, C. R. (1985). Training techniques that may facilitate generalization. In S. F. Warren & A. K. Rogers-Warren (Eds.) *Teaching functional language.* Austin, TX: Pro-Ed.

Stremel, K., & Waryas, C. A. (1974). Behavioral-psycholinguistic approach to language training. *American Speech and Hearing Association Monographs, 18*, 96–130.

Swisher, L. P. & Pinkser, E. J. (1971). The language characteristics of hyperverbal hydrocephalic children. *Developmental Medicine and Child Neurology, 13*, 746–755.

Tager-Flusberg, H. (1981a). Sentence comprehension in autistic children. *Applied Psycholinguistics, 2*, 1–24.

Tager-Flusberg, H. B. (1981b). Pragmatic development and its implications for social interaction in autistic children. Paper presented at the National Society for Children and Adults with Autism. International Conference on Autism: Boston.

Templin, M. (1957). *Certain language skills in children: Their development and interrelationships.* Institute of Child Welfare Monograph No. 26. Minneapolis: University of Minnesota Press.

Terdal, L., Jackson, R., & Garner, A. (1976). Mother–child interactions: A comparison between normal and developmentally delayed groups. In E. Mash, L. Hamerlynch, & L. Handy (Eds.), *Behavior modification and families.* New York: Bruner/Mazel.

Tronick, E., Als, H., & Adamson, L. (1979). Structure of early face-to-face communicative interactions. In M. Bullowa (Ed.), *Before speech: The beginning of interpersonal communication.* Cambridge: Cambridge University Press.

Warren, S. F., & Kaiser, A. P. (1986). Incidental language teaching: A critical review. *Journal of Speech and Hearing Disorders, 51*, 291–299.

Warren, S. F., McQuarter, R. J., & Rogers-Warren, A. K. (1984). The effects of mands and models on the speech of unresponsive socially isolate children. *Journal of Speech and Hearing Disorders, 47*, 42–52.

Warren, S. F., & Rogers-Warren, A. K. (1983). A longitudinal analysis of language generalization among adolescents with severely handicapping conditions. *The Journal of the Association for Persons with Severe Handicaps, 8*, 18–31.

Warren, S. F., & Rogers-Warren, A. K. (1985). Teaching functional language: An introduction. In Warren, S. F. & Rogers-Warren, A. K. (Eds.), *Teaching functional language.* Austin, TX: Pro-Ed.

Weller, C. (1979). Improving syntactical skills of language-deviant children. *Journal of Learning Disabilities, 12*, 470–479.

Wetherby, B. (1978). Miniature languages and the functional analysis of verbal behavior. In R. L. Schiefelbusch (Eds.), *Bases of language intervention.* Baltimore: University Park Press.

Wheeler, A., & Salzer, B. (1970). Operant training and generalization of a verbal-response form in a speech-deficient child. *Journal of Applied Behavior Analysis, 3*, 139–147.

Wheldall, K. (1976). Receptive language development in the mentallly handicapped. In P. Berry (Ed.), *Language and communication in the mebntally handicapped.* London: Edward Arnold.

Wiig, E. (1983). *Let's talk: Inventory for adolescents.* Columbus, OH: Charles E. Merrill.

Wiig, E. H., Lapointe, C., & Semmel, E. M. (1977). Relationships among language processing and production abilities of learning disabled adolescents. *Journal of Learning Disabilities, 10,* 292–299.

Wolfensberger, W., Mein, R., & O'Connor, N. (1963). A study of the oral vocabularies of severely subnormal patients. III. Core vocabulary, verbosity and repetitiveness. *Journal of Mental Deficiency Research, 7,* 38–45.

Zimmerman, I., Steiner, V., & Evatt, R. (1969). *Preschool language scale.* Columbus, OH: Charles E. Merrill.

CHAPTER 25

Spinal Cord Injuries

John A. Jubala and Gilbert Brenes

INTRODUCTION

The various chapters in this handbook make it sufficiently clear that there are quite a variety of ways in which a person can be disabled in life, but spinal cord injuries are even more varied in and of themselves. A person with a spinal injury can be disabled anywhere on a continuum from a mild weakness of a single extremity to complete paralysis of all four limbs and breathing ability. Furthermore, this injury can often be complicated by other injuries that occur at the same time, such as amputations, limb fractures and head injuries. It is seldom possible for a sole health care practitioner to be able to provide for the many medical and psychological needs of the spinal-injured person. This chapter addresses a variety of professions that may need to become involved. Also reflected is the fact that the spinal-injured individual is affected in all aspects of life by this injury.

Sir Ludwig Guttman, one of the internationally acknowledged authorities on spinal cord injury, reports that on a surgical papyrus written about 5,000 years ago by an Egyptian physician, there was the follow-ing summary statement following a description of a complete lesion of the cervical spinal cord: "an ailment not to be treated" (Guttman, 1976, p. 1). Fortunately this adage no longer applies, and the treatment available for persons with spinal injury is complex and comprehensive. However, this is a relatively recent event that only began to take form in this country and in Great Britain during and after World War II (Rusk, 1972; Guttman, 1976). During World War I, the average life expectancy was only 6 to 12 months post-injury, and this increased to a 2-to-3 year span during World War II (Guttman, 1976, pp. 5–6).

Today, the spinal-injured person is able to live a very full and active life, but only after receiving thorough medical care, rehabilitation, and education. Psychological assessment, intervention, and follow-up care are essential aspects of this continuum of care. Most spinal injury rehabilitation teams include many different disciplines, including physicians, nurses, psychologists, physical and occupational therapists, vocational counselors, nutritionists, social workers, home economists and, increasingly, education specialists and bioengineers. However, there is no cure for spinal cord injury as of yet, and the processes of treatment that will be described in this chapter have *adjustment* as a goal.

DESCRIPTION OF THE DISORDER

The spinal cord serves as the major pathway of communication between the brain and the entire rest of the body with the exception of those facial functions that are primarily controlled by the cranial nerves. The spinal cord is also a reflex center in its own right, and not simply an extension of the brain. This means that it is possible that almost every bodily function can be affected by a severe spinal cord injury. The injury is usually caused by a blunt impact to the vertebral body at a particular level, resulting in a progressive insult to the fine architecture and biochemical balance of the much softer spinal cord itself. Once the primary damage is initiated, it continues its destruction of the spinal cord nerve tissue, which is similar to brain tissue. Following the blunt trauma, there is a rupture of small blood vessels and bleeding into the neighboring spaces. The area of bleeding later enlarges with inflammatory and necrosing action that begins to take place. By 4 hours post injury, this process destroys almost 40% of the nerve tissue involved.

Spinal impairment can also arise from diseases as well. The most common include the growth of tumors (either within or outside of the cord), loss of the vertebral architecture from degenerative bone-joint diseases, extrinsic blood clots, infections, ischemia secondary to surgery, and arteriovenous malformations.

The symptoms of the injury can be either temporary or permanent, complete or incomplete. An incomplete lesion means that the injured person will have only certain degrees of sensory and/or motor impairment below the level of the lesion (see section on the impairment of motor function). A complete lesion means a complete lack of sensation and motor function below the level. Any two or more individuals with lesions at the same level can

have completely different medical pictures because of these variations.

Quadriplegia or *tetraplegia* is the term for a complete injury in the cervical (neck) region. Quadriparesis means an incomplete motor injury. Injuries in the thoracic, lumbar or sacral areas will result in either paraplegia if complete, or paraparesis if incomplete. Figure 25-1 provides a comprehensive chart of the vertebral column and nerve distribution.

Impairment of Motor Function

Conventionally, the level of injury is indicated by the most distal, neurologically intact spinal cord segment. In quadriplegia, the level of impairment can range from C1 to C8 (see Figure 25-1). There is no C8 vertebra, but a functional level of C8 can be obtained that is different from either C7 or T1. Individuals with injuries at C1 and C2 will have no motor abilities below the head and will require mechanical assistance with respiration. These individuals often die before medical stability can be achieved. When they survive they are completely dependent.

C3 injuries, at times, result in the sparing of at least some shoulder function, but essentially, this level is very similar to the C1–C2 level as outlined above. At times it is possible for persons at this level of injury to control an electric wheelchair with head movements, but at least a portable respirator will be required.

At C4 it is possible for individuals to breathe on their own, but the upper extremities remain paralyzed and therefore independence of function remains severely limited. At the C5 level this improves somewhat since shoulder and biceps mobility is possible, and the individual may be able to control the electric wheelchair with arm movement. Activities of daily living remain severely curtailed.

At the C6 level and lower, the ability to become independent in living an everyday life becomes more feasible. Much depends on the motivation of the individual and the quality of treatment available, since intensive physical therapy is usually required.

Functional Activities

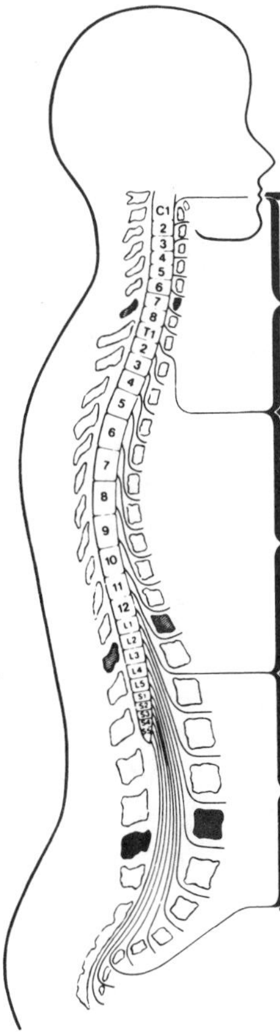

Spinal Cord Segments

Spinal Cord Segment	Eating	Dressing	Grooming	Toileting	Homemaking	Driving	Public Transportation	Wheelchair Transfers	Ambulation	Communications	Bed Transfer	Vocational	Sexual Functioning
Cervical Segments C1–T1 — Neck and arm muscles and diaphragm													
C-1	*	*	*	*	*		*			*	*	**	**
C-2	*	*	*	*	*		*			*	*	**	**
C-3	*	*	*	*	*		*			*	*	**	**
C-4	*	*	*	*	*		*			*	*	**	**
C-5	*	*	*	*	*	*	*	*		*	*	**	**
C-6	*	*	*	*	*	*	*	*		*	*	**	**
C-7	*	*	*	*	*	*	*	✓		*	✓	**	**
C-8	✓	✓	✓	✓	✓	*	*	✓		✓	✓	**	**
T-1	✓	✓	✓	✓	✓	*	*	✓		✓	✓	**	**
Thoracic Segments T2–T12 — Chest and abdominal muscles													
T-2	✓	✓	✓	✓	✓	*	*	✓		✓	✓	✓	**
T-3	✓	✓	✓	✓	✓	*	*	✓		✓	✓	✓	**
T-4	✓	✓	✓	✓	✓	*	*	✓		✓	✓	✓	**
T-5	✓	✓	✓	✓	✓	*	*	✓		✓	✓	✓	**
T-6	✓	✓	✓	✓	✓	*	*	✓		✓	✓	✓	**
T-7	✓	✓	✓	✓	✓	*	*	✓	*	✓	✓	✓	**
T-8	✓	✓	✓	✓	✓	*	*	✓	*	✓	✓	✓	**
T-9	✓	✓	✓	✓	✓	*	*	✓	*	✓	✓	✓	**
T-10	✓	✓	✓	✓	✓	*	*	✓	*	✓	✓	✓	**
T-11	✓	✓	✓	✓	✓	*	*	✓	*	✓	✓	✓	**
T-12	✓	✓	✓	✓	✓	*	*	✓	*	✓	✓	✓	**
Lumbar & Sacral Segments — Hip and knee muscles													
L-1	✓	✓	✓	✓	✓	*	*	✓	*	✓	✓	✓	**
L-2	✓	✓	✓	✓	✓	*	*	✓	*	✓	✓	✓	**
L-3	✓	✓	✓	✓	✓	*	*	✓	*	✓	✓	✓	**
L-4	✓	✓	✓	✓	✓	*	✓	✓	*	✓	✓	✓	**
Hip, knee, ankle and foot muscles													
L-5	✓	✓	✓	✓	✓	*	✓	✓	*	✓	✓	✓	**
S-1	✓	✓	✓	✓	✓	*	✓	✓	*	✓	✓	✓	**
Bowel, bladder, and reproduction organs													
S-2	✓	✓	✓	✓	✓	✓	✓	✓	✓	✓	✓	✓	**
S-3	✓	✓	✓	✓	✓	✓	✓	✓	✓	✓	✓	✓	**
S-4	✓	✓	✓	✓	✓	✓	✓	✓	✓	✓	✓	✓	**

QUADRIPLEGIA (C-1 through T-1)
PARAPLEGIA (T-2 through S-4)

Legend:
- ✓ Normal or near normal function or performance.
- * Needs some type of personal and/or mechanical assistance.
- ** It can be partially available but options need to be discussed on individual basis.
- ☐ Not practical/probable.

Figure 25-1

At C6, finger function is still absent, but wrist extension may be enough to enable the person to transfer in and out of a wheelchair and engage in many other activities of daily living. This is also true at the C7 level. At C8 there is some finger function, although it is not always well-coordinated.

All of the levels from T1 on down are considered as paraplegia, meaning essentially paralysis of the trunk and legs. Trunk paralysis, and the resulting loss of balance, is primarily seen in the T1 to T8 lesions. Ambulation is not feasible at these levels and almost all mobility is achieved by using the arms for transfers and a wheelchair for "ambulation." Walking with long leg braces becomes a possibility around the T12 level, although it requires an enormous amount of physical energy to be successful. Lumbar lesions usually allow for the same possibility of long leg brace-walking, but the energy expenditure remains great. When the lesion is in the sacral area, walking becomes more of a functional possibility, and only short leg braces are usually required.

Impairment of Sensation

Almost all spinal injuries involve the loss of at least some sensation. A complete lesion will mean that the area of sensation loss will roughly follow the same area of motor loss. The loss includes all areas of sensation, including touch, temperature, position sense, and pain. The implications of such a loss are clear, and the injured person is at risk of sustaining damage to the sensory-impaired areas without becoming aware of it until it is perhaps too late. The greatest danger posed by this loss of sensation is the risk of developing decubitus ulcerations or pressure sores. The unrelieved pressure of sitting (or resting one's feet against an object) can easily interrupt the blood flow to that area causing the death of the skin and muscle tissue. Only through vigilant weight shifts can this be prevented. Extremes of temperature must also be avoided for similar reasons.

Other Physical Consequences

The loss of bowel and bladder function is always a complication of a complete lesion. In incomplete lesions, the prognosis for control is much better, but even here there is usually some sort of ongoing care required. Permanent, indwelling catheters usually present a high risk of repeated urinary tract infections, and their use is no longer encouraged. A combination of external sphincterotomy (a surgical procedure), external catheter, urinary drainage collection, and intermittent catheterization usually can control bladder dysfunction.

Loss of bowel control is usually compensated for by establishing a bowel training program. Such programs are individually tailored to the individual's needs and consist of using suppositories, digital stimulation, proper diet and a rigidly adhered-to schedule of when to train. Needless to say, this restricts one considerably.

Sexual dysfunction is another common sequela of injury. The type of dysfunction varies considerably depending on the sex of the injured person and the level and completeness of the injury. In males, the primary area of concern for most individuals is the ability to achieve and maintain an erection. In complete injuries, only a reflex erection is usually possible, and then only in those with cervical or thoracic lesions. Physiological orgasm is not possible in complete injuries, and even a reflex erection is not possible when the lesion is in the lumbar or sacral area. Incomplete injuries increase the possibilities for physiological orgasm and full erectile ability. However, in complete and incomplete injuries alike, the possibility of ejaculating viable sperm is seriously compromised, and fertility is usually not possible. However, some advances have been made in this area in recent research projects (cf. Brindley, 1981; Ellis, 1980; Martin et al., 1983; Perkash et al., 1985).

Injured females have a different set of circumstances. Motor and sensation impairment does not necessarily restrict the possibilities of physical engagement in the sex act. However, the loss of sensation often disallows the achievement of physiological orgasm. Menstruation and fertility are usually unimpaired, although it may take several months for menstruation to occur after the onset of the injury.

The psychological issues involved in sexuality and spinal cord injury will be addressed under the Assessment and Treatment section (p. 431).

Possible Complications Following Injury

Spasticity of the muscles is by far the most common and most annoying complication of injury. Spasticity is usually absent immediately following injury because the state of spinal shock does not allow for reflexive activity below the level of lesion. However, as the state of shock recedes, those individuals with cervical and thoracic lesions are subject to the reestablishment of reflexes, and exaggeration of reflex such as is found in spasticity. This means that involuntary movement of the muscles can occur whenever the reflex is evoked through stimulation. Spasms can be severe, and can seriously interfere with the ability to engage in everyday activities.

Pain is another problem associated with spasticity as well as other conditions. Complete lesions usually produce pain only at the site of injury and usually for a short period of time. More permanent and pervasive pain is usually found only in patients who undergo extensive or multiple surgery. Spinal injuries resulting from bullet wounds also seem to produce considerable pain. Incomplete lesions that leave sensation at least partially intact can lead to a significant amount of pain almost anywhere. In addition, both parasthesias and "phantom pain" are possible and can be the source of extreme discomfort.

Higher-level spinal injuries also can cause difficulties with respiration, body temperature regulation, and a pathological reflex called *autonomic dysreflexia*. Respiratory difficulties usually center around the problems caused by paralysis of chest muscles and the resultant diaphragmatic breathing. This type of breathing is not as deep, and therefore respiratory ailments

can easily become more serious because the individual may not be able to clear the fluid buildup that accompanies such ailments.

Body temperature regulation can often be a problem for those with lesions above the T6 level. As a result, these individuals are more at the mercy of their external environment where their own comfort is an issue. Occasionally, uncontrolled sweating can also occur when the lesion lies in this area.

Since autonomic dysreflexia occurs only in high thoracic and cervical injuries, this pathological reflex can be caused by any noxious stimuli below the level of injury such as a distended bladder, pressure sore, or ingrown toenail. It is manifested by a dangerously rapid elevation of the individual's blood pressure that, if not caught in time, could result in cerebral hemorrhage. The symptoms of dysreflexia include a severe headache, sweating, chills, and a congested nose. This is definitely to be considered an emergency situation and immediate medical attention is required. Other complications include pathological fractures, urinary tract infections, cardiovasiular problems, phlebitis, and hypercalcemia.

The Psychological Experience

Unfortunately, the psychological experience of spinal cord injury is still not fully understood, even though it has been the subject of study for almost 40 years. The reasons for this are numerous, but perhaps the most common one by far is faulty research design. This problem has been well-investigated by Trieschmann (1980), and will not be addressed in any detail here. It has also been our experience that many of the researchers appear to approach the subject of spinal injury with preconceived notions of what it is like to have such an experience, and as a result begin to "force" the data they obtain into their preconceived notions.

In general, much of the literature in the past 40 years has assumed that negative reactions to injury are the norm, and that the injured person must pass through stages in adjusting to the residuals of the injury. Some of the negative stages that have been listed include denial (Wittkower, Gingras, Mergler, Wigdor, & Lepine, 1954); mourning (Dembo, Leviton, & Wright, 1975); denial, depression and anger (Siller, 1969; Kerr & Thompson, 1972); and a variety of other processes including autistic thinking, impulsiveness, explosiveness, egocentricity, frustration, ego decompensation, reaction formation, and so on. Trieschmann (1980) presents an exhaustive list of the negative reactions to spinal injury that have been noted in the literature. However, as Trieschmann also points out, all of these studies are based on the clinical impressions of the authors of the articles, not on empirical studies (1980, p.45). This trend has continued even into the most recent articles such as Ducharme and Ducharme (1984), who insist that spinal injury is an "intense, psychological, narcissistic wound" (p. 155) that almost always leads to "regressive episodes" that "reawakens early fears of abandonment and narcissistic concerns" (p. 155). No empirical evidence is offered to substantiate this assertion.

There are also those researchers who allow for a wide variety of reactions to spinal injury, depending upon the premorbid personality of the injured person. Hohmann (1975), Wright (1983), and Shontz (1971) all agree that there is no single personality type resulting from a spinal cord injury, but there seems to be a predilection for asserting the stages one must go through before the premorbid personality can once again emerge. One outstanding study did approach, in an empirical manner, the question of whether spinal injured individuals were inevitably depressed or not. Fullerton, Harvey, Klein, and Howell (1981) applied research diagnostic criteria to a group of spinal-injured patients in order to determine whether or not a depressive disorder existed. Of a sample of 30 patients, only 9 developed a verifiable depressive disorder after injury. Fullerton makes a distinction between "depression" and "despondency" (which is an everyday affective experience), when describing the emotional sequelae to injuries such as these. While the number of

actual depressive disorders was significant, Fullerton et al. (1981) did not feel that this constituted an *inevitable* reaction to injury.

Some studies have approached the spinal cord individual more naively, and seem to have achieved more complex and substantial results in terms of understanding the experience as a whole (Ray & West, 1984a, 1984b; Vargo, 1984). These researchers approached the subjects without any particular theory or clinical presupposition in mind, and simply asked the individuals to describe what they had been through. The results indicate that the spinal-injured person is capable of going through any of the emotional reactions listed previously, and is also capable of going through the experience with a minimum of negative emotional experience. Of course there are some predictable differences as to who is going to experience what, and these will be discussed in the section on psychological assessment (p. 431). Perhaps Trieschmann (1980) makes the most inclusive statement on what one can actually predict about the psychological experience of and adjustment to spinal injury:

> Studies of outcome or adjustment to spinal injury suggest that youth, a good background, interpersonal support, and financial security are important. Some independence and aggressiveness, creativity, many goals for the future all favor adjustment or productivity after spinal injury. Education and theoretical interests favor vocational success. Basically, it seems that those who were successful at coping with life prior to injury have a greater probability of coping with spinal injury. (p. 85)

Specific Psychological Reactions at Onset

Some basic facts are known about specific initial reactions to spinal cord injuries. It appears that the majority of injured individuals are aware of paralysis immediately upon injury (Heilporn & Noel, 1968). Often, those who are not aware at onset are considered to be in a state of shock, and this state is often given a psychological interpretation similar to or even equivalent with denial (Gunther, 1969; Heilporn & Noel, 1968; Kerr & Thompson, 1972).

Pain is often the overwhelming experience at the time of injury and may supercede all other possible reactions (Harris, Patel, Green, & Naughton, 1973). The same authors also state that as many as 30% of injured persons may also have a concomitant head injury, adding another dimension to the overall psychological experience. Sensory deprivation from the loss of sensation can also have a profound psychological impact. Several similar studies are summarized by Trieschmann (1980, p.40).

Also the fact that many different medications are used on the acutely injured individual, many of which, such as tranquilizers and opiate derivatives, have psychological side-effects. Add to this the possibility of the phenomenon known as *intensive care unit psychosis.*

Braakman, Orbaan, and Dishoeck (1976) found that the majority of those injured wanted to know the facts about their injuries within 2 weeks. However, Caywood (1974) makes it clear that this should not be done in a manner that takes away all hope from the injured individual. It has been our experience that all too often, the managing physician in the acute care environment will make a sweeping statement such as "you'll never walk again," or equally as distressing, "you'll be just fine in a few months," when in reality it is almost impossible to make an accurate prediction at that stage of recovery. Supplying the patient with information is very important, and the manner in which it is delivered is as important as the content.

EPIDEMIOLOGICAL FINDINGS

There are few reliable sources for statistics on spinal cord injury. A data collection center was established in 1972 by the Rehabilitation Services Administration of the Department of Health, Education, and Welfare, in order to gather data from all of the participating centers in the Regional Model Spinal Cord Injury Treatment System. This is a system of medical facilities across the United States that was established to provide proper, comprehensive care for individuals with a spinal injury. This is the first such data bank, and conclusions drawn from the data must be considered tentative as Trieschmann (1980) points out, since only about 15% of the nation's spinal injury patients are treated at these centers and the Data Bank does not include the Veterans Administration or community hospital statistics.

In 1982, the National Spinal Cord Injury Data Research Center, Phoenix, AZ, presented the following figures on these injuries (Young, Burns, Bowen, & McCutchen, 1982). The overall prevalence of spinal-injured individuals living in the United States was estimated to be about 150,000. Of these injuries, 70% were due to trauma and 30% were attributed to diseases such as cancer, neurological disease, and congenital conditions. The majority of the lesions were incomplete, with only 20% being complete. Trauma was responsible for as many paraplegics as quadriplegics.

The profile of a spinal injured individual can be summarized as a young, white male with a high school education. About 82% of those injured were male. The mean age is 28.49 years, and 80% are under 40 years of age. Where industrial accidents were the precipitating factors, the average age was 40.

The majority of precipitating causes were due to vehicular accidents (46%), with sports (16%), falls (15%), and penetrating wounds (12%) following. Sports are responsible more often for quadriplegia (94%) than for paraplegia (6%), but penetrating wounds reverse this trend with 72% paraplegia and 28% quadriplegia. Vehicular accidents and falls are evenly divided between paraplegia and quadriplegia.

Economically, the impact of spinal injury is significant. The annual care nationwide in 1979 was estimated to cost $2.4 billion. The lifetime care cost for a quadriplegic was estimated at about $500,000, and for a paraplegic it was about $250,000. The financial consequences for the family, community, and country are obvious. Much money and time are being spent on retraining, relocation, rehabilitation, and architectural modifications for a population that still has some difficulty with being productive, in the sense of being competitively employed. The 1976–1977 average annual income of the reported spinal injury cases was $10,530, with only about 7% making between $20,000 and $31,000 per year. Furthermore, about 75% of the cases only had a high school education or less, with only 6% having a Bachelor's or post-graduate degree.

DEVELOPMENTAL ISSUES

The incidence of traumatic spinal cord injury in children is very uncommon; several sources report the incidence at less than 1% of all spinal-injured patients (Melzak, 1969; Burke, 1971; Bedbrook, 1981). All sources state that no mortality data are available because of the lack of centralized record keeping. According to Bedbrook (1981), the main differences between the usual adolescent and adult injuries and those in children lie in the clinical presentation and progress of physiological recovery from injury. Evidently, it is more difficult to detect fracture or dislocation of the spine in children, and they recover from spinal shock much more quickly than adults do. However, the incidence of complete injuries is higher in children. Spina Bifida is a leading cause of spinal cord symptomatology in children (see Chapter 28 of this volume).

One other major difference between adult and child spinal injury is the higher incidence of spinal deformity with lordo-scoliosis in children. All other complications known to occur in adults can also occur in children. However, the relationship of the child to his/her family can also be considered a major difference because having a handicapped child is psychologically distinct from having disabled adolescents or adults in the family. Family therapy is called for in such cases much more than it is with the older population of spinal-injured persons.

EDUCATIONAL ISSUES

There are two forms of education that are important to the spinal-injured person. One is the formal education of the injured person; the other is the medical and self-care education usually offered through medical treatment facilities. As was mentioned in the previous section, since very few children present with spinal cord injury, not much has been written on the education of such youths. Bedbrook (1981) makes the point that such children should be educated to the highest possible level rather than simply training them for employment. It is his opinion that the ideal arrangement would be for the child to attend an educational facility where both formal education and continued physical therapy can be provided. Also, a return to the normal school environment is seen as acceptable as long as transportation is not a problem and the school building is accessible to the handicapped.

Little has been written about the formal education of spinal-injured adolescent or adults. Trieschmann (1980) quotes some studies that come to the conclusion that it takes several years after rehabilitation for the individual to feel comfortable enough to either seek employment or schooling (p. 118). However, it has been our experience that while this may be true for someone who is no longer able to return to employment to perform physical labor, it is not at all true of those who are already in school at the time of injury. In fact, it is common practice for the spinal cord injury team at Harmaville Rehabilitation Center to begin a tutoring program in conjunction with the patient's educational system immediately upon admission to the spinal cord unit.

The medical and self-care education of the spinal-injured individual has received considerable attention. This is probably because that type of knowledge is essential for survival once out of the hospital setting. The major areas of educational concern are bowel and bladder management, skin care, sexual functioning, and social skills.

If the patient has the necessary physical skills for self-care, then he or she must be instructed in proper catheterization technique as well as medications and techniques for the prevention of urinary tract infection. The same is true for proper bowel training, including instruction about nutrition and the physiological consequences of diet.

Skin care is the single most important education topic, for skin conditions are costly, time-consuming, and preventable. We have found that a graphic illustration of what a skin condition is, along with how it can be prevented, is a useful and motivating combination.

In addition to these specific medical areas, it is very useful to educate the patient in the general physiology and anatomy of the spinal cord. When this is done, the patient can become an expert on the functions of his or her own body and eventually can learn to intervene without delay as situations arise. Of course this is no substitute for continued medical follow-up and care.

Sexual education remains a very delicate matter, despite the seeming willingness of an individual to talk about this. This topic is often avoided in the acute care setting, and it is usually up to the rehabilitation team to address these issues. Since it is obvious that even very incomplete lesions will often interfere with sexual functioning (especially in the male), it is clear that this issue will at least be raised with every spinal cord patient. We have found that a presentation of at least the basic physiological information about sexual function and spinal cord injury, and the possibilities of what sort of sexual activity and sexuality in general lies ahead, to be the minimum educational experience. Some patients will express a strong disinterest in going any further with this topic, but at least the basics have been presented, and the individual has material to work with when he or she feels ready. A preprinted pamphlet is useful in augmenting this work.

Social skills are more difficult to address, since every individual has a certain degree of social proficiency that is brought to the hospital. A pragmatic approach to this area of education is to have a strong recreational therapy component in the rehabilitation setting. The recreation therapist, through the use of wheelchair sports, recreational outings, and a variety of other explicitly social situations can provide the person with spinal cord injury an invaluable chance to experience the skills needed for survival in the outside world. In addition to this, group sessions, with or without the use of prepared material on social skills, can also provide fertile ground for learning.

In general, an educational program for the spinal-injured person should be a well-prepared, inclusive set of exercises and presentations. Some examples of thorough programs can be found in Benda (1983) and McKrell (1983).

ASSESSMENT AND TREATMENT

Psychological Assessment

The two most important areas of psychological function to be assessed in the spinal-injured person are neuropsychological functioning and the general level of psychological distress or disorder. As has been mentioned, some studies have found a significant percentage of head injury in spinal-injured persons (Harris et al., 1973), and since even the best modern imaging techniques cannot always detect brain lesions, a neuropsychological battery is in order. Since this is primarily a screening measure, extensive testing is not necessarily required. We have found that the administration of the Wechsler Adult Intelligence Scale—Revised (WAIS-R) is a good general indicator of cognitive or psychomotor dysfunction. If elementary or high school transcripts are also obtained, there is often an IQ score on the student record with which to compare the WAIS-R IQ. Even if this information is not available, it is helpful to know what level of intellectual functioning the injured person is at, and this also helps the vocational counselor that may be part of the treatment team as well. For a good introduction to the use of the WAIS-R in neuropsychological assessment, refer to Lezak (1983).

In quadriplegia, standard administration of some psychological tests may have to be modified. For example, in most quadriplegics, the performance subtests of the WAIS-R simply cannot be administered. In these cases, a verbal IQ is sufficient. Also, other tests of neuropsychological function, such as the Wechsler Memory Scale, have subtests that require hand function (in this case, the visual memory subtest). It is possible to administer the rest of the test and then prorate the subtest scores for those sections that require hand function.

Once the examiner is satisfied that basic cognitive abilities are intact, then the rest of the assessment can procede. If problems are evident on the test records, then a more specialized assessment may be undertaken (e.g., Hamsher, 1984). Referral to a neuropsychologist may also be appropriate, if one is available. In any case, the possibility of neuropsychological impairment must be either identified or eliminated, for many so-called "psychological" problems of motivation, affective lability, and so forth can be directly attributable to such neurological causes, and can prove to be a significant barrier to effective rehabilitation.

The more difficult part of the assessment lies in attempting to determine the possible existence of concurrent psychopathology. Standard assessment tools, such as the MMPI, are useful in this endeavor as long as the assessor understands some of the variations that may be apparent on the test record *because* of the spinal cord injury. For example, a significant elevation on the hypochondriasis scale (scale one) of the MMPI is exceedingly common and cannot be interpreted as it would if occurring on the profile of a noninjured individual. One must also be careful with elevations on standardized depression scales, for even though a spinal-injured individual may be experiencing symptoms of depression, the symptoms may not be consistent with major forms of depressive illness.

The *Diagnostic and Statistical Manual, Third Edition (DSM-III)* (American Psychiatric Association, 1980) is a very useful guide to assessing the actual presence of psychological disturbance. Furthermore, it presents a well-ordered approach to the whole field of psychological disturbance even with its recognized limitations.

Other psychological assessment tools may, of course, also be used. One of the most in-depth tools available is the Rorschach, especially as scored and interpreted by Exner (1974; Erdberg & Exner, 1984). However, to become proficient in the scoring and interpretation of this system requires extensive training and time. Assessment tools may also be used for the more general purpose of obtaining a profile of the personality of the patient, and not only to screen for psychopathology. Many such personality profiles are available (cf. Butcher & Keller, 1984), but one must keep in mind that these tests are standardized on a "normal," not spinal injured, sample. Until we become more aware of the psychological changes wrought by spinal injury, interpretation must be cautious.

One assessment measure that has received some attention in the psychological press as being especially appropriate for spinal-injured persons is Rotter's Locus of Control Inventory (Rotter, 1966). This is a simple, forced-choice questionnaire that measures the individual's beliefs in regard to fate and/or self-control. *Internal control individuals* are those who believe that their own actions are responsible for the situation that they find themselves in, not luck or fate seen as an impersonal, external force. *External control individuals* are the opposite and feel that they are the victims of external circumstances beyond their control. Not surprisingly, those spinal injured individuals who have an internal locus of control usually achieve the highest levels of independence and overall psychological adjustment (Albrecht & Higgins, 1977; Shadish, Hickman, & Arrick, 1981).

In general, a careful psychological assessment of the spinal-cord injured individual can provide the entire treatment team with an understanding of the unique set of circumstances, personality and psychological processes that any particular individual possesses. These results can inform physicians, nursing staff, and rehabilitation personnel of the best approach towards any given individual, and can also help prevent unnecessary miscommunications between patient and staff. Symptoms of psychological disturbance can be detected early, and appropriate treatment initiated so that further complications are avoided. Furthermore, eventual vocational counseling can be informed by the results of the assessment, and an objectively based sense of direction can be established.

Psychological Treatment

For the most part, long-term, dynamic psychotherapy is of little use in the early treatment of spinal cord injury. While the patient is still in the acute care hospital, the major themes of simple survival are paramount, and the best psychological approach would be one of crisis intervention and general support. Once the injured person begins a rehabilitation program, more specific techniques of psychological intervention can be applied.

Before these techniques are addressed, one major issue should be mentioned. The use of psychotropic medication is controversial where the treatment of spinal cord injury is concerned. As Trieschmann (1980) has observed, major tranquilizers are seldom necessary, and the same is true for antidepressant medication. One exception to this rule would be in the case of someone who has a primary depression (major affective disorder), and as the result of an attempted suicide, has caused a spinal injury. Since the depression in this case is primary, and since it preceded the spinal injury, antidepressant medication is justified. The type of depression experienced by the majority of spinal cord injured persons is *not* primary but secondary (what used to be referred to as a reactive depression), and there is no justification in the current literature that these types of disorders (if they are indeed disorders) respond to psychotropic medication. Sometimes it is appropriate to be depressed.

There is little doubt that the spinal-injured person is passing through a major emotional upheaval (Dew, Lynch, Ernst, & Rosenthal, 1983), and several studies have documented the changes in general self-concept that usually occur (Mayer & Eisenberg, 1982). As a result, it is the duty of the psychologist to address these issues through a variety of modalities. One of the most popular approaches addressed in the literature is the use of group counseling

techniques. An extensive review of this literature is available in Trieschmann (1980, pp. 157–161), and will not be discussed here. In summary, most group settings emphasize the talking-through of the emotional experiences that one encounters while coping with the residuals of a spinal cord injury. Some group strategies include addressing particular themes during the session, while others are less structured and follow along the lines of traditional psychotherapy. Trieschmann dismisses most group approaches on behavioral grounds and favors direct behavioral therapy instead, since it can result in measurable changes. It is our position that this constitutes a summary dismissal of a technique that many people, patients and therapists alike, feel to be invaluable. Clearly, more research is needed.

Nevertheless, there are many behavior changes that are necessitated by a spinal cord injury. Discreet activities such as dietary control, fluid restriction or increased intake, weight shifts, aerobic and strengthening exercises, medication compliance, and the adherence to a strictly controlled daily schedule of bladder and bowel management are just a few of the new behaviors that have to be learned after spinal injury. Traditional behavioral modification methods do work in these situations, and recent examples can be found in Gordon (1982) and Carr and Wilson (1983). Trieschmann also makes an impressive case for the use of bahavior therapy in her 1980 work (pp. 161–166).

Biofeedback is beginning to be explored as a treatment for several of the physiological sequelae of spinal injury. One such study that used physiological biofeedback techniques for the control of postural hypotension is reported by Brucker and Ince (1977). We have also successfully used electromyographic biofeedback in the control of pain caused by muscle tension as well as in cases of incomplete lesions where spasticity was under some voluntary control.

Hypnosis has also been used, especially in its more indirect forms, for the treatment of some physical complications (Erickson & Rossi, 1979; Bandler & Grinder, 1975) such as spasticity and pain control. The principles of communication theory have also proven useful when applied by the spinal cord team in *all* communications with the spinal injured individual. While this has not been documented thus far in a spinal cord injury study, it has proven effective in many other such situations (Watzlawick, Weakland, & Fisch, 1974; Watzlawick, 1978).

Several sources suggest that the suicide rate is higher in spinal-injured individuals than in the general population (Wilcox & Stauffer, 1972; Trieschmann, 1980). Suicidal individuals should be seen in psychiatric consultation, and long-term follow up is recommended. Evaluation for suicidal ideation should be made a part of all psychological assessments.

Sexual counseling will most probably be required at some time in the spinal-injured individual's rehabilitation. As mentioned earlier, all such individuals should be given at least the rudimentary facts of the sexual effects of spinal injury. Some may not wish to hear more on this topic, but many will. There are many different approaches to how to actually *do* sexual counseling with spinal-injured persons (Chipouras, 1979; Schuler, 1982). Some of the methods used are individual counseling, couple counseling, group counseling, use of visual aids, and a combination of all of these. A firm grasp of the physiological conditions is necessary before the counselor can be effective and reviews of the literature exist for this purpose (Higgins, 1979; Trieschmann 1980). Since infertility is also associated with the sexual sequelae of spinal injury in males, fertility counseling must not be overlooked.

In general, the psychological treatment of spinal cord injured persons varies widely, and is dictated by the presentation of symptoms. The techniques of traditional psychotherapy, group psychotherapy, behavior therapy, psychiatry, hypnotherapy, biofeedback, and behavioral medicine all have their place, and the rehabilitation psychologist must be flexible in approach. We have found that rigid adherence to any one school of treatment philosophy can be detrimental to the patient and leaves certain problems unaddressed.

Medical Assessment

Depending on whether the individual's spinal cord injury is traumatic or pathological, the first point of assessment is either at the scene of the accident or in the physician's examining room. In traumatic injury, the first order of care is to remove the victim from the scene of the accident as carefully as possible. It is sometimes difficult to tell if a spinal injury is present when the victim is unconscious. Emergency medical personnel are well-trained in the proper procedures for removal, stabilization, and maintenance of vital functions in the injured person. Such procedures should not be attempted by the untrained unless immediate loss of life is a danger (e.g., drowning or fire).

Insidious onset of spinal symptoms is sometimes confusing, and we have encountered many patients who have been told at one point that it was "all in their head," when in reality a cervical spondylosis or spinal tumor was in progress. When spinal symptoms are presented, even in psychologically unstable persons, a neurological or neurosurgical evaluation is in order.

When the injured person is finally brought to the hospital, usually through the emergency room, further evaluation is made while life functions are stabilizing. Radiographic studies of the spine are made (including a myelogram if necessary). Physical examination starts with the arrival of the victim, and continues as much as possible while emergency measures are carried through. The decision of whether or not to surgically intervene is made as soon as all systems are stable.

A level of injury (see Figure 25-1) is determined through careful examination of the reflexes, skin sensation, muscle innervation, cardiovascular and respiratory status, and other bodily functions as needed. CAT scans can be useful in imaging the exact nature of the vertebral damage. More recently, nuclear magnetic resonancing has been used for an even clearer picture.

Bladder assessment must be made as soon as possible to avoid distention. If a residual urine of more than 500cc can be catheterized after spontaneous voiding, an indwelling catheter is inserted. Since most traumatic spinal injuries have additional injuries as well, the initial assessment must include all bodily areas of function, including an abdominal and rectal examination.

Once a diagnosis has been made, the patient (if conscious) and family should be informed so that appropriate plans can be made. If the initial assessment has been made in a community hospital or other such limited facility, plans must be made to evacuate the patient to a major medical center where the complex management that is to follow can be carried out most efficiently. The preference here is to admit the patient to a designated regional spinal cord injury center.

Medical Treatment

Medical assessment and treatment are carried on at almost the same time during the initial, emergency phases of the process. One of the first steps of treatment is the immobilization of the spine at the sight of fracture. This can be done through splinting, bracing, casting, or the application of orthoses such as Gardner-Wells tongs or a halo device. During immobilization it is essential that complications are anticipated and prevented. This applies especially to decubitus ulcers, hypercalcemia, muscle and joint contractures, and respiratory problems. Mechanical beds such as the Roto-Bed can decrease the frequency of early complications, but there is no substitute for good nursing care. The patient's position in bed should be shifted every 2 hours, 24 hours a day.

Surgical intervention is usually done during the first 10 days post-injury, if at all. There are arguments both for and against the need for surgery, since surgery may not be helpful in gaining any functional return. The surgeons argue that spinal stability is essential, and it has been our experience that a vast majority of the patients have undergone fusion of the vertebrae at the sight of fracture and the insertion of stabilizing devices, such as Harrington or Luque rods.

Post-surgically, or during the conservative treatment phase, the same attention to details mentioned in the assessment section still applies. Bladder management may now be possible on an intermittent catheterization schedule since fluid intake can be restricted. Gastric distention should be avoided, and an early attempt at initiation and facilitation of bowel movement should be made. Defecation will occur more rapidly and fully if a sitting position can be maintained, since gravity plays a role. Increasing the intra-abdominal pressure can also facilitate emptying of the bowel.

During the first 10 days post-injury, thrombophlebitis and pulmonary emboli are constant dangers. To prevent this, intermittent pneumatic pressure may be employed, as well as the use of elastic garments. The use of miniherparin for anticoagulation is debatable.

In cervical injuries, a respiratory specialist should be consulted to prevent respiratory deterioration. This may be necessary for some paraplegics as well. If the airway becomes obstructed, a therapeutic bronchoscopy can be utilized for clearing. Chest therapy and assistive coughing is mandatory during this stage.

A physical medicine and rehabilitation specialist should be consulted on day one. This will insure the complete prescription of the beginning phases of rehabilitation, and prevent numerous complications. Physical and occupational therapy should be ordered. The therapists should engage the patient in a complete range-of-motion of the affected extremities twice a day throughout the acute care stay. Strengthening of the perceived myotomes should also be initiated. Positioning is important at this stage to prevent contractures. Sitting tolerances should be slowly increased until about a 2 hour tolerance is achieved. Activities of daily living should also be started at this point.

By this stage, the patient will probably be involved in the rehabilitation process almost exclusively. He or she may be transferred to a comprehensive rehabilitation center, where physical and occupational therapy can be received on an intensive basis. This is also where a psychology program is most likely to be initiated, along with vocational counseling, nutritional services, homemaking, recreation, and a driver's evaluation.

Eventually the patient will be verticalized, either through the use of braces or a tilt or standing table. Long bone fractures can occur and should be prevented. The patient may still be losing calcium and phosphorous through the urine at this point, and osteoporosis is a continued threat. Both aerobic and strengthening exercises are important at this time so that the patient does not become sedentary. Studies have shown that sedentary patients have lower high-density lipoproteins, and are therefore at a higher cardiovascular risk (LaPorte et al., 1984).

The goals of rehabilitation are no less than to return the spinal-injured persons to the community at an optimum level of physical, emotional, vocational, and social health. They will have learned advanced wheelchair skills (if the level of injury allows) that go beyond mere propulsion, and transfer and safety techniques will have been taught. As technology expands, these individuals will be able to participate more fully in the mainstream of everyday life.

There is a definite need for long-term follow-up in the spinal-injured persons, and this follow up should not be fragmented into different specialities. One physician or team should be designated as the coordinator of care so that costly duplication of services, or contradictory medical goal-setting can be avoided.

RESEARCH

Throughout this chapter, various suggestions for treatment have been made. There are always ways to improve the existing level of care, both psychologically and medically. But the most important research that is now occuring most probably lies in the area of a *cure* for spinal cord injury. This is the first time in medical history that this

is even being contemplated, for central nervous system damage has traditionally been considered as incurable. The current research basically falls into two categories: acute and chronic phases. Acute care research is primarily concerned with controlling the immediate post-injury processes in the spinal cord such as edema, scarring, and tissue destruction (De la Torre, 1981). Progress is reported monthly in the medical and basic science journals.

Even more encouraging are the results of research in chronic spinal cord injuries. One line of work is the transplantation of the intact omentum to the traumatized spinal cord, and the return of function that follows (Goldsmith, Steward, Chen & Duckett, 1983). Embryonic tissue is also being used in this area (Bunge, Johnson & Thuline, 1983).

Central nervous system regeneration is another new approach, as is surgical transplantation of peripheral and central nervous system tissue to the damaged spinal cord (Kao, Bunge, & Reier, 1983).

Functional electrical stimulation has recently emerged as a potentially excellent treatment for increasing the active return of muscular movements, and also for using paralyzed muscles through artificial control. The work of Petrofsky is seminal in this regard (Petrofsky 1978, 1979; Petrofsky & Phillips, 1979).

Research must also be conducted in psychological areas as well, for we still do not have even a basic understanding of what it is that the spinal-injured individual really undergoes. It would be gratifying to see this knowledge accumulate to the degree that it was with, for example, the process of mourning.

SUMMARY

In this chapter, a spinal cord injury was described as a serious and disruptive experience for any individual to endure. In addition to muscle paralysis, there is also loss of sensation; bowel, bladder, and sexual dysfunction; respiratory and cardiovascular distress; and many other medical complications. Psychologically the individual can, but does not have to, experience the full range of intensive affective states and moods. Major adjustments are required in self-concept, body image, and the everyday routine of behaviors. Proper assessment should be thorough and preferably done by specialists in the treatment of spinal injury.

REFERENCES

Albrecht, G., & Higgins, P. (1977). Rehabilitation success: The interrelationships of multiple criteria. *Journal of Health and Social Behavior, 18*, 36–45.

American Psychiatric Association (1980). *Diagnostic and statistical manual of mental disorders* (3rd ed.). Washington DC: Author.

Bandler, R., & Grinder, J. (1975). *Patterns of the hypnotic techniques of Milton H. Erickson, MD* (Vol. 1). Cupertino, CA: Meta Publications.

Bedbrook, G. M. (1981). *The care and management of spinal cord injuries.* New York: Springer-Verlag.

Benda, S. (Ed.). (1983). *Spinal cord injury nursing education-suggested content.* Chicago: American Spinal Injury Foundation.

Braakman, R., Orbaan, J., & Dishoeck, M. (1976). Information in the early stages after spinal cord injury. *Paraplegia, 14*, 95–100.

Brindley, G. S. (1981). Electroejaculation: Its technique, neurological implications and uses. *Journal of Neurology, Neurosurgery, and Psychiatry, 44*, 9–18.

Brucker, B. S., & Ince, L. P. (1977). Biofeedback as an experimental treatment for postural hypotension in a patient with a spinal cord lesion. *Archives of Physical Medicine and Rehabilitation, 58*, 49–53.

Bunge, R. P., Johnson, M. I., & Thuline, D. (1983). Spinal cord reconstruction using cultured embryonic spinal cord strips. In C. Kao, R. P. Bunge, & P. Reier (Eds.), *Spinal cord reconstruction.* New York: Raven Press.

Burke, D. C. (1971). Spinal cord trauma in children. *Paraplegia, 9*, 1–12.

Butcher, J. N., & Keller, L. S. (1984). Objective personality assessment. In G. Goldstein & M. Hersen (Eds.), *Handbook of psychological assessment.* New York: Pergamon Press.

Carr, S., & Wilson, B. (1983). Promotion of pressure-relief exercising in a spinal injury patient: A multiple baseline across settings design. *Behavioural Psychotherapy, 11*, 329–336.

Caywood, T. (1974). A quadriplegic young man looks at treatment. *Journal of Rehabilitation, 49*, 22–25.

Chipouras, S. (1979). Ten sexuality programs for spinal cord injured persons. *Sexuality and Disability, 2*, 301–321.

De La Torre, J. C. (1981). Spinal cord injury: Review of basic and applied research. *Spine, 6*, 315–335.

Dembo, T., Leviton, G., & Wright, B. (1975). Adjustment to misfortune — A problem of social psychological rehabilitation. *Rehabilitation Psychology, 22*, 1–10.

Dew, M. A., Lynch, K., Ernst, J., & Rosenthal, R. (1983). Reaction and adjustment to spinal cord injury: A descriptive study. *Journal of Applied Rehabilitation Counseling, 14*, 32–39.

Ducharme, S. H., & Ducharme, J. (1984). Psychological adjustment to spinal cord injury. In D. W. Krueger (Ed.) *Emotional rehabilitation of physical trauma and disability.* New York: Spectrum Publications.

Ellis, R. G. (1980). The corona-frenulum trigger. *Sexuality and Disability, 3*, 50–57.

Erdberg, P., & Exner J. E. (1984). Rorschach assessment. In G. Goldstein & M. Hersen (Eds.), *Handbook of psychological assessment.* New York: Pergamon Press.

Erickson, M. H., & Rossi, E. L. (1979). *Hypnotherapy: An exploratory casebook.* New York: Irvington.

Exner, J. E. (1974). *The Rorschach: A comprehensive system.* New York: John Wiley and Sons.

Fullerton, D. T., Harvey, R. F., Klein, M. H., & Howell, T. (1981). Psychiatric disorders in patients with spinal cord injuries. *Archives of General Psychiatry, 38*, 1369–1371.

Goldsmith, H. S., Steward, E., Chen, W. F., & Duckett, S. (1983). Application of intact omentum to the normal and traumatized spinal cord. In C. Kao, R. Bunge, & P. Reier (Eds.), *Spinal cord reconstruction.* New York: Raven Press.

Gordon, W. (1982). The relationship between pressure sores and psychosocial adjustment in persons with spinal cord injury. *Rehabilitation Psychology, 27*, 185–191.

Gunther, M. (1969). Emotional aspects. In R. Reuge (Ed.), *Spinal cord injuries.* Springfield, IL: Charles C. Thomas.

Guttman, L. (1976). *Spinal cord injuries: comprehensive management and research* (2nd ed.). Oxford: Blackwell.

Hamsher, K. deS. (1984). Specialized neuropsychological assessment methods. In G. Goldstein & M. Hersen (Eds.), *Handbook of psychological assessment.* New York: Pergamon Press.

Harris, P., Patel, S., Green, W., & Naughton, J. (1973). Psychological and social reactions to acute spinal paralysis. *Paraplegia, 11*, 132–136.

Heilporn, A., & Noel, G. (1968). Reflections on the consciousness of disability and somatognosis in cases of acute spinal injuries. *Paraplegia, 6,* 122–127.

Higgins, G. E. (1979). Sexual response in spinal cord injured adults: A review of the literature. *Archives of Sexual Behavior, 8*(2), 173–196.

Hohmann, G. (1975). Psychological aspects of treatment and rehabilitation of the spinal cord injured person. *Clinical Orthopedics, 112,* 81–88.

Kao, C. C., Bunge, R. P., & Reier, P. J. (Eds.). (1983). *Spinal cord reconstruction.* New York: Raven Press.

Kerr, W., & Thompson, M. (1972). Acceptance of disability of sudden onset in paraplegia. *Paraplegia, 10,* 94–102.

LaPorte, R. E., Adams, L. L., Savage, D. D., Brenes, G., Dearwater, S., & Cook, T. (1984). The spectrum of physical activity, cardiovascular disease and health: An epidemiologic perspective. *American Journal of Epidemiology, 120,* 507–517.

Lezak, M. (1983). *Neuropsychological assessment* (2nd ed.). New York: Oxford University Press.

Martin, D. E., Warner, H., Crenshaw, T. L., Shapiro, C. E., & Perkash, I. (1983). Initiation of erection and semen release by rectal probe electrostimulation (RPE). *The Journal of Urology, 129,* 637–642.

Mayer, J., & Eisenberg, M. (1982). Self-concept and the spinal cord injured: An investigation using the Tennessee self-concept scale. *Journal of Consulting and Clinical Psychology, 50,* 604–605.

McKrell, J. (1983). *Learning and living after your spinal cord injury.* Pittsburgh, PA: Harmarville Rehabilitation Center.

Melzak, J. (1969). Paraplegia among children. *Lancet, 2,* 45–48.

Perkash, I., Martin, D. E., Warner, H., Blank, M. S., & Collins, D. C. (1985). Reproductive biology of paraplegics: results of semen collection, testicular biopsy and serum hormone evaluation. *The Journal of Urology, 134,* 284–288.

Petrofsky, J. S. (1978). Control of the recruitment and firing frequencies of motor units in electrically stimulated muscles in the cat. *Medical and Biological Engineering, 16,* 302–308.

Petrofsky, J. S. (1979). Sequential motor unit stimulation through peripheral motor nerves in the cat. *Medical and Biological Engineering, 17,* 87–93.

Petrofsky, J. S., & Phillips, C. A. (1979). Constant velocity contractions in skeletal muscle by

sequential stimulation of muscle efferents. *Medical and Biological Engineering, 17,* 583–592.

Ray, C., & West, J. (1984a). Social, sexual and personal implications of paraplegia, *Paraplegia, 22,* 75–86.

Ray, C., & West, J. (1984b). Coping with spinal cord injury. *Paraplegia, 22,* 249–259.

Rotter, J. (1966). Generalized expectancies for internal versus external control of reinforcement. *Psychological Monographs: General and Applied, 80,* 1–28.

Rusk, H. (1972). *A world to care for.* New York: Random House.

Schuler, M. (1982). Sexual counselling for the spinal cord injured: A review of five programs. *Journal of Sex and Marital Therapy, 8*(3), 241–252.

Shadish, W. R., Hickman, D., & Arrick, M. C. (1981). Psychological problems of spinal cord injury patients: Emotional distress as a function of time and locus of control. *Journal of Consulting and Clinical Psychology, 49,* 297.

Shontz, F. (1971). Physical disability and personality. In W. Neff (Ed.), *Rehabilitation psychology.* Washington DC: American Psychological Association.

Trieschmann, R. (1980). *Spinal cord injuries: Psychological, social and vocational adjustment.* New York: Pergamon Press.

Vargo, F. A. (1984). Adaptation to disability by the wives of spinal cord-injured males — A phenomenological approach. *Journal of Applied Rehabilitation Counseling. 15,* 28–32.

Watzlawick, P. (1978). *The management of change: Elements of therapeutic communication.* New York: Basic Books.

Watzlawick, P., Weakland, J., & Fisch, R. (1974). *Change: Principles of problem formation and problem resolution.* New York: Norton.

Wilcox, N., & Stauffer, E. (1972). Follow up of 423 consecutive patients admitted to the spinal cord center, Rancho Los Amigos Hospital, 1 January to 31 December 1967. *Paraplegia, 10,* 115–122.

Wittkower, E., Gingras, G., Mergler, L., Wigdor, B., & Lepine, A. (1954). A combined psychosocial study of spinal cord lesions. *Canadian Medical Association Journal, 71,* 109–115.

Wright, B. (1983). *Physical disability: A psychosocial approach* (2nd ed.). New York: Harper and Row.

Young, J. S., Burns, P. E., Bowen, A. M., & McCutchen, R. (1982). *Spinal cord injury statistics: Experience of the regional spinal cord injury systems.* Phoenix, AZ: Good Samaritan Medical Center.

CHAPTER 26

Stroke

Percy N. Karanjia and Jeff Smigielski

INTRODUCTION

Cerebrovascular disease ranks third as an underlying cause of death in the United States. The direct costs of treatment and caring for the afflicted exceeded $3 billion in 1976 (Baum & Robins, 1981), and the economic loss is considerably greater. Reduction of stroke incidence requires the early identification and treatment of individuals at risk. Once established, atherosclerosis cannot be substantially reversed. Stroke is often unheralded and apoplectic in onset. Little evidence exists that medical or surgical management after the stroke results in substantial reduction of the deficit.

TERMINOLOGY

Many of the definitions used in cerebrovascular terminology were devised in the 1960s before the natural history of the various stroke syndromes were well-known and prior to the comonplace use of panarteriography and cranial computerized tomography. Definitions are therefore likely to change (Millikan, 1975).

The World Health Organization (WHO) has defined *stroke* as "rapidly developing signs of focal (or global) disturbance of cerebral function, leading to death or lasting longer than 24 hours, with no apparent cause other than vascular" (Hatano, 1973). Such a definition excludes transient ischemic attack, subdural and extradural hematoma, but includes subarachnoid hemorrhage. For the purposes of the present discussion, stroke is defined as "a focal neurologic deficit of primary vascular etiology."

A *transient ischemic attack* (TIA) is an episode of focal neurologic dysfunction of vascular origin which resolves completely within 24 hours. The time from onset of symptoms to peak is rapid, usually less than 1 minute, but occasionally up to 10 minutes. Resolution is also rapid, with symptoms or signs clearing spontaneously within a few minutes and rarely lasting longer than 6 hours. TIAs are classified by the location of the compromised vascular area as either carotid or vertebrobasilar arterial in origin. In addition, transient monocular blindness (amaurosis fugax) is, by common agreement, also considered as a

TIA. When the neurologic deficit lasts longer than 24 hours but clears completely within 3 weeks, the term *reversible ischemic neurologic deficit* (RIND) is used. This usually implies a small infarct. If recent worsening of focal ischemic neurologic symptoms or signs is documented by history or by repeated examinations, a *stroke in evolution* is occurring. A stroke is regarded as *completed* when the deficit is stable for 24 hours in the carotid circulation and 72 hours in the vertebrobasilar circulation (Jones & Millikan, 1976; Jones, Millikan, & Sandok, 1980; Patrick, Ramirez-Lassepas, & Snyder, 1980).

EPIDEMIOLOGY

Considerable difficulty is encountered in the study of stroke epidemiology. The population at risk is aged, and the incidence and mortality rates are somewhat low, thereby necessitating large cohorts studied for a prolonged duration. Errors in diagnosis are common. Hemiplegia is commonly equated with stroke and stroke with hemiplegia, neither of which is necessarily correct. The involvement of neurologists with recent epidemiologic programs has corrected this error. However, considerable variation still exists between neurologists in the diagnosis of various subtypes of stroke (thromboembolic, thrombotic, lacunar, etc.).

Prevalence

As at July, 1976, there were 1.7 million survivors of stroke in the conterminous United States. Approximately 75% were in the 55–84 age range, which is a rate of 794 persons per 100,000. An increased prevalence is noted with increasing age and in blacks particularly at younger ages (Baum & Robins, 1981; Kurtzke, 1976).

Survival after stroke appears to be a function of both age and type of stroke. Younger individuals are favored over older ones and ischemia is favored over hemorrhage. Mortality is high in the first month and fluctuates downward over the next 5 or 6 months. Stabilization occurs thereafter (Baum & Robins, 1981).

The occurrence of permanent disability is considerable. The Framingham Study, a prospective, longitudinal epidemiologic study of cardiovascular disease in a free-living community (Framingham, Massachussets) has shown that 31% of stroke survivors are unable to care for themselves, 20% require some ambulatory assistance, 71% suffer vocational incapacity, and 16% remain permanently institutionalized (Gresham et al., 1979).

Incidence

The reported incidence of stroke varies widely depending on the age of the subjects, whether the sample is drawn from hospitalized or the general population, and whether only initial or recurrent strokes are included (Kurtzke, 1976). Data from the National Survey of Stroke estimate that about 297,000 persons are hospitalized annually for initial stroke (140.7/100,000) and 117,000 for recurrences (Robins & Baum, 1981). The incidence of stroke more than doubles with each decade after age 55. Men appear to have an approximately 30% greater incidence of stroke than women. This difference is more pronounced below age 65.

Frequency of Stroke by Type

Atherothrombotic brain infarction is by far the most common variety of stroke, accounting for approximately 50–60% of all strokes including TIAs (Mohr et al., 1978; Kunitz, 1984; Wolf et al., 1978). Cerebral embolism from a cardiac source probably accounts for 20% of strokes, intracerebral hemorrhage (5%), subarachnoid hemorrhage (5%), and a variety of other causes make up the remainder (10%).

DESCRIPTION OF THE DISORDER

The Stroke Syndrome

The presentation of the stroke syndrome is so dramatic that seldom is there doubt as to the diagnosis. It is no wonder that the terms *apoplexy, cerebrovascular accident,* or *stroke* have been applied to describe the disorder. What characterizes the disorder as vascular is its temporal profile — the abrupt onset with loss of neurologic function generally within minutes.

Classification

Depending on the underlying mechanism, stroke may be of either ischemic or hemorrhagic type. Ischemic stroke may be transient and brief (TIA) or permanent (completed stroke) depending on the duration and degree of ischemia. When necrosis of brain tissue occurs, an infarct is said to have occurred. Thromboembolism, thrombosis, or a hemodynamic mechanism is usual. Hemorrhagic stroke is due to rupture or leakage of blood from a vessel, usually an arteriole, but occasionally from a capillary or vein. Depending on its location, the hemorrhage may be intracerebral, intraventricular, or subarachnoid. When blood leaks into an area of ischemic cerebral softening, hemorrhagic infarction is said to have occurred.

ISCHEMIC STROKE

Transient Ischemic Attacks

Transient ischemic attacks (TIAs) have only recently been recognized as being a prelude to cerebral infarction. The probability of infarction occurring after a TIA is five to ten times greater than the age-matched general population. Probably 35% of those destined to have a cerebral infarct will do so within 4 years of a TIA (Mohr, 1978; Wolf, Kannel, & Dawber 1978), although a wide scatter of figures has been published. These differences may be accounted for by the retrospective nature of several of these studies and the varying lengths of observation. Of those who develop cerebral infarction after a TIA, a third will do so within 1.5 months and two-thirds within 3 to 6 months (Wolf, Kannel, & Dawber, 1978). Most of these will only have had a single or a few TIAs. After the first year, the incidence of cerebral infarction is approximately 6% per year compared to 1% in the age-matched general population (Hass, 1977; Whisnant, Matsumoto, & Elveback, 1973). This increased risk is carried throughout life Several studies on TIAs have shown that myocardial infarction, even more frequently than cerebral infarction, may follow a TIA. The cerebral infarct does not necessarily occur in the same distribution as the TIA. TIAs should therefore be considered an indication of diffuse generalized vascular disease.

TIAs occur twice as frequently in men as women (Wolf, Kannel, & Dawber, 1978). Whites are more frequently affected than blacks or orientals, perhaps because of their greater propensity for extracranial atherosclerotic disease. Approximately 85% of all TIAs occur in the carotid distribution, the vertebrobasilar circulation being affected in the remainder with both circulations affected occasionally.

Pathogenesis

Studies of cerebral blood flow (CBF) and metabolism in experimental animals using microelectrode, radioisotope mapping, and autoradiography have yielded important physiologic information about cerebral circulation. In humans, a variety of noninvasive brain imaging techniques, most recently positron emission tomography (PET) and magnetic resonance imaging (MRI), have done much to enhance our knowledge of the ischemic cerebrum.

Brain blood supply is maintained constant within a narrow range by a variety of mechanisms: (a) Brain areterioles may constrict or dilate depending on the arterial blood pressure within the range of 60 to 160 millimeters of mercury, and thereby maintain constant blood flow. This is known as autoregulation. If the blood pressure shifts rapidly and is outside this range, blood flow will vary directly with blood pressure (Strandgaard et al., 1973). If the artery is narrowed (stenosis) or occluded, alternate sources of blood supply (collaterals) may be found. If the pressure in these collateral vessels is at the lower limit of autoregulation, a fall in systemic blood pressure could result in focal symptoms. Once brain ischemia is established, autoregulation is suspended in the ischemic region, and CBF will vary with blood pressure; (b) Pressure sensitive receptors in the carotid bulb reflexly alter heart rate and peripheral resistance reflexively (baroreceptor reflex) and insure a constant arterial pressure head despite postural change. Age, atherosclerosis, disorders of the autonomic nervous system, and drugs, particularly antihypertensives, may interfere with this reflex; (c) CBF is coupled with cerebral metabolism. When matabolic needs rise or fall, blood flow follows. Metabolites, such as carbon dioxide and lactate, are powerful regulators of the vasculature. This is chemically mediated. Changes in the local ionic mileu of extracellular fluid, particularly hydrogen, bicarbonate, and postassium ions, also have a direct effect on the vascular smooth muscle (Betz, 1972).

Under physiologic conditions, mean hemispheric CBF is 50–60 mls/100 gm brain tissue/minute. As CBF drops, the amount of oxygen extracted by brain tissue from the blood increases. When CBF falls to approximately 20 mls/100 gm/min, the brain is significantly deprived of oxygen. Water begins to accumulate within the cells. Electrical activity ceases on the electroencephalogram. If CBF falls further to 10 mls/100 gm/min, the cell is unable to maintain its energy production and ionic homeostasis. Levels of high energy phosphates within the cell rapidly fall, and efflux of potassium ensues (Branston, Strong, & Symon, 1977). If flow is rapidly resumed, total recovery may occur. It not, the tissue is irreversibly damaged resulting in an infarct. These thresholds in ischmia have been labeled *the ischemic penumbra* (Astrup, Siesjo, & Symon, 1981).

The pathogenesis of TIAs may now be understood; a fall in blood flow such that cortical electrical activity is temporarily suspended or brief complete ischemia with rapid restoration of flow. A drop in blood pressure in brain arteries or vascular occlusion due to embolism are the principal causes.

Embolism

The idea that embolism may be the cause of TIAs stems from the observation that some emboli having once been carried into the cerebral circulation occlude the lumen, then fragment and get carried distally into smaller branches. This notion gains support from the following: (a) Angiographic data that demonstrate an occlusion which is not present on subsequent angiography; (b) Observations of the retinal blood vessels during amaurosis fugax. These have demonstrated greyish-white plugs of fibrin platelet material temporarily occluding the retinal arteriolar lumen (Fisher, 1959; Russell, 1961). Bright-orange cholesterol material has been identified (Hollenhorst, 1961) lodged at the bifurcation of retinal vessels in patients with ulcerative carotid disease; (c) Thrombi adherent to ulcerated plaques are seen by surgeons, and other similar thrombotic material has been documented within arteries (Gunning et al., 1964); (d) Attacks affect both the retina and the brain. These are two different circulations but they are within the same arterial tree consistent with embolism; (e) TIAs stop once complete vascular occlusion occurs; (f) Treatment with antiplatelet agents, anticoagulants, or surgery diminishes the frequency of attacks.

The most common cause of TIAs is artery-to-artery emboli from an atherosclerotic arterial plaque. Fibrin and platelets adhere to the surface of the plaque and form aggregates which may later embolize. Hemorrhage may occur into the plaque itself, increasing the degree of stenosis. Local arterial trauma and consequent thrombus formation (Gunning et al., 1964), bleeding (dissection) into the vessel wall (Bladin & Merory, 1975), berry aneurysms (Fisher, Davidson, & Marcus, 1980; Stewart et al., 1980), and different local arterial disease are other less common causes of TIAs.

The heart is a major source of cerebral emboli, accounting for at least 20% of cerebral infarcts (Mohr et al., 1978), but only 5% of TIAs (Yatsu & Mohyr, 1982). When the left heart chambers dilate and function poorly (either due to disease of the valves, or the heart muscle itself), clots tend to form because of stasis within the chambers. Embolism may then occur particularly if there is an associated heart rhythm disturbance. The most important of these valvular conditions is mitral stenosis (a narrowing of the mitral valve), and the most important heart rhythm disturbance is atrial fibrillation.

Hemodynamic

TIAs may occur when multiple major vessels are stenotic or occluded, since the brain may then be critically perfused by a single vessel. Occasionally, high grade stenosis of single major vessels may produce the same effect. Such TIAs tend to be highly stereotyped, incomplete, and of slower onset than when due to emboli. Vascular insufficiency appears to be more common in the vertebrobasilar than in the carotid circulation. Drops in blood pressure of any cause in such circumstances may result in recurrent focal cerebral ischemic episodes (Denny-Brown, 1960).

Another hemodynamic mechanism for TIA is the *vascular steal*, which occurs typically when the proximal subclavian artery is occluded so that there is poor blood flow to the arm. Exercise of the arm in such a case results in vertebrobasilar symptoms, since blood now flows in a reverse direction down the vertebral artery in an attempt to supply the arm muscles. The net result is brainstem ischemia (Reivich et al., 1961).

Intermittent compression of the vertebral arteries by a cervical osteophytic spur in certain neck positions may occasionally result in significant reductionof vertebral blood flow, particularly if one vertebral artery is hypoplastic and adequate collateral flow from the carotids is unavailable (Bauer, Sheehan, & Meyer, 1961).

Hematologic diseases are associated with TIAs. Polycythemia (increase in the red cell count), sickle cell anemia, and abnormalities of serum proteins result in increased blood viscosity, sluggish blood flow, TIA, and infarction. Factors other than viscosity, such as platelet activation, may be important in such individuals. Thrombocytosis (increase in the platelet count), whether idiopathic or of known cause, is associated with an increased incidence of TIAs. Hypercoaguable states, including consumptive coagulopathy and hyperfibrinogenemia, result in infarction rather than

TIA (Buonanno et al., 1980). In terminal cancer and other debilitating disorders thrombi may form on heart valves and embolies resulting in stroke (Kooikier, McLean, & Sumi, 1976).

Inflammatory vasculitides cause thrombosis of vessels, particularly in small arteries and arterioles. Microembolism may also occur.

Currently, it is believed that vasospasm plays little if any place in stroke other than association with subarachnoid hemorrhage or migraine.

CLINICAL FEATURES

Symptoms and signs of a TIA depend on the anatomic location of ischemia. TIAs occur 80% of the time in the internal carotid artery distribution and 20% in the vertebrobasilar circulation. In some cases, it is not possible to be certain which vascular territory is involved. Particular difficulty arises as the physician rarely sees the individual during the attack and has to rely on observations made by a nervous patient or excited family. The patient may perceive his deficit in a way different from that of an examiner. For instance, it is commonplace to hear a weak face or limb being described as numb. This is probably not a simple semantic error, as a weak body part probably does produce an abnormal sensation to its owner, although it is not absence of sensation or numbness. True sensory loss on the other hand is infrequent.

Motor weakness and numbness are the most common complaints in the carotid distribution. The face and arm are maximally affected. If the dominant hemisphere contralateral to the ischemic hemisphere is involved, speech may not be understood and language used incorrectly (aphasia). Such an individual is often considered "confused." Slurred speech (dysarthria) is common, but of no value in differentiating a carotid from vertebrobasilar TIA. Inability to initiate speech, or arrest during speech occurs less commonly. In both cases, vocalization is possible. Aphonia (absence of vocalization) of brainstem origin may mimic this. Specific testing is required to differentiate the two conditions.

Sudden painless temporary visual loss (amaurosis fugax) is diagnostic of disease in the internal carotid artery distribution. The symptom is often described as a *curtain descending* or a fog over one eye, and must be differentiated from a homonymous hemianopsia (visual loss in similar fields of both eyes). This may be done by covering one eye at a time and noting whether the deficit is in one or both eyes. Homonymous hemianopsia is caused by ischemia in either carotid or vertebrobasilar circulation.

Symptoms in the vertebrobasilar circulation are more protean. Unilateral or bilateral weakness or numbness may occur, sometimes shifting from side to side in different attacks. When numbness is present circumorally, particularly in association with sensory symptoms of arm and leg, it is likely to be of brainstem origin.

Staggering due to cerebellar ataxia (incoordination) is common and needs to be differentiated from weakness and labyrinthine dysfunction. Vertigo is always present in the latter. Profound vertigo is generally due to primary labyrinthine disease rather than brainstem ischemia, but lesser degrees of vertigo are common symptoms of vertebrobasilar insufficiency. Deafness is rare. Difficulty in swallowing (dysphagia), particularly to liquids, may be present. Nausea, vomiting, hiccoughs, and yawning, together with other symptoms of brainstem dysfunction (when present) indicate medullary ischemia. These symptoms are often ignored by patient and physician alike.

Double vision (diplopia) is common and is diagnostic of vertebrobasilar ischemia. Sometimes it is interpreted as blurred vision. Closure of one eye will eliminate the diplopia, proving its origin from both eyes and differentiating it from monocular diplopia which is generally a symptom of hysteria. Homonymous visual field losses are more frequently of vertebrobasilar than carotid origin, whereas total visual loss, although rare, indicates vertebrobasilar ischemia.

Drop attacks, wherein the individual suddenly loses muscle tone and briefly falls to the floor without obvious loss of consciousness, must be differentiated carefully from syncope and seizure. In the former, premonitory signs such as a lightheaded feeling, rising sensation in the epigastrium, and palpitations are present. In the latter, consciousness is clearly lost, involuntary limb movements may be present, and on regaining consciousness, confusion is noted. Loss of consciousness occurs infrequently in TIA and, when it does, is generally accompanied by other signs of brainstem ischemia.

Headache occurs in about one-third of TIAs (Portenoy et al., 1984; Grindal & Toole, 1974). It is more common in TIAs of vertebrobasilar than of carotid origin. The location of headache is frontal and retroorbital on the side of the ischemia in carotid disease and occipital in vertebrobasilar disease. It usually accompanies or follows the ischemic deficit and has no prognostic value.

The neurovascular examination is directed at determining the cause of the cerebral ischemia. Particular attention is paid to the peripheral pulses. If, for instance, the rhythm is irregular, atrial fibrillation may be suggested. Absence of a pulse indicates occlusion due to atherosclerosis or embolism.

Measurement of blood presure is of extreme importance since hypertension is a major cause of stroke. Particular attention is paid to the equality of blood pressure in the upper arms. If the subclavian artery is occluded the blood pressure will be lower in that arm. Such a condition in the presence of brainstem ischemic symptoms may suggest the *subclavian steal syndrome* (Reivich et al., 1961) as the underlying mechanism for symptoms.

Auscultation over the carotid or vertebral arteries may reveal a murmur (bruit) which, when found ipsilateral to the hemisphere with TIA, makes it probable that the two are causally related. Carotid bruits are best heard at the angle of the jaw and along the anterior aspect of the sternomastoid muscle, whereas those of vertebral origin are noted over the mastoid bone or posterior edge of the sternomastoid muscle. Murmurs radiated from the heart are best heard at the root of the neck and are thereby differentiated. Duration, intensity, pitch, and position of the bruit in the cardiac cycle, whether systolic or diastolic, are analyzed. A long, high-pitched systolic bruit, particularly one that spills over into diastole, indicates a high-grade stenosis.

Bruits are due to turbulence in the vascular stream and begin to appear once the residual arterial lumen approaches 2.5 to 3 mm. The duration, intensity, and pitch increase, with the bruit remaining systolic until 80–90% of cross-sectional lumen is compromised when a diastolic component may be added. The intensity of the bruit now diminishes, and with higher grades of stenosis (0.5–0.8 mm residual lumen) the bruit may be absent altogether (Lees & Kistler, 1978). According to Thompson (Thompson, Patman, & Persson, 1976), 75–85% of internal carotid artery stenoses are accompanied by audible bruits, but this figure may be somewhat generous. Supraclavicular arterial bruits occur in 30–40% of young healthy adults and are generally of no cons equence (Fowler & Marshall, 1965).

Recent epidemiologic data suggest a 4–5% prevalence rate of mid-cervical arterial bruits in persons over age 45 years, and increasing with age (Heyman et al., 1980; Sandok et al., 1982). A third of these are symptomatic (Sandok et al., 1982). Women are affected more than men, but the stroke risk appears to be higher in men than women. In two large epidemiologic studies a stroke rate of approximately 2% was noted in the individuals with asymptomatic bruits (Heyman et al., 1980; Hennerici, Aublich, Sandmann, & Freund, 1981). Once an asymptomatic bruit is discovered, further tests may reveal this to be due to an asymptomatic arterial stenosis. In such an event, a high probability of stroke is present once a stenosis of 80% or greater is documented (Roederer et al., 1984). When vascular risk factors are present, the risk of stroke increases further.

Attention to the general physical examination may yield clues to the cause of stroke. For instance, small hemorrhagic skin lesions (petechiae) may be noted in inflammatory disorders of the blood vessels and birthmarks (cutaneous nevi) in association with arteriovenous malformations. Visualization of the retinal blood vessels may reveal the pathology if fibrin-platelet aggregates, bright cholesterol plaques, or perhaps some unusual inflammatory disease is seen.

The neurologic examination will help pin-point the anatomic location of the lesion when particular attention is paid to the patterns of weakness, sensory loss, cranial nerve dysfunction, and cognitive dysfunction. The underlying pathology may then be inferred but laboratory investigations are usually needed for a definitive diagnosis.

INVESTIGATIONS

Knowledge of the many disorders that may manifest themselves as clinical stroke syndromes is necessary for the judicious selection of laboratory tests. When associated medical diseases are present these must be appropriately investigated as part of a complete investigation. Each patient is unique and laboratory investigations must be individualized. Commonly obtained tests and the medical disorders for which they are ordered are as follows:

Test	Disorder
Hematocrit, hemoglobin	Polycythemia, anemia
White blood cell count	Leukemia, infections
Platelet count	Thrombocytosis, thrombocytopenia
Sedimentation rate (ESR)	Vasculitis
Blood glucose	Diabetes
Serum sodium, potassium, BUN, creatinine	Electrolyte disturbances may mimic stroke or be a result of stroke

Cholesterol, triglycerides	Hyperlipidemia
VDRL	Syphilis
ECG (EKG)	Myocardial infarct, arrhythmia
Chest X-ray	Carcinoma, TB, sarcoid, heart size, etc.
Urinalysis	Bacterial endocarditis, fat embolism, general medical screen

Computerized tomography (CT) scan is obtained whenever there is any question about the diagnosis of TIA, and prior to anticoagulation. It helps to document whether an infarct, hemorrhage, or some other unsuspected cause for the TIA is present, but must be only interpreted in the light of the clinical history.

To determine the cause of the TIA, several other diagnostic tests have been advocated. These fall into two general categories: (a) noninvasive, and (b) invasive.

Noninvasive diagnostic techniques may be indirect or direct. Indirect techniques (e.g., oculoplethysmography) measure flow related variables, such as blood pressure and pulse arrival time distant from the artery being studied (Gee, 1978; Kartchner et al., 1976). Direct techniques include bruit analysis by placing a microphone over the carotid artery and subjecting it to spectral analysis (Lees & Kistler, 1978). This is an accurate way of determining the residual arterial lumen but is only of value if a bruit is present.

Duplex scanning is an elegant technique using ultrasound in conjunction with pulsed doppler. Currently it is the most accurate noninvasive method of evaluating the carotid bifurcation for disease. Noninvasive tests are useful screening procedures in the patient with an asymptomatic bruit, to follow patients with known disease who are not operative candidates or after carotid surgery, and to select patients for angiography when medical or other factors make arteriography undesirable.

Invasive techniques of visualizing the vasculature include digital subtraction, venous angiography, and conventional arteriography. The former technique was initially received with enthusiasm, since views of the carotid bifurcation and vertebral origin could now be obtained by a venous injection, thus eliminating the risks associated with arterial catheterization. However, the procedure is not risk-free and the vascular detail often inadequate, resulting in the technique falling from favor. Selective arteriography remains the best way of studying the vessels and should be performed in all patients for whom surgery is contemplated. Briefly, the technique consists of threading a catheter via the femoral artery and aortic arch into the selected vessel and injecting an iodinated radioopaque dye. X-ray films are obtained to visualize the origins of the cervical vessels using conventional X-ray or a digital technique. The procedure carries a small risk of producing a stroke if a piece of atheromatous material gets dislodged, clot forms on the tip of the catheter, air is accidentally injected, or vascular spasm is precipitated. In older individuals with poor renal function, the dye load may precipitate renal failure. Attention to adequate hydration before and after the procedure, and especially to the site of arterial puncture for bleeding after the procedure, is mandatory.

MANAGEMENT

The treatment of each patient must be individualized. The cause of the TIA must be rectified if possible, and further events prevented by aggressive management of risk factors.

Medical management consists of treatment of hyertension, diabetes, hyperlipidemia, or other cause when present. A decision is simultaneously made as to whether mdical or surgical therapy is indicated. There is general consensus that the individual who has suffered a TIA and has a high grade carotid stenosis or ulceration should have surgery (carotid endarterectomy), provided no major medical contraindication is found and a surgeon who has demonstrated a low morbidity/mortality rate for the procedure is available. If the individual is not a surgical candidate, antiplatelet aggregating agents such as aspirin or dipyridamole or formal anticoagulation with coumadin may be considered. There is considerable debate at the present time as to which therapeutic modality is superior. For further discussion on this issue the reader is referred to several recent reviews (Toole, 1974a & b; Heck, 1985; Robertson, 1985; Kistler, Ropper, & Heros, 1984a & b; Millikan & McDowell, 1978).

COMPLETED STROKE

Once a neurologic deficit is stable, a completed stroke is said to have occurred. This implies that infarction of brain tissue — death of astrocytes, glia, and the vasculature — has occurred.

Pathogenesis

Under aerobic conditions, the brain relies on oxygen and glucose for its function. Under conditions of ischemia, however, metabolism is anaerobic. Interruption of the cerebral circulation results, within seconds, in cessation of electrical activity followed within minutes by major disruption of ionic homeostasis, particularly of potassium and calcium. The net result is energy failure. Calcium-activated release of free fatty acids and tissue lactic acidosis due to anaerobic glycolysis develop and result in irreversible tissue damage (Raichle, 1983).

Brain capillaries are relatively resistant to ischemia but, when the vascular endothelium is made ischemic, the normally tight junctions between cells are loosened, allowing leakage of plasma into surrounding tissue. This results in brain swelling or "edema." If the vessel wall is necrotic, cellular blood elements, particularly red blood cells, may exit and convert a previously "pale" infarct into a hemorrhagic one.

Microscopic changes begin to appear in approximately 6 hours after the ischemic episode. Tissue necrosis occurs followed by

cavitation and glial scar formation over a period of months.

If the infarct is massive, as may occur when the entire internal carotid or middle cerebral artery distribution is infarcted, severe swelling of the brain occurs within hours, reaching a maximum by 3 to 4 days. Brain structures are displaced and compressed. The medial part of the temporal lobe (uncus) may be forced through the tentorial notch, compressing and displacing the brainstem (uncal herniation). The oculomotor nerve may be compressed as it passes through the notch resulting in an ominous sign, the fixed dilated pupil. Damage to vital brainstem structures results in death.

Infarction in the vertebrobasilar circulation results in death when vital brainstem structures are directly destroyed or indirectly by extrinsic pressure as occurs in cerebellar swellling.

Etiology

The most common causes of cerebral infarction are: (a) intra/extracranial atherothrombosis, (b) cerebral embolism from the great vessels or heart, (c) prolonged severe hypotension (global cerebral ischemia), and (d) vascular spasm due to migraine or subarachnoid hemorrhage.

Several uncommon causes are listed below:

Abnormality in	Disease
Blood cellular elements	Polycythemia vera, sickle cell anemia
	Leukemia
	Thrombocytosis
Coagulation	Disseminated intravascular coagulopathy (DIC)
	Thrombotic thrombocytopenic purpura

	Circulating agents (lupus anticoagulant)
	Homocystinuria
Viscosity	Dehydration
	Macroglobulinae-mia, myeloma
Vessel wall	Inflammatory arteritides
	Trauma
	Dissection
	Fibromuscular dysplasia
	"Moya-moya" disease

Clinical Features

Cerebral infarction is generally easy to recognize because of the abrupt nature of its onset and the permanence of its signs. However, when the onset is more gradual, the picture may evolve over several days, thereby taxing the diagnostic skills of the physician.

The nature of the symptoms and signs depend on which brain structures are affected by ischemia and by the underlying pathologic changes. Knowledge of vascular anatomy is therefore essential to localize which specific arterial territory is affected. Symptoms and signs which help to differentiate whether the arterial territory involved is carotid or vertebrobasilar are set out in the Tables 26-1 and 26-2.

Anterior Circulation Ischemia — Large Vessels

Occlusion of the internal carotid artery is commonly due to atherosclerotic thrombosis at or just above the carotid bifurcation (Fisher, 1976). Trauma, dissection, and

embolism are other causes. The occlusion can be asymptomatic when the collateral supply is adequate, but TIAs followed by cerebral infarction are the rule (Fisher, 1976).

Amaurosis fugax frequently antedates hemispheric TIAs. It indicates internal carotid artery disease in at least a third of patients (Fisher, 1959; Adams et al., 1983; Harrison & Marshall, 1985). Occasionally an embolus to the central retinal artery or its branches causes permanent visual loss.

When the infarct affects both middle and anterior cerebral artery territories, the diagnosis of occlusion of the internal carotid is certain. If, however, the middle cerebral artery territory is solely involved, as often is the case because the anterior cerebral artery receives blood from its fellow artery of the opposite side, then differentiation from internal carotid occlusion is only possible at angiography.

Ischemia of either hemisphere due to occlusion of the internal carotid or middle cerebral artery results in contralateral motor paralysis (hemiplegia) and sensory loss (hemianesthesia). Either of which may be incomplete (hemiparesis, hemihypesthesia). If these signs occur singly, they are more likely to be due to infarction in the deeper structures such as the internal capsule and the thalamus, respectively. This is because the same artery supplies both motor and sensory functions over the cortex, but not in the deep structures.

Disturbances of Motor Function

Paralysis of arm and leg may be complete, but more often, motor weakness occurs. The arm is affected more than the leg, the hand being maximally affected. Incoordination of fine motor hand movements results in the patient having particular difficulty in buttoning clothes, picking up small objects from flat surfaces, and so forth. The hand is used as a whole unit without the independent use of fingers, as does a 1-year old child. Weakness is also marked at the shoulder such that combing the hair or scrubbing the back become particularly difficult. Leg weakness affects the proximal hip flexors, flexors of the knee,

Table 26-1. Relative Frequency of Symptoms in Carotid and Vertebrobasilar Circulations

SYMPTOMS	CAROTID	VERTEBROBASILAR
Amaurosis fugax	Very common	Never
Language disturbance	Very common	Never
Diplopia	Never	Very common
Visual field loss	Uncommon as the only symptom	Very common
Vertigo	Uncommon	Very common
Tinnitus	Never	Common
Dysarthria	Common	Very common
Drop attack	Never	Common
Weakness	Very common	Very common
Staggering	Common	Very common
Numbness and paresthesia	Very common	Very common
Bilateral symptoms	Uncommon	Common
Hiccoughs	Never	Common

Table 26-2. Relative Frequency of Signs in Carotid and Vertebrobasilar Circulations

SIGNS	CAROTID	VERTEBROBASILAR
Aphasia	Very common	Never
Apraxia	Very common	Rare
Facial weakness:		
supranuclear	Very common	Rare
infranuclear	Never	Very common
Bulbar weakness:		
supranuclear	Common	Common
infranuclear	Never	Common
Oculomotor deficit:		
conjugate	Common	Common
dysconjugate	Never	Very common
Homonymous hemianopsia	Common	Very common
Hemiplegia	Very common	Very common
Quadriplegia	Never	Common
Hemisensory loss	Common	Common
Bilateral sensory loss	Never	Common
Crossed signs (ipsilateral cranial nerve with contralateral long tract)	Never	Very common
Cerebellar ataxia	Never	Very common
Loss of consciousness	Rare	Common

and dorsiflexors of the ankle maximally, a pattern common to all lesions affecting the corticospinal tracts. When the anterior cerebral artery territory is infarcted, severe leg weakness occurs.

Facial weakness affects the lower face more than the upper, so that the patient can wrinkle his/her forehead and shut his/her eye, at least partially (supranuclear palsy). Sparing of the upper face occurs because the forehead receives its motor supply from both hemispheres. If the facial nerve itself is paralyzed (infranuclear palsy), rather than its supranuclear control pathway, then the upper and lower face are equally affected. Strokes affecting the brainstem result in such a pattern of facial weakness. Saliva drools from the corner of the mouth; tears spill over the face rather than moisten the eye due to weakness of the lower lid, and together with incomplete closure of the eyelids, allow air to dry the eye; food collects in the mouth on the paralyzed side; the initial phase of swallowing is disrupted; and the speech tends to slur. Tongue and pharyngeal weakness is usually transient.

Muscle tone in the initial stages is flaccid, but gradually increases after several days to become spastic. Spasticity is useful in maintaining posture and results in the typical hemiplegic posture with the arm held abducted, flexed, and internally rotated at the shoulder; flexed and pronated at the elbow; and flexed at the wrist and finger joints. The lower extremity is maintained adducted and extended, the foot being plantar flexed and inverted.

Disturbances of Sensory Function

Since the cortex is largely concerned with discriminating functions rather than primary sensory modalities, it is these discriminating functions that suffer maximally after a stroke. Minor degrees of sensory loss are commonplace, but dense sensory loss is unusual unless the thalamus or its cortical projections are destroyed. Typically, the patient perceives touch but fails to recognize objects placed in the hand with eyes closed (astereognosis). Manipulation of the object by the fingers is faulty despite good motor movements in part because proprioception is significantly affected. If the arms and hands are held outstretched with eyes shut, the fingers will be noted to make searching, "piano playing" movements despite the absence of weakness (pseudoathetosis). Astereognosis results in the complaint that objects held in the hand are lost without awareness. Functional impairment is significantly greater than the motor weakness suggests.

Integration of all sensory information, including vision and hearing, is necessary for awareness of the body image and extrapersonal environment. This is a function of the nondominant parietal lobe. Gross disturbances of the body image may result when this hemisphere is rendered ischemic. Paralysis may be denied (denial) or the patient may even claim that his limb belongs to someone else (anosognosia). Visual or auditory space on one side may be ignored despite the ability to see and hear. Touch applied simultaneously to both sides of the body may be ignored on the affected side, a phenomenon called *extinction*. A similar effect is demonstrated by simultaneously stimulating both visual fields. Right and left body parts may be confused. Apraxia, or the inability to perform a motor act in the absence of paralysis, is common. Two frequent varieties of apraxia are: (a) the inability to copy a three-dimensional figure (constructional apraxia), and (b) the inability to dress or groom oneself, so that pajamas may be worn only on one side of the body or a shirt inside out (dressing apraxia). This complex of denial and neglect greatly impedes rehabilitation efforts.

Disturbance of Language

Ischemia of the middle cerebral artery territory of the dominant hemisphere results in a true disturbance of language (aphasia) together with contralateral weakness and sensory loss. Grammar, word choice, and word-finding errors are present. Initially, little or nothing may be said, although vocalization is possible. At other times no sense can be made of what is said and a diagnosis of "confusion" is erroneously made.

Evaluation of language must be systematic. Cerebral dominance must first be established. The hand used for writing may not accurately reflect cerebral dominance. Inquiry should therefore be made into which hand is used to throw a ball, strike a blow, flip a coin, and so forth. A family history of left-handedness is useful. The population is 90% right-handed, 99% of whom are left-hemisphere dominant for language. Of left handers, 60% are left-hemisphere dominant for speech, whereas 40% are right-hemisphere dominant (Benson & Geschwind, 1968). Spontaneous speech, comprehension, naming, reading, and writing are next examined. The aphasic patient virtually always makes errors in writing (agraphia) and usually in reading (alexia).

Global aphasia is the most common and severe form of aphasia. Spontaneous speech is usually reduced to a few monosyllabic stereotyped words (e.g., "yes-yes") or is absent. Repetition cannot be performed. Comprehension is absent or reduced to few simple word recognitions. Reading and writing are impossible. The lesion is usually large and includes both the inferior frontal gyrus (area 44, Broca, anterior speech area) and the superior temporal gyrus (area 22, Wernicke, posterior speech area). Global aphasia is almost always associated with a hemiplegia when due to stroke. The prognosis for language recovery is poor.

Broca's aphasia (expressive, motor) consists of speech that is decreased in speed and quantity of output (nonfluent) and effortful. There is considerable difficulty in "getting the words out." Nouns and verbs are used, with omission of adjectives, adverbs and prepositions such that speech appears "telegraphic" (e.g., "husband come see tomorrow"). Repetition and reading aloud are impaired in proportion to the severity of the aphasia. Paraphasias occur on naming. Auditory comprehension is intact. The normal melody (prosody) of speech is lost (dysprosody). Dysarthria and apraxia of the buccolingual musculature is present. Frustration, whether due to the difficulty in expressing oneself or due to the lesion itself, is obvious. Depression may occur. Contralateral limb weakness is usual, the lesion is located in and around

the inferior frontal gyrus. Prognosis for speech recovery is better with Broca's aphasia than that for global aphasia.

Wernicke's aphasia (receptive, sensory) is a fluent, effortless speech disturbance with retained prosody and articulation. Comprehension of verbal speech is absent. Verbal instructions therefore fail to be followed. An increased number of words are put out per minute, but few substantive words are used. Nonsense words (neologisms) or words in wrong and senseless combinations (paraphasias) are plentiful such that in the extreme case no sense can be made of the speech (jargon). No effort is made by the patient to correct the gross speech errors due to the comprehension deficit. Repetition, naming, reading, and writing are all markedly impaired. The emotional changes seen with Broca's aphasia are conspicuously absent. Instead, an indifference or even a euphoria may be apparent, or paranoia and belligerent behavior. The family and inexperienced personnel may consider such a person confused or even psychotic, particularly since hemiplegia is generally absent. The lesion is usually in the posterior part of the superior temporal gyrus when the aphasia is severe, but may be somewhat more anterior or even parietal in location in less severe aphasias. This variety of aphasia is more common in older individuals. In the severe case the prognosis is poor despite intensive speech therapy. As improvement occurs, milder Wernicke's aphasics may evolve into conduction or anomic aphasics with better comprehension.

Conduction aphasia is a fluent aphasia where repetition out of proportion to the language disorder is involved. Speech is halting with paraphasias, but there is good auditory comprehension. Reading is good, but writing shows a variety of errors. The arcuate fasciculus connecting the posterior and anterior speech areas is generally described as affected.

Anomic aphasia is a condition in which considerable difficulty is demonstrated on confrontational naming, and on being asked to point to specific objects. Auditory comprehension is otherwise intact. Spontaneous speech is fluent with few word-finding pauses, and is grammatically rich. Repetition is generally good, with variable degrees of reading and writing impairment. Anomia by itself is essentially nonlocalizing in the dominant hemisphere, but severe degrees of anomic aphasia are most frequently seen in lesions of the second and third temporal gyri. Prognosis for recovery depend on the density of the initial lesion.

Transcortical aphasias are characterized by intact repetition in the face of aphasia, because the lesion spares the inferior frontal, superior temporal and perisylvian cortices where the arcuate fasciculus runs. If the speech is fluent and comprehension severely affected, the aphasia is classified as transcortical sensory; whereas, if the speech is restricted and nonfluent, as in the Broca's aphasia, a transcortical motor aphasia may be diagnosed. Infarcts involving arterial border zones between major vessels are usually responsible, occurring posteriorly for the transcortical sensory and arteriorly for the tanscortical motor aphasias. Rarely, other varieties of language disturbance may be encountered (e.g., thalamic aphasia, pure word deafness, or alexia without agraphia, which are beyond the scope of the present discussion).

Dysarthria is a disorder of articulation caused by any disorder of the muscles of articulation. It is therefore seen when the cerebellum, basal ganglia, facial, or bulbar musculature are involved, as well as with disorders in and around the anterior speech area where motor planning of the complex movements of normal speech appear to originate.

Disturbances of Vision and Eye Movements

Monocular visual loss (amaurosis fugax) has previously been discussed (see p. 444). When visual loss is binocular, a *hemianopsia* is present. If the nasal field of one eye and the temporal field of the other are simultaneously affected, the deficit is said to be homonymous. Such a lesion causes loss of a visual field, although it may be interpreted as monocular visual loss. Generally, such a person will bump into objects on one side or miss the margin while reading. The lesion in homonymous hemianopsia is retrochiasmal, anywhere along the optic tract, radiation, or cortex. Because of the arrangement of fibers in the visual pathway, a homonymous hemianopsia due to a temporal lobe lesion affects the superior quadrant more severely than the inferior. The converse is true of parietal lesions. Associated hemiplegia or sensory loss is the rule if the lesion is in the temporal or parietal lobes. However, when lesions of the occipital cortex occur, no other neurologic deficit may be apparent.

Disturbances of ocular motility occur in the acute phase of stroke. Both eyes are deviated conjugately toward the side of the affected hemisphere (looking toward the lesion), and of voluntary gaze to the opposite side is paralyzed. With time, this disturbance usually resolves. Typically, it is seen when lesions involve the frontal eye fields for contraversive gaze and usually implies a large destructive lesion.

Disturbances of Consciousness and Behavior

Coma occurs when massive hemispheric infarction has occurred, particularly when the anterior cerebral artery territory is severely affected. After 48 to 72 hours, it is a consequence of cerebral edema. Transient loss of consciousness is rarely a symptom of unilateral carotid occlusion. Seizure, or cardiac arrhythmia, is a far more likely cause.

Apathy and lack of motivation with reduce awareness and verbal communication (abulia) are characteristic of infarcts of the anterior cerebral artery territory involving the prefrontal cortex. This is particularly marked if both frontal lobes are made ischemic, a common occurrence after rupture of an anterior communicating artery aneurysm followed by vasospasm. Often, on recovery in such individuals, judgment and insight are severely impaired. Personal hygiene may be poor and inappropriate sexual behavior may be apparent. In the extreme case, incontinence of urine and stool occurs with little concern.

Dementia is a decline of the intellect from the premorbid level sufficient to interfere with normal social functioning. When multiple infarcts occur, cognitive, dementia results. Some degree of memory loss is always present. Hachinski has devised a scoring system in an attempt to differentiate multi-infarct dementia from other degenerative dementias (Hachinski et al., 1975). An abrupt stepwise course with multiple focal deficits is the chief characteristic that labels the process as vascular.

Seizures of focal or generalized variety are common at the onset of stroke, particularly when hemorrhage or venous infarction is the cause. Months after a stroke, a permanent seizure disorder triggered by the glial cerebral scar may result.

Posterior Circulation Ischemia— Large Vessels

Vertebral Artery

Occlusion of the vertebral artery occurs most commonly at its origin from the subclavian artery (Fisher, Karnes, & Kubik, 1961). TIAs may occur, but brainstem infarction is infrequent when the occlusion is extracranial (Fisher, Karnes, & Kubik, 1961). If both vertebral arteries are occluded, or one artery occluded and the other hypoplastic or absent, brainstem infarction is likely. As the vertebral artery traverses the vertebral canal, fibrous atherosclerotic plaques may occur in a ladder-like pattern at sites of vascular compression by osteoarthritic bar (Moossy, 1966). Further up, the vertebral artery loops over the transverse process of the first cervical vertebra (C1), where it is subject to mechanical trauma often resulting in arterial dissection.

Occlusion of the intracranial portion of the vertebral artery results most regularly in brainstem infarction (Fisher, Karnes, & Kubik, 1961). Atherosclerosis is the usual cause. 70% of occlusions of the vertebral and 90% of occlusions of the basilar artery overlay atherosclerotic plaques (Castaigne et al., 1973). Embolism to the vertebrobasilar system occurs less frequently than to the carotid. This probably reflects the smaller volume of blood to the brainstem and cerebellum (20%) as compared with the cerebral hemispheres (80%). When embolism

occurs, vertebral branches, or the distal basilar bifurcation (*top of the basilar*), are most affected.

Intracranial occlusion of the vertebral artery may result in lateral medullary infarction, cerebellar infarction, or hemi-infarction of the medulla. The lateral medullary syndrome is one of the most classical in neurology. Although called the syndrome of the posterior inferior cerebellar artery (Wallenberg's syndrome), it is more commonly caused by occlusion of the vertebral artery. Intense vertigo and ataxia generally herald the syndrome, along with difficulty in swallowing, hoarseness of voice, and hiccoughs. Fluctuations of blood pressure are common in the acute stage. On examination, nystagmus (jerky eye movements); ipsilateral Horner's syndrome (small reactive pupil with eyelid droop); paralysis of soft palate and vocal cord; cerebellar ataxia; loss of pain and temperature sensation over the face and contralateral limbs and body, are noted. The syndrome develops abruptly but will often evolve further over a few days, which is a typical feature of posterior circulation disease. The prognosis is relatively benign if complications such as aspiration pneumonia, which is frequent because of paralysis of the laryngeal protective mechanism, do not supervene. Once recovery occurs, most patients do not develop recurrent posterior circulation strokes.

Occasionally the vertebral or a cerebellar branch artery is occluded, producing a pure cerebellar syndrome. Initially the gait is widebased and reeling, just like that of an intoxicated person, but gradually the base gets narrower and stability is regained. The patient may lean toward the infarcted side. Incoordination of the uper extremity results in difficulty performing such acts as feeding. Food may splatter over the face rather than finding its way to the mouth. Speech is slurred and arrhythmic with sounds, particularly consonants, having an explosive quality. These features are typical of *cerebellar speech*.

Small infarcts resolve by themselves leaving minimal or no residuum, but sometimes the volume of infarcted cerebellum is large with much cerebellar swelling (Scotti,

Spinnler, Sterzi, & Vallar, 1980). In such cases the brainstem may be compressed with life threatening consequences.

When hemiparesis, or paralysis of the tongue (medial medullary signs), accompanies the lateral medullary syndrome, a hemi-infarction of the medulla has occurred. Occlusion of the vertebral artery is the rule.

Basilar Artery

Occlusion of the long branches of the basilar artery is uncommon. The clinical findings are inconstant due to the marked variations in blood supply of the brainstem. When the anterior inferior cerebellar artery is occluded, a lateral pontine syndrome similar to that of the lateral medulla develops, but without difficulty in swallowing. Hearing loss and marked facial weakness are present and help to differentiate it from the lateral medullary syndrome. Superior cerebellar artery occlusion is rare. Vertigo, ataxia, dysarthria, Horner's syndrome with contralateral hemiparesis and loss of pain, and temperature sensation are the most constant findings.

The main stem of the basilar artery may be occluded by thrombosis, or less commonly, embolism. The onset may be abrupt, but more often evolves over several days or weeks with accumulating deficit. Cranial nerve palsies are appropriate to the level of brainstem affected. A variety of eye movement disturbances other than isolated cranial nerve palsies are frequent. Patchy bilateral sensory loss and quadriparesis are commonplace (Kubik & Adams, 1946).

Severe infarction of the pons results in coma. Minor disturbances of consciousness occur in less severe cases. If the pontine base is affected sparing the tegmentum, paralysis of all voluntary motor function may occur with intact consciousness. Such a person may be aware of the surroundings but is incapable of verbal communication. Vertical eye movements may be the only means of communication since they are generally spared (locked in syndrome).

Rostral basilar occlusion (top of the basilar) results in infarction of the thalamus, subthalamus, and midbrain. The clinical features have been reviewed in an excellent paper by Caplan (1980). Disorders of ocular motility are common. The eyes rest deviated downwards and inwards, peering at the nose. The pupils are small, eccentric, and reactive to light. Behavioral abnormalities (hallucinations, dream-like states, hypersomnia, akinetic mutism, deep coma) are frequent. Later, abnormal movements and memory disturbances are seen (Castaigne et al., 1981).

Extension of thrombosis or embolism may occur during the first few weeks of basilar occlusion before collateral circulation is established with accumulating clinical deficits. Although a few patients survive with little loss of function (Caplan, 1979), the prognosis is generally poor, death being a frequent outcome.

Posterior Cerebral Artery

Unilateral infarction. Homonymous hemianopsia results from infarction of the occipital lobe. The patient is usually aware of the deficit and may complain of seeing nothing or a blackness to one side, an unlikely complaint from temporoparietal lesions which are usually associated with visual neglect. In contrast to patients with lesions of the optic tract, the patient with an occipital infarct can read a full paragraph or copy a full diagram except in the early stages. Uncommonly, persistent multiple images are seen despite movement of the eye away from the object, and is a distressing phenomenon (*visual perseveration*). Scintillations at the periphery of the deficit are common during recovery (Caplan, 1980).

Behavioral deficits may be prominent. Amnestic syndromes (Benson, Marsden & Meadows, 1974), language disturbances with inability to name (anomic aphasia) (Caplan & Hedley-White, 1974), inability to read but with intact writing skills (alexia without agraphia) (Caplan & Hedley-White, 1974), and failure to recognize objects (visual agnosia) (Benson, Segarra, & Albert, 1974) have all been documented. Hemiplegia is uncommon.

Bilateral infarction. Occlusion of both posterior cerebral arteries is usually due to an embolus or thrombosis at the bifurcation of the basilar artery and results in bilateral occipital infarctions, with or without medial temporal lobe. Cortical blindness may result. Such a patient may deny blindness claiming sight even though a flashing light in front of the eyes cannot be identified. In less severe cases, an entire picture may not be identified although individual component parts are recognized. At other times objects may fail to be recognized (agnosia) or appear altered in their physical characteristics such as shape or size. Inability to move the eyes voluntarily sometimes occurs (visual apraxia).

A variety of unusual behavioral disorders, such as agitated delirium, frank psychosis, or severe permanent amnesia of the Korsakoff type occurs when the medial hippocampus is infarcted (Horenstein, Chamberlain, & Conomy, 1967). Of interest is the syndrome of transient global amnesia. This syndrome is characterized by a profound but transient disturbance of anterograde and retrograde memory. Its etiology is multifactorial, but it is presumed most frequently to represent ischemia in the medial temporal lobes (Logan & Sherman, 1983).

Severe sensory loss affecting the primary sensory modalities occurs when large infarcts in the posterior cerebral artery territory affect the thalamo-parietal projections. Somatosensory deafferentation results in severe proprioceptive loss which may masquerade as weakness. Objects are lost from the hand without the individual's knowledge, or the limb may appear to be "detached," or even move on its own, as in parietal lesions. Surprisingly, despite the marked proprioceptive loss, the gait is frequently normal. Loss of pain and temperature sensation although striking on examination is rarely disabling. What is often a greater problem is the burning pain in the affected limb which often occurs on recovery from a thalamic lesion (thalamic syndrome) and for which there is no specific treatment. Motor weakness is rare.

Anterior Circulation Ischemia— Small Vessels

Small penetrating arteries, 100–400 μm in diameter, arise perpendicularly from the anterior and middle cerebral arteries to supply the white matter and deep ganglionic masses. This anatomic fact makes them particularly susceptible to the effects of hypertension, which is the principal cause of lacunar disease. The vascular pathology underlying lacunes is disruption of the vessel wall with hemorrhage, focal expansion, fibrin deposition, and thrombosis (Fisher, 1969). Atheroma is seen in vessels larger than 200 μm. Infarction results in a small cavity or lacune. The putamen, thalamus, pons, internal capsule, corona radiata, and cerebellar white matter are the anatomic structures which are principally affected (Fisher, 1969).

Although lacunes are asymptomatic in some patients, characteristic clinical syndromes are described (Fisher, 1982). The most frequent type is hemiplegia without aphasia, visual deficit or sensory loss (pure motor hemiplegia). It is due to a lesion in the internal capsule. Ataxia and ipsilateral hemiparesis affecting leg more than arm occurs from lesions in the corona radiata or pons (ataxic hemiparesis) and is infrequent.

Posterior Circulation Ischemia— Small Vessels

Lacunar infarction of the thalamus results in numbness, dysesthesias or paresthesias of face, arm and leg with sensory loss, and no motor signs (pure sensory stroke). Recovery may result in a thalamic pain syndrome. Sometimes the sudden onset of dysarthria with clumsiness of the hand and ataxia may occur from a contralateral pontine lesion (dysarthria — clumsy hand syndrome).

A variety of named syndromes exist due to occlusion of small vessels originating from the basilar artery and supplying the paramedian brainstem. Typically, a cranial nerve is affected on the side of the infarct with contralateral paralysis of sensory or motor function; for example, oculomotor nerve paralysis with contralateral hemiplegia is called Weber's syndrome.

Sometimes the brain is peppered with multiple small infarcts. These accumulate over time and a characteristic syndrome results with dementia and pseudobulbar palsy. The latter is characterized by dysarthria, dysphagia, and emotional lability due to infarction of corticobulbar fibers. The face is immobile and the gait short-stepping resembling parkinsonism. Absence of tremor and signs of bilateral dysfunction of the corticospinal tracts are helpful in differentiating these two disorders. Emotional lability with inappropriate laughter and crying occurs, and is particularly distressing to the patient and family alike. One such affected individual overcome with sadness at his wife's funeral began laughing. He was so embarrassed at the event that he attempted suicide.

Recovery is the rule in lacunar infarction, even if incomplete. Recurrent infarctions are frequent.

INVESTIGATIONS

Investigations to determine the cause of the infarct are performed as discussed earlier in this chapter (p. 445). Computerized tomography (CT) will help document the infarction, but is frequently normal in the initial 24 hours even after a large cerebral infarct. If hemorrhage has occurred, it will be detected instantly. Lacunes may not be apparent for several days or weeks.

Cerebral angiography is performed only if the stroke is progressing, after recovery from a small stroke, or if an unusual cause of stroke is suspected. In each instance therapy depends on the angiographic results. Angiography is not indicated after a large infarct since it is unlikely to alter medical management and carries some risk. Noninvasive carotid studies such as the duplex scan may be safely performed in such instances to reveal information about the carotid bifurcation.

Lumbar puncture is performed if hemorrhage is strongly suspected but the CT scan reveals no blood, or when the differential diagnosis includes an unusual cause for stroke (e.g., meningovascular syphilis).

The electroencephalograph (EEG) and radionuclide brain scan add little information to the CT scan, and are not routinely performed in stroke victims today.

Course and Prognosis

The neurologic deficit after a cerebral infarct reaches its maximum generally within 24 to 72 hours, depending on whether the carotid or vertebrobasilar system is involved. If medical complications or death do not intervene, recovery will be first apparent generally within 2 weeks. Maximum recovery occurs within the first 3 months continuing thereafter at a slower pace for about a year (Wade & Wood, 1985). Significant recovery after this period of time is highly unlikely.

About one-fifth to one-third of patients with acute cerebral infarctions die within a month of the stroke (Oxbury, Greenhall, & Grainger, 1975). Most of these are massive hemispheric or brainstem infarcts. Lacunar infarcts on the other hand have a much more favorable prognosis.

Death due to cerebral infarction is rarely sudden. Increased intracranial pressure results in transtentorial herniation due to massive cerebral edema which accounts for one-third of deaths. Most of these occur in the first 3 days (Bounds, Wiebers, Whisnant, & Okazaki, 1981). Myocardial infarction and cardiac arrhythmias are also a frequent cause of death in the first week. Pulmonary embolism may occur at anytime. Pneumonia usually occurs after the first week and accounts for a third of deaths.

Coma at the onset of infarction, particularly when associated with a dense hemiplegia or conjugate gaze palsy, predicts a grave outcome (Oxbury, Greenhall, & Grainger, 1975). Similarly, a large shift of midline structures on the CT scan is an ominous sign.

For those who survive cerebral infarction, a prognosis for functional recovery must be made. The influence of several features must be considered, because no single feature alone is a strong predictor of outcome. These features are as follows:

1. *Age:* Age has little influence upon the severity of stroke, but apears to influence outcome negatively, particularly in the elderly (Kotila et al., 1984; Wade, Langton-Hewer, & Wood, 1984).

2. *Sex:* No influence on recovery has been noted (Kotila et al., 1984; Wade, Langton-Hewer, & Wood, 1984).

3. *Type of stroke:* The influence of type of stroke (hemorrhage or infarct) on recovery, is not known with certainty. It is often thought that the deficit tends to be less with intracerebral hemorrhage than infarction, as fibers tend to be split rather than destroyed. Lacunar infarcts have a good prognosis for recovery.

4. *Size of stroke:* This is the most important factor predicting outcome. With large lesions, widespread cortical and subcortical damage is likely to be present. Motor, sensory, and a variety of higher cortical functions, all necessary for recovery, are likely to be in abeyance hindering eventual recovery. Clinically, a large volume stroke may be predicted if global aphasia, anosognosia, hemianopsia, and dense hemiplegia are present. Coma is a better predictor of death than eventual functional recovery.

5. *Location of stroke:* It is generally assumed that, because of the language deficit, lesions of the dominant hemisphere are more disabling than those of the nondominant hemisphere. Others have claimed the side of the deficit makes little difference (Wade, Langton-Hewer, & Wood, 1984). Several recent authors have emphasized that visuomotor, temporal and spatial disorders, as well as disturbances of body image, result in severe permanent disability (Marquardsen, 1983; Kotila et al., 1984). Functional recovery in survivors of brainstem strokes is better than after cortical brainstem strokes because of the lack of major cognitive deficits.

6. *Clinical features:* (a) *Motor deficit:* Permanent disability is generally proportional to the severity of initial hemiparesis. Better still as a prognosticator, is the time taken from stroke to onset of recovery. Those who improve within 3 days will walk independently unaided (Gowers, 1888). If no improvement occurs within 1 month, the prognosis is unfavorable. (b) *Sensory deficit:* In the authors' experience, when major sensory deficits occur, outcome is adversely affected. However, some difference of opinion exists on this point (Marquardsen, 1983; Moskowitz, Lightbody, &

Freitag, 1972). (c) *Visual disturbances:* Hemianopsia seems to adversely affect prognosis despite perseveration of central vision (Haerer, 1973). This is probably because hemianopsia, when associated with hemiplegia, is associated with some degree of visual neglect and is usually caused by a large lesion. (d) *Higher cortical functions:* When present, dementia seriously impedes recovery. Nonadequate emotional disturbances such as abulia (or lack of motivation), indifference, and emotional lability seriously hamper recovery, perhaps even more than depression (Kotila et al., 1984). Aphasia is a major handicap but does not hamper functional motor recovery greatly.

7. *Other:* The premorbid personality and abilities are probably of great importance. The well-adjusted individual is more likely to remain so than his or her counterpart. Victims from families with strong emotional and social support systems do better than individuals who lived alone before the stroke (Kotila et al., 1984). Serious associated medical disorders will retard overall recovery.

Some two-thirds of stroke victims are likely to return home whereas the other third will need nursing care facilities. Women living with a spouse are more likely to return home than if they lived with relatives or alone. Such domestic influences seem to be less important for men. In the Orient, where families are usually more closely knit, virtually all stroke victims are returned home to be cared for by their relatives and children.

Approximately one-third of patients who are employed at the time of stroke are likely to return to work (Marquardsen, 1983).

Mortality, in the long term, is much higher than in the general population. For males, the 3-year survival rate is only 54% compared with an expected 88%; at 5 years, half the expected will survive and only a quarter at 10 years (Marquardsen, 1983; Hutchinson & Acheson, 1975). This accelerated mortality is not only present initially but persists indefinitely.

MANAGEMENT

Where to Manage

Acute stroke constitutes a neurologic emergency. If the deficit is minor or appears to be improving, the patient or family may attempt to persuade the physician that hospitalization is unnecessary. The gravity of the situation must be carefully explained, particularly the likelihood of further worsening or complication within the immediate post stroke period. On the other hand, if several days have gone by and resolution of the deficit is occurring, management may be performed in the home.

Some hospitals have specialized units for acute care; others admit patients to intensive care units or a general medical floor. If the patient is comatose, markedly hypertensive, or has cardiac arrhythmias, an intensive care setting is highly advisable. The merits of each location continue to be debated, but what is clear is that a team approach with a physician, nurses, and therapists specially trained in acute stroke care, yields the shortest hospital stay with least complications.

General Medical Care

Care of the airway is the most important feature of the management of any neurologic emergency. If the patient is comatose, a lateral decubitus or head low position is advised. An oral airway is kept in place for 24 to 48 hours, longer periods resulting in parched mucous membranes. If coma is likely to last more than a week, tracheotomy is advised. Frequent gentle suction of the pharynx with a soft polyethlene tube helps prevent aspiration.

Arterial blood gases are not obtained unless respiratory complications exist. Supplemental oxygenation has no value in the routine situation. Hyperbaric oxygenation has been tried; those that benefit return to their pretreatment state as soon as therapy is discontinued.

Carbon dioxide is a powerful cerebral vasodilator and was once used in treating cerebral ischemia. However, it was soon realized that ischemic cerebral vessels often failed to dilate with carbon dioxide whereas the normal vasculature did, resulting in blood being diverted away from the ischemic tissue (*vascular steal*). Its use was therefore abandoned.

Attention to fluid and electrolyte balance is necessary. Basic requirements of water (2000–3000 mls), sodium (80 to 120 mEq), potassium (60 to 90 mEq) and calories (2500 to 3000) must be maintained. Any additional losses through fever, vomiting or diarrhea, should be compensated. Dehydration is avoided, as it promotes thrombosis.

Many acute intracranial disasters, particularly intracranial hemorrhage, result in the syndrome of inappropriate ADH (antidiuretic hormone) secretion. Dizziness and convulsions may occur. The serum sodium and osmolality are disproportionately low to the high urine osmolality. Corrective measures must be taken immediately.

Intravenous feeding is needed when oral feeding is not posssible. If the patient is comatose and it appears that the problem is likely to last more than a few days, a jejunal feeding tube is used. However, in chronic cases, a feeding gastrostomy (a tube is placed directly into the stomach through the abdominal wall) is performed. The alert individual is encouraged to feed himself/herself as usual. Swallowing needs to be carefully evaluated, especially in patients with pontomedullary infarcts, because severe dysphagia may occur with inability to swallow secretions. Aspiration of material into the lungs is common since laryngeal protection is in abeyance. If oral feedings cannot be safely resumed within a few weeks, a cricoid myotomy, esophagostomy, or gastrostomy must be considered. More commonly, moderate dysphagia, particularly to liquids, is present. In such cases feeding with a straw or spoon is frequently successful. Thick liquids such as milk shakes or soft pureed foods are more successfully swallowed. A videofluoroscopic evaluation of swallowing will allow the correct choice of food consistency. Hiccoughs indicate dehydration, uremia, myocardial infarction, or a medullary disorder. It usually remits spontaneously within a week of the stroke onset, but occasionally persists and is then an ominous sign. Phenothiazine drugs may be of some use in its treatment.

Constipation is a frequent problem, particularly if a low residue diet is used. A gentle laxative or enema is occasionally necessary. Diarrhea due to hypertonic tube feedings may occur, requiring a change in formula. Fecal incontinence is rare. Urinary disturbances, both retention and incontinence, are frequent. Sometimes this is due to the stroke affecting the bladder control centers in the paracentral lobule and orbitofrontal brain regions, but more commonly in the elderly male, an enlarged prostate gland is the cause. Such an individual may be well-compensated when ambulatory, but is unable to void while in bed. Catheterization is then necessary until the patient can walk. If spontaneous voiding is not resumed, surgery on the prostate is performed to decrease outflow resistance. Catheterization is avoided in the incontinent since urinary tract infections are commonplace with frequent catheterization. A condom catheter is preferred for men but the regular use of a bed pan and incontinence pad are best for women.

Pressure sores are prevented by frequent turning and the use of alternating pressure air mattress or waterbed. Areas of skin breakdown must be kept clean, dry, and free of pressure.

Facial weakness results in incomplete eye closure. Tears may spill over the cheek rather than lubricating the eye since the punctum of the tear duct is everted. A dry eye, secondary infection, and corneal ulcerations may result. Methylcellulose drops, regularly placed, help to prevent these complications. In severe cases, especially when corneal anesthesia is present, a protective eyeshield must be worn. Patching the eye with a gauze pad in such cases is undesirable since the gauze may scratch the anesthetic cornea and cause ulceration.

When hemianopsia is present, it is important to approach the patient's bedside from the normal side. The bed should also be so arranged that ongoing activity in the room can be seen, otherwise the patient may constantly stare out of a window and receive little stimulation.

Blood pressure must be maintained within normal limits. Only if blood pressure is markedly elevated (diastolic greater than 110 mm Hg) should it be decreased, then only with great care making certain that the diastolic pressure falls to no less than 90 mm Hg. This is because cerebral perfusion of ischemic tissue is directly proportionate to blood pressure once arterial autoregulation has failed. Occasionally, hyertension occurs as a result of stroke. This is most frequently seen in intracranial hemorrhage or when intracranial pressure is markedly increased. Consciousness is impaired in such individuals.

Cardiac arrhythmias are frequently the cause of cerebral infarction but also occur transiently as a consequence of intracranical catastrophies. Subarachnoid hemorrhage is the most frequent cause, but cerebral infarction may also result in transient arrhythmias requiring cardiac monitoring and the use of antiarrhythmic drugs. About 4% of myocardial infarctions are complicated by cerebral embolism, most occurring within the first month after a large anterior myocardial infarct. Anticoagulants are generally recommended since the risk of a second fatal embolus is great, but carries the danger of producing hemorrhage in large infarcts. For this reason, it is often prudent to wait a few days before initiating anticoagulation.

Seizures may occur anytime after stroke. Some 5–10% of patients have a seizure during the acute event or as a sequela. The pattern of seizure may be focal or generalized. Anticonvulsants are used as in epilepsy of other causes with equal effect. Status epilepticus (recurrent seizures without regaining consciousness in between seizures) occurs rarely.

Specific Treatment

No generally accepted treatment that substantially alters stroke outcome exists. Several modalities have been tried and some physicians firmly believe in one or other therapy due to personal experience.

Cerebral edema results from cerebral infarction. Many substances have been used to treat this condition with mixed results. Corticosteroids, particularly dexamethasone, are most favored. These drugs are most frequently used in large volume infarctions where herniation (a shift of brain tissue from one compartment to another) may be anticipated. Mannitol is used only when the herniation syndrome is occurring.

Vasodilators, of which papaverine is the best studied, are ineffective. They may in fact aggravate the ischemia, as they only dilate normal arteries thus directing blood away from the ischemic zone.

Anticoagulants have a place in the treatment of progressing stroke (Carter, 1961; Millikan & McDowell, 1980), but their value is doubtful once cerebral infarction has occurred. However, if the infarct is of small volume, there is a chance that further ischemia could result in increased functional loss. In such cases, anticoagulation with Coumadin or the use of antiplatelet agents such as aspirin should be considered for secondary prophylaxis. If the cerebral infarct is caused by an embolus of presumed cardiac origin, immediate anticoagulation is desirable to prevent a second, possibly fatal, embolus. Early anticoagulation, does however, carry the risk of causing hemorrhage into the area of ischemic brain softening, particularly in large infarcts. In such cases, waiting a few days after the infarct to begin anticoagulation is probably wise.

Hemodilution decreases blood viscosity and increases blood flow, particularly in the microvasculature. Recent evidence suggests that outcome is favorably affected (Strand et al., 1984). This may mean that some who would not have otherwise survived will do so and be severely disabled whereas others will have a lesser disability (Matthews et al., 1976). Dextran 40, albumin, or hetastarch are used as diluents.

Barbiturate therapy still remains experimental. Barbiturates lower the cerebral metabolic rate and thereby decrease cerebral metabolic needs. Since blood supply is limited, it better matches the decreased metabolism. Undesirable free radicals, such as the superoxides, are also *scavenged* by barbiturates. In animal models, some benefit has been clearly shown, but human studies are awaited. Cardiovascular collapse is a serious problem with the dose of barbiturate needed for clinical use.

Surgical Treatment

Intracranial surgery is only warranted in life-threatening situations. Decompression of a large volume infarct or hemorrhage is performed in such cases to relieve the markedly raised intracranial pressure. Cerebellar infarction or hemorrhage with brainstem compression is a major neurosurgical emergency.

If good recovery occurs after stroke, methods of preventing further stroke should be considered. Such patients should be managed in a fashion similar to TIAs.

REHABILITATION

Stroke is devastating. A previously functional individual can be rendered speechless, paralyzed, and incontinent. The shock to the patient and family is total. Little can be done medically to return the stroke victim to health. The quality of the remainder of the victim's life depends on the functional recovery that occurs. The goal of the rehabilitation team is to optimize this.

The principles underlying rehabilitation include: (a) defining the clinical problem; (b) discussing the problem and its prognosis with all concerned (including the patient); (c) providing a realistic goal oriented program for home and work; (d) settling appropriate industrial and domestic issues; (e) providing a continuous treatment program; and (f) assessing requirements of aids and appliances, environmental needs, and social support.

Such a program requires a coordinated effort among the physician, nursing staff, physical occupational therapist and speech therapist, rehabilitation phychologist, orthopedic surgeon, social worker, and family.

Details of comprehensive rehabilitation management are beyond the scope of this chapter. Selected areas are briefly discussed in the remainder of the chapter.

Understanding the Deficit

The neurologic deficit produced by a stroke is far greater than would first appear. To understand this, consider a "simple" motor act such as picking up a cup. The object is first seen, visually described, recognized, and its meaning fully remembered. Next, the desire to pick up the cup is formulated. Eyes move to the object, focus, and adapt to the light, distance, and depth with coordinated head and neck movements. The center of gravity is adjusted. Synchronous coordination of muscles then allows the arm to reach out precisely and perform a smooth movement. The object is then grasped with appropriate strength. Performance of such an act requires the coordination of motor and sensory functions located in various distant sites in the neuraxis.

Damage to a specific area of the brain not only results in failure of the primary function of that area, but also affects the brain in a more widespread fashion. Blood flow and metabolic changes remote from the infarct have been documented recently (Baron et al., 1981), a phenomenon called *diaschisis*. The functional correlates of this phenomenon are not currently known. Clearly, a person suffering a "pure motor hemiparesis," is not only weak, but has a generalized disturbance of balance and coordination together with sensory perceptual, cognitive, and behavioral deficits. Successful rehabilitation requires attention to all these areas.

When Should Rehabilitation Begin?

Once the patient is medically stable, rehabilitation efforts are begun. Each patient needs to be carefully evaluated individually. The individual with a mild deficit may begin a rehabilitation program early but those with severe deficits must wait. Although several studies have emphasized that early onset of rehabilitation influences eventual outcome positively, an equally valid interpretation of the data may be that those with lesser deficits entered the program early, since no control studies have been performed. When this factor is controlled for it appears that there is no difference in those beginning a program early or late. Interestingly, the observation has been made that patients with nondominant hemisphere strokes benefit from beginning therapy later than those with dominant hemisphere strokes.

Motor Weakness

In 1895, Mott and Sherrington, two famous neurophysiologists, deafferented the limb of a monkey by cutting the sensory nerve roots. The limb was rendered useless even though the motor nerves were intact. If the lesion had been incomplete, the effect would have been much less devastating.

Brodal (1973), the famous neuroanatomist, described the value of passive movement after his own stroke. Initially, he could not move the limb voluntarily. After the limb was passively moved several times by the therapist, he was capable, albeit weakly, of making the movements. The value of passive movement may be to stimulate sensory input and is emphasized by all physical therapists.

Spasticity

After a period of flaccid weakness, increased motor tone (spasticity) begins in selected muscle groups. The result is the typical hemiplegic posture with the *antigravity muscles* predominating over their antagonists. The upper extremity is held with the shoulder depressed and adducted, while elbow, wrist, and fingers are flexed. In the lower extremity, the leg is held extended and externally rotated while the ankle is inverted and plantar flexed. The pelvis is pulled downwards.

Spasticity develops after 1 to 2 weeks in cortical strokes and earlier with subcortical or brainstem infarcts. Marked spasticity obscures residual movement. Soft tissue contractures rapidly supervene and freeze the extremities in abnormal postures. Physical therapy measures are therefore directed toward reducing spasticity. Attempts are made to inhibit the spastic muscles while facilitating the antagonists. Anxiety aggravates spasticity and must be reduced. Muscle relaxant drugs such as baclofen (Lioresal®) and diazepam (Valium®) are of limited usefulness. Frequently they reduce spasticity too much so that "useful" spasticity is lost.

PSYCHOLOGICAL SEQUELAE

General Considerations

As is the case with the physical consequences of stroke, the psychological sequelae in the individual case are dependent upon a myriad of factors, including location, extent, and etiology of insult, as well as many features of the individual, such as age and other premorbid medical and phychological history. In the following sections, commonly observed deficits in psychological functioning following stroke are reviewed, with the discussion organized by areas of functional abilities. The reader should be aware that although functional deficits may occur in a relatively isolated fashion, it is more often the case that cognitive, affective, and physical impairments are seen in varying combinations. Indeed, specific impairments may interact in such a way that functional deficits in one sphere may potentiate the disability associated with a related area of deficit. For example, a general verbal-linguistic processing deficit (e.g., aphasia) may contribute to a significant verbal memory impairment, even in the absence of substantial damage to specific structures directly associated with memory processes. It should also be noted that in considering the individual case, significant changes in psychological functioning may be seen in serial examinations, especially early in the recovery phase. Often the global and diffuse cognitive deficits (e.g., confusion and clouded consciousness), observed soon after a completed stroke, eventually give way to a less pervasive pattern of impairment associated with lateralized and localized cerebral dysfunction.

In the assessment of psychological functions following stroke, standardized psychological and neuropsychological test procedures are typically useful. However, the requirements of meaningful evaluation, particularly the evaluation expected to contribute to the planning and development of rehabilitation programs, may demand judicious modification of standardized procedures with a primary focus upon optimal patient performance. *Neuropsychological Assessment* (Lezak, 1983) presents an excellent and comprehensive review of tests, batteries, and informal clinical procedures and adaptations for evaluation of a variety of psychological functions. Such evaluations are an integral part of the development of treatment procedures for the rehabilitation of post-stroke deficits, particularly in remediation of cognitive deficits. In general, as conceptualized by Rothi and Horner (1983), cognitive remediation interventions may emphasize the recovery or restitution of impaired functions or may focus upon the training of compensatory techniques. Most typically, remediation procedures presume reliance upon both processes to some degree. At the present early stage in the scientific development of these interventions, the mechanisms of their operation in the recovery of psychological functions are, at best, incompletely understood. However, encouraging evidence is beginning to be accumulated to support the utility of selected interventions in facilitating the recovery from the psychological sequelae of stroke (e.g., Ben-Yishay, 1979; Carter, Caruso, Languirand, & Berard, 1980; Diller et al., 1974; Young, Collins, & Hren, 1983).

Against this general background, the following discussion should be viewed as a presentation of the major psychological sequelae of stroke, with the understanding that specific individuals may be expected to present the deficits described herein in various combinations and levels of severity. It should also be added that for purposes of ease of discussion, the most commonly encountered circumstance of cerebral organization wherein the left

Memory functioning

Impairment of memory functioning is a frequent consequence of many kinds of brain damage, including stroke. Most typically, the post-stroke syndrome is associated with relatively mild retrograde memory impairment, with more severe compromise of the ability to acquire, retain, and recall new information. Unilateral strokes involving the dominant (usually left) hemisphere are typically associated with impaired verbal memory functioning, while lesions affecting the nondominant hemisphere most often result in deficits in visuo–spatial memory abilities. Bilateral lesions of the temporal lobes are associated with global, and sometimes profound, memory dysfunction, especially infarctions involving selected mesial temporal lobe region structures (e.g., hippocampus).

Deficits in inattention can significantly affect memory performance, since the amount of information which is available for registration, storage, and later retrieval is severely limited. The anatomic substrate for attention is not "localizable" and is vulnerable to disruption at a variety of lesion sites. However, impairment of attention may in some cases be modality specific. That is, attention for auditory, tactile, or visual information may be selectively impaired. Clinically, it is important to distinguish disorders of memory and attention from other impairments, such as language disturbances which are sometimes mislabeled as memory or attention dysfunction.

The Wechsler Memory Scale (WMS) (Wechsler, 1945) is probably the most widely used clinical instrument for the assessment of memory; often added is Russell's (1975) modification which includes delayed recall procedures, lacking in the original version. The WMS includes memory for paragraphs, lists, and geometric designs. It is often supplemented by a list learning task such as the Rey Auditory Verbal Learning Test (Rey, 1964). Additional visual memory tasks such as

Rey-Osterreith Complex Figure Test (Osterreith, 1944) or one of the forms of the Benton Visual Retention Test (Benton, 1974), may be used.

In the remediation of memory deficits, a commonly employed approach, has been the use of repetitive practice, presumed to "strengthen" memory functioning. While such an approach may be intuitively appealing, there is as yet no convincing theoretical basis or empirical evidence to support the utility of such procedures. An alternative approach has involved the training of individuals in particular memory enhancement (mnemonic) strategies, and reports of successful interventions can be found (Podbros & Noble, 1982; Cermak & Laird, 1975; Lewinsohn, Danaher, & Kikel, 1977). Generally, the procedures employed have been elementary and unsophisticated mnemonics, and have failed to assess the utility of such procedures in daily activities. The use of potentially more powerful mnemonic systems (Higbee, 1977) has not been well studied. Schacter and colleagues (Schacter, Rich, & Stampp, 1985; Schacter & Glisky, in press) have described another potentially fruitful approach emphasizing the use of rather simple learning procedures for the development of specific training techniques for the acquisition of particular skills (e.g., computer programming) by amnesic individuals. Another alternative is the *systems approach* advocated by Poon (1980), which emphasizes the precise delineation of memory problems and the effective use of compensatory techniques. Wilson and Moffat (1984) also describe elaborate "high tech" compensatory procedures which may be useful for memory-impaired stroke patients. Such approaches focusing upon the effective use of spared cognitive abilities appears promising. Direct training of attentional abilities has also been advocated (Ben-Yishay, 1979; Wood, 1984).

Assessment of visuo–spatial abilities is performed in a limited fashion with the nonverbal (performance) scale of the Wechsler Adult Intellingence Scale—Revised (WAIS-R) (Wechsler, 1981), although individual subtest performances may be difficult to interpret, since all these tasks are timed, and most involve complex combinations of various visuo-spatial abilities. Useful supplementary tests include three-dimensional drawing tasks such as a cube, or more formal tests including the Hooper Visual Organization Test (Hooper, 1958), the Judgement of Line Orientation Test (Benton, Hannay, & Varney, 1975), and Raven's Progressive Matrices (Raven, 1960).

In the development of remediation procedures, unilateral spatial neglect has been a target symptom. Some success has been reported (Diller et al., 1974; Carter et al., 1980) with an approach which entails training in visual scanning utilizing repetitive practice with feedback. Training tasks have included paper-and-pencil activities such as cancellation tasks, specially developed mechanisms (Diller, 1980), and computer programs (Mikula, 1983). Direct training in more complex visuo-perceptual functioning has also been included as an added treatment intervention to scanning training (Young, Collins, & Hren, 1983; Weinbergy et al., 1979; Weinberg et al., 1982) and has been found to enhance treatment gains. While encouraging improvements have been observed in the clinic following these interventions, subsequent improvements in daily functioning remain to be fully evaluated.

Problem-Solving and Judgment Abilities

Impairment in complex thinking skills is not an unusual consequence of brain damage following stroke. In many circumstances, difficulties in complex cognitive activities may be viewed as the result of the combined impact of deficits in component skills such as memory or visual perception. In other instances, specific impairment of higher level cognitive processes (e.g., organizing, planning and problem-solving skills) may be seen, even when there is relative sparing of more elementary cognitive and perceptual skills. In either circumstance, functional deficits in these complex thinking abilities may have a significant adverse impact upon return to independent, productive life activity for the stroke patient. Adequate methods of assessing these deficits are unavailable at the present time (see Lezak, 1983, Chapter 16, for related discussion). Deficits in these areas may be inferred from the pattern of performance observed on the WAIS-R, or may be evaluated more directly by using such tests as the Category Test and Tactual Performance Test (both from the Halstead-Reitan Battery, Wisconsin Card Sort Test, or Porteus Maze Test. However, each of these tests involves reliance upon the integrity of certain basic intellectual processes (e.g., language, visual perception). Thus, caution must be used in reaching the conclusion that some aspect of complex reasoning ability has been compromised based on an individual's performance on one or more of these tests.

Procedures for the remediation of specific deficits in these higher level processes have been developed and are discussed in the literature (Craine, 1982; Adamovich, Henderson, & Auerbach, 1985). In general, these procedures emphasize the use of a variety of activities aimed at the remediation of skills in developing, executing and evaluating (i.e., modifying in response to feedback) strategies for the solution of complex problems of different types. As an alternative approach, others have identified deficits in component skills as the appropriate target for intervention based on the plausible notion that deficits in higher order skills simply reflect incomplete recovery of more basic abilities (Diller et al., 1974). Thus, the proponents of this approach take the position that remediation of these component skills is prerequisite to the emergence of higher-level abilities. In practice, the relative merits of these approaches are likely to depend upon the adequacy with which the specific deficit pattern of the individual patient is defined and addressed. As additional research information is gathered, the parameters relevant to the application of each approach should become better defined.

Emotional/Affective Functioning

A variety of emotional and behavioral changes may be seen following stroke. Some of these changes may be understood as secondary reactions (anxiety, depression) to the profound physical and psychological consequences of stroke. Other changes, however, may be related to the direct (or at least primary) effect of brain lesions. This latter circumstance is well exemplified by the condition of *pseudobulbar palsy,* wherein the patient displays poorly controlled, sudden, and inappropriate emotional outbursts (such as laughter or crying, with a virtual absence of internally experienced affect. Other emotional and behavioral changes secondary to brain damage are more subtle. In many cases, individuals may manifest changes in the quantity and quality of emotional response in comparison to their pre-stroke personalities, but frequently may maintain a fundamental similarity apparent to the careful observer. In cases in which changes occur, affective responses may be appropriate but shallow, or alternatively, may be excessive or even absent. For some individuals, display of emotion may represent a poor "match" with their self-described inner feeling state. For others, a primary disturbance in intrinsic motivation may be seen, as evidenced by apathy and difficulty in initiation of spontaneous activity. In contrast, others may manifest impairment of inhibitory mechanisms and may display poorly controlled social behavior and/or affective response. Psychotic reactions are rare (Lishman, 1978).

Depression is common after stroke. It may represent a secondary response to the changed life circumstances, but has also been related by some researchers to specific patterns of neurologic damage in both the right (e.g., Ross & Rush, 1981) and left (e.g., Robinson & Szetela, 1981) hemispheres. The precise nature of these putative relationships is unclear and warrants further investigation.

Cognitive and affective disorders are closely related. To understand the emotional function of an individual, knowledge of his/her intellectual strengths and weaknesses must be known. An individual with only subtle impairment of cognitive functioning may nonetheless experience significant difficulty in fully comprehending the consequences and implications of his deficit. Such an individual may appear to demonstrate a defensive denial of impairment when in fact he/she lacks awareness of his/her cognitive dysfunction. This kind of distinction is significant, and has clear implications for differential intervention; other emotional responses may be similarly influenced by cognitive limitations.

Assessment of personality and emotional functioning has typically been conducted with clinical procedures such as interviews and observations, as well as standardized psychological tests. The Minnesota Multiphasic Personality Inventory (MMPI) (Hathaway & McKinley, 1951) has been a useful assessment tool with neurologically impaired patients; abbreviated versions of this lengthy inventory have been used (e.g., MMPI-168) and have been demonstrated to have clinical utility with some brain-damaged groups (Ownby & Smigielski, 1984). Other self-rating scales such as the Beck Depression Inventory (Beck et al., 1961), Symptom Check List-90, and others also may be useful in identifying particular symptom patterns of emotional dysfunction. Projective techniques provide some information, but tend to be of limited utility for evaluation of individuals with visuo-spatial or language deficits.

Both pharmacological and psychotherapeutic interventions have been utilized in the treatment of emotional changes following stroke. While medications are used with some frequency, there is little evidence available to document that improvements in affective functioning clearly result from such treatment. Similarly, the efficacy of psychotherapy with brain-damaged patients is not clearly established. However, it seems reasonable to assert that supportive counseling or psychotherapy for both the stroke patient and family may be beneficial, at minimum, in assisting the individual and those who will live/interact with him or her, to better understand the changes that have taken place in cognitive and affective functioning, and thus facilitate adjustment to these altered circumstances. Beyond these presumed benefits, the potential utility of structured, directive psychotherapeutic interventions, such as behavioral and cognitive–behavioral approaches, would appear to be significant in work with individuals who have suffered strokes, and have in fact been suggested as appropriate approaches to treatment with other neurologically impaired patients (e.g., Trexler, 1982). The interested reader is directed to more complete discussions of affective change following brain damage (Heilman & Valenstein, 1979; Lishman, 1978; Goldstein & Ruthven, 1983).

SUMMARY

This chapter has offered a broad overview of the complex factors that contribute to the etiology, description, management, and outcomes associated with stroke. Stroke is by no means a uniform disorder, and the victim's eventual level of impairment, if any, follows a highly individualized course.

While specific clinical features of stroke are highly dependent on location of ischemia, many patients experience motor weakness and numbness, staggering, blurred or double vision, aphasia, and headache. The treatment of the manifestations and any underlying disease process requires aggressive procedures to prevent a reoccurrence. In addition to the obvious physical manifestations of stroke, a wide range of psychological sequelae may be evident also. The more typical sequelae include impaired memory functioning, complex problem-solving and judgment abilities, and emotional/affective functioning.

Once patients are medically stable, rehabilitation is begun. Because of the breadth and severity of disability that often accompanies stroke, rehabilitation is mostly comprised of a multidisciplinary effort including the physician, nursing staff, physical therapist, occupational therapist, speech therapist, rehabilitation psychologist, orthopedic surgeon, social worker, and the family.

REFERENCES

Adamovich, B., Henderson, J., & Auerbach, S. (1985). *Cognitive retraining of the head-injured patient: A dynamic approach.* San Diego: College-Hill.

Adams, H. P., Putnam, S. F., Corbett, J. J., Sires, B. P., & Thompson, H. S. (1983). Amaurosis fugax: The results of arteriography in 59 patients. *Stroke, 14,* 742–744.

Astrup, J., Siesjo, B. K., & Symon, L. (1981). Thresholds in cerebral ischemia—The ischemic penumbra. *Stroke, 12,* 723–725.

Barnett, H. J. M. (1982). Embolism in mitral valve prolapse. *Annual Review of Medicine, 33,* 489–507.

Baron, J. C., Bousser, M. G., Comar, D., Duquesnoy, N., Sastre, J., & Castaigne, P. (1981). Crossed cerebellar diaschisis: A remote functional depression secondary to supratentorial infarction of man. *Journal of Cerebral Blood Flow and Metabolism, 1 (Suppl. 1),* S 500–501.

Bauer, S., Sheehan, S., & Meyer, J. S. (1961). Arteriographic study of cerebrovascular disease. *Archives of Neurology, 4,* 119–131.

Baum, H. M., & Robins, M. (1981). Survival and prevalence: The national survey of stroke. *Stroke, 12 (Suppl. 1),* 159–168.

Beck, A. T., Ward, C. H., Mendelson, M., Mock, J., & Erbaugh, J. K. (1961). An inventory for measuring depression. *Archives of General Psychiatry, 4,* 561–571.

Benson, F., & Geschwind, N. (1968). Cerebral dominance and its disturbances. *Pediatric Clinics of North America, 15,* 759–769.

Benson, D. F., Marsden, C. D., & Meadows, J. C. (1974). The amnestic syndrome of posterior cerebral artery occlusion. *Acta Neurologica Scandanavica, 50,* 133–145.

Benson, D. F., Segarra, J. M., & Albert M. L. (1974). Visual agnosia-prosopdgnosia. *Archives of Neurology, 30,* 307–310.

Benton, A. L. (1974). *The Revised Visual Retention Test* (4th ed.). New York: Psychological Corporation.

Benton, A. L., Hannay, H. J., & Varney, N. R. (1975). Visual perception of line direction in patients with unilateral brain disease. *Neurology, 25,* 907–910.

Ben-Yishay, Y. (Ed.). (1979). *Working approaches to remediation of cognitive deficit in brain damaged person.* New York: Institute of Rehabilitation Medicine, NYU Medical Center.

Betz, E. (1972). Cerebral blood flow: Its measurement and regulation. *Physiological Reviews, 52,* 595–630.

Bladin, P. F., & Merory, J. (1975). Mechanisms of cerebral lesions in trauma to high cervical portion of the vertebral artery—Rotation injury. *Proceedings of the Australian Association of Neurology, 12,* 35–41.

Bounds, J. V., Wiebers, D. O., Whisnant, J. P., & Okazaki, H. (1981). Mechanisms and timings of deaths from cerebral infarction. *Stroke, 12,* 474–477.

Branston, N. M., Strong, A. J., & Symon, L. (1977). Extracellular potassium activity evoked potential and tissue blood flow: Relationship during progressive ischemia in baboon cerebral cortex. *Journal of Neurologic Sciences, 32,* 305–321.

Brodal, A. (1973). Self observations and neuro-anatomical considerations after a stroke. *Brain, 96,* 675–694.

Buonanno, F. S., Cooper, M. R., Moody, D. M., Laster, D. W., Ball, M. R., & Toole, J. F. (1980). Neurologic aspects of cerebral disseminated intravascular coagulation. *American Journal of Neuroradiology, 1,* 245–250.

Caplan, L. R. (1979). Occlusion of the vertebral or basilar artery: Followup analysis of some patients with benign outcomes. *Stroke, 10,* 277–282.

Caplan, L. R. (1980). "Top of the basilar" syndrome. *Annals of Neurology, 30,* 72–79.

Caplan, L. R., & Hedley-White, T. (1974). Cuing and memory dysfunction in alexia without agraphia: A case report. *Brain, 97,* 251–262.

Carter, A. B. (1961). Anticoagulant treatment in progressive stroke. *British Medical Journal, 2,* 70–73.

Carter, L. T., Caruso, J. L., Languirand, M. A., & Berard, M. A. (1980). Cognitive skill remediation in stroke and non-stroke elderly. *Clinical Neuropsychology, 2,* 109–113.

Castaigne, P., Lhermitte, F., Buge, A., Escourolle, R., Hauw, J. J., & Lyon-Caen, D. (1981). Paramedian thalamic and midbrain infarcts: Clinical and neuropathological study. *Annals of Neurology, 10,* 127–148.

Castaigne, P., Lhermitte, F., Gautier, J. C., Escourolle, R., Derovesne, C., Deragopian, P., & Popa, C. (1973). Arterial occlusions in the vertebrobasilar system—A study of 44 patients with post-mortem data. *Brain, 96,* 133–154.

Cermak, L. S., & Laird S. (1975). Imagery as an aid to retrieval for Korsakoff patients, *Cortex, 2,* 163–169.

Denny-Brown, D. E. (1960). Recurrent cerebrovascular episodes. *Archives of Neurology, 2,* 194–210.

Diller, L., Ben Yishay, Y., Gerstman, L. J., Goodkin, R., Gordon, W., Weinberg, J. (1974). *Rehabilitation monograph no. 50: Studies in cognition and rehabilitation in hemiplegia.* New York: Institue of Rehabilitation Medicine.

Fields, W. S. (1972). Collateral circulation in cerebrovascular disease. In P. T. Vinkent & C. W. Bruyn (Eds.) *Handbook of clinical neurology* (Vol. II, pp. 168–182). New York: North Holland Publishers and American Elsevier Co. Incorporated.

Fields, W. S., Bruetman, M. E., & Weibel, J. (1965). *Collateral circulation of the brain.* Baltimore: Williams & Wilkins.

Fisher, C. M. (1959). Observations of the fundus oculi in transient monocular blindness. *Neurology, 9,* 333–347.

Fisher, C. M. (1969). The arterial lesions underlying lacunes. *Acta Neuropathologica, 12,* 1–15.

Fisher, C. M. (1976). The natural history of carotid occlusion. In G Austin (Ed.), *Microneurosurgical anastomoses for cerebral ischemia* (pp. 194–201). Springfield, IL: Charles C. Thomas.

Fisher, C. M. (1982). Lacunar strokes and infarcts: A review. *Neurology, 32,* 871–876.

Fisher, C. M., Karnes, W., & Kubik, C. (1961). Lateral medullary infarction: The pattern of vascular occlusion. *Journal of Neuropathology and Experimental Neurology, 20,* 323–379.

Fisher, M., Davidson, R. I., & Marcus, E. M. (1980). Transient focal cerebral ischemia as a presenting manifestation of unrupted cerebral aneurysms. *Neurology, 8,* 367–372.

Fowler, N. D., & Marshall, W. J. (1965). The supraclavicular arterial bruit. *American Heart Journal, 69,* 410–418.

Gee, W. (1978). Clinical application of ocular plethysmography. In E. F. Bernstein (Ed.), *Noninvasive diagnostic techniques in vascular disease.* St. Louis: C. V. Mosby Company.

Goldstein, G., & Ruthven, L. *Rehabilitation of the brain-damaged adult.* New York: Plenum Press.

Gowers, W. R. (1888). *A manual of diseases of the nervous system.* London: Churchill Livingstone.

Gresham, G. E., Fitzpatrick, T. E., Wolf, P. A., McNamara, P. M., Kannel, W. B., & Dawber, T. R. (1975). Residual disability in survivors of stroke—The Framingham Study. *New England Journal of Medicine, 293,* 954–956.

Gresham, G. E., Phillips, T. F., Wolf, P. A., McNamara, P. M., Kannel, W. B., & Dawber, T. R. (1979). Epidemiologic profile of long-term stroke disability: The Framingham Study. *Archives of Physical Medicine and Rehabilitation, 60,* 487–491.

Grindal, A. B., & Toole, J. F. (1974). Headache and transient ischemia attacks. *Stroke, 5,* 603–606.

Gunning, A. J., Pickering, G. W., Robb-Smith, A. H. T., & Russell, R. W. R. (1964). Mural thrombosis of the internal carotid artery and subsequent embolism. *Quarterly Journal of Medicine, 33,* 155–195.

Hachinski, V. C., Iliff, L. D., Zilkha, E., DuBou-lay, G. H., McAllister, V. L., Marshall, J., Russell, R. W. R., & Symon, L. (1975). Cerebral blood flow in dementia. *Archives of Neurology, 32,* 632–637.

Haerer, A. F. (1973). Visual field defects and the prognosis of stroke patients. *Stroke, 4,* 163–168.

Harrison, M. J. G., & Marshall, J., (1985). Arteriographic comparison of amaurosis fugax and hemispheric transient ischemic attacks. *Stroke, 16,* 795–797.

Hass, W. K. (1977). Aspirin for the limping brain: Editorial. *Stroke, 8,* 299.

Hatano, S. (1973). Control of stroke in the community—Methodologic considerations and protocol of WHO stroke register. *WHO document no. CVD/S 73.6,* Rev. 1.

Hathaway, S. R. & McKinley, J. C. (1951). *The Minnesota Multiphasic Personality Inventory manual (Revised).* New York Psychological Corporation.

Heck, A. F. (1985). Medical management of TIAs and small strokes. In R. R. Smith (Ed.), *Stroke and the extracranial vessels* (pp. 149–158). New York: Raven Press.

Heilman, K. M., & Valenstein, E. (1979). *Clinical neuropsychology.* New York: Oxford University Press.

Hennerici, M., Aublich, A., Sandmann, W., & Freund, H. J. (1981). Incidence of asymptomatic extracranial arterial disease. *Stroke, 12,* 750–758.

Heyman, A., Wilkinson, W. E., Heyden, S., Helms, M. J., Bartel, A. G., Karp, H. R., Tyroler, H. A., & Hames, C. G. (1980). Risk of stroke in asymptomatic persons with cervical arterial bruits: A population study in Evans County, Georgia. *New England Journal of Medicine, 302,* 838–841.

Higbee, K. L. (1977). *Your memory.* Englewood Cliffs, NJ: Prentice-Hall.

Hollenhorst, R. W. (1961). Significance of bright plaques in the retinal arterioles. *Journal of the American Medical Association, 178,* 123–129.

Hooper, H. E. (1958). In H. E. Hooper *The Hooper Visual Organisation Test Manual.* Los Angeles Western Psychological Services.

Horenstein, S., Chamberlain, W., & Conomy, J. (1967). Infarction of the fusiform and calcarine regions: Agitated delirium and hemianopsia. *Transactions of the American Neurologic Association, 92,* 85–89.

Hutchinson, E. C., & Acheson, A. J. (1975). *Strokes: Natural history, pathology and surgical treatment.* London: W. B. Saunders.

Jones, H. R., & Millikan, C. H. (1976). Temporal profile (clinical course) of acute carotid system cerebral infarction. *Stroke, 7,* 64–71.

Jones, H. R., Millikan, C. H., & Sandok, B. A. (1980). Temporal profile (clinical course) of acute vertebrobasilar system infarction. *Stroke, 11,* 173–177.

Jones, H. R., Siekert, R. G., & Geraci, J. E. (1969). Neurologic manifestations of bacterial endocarditis. *Annals of Internal Medicine, 71,* 21–28.

Kartchner, M. M., McRae, L. P., Crain, V., & Whitaker, B. (1976). Oculoplethysmography: An adjunct to arteriography in diagnosis of extracranial carotid occlusion disease. *American Journal of Surgery, 132,* 728–732.

Kistler, J. F., Ropper, A. H., & Heros, R. C. (1984a). Therapy of ischemic cerebral vascular disease due to atherothrombosis. *New England Journal of Medicine, 311,* 27–34.

Kistler, J. F., Ropper, A. H., & Heros, R. C. (1984b). Therapy of ischemic cerebral vascular disease due to atherothrombosis. *New England Journal of Medicine, 311,* 100–105.

Kotila, M., Waltimo, O., Niemi, M., Laaksonen, R., & Lempinen, M. (1984). The profile of recovery from stroke and factors influencing outcome. *Stroke, 15,* 1039–1044.

Kubik, C. S., & Adams, R. D. (1946). Occlusion of the basilar artery—A clinical and pathological study. *Brain, 69,* 6–121.

Kunitz, S. C., Gross, C. R., Heyman, A., Kase, C. S., Mohr, J. P., Price, T. R., & Wolf, P. A. (1984). The pilot stroke data bank: Definition, design and data. *Stroke, 15,* 740–746.

Kurtzke, J. F. (1976). Epidemiology of cerebrovascular disease. In R. Siekert, (Ed.) *Cerebrovascular survey report. Joint council subcommittee on cerebrovascular disease, National Institute of Neurological and Communicative Disorders and Stroke and National Heart and Lung Institute* (pp. 213–242). Rochester, MN: Whiting Press.

Lees, R. S., & Kistler, J. P. (1978). In E. F. Bernstein (Ed.), Carotid phonoangiography. In *Noninvasive diagnostic techniques in vascular disease* (pp. 187–194). St. Louis: C. V. Mosby.

Lewinsohn, P. M., Danaher, B. G., & Kikel, S. (1977). Visual imagery as a mnemonic aid for brain-injured persons. *Journal of Consulting and Clinical Psychology, 45,* 717–723.

Lezak, M. D. (1983). Neuropsychological assessment (2nd ed.). New York: Oxford University Press.

Lishman, W. A. (1978). *Organic psychiatry: The psychological consequences of cerebral disorder.* Boston: Blackwood Scientific.

Logan, W., & Sherman, D. G. (1983). Transient global amnesia. Current concepts of cerebrovascular disease. *Stroke, 14,* 1005–1007.

Marquardsen, J. (1983). Natural history and prognosis of cerebrovascular disease. In R. W. Ross Russell (Ed.), *Vascular disease of the central nervous system* (pp. 25–40). Edinburgh: Churchill Livingstone.

Matthews, W. B., Oxbury, J. M., Grainger, K. M. R., & Greenhall, R. C. D. (1976). A blind controlled trial of dextran 40 in the treatment of acute ischaemic stroke. *Brain, 99,* 193–206.

Mikula, J. A. (1983, February). *A computerized approach to training visual attention and visual imagery in closed head injury.* Paper presented at the International Neuropsychological Society Meeting, Mexico City.

Millikan, C. H. (1975). A classification and outline of cerebrovascular disease. *Stroke, 6,* 564–616.

Millikan, C. H., & McDowell, F. H. (1978). Treatment of transient ischemic attacks. *Stroke, 9,* 299–308.

Millikan, C. H., & McDowell, F. H. (1980). Treatment of progressing stroke. *Progress in cardiovascular diseases, 18,* 397–414.

Mohr, J. P. (1978). Transient ischemic attacks and the prevention of strokes: Editorial *New England Journal of Medicine, 299,* 93.

Mohr, J. P., Caplan, L. R., Melski, J. W., Goldstein, R. J., Duncan, G. W., Kistler, J. P., Pessin, M. S., & Bleich, H. L. (1978). The Harvard Cooperative Stroke Registry: A prospective registry. *Neurology, 28,* 754–762.

Moossy, J. (1966). Morphology, sites and epidemiology of cerebral atherosclerosis. *Res. Publ. Assoc. Res. Nerv. Ment. Dis., 41,* 1.

Moskowitz, E., Lightbody, F. E. H., & Freitag, N. S. (1972). Long-term follow-up of the poststroke patient. *Archives of Physical medicine and Rehabilitation, 53,* 167.

Mott, F. W., & Sherrington, C. S. (1895). Experiments uopon the influence of sensory nerves upon movement and nutrition of the limbs. *Proceedings of the Royal Medicine, 57,* 481.

Osterreith, P. A. (1944). Le test de copie d'une figure complexe. *Archives de Psychologie, 30,* 206–356.

Ownby, R. L., & Smigielski, J. S. (1984, October). *The validity of the MMPI-168 with head injury patients: A preliminary study.* Paper presented at the fifth Traumatic Head Injury Conference, Braintree, MA.

Oxbury, M., Greenhall, R. C. D., & Grainger, K. M. R. (1975). Predicting the outcome of stroke: Acute stage after cerebral infarction. *British Medical Journal, 3,* 125–127.

Patrick, B. A., Ramirez-Lassepas, M., & Snyder, B. D. (1980). Temporal profile of vertebrobasilar territory infarction. Prognostic implications. *Stroke, 11,* 643–647.

Podbros, L. Z., & Noble, P. B. (1982, November). *Elaboration strategies: Their effects on memory retention in two amnesic patients.* Paper presented at the annual meeting of the American Congress of Physical Medicine and Rehabilitation, Houston, TX.

Poon, L. W. (1980). A systems approach for the assessment and treatment of memory problems. In *The comprehensive handbook of behavioral medicine* (Vol. I). New York: Spectrum Publications.

Portenoy, R. K., Abissi, C. J., Lipton, R. B., Berger, A. R., Mebler, M. F., Baglivo, J., & Solomon, S. (1984). Headache in cerebrovascular disease. *Stroke, 15,* 1009–1012.

Raichle, M. E. (1983). The pathophysiology of brain ischemia. *Annals of Neurology, 13,* 2–10.

Raven, J. C. (1960). Guide to the standard progressive motives. H. K. Lewis. London, New York Pschological Corporation.

Reivich, M., Holling, H. E., Roberts, B., et al. (1961). Reversal of blood flow through the vertebral artery and its effects on cerebral circulation. *New England Journal of Medicine, 265,* 878–885.

Rey, A. (1964). *L'examen clinique en psychologie.* Paris: Presses Universitaires de France.

Robertson, J. T. (1985). The surgical candidate. In R. R. Smith (Ed.), *Stroke and the extracranial vessels* (pp. 167–174). New York: Raven Press.

Robins, M., Baum, H. M. (1981). Incidence. *Stroke, 12 (Suppl. 1),* 145–155.

Robinson, R. G., & Szetela, B. (1981). Mood changes following left hemisphere brain injury. *Annals of Neurology, 9,* 447–453.

Roederer, G. O., Langlois, Y. E., Jager, K. A., Primozich, J. F., Beach, K. W., Phillips, D. J., & Strandness, D. E. (1984). The natural history of carotid arterial disease in asymptomatic patients with cervical bruits. *Stroke, 15,* 605–613.

Ross, E. D., & Rush, A. J. (1981). Diagnosis and anatomical correlates of depression in brain-damaged patients. *Archives of General Psychiatry, 38,* 1344–1354.

Rothi, L. J., & Horner, J. (1983). Restitution and substitution: Two theories of recovery with application to neurobehavioral treatment. *Journal of Clinical Neuropsychology, 5,* 73–81.

Russel, E. W. (1975). A multiple scoring method for the assessment of complex memory functions. *Journal of Consulting and Clinical Psychology, 43,* 800–809.

Russell, R. W. R. (1961). Observations on the retinal blood vessels in monocular blindness. *Lancet, 2,* 1422–1428.

Sandok, B. A., Whisnant, J. P., Furlan, A. J., et al. (1982). Carotid artery bruits. Prevalence survey and differential diagnosis. *Mayo Clinic Proceedings, 57,* 227–230.

Schacter, D. L., & Glisky, E. L. (in press). Memory remediation: Restoration, alleviation, and the acquisition of domain-specific knowledge. In B. Uzzell & Y. Gross (Eds.), *Clinical neuropsychology of intervention.* Boston: Martinus Nijhoff.

Schacter, D. L., Rich, S. A., & Stampp, M. S. (1985). Remediation of memory disorders: Experimental evaluation of the spaced-retrieval technique. *Journal of Clinical and Experimental Neuropsychology, 7,* 79–96.

Scotti, G., Spinnler, H., Sterzi, R., & Vallar, G. (1980). Cerebellar softening. *Annals of Neurology, 8,* 133–140.

Stewart, R. M., Samson, D., Diehl, J., Hinton, R., & Ditmore, Q. M. (1980). Unruptured cerebral aneurysms presenting as recurrent transient neurologic deficits. *Neurology, 30,* 47–51.

Strand, T., Asplund, K., Eriksson, S., et al. (1984). A randomized controlled trial of hemodilution therapy in acute ischemic stroke. *Stroke, 15,* 980–989.

Strandgaard, S., Olesen, J., Skinhoj, E., et al. (1973). Autoregulation of brain circulation in severe arterial hypertension. *British Medical Journal, 1,* 507–510.

Thompson, J. E., Patman, R. D., & Persson, A. V. (1976). Management of asymptomatic carotid bruits. *American Surgeon, 42,* 77–80.

Toole, J. F. (1984a). Medical management of transient ischemic attacks. In J. F. Toole (Ed.), *Cerebrovascular disorders* (pp. 117–126). New York: Raven Press.

Toole, J. F. (1984b). Surgical management of transient ischemic attacks. In J. F. Toole (Ed.), *Cerebrovascular disorders* (pp. 125–136). New York: Raven Press.

Toole, J. F. (1984c). Transient ischemic attacks. In J. F. Toole (Ed.), *Cerebrovascular disorders,* 3rd edition (pp. 101–116). New York: Raven Press.

Trexler, L. (Ed.), (1982). *Cognitive rehabilitation: Conceptualization and intervention.* New York: Plenum Press.

Wade, D. T., Langton-Hewer, R., Wood, V. A. (1984). Stroke: The influence of age upon outcome. *Age and Ageing, 13,* 357–362.

Wade, D. T., & Wood, V. A. (1985). Recovery after stroke—The first 3 months. *Journal of Neurology, Neurosurgery and Pyschiatry, 48,* 7–13.

Wade, D. T., Langton-Hewer, R., & Wood, V. A. (1984). Stroke: Influence of patient's sex and side of weakness on outcome. *Archives of Physical Medicine and Rehabilitation, 65,* 513–516.

Wechsler, D. (1945). A standardized memory scale for clinical use. *Journal of Psychology, 19,* 87–95.

Wechsler, D. (1981). *WAIS-R Manual.* New York: Psychological Corporation.

Weinberg, J., Diller, L., Gordon, W.A., Gerstman, L. J., Lieberman, A., Lakin, P., Hodges, G., & Ezrachi, O. (1979). Training sensory awareness and spatial organization in people with right-brain damage. *Archives of Physical Medicine and Rehabilitation, 60,* 491–496.

Weinberg, J., Piasetsky, E., Diller, L., & Gordon, W. (1982). Treating perceptual organization deficits in non-neglecting RBD stroke patients. *Journal of Clinical Neuropsychology, 4,* 59–75.

Whisnant, J. P., Matsumoto, N., & Elveback, L. R. (1973). The effect of anticoagulant therapy on the prognosis of patients with transient cerebral ischemia attacks in a community Rochester, Minnesota, 1955 through 1969. *Mayo Clinic Proceedings, 48,* 844–848.

Wilson, B. A., & Moffat, N. (Eds.), (1984). *Clinical management of memory problems.* Rockville, MD: Aspen.

Wolf, P. A., Dawber, T. R., Thomas, H. E., et al. (1978). Epidemiologic assessment of chronic atrial fibrillation and risk of stroke: The Framingham Study. *Neurology, 28,* 973–977.

Wolf, P. A., Kannel, W. B., & Dawber, T. R. (1978). Prospective investigations: The Framingham Study and the epidemiology of stroke. In B. S. Schoenberg (Ed.), *Advances in neurology, Volume 19: Neurological epidemiology principles and clinical applications* (pp. 107–120). New York: Raven Press.

Wood, R. L. (1984). Management of attention disorders following brain injury. In B. A. Wilson & N. Moffat (Eds.), *Clinical management of memory problems.* Rockville, MD: Aspen.

Yatsu, F. M., & Mohr, J. P. (1982). Anticoagulation therapy for cardiogenic emboli to brain. *Neurology, 32,* 274–275.

Young, G. C., Collins, D., & Hren, M. (1983). Effect of pairing scanning training with block design training inthe remediation of perceptual problems in left hemiplegics. *Journal of Clinical Neuropsychology, 5,* 201–212.

CHAPTER 27

Visual Impairment

Albert W. Biglan, Vincent B. Van Hasselt and Janet Simon

INTRODUCTION

The rate and extent of intellectual development will be related to the degree and quality of sensory stimulation, especially during the early years of life. An absence of or a decrease in visual sensory information may have a lasting deleterious, and sometimes irreversible, effect on development.

Defects affecting the visual system may be present at birth, or they may be acquired and occur later in life. Events leading to reduced visual acuity may be related to trauma to one or more parts of the visual system, or may be due to a genetically predetermined disease process that becomes manifested during the second or third decade of life. Frequently, a genetically transmitted defect also will be associated with other physical and developmental defects.

This chapter will describe some of the commonly occurring defects in the visual system. The list of defects presently discussed is not meant to be encyclopedic. Rather, it is intended to cover problems that represent different forms of blindness. A brief description of each will be followed by information concerning epidemiology, current methods of medical assessment and treatment, and research-related activities. Then, strategies and issues pertaining to the psychological and educational evaluation and intervention with visual impairment will be presented.

DESCRIPTION OF THE DISORDER

Anatomy and Development of the Visual System

Before each condition is discussed, it is important to review the normal development of the visual system. With this back-

Preparation of this chapter was facilitated by Grant No. G008300135 (National Institute of Handicapped Research), 086HH50003 (Special Education Programs), and Contract No. 300-82-0368 (Early Child Research Institute) from the U.S. Department of Education. However, opinions expressed herein do not necessarily reflect the position or policy of the U.S. Department of Education. The authors thank Judith A. Lorenzetty for her assistance in preparation of the manuscript.

ground, defects in development or variations in the maturation process are best understood.

The visual system can be divided into three functional areas: the eye (the sense organ), the visual pathways to the brain, and the visual cortex located in the occipital lobes of the brain.

The function of the eye is to collect, focus, and convert the image that is focused on the retina into light energy (see Figure 27-1). The image is transformed into an electrical impulse, which is then conducted from each eye in such a way that the visual field on the right side of the body is transmitted and processed by the left side of the brain (see Figure 27-2). As shown in Figure 27-3, the occipital lobe, with its specialized calcarine cortex, then recognizes the transmitted impulse. Once this occurs, the impulse is relayed to other higher cerebral centers where the impulse is remembered and integrated with other sensory inputs entering the central nervous system. Higher cerebral centers permit a person to recall or remember a perceived image even in the absence of additional stimulation by the object of regard. The process of development of the visual system occurs as a nonconditioned reflex, which matures and becomes refined over the first 8 years of life.

Normally, each person has two eyes and these must be synchronized in their move-

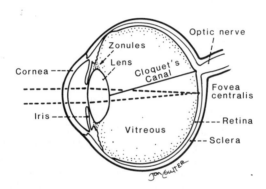

Figure 27-1. Schematic cross-section of the eye showing a beam of light focused on the fovea.

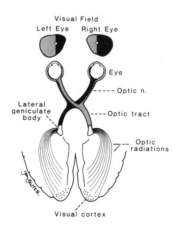

Figure 27-2. The visual fields are shown as they are projected through the visual system. The right visual field is seen by the nasal retina of the right eye and the temporal retina of the left eye. The left optic tract contains the fibers corresponding to the right side of the visual field. A relay junction of synapse occurs at the lateral geniculate body where the image is transferred to the optic radiations that go to the left occipital or visual cortex.

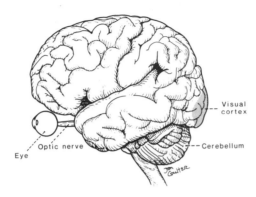

Figure 27-3. The area of the visual cortex is outlined on a schematic diagram of the brain.

ment. The ability of the eyes to move provides the capability to unify the two ocular images and, also, to increase the field of vision. The presence of two eyes facilitates the perception of depth and permits the sensation of stereo acuity. It also provides a spare if one is injured.

The anatomic development of the visual system is incomplete at birth. The peripheral retina of each eye will be incompletely developed. If a child is born prematurely, the normal development of the peripheral retina may be interrupted and vascular abnormalities may occur.

Before birth, portions of the central cavity of the eye will involute and leave an optically clear (vitreous) substance surrounding an almost totally regressed Cloquets's Canal (see Figure 27-1). Major developmental changes continue to occur after birth. In the perinatal period, blood vessels that have surrounded the lens during the first few months of gestation may persist for several weeks and then regress. An interruption or defect in this process may produce a lens opacity or cataract. The regression of blood vessels surrounding the lens is predictable to such an extent that it is one of the signs used to establish the gestational age of an infant.

The eye will rapidly grow in its axial length and circumference. At birth, the eye is 16 mm long. It will grow to 23 mm in axial length over the next 2 years of life. Over the following 10 years of life, the eye will grow an additional millimeter to attain an adult size of 24 mm. Failure of an eye to attain full growth is called *microphthalmia.* During the growth period, the refractive properties of the lens and cornea strive to keep a clear, well-focused, nondistorted image on the retina. Defects in this process produce refractive errors, myopia, hyperopia, and astigmatism.

At birth, myelination of the optic nerve is usually complete. Myelination serves as a form of insulation to separate the electrical impulses carried by each of the 1 million or so nerve fibers that are contained in this structure. The visual information is conducted by the optic nerves and the optic tracts to the visual cortex. If the nerve is small (hypoplastic) or abnormal (coloboma), fewer impulses will be able to be conducted. The optic nerves will conduct the impulses to a relay area, the lateral geniculate body, prior to transmission to the higher levels on the visual cortex (see Figure 27-3). During the first 7 or 8 years, the cells in the lateral geniculate body and the visual cortex progress in development. If the visual image is blurred or if there is a doubling of images due to eye misalignment, cells in the lateral geniculate body will undergo an arrest in development. This arrest is reversible in some instances if treatment is initiated early in life. In general, defects must be treated before age 8. The earlier defects are corrected and treatment initiated, the better the prognosis.

Visual Aculty and Assessment

Subjective tests of a child's visual acuity shortly after birth show that the vision is in the range of 20/800. By 6 months of age, a child has potential to see 20/20 as measured by a visual evoked potential (VEP). However, this probably does not represent the same quality of visual acuity as we understand it. When the maturation process is normal, a child should reflexively fixate on a flashlight at 6 months of age. By the 8th year of life, the visual system is considered to be mature and a correctable visual acuity of 20/20 should be expected.

Although the visual system has many functions, visual acuity is the most commonly accepted measurement used to grade or measure the level of development or function of the system. Visual acuity may be ascertained using subjective and objective methods. The level of visual acuity is frequently used to define the extent or degree of visual impairment. Because of its importance, a brief description of the common clinical and research methods for determining visual acuity follows.

Early detection and treatment of defects in the visual system is imperative. Examiners must be able to evaluate visual acuity in the young nonverbal child. After the first 2 or 3 months of life, acuity is estimated by assessing the quality of the fixation response. When the fixation on a light is steady and well-maintained and there is equal preference for using either eye for fixation, equal and good visual acuity can be inferred. After 6 months, a child should have a visual response to moving targets of large spatial frequency. Targets that move horizontally or vertically will produce a special form of nystagmus, known as optokinetic nystagmus (see Figure 27-4). The presence of optokinetic nystagmus indicates that the child is able to visually resolve the spatial separation between the moving objects presented by the drum or tape.

Visual acuity may be assessed in infants using the forced choice preferential looking (FPL) technique (see Figure 27-5). Presently, this method is used as a research tool, but clinical applications are antici-

pated. Visual acuity is determined by presenting targets of known spatial frequency for comparison with similar targets of equal gray scale. A child will preferentially respond to the stripes, and visual acuity can be measured.

By 2½ to 3 years of age, visual acuity can be clinically evaluated using the child's ability to recognize isolated, graphic pictures on the Allen cards (see Figure 27-6). This method permits measurement of visual acuity by comparison and recognition. Other symbol recognition tests include the E game and the Stycar tests. All of these approaches can be employed to measure visual acuity in children who are not yet able to identify Snellen letters.

Estimation of a child's visual acuity by assessing his or her activity level is unreliable. Monocular visual problems, such as tumors that render an eye blind, will frequently remain undetected because of good vision in the fellow eye. When a child has binocular visual deprivation, suspicion that the visual acuity is decreased may be evident as early as 6 months of age when a child fails to respond to his or her mother's face.

Special Diagnostic Tests to Determine Visual Function

Specialized tests can be utilized to determine the function of each component of the visual system. These procedures have become standard methods for investigating dysfunction of the individual components comprising the visual system.

The pattern-generated visual evoked potential (VEP) is an objective method for determining visual acuity (see Figure 27-7). This procedure requires an alert patient to concentrate on a flashing light or an alternating checkerboard stimulus of variable check or grid size. The electrical activity, or EEG in the calcarine or visual cortex, is averaged. The summation of electrical activity generated by the grid can then be monitored and related to the synchronized flash of an alternating checkerboard stimulus. When there is an absence of a syn-

Figure 27-4. A striped tape is being used to induce optokinetic nystagmus. A response to the moving stripes indicates that the patient has sufficient visual acuity to resolve the spacial interval of the stripes.

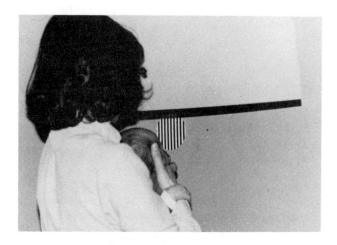

Figure 27-5. The forced preference looking technique has been used as a method to assess visual acuity in infants and young non-verbal children. A child will prefer to look at a striped target over a similar target of equal intensity (grey scale). The distance between the stripes will indicate the level of visual acuity (Photo courtesy of Velma Dobson, Ph.D.).

chronized wave form, it is assumed that the check size was not able to be resolved at the given visual size or angle. There is debate in the field of opthalmology as to whether there is a direct correlation of the visual acuity obtained with the VEP and those results obtained using the standard subjective testing methods.

The function of the retina may be ascertained via the electroretinogram (ERG) (see Figure 27-8). This test requires the temporary placement of a contact lens on the eye. An electrode in the lens measures the very small voltage potentials generated by retina tissue when it is stimulated by light. By altering techniques, the rod response and the cone response of each eye can be measured.

The electrooculogram (EOG) measures the function of the retinal pigment epi-

Figure 27-6. Allen cards being presented to a 3-year-old child. Symbols are easily remembered and can provide valuable information about visual acuity prior to learning the alphabet.

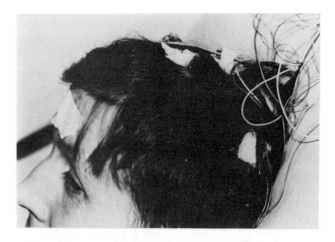

Figure 27-7. The visual evoked potential is determined by placing electroencephalogram electrodes on the scalp over the visual cortex. Averaged electrical responses over this area are correlated with visual stimulation using an alternating grid pattern of known size.

thelium layer of the retina. This layer generates an electrical potential on the front surface of the eye. This potential increases with dark adaptation and becomes reduced with light adaptation. The ratio of this change in electrical potential reflects the function of the retinal pigment epithelium.

The field of vision may be mapped-out separately for each eye using one of several methods of perimetry. The field of vision will frequently give a clue that the location of a defect is either in the eye or the visual pathway. Accurate quantitative perimetry requires a cooperative patient. The field of

vision may be estimated clinically with confrontation methods. These compare the patient's visual field to the examiner's while each faces the other.

The function of the optic nerve may be tested by alternately flashing a light into one pupil and then the other. The pupils normally will show a direct and consentual contraction when a light is directed into the pupil. The speed and intensity of contraction are observed in each eye. An equality in the response to light is a sensitive indicator of afferent visual pathway function up to the level of the lateral geniculate

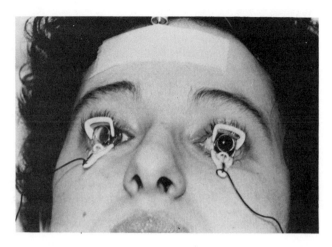

Figure 27-8. Electrodes have been placed on the eyes to determine theretinal electrical activity (ERG) generated by a bright flash of light.

body (see Figure 27-2). In children with cortical blindness, this pathway may be intact even though the child is unable to perceive light.

EPIDEMIOLOGICAL FINDINGS

The definition of legal blindness is that visual acuity is decreased in the best corrected eye to the level of no better than 20/200, or there is a reduction in visual field to the point that the central field of vision is not greater than 20 degrees.

In the United States, there are 10 million people who suffer visual impairment that cannot be corrected by eyeglasses or contact lenses. Of these individuals, 1.5 million are so severely impaired that they cannot read newsprint. There are about 500,000 legally blind people in the United States (National Society to Prevent Blindness, 1980).

The number of children who are blind in the United States is difficult to estimate since there is no centralized recording agency. The incidence of blindness in school age children is relatively constant. Over the past 2 decades, however, there has been a change in the profile of the child with a visual defect.

Blindness is rarely seen as an isolated phenomenon, but rather as a condition coexisting with one or more additional mental and or physical defects. Some of the more common causes of blindness are reviewed in the following text.

Retinopathy of Prematurity

Retinopathy of prematurity (ROP) consists of an active proliferation of blood vessels arising from the developing or immature retina. These abnormal blood vessels extend into the normally transparent vitreous cavity. With passage of time, this fibrovascular tissue may undergo contraction and in extreme cases will cause retinal detachment and blindness.

In the United States, approximately 2,100 children will be affected by this condition to some degree each year. From this group, approximately 500 will become legally blind (Phelps, 1981). The onset of blindness is usually within the first 3 to 4 months of life and is due to an irreparable traction retinal detachment (see Figure 27-9).

The exact cause(s) of ROP remain unclear. A child with the birthweight of less than 1,000 gm or the child who is born with a gestational age of less than 34 weeks is at great risk for developing this condition. Supplemental oxygen administration, pulmonary disease, and seizure

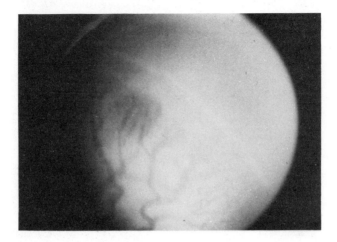

Figure 27-9. A fundus photograph that shows an area of vascular dilatation and hemorrhage at the area of retinal development in a premature infant with retinopathy of prematurity (Photo courtesy of John Flynn, M.D.)

disorders are associated risk factors (Biglan, Brown, Reynolds, & Milley, 1984). This condition may be mild and the visual acuity may be as good as 20/40 to 20/200. However, even when visual acuity is good, the eyes affected by this condition are prone to develop retinal detachments later in life (Tasman, 1979). Not all active ROP progresses to blindness. Regression is common and moderate degrees of this disease may regress, resulting in normal eye examinations with normal visual acuity. Retrolental fibroplasia refers to the cicatriciol, or late form of retinal disease characterized by scar formation on the retina surface and sometimes leading to a detached retina. Children with retrolental fibroplasia have a higher risk for nearsightedness, strabismus, and glaucoma. When myopia is present, it is treated with spectacles. The strabismus usually requires surgical correction. Glaucoma is managed with a combination of medical and surgical means.

Current research is focused on developing measures that reduce the rate of premature births. Vitamin E has been recommended to minimize the degree and extent of ROP. Blood levels for vitamin E are used to determine the degree of vitamin E sufficiency. However, the precise role that this drug has in prevention of the disorder has yet to be determined.

Treatment of the active phase of retinopathy of prematurity with cryotherapy currently is being evaluated in the United States. Opthalmologists in other nations have observed varying degrees of success with cryotreatment, or freezing of the avascular or undeveloped retina during the active phases of retinopathy of prematurity. The role that this treatment will have in the management of the early stages of this condition has not been ascertained.

Optic Nerve Hypoplasia and Coloboma

During the 7th to 8th week of gestational age, the eye begins to form a sphere by an infolding of the tissue that projects from the developing brain. At this point, the fetal fissure will close, the globe is formed, and the optic nerve and eye begin to develop. A defect in this development can either produce a small optic nerve or absence of retinal tissue (coloboma).These defects are rare, may affect one or both eyes, and have been associated with other defects in the central nervous and endocrine system. The visual acuity in patients with optic nerve hypoplasia is stable and may vary from 20/25 to 20/200. It is uncommon to have complete loss of vision. Optic nerve colobomas may extend radially to involve the retina (see

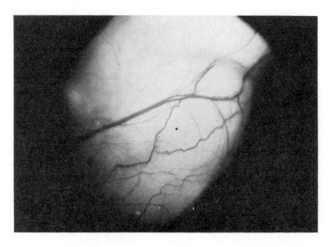

Figure 27-10. A large retina coloboma (inferior with overlying retinal vessels) has a small area of normal retina (superior and to the left).

Figure 27-10). Colobomas that involve the entire posterior aspect of the eye may still provide the child with vision sufficient for unassisted ambulation. There is no treatment for either defect.

If visual acuity is poor, near vision may be enhanced with hand-held magnifying devices. If the anterior segment of the eye is normal, the patient may achieve magnification without the use of hand magnifiers by holding objects close to the eye and employing their large amplitudes of accommodation (12 or 13 diopters). By doing this, a child may get a three to four power magnification. This unassisted source of magnification should be encouraged by instructing the child to hold printed material close to the eye.

There is a paucity of research concerning detection and prevention of these defects, although Acers (1981) discusses them in greater depth.

Leber's Congenital Amaurosis and Achromatopsia

Leber's congenital amaurosis is a rare cause of blindness. The defect is caused by a lack of function of the rods and cones in the retina. The visual acuity at birth is usually less than 20/200 and remains at that level. As with most genetically determined conditions with severely reduced visual acuity, this condition has an autosomal recessive inheritance pattern (Walsh & Hoyt, 1969). The level of visual acuity will remain constant and will be profound.

Achromatopsia is a similar condition involving a deficiency of cone cells in the retina. Night vision may be better than vision in daylight since the rod cell function is usually normal. Central vision remains decreased at the level of 20/200 or 20/400. Large-print books may be necessary in school. Printed material with smaller type should be encouraged to be held close. This will stimulate convergence and help to reduce the amplitude of the oscillation of the eyes or nystagmus.

In general, nystagmus will be present whenever defects in vision occur before 2 years of age. If blindness occurs after the second year of life, nystagmus will rarely be seen. When coarse nystagmus is present, distance visual acuity is usually not better than 20/100 or 20/400. Both of these conditions are infrequently encountered and current research is limited to family studies. There are no known medical treatments for any of the above conditions.

Retinoblastoma

Retinoblastoma is the most common intraocular tumor in children. This malignant tumor occurs at a rate of one in every

15,000 births. Because 40% of the cases have a heritable etiology and death is infrequent, its incidence in our population is increasing (Shields & Augsburger, 1981).

When this tumor is the result of a germinal cell mutation, it is transmitted with an autosomal dominant pattern. About 85% of the genetically transmitted tumors will affect both eyes and each eye will have multiple tumors which may cause bilateral blindness. Tumors that occur as a result of a somatic mutation usually affect one eye and have a unifocal presentation of the tumor (see Figure 27-11). The extent of ocular involvement will be determined by the penetrance and expression of the gene.

In third world countries, retinoblastoma is fatal due to delayed detection and treatment. With early recognition and prompt treatment, survival rates exceeding 90% can be expected. Treatment is individualized and accomplished using photocoagulation, cryotherapy, or radiation therapy, usually in combination with enucleation. The degree of sight loss with this tumor will be determined by the location of the tumor in each eye. A tumor in the macula region which is only 3 mm in size will cause visual acuity to be decreased to 20/400. Vision may further deteriorate if the eye has been treated with radiation therapy and a subsequent cataract

or radiation retinopathy develops. The genetic locus of this tumor is on chromosome 13, and much investigative attention has been directed to this chromosome using chromosomal banding techniques and esterase linkage (Halloran, Boughman, Dryja, Mukai, Long, Roberts, & Craft, 1985).

Retinitis Pigmentosa

Retinitis pigmentosa is a slowly progressing heritable disease that leads to blindness. This condition is characterized by a progressive decrease in the function of the photoreceptors in the retina. As discussed earlier, achromatopsia involves loss of cone-cell function and causes decreased central vision. Retinitis pigmentosa affects the rods, or vision cells located in the peripheral retina, that are responsible for vision in dim illumination and peripheral vision. Three modes of inheritance are recognized: autosomal recessive, autosomal dominant, and X-linked. It is common to have difficulty in establishing the exact inheritance pattern in each patient. Early diagnosis is possible by determining the dark adopted (scotopic) retina function using the electroretinogram. This test may be diagnostic even when other signs of retinitis pigmentosa are absent. Some associated findings in patients with retinitis pig-

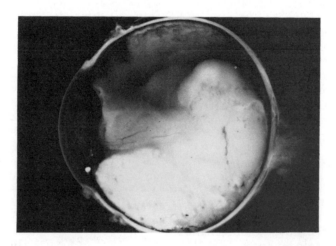

Figure 27-11. An eye that has been removed that contains retinoblastoma. The retina is destroyed by tumor and the eye was blind. Disease was treated in the fellow eye using radiation and a laser (Photo courtesy of Bruce Johnson, M.D.).

mentosa are hearing defects (Usher's syndrome) and abetalipoprotenemia (Bassen-Kornzweig syndrome). This metabolic disorder may be treated by increasing the amount of vitamin A and E in the diet. The Kearns-Sayre syndrome includes retinitis pigmentosa and heart block. Heart block may cause a serious cardiac arrhythymia. Patients with abnormal electrocardiograms may require a pacemaker. Other treatable forms of retinitis pigmentosa include defects in the metabolism of phytanic acid (Refsum's disease). A diet low in phytanic acid is beneficial.

One symptom of retinitis pigmentosa is night blindness. Opthalmoscopic examination shows a pale waxy color of the optic nerve, retinal vascular attenuation, and in later stages of the disease, a typical bone matrix change in the mid-periphery of the retina. The patient with retinitis pigmentosa usually does not have severe diminution of vision until the second or third decade of life. Typically, central vision is preserved and peripheral vision is lost.

Patients frequently demonstrate a tubular visual field defect with visual acuity that may be as good as 20/20. The patient may, however, find it difficult to ambulate because the loss of peripheral visual field.

Corneal Disease

The cornea or clear part of the eye is normally transparent at birth. A rare child may have a temporary clouding of the cornea associated with a difficult birth.

There are many closely associated defects in the development of the anterior segment of the eye. When the cornea is abnormal, there usually are defects in the iris and filtration angles, and lens. The cornea may be small (microcornea) or large (megalocornea or Keratoglobus). Axenfeld's syndrome (abnormal cornea and glaucoma), Reiger's anomaly (abnormal cornea, teeth, and glaucoma) and Peter's anomaly (abnormal cornea, iris, and lens) all represent variations of defects in the development of the anterior segment of the eye (Waring, Rodriguez, & Laribson, 1975). In extreme cases, the cornea may become completely opaque and white in color. Iris and lens

structures may be impossible to identify, even with magnification. Treatment with corneal transplantation in young patients is a major undertaking and should only be considered for select patients who have severe loss of sight. In adults, cornea transplants can be very successful procedures, but the visual result will depend on the condition of the eye lids, lacrimal system, and retina.

Another cause of blindness due to corneal disease is trauma. Because of its location, the cornea is frequently involved when the globe is injured. The healing of a lacerated cornea leaves an optically dense scar that may distort light entering the eye. Fortunately, trauma rarely affects both eyes.

Keratoconus refers to a thinning of a portion of the cornea. This condition usually begins after adolescence and rarely leads to blindness. Patients with Down syndrome have an increased incidence of keratoconus. Complete thinning of the entire cornea or keratoglobus is rare. In this condition, the cornea becomes extremely thin and prone to rupture.

The level of visual acuity in patients with corneal disease will depend on the degree of distortion and clarity of the cornea. Advances in surgical techniques, suture material, and more complete understanding of corneal transplantation and management of graft rejection has greatly expanded the ophthalmologists ability to treat corneal disease, even conditions that were once considered impossible to correct.

GLAUCOMA

Glaucoma in children is very rare. However, when it occurs, it is frequently difficult to control and it has devastating visual implications. Glaucoma may be present at birth or noted shortly thereafter, or it may be acquired secondary to ocular inflammation or trauma. The symptoms of glaucoma in children include tearing, enlargement of the cornea, and light sensitivity.

Primary infantile glaucoma is an infrequently occurring defect in the outflow of fluid from the anterior chamber.

Treatment consists of surgically opening the abnormal filtration angle (goniotomy). If a goniotomy is not performed or is unsuccessful, the cornea may enlarge, become distorted and cloudy, and visual acuity may decrease to 20/200 or 20/800.

Other forms of glaucoma are associated with cataracts, uveitis, Rubella, Sturge-Weber syndrome, trauma, and Lowe's syndrome. The later condition affects male children and is fatal before 2 years of age.

Glaucoma causes blindness by causing cloudiness of the cornea and by destruction of the neurosensory retina. Characteristic defects in the visual field include constriction of the peripheral field and accurate scotomas. Sequential visual fields may be used to monitor progression of disease. Measurement of the visual field in children is difficult since most children are unable to cooperate for a formal determination before their tenth birthday. Unlike adults, children have a poor response to medical treatment of glaucoma. When intraocular pressure is elevated in an adult, it may be controlled with medication, laser trabeculaplasty, and filtering procedures. Laser trabeculaplasty is successful for managing adult glaucoma but it has not been as successful for the management of glaucoma in children.

The future is encouraging. Much research is being conducted to develop ways to maintain filtration of the eye using setons, tubes, and other devices to maintain filtration of the aqueous humor from the anterior chamber. New topically applied eye medications are becoming available that offer effective means for controlling intraocular pressure.

Cataract

Cataracts are opacities of the crystalline lens. They may be present at birth or they may develop as a child gets older. The degree of opacity varies. Some cataracts may be punctate and not affect visual acuity. Others are complete and totally eliminate formed vision. Cataracts may involve one eye or both eyes. When visual acuity decreases to the 20/70 level, or the child is unable to function in school, cataract surgery is recommended. If a child has good vision in one eye and a complete cataract in the fellow eye, cataract surgery is recommended. Optical correction will be necessary following surgery. This is achieved with a contact lens or in select cases, an intraocular lens or an epikeratophakia graft. Children with bilateral cataracts do well with aphakic spectacles or contact lens after cataract surgery.

The technique for cataract removal in children differs from that used in adult cataract operations (see Figure 27-12). An extracapsular technique is usually used and this method of removal of the lens opacity leaves the posterior lens capsule intact. The capsule may develop a secondary opacity. This is treated with a discission or opening of the membrane with a discission knife. With the anticipated improvement of delivery systems, a YAG laser will probably be employed to manage the opacification of the residual lens capsule as it is currently being used in adults.

Unlike the adult who has a mature visual system, the child with a cataract has a condition that may prevent the normal development of the visual system. Therefore, it will require prompt attention. There is a critical point of development sometime within the first month or two of life. Because of this, cataracts detected early in childhood involving both eyes, should be treated with cataract surgery as soon as possible. In patients with bilateral cataracts, the fellow eye is operated on as soon as the first eye has recovered so the brain can receive equal visual stimulation and amblyopia can be treated. If the eyes are not provided with a well focused sharp image, the eye will be suppressed and irreversible amblyopia can occur.

A cataract is usually not an isolated ocular defect. Frequently, there are coexisting retinal or anterior segment of the globe defects that preclude achievement of a good visual result. Optical rehabilitation of the pediatric patient or a patient with a disability who is aphakic can be a challenge. Glasses and contact lenses are the first methods used. Recently, the extended-wear contact lens has been available for

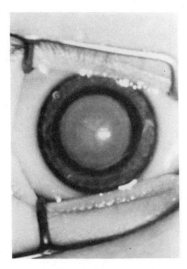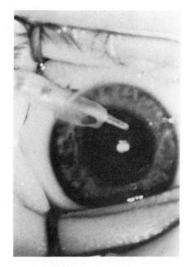

Figure 27-12. *a,* Complete cataract in the eye of a one month old infant. *b,* The cataract is being removed with an aspiration-irrigation instrument.

correction in older children. The difficulties encountered in rehabilitation arise from the fact that removal of the human lens leaves the eye without one of its more powerful refracting elements. Additionally, there is the loss of the ability to accommodate. Duplication of the optical properties of the human lens is difficult. The optical correction of the aphakic patient often will cause distortion and magnification of the image. Distortion can be minimized by placing the lens system close to the eye or within the eye. Correction with spectacles is difficult because the lenses are thick and a child's nose and ears are frequently not capable of supporting the weight of the spectacles.

Cortical Blindness

Some children are born with normal eyes and optic nerves, but the visual cortex is defective. A common cause of cortical blindness is a period of anoxia surrounding birth. The visual cortex has poor collateral blood flow and the tip of the occipital cortex of the brain is one of the more susceptible areas for anoxic damage. Cortical blindness is frequently associated with cerebral palsy, seizure disorders, cerebral vascular accidents, and untreated hydrocephalus. The loss of visual acuity in patients with cortical blindness may be complete. If there is a visual-field defect present, its extent will be determined by the portion of brain affected by the abnormal circulation. The visually evoked response and the CT scan are helpful to confirm cortical blindness (see Figure 27-13). These tests are, however, unable to predict the degree of cortical visual deficit in a reliable fashion. Some infants with seemingly profound visual loss due to perinatal asphyxia may seem to have almost absent visual functioning during the first year or two. These children may return later in life with only modestly decreased visual acuity. There is no treatment for cortical blindness.

Two disabling conditions that are frequently associated with visual problems are spina bifida and cerebral palsy.

Ocular Complications of Meningomyelocele

Eye findings that are frequently associated with meningomyelocele or spina bifida include: strabismus 34% (both acquired or paralytic and congenital forms), optic atrophy, amblyopia, refractive errors, orbit dysplasia, nystagmus, and palpebral fissure anamalies (Clements & Kaushal, 1970; Rothstein, Romano, & Shoch, 1973).

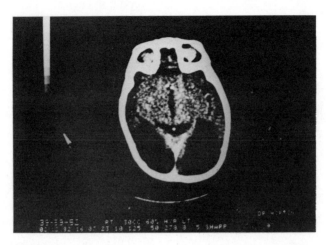

Figure 27-13. A computerized tomographic study of the head of a child who had cortical blindness. The eyes are at the top of the scan, the occipital lobes are on the bottom of the scan. There is absence of the occipital lobes (black cystic areas) on both sides of the brain.

Many defects are due in part to the frequent association of an Arnold-Chiari defect that produces an increase in the intracranial pressure. Therapy is directed toward normalization of the intracranial pressure with shunting procedures. Once 6 months of stability of the intracranial pressure has been achieved, paralytic strabismus can be corrected using conventional strabismus surgery techniques. Amblyopia is treated with occlusion and spectacles. Optic atrophy is prevented by maintaining constant and normal intracranial pressures. Anatomic changes of the orbits are minimized when intracranial pressure is normalized and enlargement of the head is controlled.

The life expectancy of patients with spina bifida has improved greatly over the past 2 decades. Defects of the visual system should be treated using the previously mentioned guidelines. Prompt attention to defects early in life will prevent the blindness that was so frequently encountered decades ago.

Cerebral Palsy

Ocular findings are commonly associated with cerebral palsy. Unlike spina bifida, where a frequent cause of the defect is due to the periodic fluctuation of the intracranial pressure, the defect in cerebral palsy is static and occurs early in life.

Eye findings include strabismus, nystagmus, optic atrophy, gaze palsies, and dyskinetic eye movements of the eyes (Buckley & Seaber, 1981; Hiles, 1975). Patients with stable ocular deviations respond well to strabismus surgery. When ocular alignment is unstable, nonsurgical management is judicious.

DEVELOPMENTAL ISSUES

All parents desire and expect an intact infant without physical or mental disabilities. Whenever the outcome deviates, parents are caught in the dilemma of resolving their own feelings about raising a handicapped child, as well as creating an environment which will encourage the child to develop. This observation clearly extends to families with visually handicapped youngsters.

Blind children progress through developmental phases similar to those for all children. Since interpersonal relationships and environmental factors are keys to promoting development, it is imperative that a sensitivity to the child's special needs be established as soon as possible within the family unit.

Blind infants respond to their mother's touch. However, their lack of vision may render them more passive than a sighted child in the mother/infant relationship. Also, the relatively low rate of smiling and eye contact in blind infants may be interpreted as indicating that the child is unresponsive. An intuitive mother must seek indicators for pleasure and continue to stimulate the child, rather than allow it to fall into patterns of isolation.

While quiet recreation might seem to be appropriate for a blind child, parents should be encouraged to actively engage in physical play. Through movement, the blind child can begin to orient to space and gains increased confidence in his or her own abilities. Since blind children require extra time to perform tasks, there appears to be a natural inclination to "do things for them," whether in play situations or at other times. Parents and others providing care to the child need to recognize the value in allowing the child opportunities for independence even when the time involved is considerable. Blind children can develop basic concepts through hands-on experience with the environment. A skilled care giver maximizes these encounters in simple natural ways.

The significance of toys to blind children is important. Manipulatives help to spur development (Barraga, 1976). Many commercially available toys are suitable for the blind child. Adults can explore the market to select those items which have appeal to the visually impaired child. Toys with an auditory component are especially appropriate. However, other innovative items may be interesting to the child as well. Boys and girls with some sight respond positively to color and shape. Therefore, bright, festive objects are a good choice.

Three aspects of development are considered critical to a blind child: affective, concept/language, and psychomotor. All three areas warrant attention. Cratty and Sams (1968) emphasize the need for the blind child to develop body image as a prerequisite to movement and mobility. Constant use of words to identify body parts assists the child in establishing a sense of self.

There is a natural tendency for adults to care and protect the visually handicapped child. Most certainly the blind youngster routinely encounters more potential dangers than his sighted counterpart. The wise parent balances issues of safety against the child's growing need to move about and explore. Kratz (1973) suggests a variety of physical activities and games that are useful for the blind child. Before the child achieves any true independence, he or she must learn to map space in relationship to his/her own body.

Parents' interest in developmental milestones often focuses on basic skill development. Indeed, learning to eat independently, toileting, dressing, and play are important areas. Lowenfeld (1971) suggests various strategies for maximizing the blind child's independence. While learning may be slow, achievements definitely are possible. A myriad of recommendations useful in the rearing of blind toddlers have been made. However, even the most conscientious parents often observe developmental lags as their child approaches school age. Delays may not be significant in themselves, and parents should be encouraged to modify expectations in relation to the child's potential.

EDUCATIONAL ISSUES

The educational and rehabilitative adjustments that must be made to accommodate blindness will depend on the age of onset and degree of blindness. Further, the expected progression or regression of the defect will determine the method of education to be used. For example, when blindness is congenital or occurs shortly after birth, such as a patient with cortical blindness due to neonatal asphyxia, there will be difficulty in grasping concepts of relative size and color and patterns or visual recognition. This may be contrasted with the patient who has an onset of blindness occurring at a later age (e.g., those with low vision due to retinitis pigmentosa or trauma). These patients have developed and can recall a former visual impression of concepts such as color or facial image. They also possess the concept of the relative size of objects (e.g., a tall building). It is unusual for a congenitally blind child to understand such basic ideas.

From an educational standpoint, it is important to determine the nature of the defect whether it is progressive or not. A child who has a defect which is expected to progress over 5 to 10 years with a gradual diminution of visual acuity, such as retinitis pigmentosa or the slow formation of a cataract or uveitus (ocular inflammation), may acquire skills in reading and sight recognition. Patients may have periods where the vision is relatively good when the uveitus or glaucoma is under control, and they may have periods of time where the sight is impaired or deteriorating. The degree of fluctuation of the visual acuity and final prognosis will determine which educational methods or learning aids are best suited. Discussions involving the physician, child, parents, teachers, and other professionals are important to examine realistic visual expectations and to project the child's educational needs and career selection.

For the purpose of education, there are three categories in which blind children are placed. The first is composed of those with low vision or best-corrected visual acuity of less than 20/400. The second group includes partially sighted children with visual acuity of 20/70 to 20/200. The third group are the children with multiple handicaps and decreased visual acuity. Children with sight of 20/70 to 20/200 may require hand magnifying devices to read newspaper print or other typing optical areas. The person with blindness associated with multiple handicaps has a more devastating problem. Cerebral palsy, infectious processes such as rubella or meningitis associated with deafness, seizures, and other neurologic sequelae present difficult challenges to the educational system.

The history of blind education in the United States chronicles 200 years. The original school concept modeled education of the blind in western Europe dating to the 18th century. Originally, community leaders in Massachusetts organized a school to train blind children from the state. The first attempt to institute educational opportunities was philanthropically supported. From Massachusetts, the idea spread to the mid-Atlantic states.

The first schools for the blind were all privately financed. The curriculum was geared toward basic training rather than academic development. Since the incidence of blindness is low, these schools often served a large geographic area in order to identify a larger population. Consequently, the schools provided residence to the pupils who attended. The basic organization of these special schools remained very similar as new schools, including those which were state controlled, developed around the country. By the middle of the 20th century, over 50 residential schools, located throughout the United States, provided education to the majority of the nation's school-age blind children. This is not to suggest that all blind youngsters attended residential schools. From the turn of the century, some resourceful public school systems engineered placements for visually handicapped pupils. Integration of blind and sighted students became a more appealing notion during the 1960s. More and better-trained vision teachers were available. Improved staff, coupled with a desire for normalcy, led to the placement of increased numbers of blind pupils in the public sector.

Passage of Public Law 94-142 in 1975 formalized the movement from residential to public schools. This legislation addresses the issue of school placement by providing enrollment in the least restrictive environment. The spirit of the law suggests educating handicapped students alongside nonhandicapped pupils whenever possible. Since many blind children have average or above intellectual potential, entactment of PL 94-142 significantly impacted on their school placement. At the same time, the residential schools have accepted many more blind children with moderate or severe concomitant disabilities.

Decision making around school placement for the blind child can be a confusing experience for both parents and professionals. In discussing school placement, it is important to consider various aspects of the curriculum. One of the premises behind placement in the public sector or *mainstreaming*, the term commonly used to describe the placement, is the notion that the cirriculum should parallel that of the regular public school as much as possible. Given this tenet, blind children study academics, related arts and crafts, and physical education. Program emphasis changes from district to district. Some areas provide training in orientation and mobility. Goals for travel training may be narrow or broad, depending on the philosophy of the school system.

Basic academic materials are adapted to the child's preferred medium. Braille or large print usually are available. Recently, the field of education for the visually handicapped has been enhanced through the development of technical reading aids. Many school systems are providing blind children with instruction on the optacon, versabraille and Kurzweil reading machine. Each of these devices translates print to a mode that can be interpreted by a blind individual without assistance. Although braille is commonly associated as a tool for the blind, relatively few visually handicapped students read braille.

In planning school programs for blind youngsters, it is important to consider individual needs. Adequate assessment and evaluation are critical prerequisites to program planning for blind children.

PSYCHOLOGICAL ASSESSMENT AND TREATMENT

Systematic approaches to the psychological assessment and treatment of blind and visually impaired persons dates back nearly half a century. Most of these early efforts focused on intellectual and social functioning. More recent activities have encompassed a wide range of areas, most notably, adaptive and independent living skills. Major strategies utilized in psychological evaluation and remediation of the visually impaired are to be discussed.

Assessment

Sisson and Van Hasselt (1987) recently identified several trends in the assessment of visually impaired persons. First, while early assessors (e.g., Hayes, 1929; Irwin & Goddard, 1914) tended to examine intelli-

gence and academic achievement in blind but otherwise normally developing school children, the emphasis has shifted to younger children, adults, and blind multi-handicapped persons. Second, evaluation is now conducted by a diverse group of examiners affiliated with public schools and community organizations. This is largely due to PL 94-142, which mainstreamed many visually impaired pupils previously in residential schools or institutions, into regular classroom settings. The movement toward deinstitutionalization in the 1960s and 1970s also forced community groups to assess and treat visually impaired children and adults.

Finally, the range of areas examined in visually handicapped clients has broadened to include: (a) intellectual functioning, (b) educational and vocational skills, (c) social competency and adaptive living skills, and (d) emotional adjustment and behavior disorders.

Intellectual Assessment

The most commonly employed procedure for obtaining information concerning intellectual functioning in the visually impaired is through standardized tests. Early testing of school-aged children involved several versions of the Binet Intelligence Scales, with the Perkins-Binet (Davis, 1980) being the most recent. This instrument provides separate forms and norms for children with usable vision (Form U) and no usable vision (Form N). Approximately 25% of the items are perceived through tactual versus auditory modes. Preliminary investigations of psychometric properties of the Perkins-Binet have shown acceptable split-half reliability (Coveny, 1972) and high correlations with verbal scales of the Wechsler Intelligence Scale for Children—Revised (Teare & Thompson, 1982).

The Wechsler Intelligence Scale for Children (WISC) and the Wechsler Adult Intelligence Scale (WAIS) are useful for visually impaired individuals (Bauman & Kropf, 1979). Typically, only the verbal scale is administered. However, many assessors also administer the performance scale when the client has useful vision. Bauman

(1973) suggested that some items may be inappropriate for the blind examinee and should, therefore, be rephrased. For example, the item, "What should you do if you see a train approaching a broken track" may be restated as, "What should a person do if a train is seen approaching a broken track?"

Major limitations of the Wechsler scales as they are typically applied with the visually impaired are the lack of norms on visually impaired individuals and the paucity of data on parametric properties of the tests with this population. While investigations of the Wechsler Verbal scales with the visually impaired have shown adequate reliability (Tillman, 1973), much less is known about their validity. For example, comparisons of the WISC Verbal scale and the Hayes-Binet (a predecessor of the Perkins Binet) with visually impaired children have yielded equivalent IQ scores in some cases (Gilbert & Rubin, 1965; Lewis, 1957) and disparate scores in others (Hopkins & McGuire, 1966, 1967).

Efforts also have been made to modify the Wechsler Performance scale for use with the visually impaired. One of these adaptations is the Haptic Intelligence Scale for the Adult Blind (HIS) (Shurrager, 1961; Shurrager & Shurrager, 1964) which consists of six subtests, four of which resemble the Digit Symbol Block Design, Object Assembly, and Picture Completion tests of the WAIS Performance scale. Additional subtests include the Pattern Board and Bead Arithmetic, the latter involving the use of an abacus. The HIS has normative data on a sample of blind adults and high reliability. Shurrager and Shurrager (1964) report a coefficient of 0.65 in a correlation with the WAIS Verbal scale.

Educational and Vocational Skills

The initial application of educational achievement tests to the visually impaired students was at the end of World War I when such measures as the Metropolitan Achievement Tests, the Myers–Ruch High School Progress Test, and the Stanford Achievement Tests were adapted for this population through braille translation or large print (Bauman, 1972, 1973). Tests required for admission to college or graduate level programs (e.g., Scholastic Aptitude Test, Graduate Record Examination) have been administered to visually impaired students with extended time periods provided to allow test completion.

The time required for administration of adapted forms of such tests is considerably greater than the regular print versions employed with the sighted. Moreover, content and procedural equivalence, as well as the predictive value of modified forms have yet to be empirically demonstrated.

Vocational aptitude in the visually impaired traditionally has been assessed through tests of manipulative skills, such as the Minnesota Rate of Manipulation Test, the Crawford Small Parts Dexterity Test, and the Pennsylvania Bi-Manual Work Sample (Bauman & Kropf, 1979). Inventories employed to evaluate this area are the Strong-Campbell Vocational Interest Blank and the Kuder Preference Record. One problem with these instruments is that they contain some items pertaining to positions not readily held by the blind. Bauman (1973) developed an interest inventory which refers only to activities potentially carried out by visually impaired persons.

Social and Adaptive Living skills

A number of social competency scales have been developed to examine level of social functioning in the visually impaired. The Maxfield–Buccholz Scale of Social Maturity for Pre-School Blind Children (Maxfield & Buchholz, 1958) is an adaption of the Vineland Social Maturity Scale (Doll, 1953). It is utilized for developmental screening of children in the birth to 6-year-old range to evaluate socialization as well as dressing, feeding, locomotion, motor development, and communication.

The Overbrook Social Competency Scale (Bauman, 1972, 1973) is an upward extension of the Maxfield–Buchholz. It starts at age 6 and continues through the high school and young adult period. This scale provides information on aspects of development related to independence in daily living, interpersonal skills, mobility, and aspects of group activity. Both of the aforementioned instruments are typically completed by informants (e.g., parent, teacher, counselor) and yield summative scores referred to as a social quotient (SQ). The SQ presumably reflects social competence relative to normative data on maturity level. However, as Ammerman, Van Hasselt, and Hersen (1986) point out, the association between SQ and specific aspects of social functioning, such as peer interaction, has yet to be documented.

In response to the need for more empirically derived social competence assessment strategies, Matson, Heinze, Helsel, Kapperman, and Rotatori (in press) examined the psychometric properties of the Matson Evaluation of Social Skills with Youngsters (MESSY) (Matson, Rotatori, & Helsel, 1983) with visually impaired children. The MESSY, which is in a Likert format, was originally constructed for sighted children with severe behavioral disturbances. It includes both a self-report and a teacher-report version which consist of 62 and 64 items, respectively. Examples of self-report items include: "I like to be alone," "I feel good if I help someone." The measure was adapted for the visually impaired by providing information in large print and on audio cassettes. Matson et al. (in press) report an internal reliability on Gottman Split-Half and Spearman-Brown of 0.78 or higher on both forms.

To provide a more fine-grained analysis of social functioning, Van Hasselt, Kazdin, Hersen, Simon, and Mastantuono (1985) designed a role-play test with items relevant to the visually impaired client's social environment. This test is comprised of 39 items which assess conversational and assertion skills. An example of a conversational skill role-play scenario is provided as follows:

Narrator: You are walking towards a classroom. The door is partially open and a small group of people is gathered in front of the door. You are new in class and don't know anyone. You would really like to get to know them. You hear/notice one of them walking over to you.

Participants' responses to role play items are videotaped and rated retrospectively on a number of verbal (e.g., speech duration and disturbances, response latency) and nonverbal (e.g., direction of gaze, smiles, posture) behaviors implicated as requisite to interpersonal effectiveness in the social skills and vision literatures (e.g., Bonfanti, 1979; Eisler, Hersen, Miller, & Blanchard, 1975; Sanders & Goldberg, 1977). Van Hasselt et al. (1985) found that the role-play test discriminated between samples of visually handicapped and sighted adolescents on several of these components.

Emotional Adjustment and Behavior Disorders

Several devices originally designed to examine personality traits in the sighted have been adapted for use with the visually impaired. For example, the California Psychological Inventory (CPI) and the Minnesota Multiphasic Inventory (MMPI) both have been administered to visually impaired samples. The CPI includes 480 true–false items and yields 18 scale scores. Some of these scales are: sociability, self-control, dominance, flexibility, and sense of well-being. The MMPI is the most widely used psychopathology assessment device. It consists of 566 affirmative statements requiring responses of either "true," "false," or "cannot say." The MMPI provides scores on 10 clinical scales (e.g., depression, paranoia, hypochondriasis, schizophrenia) and three validity scales. Cross (1947) developed a braille version of this instrument.

Unfortunately, neither the CPI nor the MMPI have been standardized for the visually impaired. While most existing research consistently has revealed evidence of more deviance scores in this population, the meaning of these data has been disputed. In a recent investigation of the adequacy of both the CPI and MMPI for the visually impaired, Adrian, Miller, and DeL'aune (1982) concluded that dysfunctional patterns of responding "may be indicative of the unique adaptive processes used by individuals who have experienced blindness or severe visual impairment from birth, infancy or childhood. Interpretations of test scores for a congenitally blind or early visually impaired person based on deviations from normative scores of a sighted group . . . could be totally irrelevant and result in inappropriate clinical judgements" (p. 178).

Some instruments developed specifically for the visually impaired are the Emotional Factors Inventory (EFI), the Adolescent Emotional Factors Inventory (AEFI) (Bauman, 1972, 1973), and the Anxiety Scale for the Blind (ASB) (Hardy, 1968). Both the EFI and AEFI assess visually impaired adolescents and young adults and are comprised of the following subscales: depression, attitudes of distrust, sensitivity, social competency, somatic symptoms, and attitudes regarding blindness. Measures of adjustment specific to school, family, and heterosocial relationships also are included in the AEFI. The ASB is a 78-item true–false inventory standardized on visually impaired adolescents and young adults (Hardy, 1968). Acceptable correlations (r = 0.60 to 0.79) between this instrument and the Taylor Manifest Anxiety Scale have been reported.

Treatment

A number of intervention strategies have been utilized to deal with difficulties in visually impaired persons. Most of these are from clinical research involving a variety of behavior modification techniques (see reviews by Matson & Helsel, in press; Van Hasselt, 1987). Major categories that have been the focus of treatment are: (a) social skills, (b) maladaptive behaviors (e.g., stereotypies, self-injury), and (c) adaptive living skills.

Social Skills

There is a consensus among professionals in the fields of psychology, special education, and rehabilitation that many visually impaired children and adults evince problems in social adaptation (see review by Van Hasselt, 1983). Indeed, early research using global indices of interpersonal deficits carried out almost half a century ago showed significant lags in social maturity among blind children (Bradway, 1937; Maxfield & Fjeld, 1942;

McKay, 1936). Studies of social functioning in visually impaired adolescents and adults have yielded evidence of poor adjustment in these groups as well (Bonfanti, 1979; Van Hasselt, Hersen, & Kazdin, 1985). Consequently, several social-skills training programs have been implemented with visually impaired individuals. With children and youth, a number of treatment approaches have focused on discrete social behaviors. For example, Yarnell (1979) administered tangible (bright light, food) and social reinforcement (praise) to increase eye contact in a 6½-year-old female with visual and hearing impairments. After 51, 10-minute training sessions, the child emitted over 300 seconds of appropriate eye contact per session in contrast to an average of 36 seconds per session during baseline. Further, generalization to extra-classroom activities was promoted by teaching reinforcement procedures to school aides.

Differential reinforcement (braille-coded tokens exchangeable for back-up reinforcers) of appropriate interpersonal behaviors was employed by Farkas, Sherick, Matson, and Loebig (1981) to improve social functioning in a 12½-year-old blind girl. Results of a multiple baseline analysis demonstrated the effectiveness of this intervention in reducing a variety of stereotypic responses (hand-flapping, tapping, rocking). Further, gains were maintained at a one-month follow-up.

In an effort to promote prosocial behaviors, Van Hasselt, Hersen, Kazdin, Simon, and Mastantuono (1983) applied a social skills training package (modeling, direct instructions, behavior rehearsal, performance feedback, manual guidance) to enhance assertive skills in visually impaired female adolescents (14 to 20 years of age). At least three behavioral components of assertion (e.g., direction of gaze, posture, voice tone, requests for behavior change) were modified in each participant. Results of a multiple baseline analysis across behaviors for one of the subjects (SL) are provided in Figure 27-14. These data were representative of all cases with the controlling effects of treatment documented across subjects.

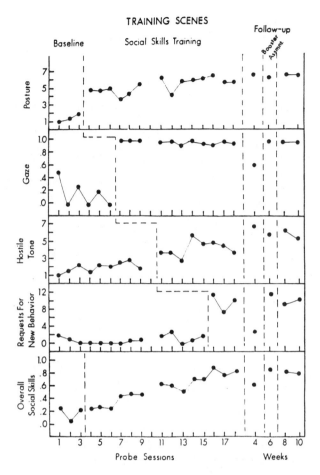

Figure 27-14. Probe sessions during baseline, social skills treatment, follow-up, and booster assessment for *SI*. A multiple baseline analysis of posture, gaze, hostile tone, requests for new behavior, and overall social skills. (Figure 1, p. 201, from Van Hasselt, V.B., Hersen, M., Kazdin, A. E., Simon, J., & Mastantuono, A. K. (1983). Social skills training for blind adolescents. *Journal of Visual Impairment & Blindness, 75,* 199–203.

In an examination of the utility of social skills training with blind multihandicapped children, Sisson, Van Hasselt, Hersen, and Strain (1985) designed a peer-mediated intervention to increase frequency of social initiations and positive social responses in four blind children who had at least one additional significant handicap (e.g., mental retardation, hearing impairment). Two nonhandicapped peers were trained to elicit appropriate social responses from the handicapped subjects during a free-play situation. A multiple baseline design across subjects showed that play initiations by nonhandicapped peers led to increased social behaviors in multi-handicapped subjects. The durability of gains was demonstrated at a 3-month follow-up.

Several social skills training programs also have been carried out with visually impaired adults. In one study, Toonen and Wilson (1969) taught a 45-year-old visually impaired male to direct his gaze toward sound sources (buzzers stationed at different angles and locations) using verbal reinforcement and performance feedback. Tracking of eye movements via infrared detection showed that the subject learned to accurately direct his gaze to the auditory stimuli. Sanders and Goldberg (1977) also attempted to improve eye contact using performance feedback and positive reinforcement with an almost totally blind, 26-year-old mentally retarded male. The results of 25 treatment sessions were an increase from a 30% (baseline) to an 80% rate of eye contact. This improvement was maintained at a 10-month follow-up evaluation.

A number of reports have described skills interventions designed to improve multiple social skill components in visually impaired adults. Bonfanti (1979) simultaneously targeted several behaviors (voice quality, eye contact, physical gestures, posture, facial expressions) in four congenitally blind adults using skills training (instructions, feedback, behavior rehearsal, modeling) in a group format. Results showed significant improvement on behavioral checklist ratings for treated participants relative to control groups of congenitally blind and adventitiously blinded subjects.

Ryan (1976) described one of the first attempts to enhance assertion skills within the context of a leisure counseling program. The importance of role playing and behavior rehearsal in training assertive behaviors, such as facial expressions, physical gestures, and response content was underscored. Everhart, Luzader, and Tullos (1980) combined assertion and relaxation training to blind subjects (17 to 42 years) in a group format over a series of six weekly 2-hour meetings. Staff noted positive behavior changes in participants. However, no empirical data were obtained to corroborate these observations.

In a more recent endeavour, Ruben (1983) applied a combination of modeling, homework assignments, prompting, role playing, and desensitization exercises to enhance assertion skills in 13 blind rehabilitation students ranging from 15 to 40 years of age. Instructional materials were presented using audiotape, large print, or braille, and covered such topics as "Why society discriminates against blind persons," and "What assertiveness is." Results of pre-/post-treatment scores on Ruben's (1983) *Assertive Behavior Survey Schedule* showed substantial increases in assertion level as a function of the 4-week training program.

Maladaptive Behavior

In recent years, increased attention has been directed to the elimination or reduction of various forms of maladaptive or disruptive behaviors in visually impaired and blind multihandicapped persons. Most of this work has involved children. In particular, stereotypic responses (i.e., repetitive motor behaviors or action sequences that appear to lack an adaptive function), sometimes referred to in the vision literature as *blindisms* or *mannerisms*, are common in blind individuals, especially those with multiple handicapping conditions. Examples of stereotypies include hand-flapping, head-weaving, eye-pressing, body-rocking, and unusual body postures. These may occur at high rates in some cases and interfere "with most, if not all, functional interactions with the environment and effective learning" (Hoshmand, 1975, p. 57). In addition to the high potential for injury to oneself or others, self-injurious and aggressive behaviors also interfere with acquisition of academic skills, and result in avoidance by others. Van Hasselt (1983) reviewed treatment studies which have applied behavioral techniques to such problems. A description of targeted behaviors, interventions employed for their amelioration, and treatment outcome is presented in Table 27-1. As the table illustrates, a wide variety of behavioral disturbances have been treated although reduction of self-injurious responses was most common (68% of the reports). Van Hasselt (1983) found that most (76%) of these investigations involved intervention with multiple disabled persons. In most cases, subjects were mentally retarded as well as visually impaired. Of the 25 reports he reviewed, 5 (Barton & Lagrow, 1983; Harris & Romanczyk, 1976; Luiselli, Myles, & Littman-Quinn, 1983; McDaniel, Kocim, & Barton, 1984; Rapoff, Altman, & Christopherson, 1980b) included individuals with a significant hearing impairment.

Table 27-1. Behavioral Treatment of Stereotypic, Self-Injurious and Disruptive Behaviors in Visually Handicapped and Multihandicapped Persons

REFERENCE	SUBJECT(S)	TARGET BEHAVIOR(S)	TREATMENT(S)	OUTCOME	FOLLOW-UP(S)
Barton & Lagrow (1983)	21-year-old mentally retarded, deaf-blind female Two mentally retarded, deaf-blind females (5 and 9 years of age)	Self-hitting of face and eyes; pinching and punching others	Overcorrection	Decrease in rates of SIB and aggressive acts for all subjects	14 weeks for adult: 3 weeks for one child
Belcher, Conettar, Cale, Ianettin, & McGovern (1982)	19-year-old severely retarded, visually handicapped male	Violent and disruptive tantrums	Behavioral interruption (verbal prompt and 360° guided turn)	Decrease in frequency and duration of target behavior to near zero levels; increased sociability	9 months
Blasch (1978)	Four female and two male visually handicapped adolescents (16–20 years of age)	Rocking; head rolling, eye poking	Punishment (recording of screeching chalk) and positive reinforcement	Decrease in rate of stereotypic acts and SIB; some reduction in untreated responses and generalization to nontreatment setting	10 days
Caetano & Kauffman (1975)	Two visually handicapped females (9 and 10 years of age)	Rocking	Elements of overcorrection (feedback and reminders) and positive reinforcement	Reduction of rocking with some generalization to nontreatment setting	Intervals not reported
Conley & Wolery (1980)	7-year-old mentally retarded, blind female and 5-year-old mentally retarded, blind male	Eye gouging	Overcorrection and positive reinforcement	Rapid deceleration in SIB for both subjects	3 weeks for female and 7 weeks for male. Treatment resumed for male after 9 month follow-up
Drabman et al. (1978)	2½-year-old profoundly retarded, blind male	Sucking and chewing on fingers	Punishment (icing procedure) and hands down carried out by mentally retarded peers	Decrease in targeted responses in treatment sessions; generalization across time with specific programming	None reported
Greene & Hoats (1971)	Two, 13-year-old mentally retarded, blind adolescent females	Head banging, aggressive behavior	Punishment (aversive tickling)	General reduction in target behaviors although considerable variability in response rate during treatment	None reported

Table 27-1 continued

REFERENCE	SUBJECT(S)	TARGET BEHAVIOR(S)	TREATMENT(S)	OUTCOME	FOLLOW-UP(s)
Green, Hoats & Hornick (1970)	15-year-old mentally retarded, blind male	Rocking; hand shaking	Punishment (music distortion)	Rapid deceleration of rate of target behaviors	None reported
Harris & Romanczyk (1976)	8-year-old mentally retarded, visually and hearing impaired male	Head banging	Overcorrection	Decrease in SIB in both laboratory and clinical settings	9 months
Kelly & Drabman (1977)	3-year-old visually handicapped male	Eye poking	Overcorrection and positive reinforcement (verbal praise)	Reduced rate of SIB in treatment and generalization settings	None reported
Lovaas & Simmons (1969)	8-year-old mentally retarded, visually handicapped female	Self hitting and scratching of face and body	Punishment (electric shock)	Immediate suppression of SIB although effects specific to trainer and setting	None reported
Luiselli & Greenidge (1982)	12-year-old mentally retarded, visually handicapped female	Slapping and punching others	Three time-out procedures and positive reinforcement	Rapid elimination of target behavior with isolation time-out	7 months
Luiselli & Michaud (1983)	19- and 11-year-old mentally retarded, visually handicapped females	Self-biting of arm; face and head hitting; aggression toward others	Overcorrection and positive reinforcement	Decrease in SIB for both subjects	4 months for first subject and 1 month for second child
Luiselli et al. (1983)	15-year-old visually and hearing impaired male	Punching and slapping others; damage to property; throwing of objects	Time-out and positive reinforcement	Rapid elimination of target responses with combined use of time-out and reinforcement	4 months
Martin & Iagulli (1974)	4-year-old mentally retarded, visually handicapped female	Middle-of-the-night tantrums	Extinction: keeping child awake until midnight	Elimination of tantrums	3 and 6 months
McDaniel et al. (1984)	4-year-old deaf blind female; 4- and 7-year-old deaf blind males	Inappropriate mouthing; self-biting; finger-sucking	Positive reinforcement, lemon juice treatment, verbal prompts	Combination of treatments most effective in reducing mouthing	5 days for one child only
Measel & Alfieri (1976)	14- and 16-year-old mentally retarded, visually handicapped males	Head slapping and banging	Overcorrection and positive reinforcement	SIB eliminated when overcorrection and reinforcement applied to first subject; reinforcement alone and in combination with overcorrection led to increased SIB in second subject	4 months for first subject only

Study	Subject(s)	Target behavior	Treatment	Results	Follow-up
Miller & Miller (1976)	13-year-old visually handicapped female	Head wagging	Positive reinforcement, modeling, self-monitoring, and peer feedback	Reduction in head wagging with multiple treatments	4 and 11 months
Myers & Deibert (1971)	11-year-old mentally retarded, visually handicapped male	Head hitting	Positive reinforcement, time-out and shaping of incompatible feeding response	Decrease in frequency of SIB	9 months
Rapoff et al. (1980a)	7-year-old mentally retarded, visually handicapped male	Head hitting	Response-contingent brief restraint	Elimination of SIB: increased compliance in classroom	2 months
Rapoff et al. (1980b)	5-year-old mentally retarded, deaf blind male	Head hitting	Positive reinforcement, overcorrection, punishment (lemon juice and aromatic ammonia	Sharp reduction in frequency of SIB: greatest response suppression with ammonia treatment	None reported
Rotatori, Kapperman, & Schryvery (1979)	33-year-old mentally retarded, visually handicapped male	Self-induced vomiting	Overcorrection, physical guidance, and positive reinforcement	Significant decrease in frequency of SIB	5 weeks
Simpson, Sasson, & Bump (1982)	7-year-old visually handicapped male	Eye gouging and head weaving	Time-out and positive reinforcement	Reduction in both target behaviors to near zero levels; improved social and academic performance	None reported
Tate & Baroff (1966)	9-year-old visually handicapped, psychotic male	Head banging and face slapping	Time-out from physical contact and punishment (electric shock)	Both treatments effective in reducing SIB and stereotypic acts	6 months
Wesolowski & Zawlocki (1982)	6-year-old mentally retarded, visually handicapped twin females	Eye gouging	Time out from auditory stimuli; response interruption; auditory time-out plus DRO; overcorrection plus DRO	Substantial decrease in SIB for both subjects with multiple-treatments; Over-correction plus DRO effective in reducing SIB one year after initial treatment	2 and 12 months

The table also shows that numerous behavior modification approaches (often in combination) have been utilized to deal with maladaptive responses. Van Hasselt (1983) found that significant improvement in treatment targets was reported in most of the studies. However, with few exceptions (e.g., Drabman, Ross, Lynd, & Cordua, 1978; Harris & Romanczyk, 1976; Kelly & Drabman, 1977), little effort has been expended to promote generalization of gains beyond immediate treatment settings. Also, follow-up intervals have varied considerably across investigation ranging from no follow-up at all (in 28% of the reports) to 1-year intervals.

Adaptive Living Skills

Acquisition of adaptive living skills is crucial to independent functioning in the community. A number of these skills have been trained in handicapped populations, most notably, the mentally retarded (see Marchetti & Matson, 1981; Watson & Uzzell, 1981). Examples of adaptive living skills include cooking, shopping, money exchange, cleaning, public transportation usage, and emergency safety skills (e.g., telephone dialling, fire evacuation). Few reports are available in which efforts have been made to teach such behaviors to the visually impaired. The two areas that have received some attention are mobility and fire-safety skills. With regard to the former, Johnston and Corbett (1973) describe a multiple component mobility training program for blind mentally retarded persons. A combination of concept-building exercises, body orientation, instructions, feedback concerning straightline travel, and homework assignments were used to enhance orienting and navigating abilities.

McGlinchey and Mitala (1975) developed a procedure to improve both mobility and a number of adaptive living skills (e.g., bathing, dressing, toileting, tooth-brushing) in profoundly retarded blind males in a state institution. These investigators placed tactile cues (various carpet textures) in different rooms of the unit to facilitate movement. In a backward-chaining strategy, patients were positively reinforced for trailing the carpet into the toilet or shower rooms at gradually increasing distances.

While the reports discussed previously described innovative approaches with considerable potential, no empirical data were obtained to document their efficacy. In contrast, Kennedy (1982) tested the relative effectiveness of three reinforcers (touch, verbal praise, vibration) in increasing mobility skill in a 28-year-old, mentally retarded blind male using a multielement baseline design. This included the three reinforcement conditions plus a no-treatment control. Results indicated the greatest decrease in time required to walk a 20-foot course when vibration was the reinforcer. In another experimental analysis incorporating a multiple component intervention (positive reinforcement, instructions, performance feedback, manual guidance), mobility skills were targeted in a 15-year-old blind male. Training was conducted over 10 months on a 104-yard path resembling a question mark. Results of a B–A–B design revealed a sharp reduction in travel time during treatment phases.

An area that has only recently been the focus of psychological intervention in the visually impaired is emergency safety. As Van Hasselt (1987) points out, their inability to utilize visual cues, along with their decreased mobility make the blind and visually handicapped particularly at risk for dangers such as accidents and fire emergencies. The latter was targeted in two studies by Jones and his colleagues (Jones, Sisson, & Van Hasselt, 1984; Jones, Van Hasselt, & Sisson, 1984). Jones Van Hasselt & Sisson (1984) applied feedback, social and external reinforcement, behavior rehearsal and training in self-control strategies (self-evaluation and self-reinforcement) to teach four blind adolescents in a residential school to respond correctly to simulated emergency fire situations. A multiple baseline design across subjects showed improvement in emergency fire safety responses in three of four subjects. However, few trained behaviors were found to generalize to actual nighttime fire drills.

To increase generalization, Jones, Sisson, & Van Hasselt (1984) included three children from their previous study in a group training procedure. Participants were taught to provide instructions and cues regarding appropriate fire safety responses to their roommates. Multiple baseline analyses across subjects indicated high levels of skill acquisition in all participants during nighttime fire drills.

SUMMARY AND FUTURE DIRECTIONS

There have been many advances in the field of opthalmology over the past 15 years. These have involved improvement in the methods and instrumentation for surgical correction and rehabilitation of ocular defects. Cataract surgery is now performed in 1 day using smaller incisions and, in most cases, an intraocular lens is used to rehabilitate the eye. Many opthalmology procedures are now being performed in surgical centers dedicated to opthalmology care. The YAG laser is being used to disrupt membranes that obstruct or diffuse light entering the eye. Lasers are also used to arrest diabetic retinopathy and to treat some forms of glaucoma. Diagnosis has been facilitated by the use of computer-enhanced tomography of the orbit and central nervous system. Invasive diagnostic studies rarely are necessary. Exciting advances have taken place in understanding the genetic transmission of tumors such as retinoblastoma. There have been improvements in the new pharmacologic agents used to treat infections, glaucoma, and allergic conditions. More effective and specific drugs have enhanced the capability of the opthalmologist to medically control disease and preserve vision.

The future for opthalmology is anticipated to be even more exciting. Over the next decade, surgical techniques will undoubtedly undergo further refinement. The alteration of refractive errors should become a safe, predictable procedure not only following cataract surgery and trauma, but for the correction of myopia and anisometropia. The eximer laser seems to show exciting promise in this area. We can expect further application of lasers for removing tumors in the eye and in the orbit.

Advances will take place in the medical management of eye conditions with development of newer, more specific, and potent pharmacologic agents administered using improved delivery systems. Diagnostic capabilities will be further enhanced by proliferations and the development of second and third generation nuclear magnetic resonance scanning. This instrument may replace all conventional diagnostic X-rays.

The recent ability to grow cells in culture and expansion of chromosome analysis techniques will increase our understanding of genetic transmission of disease. It is very probable that a cell's genetic code may be able to be altered, thus permitting the opthalmologist to treat some of the storage and deficiency diseases that remain so elusive at the present.

The pathophysiology of conditions causing blindness by proliferation of the retinal vessels within the vitreous cavity will become better understood. Diseases frequently leading to blindness such as diabetes with proliferative retinopathy and retinopathy of prematurity may be controlled as the identity of the substance or substances that cause blood vessels to grow abnormally is identified.

The future of educational services for the blind appears to be promising as well. Institutions such as the American Printing House for the Blind (Louisville, Kentucky) have engaged actively in instructional research to improve curriculum and curricular materials for severely visually impaired pupils. This effort, coupled with advances in the development of technical aids, will provide blind students with increased opportunity for access to typical instructional materials.

Recent studies regarding funding for special education (Kakalik, 1981) report that programs for the visually impaired are the highest per capita rate for all handicapped categories. This situation suggests that advocates for education of the visually handicapped will need to promote accountability for services in order to secure the level of funding which is necessary for adequate training. Combined with this effort will be the need to strive to obtain accurate child counts for the blind. Current methodology yields weak data in that blind children with concomitant disabilities often are categorized by a handicap other than blindness. Discrepancies in child count could adversely affect program funding for the visually impaired. Consequently, accurate census methodology must be emphasized.

In all likelihood, placement options will continue to be available to the visually handicapped. Residential and public school enrollment will be open. If the trend continues, it is expected that the traditional boarding school for the blind will adapt curriculum for those blind children with multiple impairments. More cognitively able visually handicapped children will be placed in public systems. However, in rural areas, blind children of average or better ability might continue in the residential school since that placement is practical and affords delivery of the most comprehensive programs.

The importance of early intervention and pre-school training to blind children is being widely documented. In light of the success of these programs and the movement toward infant services, it is expected that more and better programs will be developed for visually handicapped children under 5 years of age. Such "first starts" will be critical in preparing children for subsequent school experience.

Educators of the blind will continue to advocate for specialized professional training. Because of the unique nature of teaching blind children, it is important to have qualified specialists who understand broad-range programming options for the visually handicapped. In order to maintain excellence in education, it will be necessary to produce educators who can creatively meet the interests, needs, and abilities of blind children.

Advancements also are anticipated in future psychological assessment and treatment efforts for the visually handicapped.

Further progress is expected in the management of maladaptive response categories (e.g., stereotypic acts, self-injury) largely due to the considerable strides made in the field of behavior modification. Future endeavours undoubtedly will focus on refinement of techniques to enhance generalization and maintenance of treatment effects.

The area of social skills training for the visually impaired appears particularly promising. Indeed, adequate social development in blind children is critical given the plethora of research documenting the relationship between interpersonal effectiveness in childhood and functioning later in life. However, future skills intervention programs will need to improve a wider range of social behaviors, such as those requisite to effective interpersonal performance in vocational and leisure settings. This is important if adequate community adjustment is to be achieved. Also, skills initially trained in the laboratory will have to be evaluated in more naturalistic settings if the social validity of these approaches is to be ascertained.

Another area warranting further attention by psychological researchers and clinicians is the adjustment of families with visually handicapped children. Evidence from numerous reports supports the notion that many of these families exhibit disturbed interaction patterns (see review by Van Hasselt & Hersen, 1986). Two projects currently conducted at the Western Pennsylvania School for Blind Children (Pittsburgh, Pennsylvania) are attempting to remediate some of the problems in these family systems. The first is the Parent and Toddler Training Project (PATT), which provides early intervention for visually handicapped infants (or toddlers) and their families (Klein, Van Hasselt, Trefelner, & Snyder, 1986). PATT uses a variety of behavioral treatment approaches (e.g., problem-solving skills training, parent management training, self-management of infant care-giving skills) to: (a) enhance the social responsivity of visually handicapped infants, (b) provide a training program to develop adequate parenting skills in families, and (c) initiate strategies with parents to reduce psychological distress and improve the quality of family life. Preliminary data indicate that PATT project goals are being achieved (Klein et al., 1986).

In another project, Van Hasselt, Hersen, Moore, and Simon (1986) developed a comprehensive evaluation and treatment approach for visually handicapped adolescents and their families. The assessment component includes a number of self-report and direct observation methods to obtain data concerning social and emotional adjustment of all family members and to identify dysfunctional family interactions patterns. This information subsequently is employed to design individually tailored treatment programs. Behavioral family intervention in this endeavor consists of a combination of problem-solving and communication skills training conducted through several procedures (direct instructions, modeling, behavior rehearsal, performance feedback).

It is hoped that projects such as the aforementioned "will be of both immediate and long-term benefit to this population. Specifically, comprehensive assessment and efficacious intervention will have the immediate result of improved family relations and decreased family distress. At the same time, early amelioration of maladjustment may prevent social and emotional problems in the blind child later in life" (Van Hasselt et al., 1986, p. 634).

REFERENCES

Acers, T. E. (1981). Optic nerve hypoplasia. *Transactions of the American Opthalmological Society, 79,* 425–457.

Adrian, R. J., Miller, L. R., & DeL'aune, W. R. (1982). Personality assessment of early visually impaired persons using the CPI and the MMPI. *Journal of Visual Impairment and Blindness, 76,* 172–178.

Ammerman, R. T., Van Hasselt, V. B., & Hersen, M. (1986). Psychological adjustment of visually handicapped children and youth. *Clinical Psychology Review, 6,* 67–85.

Barraga, N. C. (1976). *Visual handicaps and learning: A developmental approach.* Belmont, CA: Wadsworth.

Barton, L. E., & Lagrow, S. J. (1983). Reducing self-injurious and aggressive behavior in deaf–blind persons through overcorrection. *Journal of Visual Impairment and Blindness, 77,* 421–424.

Bauman, M. K. (1971). Tests and their interpretation. In G. D. Carnes, C. E. Hansen, & R. M. Parker (Eds.), *Readings in rehabilitation of the blind client.* Austin, Texas: Austin Publishing.

Bauman, M. K. (1972). Special problems in the psychological evaluation of blind persons. In R. D. Hardy & J. G. Cull (Eds.), *Social and rehabilitation services for the blind.* Springfield, IL: Charles C. Thomas.

Bauman, M. K. (1973). Psychological and educational assessment. In B. Lowenfeld (Ed.), *The visually handicapped child in school.* New York: John Day.

Bauman, M. K., & Kropf, C. A. (1979). Psychological tests used with blind and visually handicapped persons. *School Psychology Digest, 8,* 257–270.

Belcher, T. L., Conetta, C., Cole, C., Lannotti, E., & McGovern, M. (1982). Eliminating a severely retarded blind adolescent's tantrums using mild behavioral interruption: A case study. *Journal of Behavior Therapy & Experimental Psychiatry, 13,* 257–260.

Biglan, A. W., Brown, D. R., Reynolds, J. D., & Milley, J. R. (1984). Risk factors associated with retrolental fibroplasia. *Opthalmology, 91,* 1504–1511.

Blasch, B. B. (1978). Blindisms: Treatment by punishment and reward in laboratory and natural settings. *Journal of Visual Impairment and Blindness, 72,* 215–230.

Bonfanti, B. H. (1979). Effects of training on nonverbal and verbal behaviors of congenitally blind adults. *Journal of Visual Impairment and Blindness, 73,* 1–9.

Bradway, K. P. (1937). Social competence of exceptional children III. The deaf, the blind, and the crippled. *Exceptional Children, 4,* 64–69.

Buckley, E., & Seaber, J. H. (1981). Unique ocular findings in cerebral palsy patients with strabismus. *American Orthoptic Journal, 31,* 53–59.

Caetano, A. P., & Kauffman, J. M. (1975). Reduction of rocking mannerisms in two blind children. *Education of the Visually Handicapped, 7,* 101–105.

Clements, D. B., & Kaushal, K. (1970). A study of ocular complications of hydrocephalus and meningomyelocele. *Transactions of the Opthalmic Society of U.K., 60,* 383–390.

Conely, O. S., & Wolery, M. R. (1980). Treatment by overcorrection of self-injurious eye gouging in preschool blind children. *Journal of*

Behavior Therapy & Experimental Psychiatry, 11, 121–125.

Coveny, T. E. (1972). A new test for the visually handicapped: Preliminary analysis of reliability and validity of the Perkins–Binet. *Education of the Handicapped, 4*, 97–101.

Cratty, B. J., & Sams, T. (1968). *Body Image of blind children*. New York: American Foundation for the Blind.

Cross, O. H. (1947). Braille edition of the Minnesota Multiphasic Personality Inventory for use with the blind. *Journal of Applied Psychology, 31*, 189–198.

Davis, C. (1980). *Perkins–Binet Tests of Intelligence for the blind*. Watertown, MA: Perkins School for the Blind.

Doll, E. A. (1953). *A measure of social competence: A manual for the Vineland Social Maturity Scale*. Princeton, N.J.: Educational Test Bureau.

Drabman, R. S., Ross, J. M., Lynd, R. S., & Cordua, G. D. (1978). Retarded children as observers, mediators, and generalization programmers using an icing procedure. *Behavior Modification, 2*, 371–385.

Eisler, R. M., Hersen, M., Miller, P. M., & Blanchard, E. B. (1975). Situational determinants of assertive behaviors. *Journal of Consulting and Clinical Psychology, 43*, 330–340.

Everhart, G., Luzader, M., & Tullos, S. (1980). Assertive skills training for the blind. *Journal of Visual Impairment and Blindness, 74*, 62–65.

Farkas, G. M., Sherick, R. B., Matson, J. L., & Loebig, M. (1981). Social skills training of a blind child through differential reinforcement. *The Behavior Therapist, 4*, 24–26.

Gilbert, J. G., & Rubin, E. J. (1965). Evaluating the intellect of blind children. *New Outlook for the Blind, 59*, 238–240.

Greene, R. J., & Hoats, D. L. (1971). Aversive tickling: A simple conditioning technique. *Behavior Therapy, 2*, 389–393.

Greene, R. J., Hoats, D. L., & Hornick, A. J. (1970). Music distortion: A new technique for behavior modification. *Psychological Records, 20*, 107–109.

Halloran, S. L., Boughman, J. A., Dryja, J. P., Mukai, A., Long, D., Roberts, D. F., & Craft, A. W. (1985). Accuracy of detection of the retinoblastoma gene by esterase D. linkage. *Archives of Opthalmology, 103*, 1329–1331.

Hardy, R. D. (1968). A study of manifest anxiety among blind residential school students. *New Outlook for the Blind, 62*, 173–180.

Harris, S. L., & Romanczyk, R. G. (1976). Treating self-injurious behavior of a retarded child by overcorrection. *Behavior Therapy, 7*, 235–239.

Hayes, S. P. (1929). The new revision of the Binet Intelligence Tests for the blind. *Teachers Forum, 2*, 2–4.

Hiles, D. A. (1975). Results of strabismus therapy in cerebral palsy children. *American Orthoptic Journal, 25*, 46.

Hopkins, K. D., & McGuire, L. (1966). Mental measurement of the blind: The validity of the Wechsler Intelligence Scale for Children. *International Journal for the Education of the Blind, 15*, 65–73.

Hopkins, K. D., & McGuire, L. (1967). IQ constancy and the blind child. *International Journal for the Education of the Blind, 16*, 113–114.

Hoshmand, L. T. (1975). "Blindness": Some observations and propositions. *Education of the Visually Handicapped, 7*, 56–60.

Irwin, R. B., & Godard, H. H. (1914). *Adaptation of the Binet–Simon tests*. Vineland, NJ: Educational Test Bureau.

Johnston, B. C., & Corbett, M. C. (1973). Orientation and mobility instruction for blind individuals functioning on a retarded level. *New Outlook for the Blind, 67*, 27–31.

Jones, R. T., Sisson, L. A., & Van Hasselt, V. B. (1984). Emergency fire-safety skills for blind children and adolescents: Group training and generalization. *Behavior Modification, 8*, 267–286.

Jones, R. T., Van Hasselt, V. B., & Sisson, L. A. (1984). Emergency fire-safety skills: A study with blind adolescents. *Behavior Modification, 8*, 59–78.

Kelly, J. A., & Drabman, R. S. (1977). Generalizing response suppression of self-injurious behavior through an overcorrection punishment procedure: A case study. *Behavior Therapy, 8*, 468–472.

Kennedy, A. B. (1982). The effects of three reinforcers on the mobility of a severely retarded blind women. *Education & Treatment of Children, 5*, 337–346.

Kratz, L. E. (1973). *Movement without sight*. Palo Alto, CA: Piek.

Lewis, L. L. (1957). The relation of measured mental ability to school marks and academic survival in the Texas School for the Blind. *International Journal of Education for the Blind, 66*, 56–60.

Lovaas, O. I., & Simmons, J. Q. (1969). Manipulation of self-destruction in three retarded children. *Journal of Applied Behavior Analysis, 2*, 143–157.

Lowenfeld, B. (1971). *Our blind children*. Springfield, IL: Charles C. Thomas.

Luiselli, J. K., & Greenidge, A. (1982). Behavioral

treatment of high-rate aggression in a rubella child. *Journal of Behavior Therapy & Experimental Psychiatry, 13,* 152–157.

Luiselli, J. K., & Michaud, R. L. (1983). Behavioral treatment of aggression and self-injury in developmentally disabled, visually handicapped students. *Journal of Visual Impairment and Blindness, 77,* 388–392.

Luiselli, J. K., Myles, E., & Littman-Quinn, J. (1983). Analysis of a reinforcement/time-out treatment package to control severe aggressive and destructive behaviors in a multihandicapped, rubella child. *Applied Research in Mental Retardation, 4,* 65–78.

Marchetti, A., & Matson, J. L. (1981). Training skills for community adjustment. In J. L. Matson & J. R. McCartney (Eds.), *Handbook of behavior modification with the mentally retarded.* New York: Plenum Press.

Martin, J. A., & Lagulli, D. M. (1974). Case Reports: Elimination of middle-of-the-night tantrums in a blind, retarded child. *Behavior Therapy, 5,* 420–422.

Matson, J. L., Heinze, A., Helsel, W. J., Kapperman, G., & Rotatori, A. F. (in press). Assessing social behaviors in the visually handicapped: The Matson Evaluation of Social Skills with Youngsters (MESSY). *Journal of Clinical Child Psychology.*

Matson, J. L., & Helsel, W. J. (in press). Psychopathology of sensory impaired children. In B. B. Lahey & A. E. Kazdin (Eds.), *Advances in clinical child psychology* (Vol. 9). New York: Plenum Press.

Maxfield, K. E., & Buchholz, S. (1958). *The Maxfield Scale of Social Maturity for use with preschool blind children.* New York: American Foundation for the Blind.

Maxfield, K. E., & Fjeld, H. A. (1942). The social maturity of the visually handicapped preschool child. *Child Development, 13,* 1–27.

McDaniel, G., Kocim, R., & Barton, L. E. (1984). Reducing self-stimulatory mouthing behaviors in deaf-blind children. *Journal of Visual Impairment and Blindness, 78,* 23–26.

McGlinchey, M. A., & Mitala, R. F. (1975). Using environmental design to teach ward layout to severely and profoundly retarded blind persons. *New Outlook for the Blind, 69,* 168–171.

McKay, B. E. (1936). Social maturity of the preschool blind child. *Training School Bulletin, 33,* 146–155.

Measel, C. J., & Alfieri, P. A. (1976). A treatment of self-injurious behavior by a combination of reinforcement for incompatible behavior and overcorrection. *American Journal of Mental Deficiency, 81,* 147–153.

Miller, B. S., & Miller, W. H. (1976). Extinguishing "blindisms": A paradigm for intervention. *Education of the Visually Handicapped, 8,* 6–15.

Myers, J. J., & Deibert, A. N. (1971). Reduction of self-abusive behavior in a blind child by using a feeding response. *Journal of Behavior Therapy & Experimental Psychiatry, 2,* 141–144.

National Society to Prevent Blindness. (1980). *Vision problems in the U.S.: Facts and Figures.* New York: National Society to Prevent Blindness.

Phelps, D. L. (1981) Retinopathy of prematurity. *Pediatrics, 67,* 924–925.

Rapoff, M. A., Altman, K., & Christophersen, E. R. (1980a). Elimination of a retarded blind child's self-hitting by response-contingent brief restraint. *Education and Treatment of Children, 3,* 231–236.

Rapoff, M. A., Altman, K., & Christophersen, E. R. (1980b). Suppression of self-injurious behavior: Determining the least restrictive alternative. *Journal of Mental Deficiency and Research, 24,* 37–46.

Rotatori, A. F., Kapperman, G., & Schryven, J. (1979). The elimination of self-induced vomiting in a severely retarded visually impaired female. *Education of the Visually Handicapped, 11,* 60–62.

Rothstein, T. B., Romano, P., & Shoch, D. (1973). Meningomyelocoele-associated ocular abnormalities. *Transactions of the American Opthalmologic Society, 71,* 287–295.

Ruben, D. H. (1983). Methodological adaptations in assertiveness training programs designed for the blind. *Psychological Report, 53,* 1281–1282.

Ryan, K. A. B. (1976). Assertive training: Its use in leisure counseling. *New Outlook for the Blind, 70,* 351–354.

Sanders, R. M., & Goldberg, S. G. (1977). Eye contacts: Increasing their rate in social interactions. *Journal of Visual Impairment and Blindness, 71,* 265–267.

Shields, J. A., & Augsburger, J. J. (1981). Current approaches to the diagnosis and management of retinoblastoma. *Survey of Opthalmology, 25,* 347–372.

Shurrager, H. C. (1961). *A haptic intelligence scale for adult blind.* Chicago: Illinois Institute of Technology.

Shurrager, H. C., & Shurrager, P. S. (1964). *Manual for the haptic intelligence scale for the blind.*

Chicago: Psychology Research Technology Center, Illinois Institute of Technology.

Simpson, R. L., Sasso, G. M., & Bump, N. (1982). Modification of manneristic behavior in a blind child via a time-out procedure. *Education of the Visually Handicapped, 14,* 50–55.

Sisson, L. A., & Van Hasselt, V. B. (1987). Visual impairment. In V. B. Van Hasselt & M. Hersen (Eds.), *Psychological evaluation of the developmentally and physically disabled.* New York: Plenum Press.

Sisson, L. A., Van Hasselt, V. B., Hesen, M., & Strain, P. S. (1985). Peer interventions: Increasing social behaviors in multihandicapped children. *Behavior Modification, 9,* 293–321.

Tasman, W. (1979). Late complications of retrolental fibroplasia. *Transactions of the American Academy of Ophthalmology and Otolaryngology, 86,* 1724–1740.

Tate, B. G., & Baroff, G. S. (1966). Aversive control of self-injurious behavior in a psychotic boy. *Behavior Research and Therapy, 4,* 281–287.

Teare, J. F., & Thompson, R. W. (1982). Concurrent validity of the Perkins–Binet tests of intelligence for the blind. *Journal of Visual Impairment and Blindness, 76,* 279–280.

Tillman, H. M. (1973). Intelligence scales for the blind: A review with implications for research. *Journal of School Psychology, 11,* 80–87.

Toonen, B. L., & Wilson, J. P. (1969). Learning eye fixation without visual feedback. *Research Bulletin, American Foundation for the Blind, 19,* 123–128.

Van Hasselt, V. B. (1983). Visual impairment. In M. Hersen, V. B. Van Hasselt, & J. L. Matson (Eds.), *Behavior therapy for developmentally and physically disabled persons.* New York: Academic Press.

Van Hasselt, V. B. (1987). Behavior therapy for visually handicapped persons. In M. Hersen, P. Miller, & R. M. Eisler (Eds.). *Progress in behavior modification* (Vol. 21). Newbury Park, CA: Sage.

Van Hasselt, V. B., Hersen, M., & Kazdin, A. E. (1985). Assessment of social skills in visually handicapped adolescents. *Behaviour Research and Therapy, 23,* 53–63.

Van Hasselt, V. B., Hersen, M., Kazdin, A. E., Simon, J., & Mastantuono, A. K. (1983). Training blind adolescents in social skills. *Journal of Visual Impairment and Blindness, 77,* 199–203.

Van Hasselt, V. B., Kazdin, A. E., Hersen, M., Simon, J., & Mastantuono, A. K. (1985). A behavioral-analytic model for assessing social skills in blind adolescents. *Behaviour Research and Therapy, 23,* 395–405.

Van Hasselt, V. B., Hersen, M., Moore, L. E., & Simon, J. (1986). Assessment and treatment of families with visually handicapped children: A project description. *Journal of Visual Impairment and Blindness, 80,* 633–635.

Walsh, F. B., & Hoyt, W. F. (Eds.). (1969). *Clinical neurophthalmology.* Baltimore: Williams & Wilkins.

Watson, L. S., & Uzzell, R. (1981). Teaching self-help skills to the mentally retarded. In J. L. Matson & J. R. McCartney (Eds.), *Handbook of behavior modification with the mentally retarded.* New York: Plenum Press.

Wesolowski, M. D., & Zawlocki, R. J. (1982). The differential effects of procedures to eliminate an injurious self-stimulatory behavior (Digito-Ocular Sign) in blind retarded twins. *Behavior Therapy, 13,* 334–345.

Yarnall, G. D. (1979). Developing eye contact in a visually impaired, deaf child. *Education of the Visually Handicapped, 11,* 56–59.

Author Index

AAMD, 337, 338, 354, 355, 356
Abate, F., 301
Abbott, D., 415, 421
Abeson, A., 161, 164, 172
Abikoff, H., 306, 307, 309, 311, 315
Abissi, C. J., 444, 469
Abrams, A. L., 321, 331
Abramson, P., 182, 188, 191
Abuelo, D. N., 355, 364
Accardo, P. J., 215, 222, 226
Acers, T. E., 479, 499
Acheson, A. J., 457, 468
Achterberg-Lawlis, J., 243, 244
Ackerman, A. B., 196, 203, 208, 212
Adamovich, B., 464, 466
Adams, A. E., 241, 244
Adams, D., 296, 299, 304
Adams, H. P., 448, 466
Adams, L. L., 436, 438
Adams, P. E., 321, 334
Adams, R. D., 454, 466
Adamson, L., 396, 421
Adelman, H. S., 30, 33
Adesso, V. J., 27, 33
Adkins, J., 360, 367
Adrian, R. J., 489, 499
Affleck, G., 12, 18
Agosta, J., 360, 368
Agran, M., 153, 154, 157
Ahern, D. K., 236, 241, 244
Aiello, J. R., 362, 365
Albert, J., 306, 311
Albert, K., 43, 51
Albert, M. L., 454, 466

Albin, J. B., 360, 365
Albin, J. M., 107, 127
Albrecht, G., 432, 437
Albright, F., 43, 54
Alcorn, D. A., 101, 103
Alexander, A. B., 188, 191
Alexander, D., 43, 51
Alexander, M., 389, 394
Alexander, M. A., 215, 216, 221, 223, 224
Alfieri, P. A., 494, 501
Alford, B. A., 144, 148
Algozzine, B., 22, 23, 24, 26, 27, 28, 30, 32, 37, 119, 133, 316, 331, 335
Alkus, S. R., 296, 299, 304, 315
Allan, J. D., 42, 51
Allderdice, P. W., 42, 55
Allen, F. H., 42, 55
Allen, H. A., 92, 104
Allen, J., 200, 208, 210
Allen, P., 360, 366
Allen, R., 295, 303, 314
Allen, T. W., 300, 313
Alley, G. R., 329, 330, 334
Almond, P. J., 201, 212
Aloia, G. F., 119, 131
Alpern, G. D., 200, 208, 210
Alpert, C. L., 395, 398, 413, 415, 417, 418, 420
Als, H., 396, 421
Altman, K., 492, 495, 501
Altshuler, K. Z., 291, 293, 294
Aman, M. G., 345, 346, 351, 358, 359, 365
Amatruda, C. S., 46, 53

Subject Index

About the Editors

Vincent B. Van Hasselt, Ph.D., is Assistant Professor of Psychiatry at the University of California Irvine Medical Center. He is the recipient of grants from the March of Dimes Birth Defects Foundation, National Institute of Handicapped Research, Handicapped Children's Early Education Program, and Special Education Programs (U.S. Department of Education) for research projects focusing on the social and emotional adjustment of developmentally and physically disabled children. He is the author of numerous scientific journal articles and book chapters concerning psychological assessment and treatment approaches for emotionally disturbed and disabled children and adolescents.

Phillip S. Strain, Ph.D., is an Associate Professor of Child Psychiatry and Director of the Early Childhood Research Institute at the Department of Psychiatry, School of Medicine, University of Pittsburgh. He has published extensively on behavioral treatments for a variety of childhood disorders. Current research interests focus on long-term outcomes for autistic children who are treated in their preschool years.

Michel Hersen, Ph.D., is Professor of Psychiatry and Psychology at the University of Pittsburgh. He is a Past President of the Association for Advancement of Behavior Therapy. He has co-authored, edited, and co-edited 55 books, including: *The Clinical Psychology Handbook, Handbook of Psychological Assessment*, and *Handbook of Child Psychopathology*. He is co-editor and co-founder of the *Clinical Psychology Review, Behavior Modification, Progress in Behavior Modification, Journal of Family Violence, Journal of Anxiety Disorders* and *Journal of the Multihandicapped Person*. In collaboration with his colleagues, he has received numerous grants from funding agencies, including the National Institute of Mental Health, the National Institute of Handicapped Research, the Department of Education, and the March of Dimes.

About the Contributors

Michael A. Alexander, M.D., is a Clinical Associate Professor of Pediatrics at the University of Pittsburgh. He is a diplomate of both the American Board of Pediatrics and the American Board of Physical Medicine and Rehabilitation. He has published in several areas relevant to the rehabilitation of infants and children. His research interests include outcome studies and the application of technological advances to children.

Cathy L. Alpert, Ph.D., is a Research Assistant Professor of Special Education at Peabody College of Vanderbilt University. Her major research interests include incidental language teaching strategies and social interaction training for young handicapped children. She has conducted studies on training parents and teachers to apply incidental teaching procedures with language-delayed children and currently is investigating the effectiveness of incidental teaching procedures for training handicapped children to communicate using a nonvocal communication mode. She has published chapters and articles on language development and language-related intervention and assessment strategies.

Roberta E. Bauer, M.D., is a developmental pediatrician with Pediatric and Neonatal Associates of Pittsburgh, Pennsylvania. After fellowships in Child Development and in Pediatric Rehabilitation at Children's Hospital of Pittsburgh and D. T. Watson Rehabilitation Hospital, respectively, she served as a staff pediatrician and medical director of the Infant and Development Program at D. T. Watson, as medical consultant to the Early Childhood Therapies Program at Allegheny General Hospital, and as a Clinical Instructor in pediatrics and staff pediatrician to the Cerebral Palsy Clinic at Children's Hospital of Pittsburgh and the state cerebral palsy clinics in Western Pennsylvania. She is presently active in the Neonatal ICU and High Risk Infant Follow-up Clinic at West Penn Hospital, where her interests are promoting healthy parenting and optimal development of families.

Henry A. Bersani Jr. is presently an Assistant Professor of Special Education/Mental Retardation at Syracuse University and Project Director of the Research and Training Center on Community Integration. Active in several national organizations, he is currently President of the Community Living Division of the American Association on Mental Deficiency (AAMD) and chairs a Community Living and Medicaid Committee for the Association for Persons with Severe Handicaps (TASH). In 1985 he was the Joseph P. Kennedy, Jr. Foundation Fellow in Public Policy and Mental Retardation. He spent the Fellowship year assigned to Senator Chafee working on the Community and Family Living Amendments.

Albert W. Biglan, M.D., F.A.C.S., is a Clinical Associate Professor of Ophthalmology at the University of Pittsburgh School of Medicine. He is Chief of the Ocular Motility Service at St. Francis General Hospital and is an active participant at the teaching program for Pediatric Ophthalmology and Strabismus at the University of Pittsburgh. He is an active staff member at Eye and Ear Hospital, Children's Hospital Pittsburgh, West Penn Hospital, and St. Francis General Hospital. Doctor Biglan is a consultant for the Western Pennsylvania School for Blind Children, Pittsburgh Blind Association, Magee Women's Hospital, and is the Scientific Chairman for The Pennsylvania Academy of Opthalmology and Otolaryngology. He also serves as the Executive Director for the American Diopter and Decibel Society, and is the author of several articles and book chapters dealing with Pediatric Ophthalmology and Strabismus.

Richard C. Birkel, Ph.D., is an Assistant Professor of Human Development at Pennsylvania State University. He maintains an active involvement in human services as a consultant and Community Psychologist. His research interests include the effects of various types of dependency on family functioning and household organization.

Gilbert Brenes, M.D., is the Director of the Spinal Cord Injury Program at Harmarville Rehabilitation Center, and Clinical Instructor at the University of Pittsburgh School of Medicine. He is a member of the Council on Education and Science of the Pennsylvania Medical Society. He is on the Doctoral Committee of the Department of Epidemiology at the University of Pittsburgh. He is also a member of the Western Pennsylvania Keystone Regional Spinal Cord Injury System. He has published several articles on cardiovascular risk factors in spinal cord injured individuals, high density lipo-protein cholesterol concentrations in physically active and sedentary spinal cord injured persons, objective assessment of spasticity in spinal cord injured persons, and activity in the spinal cord individual.

Edward G. Carr, Ph.D., is Professor of Psychology at the State University of New York at Stony Brook and a research consultant at the Suffolk Child Development Center in Long Island, New York. His research interests include experimental child psychopathology, language acquisition, severe behavior problems, and developmental disabilities.

John D. Cone, Ph.D., is a Professor of Child Clinical Psychology in the Department of Psychology at West Virginia University. His research concerns various aspects of assessment, prevention, and intervention dealing with handicapping conditions in children. He is Director of the Prevention Research Program funded by the National Institute of Handicapped Research. Editor of *Behavioral Assessment,* he has published books, chapters, and journal articles dealing with his research interests.

Thomas L. Creer, Ph.D., is Chairman of the Department of Psychology and Director of Clinical Training at Ohio University. His major area of interest in the psychological and behavioral aspects of chronic respiratory disorders, particularly asthma.

Bindu T. Desai, M.D., is an Attending Physician in the Division of Neurology, Cook County Hospital, Chicago. She has been part of the Epilepsy and the Urban Environment research project of Northwestern University and published with this group on the epidemiology of epilepsy and head injury and issues related to violence and epilepsy.

V. Mark Durand, Ph.D., is an Assistant Professor in Clinical Psychology at the State University of New York at Albany. His major areas of interest include developmental disabilities, severe behavior disorders, and sleep disorders in children.

Barbara Edmonson, Ed.D., formerly Adjunct Associate Professor of Psychology at the Ohio State University, works independently as a Habilitation Consultant in California. Her years of involvement with the mentally retarded has spanned the full spectrum of ages from preschool through adulthood, and her major interest has been the development of social perception and social competence. Her curriculum *Social Perceptual Training for the Mentally Retarded* has been widely used, and she is co-author of the *Socio-Sexual Knowledge and Attitudes Test for the Mentally Retarded.*

Judith E. Favell received her Ph.D. in Child Development and Psychology from the University of Kansas. She is currently Director of Psychology at Western Carolina Center and Senior Research Associate in the Research and Training Institute co-sponsored by the University of North Carolina and Western Carolina Center.

Her clinical and research emphasis has been on analysis and treatment of severe behavior disorders, particularly self-injury and aggression. Her work has specifically focused on the analysis of motivational mechanisms underlying the development and maintenance of behavior problems; research on rearrangements of natural and benign contingencies as methods of treatment; the effects and side-effects of behavioral and pharmacological interventions; and the redesign and evaluation of living environments for persons with developmental disabilities.

Karen M. Gil, Ph.D., is Assistant Professor of Medical Psychology in the Department of Psychiatry at Duke University Medical Center. She is also a staff member of the Pain Management Program—a research and clinical program concerned with the behavioral assessment and treatment of patients having chronic pain. She has published articles in the area of chronic and acute pain as well as in other areas of behavioral medicine.

Deborah L. Harm received her Ph.D. from Ohio University, and was a recipient of the University Doctoral Fellowship. As a graduate student she was actively involved in an NIH supported research program for behavioral management of childhood asthma. She has published in major journals on topics in prediction of asthma, respiratory psychophysiology, and cardio-respiratory psychophysiology. Currently, she is a Research Physiologist in the Space Biomedical Research Institute at the Lyndon B. Johnson Space Center.

Verna Hart, Ed.D., is a Professor of Special Education at the University of Pittsburgh. She formerly was on the faculty at Peabody College, where she coordinated the Program for Multiple Handicaps, including Deaf-Blind.

Her major interests are medically fragile and multihandicapped infants, toddlers, and preschoolers, particularly those with physical and sensory handicaps.

Bruce P. Hermann, Ph.D., is a neuropsychologist at the Regional Epilepsy Center at Baptist Memorial Hospital and Clinical Associate Professor in the Department of Psychiatry at the University of Tennessee Medical Center.

John A. Jubala is the Assistant Director of the Psychology Department at Harmarville Rehabilitation Center, a private, 200 bed hospital located in Pittsburgh. He is also a member of the Spinal Cord Team, and has been for the past eight years. He is currently completing his doctoral dissertation at Duquesne University, the topic being a psychological investigation of the experience of having a right hemisphere cerebrovascular accident. His Master's degree is also from Duquesne, and he obtained his Bachelor's degree in Psychology at Illinois Benedictine College.

Ann P. Kaiser, Ph.D., is an Associate Professor of Special Education and Psychology and Human Development at Peabody College of Vanderbilt University. For the last ten years, she has researched issues related to children's language learning and interventions to teach new language skills to handicapped children. She is the co-editor of *Teaching Functional Language* and the author of over 20 incidental teaching and comparative studies of mother–child interaction related to language learning in families with normal and handicapped children.

Percy N. Karanjia, M.D., M.R.C.P., is a Staff Neurologist at the Marshfield Clinic, Wisconsin and Clinical Assistant Professor of Neurology, University of Wisconsin, Madison. He currently runs the Cerebrovascular Service at the Marshfield Clinic and is actively involved in cerebrovascular research. He has published several articles on the subject. He is actively involved with the Stroke Council of the Wisconsin Heart Association.

James M. Kauffman, Ed.D., is Professor of Education, Curry School of Education, and a faculty member in the Institute of Clinical Psychology at the University of Virginia. He is the author or co-author of numerous publications, particularly in the areas of special education for emotionally disturbed and learning disabled children.

Francis, J. Keefe, Ph.D., is Associate Professor and Director of the Pain Management Program in the Department of Psychiatry at Duke University Medical Center. Dr. Keefe has published extensively in the areas of behavioral assessment and treatment of chronic pain. He is currently on the Editorial board of several journals and is Editor of *Behavioral Medicine Abstracts.*

Thomas R. Lagomarcino is a Doctoral Candidate in Special Education at the University of Illinois. He has been actively involved in developing model employment training programs for persons with moderate and severe mental retardation. He is currently directing a USDOE project. His research interests are in the areas of self-control and generalization.

Ronald A. Madle, Ph.D., is Director of Staff Development and Program Evaluation at Laurelton Center and Adjunct Assistant Professor of Human Development at The Pennsylvania State University. His major research and applied interests are in the areas of mental retardation, behavior therapy, staff performance management, and program evaluation.

Richard J. Marion is a Doctoral Candidate in Clinical Psychology at Ohio University in Athens, Ohio. He recently completed his internship at Good Samaritan Medical Center in Phoenix and currently works in the Institute of Behavioral Medicine at the same institution. He helped develop "Living with Asthma", an asthma self-management program, while working at the National Asthma Center in Denver. His research interests, include self-management of chronic diseases and medical decision-making.

Douglas Marston, Ph.D., is the Coordinator of the Experimental Teaching Project, Department of Special Education, Minneapolis Public Schools and an instructor in the Special Education Program, University of Minnesota. He has published several articles and book chapters on topics covering behavioral assessment, standardized testing, and the effectiveness of special education.

Johnny L. Matson, Ph.D., is Professor of Clinical Psychology at Louisiana State University in Baton Rouge, Louisiana. Formerly he held a position in psychiatry and clinical psychology at Western Psychiatric Institute and Clinic at the University of Pittsburgh and as Professor of Special Education at Northern Illinois University. Dr. Matson is the author of over 220 publications including 10 books. His *Handbook of Mental Retardation* won the award as the best book in the behavioral and social sciences in 1983, awarded by the American Association of Publishers. He is Editor-in-Chief of *Applied Research in Mental Retardation* and is on the editorial boards of 12 journals, including *Behavior Therapy* and the *Journal of Educational Psychology*. He has had numerous consultantships, including N.I.M.H., the U.S. Justice Department and the President's Committee on Mental Retardation.

Scott R. McConnell, Ph.D., is an Assistant Professor of Educational Psychology for the Psychology in the Schools Training Program at the University of Minnesota. Previously, he was an Assistant Professor of Child Psychiatry at the University of Pittsburgh and Principal Investigator of Project PREP, an integrated model demonstration treatment program for preschool children with behavior disorders. His research interests lie in the area of behavioral entrapment and generalization effects across time and settings for young children with disabilities, and in the assessment and treatment of critical skills for integration into less restrictive educational placements.

Susan M. McHale, Ph.D., is Associate Professor of Human Development at the Pennsylvania State University. Her research interests focus on the family relationships of disabled children as well as family caregiving for dependent family members and its effects on the well-being and development of caregivers.

Luanna H. Meyer, Ph.D., is Associate Professor of Special Education and Rehabilitation at Syracuse Univesity, where she teaches courses in assessment, curriculum design, and behavior management. She has been involved in collaborative projects with public schools and other agencies to facilitate the integration of children with severe disabilities for more than 10 years, and has published several books as well as numerous book chapters and journal articles on these research and curriculum development activities.

Thomas Nerney is a former Mary Switzer Fellow with the National Institute on Handicapped Research for the fiscal year 1985–1986. Prior to that he served for over two years as an expert consultant to the Assistant Secretary for Special Education and Rehabilitative Services and was the first program director for the Legal Services funded Legal Center for Medically Dependent Persons. Prior to that as a Kennedy Fellow in public policy, he served on the staff of the U.S. Senate Special Committee on Aging, analyzing public policy issues surrounding SSI, SSDI, and Medicaid. He also served as an executive with the Association for Retarded Citizens for over eight years and as a licensed special education principal and vocational rehabilitation director for an agency serving approximately 200 persons. In 1982, he received the Emma Cabot Lyman Award for his efforts to restructure Medicaid.

John J. Nicholas, M.D., is Professor of Orthopedic Surgery, Division of Rehabilitation Medicine and Professor of Internal Medicine, School of Medicine, University of Pittsburgh. He is Director of the Arthritis Rehabilitation Unit of the Presbyterian University Hospital and Liaison Officer from the American Rheumatism Association to the American Academy of Physical Medicine and Rehabilitation. His major interest is in the rehabilitation of musculoskeletal disorders.

Edward J. Nuffield, M.D., D.P.M., is Assistant Professor of Child Psychiatry and Pediatrics at the University of Pittsburgh School of Medicine. Currently acting as Medical Consultant to the Planning Section of the Office of Education and Regional Programming at Western

Psychiatric Institute and Clinic (WPIC), Pittsburgh, he was first a child psychiatrist and then Medical Director of the John Merck Program for Multiply Handicapped Children from 1975 to 1984. He has published book chapters on psychotherapy and counseling for the mentally retarded and has conducted investigations on peer play therapy in handicapped children.

JoAnne W. Putnam, Ph.D., is an Assistant Professor of Special Education at the University of Maine at Farmington. Her major interests are in social integration of individuals with disabilities, cooperative learning, and the disability Down syndrome. She has published articles and book chapters on topics relating to the education and community integration of persons with mental handicaps.

Mark D. Rapport, Ph.D., is an Associate Professor of Psychiatry and Psychology in the Department of Psychiatry and Behavioral Science at the State University of New York at Stony Brook. He is the past director of the Children's Learning Clinic at the University of Rhode Island and has published extensively on topics in psychopharmacology, behavioral interventions, assessing drug effects in children, and childhood psychopathology. His major areas of interest are pediatric psychopharmacology, attention deficit disorder/hyperactivity, and computerized assessment of drug responsivity in children.

Ronald E. Reeve is an Associate Professor and Coordinator of the School/Clinical Child Psychology program in the Institute of Clinical Psychology at the University of Virginia. He previously was involved with the Learning Disabilities Research Institute at Virginia as Assessment Coordinator. In addition to learning disabilities, he has interests in preschool programming for educationally at-risk children.

Frank R. Rusch, Ph.D., is a Professor of Special Education and Director of the Transition Institute at the University of Illinois. Professor Rusch is the author of several texts, numerous chapters, and approximately 100 research articles on topics related to mental retardation, employment, and experimental design. He is on the editorial boards of several journals; his research program has been externally funded for 10 years. All of his graduate students have assumed professional roles in universities throughout the United States.

Diane M. Sainato, Ph.D., is the Research Coordinator for the Early Childhood Research Institute at Western Psychiatric Institute and Clinic, University of Pittsburgh, and the Co-Director of Infant and Preschool Project for the Mathilda Theiss Children's Center. Her research has focused on preschool and elementary school students with various disabilities; most recently, she has investigated factors that will promote independent classroom performance for young children with severe behavior and language disorders.

Janet Simon, Ph.D., is the Executive Director of the Western Pennsylvania School for Blind Children. Her major areas of interest are curriculum development, systems for the delivery of special education services, and school administration.

Michael A. Smyer, Ph.D., is Associate Professor of Human Development and Professor-in-Charge of the Department of Individual and Family Studies at The Pennsylvania State University. His research interests focus on the design, implementation, and evaluation of health-related interventions for older adults and their families. He is on the editorial board of *Psychology and Aging* and serves as editorial consultant for several other journals.

Laszlo K. Stein, Ph.D., is Director of the David T. Siegel Institute, Michael Reese Hospital and Medical Center and Associate Professor, Department of Surgery (Otolaryngology) University of Chicago. He has published extensively on topics in auditory testing, hearing aid performance, infant hearing testing, identification of hearing loss in the multiple handicapped and retarded, auditory electrophysiological measures, and the psychiatric and psychological aspects of deafness. He is the editor of a book on deafness and mental health and currently serves as the editor of the section on electrophysiological techniques for the *Journal of the American Auditory Society.*

Jean Ann Summers is a Doctoral Candidate in Special Education at the University of Kansas. She is currently the Acting Director of the Kansas University Affiliated Facility at Lawrence. She is the author or co-author of a number of books, chapters, and articles on a variety of topics in the area of developmental disabilities, with an emphasis on adult services and on families with a relative with a disability. She has been involved in several research and/or demonstration projects related to families, including parameters of impact of disability, family problem-solving, assisting families in planning adult futures, developing a statewide family information network, and developing self-help family support groups.

Madalyn E. Tyson, Ph.D., received her doctorate from the University of Massachusetts, Amherst in 1983. She is a partner in Blue Ridge Behavior Systems, and consults to numerous agencies, schools, day and residential treatment programs in Western North Carolina. She specializes in program development with developmentally disabled children and adults.

Bonnie L. Utley, Ph.D., is an Assistant Professor of Special Education at the University of Pittsburgh, where she is responsible for training teachers and researchers to work with children with disabilities. Along with Scott McConnell, she directed the treatment and research activities of Project PREP, a classroom-based treatment program for children with behavior disorders. She has conducted extensive research with infants and young children who have profound sensory and cognitive deficits, and has actively participated in the dissemination of effective procedures to direct service agencies.

Steven F. Warren, Ph.D., is an Associate Professor of Special Education and Psychology and Human Development at Peabody College of Vanderbilt University. His research interests include generalization of newly-learned language and incidental teaching strategies. He is the principle investigator of a project examining the generalized effects of incidental teaching on language learning by children with Down syndrome. He is the co-editor of *Teaching Functional Language* and author of over 20 articles and chapters on language intervention.

Steven Whitman, Ph.D., is a Research Associate at the Center for Uurban Affairs and Policy Research at Northwestern University. He has been director of the Epilepsy in the Urban Environment Project for the past nine years. He has conducted research about the epidemiological aspects of epilepsy and is co-editor of the recent book: *Psychpathology In Epilepsy; Social Dimensions* (Oxford University Press, 1986).

Kenneth Carr Wright, M.D., is Assistant Professor in the Division of Rehabilitation Medicine, Department of Orthopedic Surgery at the University of Pittsburgh Medical School. He has a secondary appointment in the Department of Neurology. His major interests include electrodiagnosis and the rehabilitation of patients with complex musculoskeletal and neurologic disorders.

James E. Ysseldyke, Ph.D., is Professor of Educational Psychology at the University of Minnesota. His major teaching and research interests are in improving the psychoeducational assessment and decision-making process, and improving the quality of assessment for mildly handicapped children. He is the Editor of *Exceptional Children.*

Pergamon General Psychology Series

Editors: Arnold P. Goldstein, Syracuse University
Leonard Krasner, Stanford University &
SUNY at Stony Brook

549

* Out of print in original format. Available in custom reprint edition